ENCHANTED EUROPE

ENCHANTED EUROPE

SUPERSTITION, REASON, AND RELIGION, 1250–1750

EUAN CAMERON

OXFORD
UNIVERSITY PRESS

OXFORD
UNIVERSITY PRESS

Great Clarendon Street, Oxford OX2 6DP

Oxford University Press is a department of the University of Oxford.
It furthers the University's objective of excellence in research, scholarship,
and education by publishing worldwide in

Oxford New York

Auckland Cape Town Dar es Salaam Hong Kong Karachi
Kuala Lumpur Madrid Melbourne Mexico City Nairobi
New Delhi Shanghai Taipei Toronto

With offices in

Argentina Austria Brazil Chile Czech Republic France Greece
Guatemala Hungary Italy Japan Poland Portugal Singapore
South Korea Switzerland Thailand Turkey Ukraine Vietnam

Oxford is a registered trade mark of Oxford University Press
in the UK and in certain other countries

Published in the United States
by Oxford University Press Inc., New York

British Library Cataloguing in Publication Data

Data available

Library of Congress Control Number: 2009939955

Typeset by Laserwords Private Limited, Chennai, India
Printed in Great Britain
on acid-free paper by
CPI Antony Rowe,
Chippenham, Wiltshire

ISBN 978–0–19–925782–9

1 3 5 7 9 10 8 6 4 2

For Ruth, again

Preface

Although this book has been slightly less than two years in writing, its origins go back much further. After completing *The European Reformation* (1991) I soon realized that the challenge of understanding 'popular religion' in the pre-Reformation and Reformation worlds required more extensive research and reflection than the few pages that were assigned to it in the earlier book. Some preliminary research and a few experimental conference papers later, it became clear that a specific genre of religious writing, the theological analysis and critique of 'superstition', offered a fruitful and interesting territory to explore. Historians who sought to unearth from refractory and difficult sources the putative 'reality' of popular belief habitually left on the editing-room floor many pages of unwanted theological reflection. This processing, this analysis, this effort to make doctrinal sense of what 'superstition' was and to say why people ought not to engage in it, yielded all sorts of fascinating insights, and it forms the heart of this book.

In a long project one incurs many debts of gratitude. One of the earliest and most significant must be to the Leverhulme Trust, which elected me to a research fellowship for 1996/7. That precious academic year of research time launched this book project by making possible the uninterrupted study of difficult texts in a range of languages. Four other book projects then supervened, and required the research on the critique of superstition to be kept on hold, but the project continued. A second major debt is owed to the University of Newcastle upon Tyne, which assisted with my Leverhulme fellowship year and allowed me a further semester's sabbatical leave in the autumn of 2001, vital for shaping the project. Newcastle University Library willingly acquired a set of key microfilm texts for my use and facilitated this work in too many ways to mention.

Union Theological Seminary, its faculty, president and trustees, invited and welcomed me and my family to New York when they asked me to take up the Henry Luce III Chair of Reformation Church History in the summer of 2002. This appointment placed the astonishing theological riches of the Burke Library, at that time the exclusive responsibility of the seminary, at my disposal. Union also, by allowing me a semester's sabbatical leave in the spring of 2008, contributed much-needed time for the completion of the first draft of this book.

Columbia University, by affording me membership of the departments of religion and history and by inviting me to advise students in the doctoral programme, has been similarly gracious and supportive. Since taking responsibility for the Burke Library, Columbia University Libraries have enriched this project in many ways, through additional resources both in paper and electronic form, and through the continuing and ever-valued assistance of the staff of the Columbia Libraries system.

A further stimulus and encouragement to this work came when the Folger Institute, based in the Folger Shakespeare Library in Washington DC, invited me to lead a seminar in the fall semester of 2006 on 'Martin Luther and the sixteenth-century universe'. Those ten weeks of energetic discussion on Friday afternoons afforded some of the most fruitful and exciting teaching experiences of my life. The helpfulness and appreciation of the Folger Institute staff made the leading of that seminar a pure joy.

Successive generations of students have by their input and responses shaped this book profoundly. Those who participated in my final-year special subject seminar at Newcastle, and in a related MA programme, required me to refine and order my thoughts and address many theoretical issues. The participants in my 'popular religion' course at Union have again and again brought the breadth and depth of their theological questioning to bear on the material. The sheer commitment, expertise, and diverse interests of the participants in the 2006 Folger Institute seminar played a key role in shaping the ideas that have now emerged: I gratefully acknowledge here the roles of Sara Brooks, Jennifer Clement, Ruth Friedman, Genelle Gertz, Phil Haberkern, Michael Meere, Esther Gilman Richey, Jennifer Waldron, and Jennifer Welsh. Several doctoral students, as they developed their own distinctive and individual projects and perspectives, have contributed more than they know to my own growth, especially Lisa Watson and John Schofield at Newcastle, Susan Greenbaum and John Reynolds at Union, and Matt Pereira, Sarah Raskin, and many others at Columbia University.

Colleagues in all the places where I have worked have been generous with their support and encouragement. I gratefully record the contributions made by many historian colleagues where I have worked, especially Jeremy Boulton at Newcastle and Daisy Machado, John McGuckin, and Robert

Somerville here in New York. To all my Union colleagues, faculty and staff, who have watched me try, with limited success, to balance the demands of deanship, seminary teaching, and research, I extend my thanks for their understanding and patience. More specifically, those fellow historians who have talked through the rapid emergence and growth of 'superstition' as a subject distinct from magic and witchcraft have aided me considerably: in the United Kingdom, Robin Briggs, Patrick Collinson, Eamon Duffy, Bruce Gordon, Diarmaid MacCulloch, Peter Marshall, Andrew Pettegree, Richard Rex, and Alison Rowlands; in the United States, Michael D. Bailey, Caroline Walker Bynum, Michelle Gonzalez Maldonado, Nathan Rein, and Amy DeRogatis, from the History of Christianity section of the American Academy of Religion, and Randall Styers. Two expert and gracious readers for Oxford University Press made extremely helpful and constructive suggestions towards the final stages. Working with the astonishingly patient and professional staff of Oxford University Press has been a pleasure as always.

Two tributes require particular emphasis. In the 1980s and 1990s I had the privilege of coming to know Robert W. Scribner quite well, and though not a student of his myself, shared with his former students in the profound sense of loss felt at his premature death. Bob was an outstanding scholar and an unfailingly gracious, witty, and astonishingly modest person. Although my approach differed and still differs in some respects quite radically from Bob's, he encouraged me with unfailing kindness throughout our too brief acquaintance. Secondly, this work, as must be quite obvious, owes a vast amount to the formative influence of Keith Thomas. Again and again, when one wrestles with a problem in early modern thought, one returns to *Religion and the Decline of Magic* only to find what one imagined was a new idea already foreshadowed in that remarkable book. Those of us who benefited from Keith's attentiveness, patience, encyclopaedic knowledge, and penetrating intellectual insight recorded our thanks in the Festschrift volume published in 2000. This project approaches the material of early modern beliefs from a substantially different angle, but its debt to Keith's work is self-evident and willingly acknowledged.

More than I can possibly ever express is owed to my family, to my parents, my wife Ruth, and our daughters Alexandra and Sarah. They have lived through with me the consuming and obsessing effects of one book after another, and have responded with constructive advice, help, and support at every imaginable level.

This book offers, obviously, only a partial essay in addressing its material. It is both by necessity and by intention highly selective. Many other texts could or even ought to have been read, and it is quite possible that the picture that I have drawn would then have appeared somewhat different. However, the scope and range of the project precluded anything resembling scholarly comprehensiveness. This work intends to contribute to a growing area of discussion, and never to claim anything like the final or definitive word on any question.

Finally, a brief explanation is owed of the title, which intentionally nods towards a much earlier book on the subject. In the early 1690s the Dutch reformed minister Balthasar Bekker published his notoriously sceptical work entitled *De betoverde weereld*, or 'the enchanted (or bewitched) world'. Bekker attempted, at great professional cost, to subject the belief in spirits and demons in several leading religions to comparative historical analysis. Bekker's history-of-religions approach ran far ahead of much of its evidence; his confessional partiality and value judgements were all too obvious. Few if any scholars of religion would attempt such a thing today. Nevertheless, the attempt to view the belief in spirits and their associated activities as a cultural and historical phenomenon anticipated, if somewhat prematurely, the critical thinking of later centuries. To locate actual religious ideas and beliefs in their appropriate and proper historical setting is, I insist, the only means to set belief itself on a sound footing.

E. K. C.

Union Theological Seminary, New York City
July 2009

Contents

Introduction

I n March 1495 Cardinal Giuliano della Rovere, the future Pope Julius II, organized an unsuccessful assault on Genoa and Savona in support of the French campaign in Italy, during the first phase of the long and disastrous saga of the Italian wars.[1] While these manoeuvres were taking place, the Dominican preacher and regent master Silvestro Mazzolini of Prierio (c.1456–1527), the future Master of the Sacred Palace and theological controversialist, was travelling across the Piedmontese and Ligurian hills towards Savona, to deliver a Lenten sermon. On the road he met an infantry captain called Marzocchio, and the two of them agreed to head for Genoa together. The soldier's mule injured itself and started to bleed from one leg. The soldier, concerned because this was a fine animal (and a borrowed one into the bargain), asked Mazzolini if he knew how to pronounce a blessing on it. Mazzolini blessed the animal in the name of the Trinity, and the bleeding stopped. However, the soldier was evidently not satisfied, since when they met another soldier on the road he asked this second soldier to pronounce a healing blessing on the mule as well. The other soldier grumbled when he heard that a priest had blessed the animal, and pronounced a second charm or spell over the mule. Mazzolini related with ill-suppressed glee that after this second, less orthodox blessing the bleeding restarted and continued until the party reached Genoa.[2]

In 1553 the Lutheran theologian Kaspar Peucer (1525–1602), son-in-law of the great Protestant educator, philosopher, and theologian Philipp Melanchthon, issued the first edition of his *Commentary on the Various Types of Divinations*.[3] The study of meaningful prodigies, which he called 'teratoscopia', Peucer regarded as one of the legitimate and necessary forms of divination. Peucer listed a series of marvels, including various misbirths.

Besides the relatively common conjoined births, he described how in 1531 at Augsburg a woman had given birth to three offspring, one a head wrapped in membranes, the second a serpent with two legs, the body and the feet of a toad, and the tail of a lizard, the third a perfectly normal pig. Again, on 25 January 1543, an infant was reportedly born in Belgium with blazing eyes and a terrifying aspect, with nostrils in the shape of a cow's horns, and dog-hair on his back. The faces of monkeys were visible on his chest, where there were cats' eyes instead of nipples. He also had webbed feet like a swan, and a tail. He lived for four hours and after saying 'be watchful, your lord God is coming', he died.[4]

Both these stories testify to a world of thought in which matter and meaning were closely entwined. In one story a friar applies spiritual power to a physical (in this case veterinary) problem; in the other a physician-theologian discerns meaning in bizarre occurrences outside the normal course of nature. Both these stories came from the pens of extremely accomplished theologians, fully grounded in the intellectual culture of their time. Neither, however, conforms to the standard of post-Enlightenment rationalism. In each case observers in more recent centuries would probably have called their beliefs 'superstitious'. More recently, historians have become more cautious and more relativist in our outlook; we are more likely to stress how observers like these held beliefs that were 'rational' by the standards and beliefs of their time; or to deconstruct the whole idea of the 'rational' as hopelessly contaminated by social inequality or linguistic aberration.

Here is the irony. Both Mazzolini and Peucer used the concept of 'superstition' in their own writings. Both believed that it was very important to distinguish 'superstition' from the legitimate use of spiritual and religious rituals and symbols. They differed and indeed disagreed vigorously over where to draw the line between superstition and religion; but they both believed fervently that such a line existed. In no way were these theologians postmodern relativists. Both these authors, and dozens if not hundreds of others, engaged in detailed analysis and often fierce debate over what superstition was, how to identify it, how to distinguish it from acceptable religious custom, and how to dissuade less thoughtful or less educated people from engaging in superstitious practices.

Until the middle of the eighteenth century and possibly for longer, most thinking people in Europe believed that the physical matter of the cosmos was full of meaning. Gestures and rituals might somehow or other lead to physical effects or material transformation. The disposition of matter was rarely if ever purely accidental; the appearance of living beings, both their normal and their abnormal manifestations, could contain messages from the divine. Yet—and this part is least often recognized—these interpretations of meaning did not derive from random or undisciplined thinking or loose nature-mysticism. On the contrary, some of the most rigorous studies of causation in pre-modern Europe derived from the attempt to discern why things happened and what they meant, in the context of the theological analysis and critique of 'superstition'. This analysis provoked some crucial reflection upon what ritual could or could not achieve in the physical world. At one level, then, this book offers an essay in intellectual history. It narrates a debate, or rather a long series of debates, over the nature of religion and its place in the universe. It proves, if anything, that careful theoretical reflection over the proper uses and potentialities of religious practice is as old as Christianity itself (or older). Thirteenth- and fourteenth-century scholastic theologians were just as concerned to delimit the relationship between ritual causes and physical effects as their sixteenth- or eighteenth-century successors, though the answers varied at different periods.

At another level, the critique of superstition addresses the setting *par excellence* where academic theology confronted the realities of life and the irreducible, instinctive patterns of mass culture. In this genre of writing churchmen were not writing about themselves, nor meditating on arcane mysteries celebrated on altars concealed behind beautiful screens from the profane laity. They confronted the brutal facts that children fell sick and died; that cows mysteriously failed to give milk; that horses either bolted or suffered from unexplained exhaustion; that summer storms came from nowhere to devastate the crops; and that less educated people persisted in believing in the existence of a huge, amorphous variety of semi-visible or invisible spirit-creatures who might influence their lives. Ecclesiastical authors struggled to make sense of these mysteries and, even more, to analyse the exotic variety of remedies and prophylaxes that people trad-itionally used against them. The superstition-critique presents pastoral theology at its most practical, specific, and applied. Moreover, since pastoral theologians participated in the broad culture of their birth as much as in the formal intellectual habits of their professional training, the ana-lysis of 'superstition' challenged them repeatedly to navigate their own way between custom and instinct on one hand and intellectual formation on the other. Occasionally—as perhaps in the story just told above by Silvestro Mazzolini of Prierio—the mask slipped. Sometimes it fell away altogether.

'Superstition': an elusive and slippery term

Probably for as long as human beings have engaged in religious activities, there have been disputes about the right and wrong ways to practise one's beliefs. Early in Christian history, various opprobrious terms were coined to classify the 'wrong' ways to conduct divine worship. Idolatry was the worship of the wrong god, or whatever was not God. Heresy was the worship of the true God, but according to beliefs that contradicted received authority, according to personal choice rather than community consensus. Superstition came to mean the worship of the true God by inappropriate and unacceptable means. All of these were labelling expressions: none had a secure frame of reference apart from the values, presuppositions, and preferences of those who used them. However, the way that they were used tells us a great deal about the dynamics of power and authority in the history of religion. The changing shape of the controversies which they evoked forms a powerful document in the history of European culture.

The term 'superstition' derived from classical antiquity, and nearly always contained a pejorative sense—it implied 'bad' as opposed to 'good' or 'correct' belief or practice in the realm of religion. Though its etymology was never clear, it always presupposed an opposite, or even a cluster of opposites.[5] In the late Roman Empire pagans described Christianity as superstition in one sense; Christians described paganism as superstition in another.[6] In general 'superstition' could be opposed to other forms of putatively 'wrong' religion, such as idolatry, heresy, or fanaticism. It could also be opposed to putatively 'right' or valid religion, to terms such as 'piety', 'true religion', 'orthodoxy', or 'reasoned faith'. Finally, it can be used as it is typically used in modern secular society: as a pejorative term to describe *any* belief system that falls short of the speaker's chosen standard of 'rationality'. At the high water-mark of modern confidence in scientific rationalism, 'superstition' has become the preferred term of abuse used by any secular atheist to describe religion of any kind. The resurgence of religion as a factor in world politics, and postmodern aversion to the condescending attitudes of Western rationality towards the rest of humanity, have made such aggressive uses of the term rarer; but the connotations persist. However it is used, the term has the effect of driving sharp distinctions, where the need may be more for subtle shades than hard lines.

Superstition is a flexible designation, and can be aimed at a range of targets at different times and by different people. In the most general sense, it has commonly been used to refer to a fairly disorganized bundle of beliefs and practices rooted in tradition: attempts to *discern* the unknown through *divination*, and to *control* it, or at least protect against it, through simple use of *charms*. Such traditions made claims about the access to and use of an invisible reality, whose existence was assumed rather than theorized in a structured way. These beliefs privileged experience over analysis. They located spiritual power, causality, and meaning arbitrarily and conventionally in particular things, places, peoples, times, and circumstances. Often they served to address particular physical and existential needs and concerns, rather than giving an overall transcendent interpretation to the meaning of existence. In general, 'superstition' has tended to be ethically ambiguous or neutral. The criterion of a valuable practice or piece of knowledge was whether it achieved the effect desired by the person using it, rather than whether or not it was 'right' in any ultimate sense. Incoherence and inconsistency are to be expected in so-called superstitious belief systems, although they can also show surprising dimensions of similarity and parallel evolutions within different cultures. In these very general terms—which will be unpacked and analysed much more fully in Part I—'superstition' was described and subjected to theological critique from very early in Christian history, and more or less continuously since then.[7]

Between the thirteenth and the eighteenth centuries, the debate over 'superstition' grew more intense than at almost any time before or since. Nearly all the major movements in ideas in this period somehow or other impacted on this issue. The fragmentation of medieval academic theology in the so-called strife of the ways entailed a diversity of views over how to distinguish religion and superstition. The Christian humanism of the European Renaissance built itself on an explicit critique of the allegedly 'superstitious' quality of everyday Christianity as practised by the uneducated. The sixteenth-century Reformation adapted, distorted, and transformed the late medieval rhetoric over 'superstitions' with its charge that Catholicism was itself *inherently*—and not just accidentally, or when misunderstood—a particularly pernicious form of superstition. Roman

Catholicism, as it defined its 'reformed' identity in the latter part of the sixteenth century, resolved to disown those parts of its own heritage that seemed unsuitable in the eyes of its own leadership. At the same time, it vigorously resisted the charge that its 'core' rituals and customs were superstitious, and even rehabilitated some practices that had been cast into doubt in previous centuries. In the era of confessional orthodoxy from the late sixteenth century to the end of the seventeenth, the rhetoric that had traditionally condemned superstition and magic in the eyes of the devout became a crucial part of the intellectual armour used to prosecute sorcerers, magicians, and witches. Then, in the early Enlightenment, 'superstition' took centre stage in religious discussions to an even greater extent than before. 'Superstition' and 'reason' became the poles around which the religious and ethical theorists of the early Enlightenment debated the proper claims of religion on the human mind.

In this area above all else, it is vital to remember the distinction between theory and practice. Much writing on the area of superstitions has been bedevilled by a failure to distinguish adequately between what people were instructed to think and do on one hand, and what evidence suggests they thought and did on the other, between norms and reported realities. Most of the literature that forms the heart of the evidence for this book is essentially theoretical. It derives from the pens of trained theological intellectuals. Theologians and their kind wrote long and often about superstition, either in order to critique and challenge the beliefs and practices of those who were not theologians, or to continue a debate with others of their own kind who held differing opinions. They wrote in Latin and in a variety of vernaculars. They employed a range of genres from the theological *summa* to the popular sermon and pamphlet. Nevertheless, while the authors of the learned critique of superstitions wrote for a varied range of audiences and readerships, they spoke for themselves, and for much of the time for themselves only. Each source, each text used in the following pages represents an interpretation of a complex and confusing state of affairs from one, usually highly trained mind. It does not speak for the culture as a whole.

Some theoretical questions

Various consequences follow, and it is important to set these out at the start. First and perhaps most obviously, the historian must not pretend to

determine what 'actually' constituted 'superstition' versus 'true religion'
at any period. Since the whole point is to show how these loaded
terms evolved and acquired new and often contested meanings, a degree
of relativism is essential. The terms superstition and superstitious must
hereafter be read as though in perpetual, though usually invisible, inverted
commas, always as used by this or that author in the past. Quoting or
paraphrasing such a source implies no verdict on whether the views held
by that source should be adopted or rejected by author or reader.

Secondly, one needs to shed any casual assumptions about culture and
class as applied to the literature on superstition. Again, much confusion
has entered this subject because historians have imported into the Middle
Ages or early modern period unexamined assumptions about where to
draw the line, culturally and economically, between the more and the
less educated. Even—perhaps one should say especially—in the Church
of the late Middle Ages, one cannot assume that 'the clergy' held shared
and representative views about what was 'superstition', or that those views
differed from the views of 'the laity' in any clear-cut way. Still less can
one assume that clear lines were drawn between literate versus illiterate,
urban versus rural, bourgeois versus proletarian. Nor can one assume that
most people on the more privileged side of those divides shared the views
of the theologians, normally our primary sources, about what 'superstition'
was or how to respond to it. As a starting point, this study assumes only
that most of the theological authors participated in a culture which allowed
them to exchange texts and debate points with each other on the basis of
certain shared assumptions. Such people constituted what I refer to below
as the 'theological academy'. By this term is meant a culturally defined
group of literate, Latin-reading scholars who knew the basic concepts and
tools of scholastic theology and embraced the application of formal logic
as a tool to make sense of their religious experience. These people were,
evidently, an extremely small subset even amongst that pre-modern elite,
the professional clergy. More career clergy were educated as lawyers than
theologians, and few of either had profound or regular contact with the
majority of the population, unless, like some of the authors reviewed in
this book, they served as popular preachers. Some people outside this
theological academy, clerics and laity, may indeed have shared the culture
of the authors of the critique of superstition. The number and social
location of those who shared those views will have changed over time, as
successive waves of religious reform and philosophical development washed

over Europe. However, we shall probably never know *exactly* how widely the views of the writers analysed in this book were shared. At all costs the narrative in what follows should not be read as an intellectual history of European attitudes as a whole.

This raises a third question in its turn. How far does the literature on superstition describe something that might have been observed as a lived reality? How widespread or pervasive were the beliefs and practices that it denotes? To what extent might the learned literature be used as evidence for anything beyond the minds of its authors? Some scholars would prefer to avoid the question entirely. It would certainly be possible to take a rigidly postmodern stance, and to describe the superstition literatures as a series of discourses that had no necessary connection to any 'reality' whatever. However, most historians, let alone general readers, will find that enclosed, elliptical approach very unsatisfactory. They will wish to know how far the material reviewed in this book described anything that would have been observable in everyday pre-modern society, and how accurate or misleading that description may have been. There is no obvious or self-evident answer to these questions. At the most extreme, one historian has argued, with considerable evidence on his side, that the 'superstition-literature' of the early and high Middle Ages reflected little if anything more than the self-affirming continuation of a literary tradition. Theologians, in this account, quoted each other irrespective of whether the texts that they quoted described or denoted anything in the world outside their studies and libraries.[8] Most historians would not be so extreme: and indeed, there are strong reasons for rejecting an approach that dismisses entirely any relationship between the literature and the real-world phenomena of 'superstitions'.[9] However, the epistemology of medieval and early modern theologians differed from that of modern ethnographers. In general, medieval authors showed a strong preference for 'authority', first and foremost in the form of sacred texts, but also secondarily in the form of texts of antique and canonical wisdom. Historians of heresy are familiar with a literature on heretical movements that interpreted, or distorted, the empirical evidence of trial testimony to make it conform to texts of canonical authority. Experience would be shoe-horned into an ill-fitting tradition, before a supposedly 'authoritative' tradition would be adapted and revised in the light of experience.[10]

The literature on superstitions, though in some respects similar, is different in one critical respect from the literature on heresy. Heresy-writers were usually, with rare exceptions, describing a movement of people who formed a self-conscious group, even if such people would not necessarily have recognized themselves in the ecclesiastical labels of Waldenses, Lollards, or Hussites.[11] In the case of those portrayed as holding 'superstitious' beliefs, there was no such collective identity. Ecclesiastical writers depicted an amorphous and constantly shifting mass of people, including men and women, the learned and the unlearned, physicians, soldiers, and ecclesiastics as well as the more readily stereotyped folk-healers using charms and spells. Consequently, the literary image runs an even greater risk than do the heresy-treatises of homogenizing and so distorting the material that it depicts. Moreover, there is even less likelihood than with heresy that one will discover literature that explicitly argues for or justifies allegedly 'superstitious' practices (although, as will be seen, some such literature does in fact exist).

There is a second layer of conceptual difficulty with the superstition-literature. Since theologians and other ecclesiastical writers on the whole wrote normatively and pastorally, rather than ethnographically, their descriptions constantly 'read' the phenomena that they witnessed in the light of certain core presuppositions. Their descriptions are the very opposite of neutral, disengaged description. To anticipate a little, this disjunction between the assumptions of the learned and the material appears most glaring in the area of demonology. Most theological writers in the pre-modern era were post-Thomist Aristotelians: they believed that there were spirits in the world, and that those spirits were rigidly, cosmically divided into the good angels and the evil demons, the loyal and fallen spirits respectively.[12] On the other hand, we can infer that in pre-modern Europe there persisted a resilient folk-belief, according to which the invisible world was densely populated with both personal beings and impersonal forces that were morally ambiguous. These beings and forces were capable of friendship, enmity, and mischief—in fact they partook of the same moral ambiguity as people, something which academic theology stubbornly denied to the spiritual realm.[13] Theological writers could not help themselves, and had no wish to restrain themselves, from describing the spirit-world of folk-beliefs in the language of the ethically polarized cosmos of scholastic Christian philosophy. The impersonal occult force of a folk-belief became, in the theologian's eyes, the 'demon' seeking to seduce the weak-minded by offering spurious help. The historian who wishes to use this material is constantly challenged to unravel a tangled skein made up of different cultural elements. Only by establishing some rough-and-ready methodological filters, and then treating the results with great caution and scepticism, can the historian claim to infer any provisional data about the phenomena behind the distorting and perpetually coloured glass of the sources.

One final question is absolutely critical for the context of this inquiry. It relates to the evolution of so-called popular belief over the long centuries of the pre-modern era in Europe. The history of 'superstition' and the responses to it becomes inextricably tangled with questions of the rise of the 'rational' and the supposedly 'modern' in European cultural history. How, and why, if ever, did European people cease to be 'superstitious' in the sense that this book describes them? Even though this work does not presume to take a view on the broad questions of the rise of 'modernity' or 'rational religion' in Europe as a whole, it is vital to sketch out these debates, since the arguments around superstition inevitably touch on these questions at multiple points.

In German idealistic philosophy, the Reformation was assumed almost without question to have played a critical role in inaugurating the modern world of rationally restrained faith and rationally unrestrained inquiry. Wilhelm Dilthey argued that the Reformation was quite simply the German equivalent of the Renaissance elsewhere in Europe. It reacted against medieval obscurantism and freed the national spirit to discover its place in the universe.[14] The liberal theologian Adolf von Harnack claimed around 1900 that the primary and decisive importance of the Reformation consisted in the fact that it stripped away from Christianity so many of its encrustations of superfluous ritual and priestcraft.[15] His pupil Ernst Troeltsch set rather higher standards for 'modernity' than his teacher. Troeltsch recognized that the essentially medieval pursuit of dogmatic certainty lingered in the Reformation, even though its essence contained the seeds of modernization.[16] Troeltsch's colleague and associate Max Weber contributed the most influential, and to some the most notorious arguments for reformed modernity. In his classic *Protestant Ethic and the Spirit of Capitalism* of 1904 Weber reasoned that the psychic ideal-type created by Protestantism, especially in its Puritan forms, tended to espouse a pragmatic and functional, rather than a sacral, approach to the business of life. In his *Sociology of Religion* Weber developed a typology of religious development according to which religions gradually ascended from magical cults towards a rational concept of a transcendent divinity.[17] Weber developed the thesis that the process of 'disenchantment of the world' (*Entzauberung der Welt*), in which magical and supernatural beliefs lost credibility with the rise of modernity, science and commerce, reached its climax in the form of Puritan Protestantism.[18]

As idealism and liberalism waned, other historical philosophies emerged that sublimated the supposedly modernizing effects of the Reformation into other intellectual modes and keys. The Reformation, or some part of it, became the moment when a new urban bourgeoisie took control of its economic and political destiny, even when it thought it was only taking control of its civic religious and welfare institutions.[19] Even as the drivers of change shifted from a Hegelian to a Marxist mode, the 'modernizing' theme in the history of the Reformation era persisted as an axiom. In the final decades of the twentieth century, social historians sought to discern in the Reformation and confessional eras the rise of the bureaucratic state, administered by systematic record-keeping and characterized by social discipline.[20] Religious historians in this mode postulated that in the early modern centuries Europe was 'Christianized', as the highly organized and disciplinarian political and ecclesiastical machinery of confessional orthodoxy investigated, controlled, reformed, and ultimately abolished the popular culture of magic and superstition.[21] The alleged rise of 'modern man' depended either upon a campaign by the early modern professional and typically bourgeois clergy to suppress the customs of rural society, or on a progressive self-imposed isolation by the intellectual bourgeoisie from the customs of traditional folklore.[22] If the result of this campaign was a success, it was 'acculturation'; if it failed, it signalled the separation of the bourgeois from the masses, a 'civilizing process' with clear economic and class implications.[23]

The late twentieth century in Europe and America witnessed a wave of intellectual disenchantment (as one might call it) with the whole notion of 'progress' towards 'modernity'. The Enlightenment was not enlightened, especially if one were mentally disturbed. The thesis of ever greater secularization and rationalization was mocked by the recrudescence of fierce religiously motivated movements across the world, whose fervour overturned any assumption that the products of Western 'modernization' were either universally desired, privileged by history, or technologically invulnerable. It has appeared that Edward Gibbon was wrong to assume that for the barbarians to conquer Rome again, they would need to cease to be barbarous.[24] The social history of late medieval and early modern

Europe has quite naturally and inevitably shared in this abandonment of old assumptions about the linear rise of rationality and a 'disenchanted' world. Numerous scholars have tested the evidence for the rise of 'rational' early modern humanity and found it seriously wanting.

First, historians have reminded us that after the Reformation intelligent Protestants emphatically continued to believe in demons and spirits and in special interventions of the divine in their universe. The Reformation did not abolish the world of fallen angels nor remove the threat of witchcraft and hostile sorcery. Demonic magic suffered no incompatibility whatever with the Protestant world-view. Secondly, intelligent Protestant writers saw nothing improper in documenting extraordinary manifestations of the sacred in everyday life. Strange apparitions or manifestations within the natural order, like that just quoted from Peucer (see n. 4), were quite appropriate objects of study and meditation. While God might no longer work 'miracles' in the narrow technical sense, the hand of the divine was repeatedly to be discerned in the 'special providences' that might occur from time to time to warn people of their predicament and their religious and ethical duties.[25] There are absolutely no grounds for challenging either of these arguments. The evidence of continuing Protestant belief in a meaningful cosmos is copious and indisputable; and indeed this book will add further to the documentation of several of these points.

Slightly more debatable are the claims made in his later works by the brilliant social historian of early modern German religion, the late R. W. Scribner. In a key article issued in 1993, Bob Scribner argued that the Protestant Reformation *inherently* had no plan to demystify or desacralize the cosmos.[26] He identified parallels to the supernaturalism of traditional Catholicism in many aspects of Protestant culture. Protestant Bibles and even images of leading reformers were allegedly imbued with ritual and apotropaic potencies similar to those attributed to Catholic relics or sacred images.[27] Protestants might no longer expect to see visions of saints, but they could see visions of angels whose moralizing messages differed hardly at all from the apparitions of earlier centuries.[28] The rites of worship in the reformed world might be viewed by their believers in terms hardly different from those of Catholics of earlier centuries. Scribner's argument has found many followers among the many highly gifted historians of succeeding generations, including several of his pupils. It is not uncommon now to read of a 'distinctively Protestant popular religion and magical culture', or to find the traditional arguments about Protestant metaphysics turned on their head by ingenious deployment of unusual sources.[29]

The challenge posed by Scribner's and his pupils' arguments lies not in any shortcomings in the scholarship (which is invariably excellent) but in questions over method and approach. Bob Scribner developed to an exceptional level of refinement the strategy of writing the social history of the Reformation from the perspective of the local archival records of village communities in early modern Germany. He discovered many fascinating and hitherto unknown documents in the course of numerous visits to archives.[30] The inevitable price paid for this tactic lay in the consideration given to the traditional theological sources. In this style of historiography the theological writings of the reformers are minimized, when they are not entirely absent. One could quite reasonably argue that far too much attention was paid in the past to the theoretical ruminations of theologians, and relatively too little to the everyday experiences of the ordinary people.[31] However, when the role of the theological sources is so far minimized, it becomes much more difficult to distinguish between the intentions of the reformers and their failures: the latter may easily be confused with the former. Transitional phenomena such as the temporary survival of monasteries in Lutheran cities may be emphasized at the expense of the long-term reality of their abolition.[32] Scots Protestants might have continued to visit holy wells after the Reformation, but there is clear evidence that their kirk sessions disapproved of their doing so.[33] It would be bizarre to suggest that holy wells formed an inherent part of the Scots Calvinist belief-system: yet very much that kind of argument has been applied to parts of Reformation Europe.

Ultimately, the debate becomes a question of who speaks for the Reformation as a whole. The prudent answer might be that no one does so absolutely or exclusively. The leading reformers represented one voice, the secular politicians another, the ordinary believers in towns and country yet another. When one is speaking of the *intentions* behind the movement, however, it makes more sense to dwell on the dynamic forces of change rather than the reluctant voices of tradition; provided always that one maintains a degree of reserve over how far the intentions were realized in practice. There are also reasons to suspect that, even apart from his distinctive research methodology, Professor Scribner had reasons of his own, not always acknowledged in the historiography, to resist the inference that Protestantism was inherently more 'modern' than the Catholicism that it rebelled against.[34]

Historical revisionism has also come to the world of the late seventeenth century and the early Enlightenment. It has become increasingly clear that in the late seventeenth and early eighteenth centuries there arose in the culture of the intellectual elites a taste for rediscovering the spiritual and the supernatural. This phenomenon emerged particularly clearly in England, but was also manifested in other countries of Europe. Fellows of the Royal Society took a keen interest in portents and omens, apparitions of ghosts, and the dwindling number of trials for witchcraft. Despite the fact that modern historians tend to minimize the amount of actual 'atheism' or 'mechanism' in the thought of the early Enlightenment, there was clearly sufficient *fear* of the rise of mechanical philosophy to provoke an energetic quest for evidences of the 'invisible world' in order to rebut the supposed atheists. In a brilliant and important historiographical review article, Professor Alexandra Walsham has argued that this wave of 'resacralization' in the late seventeenth and eighteenth centuries demonstrates a tendency for the 'desacralization' of religion and culture to ebb and flow in a series of cycles rather than a single linear progression.[35] This book will suggest a somewhat different explanation, rooted in the disintegration of early modern metaphysics. However, Professor Walsham and the works that she describes demonstrate the presence of this wave of intellectual supernaturalism beyond any possible cavil.

Finally, some histories of the post-urbanization, post-industrialization world argue that a culture of 'superstitious' reading of the universe persisted there also, well into the nineteenth century and beyond.[36] This work will also suggest an explanation for that phenomenon. The 'critique of superstition' occupied a particular niche in the social history of European thought. Between the rise of the superstition-treatises and the onset of Romanticism, religious intellectuals believed it was both possible and necessary to try to rein in and to guide the attitudes and beliefs of ordinary people. By the nineteenth century such an aspiration appears to have largely dissipated. The urgency felt by earlier pastoral theologians to moderate the beliefs of ordinary people had been replaced by other concerns. Therefore, it is not in the least surprising if evidence survives of popular 'superstitions' long after the supposed 'decline of magic'. What had declined was the *fear* of magic.

The case for reading the theological texts on superstition

A consistent problem with modern 'revisionist' histories of Protestant meta-physics lies in the simple fact that for most historians, and nearly all students, the theological literature on superstitions has remained profoundly inaccessible and unknown. The debate over superstition and 'disenchantment' was played out, with great vigour, intellectual toughness, and some subtlety, within the theological establishment of early modern Europe itself. As a prelude to making any claims as to what happened to 'popular belief', it is vital to clear the mind about what Europe's thinkers and teachers were saying about it at the time. This work is intended to bring a body of theological literature into focus on the subject. Most of the texts analysed and deployed in this book consist of 'superstition-treatises', that is, pieces written either as occasional discussions or as part of a more systematic theological investigation into belief or a text of pastoral catechesis. This literature had existed in some form or another since the early days of the Church. Important antecedents were certain key works of Augustine, and also the sermons of Caesarius, sixth-century bishop of Arles, which offer a particularly rich set of insights into the pastoral work of a bishop in late antique Gaul.[37] Important contributions to the genre were made in the early medieval penitentials and the collections of early-to-high medieval canonists, such as Regino of Prüm and Burchard of Worms.[38] However, neither in these early writings nor in the works of the high-point of medieval scholasticism do we regularly find anything to compare with the late medieval superstition-treatises. In general the thirteenth-century scholastics discussed popular belief only when it encountered a key text in their canon of systematic theology. Peter Lombard's *Book of Sentences* almost inevitably provoked some such discussion around book 4, distinction 34, where Lombard discussed the issue of a couple made impotent in respect of each other by sorcery. Inevitably all his many commentators followed suit to some degree or other.[39] Most scholastic demonologies were preoccupied with first principles, only occasionally descending to practical applications.[40]

From *c.*1350 onwards, across Europe from England and France to eastern Germany and into Spain, a series of theological writers penned treatises that quite specifically addressed issues of pastoral teaching in the area of superstitions. In many cases these were expositions of the Ten Commandments: the first commandment against 'strange gods' and idolatry generated a fertile literature on mistaken religious practices.[41] Others were occasional pieces that responded to particular cases of conscience, like the detailed pastoral challenges discussed by Jean Gerson in his short works of pastoral advice, or by Heinrich von Gorkum's *On Certain Cases of Conscience Relating to Superstition*, both from the early fifteenth century, or somewhat later in Isidoro Isolani's *Book against Magicians and Diviners* of 1506 or Martín of Arles y Andosilla's *Treatise on Superstitions* of 1517.[42] By the sixteenth century one finds printed vernacular treatises that addressed superstition in and for itself, such as Martín de Castañega's *Treatise on Superstitions and Sorceries* (1529), and Pedro Ciruelo's *Reproof of Superstitions and Sorceries* (1539). Both appeared in Spanish, and in the latter case in multiple editions.[43] It is not entirely clear why this genre of writing should have come into existence in such relative abundance when it did. To some extent, there were simply more books being written on more subjects anyway. However, some historians have detected a tendency for the theology of the later Middle Ages to adopt a more pastorally oriented strategy in a conscious way. Certainly the literature of this period acquired a degree of contact with the earthy realities of everyday life that had been much rarer hitherto.[44]

The superstition-literature also overlapped at many points with the literature on magic and, in due course, on witchcraft also, but was not quite identical with either of those sub-genres. As has already been demonstrated by Michael D. Bailey, two fifteenth-century works traditionally linked with the genesis of the witch-hunt, Johannes Nider's *Formicarius* and Heinrich Krämer's *Malleus Maleficarum*, were largely devoted to broader questions of superstitious practice.[45] Some works contained several different genres within them: Johann Weyer's *On the Illusions of Demons*, a work that has previously been studied almost entirely for what it contains on the subject of witchcraft, contains in fact a great deal more superstition-lore that the traditional witchcraft literature tended to neglect.[46] Martín Delrio's *Six Books of Magical Disquisitions* is a particularly clear instance of this sort of hybrid work.[47] A few examples of these treatises are already available in English, in either complete or partial translation; these will be cited and referenced here in the most readily accessible editions where appropriate.[48]

The sources for this work include medieval Catholic, reformed and post-Reformation Protestant, and early modern Catholic writings, as well as selected texts from the Enlightenment. It is conventional in studies of witchcraft to argue that dogmatic religious difference was of little or no consequence where the theory of witchcraft was concerned.[49] That simple bracketing of theological concerns will not, of course, work for the superstition materials at all. Writers either side of the Reformation divide did share many important presuppositions, both philosophical and cosmological. However, the differences between medieval Catholics, Protestants, and Roman Catholics made systematic and absolutely crucial differences to the way in which they processed their material. Often the Protestant 'superstition treatises' amounted to polemical pamphlets with a strong confessional agenda, such as Andreas Althamer's published sermon on the devil from 1532, or Johann Spreter's treatise on blessings and enchantments of 1543.[50] Sometimes Protestant and Catholic writers took part in complex rebuttals of each other, as in James Calfhill's and John Martiall's competing treatises on the religious significance of the cross from 1560s England, or Johannes Heerbrand's and Albrecht Hunger's rival sets of theological theses on magic from 1570s Germany.[51] At various points important borrowings and derivations of material will be indicated, since writers copied from each other both within and across the confessional and chronological divisions. The Jesuit Martín Delrio borrowed from the Lutheran Johann Georg Godelmann: both used material freely from Johann Weyer with or without acknowledgement.[52] But even as they copied from each other, even as they shared many cosmological assumptions, these writers read the divine dispensation for the created order differently.

The inquiry will demonstrate that the pastoral struggle to transform 'popular belief' started much earlier than the first exponents of 'Christianization' and 'disenchantment' imagined. Against the background of that medieval pastoral tradition, the decades of the Reformation functioned more as an interruption and a distraction than as the key moment in the assault on folk-beliefs. In a way, the most revealing point in the story is the one at which Europe's intellectual intelligentsia lost its *fear* of popular beliefs. The key stage in the process of 'disenchantment' may prove to have occurred when transforming the beliefs of ordinary people ceased to generate such desperate evangelical urgency in the minds of the clergy. Religious intellectuals who had undergone the 'disenchanting' process in their own worlds of faith and theology felt themselves free to abandon the long-standing and largely failed attempt to disenchant the rest of society. In the process they ceased to worry when poets, dramatists, and folklorists 're-enchanted' the European world in the service of art, culture, or indeed popular entertainment.

This is an appropriate point to confess that I am not entirely sure whether 'superstition' itself, in the sense of the great amorphous body of arbitrary and disjointed beliefs that people hold about their world, has a history in the strict sense of that term.[53] That is to say, I am uncertain whether one can construct any meaningful or useful explanatory narrative that demonstrates how one form of 'superstitious' mindset transformed itself into another across time. The difficulty may be evidential. It may simply not be possible to reconstruct beliefs that lack an analytical framework or literary record with sufficient detail. It may also be that traditional belief-systems partake too much of the bedrock of the human psyche to be truly susceptible of historical analysis. Beyond all doubt, on the other hand, the intellectual *response* to superstition has a history. The critique of superstition played itself out against the major trends and themes in Europe's intellectual life over a period of several centuries. Arguments were discovered, refined, adapted, and transformed in response to the religious, philosophical, and scientific changes in the broader culture of Europe from the late Middle Ages to the Enlightenment. Superstition may, or may not, have a history in this strict sense; the response to superstition certainly does have one. The latter history, the story of the response to superstition rather than the story of superstition itself, forms the theme of the chapters that follow.

Structure and limits of the book

The first two major sections of the book attempt to separate things that cannot be absolutely differentiated one from another, and yet must be distinguished if the subject is to be comprehensible. Part I (Chapters 1–4) discusses the phenomena of popular superstition as reported in the literature, predominantly the literature from the last two centuries or so of the European Middle Ages. Writers and preachers expended a great deal of time ostensibly describing the things that people did, or tried to do, to improve their lot in a fickle and dangerous world. Although those descriptions were never fully free from either constructive interpretation or normative judgements, they did present an image of the mind of the

'superstitious' that contained a range of common factors. In the first place
this image must be analysed and studied as just that—an image, whose
relationship to anything we might call 'reality' is at best suspect. At the
end of the fourth chapter, an attempt will be made to review the written
material in conjunction with the surviving codicological, physical, and
archaeological data. This will offer suggestions—if nothing more than
that—as to how far the image of 'superstitions' reflected the life of people
in the past.

Since the subject of this chapter is the late Middle Ages, the intersection
between the practices called 'superstitious' and those of traditional Catholic
Christianity demands particularly careful attention. Here one needs to keep
two principles in constant tension. On the one hand, medieval Christianity
was startlingly inclusive: it formed a vast, diverse, and seamless texture
where the exalted speculations of the mystics and the refined subtleties of
metaphysicians touched on devotional and pastoral theology and practice,
the strands reaching right across the spectrum to the most materialistic
and apparently 'mechanical' procedures of protective prayer and ritual. It
is entirely understandable that some historians steadfastly refuse to try to
draw lines of demarcation between different parts of medieval religious
culture, including it all under one umbrella of 'traditional religion'.[54]
However, in the minds of preachers and moralists *at the time*, this all-
inclusive coexistence of disparate elements seemed neither attractive nor
even acceptable. In fact, medieval writers did include among 'superstitions'
a significant proportion of what were sometimes called 'vain observances'.
Such things were practised largely or wholly within the Catholic religious
culture, but were also unacceptable to some theological opinion within it.
It is not that no distinction existed between acceptable and 'superstitious'
religious practices: rather, it was that clergy constantly debated over where
the distinction was to be drawn. Therefore, this chapter will include
a number of things that might, then and since, have been regarded as
perfectly acceptable 'folklorized' religious practice.

In the second part one remains with the Middle Ages, but moves
into the area of theological critique and censure of popular belief as the
theological writers portrayed it. A strong tradition of anti-superstitious
writing originated with Augustine and earlier writers, which the Middle
Ages inherited and modified. Chapters 5–9 explore the demonological
tradition in medieval ecclesiastical writing. The presence and activities of
evil spirits in the natural order served as the primary theological explanation

for nearly every effect allegedly claimed for 'superstitious' activities. On one hand, since demons occupied a distinct and agreed space within the natural order of created beings, there were limits to their power. A whole range of things lay beyond the power of demons, though God could and might chose to do such things and demons might aspire to mimic the divine. On the other hand, demons were conventionally credited with the power to generate illusions: so any reports that appeared to endow them with greater powers than scholastic demonology allowed could be 'explained away' as the result of artificially generated illusions playing on fallible human senses and minds.

In Chapter 8 some of the fault-lines and differences between the theological writers on superstitions will be excavated and explored. Although there was much shared culture among the theological critics of superstition, significant differences of approach also emerged, over major issues as well as details. This book suggests that, at heart, many of these differences resolved themselves into questions of theodicy, the great intractable dilemma of the origin of evil. Very broadly, theologians divided themselves into two groups. First, some writers portrayed God as the arbiter of a cosmic gymnasium or military training camp, where individual souls were pitted against demonic adversaries, equipped with a variety of resources, spiritual and physical, for their own protection, and more or less left to get on with the struggle. On the other hand, another group of theologians consisted of providentialists. They envisaged God controlling the malice of evil spirits with constant vigilance, only permitting human beings to suffer misfortune for specific reasons at specific times. This highly abstract question impacted on the practical advice that pastoral theologians gave clergy and laity. Broadly speaking, the more freedom demons had to do harm, the more leeway theologians would give ordinary people to use (approved, ecclesiastical) 'counter-magic' to protect themselves. The more providentialist writers tended to be more restrictive: if bad things happened to people for good reasons, then protecting oneself against misfortune was almost beside the point. This debate (often identified as an issue in the Protestant versus Catholic controversies of the early modern era) was closely anticipated in the diverse writings of the later scholastics.

Demonology provided the intellectual mechanism by which ecclesiastical writers converted folkloric beliefs and customs into something that was putatively, and in theological eyes actually, evil. The pastoral challenge for preachers and parish clergy was to 'convince' their audiences that something that they called a 'superstitious' activity, and which many ordinary people practised in the firm belief that it was harmless or beneficial—and even religious—was really part of a demonic conspiracy to destroy souls. In the encounter between pastoral theology and folklore, two rival interpretations of the invisible universe clashed. The paradoxes of studying this literature are many. The demonological treatises are copious and abundant, and present by far the fullest insight that we are likely to gain into the 'enchanted' mindset of medieval Europe. Yet it seems almost certain that their particular reading of the phenomena, their anxious, fervent conviction that superstitions were really the 'novitiate of the devil', convinced very few people beside themselves and their closest supporters. Even many clerics seem not to have been persuaded. Chapter 9 enters into the challenging question of how far the 'critique of superstition' actually impacted the pastoral work of Europe's clergy. To take either of the extreme positions, to claim that the pastoral campaign was either extremely effective or failed utterly to have any impact, would be equally mistaken. There is enough evidence to infer that the pastoral campaign to manage and control 'popular culture' began well before the Reformation; but there is also evidence of sufficient fragmentation, disagreement, and divided voices to explain many of its limitations.

With Part III the survey moves into the eras of the Renaissance and Reformations. The Christian humanists form an important prelude to the Reformation controversies, not least because so many of those who shaped the religious destiny of the sixteenth century were schooled in Christian humanism of some kind or another. The humanists radically shifted the emphasis in pastoral piety away from the correct performance of ritual towards ethics and personal spirituality. They did so principally for their own adepts: but they also had an impact on the pastoral language of the broader Church. 'Superstition' suddenly broadened its ambit to include not just wrong beliefs or wrong ceremonies, but wrong *attitudes* to rites and ceremonies: it was 'superstitious' to expect benefits even from an impeccably orthodox ritual if the appropriate ethical commitment were lacking. In the critique of 'superstition' the Renaissance constituted a paradoxical but vital prologue to the Reformation debates. In the area of theological responses to folk-beliefs (as elsewhere) Martin Luther stands as the Janus-figure, the transitional thinker who embraced an older world-view thoroughly, only to break it apart and build something new. Luther struck out on his own in many different and often contradictory respects.

He took evil, and the power of demonic evil, very seriously indeed. He enlarged the consequences of the fall to include not just human sinfulness, but the disordered nature of the entire creation. Yet no-one did more than Luther to discredit the notion that one could clamber up to heaven by a sequence of diligently performed religious rituals. The paradoxes of Luther's insights in this area demand a chapter to themselves (Chapter 11).

When speaking of the contributions of the wider Protestant Reformation on this subject, it is important to do full justice to a phenomenon that many other historians have already noted. The Protestant reformers cultivated a keen sense of the active role of God in the created order, and a vigorous and articulated demonology. They collected evidence of prodigies, portents, and 'special providences'. Their 'critique of superstition' certainly did not extend as far as nineteenth-century liberal theologians might have wished. Their cosmos was as spirit-filled and as ethically driven as that of their medieval predecessors. Chapter 12 explores these aspects of the picture in some detail. It also points out some important shifts in attitude that lay embedded within the sixteenth-century context. Special providences and portents were definitely to be expected: apparitions of the dead or miraculous exorcisms of spirits were not. One hypothesis about the inner logic of the Protestant critique may help to explain the disagreement between recent and older historians. It is perfectly possible for a religious movement to contain within it the seeds of a later development: but for those seeds not to germinate in the first, second, or third generation, because other factors in the cultural environment prevent them from doing so. To put it bluntly, those historians of 'ideal-types' who postulated something inherently modernizing in the ideas of the Reformation may have been conceptually correct: but the modernizing potential that they discerned may not have been realized in fact, because too many other cultural assumptions stood in the way. Although Protestantism was clearly not 'modern' in any absolute sense, it may in some way prove to have been modern *manqué*.

Pursuing this possibility, Chapter 13 argues that the differences that separated the reformers from medieval Catholicism on the 'superstition' issue were profound and critical. The reformers argued that Catholic ceremonies, which claimed to protect the faithful from demonic malice and misfortune, essentially suffered from the same error as the popular superstitions that they criticized. In particular, a chorus of Protestant thinkers denounced the notion that rituals of consecration could modify or transform physical objects—water, salt, oil, candles, parchment, and so forth—by giving these things spiritual potency to resist evil. This was, for Protestant thought, magical thinking pure and simple. So, by a bizarre switch of rhetoric, Protestant writers denounced the things that medieval Catholicism had called into being as *preservatives* against evil, deploying against these consecrated objects exactly the same arguments that medieval Catholics had in their turn used against the rituals and objects of popular magic. The same demonological argument that medieval pastoral theologians used against magical charms now applied to Catholic rites. If a Catholic ritual 'worked', it was only because the devil made it appear to work, in order to seduce people further into error. To expect to manipulate the universe supernaturally through ritual amounted therefore to diabolical magic or, at best, the false expectation of a miracle. Miracles, which had been a resource in the earliest ages of the Church, were now ceased and no longer to be expected. It was simple blasphemy to claim that the Church could deploy supernatural power ritually and at will to protect people.

Beyond these arguments, the now conventional postulate that Protestantism was as 'enchanted' and devil-ridden as its medieval predecessors proves to require some important qualifications. Chapter 14 considers how reformed thought addressed the perennial question of theodicy. The reformers inclined, for the most part, to the extreme providentialist view that evil occurred through an ultimately wise, though deeply hidden and mysterious, decision of God. Consequently, all the resources to resist misfortune that had been zealously cultivated in the old Church were beside the point. More deeply still, the reformers' providentialism cast the role of the devil and evil spirits in general into a very different role. The devil was, at best, an entirely captive instrument of the divine purposes. The most dangerous thing that the devil could do to people was, in truth, to persuade them of wrong opinions.

Chapter 15 explores the diversity of responses to the debate over superstition found among the theologians of the Catholic reform. The debate over superstition illustrated almost more poignantly than anything else the variety of possible directions that Catholic polemic needed to take in order to sustain and defend the Roman Catholic Church in the era of confessional diversity. On one hand, Catholic theologians argued that nothing had changed since the Middle Ages: superstitions were wrong for exactly the same reasons as they had been before. On another, the reformers of Catholic Christendom aspired to purge, to purify, and to some extent to homogenize the liturgical resources of Christianity, although their desire for homogeneity has sometimes been exaggerated.[55] Thirdly, Catholic theologians responded with outrage to the Protestant arguments that equated Catholic liturgical practice with superstitious magic. They defended the authenticity and value of the officially approved rites by which the Church defended people against hostile forces and powers. These last two objectives tended to counteract each other. The potential existed for real conflict at the heart of the Counter-Reformation; that such conflict was not generally realized owed much to the fact that different arguments could be deployed in different contexts according to the pastoral need in a given area.

In Part IV the book begins to consider the breakdown of the consensus over Aristotelian cosmology and demonology in the seventeenth century, and the theological implications of that breakdown. Within various traditions derived from the Reformation, first nearer the radical margins and subsequently more in the mainstream, views arose which challenged the traditional view of the cosmos and the presence of spirit-beings within it. This trend derived as much from growing religious diversity as from new scientific theories about matter and the universe. In either case the effect was the same. The consensus over demons, and therefore over the possibilities, causes, and limitations of magical and 'superstitious' activities, broke down. It now became possible to argue, with greater clarity and conviction than before, that certain reported phenomena simply could not and therefore did not happen. It became possible to dispute the traditional explanations for the supposedly occult causes and connections between things.

A second critical change occurred towards the end of the seventeenth century in most, though not all, of the countries of Europe. The restraints of confessional discipline over religious thought and practice slackened very perceptibly. As a consequence, forms of deviant belief that might previously have been feared as the result of demonic threats were now treated with indifference or even with mockery.[56] The strict religious restraints that had been characteristic of the confessional age broke down, as new generations saw and were appalled by the catastrophic effects of dogmatically driven community strife. In this age also, though not at once and certainly not everywhere, belief in witchcraft began to lose the support of criminal justice systems in Western Europe. However, there was also an important contrary drift. As confessional dogma and Aristotelian physics alike lost their grip, many thinkers feared their world was slipping into pure materialism and atheism. Consequently, as Chapter 17 demonstrates, a sudden, anxious quest began to validate the 'supernatural'. Things that would in the past have been feared as the delusions of devils were now anxiously sought out in order to prove the existence of the 'invisible world'. The sceptical and the credulous movements of thought responded to each other, and in a sense needed each other. There would not have been the same urgency about the attack on 'Saducism' and the rediscovery of the spiritual world, if that world had not been believed to be under real attack.

In Chapter 18 the frame moves on to the early eighteenth century and the first decades of the Enlightenment. Ultimately the scope of reference for the term 'superstition' was enlarged to include all 'irrational' aspects of religious practice, discipline, or custom. The antithesis between superstition and 'reason' did not first appear in the Enlightenment, as many might suppose. Late scholasticism, especially of a nominalist variety, had repeatedly referred to the 'unreasonableness' of a superstitious practice as grounds to reject it. However, in the eighteenth century the criterion of reason took centre stage. 'Reason' is of course a flexible and variable concept, determined by perspective and assumptions. Some historians have argued that an early Enlightenment figure like Pierre Bayle derived much of his critique of contemporary religion from his own Calvinist religious roots, rather than from any abstract 'reason' divorced from religious thinking.[57] The revisionist view that highlights the religious background of such early Enlightenment figures as Bayle is helpful to this project. It shows how the eighteenth-century critique of 'superstitious' religion did not spring from nothing, nor did it break absolutely with what had been said and written before it. It is also important to register the contribution of baroque Catholic authors in this area such as Jean-Baptiste Thiers and François LeBrun, whose works appeared in a large composite edition in the 1730s.[58] Here again, one finds considerable elements of continuity as well as evidence of gradual modernization in the presentation of the traditional superstition-critique.

Nevertheless, there were important disjunctions as well as continuities between the confessional era and the Enlightenment. A significant shift took place in the vocabulary of intellectual discussion of religion. 'Superstition' ceased to be something putatively external, anathematized from *within* the theological establishment. The term now meant something *about* the way Christianity itself was practised that appalled the *philosophes*, whether they were actively religious or not. The moral outrage of Enlightenment thought focused consistently on certain targets: religious intolerance and violence from the elites, ignorance and primitivism on the part of the majority. Such a reordering of priorities could not fail to alter the way in which the discourse around 'superstition' was conducted. An important consequence of Enlightenment critiques of religion 'gone wrong' was the rise of historical interpretations of the evolution of Christianity itself. Such historicist readings of the religious past were not new. Some of the historical critiques previously assumed to be typical of the eighteenth century were in fact adumbrated by the Protestant reformers two centuries earlier. Nevertheless, the *philosophes* adopted some of the rhetoric and logic of the Protestant reformers only to direct it towards a very different goal.

Most historians now revise the traditional reading of the Enlightenment by taking its overall commitment to 'reason' with a significant pinch of salt. Even amongst those who participated fully in the cosmopolitan literary and philosophical culture of the mid-eighteenth century, many had a taste for the exotic, the bizarre, and the outré. Such tastes sat very ill with some of the propaganda about rationality and ethical sense set forth by Voltaire and his kind. One should take full account of the ways in which the Enlightenment may have been gently subverted by some of its own exponents. As with the potentially modernizing effects of the Reformation, there may have been a credibility gap between intention and achievement. The religious philosophers of the eighteenth century inhabited a world where most people still lived in a profoundly pre-modern mindset. Witch-trials continued in some parts of Europe, Protestant and Catholic, into the eighteenth century. Demonology and exorcism remained serious subjects for discussion among religious leaders of all kinds. The response to miraculous occurrences was not always one of unrestrained intellectual scepticism.[59]

The final chapter will conclude with a brief look forward to the era of Romanticism, in which the intelligentsia of Europe finally lost not only its fear but also its disdain for popular legend, folklore, and ritual. After decades of rather brittle propaganda for rationalism, Europe's intellectual and spiritual life rediscovered tradition in the name of national and ethnic particularity. The folklorists of post-Enlightenment France and Germany treated the popular legends of supernatural power neither as evidence of demonic seduction nor as embarrassing primitive relics to be discarded. Rather, they collected them as the fragile pressed flowers of a pre-modern cultural identity under threat of modernization and urbanization. It may be that, in order to treat the lore of spirits and occult causes with the curiosity of the collector, one must first be utterly removed from the world where these things are sources of fear or alarm. The interest of Romantic-era folklorists in the subject matter of European superstitions and their accompanying beliefs may represent the moment when the magical and the demonic finally lost the power to frighten those who studied it.

It is important, finally, to identify certain things that this book deliberately and intentionally either does not attempt to address at all, or at least declines to try to cover comprehensively.

1. This book presents an analysis of a body of literature. No systematic attempt is made to evaluate the institutional or legal impact of the ideas discussed here. In various parts of Europe, the critique of superstition was sometimes translated into concrete judicial procedures, by consistories and kirk sessions in Reformed countries or offices of the Inquisition in Italy or Spain. Pastoral visitations conducted under the inspiration of the Council of Trent and its programmes often included in their questionnaires inquiries about 'superstitious' practices. However, the institutional implementation of the critique forms a whole vast subject on its own, and is excluded from this study for reasons of space and coherence. Consequently, large-scale socio-historical questions about the 'acculturation' or 'social control' of the mass of Europe's people are not posed except insofar as they emerge from the theological and philosophical written sources.

2. The book focuses primarily on superstitions and the learned response to them. Even though 'superstition' had a distinct and relatively consistent 'core' in the shape of healing and protective charms, folk-beliefs about spiritual beings, and the arts of divination, it still proved an extremely elastic term, especially when used collusively as a term of abuse or opprobrium. While the dividing line between superstition and obviously related subjects such as magic, witchcraft, possession, and astrology is hazy at best, some limits have to be set to the study. So intellectual magic, as practised by learned adepts with the use of grimoires or occult manuals like the *Key of Solomon*, is largely excluded. The present book does not seek to add in any substantial way to the already vast and prodigious literature on the witch-hunting manuals, except in so far as these may also have contributed to the superstition-critique. Neither does it discuss actual records of trials for witchcraft, nor the reasons for the decline and end of witch-hunting in Europe. Possession and exorcism figure only in so far as they came to

be included in the discourse of the power of demons, and later in the debate over the putatively 'superstitious' character of Roman Catholicism. Learned astrology figures only as reflected in the critiques of theological writers: it is not evaluated or described in detail for itself. To have treated all such tangential subjects adequately would have made for a vast book.

3. This book presents arguments rooted in history, not in anthropology, philosophy, or religious studies. Consequently it uses terms as they are found in historical sources, without seeking to relate these to any more absolute or abstract nomenclature or set of concepts. The terminology used in this book is not intended to bear transfer to or automatic comparison with that used on evidence found in other parts of the Christian world beyond Western Europe, or indeed in other faiths. The outcomes of this study may well be suggestive for, and receive illumination from, comparison with entirely different fields of inquiry into the religious mind. However, once again a limit has to be set to the present study: that limit is set by the fairly broad parameters of the sources discussed in the following pages.

This work claims that only by understanding the complex rational structures that the thinkers of pre-modern Europe erected to try to understand their world, can we begin to write a satisfying account of pre-industrial European culture. Medieval and early modern Europeans read their world theologically, and we must take their theological readings of it seriously. At the same time, the relationship between theological culture and the cultures of the less educated remains constantly problematical. We cannot assume either that these cultures integrated seamlessly with each other, any more than we can postulate rigid unbridgeable divides between them. Finally, this book does imply—to say the least—that the origins of 'modernity' are inextricably tied up with the complex business of faith seeking (rational) understanding. Europe's people found that the landmarks by which they marked out the approved and received understanding of their universe were subtly but decisively shifted in the course of the later Middle Ages and the early modern period. The story is a complex one and demands all the ingenuity of historians to chart it. There is, however, a very important story to be told.

PART

I

Discerning and Controlling Invisible Forces: The Image of 'Superstition' in the Literature

No issue in medieval theological thought was more closely tied down to the elemental physical realities of life than the debate over superstitions. When Christian thinkers challenged the beliefs of ordinary people about their universe, they confronted certain life-threatening and life-changing aspects of human life. They also engaged in theological analysis of beliefs and processes that were at heart instinctive and traditional. Part I of this book attempts to represent, describe, and in some modest degree to analyse the image of the folkloric world of pre-modern Europe presented by the literature on superstitions. The people of the later Middle Ages, according to the writers on superstition, lived in a world beset by insecurities and dangers. Beside the obvious and entirely natural threats to their physical well-being and security, they also feared the effects of a range of hostile or harmful occult activities, many of which do not sit comfortably within the catch-all category of 'witchcraft' used then and since to describe them. They believed in the existence of a whole range of invisible beings and forces, which could not be incorporated at all easily into the cosmology of religious orthodoxy. They attempted to control, or just to safeguard, their destinies through an array of procedures. Some of these were entirely orthodox in the majority view of the Church of the time, while others would have aroused alarm in many and outright condemnation from the theologically literate. By far the greatest and most interesting proportion of these putatively 'helpful procedures' belonged in a debatable grey area, where some people—even among the clergy—approved and others disapproved. In short, the people depicted by superstition-writers supposedly believed that their lives were pushed this way and that by a variety of forces that could not be easily discerned, and which could only barely be controlled by the use of the appropriate rituals. Finally, they tried to gain insight into the mysteries of their world by a variety of techniques of divination. They identified meaning and insight in the otherwise arbitrary and random chances and coincidences of life, to foretell the future, explain the mysterious, and plan against misfortune.

The following four chapters will unpack the various parts of the image described above. The material chosen will largely date from before the impact of the sixteenth-century Reformation movements, although occasionally it is desirable to include material from a later date for the sake of clarity and effective illustration. When all these aspects of the allegedly 'superstitious' mindset are heaped together, the effect must be admitted to be just a little implausible. How many people could really have been so concerned by and with invisible forces? While theologians from time to time wrote about 'the superstitious' as though they were a separate class of people, it is probably more likely that fragmentary aspects of this world-view affected different sorts of people, and different individuals, at different times. In any event, towards the end of this part of the book some attempt will be made to evaluate the theological picture of superstitions and to gauge, however provisionally, where it may have touched some kind of reality.

I

The Problems of Pre-modern Life

M edieval and early modern life was precarious. An earlier generation of family historians used to surmise that pre-modern people must have been so cauterized by the dismal sequence of troubled and dangerous childbirths, infant and child mortality, and premature death through accident, misfortune, and unexplained diseases that they would have learned to suppress feelings of emotional warmth towards their family members.[1] Subsequent studies in all kinds of sources have largely discredited these assumptions. There is no reason to think that the pain and bitterness of life afflicted people in the past with any less visceral feelings of insecurity and grief than their modern counterparts experience.[2] Moreover, the theological analyses of superstition identify a range of areas where people were believed to feel particularly vulnerable. People could expect to suffer harm, wrote a variety of Thomist commentators, in their possessions, their reputation, their body, their use of reason, and their life.[3]

Bodily illness, disease, and injury

While many of these areas of potential misfortune may seem obvious, it is useful to enumerate them more or less schematically and to explain what are represented as being the greatest sources of worry. First and foremost, people feared sickness and disease.[4] Obvious as this may seem, it is striking how little discussion of physical illness occupies the superstition writers. On the whole it is assumed that people fall sick, children especially, and that most of their illnesses are of physical rather than supernatural origin. Surprisingly perhaps, a fairly clear conceptual distinction existed in the minds of pre-modern physicians and theological observers alike between natural and supernatural illness. Most illnesses were assumed to be caused naturally (even when a prior cause in the form of divine providence was inferred) and therefore called for natural medical remedies. Theological commentators on superstitions on the whole left what they deemed 'natural' medicine with a fairly clear territory to work in. Believers were expected to 'honour the physician for the need thou hast of him', as the text of Ecclesiasticus, or the Wisdom of Jesus son of Sirach advised.[5] This text was regularly taken to mean that physical illnesses should be treated with physical remedies, accompanied doubtless with patience and prayer, but not to the exclusion of the natural means of relief.[6] Theologians could from time to time censure physicians who strayed outside what the former took to be the proper realm of 'natural' medicine: but that realm was of itself privileged and respected.[7]

There existed, however, a second class of illnesses which appear also to have been feared, and in a fairly distinct way. These were the illnesses that supposedly had been inflicted by hostile sorcery. Physicians sometimes diagnosed and distinguished between the two categories of illness, though they often disagreed with each other in applying the distinction. The criterion could be as vague and as flimsy as the fact that a disease resisted normal treatments. However, more commonly magical illness was diagnosed by the presence of inappropriate foreign matter appearing mysteriously in the body. Several writers remarked on peculiar episodes in which hairs or pig's bristles appeared within the body without the skin being broken.[8] Others remarked on the appearance of needles, keys, and bones within the body.[9] The most notorious—but by no means the first—writer to describe this sort of problem was the maverick empirical physician Theophrastus Paracelsus. He noted that illnesses inflicted by sorcery tended to introduce by occult means ashes, hairs, fishbones, and other foreign matter into the body. He recommended the use of sympathetic magic learned from Gypsies to deal with it.[10] The more rationalistic Johann Weyer, meanwhile, regaled his readers with horror-stories of Paracelsian doctors who artificially introduced noxious foreign bodies into their patients' wounds and sores. By this means they hoped to make ordinary infections appear to have been caused by sorcery, and so to justify the use of their peculiar remedies.[11]

One genuinely popular fear, found especially but not exclusively in southern Europe, concerned 'fascination' or the 'evil eye'. The best evidence for the popular character of this fear is the fact that, despite the literary traditions surrounding it, theological writers interpreted it differently. In essence 'evil eye' consisted of the belief that an ill-intentioned person could cause sickness in another person, especially a child, simply by looking at them.[12] Theologians became involved because the Latin term used to denote the phenomenon, *fascinum*, inevitably came under discussion whenever Galatians 3 was expounded.[13] Thomas Aquinas contributed a key exposition of evil eye, which nearly every superstition-writer quoted. He cited the *Glosa Ordinaria* to the effect that 'some people have burning eyes, and by their look alone can harm others, especially children'.[14] He then contributed a complex physiological-theological explanation: the subtle spirits gathered in the eyes and were exuded into the air; when those spirits were poisonous and noxious they penetrated and caused sickness in those with thin skins, especially children. Aquinas then rather spoilt the point of this physical explanation by suggesting that some pact between sorcerers and demons was also involved.[15] Most authors followed Aquinas, including his final point that associated this effect with sorcery.[16] However, Martín de Castañega argued quite the contrary, that the effect of the evil eye derived from noxious humours in post-menopausal women and was entirely natural. Therefore the protection conventionally used, of hanging a piece of mirror between the child's eyes to reflect the 'rays', was a thoroughly natural and appropriate remedy.[17] Pedro Ciruelo argued both ways, suggesting that there was one form of *aojamiento* caused by natural transmission of humours and another caused by hostile sorcery.[18]

Accidental injury provoked as great a concern as illness. While pre-industrial people were spared the scourge of automobile accidents, the horse was still a dangerous and temperamental form of transport. The risks of a fall from horseback figure several times in the literature.[19] At a time when men above a certain social rank habitually went around armed, the risks of accidental injury from swords, or even more from firearms, were a regular source of worry. Several sources report that it was customary to enchant one's own weapons so that one could not be harmed by them. Martin Luther even recalled seeing a young man bend his sword double against his own chest to prove the point.[20] Given the amount of emphasis that has been placed—by medieval writers as well as modern commentators—on the alleged propensity of women to engage in superstitious practices,[21] it is interesting to note that soldiers also figured quite prominently in the stories of superstitious activities.[22] There could hardly be a lifestyle more at risk of unpredictable and critical injury, whether accidental or deliberate, than that of the soldier. Wounds—whether acquired in battle or otherwise—required a specialized form of treatment and even a specialized category of practitioners, the so-called *Wundtsegners*, who would claim to heal wounds by the ritualized application of plain cloths without plasters or bandages.[23] The custom also developed of healing injuries by binding up the weapon that had inflicted the injury rather than the wound itself (supposing that the weapon could be retrieved).[24] It goes without saying that accidental death also often meant sudden death. For those who took seriously the claims of the medieval Church about the vital importance of deathbed confession, the risks of sudden death were a real and, as far as we can see, a serious worry. A whole range of protective devices—usually in this case wrapped around the ceremonies of the Church—were supposed to guarantee escape from sudden death for at least the current day, or in exceptional cases for life.[25]

Mysterious reproduction and fragile childhood

The mysterious and often dangerous business of human reproduction generated a whole set of fears and concerns that are amply documented in the literature.[26] Some of the earliest evidence for this concern occurs in Burchard of Worms's work of pastoral guidance, the 'Corrector' which forms book 19 of his canon law collection dating from the early eleventh century.[27] In one of the sample interrogations to be made of women, he asks:

Have you done as some adulterous women are accustomed to do? When they first learn that their lovers wish to go back to their lawful wives, then by some craft of sorcery they suppress the men's desire, such that they are of no use to their legitimate [spouses] and cannot have intercourse with them. If you have done this or taught others to do so, you must do penance for 40 days on bread and water.[28]

Burchard thus established as canonical the theory, already adumbrated in a discussion by Hincmar of Rheims,[29] that men could be made impotent—and selectively impotent, towards one woman but not another—by acts of sorcery. In due course this principle found its way into Peter Lombard's *Book of Sentences*, where it formed one of a series of debatable points on the nullity of marriage discussed in book 4, distinction 34, and similarly into Gratian's *Decretum*.[30] By the late Middle Ages it was conventional to suppose that sympathetic magic, in the form of a bent needle placed in the man's bed to represent a failed erection, could be used to cause impotence. An important piece of casuistry attributed to Duns Scotus declared that it was quite acceptable to destroy the 'token' of the impotence in order to break the spell.[31] It is difficult to tell in this case whether the increasingly elaborate discussion of impotence through sorcery in scholastic theology reflected any increase in the real concern at local level. We may be observing nothing more than the innate tendency of scholastic analysis to become every more 'subtle' and multi-branched.[32]

However, the fear of unexplained impotence afflicting husbands was only the mildest and most predictable of these concerns. By the later fifteenth century, at the very latest, theological sources were reporting that men sometimes experienced, or feared they experienced, the complete disappearance of the phallus through sorcery. The conventional theological analysis of this emasculation insisted that the male member was merely occluded by a demonic illusion and would reappear as normal when the illusion was removed.[33] A humorous tale told by the Swiss cleric Felix Hemmerli confirms that this notion of illusory removal was known, at least to the tellers of amusing anticlerical stories, in the mid-fifteenth century.[34] However, the folkloric treatment of the subject is somewhat different. The legend circulated in late medieval Germany that someone who had suffered this form of emasculation was taken by a sorcerer to a nest in a tree where a large number of phalluses were gathered, moving around like small birds. The implication in the folk-tale is that the male members had really disappeared and been transported elsewhere, rather than just disappearing through illusion.[35] This combination of theology and folklore suggests that some men felt their sexual identities to be under threat in the later Middle Ages. Whether sorcery was the primary source of this fear or a convenient second-order explanation remains to be explored.[36]

The processes of pregnancy and childbirth posed constant risks to the life of both mother and child. The circumstances of medieval and early modern childbirth and lying-in remained an almost entirely female realm, from which male medical practitioners (and indeed male family members also in many cases) were excluded. From Johannes Nider in the fifteenth century to Laurent Joubert in the later sixteenth, an intellectual convention assumed that pregnancy and childbirth attracted more than its share of traditional lore, supposition, and custom.[37] Given the condescension with which male ecclesiastical writers habitually treated female cultural zones, one may feel tempted to exercise some scepticism on this point.[38] However, it is reasonable to mark childbirth as a primary area of human vulnerability that would naturally provoke the search for ritual assistance. While some older writings on witchcraft implied that midwives were either particularly prone to be superstitious or particularly exposed to accusations of sorcery, this suggestion simply does not match the evidence for much of early modern Europe. Midwives were, at least in the more structured polities of Europe, a relatively privileged class of women whose quasi-professional credentials and obligatory reputation for piety distanced them from the traditional image of the superstitious 'old wife' cultivated in some ecclesiastical lore.[39] On the other hand, the lying-in maids, much less experienced and usually younger or poorer women who attended new mothers during the very vulnerable early days after birth, might well incur suspicion and arouse fear.[40]

But what if the child did not thrive? Obviously children were even more exposed to the dangers of disease and premature mortality than the rest of the population. Like illness in general, illness in children was so axiomatic a fact of life that the superstition-literature seldom dwelt upon it. Martin Luther did identify and describe some diseases of childhood that were supposedly talked about in his region of Saxony, diagnosed according to tradition in various strange ways.[41] However, one particular form of childhood under-development attracted a significant amount of lore, both intellectual and popular. The thirteenth-century encyclopedist William of Auvergne was one of the first writers in the high Middle Ages to document the belief in the 'changeling' child, the weak, feeble, pale child who would not thrive, supposedly consumed vast amounts of nourishment without gaining much substance, and eventually disappeared altogether.[42] The term 'changeling' referred to the belief that the real child had been substituted by a spirit-child without the parents' knowledge, only to prove as insubstantial and incorporeal as its origins dictated. William of Auvergne's description of the phenomenon was duly copied by Jakob of Jüterbogk, Johannes Nider, Johannes Geiler von Kaisersberg, and Silvestro Mazzolini of Priero, among others.[43] Martin Luther also included the changeling story in his account of German folk-culture.[44]

Loss of reason

It was not just children who might fail to develop and behave as expected. Adults also supposedly lived in fear of the loss of their reason, which could damage their reputations or change their personalities altogether. While it is conventional to suppose that possession by evil spirits or demonic forces was the normal pre-industrial explanation for psychiatric disorders, the situation depicted in the ecclesiastical literature of the later Middle Ages appeared somewhat more complex. Contemporary literature referred to people suffering from 'frenzy', in which their ability to be spiritually responsible was diminished. In such circumstances the sacrament of extreme unction was believed to be capable of inducing a period of calm and reflection in which the sufferer might make proper preparation for death.[45] In contrast to 'frenzy' or mental distress stood the relatively rare and sometimes spectacular phenomenon of demonic possession. In this instance the personality of the individual was supposed to be taken over entirely by a demon. The demon then spoke through the voice and body of the individual, but expressed a quite different personality. Clerical writers habitually diagnosed demonic possession by the fact that sufferers not only lost their natural characteristics, but sometimes gained whole new abilities as well as personalities. A case in point was related by Johannes Nider. Heinrich Kalteisen of Coblenz, the celebrated Dominican inquisitor and Nider's contemporary, had reported that in the Dominican house in 's-Hertogenbosch a young novice found in the garden a white cabbage: he ate it without saying a blessing and unknowingly consumed a very dangerous demon. He started to suffer fits during the prayers; when he recovered he could speak Latin and French, and knew many passages of the Bible by heart, none of which abilities he had possessed before. He said that he had seen wonderful things in the heavens. The brothers suspected that he was possessed with a demon, which they confirmed to their own satisfaction when he refused to take the Eucharist. After exorcism he was left as stupid and ignorant as he had been previously.[46]

However, human beings might act inappropriately and unexpectedly for other reasons. A range of fears and embarrassments surrounded human sexual attraction. Extreme or inappropriate attraction between those who were not married, or repulsion between those who were, could be attributed to hostile magical practices.[47] Priests also reportedly feared the damage to reputation that might ensue from liaisons or attractions they felt themselves unable to control. Inordinate passions would be troubling to the ecclesiastical writers, and not just because they might afflict members of their order more than others, or because they had more to lose from loss of reputation than laymen. The intellectual difficulty was that, as will be clarified later, theological orthodoxy absolutely rejected the idea that the devil could control the will of a conscious person. (A possessed person, in contrast, supposedly lost the control of his or her body entirely.) If anyone could claim that 'the devil made me do it', the whole issue of personal responsibility for sin would have been cast into doubt.[48] So, the anxiety demonstrated in the literature about inordinate passions does not appear, in this instance, to spring chiefly from clerical concerns. If anything it was rather a conceptually embarrassing issue.

Agriculture

So far this review has concentrated on direct threats to the body or the mind of human beings. According to the literature people also feared indirect threats to their well-being, in the form of damage to the fragile systems of nutritional support on which Europe's people depended.[49] Farmers depended on the health of their livestock as much as on their own strength and well-being. The mid-fifteenth-century canonist Felix Hemmerli began his *Treatise on Exorcisms* with a sympathetic discussion of a farmer's concern over his sick cow.[50] Animals might fall sick purely and simply, but they might also fail inexplicably in their agricultural role. Geiler von Kaisersberg described how cows supposedly went dry of their milk, because witches were spiriting the milk away to an axe-head planted in a wooden post, from which they milked the axe and 'stole' the milk.[51] Heinrich Krämer, and following him Silvestro Mazzolini, reported a peculiar method by which countrywomen supposedly used the cow to detect where the witch lived who had stolen its milk.[52]

The health and welfare of crops was if anything even more precarious than that of livestock. The classic form that this problem assumed, in the superstition literature, was the summer hailstorm that came out of nowhere, flattened the crops, and caused the harvest to rot just as it was approaching maturity. A number of writers and illustrators referred to the possibility that such hailstorms were generated by hostile magic. Apart from demonstrating the resilience of literary tradition, this explanation may reflect the fact that such storms seemed not only particularly damaging but also particularly mysterious and unexpected.[53] Even in relatively dry Spain, one reads of 'storm-charmers' trying to move storms by ritual away from their community and its fields.[54] In arid parts of Europe, drought might arouse as great a fear as hailstorms. The whole of Martín of Arles's treatise on superstitions was provoked, he claimed, by a folklorized religious practice used to bring rain in the dry season in his home territory of Navarre.[55]

Challenges to crops could also come in the form of pests or predators. In many different circumstances commentators referred to fears about damage to livestock and crops from the hostility of nature. Wolves might ravage flocks of sheep, and ritual means would be sought to prevent this.[56] Mice and insect pests might gnaw their way through whole fields of grain. According to Felix Hemmerli, in his own time a bishop of Lausanne caused exorcisms drawn from scripture to be uttered and pronounced for a certain number of days against leeches which were attacking the salmon in Lake Geneva, biting them lethally and driving them to the shore. The fear of pests was not limited to land-based harvests.[57] In this instance some clerical ingenuity was employed to justify and make coherent sense of the long-standing ecclesiastical practice of exorcizing pests.[58] In a celebrated episode in the sixteenth century, a secular judge of Autun, Barthelemi Chasseneux, wrote a long legal opinion as to whether the mass trial in absence of the local rats for devouring the corn was legitimate or not.[59] Another form of misfortune that provoked special discussion was unexplained exhaustion or sickness in horses. According to Geiler von Kaisersberg, horses commonly exhibited signs of having been harnessed up and ridden hard at the end of what should have been a quiet night's rest in their stables. Folklore apparently blamed these symptoms on witches riding the horses as the result of some sorcery. Interestingly, Geiler was sceptical about this claim and suspected grooms of riding the horses without permission.[60]

Lost goods

One final category of misfortune called forth comments from the theological writers and, if we are to believe them, a quest for supernatural remedies. Lost property, or stolen property, was a regular concern of pre-industrial people when houses could not be made secure and locked strong-boxes were a prerogative of the relatively wealthy. Animals could stray, small household objects could be misplaced, and anything large or small could be stolen by neighbours or servants. The variety of procedures for 'finding thieves' was quite exotic. One interesting aspect of this form of misfortune was that nothing remotely supernatural was involved in the problem, even if ritual means were invoked for a cure.

It would be tempting to separate out the misfortunes described above into those that absolutely anyone could experience regardless of their beliefs, versus those where the misfortune was to some extent in the eye and the mind of the sufferer. Anyone can suffer physical illness, accidental injury, or the loss of goods through the caprices of nature or the malice of neighbours. Only those disposed culturally or temperamentally to see things thus, however, would perceive themselves to experience hostile sorcery, demonic possession, or the mysterious joy-riding of their horses by witches in the night. However, it would almost certainly be a mistake to imagine that one class of pre-modern people feared only natural misfortune and that a second class, the 'superstitious', also feared harm from occult sources. In fact, popular myth and ecclesiastical lore agreed that misfortunes could have either natural or occult causes, though these causes were differently understood from within theological culture as opposed to from outside it. One of the chief dividing-points between these two cultures was the invisible population of the universe. What sort of creatures besides God and people were at work in the cosmos? The answer proved more complex than theologians would have wished.

2

A Densely Populated Universe

With this chapter the lineaments of 'popular' belief suddenly become much less clear. In the case of misfortunes there appears to have been considerable consensus between the culture of the theologians who wrote the bulk of the surviving literature, and the rest of the population who coped with such matters in their everyday lives. In the case of the invisible creatures of the world there was a real and vital rift between the two cultures. Yet discerning the beliefs of non-theologians about the spirit world challenges the skills of critical analysis. Only as a last resort will this survey review works of imaginative literature or the output of folklorists. In the case of the former, it is impossible to know how seriously to take the imaginative world of, say, *The Tempest, A Midsummer Night's Dream,* or *The Faerie Queen.* In the case of folklorists' inquiries it is sometimes difficult to date the stories precisely, and the problem of constructive imagination arises there also. For preference, the approach used here will be to read the theological treatises (as it were) against themselves. Where they criticize a belief as something people believed and ought not to have done, it will be assumed, provisionally, that they were not attacking an imaginary foe and that some people did hold the views criticized.

Morally ambiguous fairies

At a special meeting of the Faculty of Theology of the University of Paris held at St Mathurin's on 19 September 1398, the Faculty adopted the definition of certain 'errors' that were commonly held in relation to magic. The 'errors' were almost certainly codified by the chancellor of the university, Jean Gerson. Gerson then expanded this list of errors with a discursive treatise *On Errors Regarding the Magic Art and the Condemned Articles*, subsequently published in his collected works and elsewhere.[1] Most of the 'errors' refuted in the articles stated that it was permissible to conjure demons, to use them for divination, and to achieve magical effects. Included within them was this statement: '22. That some demons are good, some are benign, some know all things, some are neither saved nor damned. *Error*.'[2] Gerson felt it was necessary to refute the belief that invisible spirits were morally diverse or ambiguous. This belief (as Chapters 6 and 7 will explain) rejected centuries of theological orthodoxy. If such a belief was current in the years around 1400, it was not derived from the teachings of the theologians.

A working hypothesis can be extracted from the superstition-literature. In the popular mind (as well as in certain forms of neoplatonic thought current in the Renaissance derived from Iamblichus and Proclus) spiritual creatures were believed to be diverse and varied in their characters and moral significance. The world was liberally and abundantly populated with creatures who did not fit into the Christian-Aristotelian-Thomist categories of God, people, angels, and demons. These creatures could interact with people in a range of ways, sometimes as friends or helpers, sometimes as sources of threats or mischief. Generally speaking the theological literature classes them, as it were by elimination, as 'demons'; but it also testifies, through the beliefs that it rejects, to a more complex classification.

It would seem that pre-modern people were relatively comfortable with the idea of spirit-creatures being around them, even in their households. From various parts of Europe come stories about 'ladies of the house', mostly female spirits supposed to take part in the housekeeping and reward good housewives. In Alfonso de Spina's work they were called 'duen de casa'. In the Sicilian fairy cult discovered in inquisitorial papers by Gustav Henningsen, they were known as the 'ladies from outside', and described as brilliantly dressed, small female creatures with paws rather than feet.[3] In Germany they went (and in some circles still do) by the name of 'Wichtelin'. Martin Luther reported that

some people have certain domestic demons, in the same way as there used once to be *lares familiares*, who sometimes appear by day. Some people in the vernacular call these *Vichtelen*, others *Helekeppelin*. It is believed that a house is most fortunate, if it is occupied by these illusions of demons; people are more afraid to give offence to those demons than to God and the whole world.[4]

Clearly these creatures were not feared as the ecclesiastics thought they should be. Johann Weyer, who stood somewhat outside the preoccupations of ecclesiastics in this respect, made similar comments:

Some of them are gentle and deserving of the title *Lares familiares;* they are active in households especially at night during the first period of sleep, and, by the noises that they make, they seem to be performing the duties of servants—descending the stairs, opening doors, building a fire, drawing water, preparing food, and performing all the other customary chores—when they are really doing nothing at all. Many of these gentle spirits, having foreknowledge of the future on the basis of hidden signs, can be heard ahead of time tending to things which we find actually being done a little later. They will even announce ahead of time, by signs, that merchants will soon arrive to offer their wares for sale. As a boy, I witnessed this phenomenon on several occasions, quite in fear, along with my brothers Arnold and Matthew, in the house of my parents Theodore and Agnes (may God in His ineffable mercy remember them at the resurrection of the just). Sometimes—when the hops lay heaped in great quantities upon the floor, and the buyers were about to come—on the night before their arrival we would hear the sacks being thrown downstairs—just as in truth happened on the following day.[5]

We are here dealing with the archetypes of the pixies and fairies of the folklorists, but reported in an era when 'official' religious culture was very hostile to such stories. It is therefore surprising to discover even the scraps of information that are forthcoming. De Spina depicted, in a way worthy of Disney, female 'fates' attending the birth of children and influencing their destinies in the rest of their lives.

Scandinavia reputedly produced a particularly rich source of lore on such creatures. The Catholic archbishop of Uppsala, Olaf Magnusson (1490–1557), published in 1555 his *History of the Northern Peoples*, including a great deal of Nordic myth and folklore.[6] On the whole Magnusson's approach resembled that of other superstition-writers: he expressed great hostility to the pagan mythologies that had only been overtaken by Christianity, in some parts of the Baltic, within the previous two centuries. He muddied the waters considerably by drawing cross-cultural analogies between Nordic and Graeco-Roman spirits and minor deities, and citing the commentaries of classical authors on them. However, he quoted some interesting local legends about 'nymphs' dispensing good or bad fortunes to young boys.[7] Although he treated the legends of the dances of elves and spectres as demonic apparitions, he believed that they took place and described them as realities. He even reported that the hero Høther had tracked such creatures down by following their footsteps in the dewy grass.[8] In general he oscillated between reporting the beliefs of the northern peoples, and confining them within Christian demonology like a good churchman.[9]

Magnusson was liberally quoted by other writers as describing demons who acted as household servants for ordinary people in Scandinavian countries. Here the story improved somewhat in the telling: Magnusson's own text was far less interesting than the paraphrases of it that were reported by others. Several commentators reported that demons were used as domestic servants in the northern countries, citing Magnusson as a source.[10] However, the idea that demons might work as domestic servants appeared in other texts, and seems to have been something of a constant factor in Germanic folklore. In the Latin literature these became 'familiar spirits', ultimately the source of the demonic 'familiars' of the English witch-trials. Johann Weyer reported a remarkable tale from Trithemius of Sponheim of a spirit-creature called 'Hutgin' (also spelled Hudgin or Hödecken) who reportedly served for some time in the household of the bishop of Hildesheim, sometimes helping him enlarge his diocese, at other times quarrelling with the other servants in the kitchen and causing mayhem in the castle.[11] Like the 'Friar Rush' of English folklore discussed by Reginald Scot, Hutgin assisted an absent husband by frustrating his wife's attempts to have adulterous affairs in his absence. Intriguingly, that motif in his legend may derive ultimately from a sermon by Jacques de Vitry which only later petrified into folklore.[12] Weyer also reported the beliefs about mountain spirits, who were essentially no more nor less than the antecedents of the mining dwarves of the folk-tales. Various kinds of spirits were said to haunt the mines of the Anneberg, the Schneeberg, and elsewhere. Sometimes they were helpful; at other times they terrified the miners and were blamed for the abandonment of mines. More typically they were reported to be merely harmless or mischievous.[13] All kinds of environments had their spirit-creatures: Johannes Nider referred ambivalently to the 'sylvestres', forest-creatures or sylphs, quoting Albertus Magnus on the subject.[14]

Spirit-partners, poltergeists, and 'teasers'

In other words, the popular lore about spirit-beings, as we can glean it from the theological texts, appears to have treated them in some sense as surrogate human beings, with bodies and passions and moral ambiguities. The most potent proof of this appears in the stories of romantic or sexual relationships between spirits and ordinary people. Many stories of this kind either set forth moral exempla to warn their hearers against lust, or proposed complex scholastic analyses of the phenomena of incubi and succubi (of which more later). However, as early as Burchard of Worms's *Corrector* in the early eleventh century, penitents were to be asked if they had believed 'that which some people are accustomed to believe, that there are women in the woods, called sylphs, whom they say are corporeal creatures and can when they wish show themselves to their lovers, and with which they say they have had pleasure, and who can when they wish, hide themselves and disappear?'[15] Johannes Nider was one of the first to refer to the legend of the 'Venusberg' (since made famous by Wagner's opera *Tannhäuser*) in his *Preceptorium*, obviously expecting that these tales of a mysterious realm of sexual delights with spirit-women would be known to his readers. Geiler von Kaiserberg quoted this passage in his sermons, evidently with the same assumption. By that stage the legend of Tannhäuser that would form the basis of Wagner's opera was already taking shape.[16] Theophrastus Paracelsus reported in his tract *On Nymphs, Sylphs, Pigmies, Salamanders, and Other Spirits* a tale which fits the mould of Burchard's warnings. A nymph who was an undine or water-spirit met and married the knight Peter von Stauffenberg, and lived with him some time until he grew discontented with her and married a human woman. The undine gave him a sign that he would die three days after the wedding, which he duly did.[17] The strange and perfunctory way in which Paracelsus tells the tale suggests that it was not his own invention, and indeed it is generally recognized as the theme of a Middle High German poem. As such it would have a long afterlife. It was issued as a separate pamphlet in German later in the sixteenth century.[18] The lyric was included in Achim von Arnim and Clemens Brentano's *Des Knaben Wunderhorn* (1805–8). After some transformations it became the basis for the libretto written by Czech poet Jaroslav Kvapil for Dvořák's opera *Rusalka*.[19] The von Stauffenberg story appears, in fact, to be one version of a common motif. Paracelsus went on to refer, in a rather clumsy way, to the story of Melusine, a freshwater mermaid whose lower half turned into a serpent at certain times of the week. With some difficulty he tried to fit the story into his highly unorthodox system.[20] He insisted, against the objections of theologians, that it was possible for men and nymphs to have sexual relationships and bear children: all such creatures he bracketed with the 'non-Adamic' part of creation.[21]

Spirit-beings also made their presence felt in the home in the form of poltergeists. The idea and the name are alike medieval in origin, if not earlier. Jakob of Jüterbogk referred to noisy spirits that did not harm people, although he was unsure whether they were demons or ghosts seeking prayers.[22] Nider referred to stories of spirit-creatures who made noises and disturbance in the household but were discovered in the morning to have done absolutely no harm to anything. Geiler von Kaisersberg reported the same stories from the same source. Alfonso de Spina told a particularly interesting tale of his own experiences of such a spirit during his youth.[23] Nider unbent from his traditional Dominican theological stance enough to say that some of these creatures were just 'teasers' who did relatively little harm. Even the theologians gave the impression that we are here dealing with a disorganized folk-belief that needed some careful interpretation.

Humans enter the spirit-realm

In the stories and motifs discussed so far, it was the spirits who came into the human world and took part in its activities. However, there are also fragments of evidence to suggest that early modern people believed that they might witness the realm of the spiritual creatures, or even become in some way a part of it. One part of this bundle of beliefs consisted of extraordinary visions. Nearest to ecclesiastical concerns were the reports that some women, at particular times of the year, could experience visions of the souls in purgatory. These visions were traditionally associated with the Ember days, according to Johannes Nider and others who followed him. Interestingly, such women were believed not only to see the souls in purgatory during a trance-like state, but also to be able after they woke from their trance, to identify lost goods.[24] Another form of vision was accessible to everyone. According to a range of ecclesiastical writers, sometimes at times of particular crisis images of armies would be seen fighting in the sky. This story was remarkably resilient and widely distributed. Nider claimed to draw on William of Auvergne, though he also confused the issue by referring to St Thomas's analysis of how souls might be temporarily released from purgatory to appear to people.[25] Alfonso de Spina also cited such visions, as did Geiler of Kaisersberg and, much later, the Philippist Lutheran writer Kaspar Peucer in his *On Divinations*.[26]

However, the most spectacular and resilient belief regarding entry into the spirit-realm was the so-called wild ride. From early in medieval European history, certain women were believed to be capable of experiencing, in a trance, an out-of-the-body flight in which they travelled great distances at night in the company of other women and a pagan goddess, sometimes called Diana, Herodias, or Hulda, to engage in a variety of activities involving sorcery and self-indulgence. This belief is most famously documented in the 'Canon Episcopi', a text debated almost as furiously by modern witchcraft scholars as by late medieval theologians. The Canon emerged first in the *Liber de Synodalibus Causis* edited by Regino of Prüm around 900.[27] A truncated version of the story appeared in Burchard of Worms's *Corrector*.[28] The full text of the canon was incorporated into Gratian's *Decretum* and thereby effectively made authoritative for the later Middle Ages.[29] The key point made by the Canon—which would later be the source of much controversy—was that the experience of flight was pure illusion, but that the women who experienced it often believed it to be real. Johannes Nider, so often seen in many ways as a forebear of the witch-myth, adhered scrupulously to the traditional view in this area. In *Formicarius* he reported how a Dominican friar had been counselling a woman who was quite convinced that she travelled with Diana by night. He asked to watch, and in due course saw her sit in a tub and anoint herself with ointment, after which she fell into a trance and had intense, dramatic dreams. These caused her and the vessel in which she was sitting to fall over: when she awakened from the trance the friar was able to convince her that all had been illusion and that she had not left the room. Interestingly, Nider located this story not in book 5 of the *Formicarius*, where he discussed magic, but in book 2 in a discussion of dreams and visions.[30] He summarized the same story in his *Preceptorium*, and it was duly popularized by Geiler in his sermons.[31] Martín of Arles did not quote the Nider story, but related how a 'respectable woman' had had an intense, sexually charged dream of a night journey, which he connected with the legends in the Canon Episcopi. She confessed it to her confessor, who asked Martín for advice.[32] As in so much of this material, it becomes very difficult here to discern literary tradition from empirical experience. However, the experiences reported both by Nider and by Martín of Arles derive, if we believe the authors, at only one remove from the surviving text. Each argued that the belief in flight was an important experience to the woman concerned (for good or ill) but that the clergy observers wished to play it down and explain it away. In neither case was the story linked to intentional witchcraft.

In other circumstances medieval people might also believe themselves privileged to have out-of-the-body experiences. Johann Lagenator of Dieburg, also known as John of Frankfurt (d. 1440), made a tantalizing reference to such a belief in a work on demonology written in 1412. 'If a child is born in a membrane, they say that he is one of those, who travel over a great distance in one night, commonly called "die farn leude".'[33] This elusive reference would probably have remained mysterious but for the discovery in the 1960s by Carlo Ginzburg in northern Italian archives of a similar belief.[34] The 'benandanti' of Friuli were men marked out at birth by having been born with part of the amniotic membrane still adhering to their heads. They believed that in a trance, at certain times of year, they flew out at night to do battle with evil spirits, to determine whether the harvest that year would be good or bad. The coincidence of similar beliefs from such different parts of Europe provokes many speculations about parallels and homologies in popular belief, though proving these from the medieval material is well-nigh impossible. However, there is no reason whatever to suppose that Ginzburg's inquisitors were familiar with the phenomenon described in John of Frankfurt's text nearly two centuries before. In these references it appears that the mostly hidden iceberg of folk myth occasionally breaks the surface.

Human beings as animals

At the opposite extreme, people might believe themselves liable to descend from the human to the animal realm. There were current in the medieval superstition-literature many stories of people who had supposedly been turned into animals by acts of demonic malice or hostile sorcery.[35] From the stories in Ovid's *Metamorphoses* to many of the legends of saints, it was something of a cliché that people, especially those lacking special insight, could be, or appear to be, turned into animals. According to a story originally derived from Palladius's *Lausiac History*, St Macarius of Egypt dispelled an illusion by which a woman had been apparently turned into a horse by sorcery, at the request of a man who wished to obtain her favours by alienating her husband.[36] Like many other theologians, Martin

Luther knew the story and referred to it in his sermons.[37] However, usually clergy retold these patristic stories for one reason only: to discredit what seems to have been a stubborn folk-belief that transformation into animals was really possible and did really happen. The secular judge Peter von Greyerz, who was identified as a key source for Nider's information about magic in the region of Bern, claimed that sixty years earlier a magician called 'Scavius' was able to escape from all his enemies by turning himself into a mouse.[38] The most spectacular form of animal transformation was of course lycanthropy. Johannes Nider in his *Preceptorium* went to some lengths to explain that the notion of witches being turned into animals was an impossibility. He suggested that real wolves might be stirred up to attack people in order to sow the belief that these were really werewolves.[39] When Geiler preached this material from Nider in Strasbourg in 1508, he supplemented Nider's material with stories from earlier medieval sources that claimed to prove that the lycanthropy was an illusion suffered by a demented individual.[40]

The image of spirits and non-human intelligences appears through the superstition-literature as through a distorting prism. Mostly we reconstruct the beliefs of non-theologians through the contradictions of the pastoral theologians. Those contradictions, however, are eloquent and at times copious. Theologians feared that ordinary people believed in a universe with a complex, ambiguous, folkloric hidden side, where the writ of organized religion did not run. They feared people's belief in their power to contact that spiritual realm in defiance of the proscriptions and requirements of Christianity. From that point of view, people's beliefs in good spirits were as dangerous, if not more so, than their beliefs in hostile or evil spirits. After all, the Church could far more easily accommodate the latter than the former. Above all the theologians feared the dependence of the popular mind on benign rituals, which form the next subject.

3

Helpful Performances: The
Uses of Ritual

The Dominican theologian and inquisitor Jakob van Hoogstraten
published in 1510 a *Treatise... declaring how gravely those people sin
who seek help from sorcerers and witches.*[1] On the face of it this title seems
paradoxical. Why on earth would anyone seek help from those whose
very name, *maleficus* or *malefica*, implies someone who does harm? In
fact, the literature on superstitions manifested constant concern with ritual
performances intended to achieve beneficial effects. Good magic, like good
spirits, was a much more fearsome adversary for the theological writers
than evil magic or evil spirits, because so much more obviously seductive
to ordinary, well-intentioned people. If we are to take even some of the
claims of the superstition-writers at face value, it appears that many people
in medieval Europe routinely expected to make use of various ritual means
to cure their illnesses, protect themselves from misfortune, and indeed to
remedy the perceived consequences of hostile sorcery. Moreover, a vast
area of shifting tidal sands stretched between approved ecclesiastical rituals
and forbidden ceremonial magic. In this liminal space all kinds of rites
and customs could develop that were neither approved nor absolutely
forbidden. Even the theologians themselves admitted that such an area
existed. As Jean Gerson wrote in 1417:

Some rites concerning God and the saints are lawful and obligatory; some are
entirely unlawful, expressly forbidden by the Church; some are in between, neither
good nor bad in themselves... [and] may be morally good or bad according to
the circumstances, especially the intention and purpose behind them... On the
first and second classes of rites one may preach with certainty, because the Church

has resolved them; on the third [*category*] one must be careful, not to approve or condemn them too absolutely.[2]

Gerson's point was even stronger than he admitted. Not only were there rites unresolved by the Church: there were also those which different ecclesiastics treated differently. This area of pastoral advice was riddled with disagreement: disagreement between laypeople and clergy, but also between clerics and other clerics.

Segenspruch and magical healing

By far the commonest kind of beneficial performance found in the literature was the ritual verbal formula—variously called a blessing, charm, spell, or enchantment—designed to heal some manner of illness, and often accompanied by some gesture or physical accessory. The German language described these formulae by the almost untranslatable term *Segen*, which embraces all of the above equivalents and more besides. Spanish has the term *ensalma*, which nowadays is taken to mean a quack healing spell, and secondarily the setting of bones. Both terms were used in the superstition-literature of early modern Europe to describe the healing charm.[3] Moreover, in this instance exceptional evidence suggests that ecclesiastical writers defended, as well as attacking, the practice of the healing spell. On 30 January 1405 Werner of Friedberg, lector in theology in the Augustinian house at Landau, was interrogated in the court of the bishop of Speyer. His interrogation rapidly assumed the character of an ad hoc heresy trial, and was in due course transferred to Heidelberg. Werner was interrogated on eight articles, of which articles four, five, and six related to issues of superstition. In the fourth article, Werner was accused of having preached that *Segen* could be used lawfully and without sin. In the fifth, he was alleged to have said that anyone who pronounced the names of the three Magi would be free from epilepsy. According to the sixth article, he had said that anyone who wore the words 'the Word was made flesh' as an amulet could not suffer from demonic illusions.[4] Most interestingly, Werner does not appear to have been particularly contrite in his responses to this interrogation. In most instances he explained his reasons for the alleged statements in his sermons with a confidence that suggests stubborn self-defence rather than contrition. On the issue of *Segen*, he argued that 'if all blessings were false, then why does one bless food, palms, eggs, and meat at Easter?' He also cited instances of healing charms which had worked, despite knowing that some clergy criticized them very much. For the other two 'superstitious' articles, he claimed to have heard or read these on sufficient authority.[5] Werner's stubborn stance on the matter of *Segenspruch* provoked the writing of one of the first dedicated superstition-treatises, Nicholas Magni of Jauer's *Treatise on Superstitions*, which consisted partly of a thorough rebuttal of Fra Werner.[6] Nor did the debate end there. A few decades later the Swiss canonist Felix Hemmerli (also known as Malleolus) wrote two short tracts on 'exorcisms' which debated the value and legitimacy of the healing charm. He knew of the travails of Friar Werner and argued that his trial, and the requirement that he recant, had been unreasonable. He spoke slightingly of the theological writers who had made sweeping condemnations against *Segenspruch* without making distinctions between a good charm and a bad one.[7] Hemmerli expressed considerable sympathy with ordinary poor people, who feared the loss of health or property and sought whatever remedies might work.

Healing charms or *Segen* combined a range of elements: they followed no particularly standard pattern, although certain recurring motifs can be seen. Many of the motifs and themes occurred in two different but related genres of ritual performance: the healing spell, designed to remove sickness or misfortune when it had arrived, and the amulet or talisman, designed to prevent sickness or misfortune from occurring in the first place.[8] At one level, many healing charms used simple rhyming poems in the vernacular. Werner of Friedberg got himself into trouble through use of one example of the rhyming formula: 'Christ was born, Christ was lost, Christ was found again, he who blesses these wounds in the name of the Father, the Son and the Holy Spirit'.[9] Felix Hemmerli reported a similar rhythmic saying used by a farmer on a diseased animal: 'if it were so, that the Virgin bore the child Jesus, so may the disease leave this animal, in the name of the Father, the Son and the Holy Spirit.' Likewise, he claimed to have heard from an aged peasant this exorcism for pests: 'I adjure you worms, by almighty God, that this place may become as detestable to you, as is to God the man who knows a right judgment and speaks a false one, in the name of the Father, the Son and the Holy Spirit.'[10] In this kind of healing spell or charm the emphasis was clearly laid on ease of accurate memorization by the presumably illiterate user. As Hemmerli remarked, even the Church used versification for the same reason.[11]

Secondly, many of the charms made reference to, or quoted from, some particularly potent or memorable piece of scripture. Supremely powerful in the minds of the casters of spells was the first chapter of St John's Gospel, used alike in incantations and in amulets.[12] However, other passages might also be used for their appropriate messages. Johann Weyer cited the use of texts such as Psalms 33, 90/91, 118, 137, 145, or Exodus 12: 46 and John 19: 6. In each of these cases the assumption appears to have been that the intention or reference in the text would aid the effectiveness of the charm or spell.[13] Other authors cited the use of Christ's words from the cross, *eli eli lama sabachthani*.[14] Even where no text was cited verbatim, often spells would make allusions to some event, such as Christ's birth, Christ's disappearance during his early visit to Jerusalem (as in Werner of Friedberg's spell), or more commonly his passion. The implication was fairly clear: the stories, texts, and events of scripture were assumed in some sense to contain palpable and negotiable spiritual potency. Their 'power' could be applied at need to the particular intention stated in the charm.

More explicit still was the invocation of 'mighty names of God'. Here the popular charm or spell wanders into the realm of the occultist grimoire or spell-book of the intellectual magician. Indeed, many of the 'powerful names' found as examples in the superstition-literature can be paralleled in medieval magical handbooks such as the *Key of Solomon*.[15] Again the assumption appears to have been that the more holy and divine names were invoked, the greater was the spiritual power tapped in the exercise of the spell. Martín of Arles y Andosilla quoted at particularly great length from a book of spells which he found in a parish of his Navarrese archdeaconry during one of his visitations. Examples included 'I conjure you, I send you out by elim, by olin, by saboan, by elion, by adonay, by alleluya, by tanti, by archabulon, by tetragrammaton'; and again, 'be you bound and fastened by these holy names of God, Alleluya, hirelli, habet, sat, mi, filisgie, adrotii gundi, tat, chamiteran, dan, yrida, fat, Sathan, Great God Almighty of the 70, Jesus Christ, Aquila.'[16] These confections of names were, of course, highly eclectic. Some were merely versions of the liturgical words of the Church, slightly misunderstood or mistranscribed. In one instance an entirely orthodox invocation of God, the *Trisagion*, was treated as though it were a list of the names of God: quoting Paulus Grillandus, the Observant Franciscan Girolamo Menghi remarked 'there are besides these many other unknown names, which . . . if they were well considered and pondered . . . would be judged none other than holy names:

as are these Agios, Otheos, Ischiros, Athanatos, of which Paolo Ghirlando in his treatise on sorceries says that many times he has taken these from the hands of sorcerers.'[17] This notion of 'powerful names' was not particularly unorthodox, nor was it restricted to the world of the folkloric charm. As will be seen below in Chapter 15, the friar Girolamo Menghi would, late in the sixteenth century, draft prayers of exorcism that exorcised demons 'by the power of all the holy unspeakable and most mighty names'; and again, 'by the power of all those ineffable names'.[18] His *Compendio*, however, differed from the typical popular spell in that, rather than appealing to the strangeness of the names, he deliberately explained their meaning.[19]

In general, charms seem to have made copious use of the mysterious power of incomprehensible words, even when these were not names. Often spells included a euphony derived from the repetition of syllables: Johann Weyer quoted phrases such as 'Sepa, sepaga, sepagoga', 'podendi … pandera … pandorica', 'danata, daries, dardaries, astararies', or 'galbes galbat galdes galdat'.[20] These do not appear to have had any fixed meaning, and certainly not any that would have been known or recognized by the user. The words were totemic gestures rather than meaningful expressions. The supreme example of a totemic meaningless word, however, was *Ananisapta*. This word was widely used as a preservative against plague and other misfortunes in the later Middle Ages. It has been found, in slightly variant spellings, on the gates of the town of Ingolstadt, on a variety of rings and jewels, on armour, in the prayer books of Emperor Maximilian I, and on church bells in Ulm and Strelln in Saxony.[21] Felix Hemmerli insisted that the word was a divinely revealed mystery, an *Arcanum dei*, bequeathed to humanity for its preservation.[22] Most commonly it was used as an amulet, sometimes associated with a three-line verse in Latin, which was quoted by both Martín of Arles and Johann Weyer:

> Ananisapta strikes down death, which seeks to harm.
> Evil death is held captive, when ananisapta is pronounced.
> Ananisapta of God, now have mercy upon me.[23]

Theological writers puzzled over where the word actually came from. Martín of Arles quoted Guarinus as claiming that the word was an acrostic for the power of the death of Jesus mediated through the Eucharist (the Latin interpretation of the acrostic that he quoted is still current in certain occultist circles). Martín Delrio believed that the term was Kabbalistic in origin, and believed that it derived from Hebrew terms that denoted a spirit presiding over divination. His scholarly philological interpretation would later be taken up by the Encyclopedists.[24] The key point to emerge must be that no-one knew for certain what the word meant or what it expressed, and in that rested some or even all of its attraction. The instinctive metaphysics of *Segenspruch* rested on the belief that some words simply *contained* spiritual power through the mere fact of being uttered or written down. They did not need to express an idea for the apprehension and understanding of another intelligent being, though theologians would insist on that assumption about their working, as will be discussed later.

Healing incantations or spells were usually accompanied with some sort of ritual gestures. By far the commonest gesture to be used was the sign of the cross. Many spells as reported in the literature include a × or + sign, to indicate that the sign of the cross was to be made at that point, just as would have been the case in a missal or other liturgical text. Johann Weyer even used this practice as an excuse to explain an otherwise incomprehensible spell:

I know a gentleman of high station who is famed for a similar type of cure. He writes '*Hax pax max Deus adimax*' upon an apple slice and then gives it as food to a person infected by a rabid dog. But these words are corrupted because of ignorance of the Latin tongue and Latin literature. The nobleman probably read a piece in German and discovered that the Latin words hoc † *po* † *mo* † *Deus adiuvet* † [May God help you by means of this apple] were effective for a cure of this sort; the words were interspersed with crosses as is usual in such superstitious 'mysteries.' Thinking the crosses to be the letter x because of the similarity of form, he read *hax pax max Deus adimax* and so inscribed the apple. I hear that he asked each client for half a stuiver, in the currency of Brabant. By accumulating this money, he built a chapel next to his castle, a chapel supposedly graced by many Masses paid for by these wages of impiety. To lend weight to this 'mystery,' the gullible are persuaded that this power to cure is passed on to the eldest of the progeny as though by hereditary right.[25]

In contrast to the grander and more exalted ceremonial magic, one generally does not read of other more elaborate choreographic gestures to accompany the healing spells used in popular 'superstitions'. However, it was common to use other physical attributes or pieces of apparatus, and these would be specified with increasing precision as time passed. Nikolaus von Dinkelsbühl (*c.*1360–1433) quoted a simple example of this phenomenon: 'they take a toenail and a piece of paper, and strike holes in the paper three times, and say to the sick person, with the first it is still woe to you, with the second likewise, and with the third you will be

healed.'[26] One of the most common circumstances related to the material
on which charms or amulets were to be written. One reads references,
for instance in Jean Gerson, to the use of 'virgin parchment', which could
mean simply previously unused parchment, but may also (as in the Key of
Solomon) mean parchment made from an animal too young to have been
mated.[27] Nikolaus von Dinkelsbühl referred to amulets being made 'when
the sun is either above or below a nut-tree; attaching it or hanging it in
a particular fashion; stringing it with red or green thread, or with thread
which has been spun by a virgin; or for the written text to be on a little
disk in a circle, or of a specific length, or a particular material'.[28] In general,
popular magical practice tended to regard virginity, whether in animal skins
or practitioners or adepts, as a helpful circumstance, by obvious association
with the Church's own insistence on the ritual purity of its priesthood and
its religious men and women.[29]

Marginal and hybrid practices

Some aspects of the popular healing spell partook of, and overlapped
with, what one might loosely call empirical medicine. Many healing
rituals involved the use of herbs, although the use of such herbs might
depend on particular circumstances as to their gathering or harvesting.[30]
Since everyone, including the theologians, agreed that medicinal herbs had
entirely natural properties to bring about healing, the presence of medicinal
herbs acted as it were as an 'excusable circumstance' in the practice of
superstitious healing. Several writers dealt with the objection that the use of
healing herbs in a healing ritual was perfectly natural and acceptable. Jakob
van Hoogstraten even claimed to have made inquiries into this topic. He
insisted that 'such servants of Satan are ignorant of the natural properties
of plants. They use them only so that the cure may be ascribed to the
power of the herbs, so that their own wickedness may be concealed, and
that other people may be less afraid of associating with them.' He claimed
to know this for certain, because 'one most pernicious scoundrel, who
was interrogated by two most excellent doctors of medicine, could not
assign any virtue or natural quality to the herbs which he gave to the sick.
No wonder, because he admitted that he used the same herbs for all the
diseases which he took it on himself to cure.'[31] One does not need to
share van Hoogstraten's judgemental attitude to find his analysis somewhat

persuasive. The herbs may have functioned as a symbolic apparatus to ritual healing, just as the words and 'powerful names' did.

One cannot discuss the 'helpful performances' found in the descriptions of popular belief without including those that hovered on the margins of acceptable orthodoxy, and those that were to medieval people securely inside those margins. These were not necessarily seen as 'superstitions' in the Middle Ages, but claimed such a large part of the later debates that it is essential to include them in this review. One of the most interesting examples of policing the margins of orthodoxy came from the pen of the Cologne theologian Heinrich von Gorkum (c.1378–1431). His *Treatise on Certain Superstitious cases* addressed a series of practices that hung around the edges of ecclesiastical ritual but incurred the suspicion of the professional theologian. The theologians' reservations will receive discussion later: here the point is to stress the apparent 'hybridity' of the rituals practised. Heinrich von Gorkum reported that wax from the candles consecrated on the day of the Purification of the Blessed Virgin (otherwise known as Candlemas) were inscribed during mass on St Agatha's day with certain words. Because of Saint Agatha's association with putting out fires, these inscribed pieces of wax were believed to have the power to preserve the building in which they were kept from being burned by fire.[32] Likewise, as a consequence of the practice of blessing foods in church during Holy Week, people would enclose joints of meat within the altar for Holy Week while the masses and readings of the Passion were being said at the altar. Thereafter it was believed that if the bones from the meat were fashioned into crosses, these crosses would protect those who wore them from shipwreck, robbery, and other misfortunes.[33] Less elaborately, Heinrich von Gorkum also cited the practices of wearing amulets with the names of the three Magi for protection (usually from epilepsy, although von Gorkum did not say this); he also referred to people who used palm-crosses to protect the fields from hail and storms, or carried them in their belongings to be safe from bad air and bad weather.[34] Finally, von Gorkum described how in some churches, after a child had been baptized, the priest would take a consecrated host and elevate it in the sight of the godparents. After that he would wash the hands that had touched the host, and the water would be given to the newly baptized child to drink.[35] Von Gorkum argued that for all these practices there was a proper and an improper way to regard them. If they were understood in a 'non-superstitious' way, as a form of devout prayer rather than as an attempt to control destiny, they could be quite acceptable.

Other examples emerge from the literature of ablution-water being used as a 'contact relic' through its association with something holy. Martín de Castañega remarked how 'the water used to wash out the chalice or to wash relics may be drunk or sprinkled on animals; [just as] sometimes for devotion people ask for the oil from the lamp which burns before the image of a saint or the sacrament, and the water from the wounds of the image of St Francis, not to make an evil use of it, but to use it with great devotion to cure illnesses of oneself or animals.'[36] The association by use of proximity with a holy object was, it seems, believed to confer a negotiable and transferable holiness into the objects so used, and this holiness could be used as protection against either general or specific misfortunes. Secondly, given the reservations expressed by a number of theologians, it appears to have been assumed by the users of such amulets or devices that their protective or apotropaic effects were certain and guaranteed. Thirdly, pre-modern people could think by analogy. When they witnessed clergy promising specific benefits to those who used the ceremonies and rituals approved by the Church, they tended to assume that the same logic must work for ceremonies sanctified by custom and experience and by association with the conventionally holy.[37]

Sacramentals and exorcisms

The argument from analogy brings us to the whole panoply of ecclesiastically approved consecrated objects and materials. The Church disposed of a range of consecrated things known collectively as *sacramentalia*, 'sacramentals'. These were distinguished quite sharply from the sacraments, the seven holy rites which ordinarily only priests could administer.[38] Sacramentals were, in contrast, intended to be used by the faithful for their benefit and protection in their ordinary lives: not only might ordinary laypeople handle and use them, but they were positively encouraged to do so. The most significant sacramentals included Holy Water, consecrated salt, Candlemas candles (those prepared with wax derived from the service of the Purification of the Virgin Mary), palm branches consecrated for Palm Sunday (and often fashioned into crosses), candles consecrated on Easter Eve, and herbs blessed on the eve of the Feast of the Assumption of the Virgin.[39] Pastoral theologians vigorously touted the benefits of these things to the people, not least in the hope of encouraging them to use only the approved ecclesiastical remedies and not the unlawful non-ecclesiastical ones. Martin Plantsch preached them to his people in Tübingen: a year or two later Geiler von Kaisersberg incorporated Plantsch's material almost unaltered in two of his sermons in the cycle *De Emeis*, preached at Strasbourg.[40] Plantsch, and Geiler following him, also described certain 'relics' as having the same benefits as sacramentals. While some of these were unique objects, a number were 'contact relics' which could in principle be multiplied for the use of the faithful without either miracle or fraud. These included special versions of holy water consecrated in the name of Saints Antony, Rupert, or Peter Martyr, to each of which a specific benefit was assigned. Similar benefits were claimed for so-called Agatha-bread, St Blasius's candles, or offerings made to St Valentinus, the saint most responsible in Germany for assisting with cases of epilepsy. Even a text, the apocryphal letter believed to have been written by Jesus to King Abgar of Edessa, was claimed to have a protective function.[41]

Consecrated objects could be used in a variety of settings. Some had specific customary uses; for example, palm crosses could be burned on the household fire to ward off storms. Others, most especially holy water, could be sprinkled on human beings, animals, and buildings under a whole range of circumstances. They might be used on their own, carried on the person for protection, or left in the home. However, sacramentals also performed vital functions in the practice of ecclesiastical exorcism. The term 'exorcism' needs a great deal of interpretation in the later Middle Ages (and indeed subsequently). In the fifteenth century it meant far more than the ritual expulsion of evil spirits from the body of a possessed person. Exorcism was, in general, taken by the superstition-literature to mean the orthodox use of ecclesiastical ritual to detect, protect against, or repel the forces of evil assailing the bodies and goods of the faithful. Since—as will be seen below in Chapters 5 to 9—all sorts of misfortune and mischief could be blamed on demons, it followed that everywhere demons were detected, exorcism could appropriately be used against them. Ecclesiastical writers would commonly tout the value of exorcism as the acceptable alternative to unlawful or dangerous *Segenspruch*, and complain that people did not distinguish between the two practices with sufficient clarity.[42] Several writers agreed that improper charms and spells derived from a degradation or depravation of what were formerly legitimate exorcisms.[43]

Exorcism, before the Council of Trent and the consequent drive to introduce some level of homogeneity into Catholic rituals, was a very flexible and varied business. Silvestro Mazzolini concluded the second book of his work on witchcraft with detailed prescriptions for exorcisms. Some of his warnings—the sort of circumstantial prohibitions that are often so useful to the historian—suggest a few of the things that exorcists, lay or ecclesiastical, might have been tempted to do. Exorcists were not to use 'unknown names' or meaningless shapes or symbols, and were not to place particular significance in the shape or manner of binding any amulets used.[44] They were not to show off their powers, or mix jokes with their exorcisms (like the priest who told a demon to depart and live in his privy: it did so, and attacked the exorcist there). They were to command demons, but not to invoke them or ask them anything.[45] However, even the rigorous Dominican Prierias seemed to suggest that one might call on a greater demon to command a lesser demon to depart. Exorcisms consisted essentially of formulaic prayers in Latin, although theologians would insist—again, rather against the grain—that the precise form of words was not important. Prierias's core exorcism prayer ran as follows: 'I exorcize you N. sick man or woman, but regenerate by holy baptism, by the Living God + the True God + the Holy God + the God who redeemed you with his precious blood, that you may be an exorcized person, so that there may depart from you all fantasy and wickedness of diabolical deceit, and any unclean spirit so adjured; through him who is to come to judge the living and the dead, and the world by fire. Amen.' Many other prayers were added; but in addition, the patient was to hold a candle if able, and to have a consecrated candle attached to the body; holy water was to be sprinkled 'liberally'; Gospel texts might not only be read aloud, but also attached to the suffering person as amulets.[46]

Silvestro Mazzolini Prierias's collection of exorcisms, although somewhat exotic, was a fairly chaste affair compared to the manual of exorcisms published later in the sixteenth century by the Observant Franciscan Girolamo Menghi. Although derived from a period later than most of the subject matter of this chapter, Menghi's exorcisms can fairly be supposed to reflect earlier as well as contemporary practice. Moreover, since Menghi derived his demonology substantially from Mazzolini, whom he quoted extensively, it is clear that the two formed part of the same cultural world. In 1589 Menghi published his *Scourge of Demons, containing fearful, most powerful and effective exorcisms, most approved remedies, both for expelling evil spirits and for chasing away sorceries from possessed bodies.*[47] The latter part of the work consisted of seven highly elaborate exorcism prayers, employing a range of names of God, names of the Virgin, and invocations of the detailed account of Christ's passion as a means to expel demons. Air, Earth, Water, and Fire were all to be conjured that they might not retain the evil spirit but drive it down into hell. The exorcist was to draw an image of the demon, then write the name of the demon (elicited by interrogation of the possessed person) over the picture. Fire was to be lit and conjured, and into it the exorcist should cast a variety of consecrated herbs and minerals, adjure all the principal demons by name, and finally cast the image into the fire.[48] Annexed to this volume was a further set of exorcism formulae, which included the prayers for consecrating the water, oil, salt, and herbs to be used in healing those who were afflicted by sorcery.[49]

Two key points emerge from reading these exorcism formularies. First, while theologians distinguished in theory between demonic possession and affliction by sorcery, both kinds of problem derived from demons, and exorcism of demons could be used against them. Secondly, the *implicit* assumptions between ecclesiastical exorcisms and popular *Segenspruch* suggest a considerable degree of commonality between them. In both cases words were powerful, and holy names contained hidden potency that could be tapped by the user. In both cases success depended on the correct performance of ritual, and the possession of an impressive and effective formula. Some of the rituals used—especially the sign of the cross—were the same in each case. In both instances the primary purpose of the ritual was to assist people suffering from evil forces. The main difference was that in ecclesiastical rituals the source of evil was routinely conceived of in terms of an intelligent and inflexibly hostile spiritual being or beings, whereas the popular mind appears—on the evidence discussed above—to have interpreted the source of evil in a more complex way. Given this level of overlap, it is not entirely surprising that medieval theologians were already accusing members of the clergy of acting as magical practitioners, long before anticlerical rationalists like Weyer and explicitly Protestant critics did so later in the sixteenth century. Martín de Castañega commented that 'poor women *and needy and covetous clerics* make a profession of being conjurers, sorcerers, necromancers, and diviners'.[50] Martín of Arles insisted that 'one must not have recourse to Magi, necromancers, and sorcerers for a solution and a remedy, as in these troubled times of ours the common people everywhere are not ashamed to run to such infamous priests'; again, 'who indeed are those lying prophets, if not the abominable priests, soothsayers, and necromancers, to whom the stupid and ignorant rabble have recourse everywhere?' He also condemned 'superstitious conjurations, as for instance to throw pebbles at the clouds while making an incantation, thinking that by this means one may drive away a storm, *as I confess I have once seen a priest to do.*'[51] It is a reasonable conjecture, therefore, that for ordinary people in later medieval Europe the different forms of beneficent supernatural power overlapped and intermingled in their minds.

For the theologically literate clergy, especially those whose theology had a pastoral bent to it, two forms of highly distinct and opposed supernatural power competed in a cosmic conflict for the allegiance of the faithful. For the majority—including many within the clergy itself—that cosmic conflict simply did not take place. Rather, a multitude of overlapping and mutually supporting modes of spiritual energy were available to see them through the awful perils of life. If one did not work, one could turn to another. From the stories of the miracles of saints, there appears to have been little difference between the ailments or threats that elicited an appeal to the miracle-working saint, and those that provoked the use of superstitious means. The same things made life precarious, and the same kinds of transferable cosmic energy could be deployed to guard against them or repel them.[52] Jean Gerson imagined some people saying to themselves, 'what do I care as to who heals me, or who gives me victory, honour, riches, or helps me? Let it be God or the devil, just so long as I get what I want.'[53] The declaration was doubtless over-dramatized, but the sense that the outcome was more important than the choice of means rings very true.

4

Insight and Foresight:
Techniques of Divination

The alleged craft of divining

Divination served as the automatic and constant accompaniment to attempts to influence or control the cosmos through ritual. 'Divination' refers to a range of techniques employed to discover things otherwise obscure or to predict the outcome of future actions and future events.[1] In theory, theological orthodoxy was fairly unambiguous on the subject. One could not truly learn future events from random coincidences, natural events, or demonic revelations, and in any case it was wicked to try to do so. However, even in this area there was a muddy marginal zone—perhaps not so wide as in the case of healing performances—where 'divination' and 'revelation' met and merged. Pastoral literature was full of discussions of 'revelations' that might or might not be trustworthy, might be divine or might be demonic.[2] The study of these special forms of discernment is more than usually bedevilled by the literary tradition. In the Middle Ages theologians endlessly copied and recirculated a list of divinatory techniques derived ultimately from Isidore of Seville's *Etymologies*.[3] Thomas Aquinas allowed himself an unusually long and discursive paragraph in the *Summa Theologica* in which he sorted out and unpacked Isidore's categories of divination. Demonic divination could occur through waking apparitions, or dreams, or the appearances of the dead (the true meaning of the word 'necromancy'), or the words of soothsayers. It could also function through the appearances of images in wood, iron, stone, water, air, fire, or the entrails of animals. Divination without express demonic agency could involve the motions of the stars, the chattering of birds, or lines appearing in human hands or the bones of animals; also patterns appearing in molten lead poured into water. Other forms of divination could involve versions of the casting of lots, such as the drawing of straws or the throwing of dice.[4] Each of these techniques had its own name, usually combining a Greek or Latin word for the key element with the suffix 'mantia', derived from the Greek μαντεία (manteia), meaning divination.

This list was so often copied and repeated by other writers that it becomes all but impossible to tell how many of these techniques were really practised in the Middle Ages and how many simply represented scholarly throwbacks to classical antiquity.[5] The early thirteenth-century encyclopedist William of Auvergne supplied a list of divinatory techniques which was later copied by Jakob of Jüterbogk: this included divining by asking children to inspect mirrors, children's nails, eggs, ebony handles, or polished swords, and other shiny objects, to which ointment made from oil would be added to increase their lucidity.[6] In the sixteenth century the Philippist Lutheran medical and theological writer Kaspar Peucer would expand considerably on this corpus of lore in his large and often-published monograph on divinations.[7] Whereas Peucer's list was heavily influenced by classical lore, Johann Weyer, on the other hand, seemed to present a fairly fresh list of techniques of divination. He described a variety of methods involving dishes dunked in water; vessels of water used as mirrors and examined by virgin boys or pregnant women; mirrors, crystals, and finger-rings; rings suspended in ladles of water; images formed in soot on fingernails; axes balanced on end; the (relatively well-documented) use of a sieve and shears to find a thief; the head of an ass; molten wax dropped into cold water; clouds, flour, cheese, fish, smoke, herbs, incense, laurel burned in a fire and expected to crackle, and ashes cast on the ground in certain shapes. This rather chaotic grab-bag of methods, so far removed from Isidore, may at least suggest some of the divinatory techniques that were current in north-western Germany in the mid-sixteenth century.[8]

Doubtless some practitioners used one or another of the techniques found in Isidore's list and its derivatives, especially among those who offered to find lost goods. The late medieval theological literature rarely described such techniques in detail for the obvious reason that this would tempt people to use them. As *Dives and Pauper* put it, 'ther ben al to many that knowyn these and many mo therto and practysyn newe yer be yer at the fendys techynge tyl mychil of this lond is blent and schent with swyche folye.'[9] By the sixteenth century one finds authors becoming markedly less reticent. Johann Weyer documented in quite precise detail a variety of rituals for identifying thieves: some partook of elaborate ceremonial magic, but others did not. One method involved a cross applied in olive oil on a crystal, and an invocation to St Helena to give a revelation in the crystal to a 'chaste young boy'. Another method involved several stones from a river baked in a fire and then buried in the ground. The stones were disinterred, and then placed in a basin of water with the mention of the name of each of the suspects: the water would seethe when the stone assigned to the name of the thief was placed in the water. This method Weyer claimed to have 'copied secretly from a priest's book'.[10] As an alternative to simply identifying a thief, one could injure the thief by a variety of ritual incantations, including a most elaborate and lengthy curse known as the Anathema of St Adalbert. The curse would supposedly cause the thief so much illness that the crime could be easily detected, or in any case avenged. Interestingly, the 'liturgical curses' of thieves and robbers derived originally from formal measures taken by monasteries in the high Middle Ages to curse predatory nobles who ravaged their estates. By implication, some of these texts were allegedly used against commonplace thieves by the late medieval and early modern periods.[11]

Omens and portents

For more everyday techniques of divination available to all kinds of people, one ought to look rather at the quest for meaning among the random events of life. According to the literature on the subject, people were ready to see meaning and guidance for the future in a wide range of apparently casual occurrences. Most of these customs can be grouped under the heading of omens rather than divination properly so called, but their function for the users was basically similar. One of the most necessary forms of prediction—then or since—was weather- and harvest-forecasting. Here a custom had developed of regarding certain days in the religious calendar as particularly significant. Good weather on the feast day of St Vincent indicated a rich grape vintage; good weather on the day of the Conversion of St Paul indicated a rich grain harvest.[12] Each country of Europe had its weather-saints to foretell the duration of

summer rains, from St Swithin of Winchester in England to SS. Medard
and Gervasius and Protasius in France, St Godelieve in Flanders, and
St Urban or the Seven Sleepers of Ephesus in Germany.[13] In fifteenth-
century England, the weather on the day on which Christmas or the New
Year (March 25) fell was sometimes thought to be predictive of the weather
for the rest of the year. Alternatively, the weather on the twelve days of
Christmas was observed as a guide for the weather of the coming year.
As the friar who wrote about these customs observed, this was particularly
absurd since all twelve days of the Christmas season might have the same
weather.[14]

In general, the calendar, that curious document that combined the
religious, the cultic, and the practical, formed the basis for a large body
of superstitions in regard to discerning the future. Ecclesiastical calendars
frequently included such beliefs, as Pedro Ciruelo complained in the
mid-sixteenth century.[15] One of the most frequently quoted instances of
ill-fated times comprised the series of so-called Egyptian Days, scattered
through the year at the rate of two to a month. On these dates it was
considered extremely unfortunate and ill-omened to begin anything. One
of the earliest references to these days occurred in Augustine's commentary
on Galatians, with reference to Galatians 4: [10–11]. Despite the warnings
in the epistle against divination, 'our congregations are full of people
who obtain the times for their activities from astrologers. Moreover, these
people often do not hesitate to warn us as well against starting work on
a building or other structure on one of the days they call "Egyptian".'[16]
These days were mentioned, along with other forms of calendar-divination,
in a questionnaire for the interrogation of those suspected of superstitious
practices found in a southern French inquisitors' manual from c.1270.[17]
Thereafter they would recur as allusions in the later medieval superstition-
treatises, although it would not be until Martín Delrio's work at the very
end of the sixteenth century that a theological authority would actually
list which the days were (and that he derived from a secular source).[18]
The days were supposedly called 'Egyptian' from some association with the
plagues of Egypt, although, given that Augustine had associated them with
paganism, it seems improbable that they would have an Old Testament
origin. In any case, these were thought to be supremely bad days on which
to begin anything new and to expect a good outcome. Rather similar was
the superstition attaching to Holy Innocents' day. Jean Gerson devoted an
entire short treatise to the belief that the day of the week on which the

Feast of the Holy Innocents fell would be an unlucky day for the whole of the following year.[19] Martín of Arles quoted similar beliefs surrounding the days of the martyrdoms of John and Paul, and also St Martial's day.[20]

Besides the attention paid to the calendar, and the weather on supposedly significant days, people would reputedly take account of a wide range of other omens. One of the most curious (and to theological eyes one of the most offensive) was that across Europe many people seem to have thought that meeting a member of the clergy or the religious orders on the road was unlucky. Martín of Arles remarked that hunters who met a priest would abandon hunting for the day as a waste of time.[21] As a variant of this, the author of *Dives and Pauper* reported that in England some people deemed it vital to pass priests or friars on the left hand, and described a traffic accident caused when a man on horseback tried to insist on this with a friar that he met.[22] Erasmus of Rotterdam would remark, as a casual reference that his readers would pick up, that the clergy, and especially mendicants, were so generally detested that even to meet with one was regarded as a bad omen.[23] However, omens were more commonly attached to meeting animals rather than particular kinds of people. In late medieval England meeting a toad or a marsh-harrier was regarded as good luck.[24] Nikolaus von Dinkelsbühl supplied a particularly thorough coverage of such beliefs: how things began would be a sign of how they would turn out; finding a bird's nest, a little iron, or a halfpenny coin was very good luck.[25] Martín Delrio would later append to his encyclopedic treatment of such beliefs a fold-out table of a vast range of things, animate or inanimate, which one might find or meet with and discern good or bad luck from.[26] Many such beliefs will have derived from literary traditions reaching back into classical antiquity, or at least to Augustine's critique of such things in *On Christian Doctrine*,[27] and it is not always easy to discover which beliefs were truly current in the absence of some circumstantial story to confirm them.

Lot-casting and astrology

As Thomas Aquinas remarked, divination included the casting of lots in various forms. One of the most recurrent forms of sortition was the *sortes Apostolorum* or the Apostles' lots. This technique was described in a thirteenth-century formula of interrogation and was alluded to as something generally known by *Dives and Pauper* in the early fifteenth

century.[28] It used to be assumed that phrases of this kind regularly referred
to the random searching of a verse of the Bible for guidance, the practice
also known as *sortes biblicae*, derived by association from the classical and
neoclassical practice of taking *sortes* from the text of Virgil or Homer.
However, recent research suggests that the 'Apostles' lots' may refer to a
divinatory text, one that was condemned by this title for the first time in
the *Decretum Gelasianum* from the early sixth century.[29] This text consisted
of a hierarchy of fifty-six responses to questions to be chosen by the
throwing of three dice. By the late Middle Ages the text containing these
responses had crystallized into a relatively fixed form identified by the
opening phrase '*Post solem surgunt stellae*', although the text is likely to
have varied considerably over time.[30] Sortition, therefore, could combine
written or traditional text, instruments such as dice, and ritual prayers. It
is likely that many more people used some simpler fokloric method than
the elaborate *sortes* contained in a written manuscript. Lot-casting posed
a problem for the pastoral-theological writers, since there were clearly
legitimate and illegitimate uses for it. It might be a perfectly appropriate
way to apportion things that could not be divided between people or to
make other random decisions (after all, even city-states such as Venice and
Florence apportioned some of their magistracies by lot); but to use it as a
means of insight into hidden truths was clearly very suspect.[31]

One ought to close this chapter with a brief discussion of one of the
most problematic and marginal of all the divinatory techniques, judicial
astrology. Astrology was a learned practice, and depended on command
of a literary corpus and careful observation. Nevertheless most of the
superstition-writers felt compelled to include it in their discussions of
popular belief. Many writers, even among the theologically learned, were
ambivalent about how far it might be tolerated without infringing divine
providence or risking the involvement of evil spirits. Jean Gerson and the
author of *Dives and Pauper* both warned their readers at some length against
the kind of astrology that either (i) imposed necessity upon human destinies
or (ii) attempted to discern the future for specific individuals rather than
large groups of people. On the whole, the lower down the social scale
the astrology was practised, the more likely it was to incur the criticism of
theological writers. Jean Gerson allowed that astrology was at some level
a true science, to which theology should not be opposed. However, he
opined that the mechanisms of natural government in the universe were
so complex, and their operations so disrupted by the fall, that to claim

specific relationships between celestial conjunctions and human events was just impossible. In this respect Gerson did not hesitate to criticize not only classical and Arab astronomers but also Albertus Magnus, who, he said, had 'inclined too much to the side of superstitions lacking reason'.[32] Gerson also quoted the rules of astrology in order to refute the cruder forms of divination, arguing that primitive calendar-divination was excluded by the rules of astrology 'according to their rules, if indeed they are true'. To affirm free will, he pointed out that 'in those things which concern free will, the stars do not impose any necessity, according to the saying of Ptolemy, that a wise man will have dominion over the stars'.[33] Theologians therefore handled astrology slightly differently from purely 'superstitious' practices, and this may say something about its social context. If it were practised at the most intellectual, academic level, with full awareness of its mathematical complexities, then (it was reasoned) such astrologers would be sufficiently wary of its subtleties not to indulge in individual prognostications. In fact, of course, they did cast horoscopes for individuals, sometimes even for those who would grow up to be theologians.[34]

'Superstitions': image or reality?

The late medieval literature on superstitions conjured up (if that is not too inappropriate a metaphor) an image of a European folk-culture where Christian orthodoxy did not have everything its own way. Faced with a host of natural and supernatural threats to their existence, ordinary people were tempted to be pragmatic rather than ethical, and to rely on tradition rather than prescription. They would pass on the tales of helpful or ambivalent spirit-creatures who were supposed to have the same emotional needs and flexibilities as themselves. They would look for assistance from whatever kind of ritual and ceremony they could find, irrespective of whether it fell within the scope of orthodoxy or not. They believed in a cosmos which resonated with meaning and potential messages for the attentive and open-minded person. This image, as was said earlier, was no more than that. It was a trope required by a particular kind of pastoral rhetoric. The incoherence, inconsistency, and folly of the ordinary uneducated layperson need to be remedied and restrained by the learned pastoral intelligence of the theological writer and those better-educated priests formed through his writings. Nothing intrinsic to the pastoral superstition-treatises proves that any identifiable group of people actually practised the activities that it condemns. One could argue that such an outpouring of literature, much of it printed either immediately or (for the older works) in the decades after its appearance, could hardly have been written and distributed for no purpose. Unfortunately this argument has a critical and fatal flaw. The extensive literature on witchcraft, which overlaps with that on superstition although it is not identical with it, did develop into a vast body of texts about a purely imaginary activity. The very argument proposed above—that the literature would not have existed without some reality to reflect—was one of those used to refute sceptical views of the witch-myth. One could argue, on the other hand, that the superstition-literature does not postulate absurdities or impossibilities as the witchcraft textbooks did. When it describes popular belief, it displays an innate plausibility that the witchcraft theory signally lacked. This is true, but of itself inconclusive. The only way to test the image of popular belief and practice is to invoke other sources of evidence. None of this proves absolutely beyond doubt that 'superstitions' formed a core part of the life of every medieval Christian, nor should we expect it to. The most that it can demonstrate is that the theologians were not arguing against shadows.

First, we do possess some texts that actually defend, support, and describe what the theologians called 'superstitious' practices. Thanks to the insatiable appetite of late sixteenth-century publishers for copy, these works were widely disseminated despite the appalled reactions of theological critics. Felix Hemmerli's three short pieces entitled *A First Treatise of Exorcisms, A Second Treatise on Exorcisms or Adjurations,* and *A Third Treatise on Whether One Should Give Credence to Demons,* constitute the best evidence of a coherent counter-argument against the theologians' consensus on the subject of superstitious charms and incantations. Hemmerli quoted a range of charm formulae in German, not visibly derived from the written traditions. He referred to an incident, the trial of Werner of Friedberg in 1405 (documented from other sources) and argued that the condemnation of Werner's practices was misguided. He included many arguments, including the analogy with blessings performed by the Church, that were commonly used (as one reads elsewhere) by those used to defending superstitions. He quoted or referred to a number of the legends about Moses' use of magic, and about the transmission of Magic from Solomon to Virgil and thence to Latin Europe, that are also known through the refutations of them written by more conventional ecclesiastical writers.[35] In short, Hemmerli appears to represent the world-view of the magical subculture among the clergy about as well as anyone could have done. Martín Delrio felt it was worthwhile to devote a whole section of his *Magical Disquisitions* to refuting his claims, calling him 'a patron of these sorts of prayers and medicaments' and noting that his works had been placed on the Index of Prohibited Books.[36]

Secondly, the much more eloquent and copious works of Theophrastus Paracelsus, though very individualist and eccentric, challenge the theologians' critiques about ritual healing in the same way that Hemmerli did. Paracelsus presented himself as an empirical experimenter, who would try out anything to see whether it worked. Somewhat aggressively, he refused to be hidebound by previous literary authorities. This open-minded approach has earned Paracelsus some esteem among historians of science and medicine, given that so much of the literary tradition in these areas was subsequently proved to be wrong. However, for the purposes of this inquiry Paracelsus figures chiefly as an outspoken defender of the use of ceremonial and magical healing, spells and amulets. In the *Opus paramirum*, which defended healing with characters, he repeated the argument for medical experiment that so many theologians claimed to have encountered: 'Our health and fortune emerge from our enemies, and from the hands of those who hate us . . . necessity, according to scripture, counts as an excuse. It is fair to respond to a desperate situation by whatever means are to hand, whether it is a devil, a spirit, a physician, or a thief, or whatever other thing happens to be available.'[37] In his *On Occult Philosophy* Paracelsus likewise insisted that the *only* effective remedy for certain kinds of illnesses was to be sought from those outside the academy:

The method of cure ought to be the same as was the infliction of the disease and the pain, that is, through the faith and the imagination . . . For not everything that a physician needs to know is taught and learned in academies. Sometimes one has to turn to old women, to the Tartars known as *Zigeuner* [Gypsies], to travelling magicians, to old country people, and to other marginalized people: it is in their schools that a great deal must be sought out and learned. For these people possess more knowledge about those matters than all the Academies.[38]

With his idiosyncratic theology as well as his idiosyncratic science, Paracelsus could argue that God knowingly and willingly made demonic and superstitious magic accessible to people to use for their own benefit. He also seems to have believed that enchantment worked through the power of the imagination of the person expressing it. He did not accept the theologians' Aristotelian assumptions that rituals and symbols could only work by communicating with demons. Obviously Paracelsus did not precisely represent anyone but himself. His cosmology, his physics, and his chemistry were all distinctive, and gave a putative coherence to his 'system' that more folkloric superstitious schemes would neither have needed nor wished for. However, he does document the currency of beliefs and arguments that are otherwise known only through their critics.

Paracelsus also provided examples of a second kind of evidence, the manual or guide to the practitioner of superstitious healing. In his *Seven Books of Archidoxis of Magic*, Paracelsus first argued for the power of symbols and formulae, then gave examples of how to construct and use them:

Signs and characters have their own properties and effects, as do letters. Indeed, if the nature and properties of metals, the influence and working of the heavens and the planets, and finally the meaning and condition of symbols, signs, and letters all are in accord and agreement, why ever, I ask you, should a sign or seal made in this manner not have its own force and property of working? Why should this one not in its own time help for the head, or that in its own time be useful for the sight?[39]

Paracelsus's *Archidoxis* contained a large number of prescriptions for amulets and medallions supposedly specific to particular diseases or parts of the body. These amulets might include combinations of precious or rare materials together with precious metals, imprinted with complex and unfamiliar symbols. The words used were mostly nonsense-words in a combination of the Latin and Greek alphabets; the symbols were sufficiently exotic to require the printers of Paracelsus's works to represent them by engravings. There were cures for epilepsy, diseases of the brain, paralysis, kidney stones, excessive menstruation, leprosy, vertigo, spasms, heart palpitations, broken bones, and, of course, impotence. Different medallions were prescribed for the last depending on whether the impotence was of natural origin or the result of demonic sorcery.[40] As with his cosmological speculations, Paracelsus's works proposed a far more virtuoso and sophisticated version of the manipulation of invisible forces by tokens and symbols than most of his counterparts would have been concerned with. Paracelsus should not in any sense be read as depicting 'typical' symbolic healing. What he does show is that these techniques were taken seriously and recognized by contemporaries; that a culture existed on which such an extravagant personal confection could be built up.

Rather surprisingly, some fragmentary but cumulatively impressive evidence does survive of the physical materials used in 'superstitious' practices, despite the best efforts of ecclesiastical disapproval, and subsequently of changing intellectual fashions, to obliterate them. Physical evidence of charms and amulets proves to be almost as old as Christianity itself. From the first millennium of the Christian era, a collection of over 130 texts survives, written on a variety of materials, that contain texts calling for 'ritual power' to assist with precisely the kinds of challenge discussed in the previous chapters. These texts survive mostly in Coptic, with some Arabic and Greek elements as well. While they will surely have differed from their medieval European counterparts in some respects, obvious parallels suggest themselves both in the subjects (health, protection from harm, sexual success) and the appeals to strange strings of names or unknown words.[41] A surprisingly large body of very similar inscribed amulets, shaped in a variety of metals and apparently intended to be worn for protection, has survived from the world of Byzantine Christianity in the high Middle Ages.[42] From medieval Europe itself, just sufficient numbers of textual amulets survive to demonstrate with more than enough plausibility that such protective devices were indeed made and used. Typically, the surviving 'textual amulets' tend to display more erudition than was probably the norm: they contain quite extensive texts with elaborate symbols. However, the basic principles of the elaborate textual amulets seem to have resembled their simpler, cruder, and mostly lost counterparts.[43]

A focus on the relatively simpler, shorter texts ensures that one verifies relatively popular and simple 'superstitious' rites, rather than the elaborate and esoteric magical texts and grimoires. The latter, of course, survive in considerable abundance, but remained the preserve of a small elite of occult practitioners.[44] There also survive, however, some items that lurk around the boundaries of the two classes of material. Only relatively recently has serious study been given to the text of a fifteenth-century copy of a 'necromancer's manual' that survives in Munich. This manuscript formulary supplies prescriptions for the invocation of spirits by a variety of exotic names, closely comparable to those criticized in the superstition-treatises. This rarity shows that, at the very least, the theological writers who condemned such things aimed at a real target.[45] Other surviving objects testify to the reality of the beliefs described above. A charm-ring from Donauwörth includes emblems entirely recognizable from the superstition-literature.[46] The 'Middleham jewel', a gold reliquary or amulet from late fifteenth-century Yorkshire, contains inscribed around the edge of one of its faces the words 'ecce agnus dei qui tollis peccata mundi miserere nobis tetragramaton ananizapta'. On the Middleham jewel one sees exactly the combination of entirely orthodox prayers with divine names and a mysterious word used as a totem that the descriptions in the superstition-literature would lead us to expect.[47] Ecclesiastical calendars, primers, and collections of prayers survive which attest the calendrical beliefs described earlier, and demonstrate much of the ambiguity that surrounded the distinction, never clear at the best of times, between an incantation and an orthodox prayer.[48]

Finally and with great caution, one may consider the persuasive role that imaginative literature could play in documenting these beliefs and phenomena. The reasons for such caution become clear if one considers the vast amount of literature devoted in the present day to themes of magic and sorcery. No-one would be justified in inferring from the *Harry Potter* corpus a widespread popular belief in the actual power of magic in the early twenty-first century. Clearly the same reserve ought to apply in the case of the stock character of the changeling in sixteenth-century drama, or Shakespeare's deployment of fairies, ghosts, and witches through many of his plays.[49] The literary evidence demonstrates that 'superstitious' beliefs functioned as highly recognizable cultural referents for early modern audiences and readers, not that they were taken seriously as everyday experience. However, they were highly recognizable—just as were the legends of Tannhäuser at the *Venusberg* or of Peter von Stauffenberg's nymph bride—and that is far from insignificant. When a dramatist could play on the different theological readings of magic and sorcery, as Marlowe did in *Doctor Faustus*, he testified to the currency of a religious and intellectual conundrum to the public mind of his era.[50]

So far this account has treated the popular beliefs and cosmology of the later Middle Ages and early modern period as a whole, avoiding the question of whether there can be discerned any significant processes of change or development. It is, as was discussed earlier, an open question as to whether the raw material of superstitious beliefs actually has a history. Over the extremely *longue durée* it must have, of course. The Christianization of late antique and post-Roman Europe will have generated countless instances of the transmutation, evolution, and re-expression of old beliefs in new cultural garb: classical minor deities will have become the fauns and nymphs of legend.[51] Similarly, industrialization and urbanization on the one hand will have made rural folkloric beliefs less plausible, while the work of the folklorists and the freeing-up of publishing in these areas may actually have assisted in disseminating those beliefs as secondary cultural artefacts, as decorative elements or hobbies in people's lives. It remains to be clarified what changes, if any, might have been witnessed between, say, 1250 and 1550. It seems probable that the greater elaboration and materialization of late Gothic piety will have infused the folklorized religious beliefs of the era with even more elements from religious legends and tales than previously: miracle-stories of saints, cults of localized holy objects, beliefs about the supposedly reliable effects of certain rituals. If the proliferation of the superstition-treatises suggests anything, it is that this popular or folklorized Christianity was becoming more complex and many-branched than ever before. In the meantime one must turn to the theological critique of popular belief. As with so many other areas of human activity, from the lending of money at interest to married couples' sexuality, medieval scholastic theology deployed vast subtlety and intellectual skill in analysing and evaluating what it called 'superstitions'.[52] That analysis needs to be explored somewhat independently of the beliefs that it criticized.

PART

II

The Learned Response
to Superstitions in the Middle
Ages: Angels and Demons

The superstition-literature often yields particularly frustrating insights into the popular mind of the later Middle Ages. While occasionally the theological writers betrayed—usually by what they challenged or rejected—some plausible lineaments of pre-modern popular belief, for most of the time they sought to reinterpret those lineaments as something else. Through the late Middle Ages a small group of philosophical and pastoral theologians, well-grounded in Aristotelian metaphysics, struggled to impose their metaphysics on the beliefs of the majority through the 'superstition-literature'. The treatises and sermons that they left behind give powerful testimony to their efforts, and the sheer volume of their surviving output gives the impression that they won the argument. Moreover, the degree to which the theological writers quoted from a range of shared patristic and medieval sources, and also from each other, can give the impression that they were unified in their approach to a quite striking degree. Both impressions are at least partly misleading. The scholastics, with their love of disputation and 'subtlety', did not manage to write or speak with exactly the same accents when they addressed this topic, any more than anything else. On the contrary, some of the differences between them on key points reveal very important nuances of interpretation not only about superstition, but about the relationship between human worship and the divine government of the cosmos, about the origin of evil, and about religion in general. As to whether the scholastic analysts of superstition won their arguments, that verdict was ultimately up to their readers and audiences. It would be well not to assume the minimalist conclusion, namely that they had no impact at all, given the time, trouble, and ink they expended on transmitting their critique to the laity and the readiness of publisher-printers to invest in the texts they created. However, one can ponder how far the complexities and fine distinctions of the theological critique may have made its message harder to receive and absorb, or may have blunted theologians' efforts to reform the pastoral practice of their less educated clerical colleagues.

This part of the book will break down this complex material into five chapters. First, it is necessary to set out some of the inherited wisdom on this subject. The later Middle Ages approached the issue of 'superstitions' in the light of a long heritage of theological discourses derived from late antiquity. Not all of these sources remained continuously in use, but those that were—especially when mediated through a key collection such as the Decretum—*could be deployed as authorities. Second, two chapters will depict the areas of overall consensus in the medieval theological analysis, first in high medieval demonology, then in its pastoral applications in the fourteenth and fifteenth centuries. Theological minds dissected popular beliefs about the cosmos through the lenses of patristic scepticism about 'relics of paganism' and Aristotelian metaphysics. The latter, in particular, equipped the writers on this subject with a reasonably stable and authoritative guide to how things happened, as well as what could and could not happen in the supernatural realm. (In fact, the term 'supernatural', though useful in many ways, is a misnomer in this context: scholastic metaphysics located spiritual beings firmly within the world of nature.) The next chapter will explore some of the fault-lines in the scholastic analysis. In this—as in other areas—theologians of the later Middle Ages anticipated, in small but significant ways, some of the disagreements over worship and divine agency that would burgeon into huge debating points at the time of the Reformation. Finally, some suggestions will be made as to the impact of the theological critique on pastoral realities. Almost inevitably, most of the evidence of impact has to come from the internal evidence of the treatises themselves; although the few other sources that survive may be of some use here as well.*

5

The Patristic and Early Medieval Heritage

M edieval writers approached the question of superstition, like any other issue in theology, from an epistemological perspective dependent on the inherited wisdom of previous authorities. Credible scriptural or traditional testimony usually seemed more convincing to the minds of that era than empirical data, which could be mendacious, misleading, or illusory. Consequently, one cannot treat the post-1250 critique of superstition as though it started *de novo*. However, since the genre of the superstition-treatise was largely a late medieval creation, the authors of the treatises had to draw upon precedent authorities who had written in different formats and for different reasons. Their sources included canon law treatises, penitential canons, and guides for hearing confessions, and theological *summae* and encyclopedias of a variety of shapes and sizes. They made occasional and highly selective use of stories from the corpus of classical antique literature. The scholastics constructed a *bricolage* of materials from a variety of traditions and genres as they sourced the authoritative 'sentences' with which to respond to superstition.

Augustine

One of the earliest, most copious, and most important contributors to this enterprise was Augustine of Hippo (354–430 CE). Augustine's thought may best be understood in the light of his spiritual career and multiple conversions. He was raised in the school of pagan Roman rhetorical virtuosity in North Africa, flirted with and eventually abandoned Manichaeism, then learned a considerable amount of Neoplatonism before turning, under the influence of Ambrose of Milan, to a particularly ascetic and earnest mode of Christianity.[1] After abandoning paganism as a cultural system, he remained captivated and to a considerable degree loyal to Neoplatonic philosophy: numerous debts to the system of the pagan Plotinus have been discerned in Augustine's spiritual autobiography, *The Confessions*.[2] Thrust into the episcopate, he took on the responsibility of defending Christianity from the charge of weakening the empire and exposing it to the onslaughts of barbarian tribes from the north. He argued for the greater merits of Christianity, and rebutted the accusation that it had weakened Rome, in his polemical masterpiece *The City of God against the Pagans*.[3] Much of his work entailed polemical attacks against the Christian 'heresies' of Donatism, Manichaeism, and Pelagianism, movements which retained considerable influence through Augustine's lifetime even though his own mode of Christianity later came to be viewed as the 'correct' and authoritative version.[4] Augustine was conditioned by his career and early training to see the cosmos in terms of binaries: God and the devil, the city of God against the city of Satan, truth against falsehood, the Catholic Church against the heretics' Church.

This taste for binary oppositions clearly shaped the way that Augustine viewed the encounter with the classical mythologies and religious practices that still held sway in parts of the Roman Empire in his lifetime. First, Augustine quite unhesitatingly described the deities of Graeco-Roman mythology as 'demons'. The word 'demon' derived from a Greek word, δαίμων (daimōn; and its diminutive δαιμόνιον, daimonion) that had in origin, and especially in Neoplatonic thought, been taken to mean a neutral or good spirit, a tutelary demigod.[5] Over time and with the critical comments of Church Fathers such as Cyprian,[6] the term 'demon' acquired, at least among Christians, the uniquely negative connotations found in Augustine. The spirits of antique paganism were now to be equated with the Satan that tormented Job and tempted Jesus, and with the evil spirits that Jesus and his disciples drove out from the bodies of the possessed. Much of books 2 and 3 of Augustine's *City of God* was devoted to showing that the multiple deities of classical paganism were forces of evil, and therefore demons in the pejorative sense. The ancient gods, Augustine repeatedly argued, spread legends about their own unchastity and immorality, and required to be worshipped with 'obscene spectacles'. 'The malignant spirits whom the Romans suppose to be gods are willing to have even iniquities which they have not committed attributed to them.'[7] At some length he discussed how the Romans were sufficiently disgusted by the religious plays performed in honour of their gods that they would not allow actors the rights of political participation allowed to other citizens.[8] It was not Christianity, but the moral depravity caused by the legends and cults of paganism, that brought Rome's moral character down so low.[9] The 'demons' gave visions and prophecies, but these miserably failed to have edifying moral content. They predicted victories but did not encourage virtue. They may even have given signs that were designed to make moral atrocities like civil war more palatable.[10] What Augustine argued polemically in *City of God*, he presented more systematically in his doctrinal works, such as *On the Holy Trinity*. Christ was the Mediator of Life, the Devil of death: the devil mediated human mortality by provoking the fall of Adam, whereas Christ became the mediator who undid the harm that the devil had done.[11] The Devil acted as the antithetical mirror-image of Christ, although weaker and more limited in his abilities.

As a thinker deeply formed by Neoplatonism, Augustine embraced a fairly sophisticated doctrine of spirits, although in many respects the articulation of this doctrine was very different from that in later medieval thought. Angels, including fallen angels, were spiritual creatures with remarkable gifts. A spiritual nature was more excellent than a corporeal nature, even if the will in the spiritual creature was depraved. Angelic spirits were the normal mediators between God and humanity, as Augustine argued with some rather strained exegesis of texts from Genesis.[12] However, Augustine expressed some uncertainty about the differences between the spiritual bodies of spirit-creatures and the physical bodies of human beings. Whether discussing the alleged cohabitation of pagan gods with mortals and the resulting mixed-parentage figures such as Aeneas, or the passage in Genesis 6 that referred to the Angels breeding a race of giants on human women, Augustine seemed unsure whether a spiritual body could have physical and sexual experiences with a mortal person. He even unbent sufficiently to recall the belief that the spirits called *dusii* in Gaul 'constantly attempt and achieve this impure feat; and so many persons of good character have asserted this that it would seem an impertinence to deny it.'[13] Augustine evidently found the idea of physical demonic lust too useful to his moral argument against the wickedness of demons to set it aside for any purely theoretical reason.[14]

Augustine took a slightly different attitude to the miraculous from that which would become normal in medieval Europe. All remarkable effects produced in nature derived ultimately from the power of God manifested in the physical universe. The difference between a 'miracle' and a natural occurrence consisted only in the way that God produced the former. Miracles appeared suddenly, clearly, out of the normal sequence of events, for the edification and benefit of humanity. On the other hand, whether flowers appeared slowly and naturally, or suddenly like the flowering of Aaron's staff, the ultimate cause was the same, the will of God. The 'miracles' produced by the arts of magic, and therefore those achieved by demons, were miraculous only in appearance. By divine dispensation, demons and sorcerers were able to manipulate certain hidden causes and powers within nature that God had placed there. The power to achieve 'miracles' was embedded within nature, and its original was God:

For as mothers are pregnant with young, so the world itself is pregnant with the causes of things that are born; which are not created in it, except from that highest essence, where nothing either springs up or dies, either begins to be or ceases. But the applying from without of adventitious causes, which, although they are not natural, yet are to be applied according to nature, in order that those things which are contained and hidden in the secret bosom of nature may break forth and be outwardly created in some way by the unfolding of the proper measures and numbers and weights which they have received in secret from Him 'who has ordered all things in measure and number and weight': this is not only in the power of bad angels, but also of bad men.[15]

In short, the 'miracles' that demons performed amounted to nothing more than manipulating the potentialities that lay latent in the physical world.

This naturalistic interpretation of the miraculous would be superseded in later thought by a more complex argument about 'miracles' and 'wonders', as will be shown below. However, more durable would be Augustine's reading of the supposed power of divination and foresight exercised by demons. To divination Augustine dedicated a short treatise *On the Divination of Demons*, apparently provoked by the claim that the pagan deities had foretold the demolition of the temple of Serapis at Alexandria.[16] Augustine insisted that God allowed such things to happen without either divine approval or divine support. Demons were able to 'divine' apparently future things for a range of entirely 'natural' reasons'. As spiritual creatures they had much more subtle and refined senses than corporeal human beings. Being extremely rapid in their movement, they could know things occurring a great distance away sooner than people could. With their vastly longer lives, they had gathered greater experience of things than mortals.[17] Human beings ought not to feel inferior to them in these gifts, insofar as birds and animals also had qualities that humans lacked. Even if they could achieve 'miracles', that made demons no better than, say, a skilful craftsman who might be morally inferior to one who lacked his skill.[18] Their apparent 'foreknowledge' Augustine explained partly from their knowing what they themselves intended to do, partly from their identifying natural signs of things to come that human beings lacked the skill to recognize. Because their divining power was essentially natural and not divine, their predictions were often misguided and misleading.[19] The key point of all this, of course, was to contrast the entirely natural abilities of the 'demons' who presided over the pagan oracles with the genuine prophecies of the one true God. The claims of the former, Augustine argued, were spurious and overblown compared with the absolute and eternal powers of God.

Augustine took another angle with pagan learning and lore in his *On Christian Doctrine*, a work that profoundly influenced later medieval commentaries on omens and other related subjects.[20] At heart, *On Christian Doctrine* argued for a mode of biblical exegesis through semiotics; it proposed an appropriate way to handle the figurative and image-laden qualities of scripture. To understand some of this figurative language, the exegete needed some of the scientific and literary techniques of the classical pagans. However, some skills taught in classical paganism were entirely worthless, and Augustine sought to sweep these aside in part of book II of the work. Included in these pernicious arts were the lower-order techniques of discernment associated with pagan 'superstitions', including divination by signs and omens. Augustine used this warning against pagan knowledge to enumerate a range of practices that were in his eyes pointless and fatuous: medical incantations and amulets, superstitions about children or dogs walking between friends being a sign of the disruption of a friendship, or beliefs that sneezing when tying shoes or tripping over the threshold were bad luck.[21] Augustine then embarked on a complex assault on judicial astrology as practised in the Roman world of his day. He demonstrated that most of the characters with which the heavenly bodies were associated in astrology were merely conventional; some dated from very recent times. Like many after him, Augustine argued that the different destinies of twin brothers such as Jacob and Esau demonstrated the falsity of casting horoscopes from nativities.[22]

Augustine's rhetoric on this point inaugurated what would become clichés of medieval superstition-critique. He argued that the business of superstitious observances entailed a contract or pact with demonic spirits: all superstitions 'come from some pestilent association of people and demons, as it were established by a contract of unfaithful and treacherous friendship'.[23] Augustine doubtless intended the oxymoronic concept of a 'pact of unfaithfulness' for rhetorical effect; but it would become a core concept in the medieval explanation of what happened when superstitious rites were used. Augustine exploited this notion, that converse with demons could account for the apparent effects of magical practices, in several settings, including his attack on the 'theurgy' advocated by the Neoplatonist Porphyry.[24] Secondly, Augustine argued that superstitious practice was inherently seductive. Those who engaged in such practices tended to find that, to some extent, they 'worked', and as a divine punishment they tended to become more and more entangled in these kinds of activities. As he pointed out, the wrongness of using soothsayers lay not in the fact that they were always wrong: rather, even when they were right, the spiritual consequences of associating with them were always pernicious to those who used their services.[25]

Augustine therefore contributed to the theological heritage of the Western Middle Ages some key concepts in handling superstitions. Superstition derived from association with and provocation by 'demons'; demons were entirely evil creatures, intelligent, crafty, experienced, and malicious; the cosmos was rigidly divided into the domains and powers of light and darkness, of God and the devil. However, though many of these propositions would be repeated by the scholastics, it is important to note dissimilarities between Augustine and his medieval admirers. Augustine wrote in an era where classical paganism was still a real option for intelligent people. His literal 'demonizing' of pagan spirits and minor deities aspired to draw hard and fast boundaries, where contemporaries might have been tempted into a miasma of syncretism. Augustine, like many of his opponents, was enough of a Neoplatonist to view spiritual beings, and causation in the cosmos, in a different way from medieval Aristotelians even as he insulted and deplored the pagan Neoplatonists for their religious views. In short, Augustine's religious and intellectual contexts differed in significant ways from those of the high and later Middle Ages. However, since he tended to be quoted in short encapsulated extracts or 'sentences' anyway, that difference largely remained hidden from those who used his works.

In so far as Augustine was quoted in extracts that then found their way into canon law collections and especially Gratian's *Decretum*, his impact remained confined to those areas where his metaphysics did not conflict with those of the prevailing Aristotelian orthodoxy. Through the Western Middle Ages a few authors conserved a more Neoplatonic approach to the spirit world, but their influence remained somewhat marginal. A work circulated in the West under the name of the Byzantine theologian and philosopher Michael Psellus (1018–81), a dialogue entitled *On the Workings of Demons*. This short work (now thought by many to have been written by another anonymous author, slightly earlier than Psellus) argued, amongst other things, 'that not merely the daemons, but even the pure angels have bodies, being a sort of thin, aërial, and pure spirits . . . for these effects could not be accomplished otherwise than through the medium of a body.'[26] Marsilio Ficino translated the work into Latin, and it was published along with Iamblichus of Chalcis's *On the Mysteries of the Egyptians* several times from 1549 onwards, bundled with either the works of Ficino or those of Iamblichus.[27] However interesting the Neoplatonic strain in Western thought is for the history of philosophy, it amounted to only a very minor footnote in the analysis of superstition. Neoplatonists generally expended most effort defending their own sometimes esoteric pneumatology and psychology, a task which was more easily accomplished if it was firmly distinguished from popular beliefs. On the other side, Aristotelians who critiqued popular superstitions usually ignored the Neoplatonists, who complicated an image of otherwise broad consensus on the issue of what spirits actually were.

From Late Antiquity to Gratian's *Decretum*

In the declining centuries of Christian late antiquity several pastoral writers contributed significantly to the critique of the popular beliefs of their less educated contemporaries, recently converted from paganism, if at all. Caesarius, bishop of Arles (*c.*470–542), worked as both a pastoral preacher and a monastic leader in southern Gaul. His sermons both documented and criticized many of the folkloric practices still to be found in the society of his time, chiefly because the lines of allegiance in rural society between pagans and Christians were not clearly drawn.[28] Martin, archbishop of Braga in present-day Portugal (*c.*520–80), similarly embarked

on missionary campaigns to convert the remaining pagans of the northern
Iberian Peninsula in the sixth century. He wrote an interesting and much-
studied sermon under the title *On the Correction of the Rustics* criticizing
the superstitions still prevalent among the country people with whom he
worked.[29] The works of Caesarius and Martin were excerpted and quoted
by later writers, to such an extent that it has even been suggested that
the high medieval superstition critique depended essentially on a literary
rather than an empirical tradition.[30] However true this may be of the earlier
writers, by the fourteenth and fifteenth centuries these late antique sources
were overwhelmed by a much more recent corpus of canonical literature,
where they played a minor role.

Much the most important contributors to the medieval heritage of
superstition-lore came from the collectors and encyclopedists of the early
Middle Ages. One of the earliest and most influential was Isidore, archbishop
of Seville (560–636). His *Etymologies* amounted to an encyclopedia of
contemporary learning. His discussion of techniques of divination became
virtually the definitive statement on the subject until it was superseded by
the advent of greater biblical and scriptural erudition in the later sixteenth
century.[31] Isidore's work, along with Augustine's, then contributed to the
erudite if compressed discussion on magic in book 15 chapter 4 of the work
entitled *De rerum naturis*, also known as *De universo*, compiled by Hrabanus
Maurus, archbishop of Mainz (c.780–856), probably in the 840s.[32] The
distillation of Isidore and Hrabanus on this (and other) subjects in due
course fed into the collections of the early collectors of canon law, Regino,
Abbot of Prüm (c.840–915), Burchard, bishop of Worms (d. 1025), and
Ivo, bishop of Chartres (c.1080–1116).[33] The ultimate product of this
process of accumulation of testimonies was seen in the *Decretum* of Gratian
of Bologna, compiled definitively in the middle of the twelfth century. Part
II, case 26 of the *Decretum* was dedicated to a systematic compilation and
reconciliation of the authoritative texts on sorcery and all its branches.[34]

Gratian began his digest on this subject with *Sortilegium*, which could
mean both sorcery in a general sense and, more specifically, the casting of
lots. Gratian argued that the use of lots to make a decision in a sacred story
(e.g. the decision to throw Jonah out of his ship or the election of Matthias
as an apostle) could not be turned into an argument for sortition in ordinary
circumstances. He then incorporated extracts from Augustine against pagan
practices in general.[35] There followed an extended discussion of divination,
drawn from Isidore and Augustine. Gratian then addressed the question of

how those—especially clergy—who engaged in divinatory practices should be punished. It was in this context that Gratian transcribed the famous Canon 'Episcopi' about the alleged night-ride with Diana or Herodias, which Gratian attributed to the Council of Ancyra (314), although the text certainly did not derive from that council.[36] He then repeated his insistence that all magical arts were illusory, appending an extended quotation of a collection of dicta from Hrabanus Maurus and others, fathered on to Augustine, the probable source of some of it.[37] Although the *Decretum* was intended to be a personal digest for teaching purposes, and to attempt to reconcile the jumble of conflicting or apparently conflicting canons in circulation, it rapidly became viewed as an authoritative source. However, its format encouraged the excerpting process, the ripping out of context of selected authorities, which became such a pronounced trait of medieval scholarship. What it could not contribute was a coherent metaphysical theory to explain why superstitions appeared to work, or a coherent ethic—apart from the deontological fact that the Church condemned such practices—to say why one must not use them.

An entirely different form of ecclesiastical literary inheritance helped to shape the superstition-treatises of the late Middle Ages. Certain selected legends from the vast corpus of early medieval hagiography contributed disproportionately to the body of material used by the theological writers. A case in point is the legend ascribed to the life of Germanus, bishop of Auxerre in Gaul (*c*.378–448).[38] Germanus served as a militant evangelist beyond the boundaries of Gaul, leading a celebrated mission to reclaim post-Roman Britain from the Pelagian heresy. However, he was famous in the later Middle Ages for a quite different kind of feat. According to Johannes Nider, the legend of St Germanus related an incident when Germanus had visited a village. He saw a table being prepared late at night in a house; when he was surprised he learned that this was for the 'good women' who came to eat there at night. He stayed up that night and saw a multitude of demons in the form of women sitting at the table. He ordered them not to move; he woke the family, and asked if they recognized those who were eating there. They said they were their neighbours. Then Germanus sent the people to the houses of some of those supposedly at the 'feast', and all were found to be in their beds. On being adjured the demons revealed themselves in their true shapes and confessed that they had deceived the people.[39] This story was a recension, clothed in hagiographic terms, of the cult of 'Habundia', the fokloric fertility spirit or deity who was supposedly propitiated by offerings of produce in agricultural communities.[40] This version of the legend of Germanus was cited in turn by Johannes Nider, Jakob of Jüterbogk, Geiler von Kaisersberg, Alfonso de Spina, and Martin Plantsch, to name but a few.[41]

In general, many of the saints' lives from the early Church referred quite explicitly to the role of demons in the lives of saints. The ability to detect, see, resist, repel, or exorcise demons constituted one of the most regular and potent proofs of sanctity in late antique Christianity. An obvious source for this sort of material would have been the lives of the Desert Fathers, mediated through patristic sources such as Athanasius's *Life of Antony*, Palladius's *Lausiac History* or Cassian's *Conferences*.[42] Johannes Nider, the most prolific teller of holy tall tales in the fifteenth century, cited these patristic hagiographies on several occasions in his *Formicarius*, referring to Cassian and others by name.[43] However, while it is not impossible that some of the more learned demonologists read the original hagiographic texts in the originals (or in Latin translations of Greek originals as the case may be) it is just as likely that these texts were absorbed through collections and abstracts such as Vincent of Beauvais's *Speculum*.[44] The number of late medieval genre paintings that depict the temptations of St Antony testify to a flourishing iconography of demonic tempters.[45] In a number of cases the saints' legends contained posthumous miracles, where a saint appeared to his or her devotee and promised some particular reward, usually guaranteeing ultimate salvation through a good death, as recompense for the devotion shown by the follower in life. Johannes Nider, challenged on the claim that most of these claims were found in the lives of 'new saints', proceeded to cite some earlier examples. He retold the story of the Christian martyr Potamiaena's appearance to her penitent executioner Basilides, from Eusebius; and a story of the promises made by Onofrius the anchorite, as reported by Paphnutius.[46]

The heritage of authoritative texts on superstitions, then, tended to be fragmentary and unsystematic. The early medieval accounts anticipated many of the key principles and arguments of the later medieval analysis; but there was lacking a coherent and agreed 'demonology' that would explain how superstitious practices worked and what was wrong with them. That coherent explanation would emerge, in abundance, during the most productive period of medieval scholastic theology.

6

Scholastic Demonology
in the Twelfth and Thirteenth
Centuries

Peter Lombard and the beginnings of scholasticism

The twelfth and thirteenth centuries were, among much else, a great
age of consolidation, organization and codification in Western European
Christianity. While Gratian was assimilating 'discordant canons' into a more
coherent and consistent digest, Peter Lombard (1095–1160) was attempting
something similar as he taught theology in Paris. The *Book of Sentences*,
compiled during the 1150s, represented the first great systematic codification
of Catholic theology under thematic headings.[1] Moreover, the *Sentences* set
the agenda for the vast majority of Western systematic theologians for the
rest of the Middle Ages and beyond. Nearly every major theologian wrote
a commentary on the *Sentences*, including Bonaventure, Thomas Aquinas,
Albertus Magnus, Duns Scotus, and Peter of Tarentaise (later Innocent
V).[2] The theological debates of later scholasticism were fought over the
exegesis of its short chapters, in a further array of commentaries by such
theological luminaries as Johannes Capreolus, Peter Aureoli, Pierre de la
Palud, and John Major.[3] Lombard's work had a historically very important
characteristic that encouraged this flood of commentary. Intellectually
speaking, it formed a somewhat loose collection of texts and discussions; it
did not seek to impose too much coherence or rigour on to its material.
It encouraged the collection and juxtaposition of earlier authorities and the
discussion of their relative merits on contested questions.

Lombard laid some of the ground rules for the discussion of angels and demons in a large section of the second book of the *Sentences*.[4] First he discussed when in the order of creation the angels were formed. They could not have been created before the heaven and the earth, which had been created 'in the beginning'. It was therefore concluded that the angelic natures were created simultaneously with the corporeal natures, in the very beginning of time itself, and located in the empyrean heaven.[5] Lombard stood rather at the cusp of theological and philosophical change where the nature of the angelic creatures was concerned. He quoted Augustine and others to the effect that the angels might have a sort of 'aery bodies' but also acknowledged as preferable the possibility that they were purely intellectual and incorporeal natures. These speculations led him to explore somewhat ambivalently the question of angels, and God, 'appearing' to people, and demons 'entering into' or possessing people.[6] With relative brevity Lombard sketched out the rival opinions regarding the fall of the evil angels. Some thought that these were created evil from the start; others that they enjoyed a period of free will and then fell. The preferred opinion was that they were very briefly free to choose to be either obedient or rebellious, but that some of them fell soon after.[7] Thus the angels were not created fully perfect, but were good rather than evil. Only those who stood firm in loyalty to God received the full and final beatitude, whereas the fallen ones were irretrievably condemned. Certain kinds of grace were specific to the stages in the beatitude of the good angels.[8] The chief of the fallen angels was Lucifer, who fell through pride. There was some conflict in the texts as to where the demons were located after their fall, some in the middle air and some in hell. Those in the air were probably able to tempt and harass human beings.[9] After the fall of the angels, though good and evil angels each had a kind of free will, they were nevertheless unchangeably bent on right and wrong actions respectively. Good angels had a free will which empowered them only to do good. Evil angels, meanwhile, had not entirely lost their knowledge and abilities. However, they could use physical matter for their purposes only to the extent that God permitted it. Angelic natures could not create new beings except by manipulating the 'seeds' of things in the earth by divine dispensation. In any case, the physical powers of demons were limited by divine control and providence.[10] Compared with later *summae* or indeed with many of his commentators, Lombard wrote something between an agenda for theological discussion and a fully-fledged treatise. Most of his preferred choices would, in fact, become normative for later scholasticism. However, it would take a greater intellectual confidence and certainty than Lombard deployed to form the definitive angelology and demonology of the later Middle Ages.

The rediscovery of a much larger corpus of ancient Greek and Arab metaphysical and philosophical writings transformed the intellectual life of Europe in the later twelfth and early thirteenth centuries. Perhaps the subtlest and most defining characteristic of this age was its greatly enhanced belief in the power of reason.[11] The properly trained logician, plying his skill according to the rules, could discern things about the universe that were not self-evident. Conflicting opinions and authorities could be lined up against each other and either reconciled through subtle distinctions, or tested until one was proved preferable to the other. Since a great deal of the metaphysics available in this era consisted of commentaries on Aristotle, a coincident effect of this intellectual flourishing was that Aristotelian assumptions tended to win out over Platonist ones. The triumph of Aristotle among the theologically learned of the Middle Ages, more than any other intellectual development, shaped the intellectual response to popular beliefs. It was not, of course, an unmodified Aristotle, but the Aristotle of medieval Christian scholasticism, who ruled the metaphysical roost until the middle of the seventeenth century. The assumptions of scholastic Aristotelians about spiritual creatures, about causation and evil in the universe, would not only inform the late medieval superstition-literature, but would also provide the bedrock assumptions shared by Protestant and Catholic rivals in the debates of the sixteenth and early seventeenth century. Many disagreements over the putative 'modernity' (or lack of it) in early modern thought can be resolved if one allows for the continuing role played by scholastic philosophy.

Thomas Aquinas on angels and demons

Easily the most influential of the scholastics in the area of popular beliefs and 'superstitions' was Thomas Aquinas. Aquinas did not, of course, enjoy in the Middle Ages the sort of effortless supremacy that the combined efforts of the Dominican Order and the Society of Jesus won for him between the sixteenth century and the nineteenth. He was controversial in many quarters, and until a revival of his thought in the fifteenth century suffered a relative decline in his reputation.[12] However, so many of the theologians involved in the critique of superstition were Dominicans, or at least followers of Thomas, that Aquinas acquired an ascendancy in this specialized area that he never really relinquished.[13] He contributed fairly little to the detailed casuistic investigation of particular beliefs. In fact, he rarely referred to specific details of magical or superstitious practices or thought-patterns. Where Thomas mattered was in the area of metaphysics, angelology, demonology, and the relationships between spirit and matter. He articulated a full, rational vision of how bodies, souls, and spiritual beings related to each other and to God. From this vision he deduced clear and (relatively) consistent views about what could or could not happen in the universe. All the subsequent writers who explored the subject largely took Thomas's conclusions in these areas as a given. When they disagreed, it was against a shared background of opinions about what was or was not possible.

The following exposition of Thomas's demonological system will rest chiefly on key sections of his two *summae*, the *Summa Theologica* and the *Summa against the Pagans* or *Summa contra Gentiles*.[14] The two works served different functions and followed, in this area, different lines of argument. The *Summa Theologica* offered a resolution of apparently conflicting authorities from scripture and tradition through the application of inferential logic. The *Summa contra Gentiles*, in keeping with a work ostensibly directed towards unbelievers, argued from first principles and philosophical maxims rather than sacred texts. Usually it was only at the end of a chapter that Thomas would introduce, as it were with a flourish, a quotation from scriptural or patristic authorities to demonstrate the orthodoxy of the point just reached. Interestingly, one of the most vexing questions in *Summa contra Gentiles* was how to prove that the evil angels were naturally good, but had *chosen* a path which caused them to be intractably evil: here Aquinas, most unusually, began his discussion with Christian authorities.[15] Besides these two key works of Thomas, reference will be made to his *Commentary on the Sentences*, where Thomas reflected systematically on Peter Lombard's work just discussed; to the much shorter *Quaestio disputata de spiritualibus creaturis* (*Disputed Question on Spiritual Creatures*); and to the *Quaestiones disputatae de malo* (*Disputed Questions on Evil*), composed towards the end of his life, where in the very extended question 16 Aquinas expanded the demono- logical arguments found in his earlier works. The latter treatises elaborated on Aquinas's positions in the *Summae* but did not differ substantially from them. They do, however, suggest a degree of passion for these topics in Thomas's mind.[16]

Thomas began not with the phenomena of popular belief, but with essential questions of being. Thomas speculated with more precision and consistency about the nature of spiritual beings than anyone before him. The question of spiritual creatures, angels whether loyal or fallen, formed the starting point for any theological discussion of causation in the cosmos. Theologians were fond of quoting a saying from the Eastern theologian John of Damascus (c.650–c.750): 'an angel is an intelligent essence, in perpetual motion, with free will, incorporeal, ministering to God, having obtained by grace an immortal nature: and the Creator alone knows the form and limitation of its essence'.[17] Aquinas frequently quoted Damascenus, as he did other early medieval authorities; but in truth his speculations were both more precise and more extensive than his forebears'.

First of all, Aquinas was clear that angelic natures were part of the created order. They were not in any sense participating divinities: they were part of the creation. They began with the divine creation of the primary matter of the cosmos and of time itself. They were created within time, and most appropriately located within the empyrean heaven.[18] This 'creatureliness' of angels would in practice define a great deal about what they could or could not do or know. Secondly, angels were truly incorporeal beings. The perfection of the universe, Thomas argued, required that there should be intellectual creatures. Since intellection was not a bodily function, such creatures had to be without bodies.[19] In the *Summa contra Gentiles* Thomas argued that since we knew that human souls could exist separated from the body, it was logical to infer that some intellectual substances subsisted perpetually without bodies, namely angels.[20] The essential was prior to the accidental, the simpler to the more complex. Such intellectual substances were distinguished from God by the fact that they did not simultaneously realize all their potentialities at once, and were indeed limited.[21] Thirdly, the angelic nature was naturally incorruptible, that is, it could not decay; angels were therefore created immortal.[22] The incorruptibility of angels rested on one of Thomas Aquinas's more curious metaphysical speculations about the angelic nature. Ordinary material creatures were composed of matter and form. Their differentiation within a single species derived from the degree to which the matter reflected, or did not reflect, the essential form. Corruption took place when the matter of their bodies deteriorated from the form to which they belonged. Since angels were not corporeal, they were not composed of matter and form. Since they could not therefore be differentiated by their resemblance to a form, it followed that each angel (including fallen angels) must be a separate species by itself. Material difference from the form, which caused multiples of the same species to exist in the material world, was impossible for angels.[23] Finally, the angels were very numerous, as Thomas argued against those who claimed there were only as many celestial intelligences as there were planetary spheres.[24]

Regarding the unfallen angels, Thomas theorized precisely about the nature and reason of their blessedness. They enjoyed an initial beatitude because of their vision of God, but at that first stage were capable of falling. When those who stayed loyal turned to God, this was a gift of grace, probably innate in their first creation. After their decision to turn to God, they were immediately beatified to the point where they were confirmed in their upright and holy state. Consequently, after this second beatification, blessed angels could not sin.[25] Yet even in their blessed state, there were distinctions between angels, and limits to what the entire order was capable of doing. Aquinas followed the distinction of angels into three hierarchies of three orders each that had been established by Gregory the Great and by the *Celestial Hierarchy* of pseudo-Dionysius, navigating round the slight inconsistencies between these various works about the nine orders.[26] Superior angels could enlighten inferior ones about truths known to the higher orders, although there would always be limits to what the lesser angels could comprehend.[27] In general, however, all angels acquired knowledge of things in a different way from human beings. Since they were not corporeal, they did not form their understanding of things from sense-impressions and then build up knowledge progressively. Put simply, angels did not 'learn' as people do. They knew what they knew by pure intellection without respect to space and time, although they were limited by location and knew different things only sequentially, unlike God who knew everything immediately and simultaneously.[28]

Aquinas and the abilities of spiritual creatures

Important limitations were set to the abilities of all angels, good or bad. First of all, as created beings within time, they did not and could not know the future, except as they could infer from natural causes.[29] Secondly, they could not know the inner thoughts of the human heart, except by inference in the same way that people are capable of doing.[30] Their knowledge of the mysteries of grace was partial, determined by their rank in the celestial hierarchy.[31] Perhaps most importantly for this subject, Aquinas suggested a clear distinction in the matter of miracles. Only God could cause a miracle, in the truest sense of the word, to happen. Aquinas defined a miracle as something that took place entirely against the natural order and sequence of events. In a true miracle, God caused something to happen without the proximate sequence of natural causes being required before the desired outcome occurred.[32] In the *Summa contra Gentiles* Aquinas divided miracles into three categories: those absolutely against the order of nature, as when the sun moves backwards or the sea is divided; those where something natural happens out of the normally possible order, as when the blind see, the lame walk, or the dead are raised; and those where something natural happens without the usual natural causes, as when a fever is cured by a word, or rain falls outside normal weather patterns.[33] Only God could do any of these things, though the degree of disruption to natural patterns varied. It followed that angels, good or bad, could only perform processes that lay within the natural potential of matter. Angels were faster, stronger, and much wiser than people, but they were bound like all created things to the natural potentialities of the created order. On the other hand, 'separated substances' (angels) had the power to cause 'certain marvellous things' (*aliqua mirabilia*) which were not true miracles. Spiritual beings could use the natural potential of things to cause natural events to occur out of the ordinary sequence: by the ingenuity and craft with which they worked on matter, they could cause things to happen in a surprising and amazing way.[34] Angels also could not control the human mind or will. They could, however, present images to the human senses and so influence the decisions made by people. Angels, Thomas argued, could affect the imagination by moving the humours around in the body, or by presenting images to the organs of sense. They could change the senses by interfering directly in the chemical processes of the body, in the way that a choleric person tastes everything as bitter; or they could form objects externally, as for example when angels assumed bodies for the purposes of becoming temporarily visible.[35]

For analysing superstitions, an understanding of the fall of the angels was critical. Since the entire theological explanation of the alleged efficacy of superstitious practices rested on the supposed cooperation of demons with superstitious rites and ceremonies, it was essential that there be a clear idea of why the angels fell, what powers remained to them after their fall, and how human beings might interact with them. Again, Thomas Aquinas provided two intriguing and differently ordered expositions of this problem in his two *summae*. In *Summa Theologica* Thomas argued that the perfection of the universe required that it contain all the possible degrees of goodness. One such lower degree of goodness was that which allowed for the possibility of a fall away from the good. 'Evil' could occur in that which had the inherent possibility to turn aside from good. This formula allowed God to be the creator of a *corruptible* universe while exempting the divine nature from actual responsibility for the presence of evil.[36] Angels, like any other rational creatures, contained in their nature the possibility of sinning: those that could not sin received this as a special grace, not as a natural gift.[37] They could, however, only sin in the way that was appropriate to a spiritual creature. Since they had no bodies, they could not experience the animal, bodily passions of lust or anger (as Aquinas understood these to be).[38] Therefore, the only reason for demonic involvement in people's sexual sins was their desire to offend God as much as possible. The only sin that was consistent with the angelic nature was the sin of pride and disobedience. Specifically, Thomas argued that the first angel to fall desired to attain beatitude, to be like God, by his own efforts rather than by the gift of God.[39] He went on to argue that the first angel to fall sinned almost immediately after being created, and probably was the highest of all; that this angel persuaded others to follow; but that more angels remained loyal than rebelled.[40] Since then, until the Day of Judgement some demons were trapped in the atmosphere above the earth, while others were in hell to torment damned souls. After the Last Judgement all would be finally sealed in hell.[41]

The *Summa contra Gentiles*, with its more restricted use of scriptural and patristic authorities, explained the existence of evil angels by a slightly different route. Here Aquinas actually began with magic. He argued that the rites used in magical practices must (once other options such as astral influences had been eliminated) express an appeal to an intelligent substance. Since magical rituals were often used to procure sinful or indecent things, and since they involved irrational, illusory or deceptive claims, these could not be appeals to good spirits, that is, blessed angels.[42] Magical rituals must therefore consist of appeals to evil spirits. However, it could be demonstrated a priori that intelligent spiritual substances could not be *naturally* or essentially evil. It followed that they must therefore be evil through an act of choice.[43] Once again, Aquinas argued that the only thing that could make intelligent spirits evil was the desire to pursue individual goods against the common good, that is, the sin of pride, which in turn led to hatred against God and envy of human beings.[44] In short, according to *Summa contra Gentiles*, the existence of superstitious magic proved and explained the fall of the angels, rather than the reverse.

Fallen angels were restricted in their abilities and powers as their unfallen counterparts were, but still had considerable freedom to act. They retained all their natural gifts and powers, and many gifts of grace, including their knowledge of the truth. They retained a hierarchy among them. They had the same power to affect the imagination and the senses as good angels.[45] However, they were prone to error unlike good angels, being apt to use false reasoning or to be ignorant of divine revelations: they might not know that a dead body would be resurrected, or that a man might be God incarnate.[46] They could do many surprising and astonishing things, especially in the eyes of human beings; but they could not perform true 'miracles' in the precise sense of the word. However, as Aquinas insisted, sometimes the 'marvels' that they performed were real occurrences and not just illusions, like the serpents and toads produced by Pharaoh's magicians.[47]

The most important distinction between Aquinas's demonology and the popular conception of spirits concerned the will of the demons. For Thomas, the demons were implacable, irretrievably, permanently dedicated to nothing but evil. He argued for this absolute and permanent division on the grounds of the different modes of cognition between people and spirits. People apprehend things progressively and may learn more, or change their minds; spirits learn things instantaneously and completely, and therefore their choices once made are made for ever. Thomas quoted John of Damascus's dictum that the fall of the angels was like death to human beings: it was an irreversible and cosmic change of being, after which no change of state was possible.[48] Given their obstinacy in evil, demons sought to assault people, to cause them harm, to tempt them into evil, and to bring about the damnation of souls. Thomas did not subscribe to the view that all sin derived from the temptations of demons; some sins happened simply because the flesh was corrupt and people with free will turned that way. Only in the sense that the fall derived from the first temptation of Satan in Eden, could the devil be said to be the source of all sins.[49]

Demons and human beings

The final key question for practical pastoral theology was how demons could interact and engage with human beings, and vice versa. This issue received its most important treatment in a series of questions towards the end of the second division of the second part of the *Summa Theologica*. Here Aquinas explicitly addressed the question of what superstition was, how it was subdivided, how it worked, and why it was wrong to practise it. With perhaps excessively schematic thinking, Aquinas argued that superstition represented the excess of religion, whereas unfaithfulness or disbelief represented the defect of it. 'Excess' in this case meant worshipping the wrong being, or the right being in the wrong manner. For practical purposes Thomas divided superstition into three basic categories: *idolatry*, consisting in divine reverence given to a creature; *divination*, which sought knowledge other than from God; and thirdly *superstitious observances*, where the true God was worshipped in an improper manner chosen by human invention.[50] He then expounded each of these in turn. The section on idolatry, perhaps not surprisingly for something written in the mid-thirteenth century rather than the fifth, was somewhat abstract and over-schematized, affording few insights into the matter of Thomas's concerns.[51] The sections on divination and observances, in contrast, were extremely influential on those who followed. Divination was wrong because it aspired to know things from God's perspective without God's gift or permission. As Aquinas quoted with approval from Origen (whom elsewhere he often disagreed with) 'there is a working of the demons in the service of foreknowledge, which is seen in certain arts by those who have given themselves over to the service of demons'. One can serve the demons by worshipping them as gods (in idolatry) but one can also serve them by invoking their help to learn or know something.[52] Although Thomas supplied a great list of divinatory techniques (discussed earlier),[53] his primary interest lay in the theological analysis of the implications of divination. Divination involved, as Augustine had argued, a pact with demons; but it was also harmful because of the deception intended by demonic spirits even when they occasionally told the truth.[54] Moreover, the falsity and irrationality characteristic of so many divinatory techniques virtually ensured that demons would involve themselves in such proceedings. On those grounds Aquinas argued that such things as judicial astrology, interpretation of dreams, and divination by lots were always harmful.[55]

The section on superstitious observances opened with a dismissal of something more proper to intellectual magic than popular belief, the 'notory art' where knowledge was supposed to be obtained by the performance of esoteric rituals. The key argument here, and one that would be repeated endlessly by Thomas's followers, was that where rituals and signs were used that had no natural or reasonable link to the effects they were meant to acquire (in this case, hidden knowledge) it followed that they were 'meaningless empty signs' (supervacua signa) whose only function could be that they gave a signal or prompting to an evil spirit. The art was futile because it was not a function of demons to give enlightenment to human beings, and certainly not through rituals.[56] This line of reasoning, of course, could be and was extended to any conventional set of rituals or formulae not approved by the Church: its usefulness extended far beyond the notory art. Thomas then turned to discuss rituals for healing. These were only licit to the extent that the things used had a 'natural' property to achieve the desired outcome. Of course, contemporary thinkers would differ in what constituted a 'natural' property: Aquinas's view on this was somewhat minimalist. He rejected the Platonic view that herbs and stones inscribed with certain characters could have 'natural' effects. Here he could quote Augustine against Porphyry, citing the former's conviction that such things were associated with demons.[57] Aquinas then made liberal use of Augustine's On Christian Doctrine to prove the falsity of omens. People understood omens not to be caused naturally by the things they portended, but rather as signs: since they could not be signs from God therefore (by the familiar argument by elimination) they were signs from demons.[58] Thomas then concluded the section with a detailed discussion of religious amulets. This section is perhaps the most circumstantial and detailed of these passages in the Summa. Amulets were acceptable, but only as long as they had no unknown signs or names, no falsehoods, no meaningless symbols, but only the approved prayers and symbols of the Church. Thomas's passage on amulets would become one of the most frequently cited passages in the superstition-treatises: interestingly, it was the one where he drew the finest distinctions and attempted to accommodate what must be assumed to be general practice.[59]

As was noted earlier, Thomas argued the fall of the angels from the natural inefficacy of magical ceremonies in Summa contra Gentiles.[60] The care that he took over this argument suggests, potentially, that there was real disagreement in medieval society on this point. The 'respectable' argument for the efficacy of magic claimed that its potency derived from the influences of the stars, and that it therefore belonged to the more or less respectable science of astrology.[61] Aquinas replied that a corporeal object, like a star or planet, could not achieve intellectual effects such as permitting a person to speak a previously unknown language. Magical ceremonies used incantations where the uttering of words conveyed not some natural potency, but rather *meaning*. Meaning could only be conveyed from one intelligent being to another; the clear implication was that such rites entailed communication with spirits. As Thomas went on to argue, such spirits could be inferred not to be good ones.[62]

Limitations to the Thomist analysis

Thomas Aquinas's contribution to the medieval theological analysis of superstition had enormous influence,[63] but was also curiously specific and limited. His approach focused on the schematic and theoretical issues, and did not in general apply the results of his theology to a large range of specific instances in the everyday life of people who were supposedly in danger from the assaults and seductions of demons. While he did offer some specific prescriptions in the area of amulets, Aquinas largely left the detailed application of his ideas to his successors. Secondly, he largely took the existence of magical practices in the world for granted. Only occasionally did Aquinas descend into the arena to defend his views against the sceptics who existed, at least theoretically, in his own time. As for instance when he discussed the canonical saw about impotence caused by sorcery in his *Sentences* commentary:

Some people have said, that there was no sorcery in the world, unless in the belief of people, who ascribe natural effects whose causes are hidden from them to sorcerers. But this is against the authorities of the saints, who say that demons have power over bodies, and over the human imagination, when they are permitted to by God; hence by means of them [demons] sorcerers can do something by means of some sign. This opinion derives from the root of unfaithfulness or disbelief, since such people do not believe in demons except only in the opinions of the common people. Supposedly, the fears they generate for themselves out of their own thoughts, they ascribe to the Demon; when from powerful imagination some images appear in the senses, such as people generate, then it is believed that demons are appearing. However, the true faith rejects these arguments: we believe that the angels fell from heaven, and are demons, and by the subtlety of their nature can do many things which we cannot; therefore those who cause them to do such things are called sorcerers.[64]

It is almost impossible to discern how common such scepticism about spiritual beings may have been, if indeed Aquinas were not here simply raising up a straw figure to knock down. On the whole, however, he seems to have been content to work largely within his metaphysical comfort zone, only occasionally rebutting the excesses of Peripatetic materialism or pointing out the dangers of the loose Platonic theory of spirits.

Given his explicit dependence on patristic and occasionally canonical authorities, especially Augustine, pseudo-Dionysius, John of Damascus, and (occasionally) Origen, one might ask what exactly Aquinas contributed that was new to the Church's lore of arguments around spirits, magic, and superstitions. Two things immediately stand out. First, Thomas integrated the doctrine of spirits into his metaphysic in a way that rooted the absolute evil of demons in basic theory as never before. The incorporeal nature of angels, and their specific manner of intellection, served to justify with complete cogency (if one accepted his premises) the idea that there were only two kinds of spirits in the universe, good ones and bad ones. In place of Augustine's rather loose argument from insult about the stage plays of the pagan myths, Aquinas provided a metaphysical description of an angel's essence that depended on the binary moral division of the spirit-world. This rigid binary scheme would, of course, be very hard to apply in a pastoral context. Common sense suggests that human beings will more readily imagine spirits to be broadly similar to themselves, rather than entirely 'other' in their mental processes, as Aquinas described them. However, the binary approach would determine how most of the theologians of the succeeding centuries were trained to think about spiritual beings. Secondly, Thomas contributed to popularize, insofar as he did not invent, what one might call the diagnosis of elimination in regard to the workings of charms, spells, and magical symbols. If incantations do not engage with the astral natures (which they do not) and do not have natural properties to achieve their alleged effects (which they have not), then all that remains is that a magical or superstitious ritual constitutes a sign communicating meaning to a spiritual creature. This argument from exclusion would be enormously popular in the hands of the late medieval pastoral theologians, as will be seen below.

Some important questions Thomas did not resolve in a decisive way, and his relative lack of clarity here contributed to the debates among his successors. While (as in the extract above) he referred to 'divine permission' as a necessary condition of the activities of demons, he did not specify very precisely how far that permission extended. Later thinkers would go to one of two opposite extremes. Some construed God's permission to the demons as a sort of broadly based open charter to tempt and assail; others interpreted each demonic temptation as flowing from a specific act of God's providential government of the world. While Aquinas devoted several questions of the *Summa Theologica* to providence, his main concern was to ensure that providence did not entail determinism or deny free will.[65] Secondly, one could argue that Thomas did not develop the precise operation of 'demonic pact' as clearly as some of his more pastorally minded successors. While it is possible to construe out of Thomas's writings most of the later theory of demonic pact (explicit or, more commonly, tacit and implicit) as the basis for superstitious rituals, he did not articulate the idea behind the pact, supposed or inferred, as much as many of his followers.

It remains debatable how far the Dominican Thomas Aquinas was truly 'preachable' on these questions. Some of the later efflorescence of pastoral literature suggests that a need was felt to apply his principles to particular actions and customs more than he had done himself. Certainly that was how he was used. Aquinas's massive and magisterial works became quarries from which later generations of ecclesiastical writers could source authoritative principles to apply in their own writings. Sometimes they cited him by name; sometimes not. There can be no more compelling tribute to the influence of his principles on this issue than the rapidity with which they became common currency among theological writers.

7

The Demonological Reading of Superstitions in the Late Middle Ages: Areas of Consensus

The style, manner, and diversity of theological writing changed perceptibly in Europe around the middle of the fourteenth century, for reasons not entirely clear. Scholastic theology continued to be written, and indeed proliferated into the various competing schools of the late Middle Ages. However, alongside the traditional academic analysis of dogma there arose a significant literature of pastoral advice based on *applied* scholastic premises and arguments. Whether as professional academics or simply as clergy in positions with cure of souls, a range of writers wrote an increasingly diverse array of works of ethical and practical guidance based on detailed cases of conscience. The largest corpus of such literature consisted of the *summae* for confessors. These works responded to the obvious need of pastoral clergy (and the mendicants who persistently heard confessions) for guidance through the multiple pitfalls of administering the sacrament of penance. Towards the end of the Middle Ages such works became veritable encyclopedias, and with the first half-century of printing appeared in multiple editions.[1] There also appeared a range of specialized works to address particular pastoral and ethical needs. It is to this broader range of literature that the late medieval superstition treatises belong. They testify to a belief among the clergy that even the most concrete and practical problems in priestly ministry could be analysed and explained using the categories and approaches derived from scholastic theology. Consequently, the application of superstition-theory to particular instances and circumstances, the one aspect that was lacking in the work of someone like Thomas Aquinas, is found in exuberant abundance in the pastoral writings of the fifteenth and sixteenth centuries.

Late scholastics did not all speak with a single voice. The different *viae* into which scholastic thought had fragmented by the fourteenth century gave different nuances and a subtly different vocabulary to writers from different schools. Additionally, the personalities, choices, and experiences of the various authors affected their style and accent quite visibly. This chapter will concentrate on those areas where, on the whole, there was some measure of agreement and resemblance between the various texts. In the following chapter an analysis will be offered of what appear to have been the most significant differences between them, even to the point where one might almost discern rival schools of thought in terms of pastoral advice. That discernment process requires a delicate and subtle handling of the sources, since no theologian expressed an overt wish to be a partisan or partial witness, and all shared certain key assumptions and intellectual methods.

The natural inefficacy of charms and spells

In their various ways the late medieval theologians argued first that, regardless of the means or techniques employed, superstitious rituals and performances, in themselves and by their own *natural* powers, did not achieve the effects they were supposed to do. The reason was that their physical material, whether material objects or words spoken or written, could not acquire special *natural* properties by an artificial process.[2] The same argument applied whether the intention behind the superstitious or magical rite was good or evil. As Nikolaus von Dinkelsbühl observed with some disdain, referring to the popular healing charms in use in his day, 'it is quite clear that [these performances] have no natural power to do anything useful: for who is so stupid, as not to realize that a hole in a piece of paper made with a toenail has no natural power to heal a person? . . . this is a deception [*Getewsch*] as the sick person realizes when he comes to his senses.'[3] On the other side of the ledger, Johannes Nider argued in just the same way about harmful spells: 'the actions of sorcerers do not effect those things directly, by their own proper and immediate action...the stick with which the witch strikes the water to make it rain does not cause the rain.'[4] Later in the fifteenth century, Bernard Basin argued very similarly that shapes, like the carved image of the lion discussed by Gerson, or the bronze mouse supposedly used by Virgil to drive the mice out of Naples, could not affect living creatures; and that words, written or spoken, could not affect matter in the way that magicians alleged.[5]

However, possibly the most thorough exploration of the natural ineffectiveness of superstitious rituals came from the pen of the Tübingen theologian Martin Plantsch in the early 1500s. Like Nider, Plantsch was concerned with the causes of misfortune and the attribution of misfortune to hostile sorcery. However, the logic of his critique applied to both good and bad spells. He argued that if spells were supposed to work 'naturally', then their effects must flow from the natural properties of the materials used in the spell. So,

If the charms written down produce health in me, then all written charms have this effect; but all charms are written in the same ink, of the same species, because charms are nothing other than ink drawn on parchment in various ways; but then as all drops of the same ink are of the same substantial material, so all charms written in the same ink are of the same species, wherefore, if your charms written with ink and sold in the market cure this infirmity by natural power, then my charms written in the same ink will heal the same infirmity. It does not matter if I write different words from those which you write, because mine and yours are written in the same ink, hence, notwithstanding how diversely I may have drawn the drops of ink across the parchment, those drops do not begin to be of a different species from your drops of the same ink, drawn otherwise on parchment of similar material.[6]

The same logic applied to spells spoken and pronounced by the healer or the sorcerer: words were, substantially, nothing more than 'air broken with the tongue'. Likewise, images made of wax or other materials did not acquire 'natural' power through being moulded, cast, or cut into a specific shape or pattern. Jean Gerson reproached a physician in Montpellier for using a medallion with an image of a lion engraved on it to cure diseases of the kidneys. Gerson postulated that 'symbols, shapes, or letters do not have or acquire, from purely natural and bodily causation, any physical power; just as mathematical signs, to which symbols and shapes also belong, do not belong to the active powers, and in them (according to Aristotle) is neither any [specific] good nor purpose'.[7] As Pedro Ciruelo, in his popular vernacular treatise against superstitions from sixteenth-century

Spain remarked, 'all wise men, philosophers, and theologians agree in saying that men's words have no inherent power. A word is nothing more than a puff of air emitted from a man's mouth. A word is not a natural curative which can heal any illness. It has no power to counteract choler as rhubarb does, nor, like fungus, can it purge the body of phlegm.'[8] It was not acceptable to argue that rituals or objects acquired 'natural' properties when *meaning* had been given to them through their being formed or shaped in a particular way. Truly natural effects inhered in the substantial properties of the materials used, and not in anything else. This argument ran contrary to the assumptions of many in later medieval and early modern culture, not just the Paracelsians.[9] Even in the late sixteenth and early seventeenth centuries some medical writers such as Juan Bravo of Coimbra were apparently willing to argue that charms worked 'by the natural power of words'.[10] The contrary theological opinion, therefore, should not just be assumed to be self-evident or common sense. Rather it rested on a particularly rigorous application of Aristotelian physics. The classical theological opinion distinguished between, on one hand, the natural actions of material substances upon other matter, and, on the other, the communication of meaning and intention through symbols between one intelligent being and another.

How charms work: 'implicit' demonic pact

However, because superstitious rituals did not have 'natural' effects, it did not follow that they were entirely ineffective in every sense. Curiously, theologians in the late Middle Ages and early modern period rarely if ever applied a rigid scepticism to the phenomena they encountered. Rather they took the data in the narrative sources (especially authoritative sources such as scripture) for granted, and asked only how to explain the reported occurrences. The evidence for the *apparent* efficacy of superstitious performances and magical rites appeared to be copious and irresistible, so the only question was how to explain their workings in a way consistent with theological metaphysics. By the same rigid logic as seen in Aquinas, therefore, it followed that superstitious rituals could only 'work', could only have a physical effect, by communicating with another intelligent being endowed with the power to achieve the observed effects. Moreover, those intelligent beings had, by elimination, to be evil spirits.

Theologians invented a powerful, and pastorally flexible, interpretative tool to deal with the apparent effectiveness of superstitious practices. They construed an 'implicit pact' that was supposedly entered into by the superstitious adept with a demon. According to such a pact the demon caused the desired effect, when prompted to do so by the performance of an illicit ritual. As early as Nikolaus von Dinkelsbühl's vernacular exposition of the Ten Commandments, one could read that 'in all superstitions the effect comes from a pact that someone has or makes with the devil, whether privately or publicly'.[11] Nikolaus von Dinkelsbühl here struggled to express in contemporary German the idea of 'implicit' versus 'explicit' pact. The key point about an 'implicit pact' was that the one who entered into it made no overt or conscious gesture to initiate it. It happened as a result of actions taken recklessly, rather than through a positive decision, let alone some personal encounter with a demon. Jean Gerson articulated this idea in its pastoral and psychological fullness. In 1398 he postulated that 'an observance to achieve some effect, which may not reasonably be looked for either from God working by a miracle or by natural causes, ought among Christians to be regarded as superstitious and to be suspect of an implicit or explicit pact with demons.'[12] Gerson then unpacked this basically Thomist argument as follows. Demons were subtle, and sought to seduce people rather than attack them frontally. Therefore they devised ritual means by which people might serve them in quest for their bodily desires for wealth, honour, sexual gratification, or knowledge of the future. People took up such superstitious practices because of curiosity and the desire for the forbidden. They were incurably credulous; they blamed their failures on their own carelessness or failure to perform the ritual correctly. They would believe in the power of a superstitious rite even if it worked only one time in ten.[13] Demons were in no way constrained by such rituals; rather, they chose to respond to them as a way of soliciting further respect and reverence. In a sequence of other short works Gerson similarly deployed the notion that pacts with demons to achieve magical effects might be overt or merely implicit and hidden.[14]

Early sixteenth-century writers deployed this argument with increasing sophistication. Jakob van Hoogstraten approached the question legalistically. Someone who used superstitious rites 'knew, or ought to know' that neither by natural powers nor by specific divine ordinance ought those rites to work. Therefore, someone who used them, knowing that there was neither natural nor divine sanction behind them, was in effect 'looking for such

effects to be given him from the demon, and in consequence virtually
or tacitly consenting to the service of demons. For such consent may
reasonably be regarded as a tacit pact.'[15] Martín de Castañega showed more
sympathy. Sometimes people thought themselves still to be good Christians
and not to have renounced the faith, but believed in and practised the
same 'diabolical ceremonies'. By doing so they entered into an implicit
pact, because in these ceremonies they virtually or effectively renounced
the faith. Alternatively, other people might not believe in such things, but
practised them anyway in the search for health, saying according to the
Spanish proverb *valgan lo que valieren*, 'for whatever they are worth'; this
was a mortal sin and an occult pact, 'though not as serious as the other
kinds'.[16]

A certain kind of pastoral reasoning lay behind the idea of 'implicit pact'.
The whole point of an *implicit* pact was that those who supposedly entered
into it did not know that they were doing so. Those who used superstitious
techniques believed (if they reflected on the causality behind their actions
at all) that they were either using something morally neutral, or something
(as we shall see shortly) on the outer margins of normal Christian practice
at worst. Theologians took it on themselves to persuade their hearers
and readers that such people were 'really' using the services of evil spirits
even, or perhaps especially, when the purpose was apparently benign.
The theological critique sought to corral a range of supposedly useful
practices into the enclosure of evil magic, where they could be subjected
to official disapproval and condemnation. However, all this rhetoric could
not conceal the fact that an 'implicit pact' was a purely virtual, construed,
hypothetical reality, and one of which the human participant was entirely
unaware. The nearest analogy to this sort of constructive reinterpretation of
reality lies in the canon law of marriage. In canon law, a consensual sexual
relationship, entered into by two adults not under any legal impediment,
could be construed as a canonically binding 'marriage' by consent, awaiting
only confirmation through a formal ceremony. More notoriously, previous
liaisons entered into by someone subsequently married to another person
could be cited as 'pre-contracts' if it were desired to annul the marriage.[17]
Medieval religious thought could and did reinterpret perceived realities to
make them conform to theological norms.

The late medieval theological critics of superstition pointed out with
disarming frankness how many superstitious rites were in fact deeply
entangled in popular thought with the practices of traditional Catholic

Christianity. In the early fifteenth-century dialogue *Dives and Pauper*, the questioner remarked that those engaged in superstitious divination appeared to be devout, pious, ascetic people, and impressed those who saw them with their religious character. 'Pauper', the figure of the friar who is the teacher throughout the dialogue, replied that any holy things abused in magical practice were in fact all the greater insult to God, and that religious devotions used for 'witchcraft' were 'a wol heye sacrifyce to the f[i]end'.[18] Very similarly, Gerson in his *Triologium* on astrology objected that

if someone alleges that many things are often commanded to be observed in the magic arts or sorcery which are holy and honourable: as to fast, to be chaste, to say the *Pater Noster* and the Gospel: one person used to answer truly and Catholically, that superstition is all the worse, the more good things are mingled in with it, since by that means by which God ought to be honoured, the devil is honoured.[19]

Johannes Nider, and following him, Geiler von Kaisersberg and Martín of Arles, observed similarly that sorcerers habitually made use of holy or consecrated objects, for example by drawing a thread through the chrism, or placing a wax image under an altar-cloth. This was, Nider argued, to involve the people in even greater sin by adding sacrilege to perfidy; but he also acknowledged that such appropriation of religious things served to persuade people that something good was being done.[20]

Here again two interpretations of invisible things clashed. To the theologian divine worship was being misapplied to demonic forces at the demons' own, albeit secret, provocation. To the popular mind, protective rituals simply deployed the transferable holiness inhering in sacred objects for people's material benefit. Ironically, the theologians' reasoning tried to create a vast cosmic gulf between rituals that were, in reality, divided from acceptable religious practice by a faint line drawn unsteadily in shifting sand. This paradox emerges with especial clarity in a work described earlier, the treatise *On Certain Cases of Conscience Relating to Superstition* by Heinrich von Gorkum.[21] This treatise sought to separate the acceptable from the superstitious in a range of para-liturgical practices, the use of Candlemas wax to protect against fire in the name of St Agatha, the use of crosses made from the bones of meat enclosed within the altar during Holy Week, and so forth. Generally Heinrich von Gorkum approved of the devotion involved, and endorsed the appeal to specific saints for protection against particular dangers. However, people ought to realize that the power to protect did not inhere in the objects themselves. Laypeople doubtless believed that in the amulet, or whatever else, there was an inherent power to achieve certain desired effects; 'but [such belief] is entirely vain when used with this intention.'[22] Heinrich warned against the belief that any shape or design had inherent power. Even the shape of the cross contained no potency of itself. It was not a naturally potent thing like a magnet; rather, out of respect for its significance God more often worked wonders through it.[23] To believe that wearing the names of the three Magi as an amulet would *of itself* preserve from disease proceeded from a false opinion, 'and thus is made a certain tacit contract with the ancient adversary, with whom we are committed to eternal warfare, and therefore to no agreement of friendship whatever.' People ought to be advised by their pastors against trusting in such 'fantasies' to the extent that they were frivolous, 'and invented by evil spirits who try to cover their deviousness under the appearance of goodness'.[24] In the eyes of the pastoral theologian, religious orthodoxy formed a narrow and sharply defined path, and those who strayed even slightly outside it risked entering the domain of demonic spirits via implicit pact. Moreover, the dividing line was formed not by the use or abuse of a particular ritual, but by the spiritual expectations that one brought to it. A wrong 'reading' of the rite could turn a voluntary devotion into a dangerous superstition.

Reshaping popular belief through demonology

The binary opposition between the divine and demonic economies of salvation gave some writers a whole structure for their exposition of the evils of superstition. As the inverter, perverter, and satirist of everything that God has established in the world, the devil could be expected to have his anti-sacraments, his anti-church, his rival and inverted divine dispensation. Geiler von Kaiserberg pointed out that the devil, cast out from heaven but wishing to imitate God, had established his own 'sacraments'; although, since the devil was both treacherous and not entirely master of his own domain, the demonic sacraments often failed to achieve their effects, unlike the divine sacraments.[25] Martín de Castañega pressed the antithesis further: there were two churches and two congregations in the world, the divine and the diabolical; the devil's church had its own 'sacraments' or 'execrations' in the form of superstitious rites, composed of rare materials, obscure and meaningless words, and substances very difficult to find.[26] This binary or dualistic cosmology has, of course, already been observed in relation to the literature on witchcraft, which derives so much and in many ways resembles and even overlaps with the literature on superstitions.[27] However, there is a subtle but important difference. The world of the demon-worshipping collective cult of witches was a pure fantasy and illusion, and there the language of binary opposites could be deployed without restraint. The world of the superstitious was not so evidently a matter of imagination; rather, theological writers described real activities conducted by real people, but reinterpreted them to accord with their dogmatic presuppositions.

In a number of areas scholastic demonology and popular folklore clashed. To make the reported phenomena fit with the demonological rules about what could and could not happen in the world, the writers on superstition had repeatedly to reinterpret or re-explain stories of marvellous or mysterious events or transformations. Again, they did not take the apparently simpler course of simply denying their veracity, but rather retold the stories to mesh with their cosmology. Geiler von Kaisersberg regaled his Strasbourg audience with thorough analyses of the many stories about people who had allegedly been turned into animals by acts of sorcery.[28] He related a variety of tales derived from William of Auvergne and Vincent of Beauvais, where people believed themselves to have been turned into wolves. Generally, Geiler echoed the orthodox explanation that such transformations occurred only in the disordered imaginations of the people concerned, and that to onlookers they appeared to be behaving very oddly but not to be physically transformed.[29] Geiler then turned to the range of zoomorphic transformations reported in classical mythology: Circe turning the companions of Ulysses into swine, or the companions of Diomedes allegedly turned into birds. In each case the preacher reinterpreted the story to fit with what was credible according to his theory. Since it was beyond the power of a devil or a sorcerer to change one creature into another, the explanation must be that these apparent transformations were achieved either by illusion, or by the very rapid substitution of one object for another so that a real transformation seemed to have happened. At times the explaining-away almost acquired a comic aspect. Those unfortunate people who believed themselves to have been turned into pack-horses or mules by sorcery were, in reality, still human beings: they were enabled to carry loads more appropriate to pack-animals only because demons hovered invisibly in the air above them and supported part of the weight of their loads.[30]

Theologians dwelt at some length, sometimes to their own evident embarrassment (and sometimes not) on the question of sexual relationships between demons and people. In contrast to the writers specifically devoted to the supposed witch-cult, writers on superstition chiefly focused on the sexual assaults of demons on people during sleep, and the question of whether it was possible for a child to be born through demonic intercourse with an incubus or succubus. As noted earlier, Augustine had seemed to give credence to the stories of fauns and *dusii* in his writings, and this gave the legends credibility among the scholastics.[31] Thomas Aquinas dealt with the issue only obliquely when discussing the physical capacities and limitations of angels. Aquinas insisted that even if (according to Augustine) demonic sexual intercourse might actually take place, no hybrid child could be born from this union, since demons had no bodily material. It followed therefore that any child claimed to have been conceived after demonic intercourse must have been produced with male semen stolen from a man by a demon in the form of a succubus, then implanted in a woman by the same demon acting as an incubus. In such an event the child would be entirely human.[32] This ingenious and somewhat distasteful imagery saved appearances for the theologians. In place of the jealous nymphs and lustful satyrs of classical and Gothic folklore, there remained only anaemic, emotionless, hostile demons, seeking to use yet another human frailty to harm souls and lead them to destruction. Johannes Nider developed the question of demonic sex in unusual detail in two chapters of the fifth book of *Formicarius*. He explored the stories of demonic sexual harassment from Augustine through medieval ecclesiastical lore to William of Auvergne and Thomas of Brabant. He related the story of a mysterious courtesan who had mixed among the many prostitutes at the Council of Constance, making large profits before disappearing in a puff of smoke.[33] While fully accepting Thomas's explanation of what happened in such demonic liaisons, Nider was more interested in telling stories of how such things had happened in specific instances. Some stories he believed were genuine; others were the products of seduction or fraud by unscrupulous men. He also discussed a range of possible remedies, including exorcism, confession, the use of relics, and, rather curiously, moving away from the place where the assaults had occurred. He related a series of exempla to prove these points: sacramental confession had freed a widow from molestation by one incubus; St Bernard's staff laid on a bed had released another woman from vexation.[34]

Later writers copiously and repeatedly copied or paraphrased Aquinas's interpretation of the incubus phenomenon. Jakob of Jüterbogk also included incubi among a range of problems requiring ecclesiastical exorcism.[35] Martín of Arles used the received lore on incubi to explain a disturbing dream suffered by a female penitent whose priest had sought Martín's advice about it.[36] Two preachers, Martin Plantsch at Tübingen and, following him, Geiler von Kaiserberg at Strasbourg, included stories of demonic intercourse in their sermons to the urban populace. Plantsch speculated without apparent discomfort about how a man might believe himself to be enjoying a sexual encounter with an illicit lover when he was actually sleeping with a corpse and a demon combined. Geiler, more modestly, while borrowing Plantsch's arguments, remarked that it was 'not nice' (*nicht hübsch*) to dwell overmuch on such things.[37] Martín de Castañega followed Geiler's advice and handled the material more circumspectly.[38] Silvestro Mazzolini was more preoccupied with those human beings who voluntarily associated with demons, and envisaged relations with incubi more in terms of the deliberate indulgences of witches. He insisted that 'those who deny the reality of incubi and succubi are neither good Catholics nor good philosophers'. Probably under the influence of the *Malleus Maleficarum*, which he quoted extensively, Mazzolini seemed more ready than he should have been to accept the possibility of real miscegenation between humans and demons, until he corrected himself.[39] This was perhaps a pardonable slip, given that according to Pius II a French cardinal could accuse the bishop of Arras of being 'unless I am mistaken the son of an incubus' when urging his total unsuitability for the cardinalate to the pope.[40]

Most pastoral theologians in the later Middle Ages appear to have been somewhat less troubled by the opposite problem, interference with sexual relationships between one human being and another. This problem included disordered or misdirected desire, as well as sexual dysfunction or impotence supposedly caused by evil spirits. The main issue for pastoral theologians was to ensure that while the potentialities of demonic ill will were fully acknowledged, it was vital to preserve human responsibility for sexual sins, as seen earlier.[41] There were some important exceptions to the widespread comparative reticence. Johannes Nider took great interest in this subject in one chapter of the *Formicarius*. Demons, 'Theologus' argued, could not exert force on the human mind directly, though they could alter and confuse the sense-impressions on which mental decisions were made. Nider cited one of the classic exegeses of *Sentences*, book 4 distinction 34, that written by Pierre de la Palud, a particularly subtle analysis of the pastoral response to different forms of impotence.[42] Such interference was caused, of course, not by the rituals that sorcerers used with material objects such as the testicles of cockerels, but directly by the demons at the prompting of human sorcerers and witches. Nider then explored a range of patristic and medieval legends of how saints had been able to repel or resist this form of demonic temptation.[43] In the following chapter Nider discussed at length the remedies for inordinate sexual desire. As usual he combined sophisticated scholastic theology with fanciful ecclesiastical legends about how the gift of chastity was given to saints in the past. The legends sat rather awkwardly with the theology, since they often discussed stories of saints who prayed for some special grace to be made entirely sexually incapable, rather than just to resist temptation.[44] The most persistent fascination with the mechanics of diabolical intervention in human sexuality was evinced, however, by Heinrich Krämer in the *Malleus Maleficarum*. The *Malleus* was a curiously disordered and extreme text. It displayed greater credulity and less theological discipline than most other works of the Dominican school of pastoral theology. Krämer discussed the question of male emasculation by sorcery with far greater detail than the other superstition-writers, and did not always stick to the theological line of what was or was not possible to demons. His discussion of incubi and succubi strayed very visibly outside the agreed post-Thomistic position. He copied some of Nider's tales of sorcery in the Bernese Oberland and deployed them with less scholastic exegesis than was normal.[45]

The demonological explanation intruded into more or less every area of popular and folkloric fears and anxieties. In fact, so durable and so persistent was this interpretation, so thoroughly did it suffuse the preaching and literature of instruction, that demonic readings of mysterious occurrences must have become, to some extent, part of popular belief and culture themselves. As was observed in the previous chapter, most theologians following Aquinas persistently introduced demonic pact into the explanation of the workings of the evil eye, though there were rare exceptions and qualifications to this.[46] William of Auvergne's stories of 'changelings' linked them to the lore of incubi and succubi. Such children were supposed to be children of incubi substituted by demons. Such substitution supposedly explained their abnormal responses to nutrition and inability to thrive. Above a certain age they often disappeared, and were alleged really to be demons in the form of children.[47] (Helpfully, the theological writers suggested that such afflictions occurred to punish excessive parental affection.) Of course, according to a consistent theologian like Thomas incubi could not have children of their own, and the offspring generated by incubus relationships were purely human. William of Auvergne seems here to have been trying to mediate in theological language the notion that changelings were 'fairy children', spirit-creatures literally substituted, 'changed', for the real children at birth. A similar story, roughly and imperfectly accommodated into the demonological structure, was told in the sixteenth century about a Bavarian nobleman. His wife died, but then reappeared to him after her death, offering to (re)marry him if he gave up swearing. She lived (if that is the word) with him for some years and even bore him some 'sad, pale children', until one night when drunk he swore at a maidservant, at which his demon-wife vanished.[48] Like Alfonso de Spina in his *Fortress of the Faith*, theological writers struggled to encompass within the category of 'demons' all the exotic diversity of spirit-creatures found in popular belief.[49] Occasionally the irreducible logic of folklore burst the restricting bounds of scholastic dogmas about angels and demons.

Gender and superstition

Theorists of superstition included in their treatises some conventional arguments about gender, although those arguments should be approached with some caution. According to a cliché regularly found in the superstition-literature, women were particularly prone to engage in superstitious activities and to pass on the lore regarding them. Johannes Nider was responsible here, as in so many other areas, for disseminating ideas that others copied. In this case he may have derived his arguments from earlier writers such as William of Auvergne (d. 1249).[50] Women were supposedly more prone to engage in superstitious activities because they were more credulous than men. They were naturally more impressionable, and more prone to extremes of good and evil. They were loquacious, and unable to keep silent about the things they learned from others. Those who were widowed had no ready means of physical defence against their enemies, so were more especially tempted to use harmful sorcery.[51] Secondly, the circumstances and cultural surroundings of childbirth supposedly formed a fertile ground for the spreading of superstitious ideas. New mothers were physiologically prone (it was argued) to fantasies and mental disturbances because of their condition. More importantly, they tended to be surrounded by older women steeped in superstitious lore, and to imbibe it in circumstances where such lore spread unchecked.[52] Geiler paraphrased Nider's arguments in their entirety in one of the sermons in his cycle on the subject.[53] The *Malleus Maleficarum*, though much more notorious, was again cruder and less specific in its anti-feminism than many of the contemporary works.[54] Martín de Castañega paraphrased the conventional explanations, adding a few more speculations that muddied the waters by contrasting female sorcerers with more intellectual male magicians.[55]

The gendered explanation for superstitious activities was a trope, a theme repeated derivatively over and over again by a multiplicity of writers. It had at most a very weak causal connection to the rest of their arguments. A rather different impression of the theologians' attitude to gender and superstitions emerges if one reads the literature as a whole. Certainly the treatises did refer repeatedly to women using healing charms, or to women adopting preventative measures to protect children or to ensure success in traditional female pursuits such as dairying. However, they also referred to superstitious activities being regularly practised by two other categories of people, clergy (especially those on the fringes of the clergy, those in lesser orders, and travelling irregular mendicants) and soldiers. While some authors suggested that superstition was female precisely *because* organized religion was a male preserve, in practice the same authors acknowledged, and the evidence shows, that many clerics engaged in both liturgy and superstitious practices.[56] There was hardly a less typically female activity, in that era, than the military life. Yet theory, narrative, and surviving artefacts all confirm that soldiering and weapons were thoroughly encrusted with superstitious lore.[57] The theorists of superstition made no attempts whatever to conceal the involvement of these two characteristically male professions in magical activities. No attempt was made to streamline the descriptions or the critiques of superstition according to the theoretically gender-based perceptions of this culture.

Acceptable counter-measures

One final observation needs to be made about the agreed critique of popular superstition in the minds of the late medieval theological writers. In terms of pastoral guidance as well as analysis, the superstition-treatises tried to draw hard and fast lines where popular custom and practice saw a hazy miasma of infinite variety. Pastoral theologians wished ordinary people to confine their choice of preservatives and remedies as strictly as possible to those approved and endorsed by the Catholic Church. As will be seen later, this prescription posed internal problems of its own, since it was by no means clear where orthodox practice ended and superstitious error began. However, that did not prevent theologians from engaging in much sententious rhetoric on the subject. There were, as pastoral writers as diverse as Martin Plantsch and Silvestro Mazzolini pointed out, abundant preservative rituals approved of and provided by Holy Church itself. Martin Plantsch argued that those who feared themselves to be suffering from hostile sorcery could use a range of officially approved means of protection. First was the sacrament of penance, since many afflictions might be caused by sin. Then one might use the rite of exorcism, and the array of *sacramentalia* consecrated to protect against misfortune, as described in Chapter 3 of Part One.[58] Geiler von Kaisersberg dedicated two sermons to paraphrasing very closely Plantsch's recommendations in this area.[59] The message was that laypeople ought not to think that superstitious remedies were their only recourse. Silvestro Mazzolini insisted that 'there is no shortage of preservative remedies against the spells of witches'. His remedies included confession, the use of sacramentals, indeed much the same list as Plantsch's, however much they disagreed on other areas. Later on in the treatise the two diverged when it was a question of counter-magical rites.[60]

At times, of course, the distinction between the acceptable and the unacceptable was far from clear even to relatively well-informed ecclesiastics. Here the series of conditions applied by Thomas Aquinas to amulets proved extraordinarily useful to later medieval writers.[61] So did a series of prescriptions that Aquinas offered for discerning superstitions in general:

Thus whatever a person does that pertains to the glory of God, and to that which subjects the human mind to God, and also [subjects] the body through the balanced restraint of the desires, according to the ordinance of God and the Church and the custom of those among whom someone lives, is not superfluous in divine worship. If however there is something that in itself has nothing to do with either the glory of God, nor to that which brings the human mind to God, or that restrains the concupiscence of the flesh; or if it is against the institution of God or the Church, or against common custom (which according to Augustine is to be considered as law): that thing is entirely superfluous and superstitious, since consisting only in externals it has no relationship to the internal worship of God.[62]

Johannes Nider took the passage from St Thomas and elaborated it into a set of casuistic rules for distinguishing the superstitious from that which was not. He added a few additional criteria: one should consider whether a rite was likely to produce a result by natural causes, 'which physicists, medical people and astrologers can decide better than theologians'; and one should consider whether it is likely to cause offence.[63] Nider's paraphrase was cited by others, for example by Silvestro Mazzolini and Martín of Arles.[64] The problem with criteria of this kind was that they were extremely elastic in their application. They gave no more than a series of values or principles around which a principle of selection and approval or disapproval might be discerned. In fact, as will now be seen, there was ample room in the medieval superstition-critique for difference and disagreement, even given the enormous amount of theological culture shared by these writers.

8

The Demonological Reading of Superstitions in the Late Middle Ages: Areas of Difference and Disagreement

Since one of the purposes of scholastic theology was to explore the possibilities of applied reason in theological thought through contradiction and confrontation of opposing views, it is hardly surprising to find disagreement between the scholastics on all sorts of issues. Many of those disputes have enjoyed a very poor reputation down the centuries. The satires of Erasmus depicted scholastic debates as trivial, petty, arcane, and obsessed with categories and counterfactual arguments. The case for the defence has not always helped either, since scholarship on late scholasticism has often followed the partisan loyalties of the theological movements being studied. It does not always help historical evaluation of movements of ideas if Thomists chiefly write supportively about Thomism and Franciscans argue for the importance of Franciscan theology. Nevertheless, this chapter presupposes that these debates mattered and should receive serious comparative study. Late medieval theologians used scholastic methods because they believed those techniques to be uniquely powerful tools to get at the truth. When they came to different conclusions over the issue of superstition, scholastic theologians were struggling to give advice in a way that made sense, in a world of desperate insecurity and constantly competing and eliding systems of belief. In the debates, even more than in the areas of consensus, one sees the scholastic critique of superstition engage most obviously with the lived realities. Roughly five related areas of debate will be reviewed here. The first relates to whether or not one might use 'counter-magic' against hostile sorcery, and chiefly divided Franciscan from Dominican theologians. The second, third, and fourth sets of debates chiefly divided the realists from the nominalists. These two schools of thought expressed themselves differently on whether the power of God was actually embodied within liturgical 'holy words', or whether such words achieved their effect only through covenant or convention. Thirdly, a debate surfaced over the extent and preciseness of divine 'permission' to the forces of evil to torment and harm people. Did divine permission extend to every specific act of evil spirits, or was it more akin to a general, if limited, permit to assault whomever? Linked to this was another question, regarding whether the benefits of devotional acts taken to defend against misfortune were certain and guaranteed, or subject to God's overarching providential plan. This debate ended by challenging, not just superstitious rituals, but many things commonly done in entirely accepted and orthodox religious rites. The final issue, already very well reviewed in the literature on witchcraft theory, was how the scope of the *Canon Episcopi* was understood in fifteenth- and early sixteenth-century discussions of the power of alleged witches to fly through the air in the company of pagan deities.

How far may one counteract sorcery with sorcery?

The first and most public dispute in the theological response to superstition arose over the interpretation of a remark made by Duns Scotus in his *Commentary on the Sentences*, reflecting on the passage in book 4, distinction 34, where Peter Lombard discussed impediments to marriage created by hostile sorcery leading to impotence. The Franciscan Duns Scotus discussed the question of what to do if one discovered a sign or token intended to 'cause' the impotence, for example a bent needle left in the victim's bed. Would it amount to forbidden 'counter-magic' to destroy the emblem that was instrumental in the sorcery taking effect? Scotus responded that it was a 'trifling question' to even ask whether one could destroy the token:

If the sorcery is identified and destroyed, the demon will not vex the man further, since by the pact he will not act any longer than the token remains. From this it is clear that the question is a trifling one whether one is allowed to remove the [token of] sorcery with the intention of curing the bewitched person. Not only is it lawful, but it is meritorious to destroy the works of the devil; neither in this is there any infidelity; because the one who destroys [the sign] does not assent to any malign works; however, he believes that the demon will be able and willing to strive [only] as long as the sign remains; and the destruction of the sign will bring an end to the trouble, according to the voluntary pact which [the demon] has with the sorcerer by means of that sign.[1]

Scotus's argument may be deconstructed as follows. The token of the sorcery was not the real cause of the misfortune, since it merely prompted a demon to harass the unfortunate husband. Removing the token had no causal effect in itself; so it was not an act of counter-magic or sorcery. Rather, removal of the token persuaded the demon to cease from troubling his victim, because the demon wished to keep the sorcerer or sorceress persuaded that the token was really effective, and would cease the vexation in order to maintain the illusion. There was something dangerously elliptical about this argument. More importantly, when the theological rationale was stripped away, Scotus's recommendations would lead people to behave *as though* the magical practices supposed to cause impotence were effective, and the destroying of the apparatus of those practices were helpful and even necessary.

Despite these risks, Scotus's argument about the removal of tokens to cause impotence was in itself not controversial among late medieval pastoral writers. Two of the most resolutely censorious Dominican writers on the subject, Jakob van Hoogstraten of Cologne and Silvestro Mazzolini of Priero, argued that Scotus's argument, *per se*, did not pose a theological problem. They agreed that breaking the compact between sorcerer and demon by destroying the emblem of their pact did not amount to the use of counter-sorcery.[2] However, they accused a range of other writers, sometimes rather hazily identified, of misusing Scotus or extending his arguments beyond their legitimate boundaries. It appears that some confessional theorists and some canon lawyers argued that one might employ a sorcerer to remove hostile sorcery without sin. Peter Aureoli OFM (1280–1322/30/45) reasoned that one might employ the sinfulness of another person to one's own benefit.[3] The sorcerer was quite willing to carry out the counter-magic; one was not tempting him or her into any sin that the individual was not perfectly willing to commit by choice. Aureoli argued that it was lawful to take a loan at interest from a usurer; to take the sacraments from a priest who was administering them in a state of mortal sin; or to take an oath from an unbeliever who was willing to swear on a false god.[4] If it was lawful to use the sin of another to one's own benefit in these cases, then it could also be lawful to use the sinful acts of a sorcerer to benefit oneself. Aureoli's relatively laxist argument remained a minority opinion among medieval theologians. However, it found its way into one of the most influential of treatises on confession, the so-called *Summa Angelica* of another Franciscan, Angelo Carletti of Chivasso OFM.[5] The argument was also taken up by a number of canon lawyers.[6]

It seems that for several Dominican and later for Jesuit theologians, a key question in moral casuistry was whether people convinced that they were suffering from hostile sorcery might use the assistance either of another superstitious magician, or of the person supposed to have inflicted the spell in the first place. Jakob van Hoogstraten dedicated large parts of his 1510 treatise on the remedies for magic to this specific question. He acknowledged that some of the arguments found in Aureoli's writings had force and venerable authorities to back them up. However, for Hoogstraten any recourse to the magic arts savoured of idolatry and service to the demons. Magic was not an ordinary sin like usury; it was a sin of apostasy which contaminated the client of the sorcerer as well as the sorcerer himself or herself. Hoogstraten looked back beyond the late Franciscan tradition to (predictably) Thomas Aquinas and his teacher Albertus Magnus, but also cited an early Franciscan, Bonaventure, for support for his views.[7] Silvestro Mazzolini repeated many of the same arguments as Hoogstraten some ten years later. However, despite his preference for Dominican theology Mazzolini tended to be confused and ambivalent. He condemned the use of explicitly magical remedies, but discussed and even at times allowed an intermediary category of 'tolerable' remedies, though he regarded them as only tolerable, rather than to be approved or actually permitted. He oscillated at times between merely reporting such things as 'tolerated' by others and seeming to tolerate them himself. These remedies included a peculiar form of sympathetic magic by which a dried-up cow was enchanted to identify, and charge towards, the home of the sorceress who had made it dry. Here again one suspects that Mazzolini was more influenced by some of the out-of-order remedies cited in the *Malleus* than by his own theological training.[8] Although the debate over counter-magic was essentially a late medieval issue, it received an exceptionally thorough summary and evaluation in the work of Martín Delrio at the very end of the sixteenth century.[9] Delrio came down very firmly on the rigorous,

Thomist side of the question. He insisted that any form of counter-magic was to be condemned absolutely. However, he documented a significant amount of contrary opinion in both canon law and, to a lesser extent, in theology. He resorted to character-assassination of Petrus Aureoli at one point to save his argument. He also had to challenge new foes, such as the secular jurist Nicolas Remi, who argued that procuring a sorceress to reverse a bad spell that she had cast was permitted, so long as force was used, to compel her rather than entreat her.[10]

The lesson of all this is clear. The pastoral clergy were waging a losing battle against the use of superstitious remedies by people who believed themselves to be suffering from harmful magic. Theologians experienced the pressure from the surrounding culture to accommodate their ideas and rules to the realities of pre-modern life and its multiple insecurities. They may well have felt that 'tolerating' or somehow allowing some of the less pernicious forms of counter-magic was preferable to losing all credibility with ordinary people, including many of the less educated clergy and the canon lawyers. In superstition as in marriage, it was perhaps preferable to maintain some link with the prevailing culture rather than to isolate oneself from it entirely and risk complete irrelevance.

Does divine power inhere in rituals and sacred objects?

The second issue for debate seems on the face of it a typically arcane late-scholastic logomachy; but in fact its consequences were even more practical and far-reaching than the issue just discussed. In popular belief and culture people undoubtedly behaved as though 'holy words', gestures, and rituals in general had an inherent and performative power. That is, the power to achieve spiritual effects was supposedly 'grafted into' the material objects or the ritual actions. The question for the theologians then was, 'is it true that divine power is delegated, transferred or embedded in certain forms of words or ritual gestures?' If it were, then some complex reasoning would be required to explain why the power inherent in sacramental words (say, to baptize or to consecrate the Eucharist) might not also be used for some other more secular purpose. This question about whether holiness could be ritually embedded in physical objects would become an absolutely critical shibboleth in the Reformation era. It is therefore very significant that there were real differences of emphasis in late scholasticism before the Reformation debates had even begun.

In the realist theological tradition derived from Thomas Aquinas, there was sufficient theological authority to suggest that divine power really did reside in holy words. In the critical section of the *Summa Theologica* where Aquinas discussed amulets, he responded to the suggestion that 'the divine words are of no less efficacy when they are written down than when they are spoken'; and again, 'the holy words have no less effect on the bodies of people than in the bodies of serpents and other animals.'[11] Responding to those points in the second part of the question, Aquinas accepted that 'if regard is had only to the holy words and to the divine power, it will not be unlawful.'[12] In his *Commentary on the Sentences*, Aquinas distinguished between on the one hand, words that were uttered 'merely for the reason of signifiying something' and, on the other hand, 'those that are uttered for the purpose of making something happen, which applies also to uttering words to things that have no understanding, in order that the power of the words may be applied to those things; hence for instance one says "I exorcize you creature of salt".'[13]

Aquinas was far too wise to suggest that the power in holy words might operate *apart* from the specific will of God, but he left the door open for others. Johannes Nider, in the *Formicarius*, cited Aquinas on exorcisms as proof that words might in certain circumstances be ordained to do more than just communicate meaning—that the utterance of words might itself be powerful.[14] Jakob of Jüterbogk specifically likened the power of exorcisms over snakes and animals to the power *infused* by God into the words of baptism or consecration of the Eucharist.[15] Silvestro Mazzolini likewise argued that there might be 'power in certain words, as in the sacramental [words] and blessings and certain lawful charms . . . not because they are words; rather from the institution and ordinance of God, who [according to the forms used by the Church in sacraments and sacramentals] grants a spiritual intention potency.'[16] Again, in discerning a superstitious from an acceptable ritual, he suggested that one should test a rite or charm to see whether it was an acceptable rite. To be such, the form of words must have 'from God . . . a property to achieve the effect which is looked for, as [for example] the words of consecration [have a property] towards the transubstantiation of bread and wine.'[17]

In these arguments there was no contradiction of the principle noted earlier, that power could not *naturally* exist in words and rituals. The question was only whether power might be grafted *divinely* into such words. Perhaps the clearest statement to this effect came from Jakob van Hoogstraten. In chapter 3 of his treatise he responded to the objection that might be made on behalf of folk-healers, that they used holy words, and therefore, since there would be some power in the words, there would also be genuine spiritual power in their healing charms. Hoogstraten responded to this argument by saying 'The power *which exists in the* [holy] *words* is supernaturally communicated to them by God for the spiritual health of humanity'; therefore, this power could not be used as an instrument of sacrilege, apostasy, deceit, or false accusation. He concluded that 'although there is spiritual power in these words, nevertheless, it can in no way cooperate with evil-disposed operations.'[18] Hoogstraten agreed that divine power existed in the 'holy words', but argued that it was not transferable to other purposes not instituted by God. Hoogstraten, here as elsewhere, was forced to use a legalistic rather than a metaphysical argument to repel the claim that superstitious people could use divine power in holy words.

By the end of the Middle Ages a completely different way of reasoning through this problem emerged. An early glimpse of this approach appeared in the short piece by Heinrich von Gorkum discussed earlier. As noted above, Gorkum warned his readers that no power inhered in the sign of the cross itself.[19] He went on to argue that

just as in the axe there is no permanent power of [working wood] except when the artisan actively moves the axe, so also neither in the sacraments, nor in relics, nor in the sign of the cross or in words is there active potency (*virtus in actu*) unless the motion of the supreme artisan specifically cooperates towards achieving those effects for which they are destined. And again, neither is the reading of the passions instituted to confer any such power against whatever dangers.[20]

Gorkum went on to argue that even the power of the Canon of the Mass itself was strictly circumscribed to the purposes for which it was intended: 'For example, the Mass is ordained in memory of Christ's passion, bringing to the living and the dead release from guilt and petition for grace. But if anyone . . . thinks that there is, as it were, power in the mass to cure bodily illnesses, or bring abundance of fruits . . . that incurs the guilt of superstition and abuse of divine things.'[21]

This sort of rationalist argument was taken to its greatest extreme by the Tübingen nominalist Martin Plantsch. Plantsch's argument against the *natural* efficacy of words was conventional and uncontroversial, and as such was discussed earlier.[22] However, as though carried on by the force of his own argument, Plantsch went on to say some fairly radical things about the power of words as used in entirely orthodox rituals. Sorcerers, he said, might reply to him that the power of words derived not from their nature, but from the power of the consecration or other religious rite which was being conducted when the charm or amulet was prepared. Plantsch rejoined that neither the mass, nor any part of it, nor any other consecrations or blessings had any inherent effects of themselves; they worked only by the ordinance of God who responded to the signs which he had instituted, and only in the ways and for the purposes that he had instituted. The words of consecration did not effect the transubstantiation of bread and wine; God caused the conversion. God alone caused that the substance of bread ceased to be there, and in its place the body of Christ began to exist; likewise the words of baptism did not pour grace into the one baptized, but God alone, when these words were offered by the minister and the other things necessary for the efficacy of baptism are present, and so likewise of the other sacramental words. Therefore neither the words instituted by God, nor the spells of the sorcerers, had intrinsic power to work their effects.[23] This argument aligned itself with the classic nominalist principle that the means of salvation offered to humanity by God worked not of necessity, as though they were the only possible means of salvation; but rather because of a divine *pactum*, a divine decision to confine and direct grace consistently and reliably through certain arbitrarily chosen channels.[24] Therefore divine power was never 'delegated' into holy things as the Thomists had implied; rather, the holy words had a purely conventional and covenantal effect. This analysis of the sacraments according to 'pactum theology' can be found in sources as far apart as Geiler von Kaisersberg's *Die Emeis* or Martín de Castañega's *Tratado de las Supersticiones y Hechicerias*.[25] In terms of the superstition-critique, the nominalist approach implied that there was no *functional* difference between the mechanics of a sacramental consecration and a demonic spell. The difference lay solely in the one invoked: the former was addressed to a trustworthy God who would ensure, in the case of the sacraments, the appropriate effect; the latter was addressed to a deceitful demon whose response no-one could or should rely on.

Providential God or cosmic gymnasium?

Why did it matter whether the power of 'holy words' was inherent or merely conventional? This debate was important because it connected and interlocked with another debate about divine providence, and God's permission given to evil spirits to hurt people. The two arguments together would have a significant impact on the pastoral advice to be given to those in trouble. In the perspective derived from Thomas Aquinas, divine power was assumed to be as it were 'delegated' down to the representatives and embodiments of the Almighty on earth. In the nominalist view derived from William of Ockham and his followers, all divine power remained immediately and absolutely with God, and human beings could only interact with that power to the extent and in the manner that God had covenanted to permit such interactions. The God of Dominican theology laid down the rules, provided the means of defence against evil, and (more or less) told human beings to get on with the cosmic battle. The God of the nominalists, a God who worked in the sacraments only through pact and convention, necessarily kept the divine hand firmly on the controls in respect of each individual occurrence—and was therefore naturally a providential rather than a laissez-faire deity.

The radical contrast between these two approaches appears most obviously when one compares two works on the same subject from the very eve of the Reformation era, Silvestro Mazzolini's *On the Marvels of Witch-Magicians* and Martin Plantsch's *Short Work on Witches*. Each of these works, although their titles referred to witchcraft, focused primarily on demonic misfortune, with the means to defend against it and repair its effects. They belong firmly with the superstition-treatises rather than the classical witch-hunting manuals. Mazzolini's work approached the question of demonology from a philosophical standpoint first of all. In the first book of his treatise he proved the existence of the immortal human soul (digressing at length to attack the then fashionably controversial school of Paduan Aristotelians).[26] He then demonstrated that there must be more excellent intellectual substances than the soul (i.e. angelic natures); that they had free will, and could therefore sin and be evilly disposed, and that some in fact had sinned and were so disposed.[27] The style of this section of the work obviously borrowed from Aquinas's *Summa contra Gentiles*, although Mazzolini spent even more time discussing classical philosophical alternatives than Thomas had done. The second book of the work departed substantially from Thomas. Mazzolini presented, in parallel to his discussion of angels, a discussion of the presence of witches (*striges* and *lamiae*) 'in nature'. Such creatures were blamed for associating with demons conspiratorially and sexually, and for interfering maliciously with human and agricultural fertility.[28] In the third book, in close resemblance to the *Malleus* but rather more briefly, Mazzolini proposed ways to deal with such people through ecclesiastical inquisition.[29]

The point to be observed in all of this was that Mazzolini explained human misfortunes and suffering in *philosophical* terms. The natural order was so constructed that evil intelligences, demonic and human, could cooperate to cause mischief and harm to human beings, and appropriate measures must be taken against them. There was good theological precedent for this approach. However, there was really no theodicy here. Mazzolini largely left divine permission and divine providence out of his explanatory system. He cited divine permission at only two significant moments in the book. First, when discussing sexual relations of incubi and succubi with human beings, he quoted the passage from Aquinas regarding demonic transmission of human semen, as cited earlier. However, that passage rather ran against the grain of the rest of his exposition, and even suggests an editorial interpolation after composition.[30] Secondly, he argued very late in the work that all kinds of diseases might ordinarily be inflicted by demons through witches 'with divine permission', for example leprosy or epilepsy.[31] Mazzolini presented human struggles against disease and misfortune as a battle to be waged against the forces of evil with the instruments of Catholic practice: confession, exorcism, and the use of sacramentals. The idea that misfortune might derive from the divine dispensation, that God might permit bad things to happen for specific good reasons, appeared either perfunctorily or not at all in most of his chapters. In his world, divine power was delegated and was there to be used for one's defence.

The contrast with Martin Plantsch could hardly be more striking. Plantsch's book originated with some sermons that he preached in the parish church of St George's at Tübingen in 1505, after a local witch-trial. Heinrich Bebel's dedicatory epistle to the treatise summed up its argument as an appeal to 'holy patience'. All fortune, good or bad, ultimately came from God alone, and all kinds were to be borne with equal constancy.[32] Plantsch opened his treatise with a declaration of the 'first Catholic truth' that 'no creature can cause harm to another, or produce any positive external effect, unless God is willing, consenting, giving power for the doing, and cooperating'.[33] Plantsch was aware from the start that this claim was alarming, since it appeared to make God the author of evil. He therefore embarked on a complex theological argument based on a range of scholastic authorities, but drew particularly on William of Ockham,

Gabriel Biel, and Simone Fidati of Cascia. He concluded with something closely resembling Luther's doctrine of the 'hidden God': there was 'a most righteous and most hidden cause' of evil within God, which we cannot investigate.[34] Whereas for Mazzolini divine permission remained all but invisible, for Plantsch it was so important that it came perilously close to making God the conscious author of the bad things that happened, even though Plantsch emphasized that such things always happened contrary to the revealed and express will of God.

Consequently, a Christian person should only fear God, not a demon, a soothsayer, an enchanter, or any other creature; any evil that such a person suffered ought to be ascribed first of all to the righteous will of God.[35] Plantsch then argued that the harm done by sorcery did not proceed from the material causes used by sorcerers. The means used in hostile magic were inherently ineffective, so they worked only by giving signs or prompts to evil spirits.[36] Moreover, the supposed results of hostile magic occurred sometimes in reality and sometimes only in illusion. Plantsch turned to offer complex psychological explanations of the power of illusion, partly derived from Gabriel Biel, always insisting that these operated only with divine permission.[37] He set out a (rather brutal) list of ten separate reasons why the judgement of God might permit even innocent people to suffer harm.[38] It followed that a Christian who wished to be delivered from hostile demonic sorcery must use, not counter-magic of any kind, but rather prayers scrupulously based on the rites of the Church and chosen according to severely rational criteria. Plantsch recommended the use of the sacramentals of the Church, and cited the prayers annexed to them in full. However, he warned that they had no inherent effect of their own; everything that was done with such things must be 'reasonably related to the praise of God'. The word 'reasonably' (*rationabiliter*), although already seen in Thomas, became almost a cliché in the works of the later nominalists. If people used things conducive to the honour of God, they showed love and respect to God, just as a loyal subject showed devotion to a ruler by treating the ruler's image or emblem with respect. That was why, said Plantsch, certain things were exhibited in churches 'which of themselves have no efficacy' but which were regarded as conventionally useful in invoking God for help against particular misfortunes: St Antony's water against 'morbid fire', Agatha-bread used against fires, St Blasius's candles placed round the neck for curing sore throats, the waving of a paten in front of the eyes against blindness, or ablution water from a chalice given to children for indigestion. Plantsch added that

All these things can be used with pious intention ... to cure ailments and drive away demons, so long as the hope is placed not in them, but the effect is looked for from God, because of the devotion of the person using them, or because of the intercessions of the saints whose names are invoked in the blessings and in whose reverence these things are used.[39]

Sacramentals, nevertheless, did not always work; they were not like sacraments, and the benefits must be looked for from the providence of God alone.

The critique of superstitions spills over into popular Catholicism

Martin Plantsch's severely providential approach to the causes of evil and strictly rationalist attitude to the spiritual means of self-protection did not spring fully-grown in Western European theology in 1505. His work just represents a particularly extreme and well-articulated version of a trend that had appeared in Europe with the works of Jean Gerson a century or so before. In his pastoral writings, Gerson warned against the assumption that every misfortune should be resisted and repelled by whatever spiritual means were available—even if those means were entirely orthodox. In a remarkable short work of pastoral guidance entitled *On the Direction of the Heart*, written in 1417, Gerson warned that 'too many people ... for whatever thing, howsoever profane and mean, seek from God and the saints some supernatural working, although the opposite of what they ask for might work often for their spiritual good: as for example illness, or some adversity in worldly things.'[40] He encouraged people to seek their spiritual benefit in the salvation of the soul, and in effect to leave material and physical good things to look after themselves.

   This point brings one to the final, most interesting and controversial, aspect of the nominalist approach to the critique of superstitions. Providentialist theologians such as Jean Gerson and his followers argued against expecting guaranteed or certain beneficial effects, not only from explicitly magical or demonic superstitions, but from *any* devotion, no matter how sanctified and respectable. This was the most radical contribution of the medieval critique of superstitions to the Catholic Church on the eve of the Reformation. It corroded the credibility of a whole range of liturgical or para-liturgical practices that had not hitherto fallen under the suspicion of 'superstition'. Gerson himself took slightly different tones on this topic at various stages in his career. In his *On Errors Concerning the Magic Art*, he condemned the notion of trying to 'tie God down' to responding to magical rituals in a determined way. Yet he envisaged a defender of magical practices objecting:

Are not similar things done, or tolerated by the Church in certain pilgrimages, in the cult of images, in wax [images], in holy water, and in exorcisms? Is it not said every day, if he remains nine days within that Church, if he is sprinkled with that water, or if he vowed himself to that image, or does other things of this sort, he will soon be cured, or will achieve what he desires?

Gerson responded 'that there are many things introduced under the appearance of religion among simple Christians, which it would have been more holy to have omitted'. These 'superstitious' practices were tolerated in the Church only because the ill-informed faith of the people could be corrected by that of their betters.[41] In *On the Direction of the Heart* he identified a number of forms of devotion, such as offering novenas rather than sevenfold or fivefold prayers, making different offerings to different saints for the birth of male or female children, or offering to St Humbert to cure the bite of a rabid dog. These practices he deplored as having no good reason, therefore being superstitious.[42] However, in the *Triologium of Astrology Theologized* of 1419, he seemed to draw back somewhat from his earlier strictures. Gerson wrote that these same rites concerning numbers of prayers, novenas, offerings of candles, bread, and so forth, if approved or tolerated by the Church, were not condemned *even though they appeared to have no more reason for them than the other things* (i.e. magical practices).[43]

Where Gerson had shown the way, several other intellectual critics of superstition, including some who were not formally nominalists, were ready to follow. Johann Lagenator of Dieburg, also known as Johann of Frankfurt (d. 1440), included in his superstition-treatise a condemnation of those who founded field-shrines where bogus miracles attracted devotees in search of a cure, thereby depriving their parish churches of due offerings.[44] Johann Wunschilburg included a condemnation of 'superstitious masses' in his treatise.[45] Even earlier, the author of the middle-English treatise *Dives and Pauper* (c.1410) objected to one specific aspect of new rites and rituals, namely that they claimed *infallibly* to procure certain spiritual or even material benefits. Those who promoted 'Lady Fasts', whose devotees fasted for seven years on the day of the week on which the Feast of the Annunciation fell in the first of those years, claimed that the one so fasting would thereafter be *guaranteed* not to die suddenly. 'Pauper' (the friar) objected that 'we mon nought artyn [must not bind] God ne puttyn him to no lawys, and therfor we schuldyn puttyn al our lyf and our deth only in his will.' The anonymous author resented precisely this claim to produce a *certain* result promised by the cult.[46] Martín of Arles warned repeatedly against putting God to the test by expecting guaranteed results from a particular devotion, in his case the threatened immersion of a saint's statue to produce rain in time of drought.[47] Similarly, Martin Plantsch, having insisted that *sacramentalia* worked only through the devotion of the user, denounced as a further error the belief that certain fasts, prayers, or masses said in a particular combination would ensure a good death, would redeem a soul from purgatory, or would ensure that such a person could not be damned. He regarded the attribution of such rites to popes Leo or Gregory as a falsehood.[48] The Spanish Thomist-trained humanist Pedro Ciruelo denounced such beliefs in a very similar way around 1530. Ciruelo did not even spare the ever-popular 'trental' of thirty masses for the souls of the dead from his censure; by so doing he forced his seventeenth-century editor to back-pedal furiously from some of his more radical positions.[49]

The nominalists' critique of popular religiosity, especially when it claimed to bring guaranteed or certain benefits, was not generally shared by the theological establishment, let alone by the senior clergy as a whole. On the contrary, it seems to represent another fault-line of disagreement in later medieval pastoral theology. Several writers, especially those in the Dominican tradition, warned against over-zealous criticism of respectable devotions on the grounds of alleged superstition. Johannes Nider defended from the criticism of being 'superstitious' several fashionable devotions to new saints, endowed with supposedly certain benefits.[50] Silvestro Mazzolini adopted a decidedly petulant tone when defending as orthodox the carrying of relics into the open air against storms, or the uttering of blessings over sick animals.[51]

The debate over the *Canon Episcopi*

One final, and much better known area of theological disagreement concerned the status of the *Canon Episcopi* in relation to the supposed cult of witches. This argument lacked both the theological sophistication and the wider impact of the subtler and more profound debates. It was, at best, really just a specific example of the broader disagreement over the scope and freedom allowed to demons by 'divine permission'. However, because of the sensational character of the issues involved, and their relationship to the horrendous business of the witch-trials, it became much more notorious. As was noted earlier, the *Canon Episcopi*, incorporated in Gratian's *Decretum* with a spurious attribution to the Council of Ancyra of 314, constituted the authoritative statement that night-flight with pagan goddesses was a delusion and a fantasy.[52] Right to the end of the Middle Ages many pastoral theologians continued to accept its authority on this subject. These writers continued to insist that the supposed experience of out-of-the-body flight with demonic forces was a dangerous delusion, which might be associated with demonic pacts. However, it did not take place in the physical world and therefore no descriptions of such experiences should be treated as factual.[53] Geiler von Kaisersberg, and following him Martin Luther, repeated Johannes Nider's celebrated story of the woman hallucinating in a tub, to confirm this interpretation.[54] The traditional view found exponents in the late fifteenth and into the sixteenth century. It was sustained and defended in Giordano de Bergamo's *Questions on Witches* of *c.*1460, Alfonso de Spina's *Fortress of Faith* from the 1480s, Samuele da Cassine's *Questions on Witches* of 1505, Gian Francesco Ponzinibio's *Subtle and Elegant Treatise on Witches* of 1511, and in Martín of Arles's *Treatise of Superstitions* of 1517.[55]

However, a minority view developed in the 1450s that would soon take over the ground of received orthodoxy. Various inconsistent arguments arose to explain away the *Canon*, so as to allow that real sorceresses might really fly to real meetings to meet other real creatures, demonic and human. One of the first writers to build an extended argument to this effect appears to have been Nicolas Jacquier, OP (d. 1472), who wrote a treatise entitled *The Scourge of the Enchanting Heretics* in the wake of the 'Vauderie' trials at Arras in the 1460s. Jacquier, like many of his successors, argued that the 'fascinarii' uncovered in the recent trials were substantially different from the devotees of Diana or Herodias described in the *Canon*, and therefore the provisions of the Canon did not apply.[56] Jacquier's view found echoes in a sequence of minor controversial works, and one major one. The Dominican Girolamo Visconti (d. 1477/8) argued that notwithstanding the *Canon Episcopi* it was possible for 'strie' to be transported by demons, and therefore they might be prosecuted on the basis that their activities really happened.[57] Bernard Basin (1445–1500), a Thomist and canon of Saragossa, accused the *Canon* of 'levity' and pointed out that it was only derived from a provincial council. If the decree were understood to mean that these transportations and apparitions of women *sometimes* were only imaginary, but not to deny that they *might* be true and real, that might be acceptable.[58] Vincenzo Dodo of Pavia wrote a treatise to refute Samuele da Cassine on this issue, and Bartolomeo Spina wrote a similar refutation of Giovanni Francesco Ponzinibio. Silvestro Mazzolini argued for the reality of the witches' flight on the basis of some legal arguments made in his native Piedmont.[59] Arnoldus Albertini was still pressing the argument as late as the 1520s.[60] Meanwhile, of course, the authority of the clumsily written but appallingly commercially successful *Malleus Maleficarum* had supported the thesis that the *Canon* should be set aside. Heinrich Krämer argued that the divine permission extended to demons made it perfectly possible for them to carry witches bodily, and that it was heretical to deny the possibility.[61]

Historians of scholasticism must always beware of attributing too much practical importance to the arcane and subtle debates that it costs so much labour to trace and to identify. However, in this case one may at least plausibly suppose that the incoherence of scholastic pastoral theology had a negative effect. Because the theologians disagreed among each other, their critiques could not be translated clearly and without ambiguity into the public square. Some preachers might denounce this or that practice, but a learned person could always be found to take the opposite view. The medieval Church was not complacent: it was simply divided against itself. Neither of the two schools of thought offered a wholly satisfactory response to the vulgarization of Christianity in popular piety. The neo-Thomist approach of Nider and Mazzolini 'diabolized' secular magic, but offered in its place a range of ecclesiastical exorcisms which were not essentially different in approach or in world-view from the secular magic which they condemned. The nominalist-inspired critique of Gerson, Plantsch, and others went to the opposite extreme. By its own severely rational logic, it tended inescapably to condemn a great many officially approved cults, to throw out baby and bathwater together.

9

The Pastoral Use
of the Scholastic Critique
# of Superstitions

After reading so much intricate scholastic analysis, the historian inevitably wishes to know how much, if anything, of this complex body of thought mattered or functioned outside the classroom and the debating chamber. In proportion to the vast amount of academic analysis, the evidence for the pastoral application of the critique is meagre. Nevertheless, just as there is sufficient evidence that superstitious practices did actually exist in late medieval society, so there is just enough suggestive evidence that the critiques of theologians sometimes filtered down to the clergy who had cure of souls. Two of the most copious treatments of superstitions from the early sixteenth century, one substantially derivative from the other, were based on sermons preached to urban congregations in western Germany.[1] Even more interestingly, it would seem that the theological critique caused ructions and disagreements among the clergy themselves, and generated sometimes uncomfortable discussions about tactics and the best way to proceed.

Jean Gerson offered some extremely interesting thoughts on the question of pastoral technique in *On the Direction of the Heart*, written in 1417. This text addressed, not the overtly magical or demonic practices attributed to some laypeople by the demonologists, but rather the excessively mechanical and materialistic forms of vernacular piety. Such piety included the offering of novenas rather than some other number of prayers, or the attribution of particular material benefits to particular saints. So, as Gerson wrote, 'innumerable particular observances are practised that seem to have no reason for their foundation; and so such a rite evolves into superstition, which is nothing other than vain religion. It is called vain, because it lacks reason and effect.'[2] How was one to respond to such practices in a pastoral context? Here Gerson, rather than lapsing into the usual dualistic demon-hunting approach, responded with a sensitive and nuanced evaluation of popular piety. Many people could only raise their thoughts to divine things through material means. A confident expectation of divine help, even if provoked by a material or external rite, might be helpful to someone. Moreover, Gerson argued, some practices were intermediate, neither positively endorsed by the Church nor actually forbidden. On such intermediate practices the preacher should preach with care. Towards those laypeople otherwise well disposed, it would be better to try to correct their understanding rather than change their practices, 'especially for those who are not of such great authority that they could entirely eradicate such observances without causing scandal'.[3] Gerson went on to suggest some potential, speculative reasons for otherwise arbitrary rituals: for example, novenas might be in honour of the nine orders of angels. Nevertheless, many rites could only be explained in terms that 'this was what pleased the legislator, or the custom of the Church'.[4]

Gerson then challenged the popular assumption that one might expect miraculous assistance in every kind of physical danger or misfortune through appeals to saints. In general, God should not be put to the test. But what about the beliefs that someone who says the *Pater Noster* five times before an image of the crucifix would have a thousand days', or twenty thousand years' indulgence? Or the stories of people's relatives appearing to them in dreams and asking for post-mortem masses to release their soul from purgatory?[5] Again, Gerson recommended pastoral care and caution. He seemed to suggest that parochial and lesser clergy should neither express firm approval of such beliefs nor disapprove of them too stridently. However, 'prelates and doctors ought to be more vigilant and cautious in the foresaid than the simple, so that they take care lest such piety, if it exceeds its limits and is not according to knowledge, may lapse into harm to the faith and unbearable superstition . . . In public preaching and exhortation they ought rather to restrain than encourage such things.' There were quite enough rituals without creating new ones, and anything said by a learned or senior cleric tended to be treated as absolute truth.[6] Gerson clearly assumed that preaching against superstition was a real pastoral question for the intended readers of his treatise. Moreover, he seems to have felt that theologically literate clergy faced a credibility problem in addressing this issue. Too noisy and too rationalistic a response to well-intentioned but ill-educated piety might generate the exact opposite effect from the one desired.

There certainly were disputes among the clergy themselves about the appropriate response to superstitious practices. As was noted in the previous chapter, the dispute over Werner of Friedberg's advocacy of exorcisms in 1405 led to a vigorous debate in Heidelberg and beyond.[7] Felix Hemmerli, discussing Werner's case and issues related to it, speculated that a peasant might have suffered 'terrifying correction' from his priest for using the formula 'If it were so that the Virgin bore the child Jesus, so may the blight leave this animal, in the name of the Father . . . etc.'[8] Hemmerli, that persistent defender of healing spells, conjured up the image of a host of censorious and intolerant theologians, insensitive to the dangers of agrarian life, condemning wholesale practices which were really quite benign. He went on:

Some people preaching the divine teaching, and attacking the vice of superstition, incur the charge of superstition themselves (just as an over-zealous confessor spoils the benefit of confession): so those who do not understand the 'effect of superstition' should beware of proceeding too curiously without authority, lest they incur the charge of superstition themselves . . . One who preaches that the excess of superstition is to be so generally and without distinction detested under pain of mortal sin, speaking too curiously, and not considering the power of the word, as it is subtly defined by St Thomas and the other doctors, condemns himself with his persecution of superstition to hell.[9]

Hemmerli almost certainly exaggerated; but he, like Gerson but for entirely opposite reasons, was clearly very sensitive to the possibility that over-zealous junior clergy might challenge laypeople over their favourite healing rituals. It is unlikely that either of these writers was merely striking out at thin air.

Finally, as was seen earlier, many of the late medieval superstition-treatises appeared as specific responses to specific questions. Heinrich von Gorkum wrote his entire treatise around a response to about four specific popular para-liturgical practices that arose as 'cases of conscience'.[10] In the preface to his *Treatise on Superstitions*, Martín of Arles recalled a conversation taking place amongst the clergy in his cathedral. The archdeacon of Usso had intervened and asked Martín to express an opinion about a custom in a village in his archdeaconry. It emerged that the people of Lumbier in

Navarre had the custom of carrying the image of St Peter from the altar of their parish church in procession to a river during a time of drought. Some would threaten to submerge the image if the saint did not give rain; others would offer to 'stand surety' for the saint and promised that within twenty-four hours he would bring rain.[11] In response to the archdeacon's inquiry, Martín composed his extensive and wide-ranging treatise. In the course of it he referred to pastoral tours in which he had learned of, and presumably criticized, some of the customs current in the villages of his own archdeaconry. His extensive quotations from books of charms suggest (i) that he had found them in visitations of churches and (ii) that he had confiscated them when he found them.[12]

The clergy of the Church in the late Middle Ages could never speak with a single voice. For every zealous theological rationalist who aspired to teach a more rarefied Christianity to urban or even to rural congregations, there will have been dozens who preferred to accept quietly and without protest the folklorized ritual practices of their congregations. There may also have been uncounted numbers of less educated clergy and those in minor orders who completely shared the folkloric views of the majority of the laity in the communities around them. Secondly, even those who did aspire to re-shape the beliefs and practices of ordinary Christians differed radically in both the rationale and the extent of their critiques. Some, like Johannes Nider or Silvestro Mazzolini, were content to attack only those rites that had savoured of secular magic and had no clear ecclesiastical sanction. So long as something was approved by the Church and consistent with its customs, they might not only abstain from criticism but would even defend it vigorously. Others, like Jean Gerson or Martin Plantsch, extended their criticism of popular superstitions as far and as deep as the argument would lead them. These more thoroughgoing rationalists—according to their theological lights—would question anything that lacked 'reason'. The only remaining pastoral question was how far it might be politically prudent or practically feasible to wean people away from their cherished rituals. This dissent and disagreement between theologians need not occasion any surprise. As Caroline Walker Bynum's work on the Holy Blood of Wilsnack and its field-shrine has shown, theologians could easily find themselves in total disarray over how to respond to a vigorous popular cult.[13]

Finally, a small segment of the clergy, rarely but occasionally documented, actively and noisily defended the beliefs and practices of ordinary people as vehicles and instruments of special divine grace. They protested against the excesses of the theological establishment and confirmed the less educated in their ritual and sympathetic magic. Usually such clerics did not set their opinions on paper, which is why we are limited to the occasional cases of Werner of Friedberg or Felix Hemmerli. However, it is extremely probable, to say the least, that there were many more who felt similarly but never left a record of their opinions.

This is not to say that the medieval Church was complacent about popular belief, or indeed that it was cynically self-interested in permitting such practices to continue, as some later reformers would claim.[14] The point is rather that there was absolutely no agreement on anything, beyond the obvious and usually quite unhelpful fact that the vast majority of clergy vehemently disapproved of anything that explicitly savoured of demonic magic. The theological establishment had adopted the demonological approach to refuting and denouncing popular superstitions. Yet many of the clergy seem to have found that 'demonizing' folklorized religion was too blunt and too extreme a weapon to use in the contexts where it mattered. Many people would simply refuse to accept that there was anything wrong in practices that were so obviously intended to be helpful. Even the most censorious theologians report this incredulity at many points. Individual pastoral writers like Gerson showed signs of trying to devise a more subtle programme of pastoral acculturation. However, the vast majority remained locked in an argument that revolved around Thomist beliefs in evil spirits.

Left to itself, the late medieval critique of popular belief might ultimately have achieved an equilibrium and a cohesion that would have informed the alleged 'acculturation' process of the early modern period.[15] According to some commentators, this was exactly what happened in those regions of Catholic Europe where the Reformation entirely failed to penetrate.[16] However, for most of Europe, especially north of the Alps, the advent first of Christian Renaissance humanism and then of the Reformation would completely change the terms of the debate. The charge of 'superstition' would broaden out to encompass attitudes to all kinds of rites, including the unfailingly orthodox; then it would be turned on the old Church itself. The medieval Church began to suffer assaults from the very weapons that it had itself devised to impugn popular errors.

PART III

Superstitions in Controversy: Renaissance and Reformations

The sixteenth century did not, of course, experience a gradual and steady evolution of thought and religious culture from those that preceded it. On the contrary, religious life across the continent, but especially north of the Alps, was rocked by a series of dramatic seismic shifts. The Christian Renaissance in Northern Europe challenged many of the assumptions of late Gothic religious culture. The Protestant Reformation provoked a massive re-evaluation of the whole purpose and function of ritual and religious discipline within the Christian life. The Catholic Reformation embarked on a purification and refinement of the sources and content of Catholic teaching unlike anything seen in the previous centuries.

At the same epoch, historians have traditionally detected some form of sea change in the relationship between 'elite' and 'popular' cultures. It used to be quite widely argued that early modern Europe saw the first concentrated attempt to dissuade the mass of the people from 'superstitious' belief-systems, or at least to drive a wedge firmly and consistently between orthodox Christianity and its 'folklorized' accretions. It was claimed that this campaign was waged by Protestant and Catholic reformers alike, in similar terms and with similar arguments. After the Reformation, the various Protestant and Catholic confessions embarked on a massive educational enterprise, in which each sought to inculcate a uniform pattern of belief and practice among its people, from the top down.[1] *The confessions backed up their educational work by strenuous, if often incomplete, efforts to institute pastoral and spiritual discipline. Such discipline produced the legions of visitation protocols found in reformed Catholicism, and the corresponding Protestant effort, which has been documented in the last generation by historians of German reformed confessionalism.*[2] *In so far as both Protestant and Catholic educators laid claim to the mantle of Renaissance Christian humanism, both were heirs to the tradition in which Erasmus of Rotterdam had pressed for a personal, ethical piety, in place of a religion based on 'superstitious' cults and ceremonies.*[3]

In different ways, the idea that 'superstitions' were first attacked in a thoroughgoing way in the early modern period also fits in with two models of early modern cultural change: the 'acculturation' model proposed by Jean Delumeau and, in his earlier works, by Robert Muchembled; and the model of a progressive separation of elite and popular cultures proposed by Peter Burke and in Muchembled's more recent writings.[4] *The only issue for debate appears to be whether the enterprise of dissuading the masses from their traditional beliefs succeeded or not. If it succeeded, it was 'acculturation'; if it failed, then the outcome was a separate 'elite culture'. Stuart Clark has lent further weight to the idea that Protestant and Catholic fought on a common religious front against popular magic. His monumental study of Protestant and Catholic demonologies relegates confessional differences to the sidelines. He continually stresses the shared concepts and the similar purpose behind all demonological writers.*[5]

On the other hand, a more recent generation of social historians appears to argue against the idea of any substantial change, let alone 'modernization', of popular belief and practice in the early modern period. Drawing on the later work of Robert Scribner, a series of scholarly works have argued that, in general, the people of the sixteenth and indeed the seventeenth centuries remained firmly within a medieval world.[6] *The main thrust of these works has been to argue that Protestantism, qua Protestantism, did not in any sense inaugurate the 'modern era' as an earlier age of German historiography had claimed.*[7] *However, the drift of such arguments tends to minimize the idea of any major cultural change in the early modern period. Moreover, much recent work in the eighteenth century has contributed to the argument that even the 'Age of Reason' showed a persistent interest in the occult, the miraculous, and other supposedly 'irrational' vestiges of earlier patterns of thought.*[8] *Moving forward still further, some social historians would claim that even industrialization and the modernization of the nineteenth and twentieth centuries had at best a limited impact on a culture impregnated with traditional supernatural beliefs and a great deal of wishful thinking.*[9] *The key point in all this revisionist historical writing seems to be* that changes in social history occur very slowly, and seldom at the pace suggested by high-profile intellectual debates.

These are important claims and essential debates in the subject. However, they will not form the core of this part of the book. These chapters address a separate but related question: namely, what were the theologically educated people of Europe saying about the subject? Whether or not there was a sea change in popular attitudes, or even elite attitudes, there were certainly some radical and important developments in the literature of the intellectual analysis of popular superstitions. New arguments were devised; old arguments were refocused on new targets; new rifts opened up between rival schools of thought that had not even existed before the Reformation era. It is perfectly possible to argue that all these changes in the religious literature of the period had absolutely no impact on what the mass of the people actually did and thought. If that indeed proves to be the case, it throws the changes in the intellectual response to superstitions into interesting relief. However, the putative continuity in popular thought does not abolish the changes in the theological culture, nor entirely remove their interest and their relevance for Western religious history.

Chapter 10 will begin by setting out the responses to 'superstition' found in some of the writings of the Christian humanists. Here one should neither expect nor try to construct a systematic or theologically articulated image of what 'superstition' was supposed to mean. The whole thrust of humanist thought was rhetorical rather than analytical: terms were thrown around for effect rather than defined precisely. Nevertheless, and allowing for the many differences between the various exponents of Christian humanism, certain themes emerge. 'Superstition' for the humanists constituted a materialistic attitude to worship: whether the custom or rite in question was orthodox or not in the eyes of the Church hardly mattered.

The next chapter will introduce the Protestant Reformation. Martin Luther brought to the issues raised by superstition, as to everything else, a mind of extraordinary vigour and originality. Yet his thought also had a transitional character. Luther was so thoroughly shaped by late medieval thought that his innovations can only be understood in the context of his conservative or traditional traits. Next, it is important to register the considerable amount of shared culture that continued to exist between Protestants and Catholics through the Reformation era. Given their shared background in an Aristotelian scholastic cosmology, it is not surprising that many assumptions about angels, demons, magic, and natural causation appeared in very similar terms among Protestant and Catholic authors.

Once one has duly noticed those areas where Protestants and Catholics shared a common culture, it will be time to document the real and radical differences between the confessions. For Protestant demonology intersected not just with the cosmology *of the reformed churches, but also with their philosophy of history. The Protestant reformers argued that Christian worship and teaching had been degraded over time by the deceits of the devil and the machinations of Antichrist. Consequently, Catholic rites and customs as then practised were, quite literally, diabolical travesties of true worship and manifest superstitions. It has long been well known that Protestant polemics tended to argue, in general terms, that Catholicism was merely a form of superstition.[10] However, it appears that this claim was not just a vague insult or a piece of theological abuse. Protestant theological treatises appropriated the arguments of the late medieval superstition-critique and applied them, quite precisely, to Catholic rituals and consecrations. Protestant thought on the subject of human misfortune and its remedies tended to the extreme end of one of the axes of difference already seen in late medieval scholastic theology. Protestants typically took an extreme providentialist view when explaining the causes and remedies of evil in the world. This perspective, as will be seen, meshed well with reformed disdain for Catholic ritual preservatives against misfortune. However, it also meant that evil, and specifically evil angels, became more and more the unwilling agents of divine control over the cosmos. When responding to misfortune, prayer to God became primary; defence against evil spirits became either peripheral or irrelevant. This theological perspective initiated the first stage in the long, slow decline of the devil in Western thought.[11]*

The response of the Catholic Church, so apparently centralized and yet so diverse in many ways, demands a more careful analysis at this period. Many Catholic writers on the subject of superstition echoed and copied from their late medieval predecessors. As such, they continued to transmit warnings against the demonic involvement in superstitious rituals and beliefs. However, they also sensed the need to answer, to resist, and to rebut Protestant criticisms. They defended vigorously the Catholic preservatives against misfortune, especially the consecrated objects known as 'sacramentals', and strove to demonstrate their usefulness. Moreover, Catholic apologists wished to defend the unique status of their Church not only on dogmatic or positivist grounds, but also on the grounds of its proven effectiveness. Reformed Catholicism claimed to prove the 'correctness' of its theology by abundant signs of divine favour shown in miraculous and charismatic achievements—especially miracles of exorcism—demonstrated in the mission-fields both outside Europe, in Asia and the Americas, and also in areas of confessional rivalry at home. Catholic theological writers faced a third challenge, in this area as in so many others of the Catholic Reformation. They needed to sort out the enormous disarray and disagreement inherited from previous centuries about what was, or was not, acceptable Catholic practice. It was not nearly enough to say that something was sanctioned by custom. These demands, to preserve continuity, to defend against heresy, and to harmonize conflicting traditions, give the Catholic writing of the early modern period an extremely interesting and occasionally confusing character.

Finally, in Part III, like its predecessors, it will clearly be necessary to explore at various points the relationship between the superstition-critique and the early modern witch-hunt. While much of the superstition literature touched tangentially on the supposed phenomenon of witchcraft at many points, the two phenomena remain so stubbornly different in the literature and in historical experience. Superstition was everywhere pervasive, mostly low-key, and rarely evoked a judicial response save in some cases brought before the Roman Inquisition, which were usually handled fairly leniently.[12] Even those thinkers who argued that practitioners of superstition were unwittingly working with demons rarely supposed that the 'implicit' pact in any way resembled the overt pact and quasi-sectarian demon-worshipping activities attributed to witches.[13] Witchcraft, in contrast, roused fears in specific regions at particular times, and led to sporadic and unevenly distributed prosecutions, sometimes in ones and twos and sometimes in the terrifying mass purges seen in certain fairly closely defined areas. Yet the two subjects are not fully or entirely distinct, and no discussion of the impact of the superstition-critique can or should pass by the phenomenon of witchcraft prosecution.

10

Some Renaissance Christian Humanists and 'Superstition'

The religious ideas of the Renaissance, even in northern Europe, resist any attempt to categorize them or to assimilate them into a single movement of thought. Certain tendencies, certain literary and philosophical tastes, and a particular style of writing, mark off the characteristically Renaissance figure. The style is extremely easy to recognize; it is almost impossible to define in a satisfactory or inclusive way. Any attempt to typify humanists will run up against their diversity. Christian humanists included Platonists and Aristotelians, exponents of sober ethics and devotees of esoteric mysteries, self-publicists and recluses, monastics and anti-monastics, ecclesiastical administrators and anticlerical laypeople.[1] However, certain aspects of the Renaissance programme are relevant to this subject. First, humanists as a whole regarded the individual's spiritual and ethical disposition as far more important than any value or benefit to be received from the mere fact of a religious ceremony having been performed. Secondly, they often had a low view of tradition. The characteristic desire of humanist scholars to return to the sources, the wellsprings of knowledge whether in classical literature or Christian theology, would discourage acceptance of something simply because it was part of received custom. Thirdly, many—by no means all—humanists were inclined to Platonist views. This led those who were so inclined to value the spiritual and the invisible above the earthly and corporeal. Spiritual enlightenment was to be sought above and beyond the bodily realities that infused and shaped so much popular medieval piety. Finally, many (again, not all) humanists typically belonged to highly educated societies of like-minded thinkers. At least in their own self-image, they tended to be elitist. To the extent that a Christian humanist shared some or any of these attributes, one might expect to find an attitude of hostility towards 'superstition' conceived in very broad terms. The main contrary drift, found among a minority of Renaissance figures, was their taste for the exotic, the 'ancient theology' with its nuances of mysteries to be learned, either in the form of the Hermetic Corpus or the Hebrew Kabbalah. This taste could easily lead its aficionados in a quite different direction from the stripped-down, rational, ethical piety to which other humanists aspired.

Neoplatonism, which enjoyed popularity among a small but significant and influential section of the European intelligentisia from the fifteenth to the seventeenth centuries, posed certain specific problems for the analysis of the universe and its workings that had been standard for most of the later Middle Ages. In the Neoplatonic universe it was possible for spiritual beings to be linked by networks of affinity and sympathy that did not fit into the Aristotelian categories of matter, mind, and the transmission of ideas. Neoplatonists did not automatically subscribe to the dualistic view of Thomas Aquinas and his followers, that all spiritual intelligences were either good angels or fallen angels. They did not believe that all influences between one spirit and another must operate simply by the communication of meaning. They envisaged connections between cosmic entities and their representations, in the form of signs and symbols. In some versions of the system such as that proposed by Iamblichus of Chalcis, it was possible to argue that ritual ceremonies and formal symbols might be used to control, regulate or otherwise exert influence on the cosmic powers.[2] By no means all Renaissance Neoplatonists were followers of Iamblichus; and it appears that this body of literature inspired elitist curiosity rather than anything more significant. However, to the extent that such views became more thinkable in European intellectual circles than before, they could only complicate the question of how to respond to popular superstitions. The point is not that Neoplatonists laid themselves open to the charge of being 'superstitious' themselves, whether now or in their own time. Rather, by raising alternative views of the interconnections in the universe, they potentially made the task of the superstition-critic a little harder.[3]

Jacques Lefèvre d'Étaples and Mutianus Rufus

The ambiguities of the humanist response to superstition are well, and somewhat confusingly, illustrated by the case of the French religious humanist Jacques Lefèvre d'Étaples (*c*.1455–1536). On the one hand, Lefèvre represented a particularly vigorous development of the trend noted at the end of Chapter 9. He, like many other humanists, was quite sceptical about the value and effectiveness of conventional ecclesiastical rituals, especially if these were performed mechanically and without a devout intention and committed spirit. At the high water mark of the experiment in liturgical and devotional reform inspired by Lefèvre in Bishop Guillaume Briçonnet's diocese of Meaux, near Paris, Lefèvre and his often more radical followers reportedly preached against many perceived accretions in the worship life of the Church. The sources for the Meaux experiment are problematic: they derive chiefly from the attacks mounted on its leaders by Noel Beda and the Sorbonne. However, it was alleged in those attacks that Lefèvre and his allies had argued that the cult of saints was worthless, and that prayers to saints were akin to superstition.[4] It seems fairly certain that Lefèvre's critique of contemporary cults derived not from the sort of radical nominalist critique of divine causation discussed in the last chapter, but rather from a general Biblicism. For Lefèvre, the biblical scholar, anything that tradition and custom had superadded to the witness of the primitive Church and scripture needed to be examined with care.

On the other hand, Lefèvre took certain positions which, while entirely orthodox among the intellectuals of his day, complicated his relationship to the received Aristotelianism in relation to cosmic causation. Lefèvre wrote a treatise *On Natural Magic*, which of itself is quite unproblematical. As will be seen, the theme of 'natural magic' was a staple of intellectual analysts of magic, and always referred to that type of manipulation of the physical world that depended on genuine understanding of the inherent properties of things. 'Natural' magic involved neither arcane rituals nor ambiguous relationships with spiritual beings.[5] In his earlier career Lefèvre had been a zealous Aristotelian; his paraphrases of the works of Aristotle had generated a whole new set of tools for teaching Aristotle's philosophy.[6] However, in the early sixteenth century Lefèvre found himself dabbling in Hermetism and Neoplatonism, partly through the influence of Johannes Reuchlin. In 1502 he issued an edition of Ambrogio Traversari's translation of the pseudo-Dionysian writings, including the *Celestial Hierarchy* and the *Mystical Theology*.[7] Neoplatonic traces have been found all through the programme of the Meaux circle. Lefèvre therefore presented a rare instance of a Christian humanist whose rhetorical postures in one area of his work, his pastoral attitudes to worship, appeared potentially complicated by his philosophical interests in another area.

Conrad Mutianus Rufus (1470/1–1526) offers a rather different insight into the impact of Renaissance thought on the language and problematic of superstition. A canon of Gotha until the dissolution of its chapter, he led one of the most influential circles of Renaissance humanist religious and literary culture in early sixteenth-century Germany. Mutian was somewhat typical of his generation in that, having espoused a highly critical and spiritualizing approach to religion in the first decade of the sixteenth century, he then drifted gradually back to a more and more conservative stance as the destructive potential of the Lutheran Reformation for the old ways became clear. He represented the extreme end of his movement in one respect: he was extremely private to the point of secrecy about his views. He discouraged the publication of his letters, even though many letters at this period were written expressly in order to be published. At his most radical, however, Mutian presented a significant theoretical challenge to the conventional religious practice of his age, rooted in his humanistic culture.[8] More vehemently than Lefèvre, Mutian argued that religious practices that claimed to encapsulate a spiritual grace in a physical element were 'barbarous' and crude. Taking the tonsure, or making a ritual fast, became a stupid and ignorant act if the practitioner believed that one could ensure divine favour by doing so. This critique of mechanical religious practices Mutian combined with a vigorous, if private, polemic against the moral failings of the clergy. As one of his historians remarked, 'He consistently protested against the externalization and vulgarization of spiritual meaning and values.'[9] Mutian was enough of a Neoplatonist to feel that the divine must be approached through spiritual rather than corporeal things; that growth in spiritual insight required the progressive casting away of physical helps, including (as it seemed at times) the sacraments and the physical body of Christ.[10] In their place he put an ethic of harmony and mutual love.

Erasmus

Many of these Neoplatonist humanists implicitly criticized the materialistic piety of the surrounding culture as, at least implicitly, ignorant, debased, and superstitious. There was no need to target any more gross or vulgar form of popular religion: their target was a Christian orthodoxy that seemed mired in the contemplation of physical objects, whether sacramental materials or holy relics. The author who made the criticism of vulgar 'superstition' most explicit and most widely readable was, however, Erasmus of Rotterdam (1467–1536). Erasmus was by far the most widely read and discussed of all the Northern humanists, despite the fact that he wrote only in Latin, leaving others to translate his works into the vernacular. He was by no means typical of the Northern Renaissance. The philosophical and esoteric aspects of humanism had very little interest for him. He was predominantly a literary figure: a stylist, collector of proverbial sayings, poet, educator, letter-writer, and editor of texts both classical and religious. The latter part of his career was overshadowed by the events of the Lutheran movement, which forced him to some awkward intellectual courses and a number of physical displacements.[11] Despite the fact that his particular theological positions became more and more untenable as the sixteenth century progressed, his words and his works continued to be read (especially in Protestant Europe where they escaped the censure and expurgation of the Catholic Church) well into the seventeenth century and beyond. Erasmus conjured up, and disseminated with his unique literary skill and influence, one of the most powerful images of what 'superstition' meant in the Christian context. Moreover, this image proved to be quite distinct from the laboriously constructed positions of the late scholastics.

Erasmus made his most potent contributions to the rhetorical critique of 'superstitious' religion through satirical and comic writings. However, his first and most nearly philosophical contribution to the subject appeared in the *Enchiridion of the Christian Soldier*, a spiritual manual written in 1503. Here Erasmus expressed himself in terms not entirely dissimilar to those of his more philosophical Neoplatonist contemporaries:

Let us add a fifth rule, as a kind of reinforcement to the previous one, that you establish firmly in your mind that perfect piety is the attempt to progress always from visible things, which are usually imperfect or indifferent, to invisible, according to the division of man discussed earlier. This precept is most pertinent to our discussion since it is through neglect or ignorance of it that most Christians are superstitious rather than pious, and except for the name of Christ differ hardly at all from superstitious pagans.[12]

In practice Erasmus meant something less abstract than this introduction suggested. He objected to the notion that a devotee of a relic- or saint-cult could acquire personal holiness, without seeking at the same time to cultivate the moral virtues that distinguished the saint. For Erasmus no less than Mutian, piety often focused itself on, not to say reduced itself to, the cultivation of the virtues. Any cult that implied that mechanical performance of religious duties could substitute for a good life, or transfer the merit of one person to another less deserving, was anathema to him.

Erasmus had more impact through his lighter writings than through the somewhat ponderous earnestness of the *Enchiridion*. In the *Colloquies* and the *Praise of Folly* Erasmus described, and made fun of, the vast range of contemporary Christian practices that supposedly augmented grace by the mere fact of being performed. Erasmus's critique included relics, the shrines of particular saints, the expectation of particular physical benefits from saints assigned to particular needs (he came close to the claims of later Protestants that some saints were the reincarnation of pagan deities), and the making of all kinds of religious vows, including those to enter the life of a monastic order. Erasmus first poked satirical fun at contemporary religious culture in his *Praise of Folly*, first published in 1511 but subsequently revised and extended.[13] This enormously successful *jeu d'esprit* embodied quite a complex rhetorical construct. 'Folly', the minor deity who personifies silliness and self-delusion, steps into the pulpit to deliver a mock encomium, a speech in the classical genre of frivolous parodies of the honorific speeches delivered to heroic or distinguished figures. Folly chooses to praise herself (for Erasmus identified *Moria* as female) and demonstrates with dazzling rhetorical pyrotechnics that life cannot really be lived, and certainly never is lived, without self-delusion, without ridiculous pleasure taken in unworthy objects, without the necessary mixture of self-love and self-esteem. Folly thus demonstrates to her own satisfaction that she is indispensable to the life of every mortal person. In the course of this playful exposition Erasmus made fun of the expectation that mechanical devotion to the cult of a particular saint would infallibly bring the promised benefits: that Christopher would protect on a journey, that Barbara would ensure survival in battle, or St Erasmus would guarantee wealth.[14] Johannes Nider had earlier reported that there was debate over the validity of these sort of cults and had defended their usefulness.[15] 'Folly' then made similar fun of the belief that a particular set of verses from the Psalms would ensure freedom from sudden death and therefore eventual salvation.[16] Finally, she pointed out that no-one made a votive offering of thanks for delivery from folly or an increase in wisdom—all people ever gave thanks for were the most unworthily received of material benefits.[17] Erasmus, however, did not enter into any substantive discussion of the value of these practices. 'Folly' simply pointed out how vital a role foolishness played in them: and if anyone complained, of course Erasmus could reply that it was only Folly speaking. Erasmus even appended to the text a series of footnotes attributed to a 'Gerhardus Listrius' which back-pedalled furiously on the more irreverent passages in the text.

Erasmus trespassed on slightly more dangerous ground when he made fun of other, more elevated manifestations of orthodox Catholicism. In the person of Folly he lampooned without mercy the claims made by monastics to follow Christ while practising a range of allegedly 'pharisaical' ceremonies that were not only unhelpful and unspiritual but actually ridiculous. They boasted of the filth of their garments, their exaggerated abstinence from speech or food, or their hypocritical avoidance of physical contact with money. 'Most of them rely so much on their ceremonies and petty man-made traditions that they suppose heaven alone will hardly be enough to reward such merit as theirs. They never think of the time to come when Christ will scorn all this and enforce his own rule, that of charity.'[18] Again, Erasmus was not entirely novel here. A hundred years earlier Jean Gerson, in the *Direction of the Heart*, had expressed similar scepticism about the value of monastic customs and rituals when practised to excess.[19] More audacious was Erasmus's satire of the exaggerated pride in learning to be seen among preachers and theologians. He constructed an elaborate and withering caricature of the scholastic preacher, wearing out his physical energies and faculties in constructing a hopelessly over-elaborate sermon. The sermon, it emerged, had nothing to do with inculcating Christian practice and everything to do with ostentatious parading of the preacher's learning and ingenuity.[20]

A few years after the success of *Praise of Folly*, Erasmus produced his *Familiar Colloquies*, a gradually expanded set of conversation pieces drawn from a wide range of social and cultural settings, real and imagined.[21] The *Colloquies* had the potential to influence an even larger market than the

Praise of Folly, for several reasons. The essays were not overtly satirical; they were dialogues, which meant that the views of the characters could potentially be 'disowned' by their author; but nevertheless the tone of much of the text was obviously intended to be didactic and to raise serious thoughts in its readers. These little pieces were intended to serve as educational fodder for students learning Latin, and as such they had an enormous subsequent publishing history, especially in Protestant countries where they were not censored.[22] While many of the *Colloquies* treated of entirely secular or domestic subjects (for a celibate, Erasmus showed surprisingly great interest in courtship, marital relations, and childrearing) many also included commentaries on religion as practised on the eve of the Reformation. The *Pilgrimage for Religion's Sake* of 1526 drew on the real visit that Erasmus had made to the shrine of the milk of the Blessed Virgin at Walsingham, in Norfolk.[23] Erasmus took the opportunity to represent the Virgin Mary as 'all but exhausted by the shameless entreaties of mortals' who persisted in demanding, and expecting, from the saint assistance with wishes that were not only unspiritual but in many cases immoral or indecent. The participants in the colloquy took opposed attitudes to the veneration of the relic of the Virgin's milk: with gentle sarcasm Erasmus indicated (but in an entirely deniable way) that the relics were spurious, with such items as the wood of the Cross or the Virgin's milk replicated in vast abundance all across Christendom.[24]

Erasmus took a more abrasive attitude towards the needs of petitioners in *The Shipwreck* (1523). Here he depicted the reactions of the passengers and crew on a vessel wrecked in a storm in the English Channel (again, the experience may have been close enough to some of Erasmus's friends for him to write with some realism).[25] The people on shipboard responded to the danger by calling on a variety of saints, usually with specific reference to the place where the saint was venerated (Erasmus, like later reformers, remarked on how vows made to, say, the Virgin had to specify which of her geographical avatars was invoked). Some of them made exaggerated promises to make huge votive gifts to certain shrines if they reached land safely. They had no intention of keeping such vows, yet somehow assumed that the saint could be deluded or tricked by the offer. Others actually invoked the sea itself for mercy and made flattering pleas to it. This practice provoked one of the participants in the colloquy to exclaim 'absurd superstition!' The apostrophe was safely and uncontroversially directed to a quasi-pagan invocation of the force of nature; but the accusation was left hanging in the air as a critique of the whole business of mechanical and insincere bargaining with spiritual forces when in fear for one's safety.[26]

Of all the *Colloquies*, one entitled *The Exorcism, or the Ghost* (1524) addressed most boldly and comically the issue of superstitious beliefs. A young man named Polus decides to play a trick on his credulous father-in-law Faunus. (Erasmus described Polus as the kind of trickster who would claim to see a portentous shape in the sky when out riding, just to shock his fellow travellers, and would persuade them that they see it also.) He spreads a rumour that a ghost has been seen hanging around a grove of trees on Faunus's estate. He then hides in the undergrowth and produces a horrifying howling sound, which convinces Faunus that he must prepare the most elaborate and detailed rite of exorcism to be performed by a local priest. When the priest begins the rite, Polus and a friend appear on shrouded black horses and scare Faunus away, who later relates that he has seen two terrifying evil demons. The story descends into farce as Polus stages a mock conflict between the 'demons' and the exorcist over someone claiming to be a departed soul. The exorcist hears that the soul can only be liberated if Faunus gives nearly his entire fortune for pious purposes. The 'spirit' later reassures him, by means of a letter written in archaic characters left on an altar, that it has entered paradise and needs no further alms.[27] At the end one of the participants in the conversation declares that he is now convinced that most stories of this kind are frauds concocted for fun or for greed.

Whether deliberately or not, Erasmus and his kind made a very important contribution towards rephrasing the way in which the discussion of superstition was conducted on the eve of the Reformation. Erasmus actually used the term 'superstition' (and cognate humanist terms like the Greek δεισιδαιμονία 'deisidaimonia')[28] relatively sparingly.[29] However, he repeatedly and consistently tried to educate his readers away from religious practices that consisted of mere performance. He rejected the belief that one could claim saintly or divine favour for a symbolic act of obedience or devotion, divorced from any effort towards moral improvement. Erasmus was, moreover, always on the lookout for evidence of base financial motives on the part of the clergy. In a letter in 1528 he reported the story of a cleric who had apparently fixed candles to the backs of crabs or crayfish and left them to scuttle among the graves in his churchyard. He then brought the layfolk to see the flickering lights and tried to convince them that these were the souls of the dead seeking the devotion of the living. Those who have studied animal symbolism believe that this may have been a symbolic ritual for the souls of the departed where no deceit was intended: but Erasmus naturally interpreted it as the abuse of holy things for profit.[30]

The rhetoric, and even more the satire, of Erasmus broadened the literary critique of popular religious practices outwards from the obviously and profanely magical to include the most materialistic and apparently 'mechanical' of the cults found in traditional religion. For Erasmus, it was not the precise theological configuration of the ritual that mattered: it was the intent behind it. An irreverent attitude, such as the desire for material gain, would contaminate even the most orthodox ceremony. With nothing more than his largely intuitive ethical-spiritual theology as a guide, Erasmus re-focused the intellectual critique of superstition on to things that were going on firmly under the Church's umbrella. In due course the Protestant reformers would take up that change of targets, but in a far more thorough and trenchant way than Erasmus could ever have envisaged.

11

Magic, the Fallen World, and Fallen Humanity: Martin Luther on the Devil and Superstitions

In many subjects in religious history it would be a truism to say that the Reformation marked a turning point. With the literature on superstition this claim is by no means self-evident, and needs to be carefully stated and evaluated. Nevertheless, this study does argue that something very important changed in the arguments over superstition with the coming of the Protestant Reformation, even though the effects of that change on the ground were neither immediately self-evident nor uncomplicated. This book proposes that, with the advent of Protestantism, the relationship between the performance of ritual and the saving work of God in the individual soul came to be conceived in a radically different set of ways. That re-conception could not fail to have an effect on how the rival categories of 'religion' and 'superstition' were envisaged.

In the medieval West it had become axiomatic to say that the saving work of God was in normal conditions channelled through the rites of the Church. That assumption, inherent in the essence of 'Catholic' Christianity, became explicit in the work of the Fourth Lateran Council in 1215.[1] The Spirit-led Church ministered the sacraments that reliably conferred grace on those who sought them worthily. Penitential discipline through auricular confession responded to the constant reality of human sin by ritually reconciling the penitent to the Church and, therefore, to the divine dispensation.[2] Those who participated obediently in the rites and ceremonies of the Church, and received absolution on the point of death, could be buried in consecrated ground and hope eventually to reach Paradise.[3] There were, of course, vigorous debates in the later Middle Ages over precisely how the relationship between God and the work of the Church should be understood. Even to entirely orthodox theologians it was perfectly evident that the relationship between the ideal, universal Church and the actual visible institution might be unstable.[4] Moreover, theologians of the *via antiqua* and the *via moderna* disputed whether the particular divine order for the redemption of humanity was logically necessary and capable of rational deduction, or merely an arbitrary, conventional (but stable and consistent) decision of the godhead that could have happened otherwise.[5] Nevertheless, even the most critical and edgy of medieval theologians still argued that salvation operated through the traditional procedures, however they might debate the theological rationale behind those procedures.[6]

The European Reformation and the role of ritual

The theology of the sixteenth-century Reformation did not struggle to justify the rituals and ceremonies of the Church: rather, it invalidated and disrupted them by its own inner logic. For centuries theologians had debated over how, exactly, God contrived to make a sinful soul sufficiently pure to make it fit for salvation. The debates between Ockhamists and Augustinians revolved around the relative status of the divine and human input into this process.[7] The mainstream reformers answered, shockingly, that this was asking completely the wrong question. The whole point was that God did *not* purify the soul in order to accept it. God chose out of pure grace and for Christ's sake to accept the soul *in spite of its continuing and fatal impurities*.[8] The 'righteousness of God' came to the believer in two ways. First, it was 'imputed', that is to say, in effect attributed to the believer *as though* the believer were righteous even though he or she essentially was not. Justification depended on this first act of imputation. Secondly, God's righteousness was truly 'imparted' or infused into the nature of the saved person, but in an incomplete, partial and entirely inadequate way, at least in this life. Even the greatest saints were debtors to God for their real sins.[9]

Since the process of redeeming people from their sins consisted of the reception of undeserved grace, rather than purification through rites correctly performed, the business of the Christian religion necessarily changed. Righteousness before God came through trust in a divine gift of grace, apprehended in knowing, conscious, faith. The duty of the Church was to proclaim grace, not to mediate purification. Instruction with meaning and worship in the common tongue therefore took the place of ceremonies performed mysteriously in a language known only to the learned. As the Church was no longer conceived as a single organic entity linked mysteriously to the heavenly economy, it need neither be a single centralized organization on earth, nor a sacramentally separate caste of clergy governed by distinct and different laws. On the contrary, the individual churches of each effective political entity were local manifestations of the one universal, and invisible, Church. Their ministers were the specialist servants of the community, not somehow separate from it.[10] Some social historians who confidently assert that there was nothing demystifying or 'disenchanting' about Protestantism should take into account that the core theology of the Reformed faith was *in its very essence* a process of demystification. How that message was received or adapted at popular level was of course another matter. How it worked in the culture of Renaissance Europe depended on a complex process of political and social interweaving and affiliation. Even for the educated, Protestant theology continued for many centuries to function within a world shaped by Aristotelian metaphysics.

The very schematic and simplified image of mainstream Reformation teaching offered in the preceding paragraphs manifested itself, in reality, within the very different voices, tones, and styles of the individual reforming leaders and thinkers. The core message appeared in Luther, Melanchthon, Bucer, Zwingli, Bullinger, and Calvin, but in many different accents and vocabularies. Much confusion has been introduced into Reformation history by the extreme assumptions that either (i) everything Martin Luther said and wrote ought to be normative for the entire Reformation or (ii), at the opposite end, that because Luther differed radically from other reformers on certain key issues, there was therefore no theological 'core' to the magisterial Reformation at all. In fact, of course, Luther is and was an enormously complex, ambivalent figure. He lived out in his own mind and his own psyche the viscerally painful transition between one mode of being Christian and another. Many aspects of his early life and training remained with him for the rest of his life. Some of his personal theological traits and quirks found no echo even among those closest to him in

Wittenberg, never mind in the wider reformed world. Luther's theological world contains profoundly medieval elements; but it is also suffused with his own profound individuality and personal genius.[11] Because of this individuality, not to say quirkiness, found in Luther's writings, he receives a separate and special treatment here. The purpose is to prove three distinct and apparently contradictory propositions: (i) that Luther in many respects belonged in the world of the medieval superstition-critique, though in a distinctive way; (ii) that he had a highly personal view of the fallen creation that was shared neither by the late scholastics nor by most of his fellow reformers; and yet (iii) that in important ways he inaugurated many of the arguments that would lead the Protestant critique of superstition down previously untrodden paths.

Martin Luther's *Exposition of the Ten Commandments* (1516–18)

Of all Luther's works, the one that most fully reveals his attitudes towards popular superstitions, and that best embodies Luther's Janus-like posture at the frontier of two eras, is his *Exposition of the Ten Commandments Preached to the People at Wittenberg*. This cycle of sermons on the Decalogue is believed to have been delivered beginning on 29 June 1516, though the text was probably elaborated for publication. It appeared as a Latin pamphlet published by Johannes Rhau-Grunenberg and dated 20 July 1518.[12] This work antedates the Reformation: it belongs to a period when Luther was lecturing and conducting his pastoral ministry before the storm brewed up over indulgences. Yet it also belongs to the years when Luther was working hardest to discern his distinctive theological position. It uses the shape and as it were the 'shell' of a traditional didactic superstition-treatise to put across some quite varied messages. Luther began his treatment of the First Commandment against idolatry in a way characteristic of his theology at that stage in his development. Any trust in one's own wisdom or virtue, any faith in anything other than God, inevitably caused one to break the First Commandment. 'This idolatry reigns in every person, until they are healed by grace in faith in Jesus Christ.'[13] Christians must aspire to be completely abstracted from concerns of this world, to care nothing for material things or benefits when compared to possessing Christ. This was not a 'counsel of perfection' for the elite, but a demand made of everyone;

so everyone must be penitent for their failure to attain that goal, and not be complacent.

Luther then described and challenged 'idolatry' under three quite distinct headings: those of conventional demonology, those of Renaissance humanism, and those of his emerging theology. First, he spoke with the language of the late medieval superstition-critique and criticized the popular beliefs that attempted to win material benefits through forbidden rites. However, Luther demonstrated originality even here. First, he took material from personal experience as well as from his reading; his sermons read as refreshingly original when compared with many scholastic equivalents. Secondly, he divided his treatment by age-groups, enumerating the superstitions specifically appropriate first to adolescents, then to those of young adults, then of old people. Adolescent superstitions involved such things as enchanting weapons so that they could not harm the owner, or carrying as amulets texts like the *Enchiridion Leonis papae*, a book of charms alleged to protect against injury or misfortune. They also, not surprisingly, involved love-magic to win or keep a partner, or to divine the outcome of the relationship.[14] Several of these rituals involved the abuse of consecrated objects such as holy water or wax. Despite that fact, Luther reflected that they 'are foolish rather than evil . . . seeming to be jests of the demons', though they were very dangerous if taken seriously. Luther's second category of superstitions belonged to those already married and caring for children in the household and animals on the farm. He listed a number of spurious childhood illnesses which were diagnosed and treated by superstitious means.[15] Then there were various blessings used by householders to 'sign' their animals and plants to protect them from predators and bad weather. Luther reflected ironically that the 'poor wolf' was thus being deprived of his share of the sheep assigned him by God. If Job had used such methods, he would have avoided misfortune but lost God's approval. Luther included in this section a sarcastic denunciation of the belief in omens and calendar-divination such as the 'Egyptian Days'.[16] He then devoted several pages to denouncing the bad theology implicit in the belief in judicial astrology. No 'inclination' to evil could be blamed on the heavenly spheres; human sin was the only thing to blame. Luther, ever quick to spot an inconsistency, wondered why the demons, who lived so much closer to the stars, never changed their inclinations in the least as a consequence.[17]

So far Luther had dealt in a fairly classical way with traditional superstitions. His 'third age' discussed the old women who willingly associated with demons, that is, witches.[18] This treatment covered six pages of the Rhau-Grunenberg edition, and dealt with many broader issues of superstitious beliefs other than witchcraft. Luther displayed either ignorance or rejection of the main themes of the *Malleus Maleficarum*, though he did know some older sources such as Johannes Nider, mediated through Geiler von Kaisersberg's sermons. These six pages, rarely paralleled in any of Luther's later writings, constitute the best evidence for the often repeated claim that Luther believed conventionally in witches. In fact, Luther's treatment more resembles a critique of the *belief* in the powers allegedly ascribed to witches by ordinary people, and to some extent by the 'witches' themselves. Witches could indeed inflict injuries and diseases on people, damage their crops and animals, and steal milk occultly, as theological orthodoxy agreed.[19] People also *believed* that one could learn things through divination, especially by using young virgin girls or boys; but this was deceptive. Similarly misguided, and 'forbidden to be believed' was the myth that witches rode on broomsticks to meetings, or turned into animals such as cats. Luther then described the cult of Habundia (though he ascribed it to Herodias or Hulda) and the belief in the domestic spirit-creature known as a *Wichtelin* or *Helekeppelin*.[20] Luther then listed a range of misguided beliefs about how to protect children from illness, or ensure safe childbirth, that he blamed on gullible old women. The most typical thing that 'old witches' did was to sow absurd ideas in people's minds. Never the feminist, Luther remarked, 'Who can list all the ludicrous, laughable, false, vain and superstitious ideas of this gullible sex? This trait was ingrained in them from Eve, the first woman, that they should be deceived and mocked.'[21]

Luther then dealt with a number of 'disputed points': as he claimed, areas where there was popular or even learned disagreement. Against the sceptics, Luther argued that sorcerers could indeed stir up storms and harm the crops, through the agency of demons and with the permission of God. 'It is right for Christians to know that these evils are indeed inflicted by demons and their sorcerers, but nevertheless that they are so ordained by God. God does good things through himself, but bad things through bad people.'[22] Secondly, Luther insisted at greater length that witches could not fly to meetings nor be turned into animals. He cited the *Canon Episcopi*, and related a range of entirely conventional stories of demonic illusions, to prove that such stories were mere fantasies.[23] Luther concluded the section with a number of other phenomena that he likewise ascribed to demonic illusions: incubi and succubi, changelings, and experiences of sudden transportations.[24] It goes without saying that Luther took the power of demons extremely seriously: indeed, all these deceits and illusions derived from the desire of demons to 'delude the fleshly senses and imagination, the basest parts of a person'.

Then Luther suddenly changed gear, in a way that was quite unexpected from the perspective of a scholastic theologian, but entirely comprehensible from that of a Renaissance humanist.[25] He turned to criticize those who went to excess in their devotions to relics and the cult of saints in general. Luther argued that many people venerated the saints chiefly or solely in the hope of gaining material benefits through their intercession. Such people in effect made idols of the saints and worshipped them as subsidiary deities. Luther made no doubt that he was including such people with the superstitious, albeit in a lesser category of blame:

Such people, to be sure, St Augustine does not entirely reject, but commends them only to the extent that he says they are better than those who seek worldly benefits through a pact with the devil. For it is better to seek even temporal benefits from God than from the devil. But for all that they are not to be commended; indeed they are not really Christians. Faint praise is really a great denunciation, if they are not good except unless they are compared to the very worst![26]

Human beings persisted in venerating the saints for the physical benefits that they might bring, even though those things were 'useless to us and foolish in the sight of God, and were pleasing neither to God nor to the saints'. Luther then went on to enumerate a range of the cults where a saint had become such a specialist in curing a particular ailment or averting a particular misfortune that the benefit was ascribed to the saint alone: St Antony for the disease of 'holy fire', Saints Sebastian, Martin, and Roch for the plague, St Valentinus for epilepsy, St Christopher for escape from sudden death, Saints Lawrence and Florian for house fires, St Vitus for 'that wretched dance of his', St Erasmus for money, St Louis of Toulouse for beer-brewing, and St Wendelin of Trier for shepherding.[27] Luther then noted the same specialization ascribed to female saints: St Anne according to her legend supposedly brought wealth; Barbara supposedly protected from sudden death and (with Margaret) from death in childbirth. Juliana and Ottilia were 'eye-doctors' consulted only by those with ailments of the vision; Apollonia dealt with toothache, and Scholastica with thunderbolts.[28]

Luther's challenge to the cult of saints could almost have come verbatim from the pen of Erasmus, if Erasmus had been capable of Luther's blazing intensity rather than his own dry, acidic irony. Luther remarked that not only were the saints treated as the sole donors of their benefits; people thought of them only for the material benefits, and never asked to imitate the virtues, let alone the sufferings, that made the saints famous in the first place.[29] A few pages later, Luther recollected himself a little and defended himself against the argument that appeals to saints for patronage were an established custom in the Church. Praying partly for material benefits might be acceptable, but praying *only* for material benefits was not.[30] Luther also suggested that since many of the saints' lives were spurious and sketchy, they might have become disease specialists simply because their name suggested an ailment in the vernacular: so the name of St Valentinus suggested the 'falling disease' of epilepsy in German, or that of St Vincent suggested finding things.[31] Luther was by no means incapable of humour. If St Christopher had had an image of St Christopher to look at he would not have been martyred. St Wendelin in life

tended the sheep of one man; now he is dead he is compelled to look after everyone's livestock. It still causes us Christians no shame to share out the business of worldly things among the saints, as if they had now become servants and bonded labourers: things have nearly gone back to that morass of superstitions, such that we have once again created the confusion of gods among the Romans, and made a new pantheon, and this for no other reason than in order to have a good life ourselves down here.[32]

The cult of saints was also contaminated by a range of abuses. People honoured their patrons with feasts that were nothing but occasions for drunkenness, indulgence, and lechery: this was a poor way to show honour to one's particular patron saint whom one had chosen.[33] People succumbed to pride and rivalry, wishing their own favourite festival to be valued over others. New devotions and new shrines were built out of avarice, to raise cash by encouraging people to patronize a cult that was not yet authorized.[34] However, Luther then tightened the screw one turn further. The frenzied enthusiasm for new devotions proved that they were, in truth, deceits of the devil. One could not imagine that the Holy Spirit would lead people to abandon their parish church and its regular devotions, even to abandon their household duties and families. 'This is something that it is impossible for the Holy Spirit to have done; it is most evidently an illusion of the demon. The Holy Spirit is not a spirit of rashness and rushing into things, but rather a spirit of Counsel.'[35] Luther here adumbrated an argument that would have a long history in the sixteenth century: that Catholic cults and devotions arose in the same way as more obviously superstitious practices, through the deceits of demons. Luther was, to be sure, careful to say that he was challenging spurious new pilgrimages, something about which there was already quite enough controversy in the theological academy.[36] He sufficiently foresaw the possible objections to a critique of pilgrimages to fend them off as he spoke. He ensured (in this case) that he defended himself against the suspicion of supporting the 'Pikart' heresy that saints should not be venerated at all. Luther was still enough of a conservative in 1516–18 to respect the Catholic proprieties as he excoriated what he saw as crass impiety.[37]

Having surely given enough hostages to fortune, Luther then turned his critique of 'idolatry' against those who 'worship an idol of their own wisdom and righteousness'. There were, he claimed, some people who stubbornly minimized the role of original and actual sin in human nature. Such people believed that we suffered not from sin as such, but from a 'lack of merit', and this lack of merit was remedied in Christ. Luther's argument in this section is not easy to follow, and it is even harder to discern who exactly his targets were. One can only guess what the citizens of Wittenberg made of that part of the sermon-cycle. Paradoxically—given the strongly humanist tone of the previous pages—it seems likely that Luther was here criticizing the 'idolatry' of those who held an overly optimistic anthropology, something that a few humanists were most likely to suffer from.[38] Such critiques do not belong with the theological analysis of superstition except in that Luther, from this point onwards, would increasingly regard theological error as far more serious than any other vexations of evil spirits. One of the worst things that the devil could do was to teach people bad theology.

Luther and the fallen universe

By around 1521, at the very latest, Luther's core theological insights had attained their mature and definitive form.[39] However, Luther continued to work out important aspects of the relationship between his understanding of 'the Word', 'the Gospel' (by which he meant chiefly the understanding of justification), and other parts of his theological vision, for the rest of his life. While much of Luther's training in the scholastic *via moderna* from his student days remained with him, nothing about his theology was ever completely conventional. In particular, Luther significantly reworked and rethought the relationship between theology and philosophy in relation to the cosmos, the fall, the state of humanity, and the origins of evil. This would lead Luther to say some radical and occasionally terrifying things about the devil and his power. Those statements, and the ideas behind them, call for a brief exposition before one investigates further the Protestant critique of popular superstition. Luther's cosmology was permeated through and through with his theology. Luther did not naturally conceive of the universe of the deists, in which the perfect cosmic watchmaker sets a self-correcting machine in operation and leaves it to get on with its business. On the contrary, Luther believed that the entire mechanism of the universe continued to function only through the goodness and controlling power of God. Puzzling phenomena such as the retrograde movements of the planets proved this point. Luther also suggested that the sea would overwhelm the land if it were not restrained by God.[40] Even the animals supposedly produced by putrefaction, like mice, were divine creatures: their 'pretty feet and delicate hair' showed the hand of God at work in them.[41]

On the other hand, the universe was fallen. It was not just angels and human beings that were fallen: for Luther, the fall of humanity had damaged the entire created order. He was utterly convinced that the fall corrupted every capacity, every nature, and every disposition of the universe that had previously made it useful and helpful to its inhabitants. Before the fall Adam had far greater natural, never mind moral or spiritual, abilities than he had afterwards. Before his fall he held dominion over the other creatures easily and without effort. After the fall human beings could only rule over the animals with effort and skill, and that only partially.[42] Although human beings were created to work, the pain, labour, and effort involved in work, no less than the pain of childbearing, came as a direct result of humanity's fall.[43] The whole of nature, and not just human nature, was depraved and corrupted. Luther argued (not entirely unconventionally) that the earth only produced thistles and other harmful and unproductive and useless things since the fall.[44] He suggested that the four rivers of Eden, which had flowed from a single source in their first creation, were disordered and realigned at the fall so that they now flowed from different sources and in opposite directions.[45] Even the serpent, having been the instrument of Satan's corruption of humanity, was now obliged to bear the consequences: 'Although before the curse it was a very pretty little beast, it is now more frightful and more hated than all the other animals. . . . Thus the serpent is compelled to bear a part of the curse and of the punishment.'[46]

Repeatedly Luther reflected on how the creation, having been distorted by sin, deteriorated even more as time passed. The earth was less fruitful of good things, and more productive of harmful ones. Even the air, water, and light were less generous than before: 'the entire creation in all its parts reminds us of the curse that was inflicted because of sin.' The flood then increased and aggravated the effects of the fall on the natural world.[47] The appearance of new diseases such as the 'French pox', unknown in his childhood, showed that the punishments for sin were becoming graver as the world neared its end.[48]

Compared to the scholastics, Luther took relatively little interest in speculating about the fall of the angels. There was insufficient basis in scripture for certainty;[49] it was a 'likely idea' that there was some rebellion or attempted usurpation by 'some proud angels, displeased by the meekness of the son of God'. After the rebellion of some, the remainder were confirmed in goodness, which indeed they would have been even if the rebel angels had not sinned.[50] However, it is a truism that Luther took the power of the devil extremely seriously.[51] His entire theological oeuvre contained repeated references to the power of the devil and the challenges that the forces of darkness posed to the Gospel.[52] In the light of the demon-infested quality of Luther's rhetoric, one would expect him to have a great deal to say on the themes of this book. In fact, rather fewer explicit references to the devil's power to cause physical harm appear in Luther's work than might be expected. One of the most notorious statements of this kind occurred in Luther's commentary on Galatians, completed in 1535 just before he began his Genesis commentary:

For it is undeniable that the devil lives, yes, rules, in all the world. Therefore witchcraft and sorcery are works of the devil, by which he not only injures people but sometimes, with God's permission, destroys them. But we are all subject to the devil, both according to our bodies and according to our material possessions. We are guests in the world, of which he is the ruler[53] and the god.[54] Therefore the bread we eat, the drinks we drink, the clothes we wear—in fact, the air and everything we live on in the flesh—are under his reign.[55]

This passage would earn Luther some severe reproaches for excessive language from, among others, Martin Delrio at the end of the century.[56] Luther was here expounding the passage in Galatians where Paul speaks of the people being 'fascinated' or 'bewitched' to forsake the truth.[57] Luther interpreted the text to the effect that Paul was comparing the Galatians to children suffering from bewitchment. He then told tales of children made sick by sorcery and of the changeling child, as he had described much earlier in the *Ten Commandments* treatise.[58] However, Luther then went on to do something rather unconventional. He argued that the illnesses caused by witchcraft were, in truth, illusions. The devil appeared to be able to cure the part of the body that had been damaged, which, if it were truly injured or removed, would be beyond the devil's power. 'A genuine injury cannot be healed or restored.'[59] Luther cited, as evidence of the devil's power to deceive, the story of St Macarius and the girl supposedly turned into an animal, whose true nature was only covered by a demonic illusion.[60] It was a considerable stretch from demonstrating that the devil could cause illusions—which was an entirely orthodox claim—to the much less orthodox suggestion that *all* demonic bewitchment was a kind of illusion.

Demonology and theological error

Luther insisted, with greater certainty and passion as time passed, that the most important form of 'bewitchment' was the spiritual bewitchment caused when the devil spread false doctrine to challenge and corrupt the Gospel. Temptation and delusion leading to *religious error* took over more and more in Luther's mind as the proper work of the devil. In the *Larger Catechism*, the supreme idolatry was to seek salvation through good works.[61] The mass for the dead and the whole system of belief in purgatory Luther described in the *Articles of Schmalkalden* as a 'mask' or illusion of the devil.[62] One of his final, most bad-tempered and obscene works of controversy, written in 1544, was *On the Papacy at Rome, Founded by the Devil*.[63] It would be easy to assume that this association between demonic temptation and theological error was a mere metaphor, a rhetorical flourish, a means to make a spectacular *in hominem* attack on a theological opponent. Such a reading would dangerously misrepresent Luther's intention. One can see just how seriously Luther intended his demonological reading of theological wrongdoing from a relatively early work, *That These Words of Christ, 'This Is My Body,' Still Stand Firm against the Fanatics*, written at the height of the first Eucharistic controversy in 1527 as a theological rebuttal of those Luther called 'sacramentarians' and 'fanatics'.[64]

Luther proposed a demonological reading of theological error from the very start of this treatise. The devil tried to cause general mayhem in the world, of course. 'But especially and supremely does he demonstrate his craftiness in spiritual, inward matters which concern the glory of God and conscience. How he can slither and squirm, twist and turn in all directions, and hinder and thwart us on all sides, that no one may be saved and persevere in the Christian truth.'[65] Luther then set forth a sort of demon-centred reading of Church history. After the coming of Christ laws and works were cast down, but the devil intruded his followers into Christian schools and sowed theological disputes and heresies. Thus scripture became discredited, and some external source of authority had to be identified, in the form of Church Councils, to resolve disagreements. To try to end these disputes, there arose human laws and, ultimately, the papacy itself. Now the devil was happy to further the rise of human legislation and works as far as possible. Luther, having seen the neglect of scripture and the folly of human laws, then revived the study of scripture and restored Christian freedom, 'and escaped the devil, although he stubbornly resisted and still continues to do so'. Now, however, the devil continued to try to frustrate the work of restoring scripture, by sowing dissension and disagreements over the sacraments. Luther foresaw that if these 'heresies' continued there would need to be another set of regulations as in the early Church, which would have the same fatal effects.[66]

In these apocalyptic and stressful years of the 1520s Luther came to regard the struggle with the devil for Christian truth as not merely an accidental inconvenience, but a necessary accompaniment to teaching the truth. If one wished to have the scriptures, one must wrestle and struggle with the devil; if one gave up the battle, one would have peace with the devil.[67] This interpretation of the cosmic struggle over truth led Luther to view demonic temptation and harassment in a quite different way from the medieval tradition. Whereas before such temptations and assaults might be viewed as the outcome of sin, for Luther they were sure evidence that one was struggling for the truth and had identified something important.[68] As Luther wrote in his commentary on Galatians:

It is a real advantage to us that with his plots he attacks and exercises us this way, for by this means he confirms our doctrine and increases faith in us. We have often been struck down in this battle, and we are still being struck down; but we are not destroyed.[69] For Christ has always led us in triumph, and He is still triumphing through us.[70] From this we gain the firm hope that through Christ we shall eventually emerge as victors over the devil. This hope gives us firm comfort, so that we can take courage this way in all our temptations.[71]

However, other less affirmative consequences followed for Luther's attitudes towards controversy. As Mark Edwards demonstrated many years ago, Luther came to view his struggle as being not with erring theologians in themselves, but with the 'spirit' that worked within and behind his theological opponents. This 'spiritualizing' of the struggle with theological rivals led Luther to assimilate and homogenize his opponents into a single threat, neglecting the nuances that distinguished their thought. He assumed that, for instance, Zwingli must have learned his Eucharistic ideas from Karlstadt.[72] It also, of course, disposed Luther not to negotiate in anything resembling good faith with those he saw as quite literally possessed. As Luther put it in the sarcastically entitled *Against the Heavenly Prophets in the Matter of Images and Sacraments* of 1524–5, 'It ought to surprise no one that I call him a devil. For I am not thinking of Dr. Karlstadt or concerned about him. I am thinking of him by whom he is possessed and for whom he speaks.'[73] In 1535 Luther would repeatedly explain the perversity of the sects by the fact that they had been taken captive by the persuasions of Satan: 'this bewitchment is nothing other than a dementing by the devil, who inserts into the heart a false opinion.'[74] Not only would Luther not negotiate doctrine, as the outcome of the 1529 Marburg colloquy would show. He became certain that the conversion of those who had espoused and defended theological error was actually impossible. As he wrote, again in 1527:

So I shall once more set myself against the devil and his fanatics, not for their sake, but for the sake of the weak and simple. For I have no hope that the teachers of a heresy or fanaticism will be converted. Indeed, if that were possible, so much has already been written that they would have been converted. It has never been reported that an author of false doctrine was converted. For this sin is too great, because it blasphemes God's Word and sins against the Holy Spirit. Therefore God lets it become hardened.[75]

An extremely dangerous parallel suggested itself here. As Luther had already accepted and agreed with the medieval tradition, the good angels were confirmed in their goodness and the evil angels were confirmed in their obstinacy such that they could never be reclaimed. Luther's demonological reading of theological error ran the risk that 'heretical' human beings would be assumed to be like the evil angels, so thoroughly possessed by spirits of error, dissension, and pride that they could never be reclaimed.

Since Luther saw the struggle for Christian doctrine in his own time so much as a fight between the cosmic powers of good and evil, what did he make of the debate discussed at the end of the previous chapter, between those who thought that the demons had relatively free rein to cause mayhem, versus those who argued that they were strictly constrained by divine providence? Luther's response to this question evinced some personal and distinctive attitudes. On the one hand, Luther portrayed the struggle for souls between God and the devil in more dynamic, desperate colours than late scholasticism had done. For the Middle Ages human beings were poised between God and the devil. God called; the devil tempted. Once cleansed of original sin through baptism, human beings were delicately balanced between the tinder of sin and the residual potential for goodness within them that survived the fall.[76] In Luther, human beings were not poised waiting to choose. God and the devil were fighting over each individual soul. People were like mules or horses which must be bridled and ridden: the only question was who was doing the riding.[77] This sort of language, along with the highly coloured, and repeated, description of the devil as 'lord of this world', conjures an image of a very powerful devil, an almost Manichaean rival of the good God in the struggle for souls. On the other hand, the same Luther who wrote so passionately about the power of the devil to deceive and delude, also wrote equally passionately about the all-governing hand of God. Already in the *Ten Commandments* sermon-cycle he had simultaneously pointed out the assaults of demons and yet insisted on the providence of God. 'Without the permission of God he [Satan] could not move a leaf on a tree.'[78] In *On the Enslaved Will*, his rebuttal of Erasmus's *Diatribe on Free Will*, Luther expanded at some length on God's absolute control over all that happens.[79]

It appears that Luther was trying to have both sides of the argument between the 'cosmic gymnasium' and the absolute providential control of God. In a sense he was, but only because of the remarkable sophistication of his theology. Luther was aware that God could be known, or envisaged as being, on several levels. Typically he distinguished between God revealed and God hidden. The revealed God was the God known in the sufferings of Christ and the struggles of the Church against the forces of evil. The hidden God was the inscrutable God concealed in the darkness of divine providence and predestination. The hidden God was the God who is incomprehensibly involved in the daunting, terrifying things that happen and that to our understanding make no sense.[80] We are to direct ourselves to the God revealed in the Word and leave the hidden God alone. 'After all, who can direct himself by a will completely inscrutable and unknowable? It is enough to know simply that there is a certain inscrutable will in God, and as to what, why, and how far it wills, that is something we have no right whatever to inquire into.'[81] This radical division, not in God's own nature, but between that which is knowable and unknowable by human beings, explained for Luther the paradox between contingency and providence. What appears to us to be a contingent and accidental event is, to the eyes of the eternal God whose will cannot be hindered, actually neither contingent nor accidental but necessary and immutable. Things appear contingent to us because we do not know what to expect and they seem to happen by chance.[82] This theological stratification allowed Luther to take the massive reality of evil and demonic malice completely seriously, without ultimately denying the absolute but inscrutable sovereignty of God over creation. It also enabled him to avoid the somewhat facile, and certainly insensitive, explanations for God's permitting evil to happen that had been used, for example, by Martin Plantsch or Geiler von Kaisersberg.[83]

Luther and 'the devil's sacraments'

Luther made one further, quite crucial contribution to the evolving debate over superstitions in the sixteenth century. In a startling way, he inaugurated one of the classic Protestant arguments against Roman Catholic consecrations. This rhetorical flourish appeared towards the end of a work written for a quite different purpose. In 1539, in response to the papal summons of the abortive Council of Mantua, and drawing on Pierre Crabbe's recently published Catholic history of Church Councils, Luther wrote an extended polemical pamphlet entitled *On the Councils and the Churches*.[84] For most of the work Luther challenged the claim that Councils of the Church could or should play *any* constructive role in adding to the body of Christian doctrine: councils should meet only to repress error and restore true teaching. At the end Luther explained his view of the correct theological understanding of the Church. The true Church was known by the possession of a number of 'marks' (Luther tended to cite a larger number of these than other reformers). It should not, however, be known by its spurious and unnecessary relics, rituals, and consecrations. On the contrary, the misconceived rituals in the Catholic Church formed yet another aspect of the devil's war against the true Church. The devil saw the Church being established, and set up his rival institution alongside.[85] As 'God's ape', the devil imitated the true sacraments and other external rites of the true Church by instituting sacramentals such as holy water, salt, candles,

herbs, images, and other such things. The devil instituted these 'aping' false
rituals in exactly the same way as he had done with 'rain-makers, sorcerers,
exorcists of devils, etc.'.[86] The parallelism was exact: Luther applied the
argument about the 'devil's sacraments', already well established in medieval
demonology, but applied it to Catholic consecrations and sacramentals.[87]
The true sacraments were by the power of God imbued with supernatural
power to absolve from sin or to communicate the body of Christ to
the believer; 'so too the devil wants his mummery and aping tomfoolery
to be...imbued with supernatural power.' Thus Catholic propaganda
attributed greater power to the Agnus Dei than even God would offer;[88]
bells could drive away devils during storms, some blessings heal cows
or quench fires, while amulets could give protection against all kinds of
misfortune. 'There was no need so small that the devil did not institute
a sacrament or holy possession for it, whereby one could receive advice
and help.'[89]

Luther was aware that, as usual, the devil had him in a bind. By
challenging the usefulness of the 'devil's sacraments', that is, the Catholic
consecrations, Luther had inspired some people to challenge the value of
even the true sacraments, instituted by Christ and commanded by God. So
the devil, in the shape of the sacramentarian heretics, spiritualists, and other
radicals, had attacked the true understanding of the sacraments. The crucial
difference between true and false rites, however—here as everywhere else,
for Luther—was that God had *specifically commanded* the easy, gentle and
acceptable means of grace and salvation, consisting in preaching, water,
bread, and wine, through the Word.[90] In contrast, the rituals concocted by
the devil achieved nothing except what was either fraudulent or merely
the reversal of what the devil had done first, such as causing cows to lose
their milk. Finally, Luther pointed out that the Church rightly and usefully
acquired certain physical objects for the convenience of worshippers, such
as buildings, altars, pulpits, fonts, vestments, etc. These things (Luther
did not explicitly add, 'despite having been consecrated' but that was
clearly his intent) had no more power than in their material natures, nor
were they in any way necessary to salvation. They were just practical and
useful instruments for organizing and conducting worship. Respecting such
inessentials was a matter of good order rather than theological need.[91]

Martin Luther personified in his own development much of the transition
from the classic late medieval to the Reformation response to the phenomena of 'superstition'. From the first Luther knew, as the humanists did, that

the popular quest for spiritual solutions to material and physical problems did not just resolve itself into the question whether the rites used were 'official' Church rituals, or more borderline products of the surrounding culture. To use religion of *any* kind for purely physical benefits provoked Luther's criticism, as a mendicant and a theologian. Even officially approved ceremonies were bad if they only sought physical benefits. Luther began from the same standpoint as his medieval forebears: he analysed popular belief in the terms of medieval demonological analysis. However, Luther's devil was a different kind of being from the closely circumscribed demons of scholastic theology. Luther envisaged the devil much more as a single being, enormously powerful (at least when viewed from the human plane, within the physical world) and dedicated to deceiving people and preventing their salvation at all costs. In keeping with his view that physical harm was far less important than spiritual error, Luther thought that the worst possible thing the devil could do was damage the preaching of the Gospel, and therefore the salvation of souls. As the reformer's thought developed, he became ever more convinced that the devil was actually occupying, controlling and directing the Catholic Church of his day with this purpose in mind. Consequently, Luther began, towards the end of his life, to identify those aspects of Catholicism that actually amounted to the 'devil's sacraments', demonic intrusions of inappropriate rites into the Church, designed to draw people away as far as possible from the authentic means of salvation. Luther contributed very significantly to what became, in due course, the Protestant demonology of Roman Catholicism and the use of the rhetoric of 'superstition' in this argument. However, Luther remains a marginal figure in many ways, just as the sixteenth century remains an era of transition. It would be equally foolish to expect either unbroken continuity or absolute, categorical shifts from one state to another. It is now time to look at the broader perspective of the Reformation on these same issues.

12

Prodigies, Providences, and Possession: The Sixteenth-Century Protestant Context

The Reformation constituted a vital turning point in the Western European theological understanding of worship and ritual and their role in the world. The next four sections of this chapter will set out the ever-deepening divergence between the writers who emerged from the Reformation and the continuing and developing Catholic tradition. Yet the confessional theological analyses of religion and superstition diverged, and fought each other, through the early modern period against a background of two other equally important processes. First, ideas about the cosmos and causation in the material world changed in early modern Europe, but only very gradually and quite out of step with the religious changes. For the whole of the sixteenth and much of the seventeenth century Aristotelian ideas of matter and causation retained considerable influence and ascendancy in European thought. The rivals to Aristotelian-Ptolemaic-Galenic science, especially some of the more exotic and occultist brands of Neoplatonism, appeared more disturbing and dangerous to many theologians than the orthodoxy they sought to displace.[1] Newtonian physics and cosmology, insofar as it postulated attraction between physical bodies at a distance, would be profoundly disturbing to the theological mind for many decades precisely because of its apparently occult associations.[2] Secondly, social and cultural processes conspired to make the various Protestant and Roman

Catholic polities appear remarkably similar in certain respects. The later sixteenth century witnessed wave upon wave of more or less organized 'social control' by regimes of all political and religious colours across Europe. Through the early modern period regimes sought to collect more and more information about their people, as seen for instance in parish registers or taxation records. Increasingly they took control over the care of the poor, generally striving to immobilize the indigent poor, to punish and deter vagabonds (suspected of robbery and fomenting sedition), and to inculcate habits of social cohesion, sexual discipline, and gender and class subordination.[3] These campaigns for hierarchical, rational uniformity in society could not fail to intersect with the response to popular beliefs and customs.[4]

Because the processes of philosophical development and social control proceeded alongside, but out of step with, theological changes, it is exceedingly difficult to spin these multiple and tangled threads into a consistent narrative. Some recent historians have attempted to subsume the theological debate into one or other of the other two strands of development. If religion is subsumed under cosmology and philosophy, then the Reformation era will appear at best a stubborn postlude to the medieval Aristotelian age, still mired in beliefs about demons and obsolete attitudes to physical causation. If it is subsumed under social control and the rise of the 'modern state', then religion matters—since it is a vital tool in the hands of the state-builders—but theological differences between Protestants and Catholics appear insignificant compared to the common purpose between them. When one adds to this the fact that the theological literature on superstitions is dense, polemical, complex, and often barely readable, it is easy to see why many historians in recent decades have circumvented the material by subsuming theological argument under some other intellectual heading rather than analysing it.

The present chapter will set out many ways in which Protestant descriptions of superstition drew on and echoed the ideas of many of their medieval antecedents. Neither in cosmology nor in demonology did the Reformation mark a clear, sharp turning point from what had gone before.[5] Because most theologians in the sixteenth century—and for some time after—were Aristotelians, their sense of what was possible in the world largely reflected late scholastic ideas. They believed in the presence of demons in the cosmos; they also believed that one might witness the hand of God active in the visible world. They treated magic as something deserving of serious analysis and concern by intelligent people. As an example, previous historians have remarked that the followers and students of Philipp Melanchthon took a specially strong interest in prodigies and other surprising phenomena in nature.[6] This interest embraced many subjects bizarre to modern eyes, such as misbirths or apparitions in the sky. If one takes a superficial view of such interests, it can seem as though Philipp and the Philippists suffered from a morbid fascination with the weird. Such an explanation would be a gross anachronism as well as facile. Melanchthon, unlike most reforming leaders, was a philosopher, historian, and literary scholar as well as a theologian. He remodelled the university curricula in these and other subjects more or less single-handed, in the hope that other areas of learning than theology would not be neglected in the enthusiasm of the early Reformation.[7] He persistently taught in the Arts Faculty at Wittenberg and refused all inducements to transfer permanently to theology (possibly deciding that Luther was a better colleague when kept at some distance).[8] Melanchthon cared passionately to integrate the different areas of his intellectual expertise. As a natural philosopher who was also a theologian, he tried to identify the hand of God at work in nature. While the divine creativity might most typically be seen in the ordinary workings of the cosmos, there were also special instances, cases of the marvellous or the bizarre, that could contain a particular special message, a unique significance intended to convey the divine will or meaning.[9]

Cosmology and demonology

In the late 1540s Melanchthon composed his textbook on physics and astronomy, entitled *Initiae Doctrinae Physicae*.[10] At the very outset of the work he argued that the heavenly bodies were not placed randomly or without meaning in the universe. He believed that the spheres exerted physical effects upon the rest of the 'inferior matter' of the world, causing not just changes in the weather but disturbances in human affairs.[11] Some parts of theology could not be explained without an understanding of the laws of nature; physical knowledge helped to delineate the boundaries of necessity and contingency.[12] Unusually for a textbook on physics, Melanchthon devoted most of the first book to astronomy and what he regarded as the 'correct' astrology. The second book dealt with the more conventional questions of matter and causation. As always, theological priorities were paramount:

This reducing of things to their first original serves as a demonstration of God, and convinces the mind of the doctrine of the order of causation, such that one is compelled to admit that God is the designing mind, since God has impressed his marks into the remainder of all nature. These marks show in a certain fashion what God is, and of what kind is his will, setting out a rule for discerning good and evil. This reducing of things to the first cause from the signs in nature is truly pleasant to a good mind, and confirms honourable opinions about God.[13]

Interestingly, Melanchthon displayed much less concern with the fallenness and brokenness of the physical world than Luther did. His physics was overwhelmingly based on Aristotle, whom Melanchthon cited repeatedly and at length. He dissected the varieties of causation in fine detail.[14] Apparently contingent or fortuitous events might in truth have a specific cause. While all outcomes could ultimately be attributed to the will of God, divine intervention might also occur in a special and dramatic way, as when those favoured by God were providentially preserved from danger, or those punished by God were consumed by the dramatic forces of nature. The devil might immediately and directly influence human affairs, 'sometimes as though jesting', whether by conferring spurious benefits or issuing ambiguous and deceptive oracles.[15] Thirdly, human temperaments and the heavenly bodies might influence the outcome of apparently fortuitous events. Of Melanchthon's pupils, Johann Stigel composed more elegant Latin with far greater facility than Zacharias Ursinus, who was learned and worked hard but did not have a good astral temperament for the task. Kaiser Friedrich III and François I of France were both unlucky warriors because their horoscope had Mars in a bad place.[16] This was not causation as modern philosophy would have it. However, by the standards of his time and the authorities that he used, Melanchthon reasoned in a consistent and fairly rigorous way as he sought to integrate theology and natural philosophy. Melanchthon's textbooks and his tireless educational efforts shaped the minds, not only of Lutherans across Germany, but of many who would later embrace the reformed tradition in Heidelberg and elsewhere after being trained by Philipp. In general, Protestant thinkers followed Melanchthon in seeking to fit the spiritual realm and spiritual beings into their view of the cosmos. They subscribed to a broadly Aristotelian view of causation where matter acted on matter, and intelligent minds on other intelligent minds, but intelligible symbols could not affect matter directly. This meant that most mainstream Protestant thinkers adopted a view of the existence and abilities of evil spirits very similar to that of their medieval scholastic antecedents. There was a scientific as well as a theological reason for this continuity. Aristotelian physics had some difficulty in explaining the continuous motion of bodies. Before Newton it was not obvious why celestial spheres remained in continuous (though apparently erratic) motion. The notion of incorporeal intelligences moving the spheres seemed more satisfactory than any other possible explanation.[17]

One of the most learned short essays in demonology came from the pen of the Florentine expatriate Pietro Martire Vermigli, in his posthumously published commentaries on I and II Samuel. Vermigli took advantage of the story of the apparition of the witch of Endor to write several discursive additions to his running commentary. His essay entitled 'Whether the Devil Can Appear, and Know the Future, and Give Answers' actually encompassed an extensive discussion of the various opinions in classical philosophy about the existence of demons.[18] A range of classical philosophers had denied that there was a specific demonic nature: instead they assigned the alleged phenomena of demonic activity to melancholy, delusion or misunderstanding. Platonists accepted the existence of demons but gave them 'airy bodies'. Scripture, and correct theology, agreed that demons were spirits and truly incorporeal. Their knowledge was, however, strictly limited; despite their great experience, they had no insight into the purposes of God and knew the future only by conjecture.[19] They could be seriously deceived, as they were (for instance) about the true nature of Jesus Christ, and could not introspect the human heart.[20] Vermigli's essay closely replicated the clichés of medieval demonology. Several other Protestant writers engaged in similarly conventional expositions of the qualities, natures, powers, and limitations of demons. Among the Protestant mainstream one could include the article 'On Satan, and Evil Spirits in General' in the theological encyclopedia published under the title of *Problemata theologica* by the Bernese theologian and botanist Benedikt Marti ('Aretius', 1522–74), although Aretius gave more space than usual to the Neoplatonists;[21] the first chapter of the *Treatise on Magicians, Sorcerers and Witches* written by Johann Georg Godelmann (1559–1611), a Lutheran jurist at Rostock University;[22] the first chapter of the *Christian Opinion on Sorcery* authored pseudonymously by the Heidelberg professor Hermann Wilken or Witekind (1522–1603) under the name Augustin Lercheimer;[23] and a series of chapters in *A Discourse of the subtill Practises of Devilles by Witches and Sorcerers* by George Gyfford (1547/8–1600).[24]

One expert on the lore and literature of demonology stood out from the rest in the middle of the sixteenth century. In 1563 the Low German physician Johann Weyer (1515/16–88) published his *On the Illusions of Demons*. It may well raise eyebrows in many quarters to include Weyer in a chapter devoted to Protestants. Weyer worked in the duchy of Cleves-Jülich-Berg at a time when the confessional position of the duchy was by no means clear. He has been credited in most scholarship with a neo-Erasmian reform-Catholic theological position, one that resisted incorporation into any of the Protestant confessions. His formation comprised much more than theology: he absorbed specific elements from the occultist writer Agrippa of Nettesheim, and much from his medical training.[25] Weyer crafted his work quite skilfully, and contrived to appear to write mostly against the vulgar and uneducated sort of Catholics rather than Catholicism *per se*. He carefully elided his anticlerical venom into his criticisms of popular ignorance. Nevertheless, Weyer would become an absolutely crucial figure in the emergence of a distinctively Protestant theology of superstitions. Moreover, he wrote positively about the Reformation, read Protestants with approval, and was read and quoted extensively by them.[26] The first of the six books of Weyer's magnum opus was devoted to a systematic analysis of demonology. Like others he rejected the Peripatetics and the Neoplatonists to turn to the traditions of the Church. He cited the vast literature on demons from patristic and medieval theology, then charted the work of the devil from Eden to classical antiquity.[27] He then itemized the activities of demons in detail, contriving repeatedly to include with their delusions and misdeeds quite a range of acts associated with popular Catholic piety, as will be seen below.

More problematic in the area of demonology was the Kentish landowner and amateur theologian Reginald Scot (d. 1599). Scot was notorious in his own time for his acerbic scepticism in the matter of trials for witchcraft. He was suspected of disbelieving in spirits altogether; more recently he has fallen under suspicion of adhering to the views of the Family of Love, even though he explicitly rejected their teachings.[28] Somewhat like Weyer but with a more radical daring, Scot challenged traditional beliefs about sorcery by tainting them constantly with vulgar ignorance and with popish blindness (which in Scot's eyes were closely allied). His *Discourse upon divels and spirits*, usually printed after his more famous *Discoverie of Witchcraft*, expended great energy and sarcasm in demonstrating the divergence of views over demons in late antiquity.[29] He made merciless fun of the claims of those who, like Pseudo-Dionysius, claimed to know the angelic natures in detail;[30] at the other extreme he treated with contempt the ideas of corporeal devils or 'familiar spirits' that bulked large in English vernacular witchcraft trials.[31] He took care to lean on authorities of impeccable standing in reformed Protestantism, especially Calvin, Pietro Martire Vermigli, and the English exegete Edward Dering. In the end, however, after all the sarcasm and rhetoric, Scot came up with a surprisingly conventional belief in spirits. Demons were incorporeal spirits; the devil, whether understood as singular or plural, was a creature of God, whose evil God used for God's own good purposes. The devil's nature was incurably evil; he was determined to tempt, corrupt, and destroy people.[32]

Demonic mischief

Protestant writers took a broadly similar view to their medieval forebears of the kind of things that demons might try to do to hurt people. Andreas Althamer (c.1500–c.1539), otherwise known as the organizer of the Reformation in the Margraviate of Brandenburg-Ansbach, published a sermon on the devil in 1532 that reflected both the old and new views of demonic vexation.[33] The devil was a murderer and a liar; people must regard him as the ultimate source of disorder, murder, and bloodshed, as far as he was able and as far as God allowed him. The devil took pleasure in disorders and disturbances and would overturn society if God did not prevent it.[34] Likewise, all lies, errors, fanaticisms, and false teachings derived from the devil; the devil falsified the word of God, and in so far as he was able lied, betrayed, and seduced.[35] Thirdly, the devil was the source of all the temptations to evil in the world, and as such must be resisted strenuously.[36] Melanchthon, perhaps surprisingly, struck a slightly more sardonic note. The devil sometimes tried to win people over by promising them good things, only to deceive. 'Recently at Nuremberg, in 1530, he showed a priest treasures in a crystal. When the priest dug for these near the city, with a friend there to observe, they saw the chest in the hole, and a black dog sitting on the chest. The priest went into the hole but the top then fell in and killed him, and filled up the hole.'[37] Benedikt Marti similarly reported that while some demons caused illness or insanity in people, others just engaged in mockery, such as overturning furniture and filling houses with unpleasant noises. Marti was not the first author thus to describe poltergeists.[38] Johann Weyer typically supplied far more detail than most about the range of demonic activities, from preventing milk from churning to inserting foreign matter into the bodies of sick people or removing the organs of the dead before dissection.[39] Weyer was quite rare among writers in the Protestant tradition in discussing the possibility of demonic sexual intercourse with human beings. He analysed it at length in book 3 of *De Praestigiis*; he sought chiefly to dispel the folklore of demon–human hybrids and to dismiss most of the stories of demonic intercourse as delusions.[40]

Delusions in general received fairly copious coverage in the writings of Protestant demonologists. Benedikt Marti and the Danish Lutheran theologian Niels Hemmingsen both amalgamated their discussions of demonic illusions and of 'fascination', the term more commonly used to describe the evil eye. People could be 'fascinated' when they were harmed with a mere look; they could also be deceived by illusions presented to the eyes (as in the story of the young girl and St Macarius) or to the mind (as in the case of wrong ideas such as those described in Galatians).[41] Hermann Wilken enumerated a range of crafts of illusion ('Gauckeley'), 'an operation of the devil whereby he blinds the sight of people and animals... such that they do not see what is, or see what is not'.[42] Marti, Wilken, and Godelmann amused themselves and their readers by citing some of the outrageous tales attributed to Johannes Faustus in German folklore (current in Luther's time though not printed as a single narrative until 1587).[43] Faust reputedly, when a peasant refused to give way to him on the road, appeared to swallow up his horses and cart together. On another occasion, a peasant had sold some really well-fattened pigs: the buyer was driving them home along the road and when he pushed them against a torrential stream, he saw only straw floating in the water, and the pigs had disappeared. The purchaser went back to the inn to seek out the seller (Faust) who had deceived him. He went up to him angrily and shouted 'hey, you cheat!' and grabbed him by the foot. The whole foot came away as though it had been entirely detached from his body.[44]

Demons could be particularly deceptive through the arts of divination, and Protestant lore detailed this as fully as its medieval antecedents. Protestant theology and philosophy generated a formidable encyclopedic textbook on the subject of divination, the *Commentary on the Principal Types of Divinations*, first published in 1553 by Kaspar Peucer (1525–1602) and subsequently revised several times before the author's death. Peucer studied natural philosophy, medicine and theology at Wittenberg, where he met and married Philipp Melanchthon's daughter Magdalena. His career would be blighted by the turns of electoral religious politics in Saxony: first his Philippism, then his involvement with Calvinist ideas would lead to controversy, disgrace, and some years' imprisonment.[45] Peucer shared his father-in-law's curiosity about the intersection of natural philosophy and theology, and considered that not all forms of divination might be dangerous or forbidden: some, such as medical prognostications from symptoms might be entirely reasonable; others, like judicial astrology, might exist in acceptable and unacceptable versions.[46] The demonic forms of divination figured in Peucer's chapter on magic. As magical practice had steadily deteriorated since antiquity, demons intruded themselves into the business of prediction and offered to tell magicians the future or to work desired effects for them. Diviners might use familiar spirits enclosed within crystals, or try to summon the dead to give responses.[47] There then followed a list of divinatory techniques informed by Peucer's considerable classical scholarship: these involved basins, buckets of water, mirrors, crystals or rings and polysyllabic Greek words.[48] Johann Weyer politely acknowledged Peucer's work in the subject and then appended an even longer list of divinatory techniques supposedly used and to be avoided.[49] Niels Hemmingsen offered a similar though slightly less elaborate list with picturesque Scandinavian background details.[50] Girolamo Zanchi (1516–90) delivered a series of lectures in the Strasbourg *Gymnasium* on various forms of divination. In due course these appeared as a book packaged with Thomas Erastus's treatises on judicial astrology.[51]

Possession

Some unfortunate people could also be possessed by devils. Philipp Melanchthon provided here again some of the most persuasive opinions on this subject. In his correspondence he made several observations on the subject, later collected and quoted by Johann Weyer. Melanchthon observed that while frenzy, delirium or madness might have a natural cause, it was also certain that devils entered into some people and tormented them, with or without other physical symptoms. An illiterate woman in Saxony had been attacked by a devil and afterwards could speak in Greek and Latin about the forthcoming Schmalkaldic War. Another illiterate woman, this time in Italy, while suffering from possession, was able to quote the finest verse in Virgil's *Aeneid*. A girl in Brandenburg Mark was afflicted with the ability to pluck hairs from people's clothing, which then turned into coins and which she ate: she was later healed. In the same way as for medieval writers, to these early Protestants the bestowal of extraordinary and temporary gifts on the mentally distressed proved demonic possession.[52] In general, Protestant writers acknowledged the reality of possession while they castigated Roman Catholics for the means that they used to respond to it. As will be seen below, Protestants believed only in praying for the possessed to be delivered from their afflictions. They did not regard the rite of 'exorcism' as practised in the Roman Church as lawful; indeed, it constituted some of the strongest evidence that Catholicism was itself magical. How the theory of possession was to be applied in specific cases was, of course, much more controversial.

The case of John Darrell, the puritan preacher and exorcist of late Elizabethan England, offers some interesting counter-currents to the usual theological perspective. Darrell acquired a reputation as an exorcist in Nottinghamshire from 1597 onwards: he and his friends promoted his case in print. He attracted a furious condemnation from the conformist Anglican clergyman and divine Samuel Harsnett (1561–1631), later archbishop of York. Darrell was put on trial before an ecclesiastical commission and found guilty of fraud, though Protestant opinion in England was clearly divided over his case and he was soon released.[53] Harsnett shortly afterwards opposed the exorcizing of the Catholic Weston in a vehemently anti-Catholic pamphlet.[54] The Anne Gunter exorcism case in 1600s London, following soon after the trial of Darrell, became one of the most sensational of the contestable cases of alleged possession.[55] As always, one finds Reginald Scot somewhat on the outer edge of acceptable opinion on this subject. Scot insisted, more as a point of philology than metaphysics, that often when the Bible, or indeed common speech, spoke of the devil being in a person, it meant either that such a person was diseased or evil-intentioned. Scot would allow that purely invisible and spiritual demons might enter people; but mocked the opinions of Catholics and 'some Protestants . . . more grosse than another sort' that demons could be driven away by physical cures, or could assume physical bodies at will.[56]

Apparitions and Visions

Aside from demonology, Protestant writers would also discuss a range of apparitions and events of special significance that might communicate meaning to the sublunary world. They found it entirely credible and consistent with their world-view that God might transmit, directly or indirectly, important messages to people through extraordinary occurrences. Melanchthon theorized that God worked in the universe by a twofold action. In one sense God continuously sustained the ordinary workings of things; in another the divine will made itself felt through special interventions, which while not 'miraculous' in the technical sense, occurred contrary to the ordinarily expected sequence of events. These belonged to a category of special providences, and were either intended to achieve some special end (such as the preservation of Moses in infancy) or to transmit some special meaning to people.[57] As a (somewhat modified) Aristotelian, Philipp rejected the idea that the universe was either a self-sustaining mechanism or the product of a random collision of particles (as Epicurean philosophy claimed). Rather, a constantly guiding divine hand was required; so when that divine hand did something unforeseen, it suggested that possibly, though not invariably, there was a message to be learned. This line of thinking underlay the Protestant preoccupation with marvels, prodigies, and other similarly significant occurrences. The words *ostenta, monstra, prodigia*, as Peucer remarked, essentially meant something which showed something or made a point.[58]

Melanchthon divided 'monstra', significant apparitions, into four categories. First, spirit-creatures might appear to announce dire events, as happened in classical antiquity: these could be either good or evil angels. Second were extraordinary appearances in the heavens such as comets, which were natural in origin and might have no human significance, but usually meant something. Thirdly, there were prodigious apparitions in the skies, such as apparitions of armies fighting: these were artificial productions composed of natural vapours and colours that might be made by good or evil angels. Finally there were natural creatures that somehow were born out of their proper species or endowed with some spectacular and portentous abnormality.[59] What Melanchthon had sketched out in his *Physics*, Kaspar Peucer developed more fully in a chapter of his work *On Divinations*. Peucer identified as a branch of legitimate divination the inspection of prodigies, which he called *teratoscopia*. Scripture used the term τέρατα to refer either to the direct and abnormal works of God, or to the deceptions of demons practised as a result of rivalry with God.[60] Such prodigies did not actually overturn the natural order, but reflected the power of the omnipotent God to direct nature in unusual ways. However, Peucer analysed the causes of prodigies with greater sophistication. Some derived immediately from God. Others, however, might come from intermediate causes in the angelic and human natures. Since the fall, nature had become corrupted and defective, and abnormalities appeared in it. Moreover, the devil strove as far as possible to interfere and damage natural processes, leading to prodigies and misbirths. In sum, such anomalies could occur through the work of good or bad angels, astral causes, or the corruption of natural processes.[61]

Bizarre and spectacular descriptions of prodigies and monsters therefore served as a constructive attempt to see the divine message in the 'prerogative instances' of the created order. They were none the less strange for that. In 1523 Philipp Melanchthon published in German an explanation of the two most famous misbirths of the early Reformation era, the 'papal ass' found dead in the Tiber in 1496, and the 'monk calf' born in Freiberg in Saxony in 1522. These two monstrous animals were not of identical types. Although the stories about them were doubtless improved considerably in the telling, they fitted awkwardly enough into the interpretative schemes to suggest that there was some raw truth behind the stories. The papal ass was reputedly a donkey with much of its body covered in scales, the breasts and abdomen of a woman, a human hand on one foreleg and a clawed talon on one hind leg. Its rump had the shape of a bearded human face, while its tail took the form of the head of a monstrous creature. It had been interpreted as a judgement on Alexander VI, the pope at the time of its discovery; but in the atmosphere of the early Reformation it could be read as a warning against the papacy as a whole. The 'monk calf' by comparison had no obvious features derived from other animals: but its head and front quarters were deformed in a way that suggested a monk's cowl, while its horn buds were grouped in a pair on one side of its head.[62] Melanchthon later reported a different kind of misbirth that seemed to have an obvious meaning:

Before the war [of the League of Schmalkalden, 1546–7] a baby was born in a region of France, in whose stomach, once he emerged from his mother's womb, a knife was found embedded, with the point projecting outside the stomach; shortly afterwards by suppuration it was removed. All agreed that this signified civil war. Nor could any physical cause be given for it. How would the knife have been inserted into the mother's womb? Rather by diabolical trickery the knife was implanted into the baby's stomach, to signify the mutual slaughter of citizens, who afterwards struck with their swords as though into their own entrails.[63]

Kaspar Peucer reported a larger number of prodigious children and animals. Some were relatively predictable, such as conjoined births, though it was assumed that these too could be meaningful: cases had occurred in Hesse in 1540, at Louvain in 1547, and in England in 1552.[64] Following his description of the two classic animal misbirths of the papal ass and the monk calf, Peucer described the two startling instances of human misbirths, the monstrous triplets reputedly born in 1531 to a woman at Augsburg, and the malformed but prophetic infant said to have been born on 25 January 1543 in Belgium, as described earlier in the Introduction. Peucer went on to relate the case of another animal misbirth, a calf found in a field in Bitterfeld in 1547 with parts of its face and most of its hind quarters in human rather than bovine shape.[65] Another prolific source of marvellous prodigies was the Baltic fishery. Peucer reported that in 1550 a fish was captured near Copenhagen with a human face and a tonsure like a monk's, with a scaly body and the appearance of a cowl. More famous was the fish reported to have been caught with various weapons around its body and an inscription supposedly threatening woe to Denmark.[66] In 1626 a fish was caught off the English coast and the contents of its stomach brought to England: it proved to contain several devotional treatises, badly decayed but still decipherable.[67]

More elusive, but just as interesting to many Protestant commentators, were occasional visions in the sky. Typically, armed men or ferocious animals fought each other in the clouds, sometimes in quite elaborate pictorial combinations. These apparitions usually attended either the death of some important political figure or the onset of an especially disturbing time of civil strife. They were generally taken as warnings of imminent trouble. Peucer inferred that the vision of a tree, a horse, a hunting dog, a cross, and a lightning bolt, around the time of the death of Elector John of Saxony in 1532 must have foretold the changes in the Saxon dynasty and the disasters for the churches.[68] From all across Germany in the 1530s and 1540s came reports of apparitions in the sky that in some sense foretold instability and violence. The specific significance of the images was not generally made clear, and they were usually interpreted merely as general warnings of trouble; but people clearly thought it worth the time to document, date and conserve such reports in fairly meticulous detail. An unusually detailed example was the following:

In the year '34 on the third day of July, in the town of Schleswig, at midday under a calm sky, there were seen in the air lions rushing to fight from various places;

next to them an armed horseman, carrying a spear for battle. Not far from the horseman lay a human head, without a torso, decorated with an imperial crown. A short while afterward, there was seen the head of a tusked boar, and two dragons spewing fire. Then, there shone out the image of a single very large city, placed by a lake, besieged by fleets and land-based forces, and above it, a bloody cross, which partially changed to black. Then another horseman appeared, blazing in a fiery colour, wearing an imperial crown on his head; he was followed by a horse without a rider. Afterwards, in a broad plain, two burning castles appeared, close to a high mountain, where a great eagle was perched, hiding half of its body behind the side of the mountain. Then some eagles' chicks appeared, bright white in colour; then the head of a recumbent lion, marked with a crown. A cock pecked with its beak until it appeared to separate from its body and then vanished, while the body remained visible. Other lions stood alongside, and next to the boar's head, a rhinoceros that gradually changed into a dragon, and many other animals of unaccustomed shape and size. There was also a burning castle on a high rock, ringed by two armies, and the entire region appeared, with many towns, castles, and villages. Soon the whole region in which all these things stood was consumed by fire, and a vast lake obscured the ruins of the devastated land, with only two towers standing out in the place where the city had been. By the side of the lake stood a great camel, as though drinking.[69]

Then there were the portentous forms of strange rainstorms: precipitation of blood, milk, corn, stones, sulphur, fire, and 'corn the size of hailstones' were all reported. At Bockenem near Hildesheim a river of copious blood flowed out of the ground; shortly afterwards the town was sacked and largely burned by an army. Peucer admitted that these visions could be generated by various means whether divine, demonic, or natural. The lesser abnormalities might be natural and meaningless; the major ones, on the contrary, gave warnings that ought to be heeded.[70]

Ghosts, astrology, and apocalyptic

The most alarming and potentially controversial apparitions were those purporting to be the ghosts of the dead. Nearly every Protestant writer on demonology said something about ghosts, and largely to the same overall effect.[71] Protestants were agreed, once the basic doctrinal principles of the Reformation were established and understood, that the souls of the dead were taken either to heaven or to hell after death. Before the Reformation, the most common reason why the spirits of the dead allegedly walked the earth was to inspire their surviving friends and family to endow

copious quantities of masses to speed their souls' release from purgatory.
Reformation theologians agreed that such masses for the dead were contrary
to the Gospel. God could not possibly permit such apparitions to inspire a
blasphemous form of worship: but the devil very easily could and would
counterfeit them to cause trouble. Peucer likened the stories of ghosts to
the classical myths of the shades of the dead, and added: 'Just like these are
the old wives' fables of purgatory, which our forebears used to hear trotted
out in Church, and those tales about the wandering souls of the dead, made
into clichés by constant repetition. The devil increased the trust placed
in these things so as to establish the received and idolatrous custom of
funeral ceremonies, the practice of celebrating masses for the dead.'[72] This
did not mean, of course, that Protestants denied the existence of ghosts *per
se*: nor did it exclude a variety of natural or physical explanations for the
apparitions. It did, however, mean that ghosts could not possibly be the
souls of the dead.

The Protestant stance on ghosts received its definitive statement from
the Zurich theologian Ludwig Lavater (1527–86) who was also Heinrich
Bullinger's son-in-law. Lavater published the first edition of his *On Spectres,
Apparitions and Great and Unaccustomed Noises, and Various Presages* in
German in 1569 and in Latin in 1570; it received multiple re-editions
and translations thereafter.[73] The first part of Lavater's treatise discussed
the phenomena. Lavater affirmed that apparitions known as ghosts did
actually appear, though he also gleefully reported various instances where
priests counterfeited apparitions for corrupt reasons. In the second part he
systematically dismantled the Catholic belief in the apparitions of souls in
purgatory, mocking the claims made by Jakob of Jüterbogk (Jacobus de
Clusa) in his *Tractatus de animabus erutis a corporibus*, published in the later
fifteenth century. Lavater insisted that the notions of purgatory and limbo
as destinies for souls were unscriptural and without authority from the
early Church. On the contrary, demons could and would counterfeit the
appearances of spirits in order to disorder the Christian religion: 'by meanes
of false miracles, he decreeth new Hollydayes, Pilgrimages, Chappels, and
Aultars: by conjurations, blessings, enchantments, he attempteth to cure the
sicke, to make his doings have aurhoritie'.[74] Lavater linked the apparitions
of ghosts with the portents and presages of great events and the deaths of
people, that were reported in popular literature. Most if not all of such
apparitions came from demons (here Lavater departed rather from the
Philippists) and were therefore speculative: demons did not really know

the future, so their predictions were just educated guesses.[75] The same demonological explanation of ghosts was echoed, in detail, by Weyer, Marti, and Godelmann.[76]

For Protestant scriptural exegetes, the text that posed most problems in the theology of apparitions of the souls of the dead was I Samuel 28. King Saul, on the brink of defeat by the Philistines, and having expelled most of the soothsayers from the land, goes to one of the remaining ones at Endor. He asks her to conjure the spirit of the dead prophet Samuel. An apparition of Samuel rises up at the soothsayer's bidding and foretells Saul's imminent defeat and death. This text had generated a considerable body of exegesis down the centuries. It was authoritative scripture and could not therefore be dismissed as a fable; moreover, the text referred to the apparition as 'Samuel' without any qualification or explanation. Pietro Martire Vermigli analysed and summarized a great deal of the previous discussions in his extended essay on the subject in his *Samuel* commentary, before giving his own verdict.[77] He identified the divinatory technique as a form of necromancy, that is, divination from the responses of the dead. The question was whether the apparition was really Samuel (in soul, body, or both) or a demon impersonating Samuel. Vermigli quickly dismissed all possibilities other than Samuel's soul or a demon. He noted that differing opinions had been expressed both within the Jewish rabbinical tradition and among the early Church Fathers on this point. Even Augustine appeared to contradict himself across his various utterances.[78] The later medieval exegete Nicholas of Lyra believed that the vision was the real Samuel, partly because of reading the text literally and partly because of an allusion to the incident in the praises of Samuel in Sirach 46:20.[79] Vermigli himself insisted that the apparition was a demonic illusion. The real Saul could only have appeared if God had permitted this to happen at the soothsayer's bidding, which was unthinkable. As a somewhat unusual afterthought (for a Protestant) Vermigli noted that even Gratian's *Decretum* agreed with him.[80] Vermigli's position became definitive for Protestant exegesis. Johann Weyer made almost identical points: he cited Jerome to the effect that the deuterocanonical book of Sirach was not definitive for doctrine, and quoted some of the same patristic authorities as Vermigli at considerable length.[81] There is some good reason to think that not all Protestants adjusted immediately, or definitively, to the theological view of ghosts.[82] Nevertheless, the theological argument against apparitions of the souls of the dead was strong and widely held.

Besides the ambiguous or the demonic apparitions, there remained the possibility that God might really communicate important messages to people through nature or through extraordinary revelations. Some Protestants included astrological readings among the intermediate means by which divine meaning might be expressed. There was little agreement on the subject. Melanchthon, and following him Kaspar Peucer, were relatively optimistic about the possibility of a chastened, purified, but still informative astrology. Such a practice would need to avoid the extremes of astral determinism and acknowledge the extraordinary complexity of human events. That complexity would probably make the planning of actual decisions by astrological criteria impossible.[83] Bullinger expressed a much more negative view. Arguing rather at cross purposes past the Philippists, he denounced the suggestion that astral influences were so strong that people with inclinations to evil (such as those born under Venus, supposedly destined to be sexually depraved) could not be held responsible for their sins because of their destinies.[84] John Calvin delivered a much more calculated and specific blow to the predictive science in his *Avertissement contre l'astrologie* of 1549. Calvin argued that the only credible astrology was the kind that deduced general influences of the spheres on the physical matter of the world, such as the effects of the cycle of the Moon on oysters. The judicial astrology that attempted to discern the characteristics and destiny of a person from the state of the sky at the time of their birth lacked logic even on its own terms. It would be better to infer something from the sky at the moment of conception rather than birth (supposing that could be known) but in any case regeneration by grace could completely change a person's complexion. Ultimately judicial astrology ought to be condemned along with the other forms of illicit divination.[85] There was little or nothing that was distinctively Protestant about these debates. The arguments used against astrology by Luther and Calvin corresponded fairly closely to those employed, for example, by Jean Gerson in c.1400 or by the Jesuit Benito Pereira near the end of the sixteenth century.[86]

Protestants also resorted to apocalyptic speculations for insight into future events. Following Luther, at times the most apocalyptic of all the reformers, various Protestant theologians speculated about the place of the Reformation movement in salvation history and the ultimate destiny of the universe. Philippist church historians such as Christoph Pezel speculated that world history since the time of Christ should be divided into four periods of approximately 500 years each, the last beginning with the advent of Luther and the Protestant Reformation.[87] In some instances these two thousand years of the Christian era were added to the two previous two-thousand-year eras of heathen error and Judaic law respectively.[88] Gnesiolutherans led by Matthias Flacius Illyricus believed that the 'true Church' could be tracked through the Middle Ages at a time when the Catholic Church was overwhelmed by demonic error. Historians in the reformed tradition, especially those in England following John Foxe, interpreted Christian history in terms of Revelation 20. After the thousand-year binding of Satan foretold in the Apocalypse, the devil must be let loose 'for a little while'.[89] This 'little while' was variously interpreted as the time from the Gregorian papacy to the Reformation, or to include the time after the Reformation when the reformed church was still under attack. In any event, this reformed historical understanding of Satan meant that the assaults of demons were not just part of the normal order of life in the sublunary world. These assaults now had significance in the light of the cosmic struggle for the destiny of the created order as a whole.[90]

Magic and witchcraft

For Protestants as for medieval Catholics and early modern Roman Catholics, demons interacted with human beings through the practices of magic and witchcraft. It has for some time been conventional to argue that there was almost no significant difference between Protestant and Catholic theories of magic. To a degree this is clearly correct. Writers from the Lutheran and reformed traditions presented very similar histories of magic. The rival university theses on magic crafted by the Lutheran Jakob Heerbrand of Tübingen in 1570 and the Catholic Albrecht Hunger of Ingolstadt in 1574 made very similar points for most of their length (though the disagreements were important too).[91] The *magus* had been in antiquity a careful and philosophical observer and investigator of the secrets of nature; but over time and with the depravation of everything by the devil, 'magic' had come to encompass a range of deceptive and demonic arts that tried to explain, foretell, and control the cosmic processes. In reality, such things could do nothing except endanger souls and cause harm to people. As in other areas, Johann Weyer wrote the first systematic treatment of magic in what would become the idiom preferred by Protestant theologians. Book 2 of *De Praestigiis* presented a sophisticated linguistic and philosophical analysis of 'bad magic'. Weyer inaugurated the practice of distinguishing magicians not according to the medieval Latin nomenclature but by the various Hebrew names used in the Old Testament for practitioners of various magical arts.[92] However, the distinction between the different forms of incantation, divination, and sorcery did not imply any difference in Protestant views about how magic functioned. A magician was someone who summoned or otherwise communicated with a demon using ritual forms in order to accomplish 'some deluding, deceiving, or otherwise mocking task'.[93]

Like the scholastics, most Protestant analysts of magic agreed that a pact with demons was generally involved in magical operations, whether this was explicit and intentional or merely accidental and implicit. For Thomas Erastus, 'a "magus" is therefore someone who claims to be able to know or to do supernatural things with the open or covert assistance of a demon'.[94] Both Erastus and Hemmingsen argued that, since the words and gestures of magic were *per se* ineffective, some kind of pact with a demon must be involved. Niels Hemmingsen claimed that implicit pact was the first step on a slippery slope: 'an old woman recites prayers and incantations to cure diseases, not thinking there is any impiety; she is gradually drawn further away from God by this abuse of the word, until at last, openly seduced, she makes an express pact with the devil.'[95] Johann Georg Godelmann came to similar conclusions, although he sliced and diced the question of demonic pacts more minutely than others. He distinguished between truly magical and merely superstitious healing activities: in the former there was an explicit pact, in the latter merely a tacit pact. So 'such superstitious matters, both in magical curing and in superstitious curing, are merely *the sacraments of the devil*, in which the Devil . . . does this only in order that by these means he may delude, ensnare and deceive the souls and minds of people.'[96] However, those who merely engaged in some misguided form of divination, such as casting of lots or palmistry, could not in his view be said to have entered into any sort of pact, even a tacit one.[97]

Writers and preachers from the Reformation movements all warned people in very similar terms against the temptation to use magical forms of healing and protection, especially against those types of misfortune that supposedly had magical or demonic origins. The argument remained the conventional one that even if one used a demonic device to achieve a good end, this still amounted to a dangerous and sinful engagement with diabolical forces.[98] In the course of giving this stern pastoral advice, Protestant writers took the opportunity to describe and relate a range of

weird and spurious cures. Johann Spreter, a jurist from Rottweil, and Niels
Hemmingsen both, and apparently independently, related a medieval tale
of a fictitious cure for a disease of the eyes. A woman went to a student,
and asked him to write down the contents of a piece of parchment to use it
as an amulet against cloudiness in the vision. The student could not read it,
so instead wrote in Latin: 'May the devil tear out this old woman's eyes and
fill the sockets with dung', and gave it to the woman. When the woman
wore it around her neck, she was healed; but after a year she opened the
amulet and had the words read, threw it away in a rage, and the eye disease
came back.[99] These authors, like Weyer and many others in the period,
were aware of the power of auto-suggestion in such cures, but did not
consider that placebo effect was sufficient excuse for a superstitious cure.[100]

Several Reformation era writers attacked the empirical cures of
Theophrastus Paracelsus, who had displayed a reckless arrogance in
his evident contempt for theologians' attempts to restrict the scope of
experimental medicine.[101] Here again Protestants seem to have adopted
their enraged tone from Johann Weyer. As a practising physician Weyer
had found himself picking up the pieces after unsuccessful medical
experiments by Paracelsian physicians who had 'memorized the foul
sayings of that insane man'.[102] The Palatine physician and theologian
Thomas Erastus devoted a four-part treatise to an attack on the medical
theories of Paracelsus, in the first part examining 'the things [Paracelsus]
set forth regarding superstitious remedies and magical cures'.[103] Johann
Georg Godelmann devoted a chapter to 'praestigious curers of supernatural
illnesses', chief among whom was Paracelsus.[104] He took care to cite
Paracelsus's many acts of defiance against theological orthodoxy in his own
words, and generally did so accurately.[105] Godelmann included Paracelsus's
cures within a wider discussion of curative amulets. Only those that relied
on the natural effect of the material used (such as peony, claimed by
Galen to prevent epilepsy when worn around the neck) were lawful. All
others became 'sacraments of the devil'. He then described some of the
diagrammatic and symbolic medallions included within Paracelsus's *De
Occulta Philosophia* and *Archidoxis Magicae*. (He could in fact have presented
even more exotic examples but refrained from doing so.)[106]

At this point one ought to allude briefly to the Protestant literature
on witchcraft, although that has been treated much more fully by others
elsewhere.[107] The conventional view presents Protestant and Catholic
witchcraft theory as closely allied to each other; and here again, there is good

evidence in support of this view. Lambert Daneau in France and Thomas Erastus in the Palatinate both wrote treatises on magic and witchcraft that compared closely with their medieval Catholic counterparts in many respects. Lambert Daneau even included (although he was somewhat unusual in this respect) a fairly full discussion of the diabolical gatherings or sabbats that bulked so large in Catholic discussions of witchcraft as a sect or movement.[108] Protestant and Catholic confessions both produced some relatively credulous and also some relatively sceptical treatises on witchcraft; mainstream Protestants—and even marginal ones like Reginald Scot—broadly admitted the existence of spiritual beings determined to cause mischief, to whom misguided or desperate people might ally or subject themselves. The most infamous and widely debated of sceptics, Johann Weyer, expressed his scepticism along a fairly narrow front. Weyer did not deny the reality of evil spirits; nor did he doubt that some people believed that they served them; nor did he deny that such people deserved punishment. However, he did extend the scope of demonic illusion far further into the stories of alleged witchcraft than others. He extended it to include the 'explicit pact' itself, which he regarded as 'deceptive, foolish, and of no weight'. He argued that demons, with divine permission, really caused the *maleficia* popularly ascribed to witchcraft: the alleged pact of demons with witches was entirely irrelevant, and a product of delusions and mental disorder.[109] The flight to the sabbat and intercourse with the demon he regarded as fictitious; the means alleged to cause bewitchment were ineffective and inconsequential.[110] Alleged witches, as opposed to conscious and deliberate magicians, should be treated leniently and their confessions treated with suspicion. At considerable length he argued that alleged witches ought not to be punished for acts that they simply could not have committed.[111]

Weyer was extensively and approvingly read by many Protestants, and despite what has often been written or implied, Protestant writers were, on balance, more likely than Catholics to be at least cautious and selective in which elements of the witch-myth they accepted. Hermann Wilken, in tones strongly reminiscent of Weyer, argued that witches could not really do such things as control the weather, make people sick with words or gestures, or change themselves into animals. Stories of dances with the devil originated from misunderstood Catholic sermons. Wilken questioned whether even things that were theoretically possible, such as being carried through the air by demons, actually happened other than in illusions.[112]

These women, he argued, should be treated mildly, and sent to the physician or the clergyman rather than the judge, to help them out of their unbelief and error. Conversely, much greater severity ought to be used with soothsayers, sorcerers, and illusionists.[113] In 1598 Antonius Praetorius, parish minister of Laudenbach in the Palatinate, published a treatise that closely followed Wilken's arguments.[114] An opinion of the theologians of Nuremberg, dated 26 May 1602, largely adopted the same perspective. Johann Georg Godelmann, meanwhile, rejected Weyer's and Wilken's arguments about the impossibility of most supposed acts of witchcraft. However, he brought far greater legal caution into the debate and urged extreme care on such subjects as lycanthropy, sexual intercourse with the devil, or weather-magic.[115]

This is not the point to expand further the putative distinction between Protestant and Catholic perceptions of witchcraft.[116] One difference between them does, however, cry out for attention. To a Catholic of the old or the new type, the preservatives and cures against bewitchment offered by the Church were legitimate and appropriate tools to use for one's own benefit. To Protestants such devices were just another aspect of the demonic conspiracy to delude and defraud the Christian world.[117] It is therefore time to turn to the ways in which Protestants actively, purposefully, and in detail argued that Catholicism itself was a species of superstition.

13

The Protestant Critique
of Consecrations: Catholicism
as Superstition

Whatever the similarities between Catholic and Protestant writers in their views about the world and the creatures in it, it would be absurd to deny that there were vitally significant differences between the major confessions of the Reformation era on the topic of superstitions. Significant disagreements, albeit largely hidden from view, had already emerged between realist and nominalist scholastics as to how far the critique of superstitions could be allowed to impinge upon and modify popular belief and religion.[1] Protestant reformers took those critiques several stages further; some 'radical' reformers went further still. As the Reformation progressed and hardened into militant confessionalism, it became insufficient merely to cast aside the old rites and customs as unscriptural, superfluous, or erroneous. Protestant polemics defined Catholicism as a superstition in the technical sense: Catholic rites embodied the devil's mockery and depravation of true religion.[2] One area of Catholic practice presented a safe and—in the constantly fractious world of Protestant theology—broadly agreed target between Lutherans and reformed. The medieval Church offered to the faithful an array of consecrated objects: holy water, consecrated salt, palms consecrated on Palm Sunday, consecrated wax in the form of candles or the Agnus Dei, and herbs consecrated to the Virgin Mary on the Feast of the Assumption.[3] These 'sacramentals' were supposed to defend their faithful users against demonic assaults and material misfortunes, though their benefits were not certain, in contrast to the guaranteed spiritual benefits acquired in the sacraments.[4] They constituted the Church's chief weapons against superstitious remedies and amulets; but they also seemed dangerously similar to them in many ways.

Karlstadt and Eberlin on consecrations

Protestants did not seize on the sacramentals immediately as sticks with which to beat the old Church. Compared to such obvious 'abuses' as the sacrificial mass, clerical celibacy, monasticism, ecclesiastical privileges, canon law, or the papal monarchy, consecrations seemed of relatively secondary importance in the early years. However, some few early discussions of the subject do deserve attention. Probably the first Reformation era writer to criticize the sacramentals was Andreas Bodenstein von Karlstadt, in a treatise *On Consecrated Water and Salt* published in multiple editions in various German cities in 1520, and supported by a further short treatise in 1521.[5] Karlstadt did not at this point equate sacramentals with superstition. However, he did argue that it was a gross error for priests to teach people that there was an actual spiritual benefit in the use of consecrated water or salt. He argued, in terms similar to those later used by Zwingli, that material objects used in worship were representations of spiritual things, not the spiritual thing themselves. Holy water, conventionally sprinkled on the face to remove venial sins, had no such effect. Rather, water served as a symbol of the sufferings and persecutions through which Christ passed.[6] When Christ washed the disciples' feet on Holy Thursday, it was not the water that cleansed them of sin but Christ's death on the following day.[7] If water signified suffering and, through suffering, the remission of sins, the consecrated salt, for Karlstadt, represented the reading of scripture, that ought to be available to everyone but was all too often withheld from the people.[8]

Though Karlstadt did not connect the false use of consecrated things with demonic superstitions, he did note that the rites of consecration 'give rise to various magical practices' that Christians should be warned against.[9] However, he preferred to link sacramentals to his emerging theology of the sacraments. Signs represented spiritual things in the way that a signpost showed the way: they did not contain what they represented. Karlstadt, unfortunately, suffered from a prolix, repetitive, and inelegant prose style, as evident in these pamphlets as elsewhere in his writings.[10] His reputation

suffered even more from the merciless pasting that Martin Luther gave
him in his polemical treatise *Against the Heavenly Prophets*.[11] As a result his
influence tended to be mediated through the work of others.

After Karlstadt's treatise had been attacked by some Franciscan friars of
St Annaberg, Johannes Eberlin von Günzburg (1470–1533) was provoked
to write a rejoinder on the theology of consecrations, *Against the Profaners
of God's Creatures through the Consecration or Blessing of Salt, Water, Palms,
Herbs, Wax, etc.*[12] It appears to date from the controversial pamphleteering
days of 1523, although not published until some two years later. Eberlin
advanced a much more sweeping argument that adumbrated the later
Protestant approach to the subject. The consecration of created objects was
unscriptural. All things were good in their first creation by God. They
became good or bad in practice depending only on how they were used.[13]
Eberlin then made fun of a range of consecration customs, but reserved
his greatest venom for the consecrating (conventionally called 'baptizing')
of church bells (customarily rung to drive away demons during storms)
carried out by bishops in the old church. He addressed such bishops thus:

> Oh you village idiots! . . . You know not what baptism is or what it is to baptize:
> you are not willing to baptize a child yet you baptize a bell: what fools you
> are! . . . There is no greater idol of Antichrist than bells; no greater idolatry than
> the use of bells. Will you consecrate bells? Woe to you! Do you want to turn
> away God's wrath and chase away the devil with bells? I can well believe that the
> devil arouses a thunderstorm and then disperses it, so that people will ring bells
> and sprinkle holy water, and burn consecrated palms and candles: by this means
> [the devil] promotes and strengthens idolatry among the people.[14]

Here Eberlin applied, perhaps for the first time in the emerging Reformation, the familiar argument from medieval pastoral demonological writings.
A false rite appeared to work because the devil stirred up a problem—bad
weather, disease, or whatever—and then removed it, apparently by means
of the false ritual that the same devil had himself devised. The apparent
'success' of the ritual perpetuated the misguided use of it.[15]

Eberlin went on to argue that to regard some things as blessed over others
was an insult to God; to believe that they could drive away the devil was
usurping the role of Christ, who had driven away the devil, cancelled out
sin, and brought us closer to God. So blessings as commonly understood
were 'the devil's work to seduce us'.[16] Ironically, the sacramentals were
used without reference to their natural function: water did not wash, salt
did not give taste, candles did not illuminate, and so forth.[17] It would be

perfectly proper for a Christian person to use these consecrated objects for their ordinary, everyday uses: to put holy salt in soup, or use holy oil on a wound or to lubricate a wagon wheel.[18] He enlarged his critique to include the cult of saints and the customs surrounding burials. Only in Christ do we have help, counsel, and protection for body, soul, honour, and goods against the devil and hell. Nothing truly 'consecrates' except faith; all other blessings are masks, 'serving more for seduction than for salvation, more as a sorcery than a blessing'.[19]

The classic Protestant arguments: Spreter, Peucer, Weyer

Neither Karlstadt's nor Eberlin's arguments were quoted explicitly in the mid-sixteenth-century Protestant critique of Catholic consecrations, so one cannot know how far these early pamphlets directly influenced the developing Protestant rhetoric on the subject. However, between Eberlin's works and Luther's later comments two core arguments had emerged: first, that the devil subverted true religion by instituting unscriptural and unlawful rituals within the Church; and second, that the attempt to add extra 'blessings' to material things by rituals of consecration was a futile abuse of the created order. These arguments later found fuller articulation in a series of works from both Lutheran and reformed Protestants across the middle and later part of the sixteenth century. One of the earliest statements came from the pen of Johann Spreter von Kreudenstein, the jurist of Rottweil, in his *A Short Opinion, as to What Should be Thought of the Idolatrous Blessings and Conjurations*.[20] Although he was a lawyer by training, most of Spreter's writings, all in German, related to religion in some form or other. He published several pamphlets in the late 1520s relating to the introduction of the Reformation in Rottweil;[21] in 1543 a set of editions of otherwise unknown works by Spreter were all published at Basle by the same printer, Bartholomaeus Westheimer. Spreter's printed works included treatises on the Eucharist (very much a hot topic in southern Germany), the providence and calling of God, the churches of Christ and Antichrist, and a treatise on biblical doctrines on usury and other financial questions.[22]

Spreter's *Opinion* set out one of the first coherent arguments equating Catholic consecrations with superstitious blessings. Spreter identified the key problem as *Segenspruch*, the uttering, writing, or carrying of a healing or prophylactic spell or charm. Spreter began with a thesis that would become definitive in the Protestant critique:

It is a dire abomination and real sorcery before the Lord God, that some people think through their blessings to augment, diminish, make great and small God's works, and to beware of and protect themselves against all evils, regardless of the fact that God has blessed everything in eternity. That which God once blessed, should be and remain for eternity blessed, and may not be further blessed or improved by any creature; likewise all things which are blessed by God, may not be impaired by people.[23]

Spreter then embarked on a complex philological analysis of the multiple meanings of the word *segnen*, 'to bless', found in scripture. Only God could 'bless' something in the sense of declaring it good, assigning it properties, making it fruitful. Enchanters used words to claim to overawe or expel the devil, but were in truth turning to him. There were two kinds of 'blessers and sorcerers'. The first were those who claimed to be good Christians, monks, nuns, priests, and so forth: they consecrated salt, water, and the other sacramentals, but 'the devil does not flee these things; yea, rather he has more means to deceive'.[24] On the other side there were the sorcerers, the enchanters of weapons, the diviners of future spouses, those who made amulets with strange names on them, or practitioners of the wound-salve.[25] Spreter claimed to have seen an amulet which a folk-healer had prepared, that seemed to contain nothing but the names of demons. He also described a number of agricultural superstitions: enchanting flocks to protect them from wolves, or branding animals bitten by a rabid dog with 'keys' of a particular shape named after St Rupert or St Loy. Other people, when an animal had broken its leg, left the leg unbound but bandaged a chair-leg in a form of sympathetic magic. There were even 'blessings of St John, St Quirinus, St Stephen, etc.' that were believed to remove the penalties of sin.[26] In all these things (as in the medieval superstition-critique) Spreter argued that the demon merely removed the harm that he had caused in the first place, and by so doing entangled the enchanter in superstitious practices. Spreter's distinctive contribution to this argument lay in his polemical juxtaposition of ecclesiastical consecrations alongside popular charms and spells. Exactly the same argument applied to both: these rites that claimed to drive away demonic assaults actually relied upon the devil's help.

What Johann Spreter had sketched out in a short pamphlet, Kaspar Peucer then amplified in several key passages of his work *On Divinations*. Peucer provocatively included his discussions of Catholicism in the chapters on 'Magic' and 'Incantation'. Following Luther, Peucer argued that the devil aspired always to mimic, mock, and corrupt every part of the life of the Church, and to obscure or pervert the true doctrines of Law and Gospel. Because Christ and the saints cured with the utterance of a word, the devil persuaded people that there was a 'naturally effective power' in words uttered, and that by uttering formulae one could implant power into material things such as 'water, fire, salt, oil, and other things... Hence there began the persuasion, which is the chief and mainspring of pontifical idolatry, of the power of the conversion of bread, at the pronunciation of words, into the substance of the body of Christ.'[27] Peucer might appear here to have strayed (as he subsequently did to his great cost) outside Lutheran orthodoxy in his theology of the sacraments: but not so. In fact, Peucer's argument that the power to consecrate could not lie *in the words themselves*, but in the will of God, remained quite conventional and even echoed some medieval antecedents.[28]

The devil mocked God's appearances to people in the theophanies of the Old Testament by appearing in the form of ghosts of the dead; thus the devil promoted the belief in purgatory.[29] In a complex and polemical argument about incantations and their origins, Peucer classed with sorcerers' poisons and enchanted herbs the 'papal' consecrations of oil, salt, water, bread, and herbs. 'Popish consecration takes things intended for bodily use and transfers them to another purpose, contrary to the ordinance of God... it pretends to confer power on those things to remove the stains and defects of sins, to heal up the wounds of corrupt nature, to drive away demons, and to prepare souls for the grace that is to be poured into them.'[30] In response to the stock Catholic defence that Paul called for things to be 'sanctified by the Word of God and with prayer' (I Tim. 4: 4), Peucer responded that 'to sanctify' did not mean by the power of the words to change the substances of things, or to endue them with new properties. There was no intrinsic, performative power in the words to change the properties of things: the biblical text meant only that appropriate use of such material things, combined with prayer and thanksgiving, was pleasing to God.[31] Throughout these long chapters Peucer constantly switched between denouncing vulgar magical techniques and Catholic consecrations and para-liturgical practices. He sent a clear message that both these things worked in the same way and derived from the same source.

Johann Weyer then gave even greater publicity and circulation to basically the same body of argument. Situated in a confessionally ambivalent location, Weyer was somewhat more careful to direct his satire and his critique at vulgar abuses of Catholicism rather than Catholicism *per se*: but he was only barely careful, and there was no mistaking his real intent. In book 5 of *De Praestigiis*, ostensibly directed at superstitious cures for bewitchment, Weyer entitled the third chapter 'How the "Magicians" of the Church Deceive the People with Regard to the Curing of Diabolical Ills'.[32] Priests mendaciously claimed to cure diabolical illnesses with consecrated objects such as holy water 'blessed over and above God's original consecration'. He listed a large number of cures that rested on the quoting of a text of scripture, as though the text were intended to be used as a magical formula.[33]

After listing at great length many charms and spells (which later imitators would habitually abridge to prevent their writings being used as a grimoire!), Weyer denounced the practice of wearing passages of scripture as amulets. After quoting patristic authorities who criticized the wearing of amulets, Weyer described how the Agnus Dei, the amulet made of consecrated wax and distributed by the papacy, was supposed to preserve its wearers from a whole range of evils.[34] The rhyme that Weyer quoted about the Agnus would later be quoted with outraged disapproval by other Protestant writers.[35] The author most likely to have drawn Weyer's attention to this custom was Martin Luther himself, who published the German verses in a short pamphlet in 1539.[36] Weyer linked the Agnus with magical medallions and talismans where symbols or words of scripture were imprinted. Neatly fusing the secular and ecclesiastical preservatives, Weyer insisted that 'even if the objects be decorated with an infinite number of divine marks and names for God or words from Holy Scripture, no power will be gained or lost from the substances as a result of all these figures' since 'God has bestowed upon individual substances their own marvellous powers of performing certain specific actions. And indeed no new mixture of qualities is established in them now.'[37] In chapter 21 of the same book of *De Praestigiis* Weyer again demonstrated the slippery quality of his rhetoric. He listed several physical substances believed in classical antiquity to guard against witchcraft. Sulphur, cinquefoil, and various animal body parts were all supposed to be preservatives, as well as other stones and herbs. Weyer then slid rapidly into a highly sarcastic enumeration of the sacramentals such as holy water 'which of course puts on new powers by virtue of the following words . . .'; likewise salt and the balsam gum used to make Holy Oil. Weyer quoted the prayers of consecration, with citations of sources, leaving the 'pious reader' to reach the appropriate conclusion. His rhetoric was ingeniously deniable, but the thrust of it was unmistakable.[38]

Later developments of the argument

Between the works of Spreter, Peucer, and Weyer the lines of the Protestant attack on the consecration of sacramentals were laid down. It remained only for others to follow where they had marked the path. The highly orthodox Lutheran Jakob Heerbrand, in a critical section of his Tübingen university theses on magic, attacked the Catholic clergy on exactly the same point. 'Pontiffs and priests, satellites of the Roman Antichrist, sin much more grievously in this respect than common Magicians and Enchanters.' Their grievous sin lay in thinking that by their consecrations they could confer new properties on material things. Because of the abuse of the words of scripture in the rites of consecration, these rituals constituted forbidden magic and an abomination before God.[39] Hermann Wilken's pseudonymously entitled *Christian Opinion and Reminder about Sorcery*, in a chapter on 'blessings and conjurations', addressed consecrations with arguments almost identical to those of Spreter. More methodically than the latter, though, Wilken enumerated the 'devil's work' of the canon of the Catholic mass, the consecration of sacramentals, the blessing of the Easter Eve fire, and the consecrating of church bells.[40] At the end of the century Johann Georg Godelmann quoted Heerbrand and Wilken verbatim; he then added an extract from a sermon preached by Jakob Andreae at Esslingen, where this prominent Lutheran theologian had denounced the ritual by which the oil of chrism was consecrated, and described it as in no way different from the conjurations of a magician.[41]

By the 1550s the argument likewise arose in the 'reformed' Protestantism coming from Zürich and Geneva, that the precise formulae used in Catholic worship aligned Catholicism with vulgar sorcery. As Heinrich Bullinger argued in his famous sermon-cycle, the *Decades*, widely translated in the sixteenth century:

These imaginations do rather seem more to maintain superstition than religion; as though the words, pronounced according to the form conceived, had power to call down out of heaven, to bring from one place to another, to restore health, to draw to, to put from, or to transform or change. . . . Words of themselves were instituted of God to this end, to signify; and by signifying to bear witness, and to admonish: neither have they beside any hidden force to change the natures of things, or to cause the things themselves to be corporally present; neither do we read that holy men ever used them after this manner: therefore they sin and deceive men, which otherwise use them than they were instituted.[42]

The firebrand Scottish preacher John Knox asked rhetorically when attacking the Catholic doctrine of the Eucharist, 'O Papists! is God a juglar? Useth he certane nomber of wordis in performing his intent?'[43] In the preface to the baptism rite in the 1556 Genevan Service order, the reader was warned 'that the sacraments are not ordeined of God to be used in privat corners *as charmes or sorceries*, but left to the congregation, and necessarely annexed to God's word'. In the rite itself the minister explicitly denied 'that we thinke any suche vertue or power to be included in the visible water or outward action'; the spiritual effects of baptism would follow 'in tyme convenient', not automatically or mechanically, or at once.[44] Stark antitheses were drawn by Knox, in his *Godly Letter to the Faithful in London* of 1554, between trusting in God and his word, as opposed to trusting human inventions: 'God may not abyd that our bodeis serve the devill in joyning our selves with ydolatrie.' 'Greatter iniquitie was never frome the beginning, than is containit in worshipping of an abominabill ydoll; for it is *the seill of the league whilk the Devill hes maid* with the pestilent sons of the Antichryst.' The mass, as a marginal note to this text said, was 'the devills sacrament and seale', like the 'tacit pact' of the sorcerer or witch.[45]

The German reformed cleric, Antonius Praetorius, already encountered as a sceptic on the topic of witchcraft, used the same rhetorical devices to fuse Catholic and popular preservative rituals against hostile sorcery. He denounced the 'great stupidity and heathenish blindness' in the commonly used apotropaic techniques: these included making an image in wax, over which monks or priests would say three masses on three Fridays; using the sign of the cross and sprinkling holy water; making 'cross-pennies' or preferably 'cross-ducats' with consecrated wax; hanging consecrated herbs in an animal's stall; or hanging salt and bread, or an amulet on which certain strange names and words of Holy Scripture had been written.[46] Such techniques were not only unscriptural; they were irrational. 'If Satan could be hindered in his work by crosses, herbs, salt, bread, and words, then he would be weaker and more fearful than a person, or indeed a dog or a pig; in fact he is strong and ferocious; therefore it is absurd to suppose that he would flee from these things'.[47]

Exorcism and the Passing of the Age of Miracles

One preservative ritual authorized in Catholic practice drew the Protestants' fire above all others. Catholics claimed that only in the true [i.e. Catholic] Church did the power to exorcize evil spirits remain effective. Exorcism repeatedly became a proving ground and a battleground for the rival spiritual claims of the two main confessional groups.[48] Benedikt Marti of Bern devoted a particularly intricate and learned article to the evolution and degeneration of the 'exorcist' in Christian history. In the New Testament the root verb ἐξορκίζω (exorkizō) meant simply to bind by oath. When Scripture spoke of Jesus driving out devils, it used the verb ἐκβάλλω (ekballō) meaning simply 'to cast out'. Jesus's ejecting of devils was never accompanied with verbal formulae, and those disciples who cast out demons in Jesus's name were not called exorcists. As long as the gift of miracles persisted in ordinary Christians, demons were expelled simply and without ritual, and the term 'exorcize' was gradually applied to this ministry. In the late antique Church 'exorcism' came to form part of the ritual administered in preparation for the baptism of adults. Only in the medieval and contemporary Church had the clergy begun to use elaborate technical formulae, extended quotations from dubiously appropriate texts of scripture, and lots of physical apparatus to try to drive demons from the possessed with ritual. The thirteenth-century liturgical writer Guillaume Durand had defended and explained medieval Catholic exorcism with reference to Josephus's story of Solomon having the gift of driving out demons with a root enclosed in a ring.[49] Marti responded that this proved only that Solomon had been tainted by paganism, and that Catholic exorcism was an invention of demons. False exorcisms began when Satan adjured Christ not to torment him;[50] paganism contributed the use of stones, herbs, amulets, and rituals; Judaism contributed the adjuration of spirits by the ineffable name of God. 'Papistic' exorcism used a mixture of pagan and Jewish elements: from the pagans it took ligatures, consecrated herbs, roots, waters, salts, relics; from the Jewish it took the holy names of God, the angels, patriarchs, Christ, the apostles, the martyrs. 'By these trifles, in truth, the devil deceived them; he pretends sometimes to be compelled, in order to confirm that superstition; meanwhile he openly insults them.'[51] The Lutheran Martin Chemnitz, in his *Examination of the Council of Trent*, applied an almost identical historical critique to exorcism, though more briefly.[52] Ludwig Lavater of Zurich devoted the third part of his treatise on ghosts to exhorting the faithful simply to pray if they were troubled with apparitions. He denounced the creeping superstition that had grown in the Church in the matter of exorcisms: the consecrated objects could have no power on demons, who at most would beat a tactical retreat if these were used. With a truly Swiss image, he compared the growth of superstitions to an avalanche in the Alps that brings down an even greater weight of snow with it.[53]

Protestants responded to the elaborate and sometimes psychologically impressive rituals of exorcism by mocking them as a form of magic. Heinrich Bullinger argued that 'everything that the Papists do with their conjuring of the possessed to depart' was 'ridiculous and absurd'. 'Why must one stand the possessed person naked in a bath of cold water, throttle him with the stole, sprinkle him with holy water, swipe him with sticks, cover him with the chasuble or mass-vestments, and use many other follies?'[54] Reginald Scot compared Catholic exorcists with conjurors of spirits: 'I see no difference, between these and popish conjurations; for they agree in order, words, and matter, differing in no circumstance, but that the Papists doe it without shame openly, the other doe it in hugger mugger secretly.'[55] On the same grounds Godelmann argued that papal exorcists ought to be classed with enchanters.[56]

Secondly, Protestant polemic insisted that the true exorcism, the supernatural power to cast out demons with a command, had been a miraculous gift in the early centuries of the Church, and that this gift had long since ceased. Possibly no claim about Protestant teaching has been more thoroughly challenged in recent years than the claim that Protestants argued that the age of miracles was past.[57] Certainly an abundance of evidence can be brought forward to show that ordinary people continued to look for extraordinary signs of divine intervention in the visible world.[58] Martin Luther, especially when writing in German, was often unclear about the distinction between true miracles and specious but essentially natural 'marvels', especially as the same German word *Wunder* could be used to refer to either.[59] Calvin, in a curious apologetic passage in the preface to the first edition of the *Institutes* of 1536, appeared to boast of 'miracles' among the Protestants; but the context in which he wrote this (often ignored) was a denial that miracles *per se* could or should authenticate the Catholics' claims to be the one true Church. Like Luther, Calvin remarked that Satan and magicians had their (illusory) miracles.[60] Only by stubbornly refusing to read what Protestant theologians wrote on the subject can one overlook this basic principle: developed mainstream Protestant theology insisted that true miracles were no longer to be expected in the Church. Theologians began by rejecting the claim of the Catholic Church to perform miracles at will, by institutional authority, through any of its ordained clergy. It was easy for Protestant writers to demonstrate the absurdity of imagining that spectacular spiritual gifts rested in the whole Catholic Church, as it were by hereditary right. However, they did not stop there: they argued that in the present historical location of the Church *no* true miracles were any longer to be expected. How that theological proposition would diffuse itself through society was of course another question.

As early as the reign of Edward VI, Bishop John Hooper, reforming pastoral bishop and future Protestant martyr, wrote in his *Brief and Clear Confession* of 1550 that the miracles of the primitive Church had so confirmed the Gospel that 'there is now no more need of new miracles'. However, believers ought to beware of 'the false miracles of Anti Christ . . . which miracles are wrought by the working of Satan, to confirm all kinds of idolatry, errors, abuses, and iniquities'.[61] Early in the reign of Elizabeth I, the English theologian James Calfhill argued in his *Aunswere to the Treatise of the Crosse* in 1565 that the gift of working miracles was ordained for the building up of the Church in its first years only. As he put it, one waters a tree when it is a sapling, but ceases to do so when its roots are well grown.[62] This attitude became absolutely typical of the stance adopted by theological authorities. John Calvin extended his critique of ritual healing in the Church to include extreme unction. 'That gift of healing, like the rest of the miracles, which the Lord willed to be brought forth for a time, has vanished away in order to make the new preaching of the Gospel marvellous forever . . . the Lord . . . heals their weaknesses [when] necessary . . . [but] he does not put forth these manifest powers, nor dispense miracles through the apostles' hands. For that was a temporary gift, and . . . quickly perished partly on account of men's ungratefulness.'[63] As Ludwig Lavater observed, 'the holy Apostles, and many godly men after them, were endued with this grace from God, that they could cast out unclean spirits: which gift continued a long season in the Church, to the great profit of the faithful, but afterwards it ceased as other miracles did also.'[64] Now that miracles were no longer to be expected, all that was left was a deceptive and demonic ritual. Exorcism, said William Perkins, was used by Christ and his followers when the gift was current; 'but in these daies ... that gift is ceased, and also the promise of power annexed to the use of adjuration: and therefore the meanes thereof must needs cease. And for an ordinary man now to command the Devill in such sort, is meere presumption, and a practise of sorcerie.'[65] As for miracles in general, since the rise of the papacy, there had long since been only 'delusions, and lying wonders, by the effectual working of Satan ... of which sort were and are all those miracles of the Romish Church, whereby simple people hath been notoriously deluded. These indeed have there continued from that time to this day. But this gift of the holy Ghost ... ceased long before.'[66]

Catholicism as paganism and as magic

Protestant polemic, in its developed form, deployed a number of arguments against Catholicism that were not new, but neither had they been articulated in such detail before. Erasmus and Luther had both pointed out, one in jest and the other in exasperation, that the cult of saints increasingly resembled the classical pantheon.[67] Heinrich Bullinger developed what was, for its time, a highly sophisticated historical-critical argument about the degeneration of Christianity before the Reformation in his two-part study, *On the Origin of Error*, which appeared in Zurich in 1539. The first half of this work was devoted to the rise of the cult of saints and their images. With a display of fairly impressive classical learning Bullinger hypothesized that the primitive monotheism of the pre-Christian ancients only gradually descended into polytheism, idolatry, and image-worship.[68] Among Christians, just as monasticism began heroically and then degenerated, so the veneration of saints began with a good intention and zeal: 'in the same manner first of all the superstitious cult of saints, then the error of idolatry was received into the Lord's Church.'[69] The cult of saints developed gradually with the patronage of some of the Fathers, and proliferated when Christianity was at peace in the Empire. Like some later Enlightenment authors, Bullinger speculated that the use of images of saints may have been intended to assist converts from paganism who could not do without their images and statues.[70] Towards the end of the book Bullinger insisted that 'the worship and superstition of idols among pagans is the same thing as the worship of saints and their images among Christians.'[71] He went on to argue, methodically and relentlessly, that the patronage of saints over aspects of life mapped precisely on to the care of the pagan gods for their devotees. Valesianus Theodulus was now asked to keep hail off the crops instead of Jupiter; Agatha looked after fire 'like a new Vesta'; geese were looked after by Gallus; sheep by Windelin, horses by Eulogius, cows by Pelagius, pigs by Antony. Catharine has succeeded Minerva; Gregory has succeeded Mercury; instead of Venus and Flora people turn to Aphra and Magdalena.[72] Even the images, temples and feasts of Christians resembled 'pagan superstitions'.[73] As Bullinger put it elsewhere in a passage in his *Decades*, 'the very saints themselves, triumphant now in heaven with Christ our King, shall be reputed for strange gods; the saints themselves, I say, not in respect of themselves, but to us they shall be strange gods in respect of us, which judge very fondly of them, and bestow on them the honour due to God, in worshipping and calling upon them, as we should worship and call upon our tutors and defenders.'[74] The assertion that saint-worship partook of superstition and paganism, and indeed of idolatry, became a Protestant trope. As John Hooper wrote in his *Exposition of the Ten Commandments* in 1547:

Such as trust in adversity to be holpen by any saint, and not only by God in Christ, make them strange gods, as they do that call upon the saint departed in the time of war; as in time past the Englishman upon Saint George, the Frenchman upon Saint Denys, the Scot upon Saint Andrew; which is nothing else but a very gentility, and ethnick custom; as though their private gods and singular patrons could give the victory and upper hand in the field, or Saint George favour him that Saint Andrew hateth.[75]

Protestant theologians not only linked Catholicism and superstitious magic conceptually: they also linked Catholicism and magic through guilt by association. Priests were actually and literally magicians. Benedikt Marti, followed by Johann Georg Godelmann, alleged that in the Catholic Church priests and clerics were not regarded as sufficiently learned unless they were magicians. Popes from Sylvester II through to Alexander VI and Paul III practised sorcery.[76] Johannes Weyer had made virtually the exact same accusations.[77] According to Hermann Wilken, a canon of Halberstadt named Johannes Saxonicus used sorcery to enable him to fly, and thus celebrated three masses on the same Christmas Eve, at Halberstadt, Mainz, and Cologne.[78] Godelmann wrote about a famous practitioner of the wound-salve, called 'the Monk of Chemnitz', who could heal injuries at a distance by anointing the sword which caused them.[79] The Danish theologian Niels Hemmingsen recalled how Catholic priests used a Psalter and a key to divine who had stolen lost goods.[80]

Catholicism and magic were assimilated to each other, in both directions. If clerics had practised magic, enchanters and sorcerers invariably used ecclesiastical rites and ceremonies. As John Bale said, the mass 'serveth all witches in their witchery, all sorcerers, charmers, enchanters, dreamers, soothsayers, necromancers, conjurers, cross-diggers, devil-raisers, miracle-doers, dog-leeches, and bawds; for without a mass they cannot well work their feats.'[81] Of the sign of the cross, James Calfhill argued against the Catholic Martiall, 'possible it is that, in time past, men did some good by signing them with a cross: now it is not, according to your position, "medicinable against all conjuration, enchantment, sorcery and witchcraft"; *but rather daily used in all these*'.[82]

Protestant writers asserted that Catholicism and superstition arose together, and fell together. Of the old days, George Gyfford argued that 'when the light of Gods word was suppressed, as it was in the popery, then was a way made for him, to worke all his feates. Then did conjurors and witches, and enchanters abound. Then were all manner of charmes rife and common. Then were a thousand magicall inventions and toyes.'[83] After the Reformation, things were better: Pietro Martire Vermigli recalled how Plutarch reported that around the time Christ was born all the 'loquacious oracles' of the pagans fell silent. Vermigli added that 'even today we see it happen in those countries that embrace the Gospel, that not only idolatries, but also divinations and feigned miracles at once come to an end.'[84] Hermann Wilken claimed that since the Gospel had been preached, the black arts had declined in use, and were more widely regarded as sinful; he looked forward to these things disappearing entirely.[85] Of apparitions of spirits, Reginald Scot remarked that 'which sights and apparitions, as they have been common among the unfaithfull; so now, since the preaching of the Gospell they are most rare.'[86] More pessimistically, Niels Hemmingsen agreed that superstitions had declined at the time of the Reformation; but a little later, as people grew weary of the Gospel, so they resorted to their old superstitious ways.[87]

14

The Reformed Doctrine
of Providence
and the Transformation
of the Devil

Ultimately, the theological problem of superstition resolved itself into the theological problem of evil. Superstitious beliefs and practices were used because they were believed to help predict and ward off the bad things that happened. Christian intellectuals' responses to superstition would, therefore, vary depending on their view of the nature and causes of evil. In turn, the problem of evil depended on one's view of God's providence: on the nature of God's 'permission' for evil things to happen. As was shown earlier, medieval theologians took widely varying positions on this issue.[1] Some Thomist theologians came close to allowing demonic forces free play in the sublunary world; some nominalists were such extreme providentialists that they made even sins and misfortunes depend, in some sense, on the will of God. It was to be of the greatest importance for the history of Protestant theories of evil and causation that, as the sixteenth century progressed, reformed thought took an ever clearer and more distinct view on this issue.

Protestants and Providence

Philipp Melanchthon was the first Protestant writer to speculate at length on questions of providence. He wrote a certain amount about providence in his textbook on physics, where he interpreted the relationship between God and the world philosophically. He declared that he wished to steer between the theoretical extremes of the Epicureans, who regarded the universe as the product of random and chance events and removed divine agency altogether, and the Stoics, 'who bind God with secondary causes, and pretend that neither natural agents, nor wills can do other than as they [in fact] do, and thus are called to do both by the first cause. Good instruction in physics is most useful for refuting the insanities of both sects.'[2] Given this desire to steer between extremes, Melanchthon's doctrine of providence was of a fairly soft variety. God cared for humanity by ensuring the stability and appropriateness of the seasons, by warning people of dangers to come through signs and prodigies, and by ensuring that, on the whole and in most if not all cases, the grossest criminals were punished and that good deeds were rewarded. He drew most of the arguments and evidence that he used in this text from classical antiquity: he quoted Xenophon that God was 'a lover of life', φιλοζῷον (philozoön). In Stoic thought Melanchthon objected chiefly to the fact that it (as he claimed) derived all events from an irresistible sequence of secondary causation: even God was thus not free to act with sovereign autonomy. There was, he argued, no point in intercessory prayer to a Stoic divinity.[3] A plausible and ingenious argument suggests that Melanchthon may have adjusted his teaching on providence as his career progressed to take account of his debates with the Zwinglians in Zurich (whom he regarded as the Stoic determinists of his own age). According to this view Melanchthon deduced divine providence *a posteriori* from God's benevolent interventions in daily life, rather than a priori from God's absolute sovereignty as Zwingli did.[4] Melanchthon certainly disliked Zwingli's theology very deeply, though whether he reshaped his own ideas to rebut Zwinglian Eucharistic teachings, at a time when Melanchthon was certainly not ultra-Lutheran on that subject himself, remains doubtful.

In any event, John Calvin would shortly afterwards set out a radical and highly articulated doctrine of providence in his treatises, *Of Predestination and Providence*, published in French in 1552.[5] Calvin argued that 'providence' did not refer to a deity sitting remote in heaven and unconcerned with events on earth, but to a God who was both intensely aware of all that happened and also intimately and constantly involved in regulating the affairs of the world. God not only cared for the cosmos by a general providence, but also looked after each living creature with a special care, but especially over human beings. More especially still, God took care and looked after the members of the Church: 'the Church is the great workroom of God, wherein, in a more especial manner, He displays His wonderful works; and it is the more immediate theatre of His glorious Providence.' Proper consideration of providence, Calvin argued, should keep people from presumptuous confidence in themselves, but lead them to rest secure on God's care, and to commit the outcome of all they did to God. Anyone who looked back on past events ought to reflect that good outcomes were the achievement of God; bad ones happened 'according to the good pleasure of God'.[6]

God's providence could operate within the normal 'means', that is, in accordance with the settled order of nature; but it could also operate entirely outside those means or even contrary to them, if God so willed. At this point Calvin had to address the crux—and the issue over which he had already been heavily criticized by opponents—of God's responsibility for evil. He reasoned 'that the will of God is the great cause of all things that are done in the whole world; and yet, that God is not the author of the evils that are done therein . . . those things which are vainly or unrighteously done by man are, rightly and righteously, the works of God!' Calvin rebutted the suggestion that this revived Stoic determinism. Somewhat ingeniously, Calvin explained the distinction between different types of necessity. Jesus had human bones that were prone to breaking just like ours; however, it was foretold in scripture that they would not be broken. The decree of God specified that his bones could not be broken; but as to their contingent nature, they were breakable.[7]

This interpretation of events led Calvin to take issue, once again, with his antagonist, the Netherlander Catholic theologian Albert Pighius. Pighius, Calvin argued, 'would make of God nothing more than a kind of wise manager, or a skilful general'. Pighius had (allegedly) claimed that when a man was deliberately killed by another, the will and decree of God was not involved. Calvin insisted the contrary: citing several Old Testament passages, he added 'it is a fact, universally admitted by common sense, that whatsoever men undertake, the issue thereof is in the hand of God.' Sinful and ignorant human beings, however much they strove for their ends, could not help but accomplish the will of God without knowing or wishing it, as Joseph's brothers did when they sold Joseph into slavery in Egypt. Satan himself could be used by God to a good effect, as with the 'thorn in the flesh' that Paul called a 'messenger of Satan' sent to subdue his pride.[8]

Calvin entered, as he habitually did, into the heart of the most difficult of theological questions. Did God deliberately *intend*, or merely *permit*, the evil acts of human beings? Calvin was uncompromising: God 'hardened Pharaoh's heart' actively and deliberately. However, God did not pervert the minds of those who would not otherwise have sinned: rather people whose will was already perverse willed evil intentions of their own desires, but 'by the ordaining purpose of God'. To encapsulate the paradox, those who spontaneously willed to do evil would, despite themselves, accomplish the divine plan. Therefore evil could not be said to occur merely by God's *permission*: rather, it occurred by God's ordaining plan even though sin, as such, was displeasing to God. The following passage perhaps best summarizes the logic of Calvin's position:

Now Saul acted, indeed, from his own wickedness. He exercised the malice concealed within by a voluntary action. Nevertheless, it was Satan that urged him on; and that, not while God was a mere inactive observer, but while God willed it. Indeed, the evil spirit could not, with propriety, have been said to be 'from the Lord', unless he had been the Lord's ordained minister, to execute His vengeance and to be, as it were, His executioner. Nor is Satan merely the minister of God's wrath by his instigating men's minds to evil passions and acts, but by effectually dragging them and leading them captive, at his will, into wicked actions.[9]

Calvin went on to demonstrate at some length that Augustine agreed with him on this question. Calvin then explicitly turned against the scholastic theology that gave God absolute power apart from divine justice: God could not in principle be less than just, though that justice might be hidden. It is not difficult to see why hostile critics accused Calvin of making God the author of sin. However, Calvin rejected the accusation. The God who sometimes used the forces of evil for the divine purposes was like a general who employed mercenaries to defend a people against an unjust invader. 'When the wickedness of men proceeds thus from the Lord, and from a just cause, but from a cause unknown to us, although the first cause of all things be his will, that he is therefore the author of sin I most solemnly deny.'[10] God's will was complex; towards the end of the treatise Calvin, paraphrasing Augustine, came close to the language of the 'hidden God' found in Martin Luther. The revealed will of God decreed that people should act rightly: the invisible and incomprehensible but just plan of God might require that they do the opposite in particular circumstances.[11]

For our purposes, what mattered most was that Calvin struck away the conventional prop of medieval demonology, the notion of 'divine permission' as the space within which demonic forces could do harm. For Calvin, behind every action of Satan lay the controlling hand of an ultimately benign but also all-sovereign God. No doubt Satan was the 'executioner of God', as malicious and dangerous as ever medieval demonology depicted him to be. However, since the afflictions of demons proceeded from the judgement and hidden purpose of God, since they were not just 'permitted' but actually ordained, it was no longer appropriate to seek for extraordinary, miraculous, spiritual, or ritual means to resist them. The only appropriate recourse of the faithful believer was to pray to God, in conscious awareness that God might have decreed that the misfortune should not be removed in this life.

Where Calvin led, the reformed tradition largely followed, even in theological environments where Calvin's authority was by no means definitive.[12] Benedikt Marti's article 'Providence', while starting from a similar philosophical standpoint to that of Melanchthon, contrasted the reformed theological position from that of Epicureans and Peripatetics, and indeed from earlier theologians. 'We . . . declare that the providence of God is such that nothing is removed from its governance: and one can if one wishes call this an individual, special, particular providence . . . Nothing is so minute, nothing so humble, nothing so infinitely numerous or so base in condition, that it is not by clear reasons subject to the providence of God.'[13] The apparent 'contingency' or accidental quality of events was merely a matter of human perspective. It was insufficient, Marti argued, to view providence as merely foreknowledge: it represented not just divine knowledge but divine 'administration'. Marti then divided providence into three types: the general government of the cosmos; the specific decrees by which, for example, God saved the elect; and the 'permission', the συγχώρησις (synchorēsis), by which God releases Satan or afflicts the godly. Though using the term 'permission', Marti really meant the same thing as Calvin: God 'may permit something to the evil [spirits], but nevertheless he does not remove his guiding hand nor absent himself when he is really most definitely present.' Marti concluded 'that everything is administered by the providence of God; and that God takes note of human affairs, not only in a general or universal sense, but also in individual things down to the most minimal.'[14] Heinrich Bullinger, another theologian certainly not beholden to Calvin, affirmed the same radical belief in God's meticulous oversight over creation when discussing the causes of harmful sorcery in his *Against the Black Arts*: 'God is the Lord, holds power over everything visible and invisible, and governs everything in accordance with his providence; the devil only has power over the soul, reputation, body, and goods of a person in so far as God gives permission.'[15]

The devil transformed

With the devil downgraded, as it were, to a helpless tool in the hands of the Almighty, not only were the ritual preservatives against demonic assault irrelevant: demonic assault itself began to change its character. Luther had already argued that the primary means that the devil could hurt people was by sowing wrong ideas. Luther could argue in this way without in any sense diminishing his belief in the reality of personal evil.[16] Over time, however, the devil tended gradually and imperceptibly to slide into the area of metaphor and symbol. Some representatives of the 'radical Reformation' were the boldest in taking this step, metaphorizing nearly the entire spiritual realm out of existence.[17] However, one of the earliest examples of this mode of thinking came from a close friend and ally of Calvin. Pierre Viret's *Le Monde demoniacle* of 1561 developed this use of the devil as a metaphor almost to an extreme. Black devils were open persecutors of the faith; white ones were papists who carried out some marginal token reformation. 'White devils' were also those who patronized reformation but then deprived it of its vigour by thwarting the establishment of strong, independent Church discipline. In this work Viret actually delivered a coded harangue about the disciplinary debate within the reformed churches of France, disguised as demonology.[18]

An almost comical aspect of the same phenomenon is afforded by the set of mid-sixteenth-century German *Teufelbücher*, which appeared in a collected folio volume in 1569.[19] The assembly of these obviously related works, mostly by quite minor Lutheran writers, was organized by Cyriakus Spangenberg (1528–1604), who contributed parts of several of them. Sure enough, one of them, Ludwig Milich's *Zauber Teufel* of 1563, addressed popular magic, charms, and sorcery in fairly conventional terms. But the collection also included works entitled *The House-Devil*, Joachim West-phal's *The Arrogance-Devil*, Andreas Musculus's *The Trouser-Devil* (all of c. 1565), *The Dance-Devil* of 1567, and indeed the curse-, booze-, game- or hunting-devils. Spangenberg and his collaborators presumably did not mean that their ten sorts of bad wives were literally representatives of the demons on earth. They here adapted the pre-existing genre of the *Teufelbuch* to put across a wholly conventional message on the proper social conduct expected of good Lutherans within the sublunary universe. The demonic had become a metaphor, and a very transparent one at that.[20]

More seriously, Reginald Scot began to address the metaphorical meaning of the word 'spirit' in the Bible itself. In his *Discourse of Divells*, he pointed out that 'spirit' might be used in scripture to refer to bodily infirmities or mental disorders; and that it could also be used in a good sense, as meaning the gifts or the presence of God in a person. It could even describe a psychological state: 'Where it is written, that God sent an evil spirit between *Abimelech*, and the men of *Sichem*, we are to understand, that he sent the spirit of hatred, and not a bulbegger.'[21] In his remorselessly sarcastic attacks Scot chiefly targeted the folkloric English belief in 'familiar spirits' that took permanent bodily form, as explained earlier.[22] As a practised reader of Calvin, Scot readily remarked that 'evermore spirits are spoken of in scripture, as of things spirituall, though for the help of our capacities they are there sometime more grossely and corporally expressed, *either in parables or by metaphors*, than indeed they are.'[23] The language of spirits was the language of divine 'accommodation' to human capacities.[24] Of the Old Testament story of the 'lying spirit' sent to persuade the kings of Israel and Judah to go to military disaster at Ramoth-Gilead, Scot remarked 'this story is here set forth in this wise, to bear with our capacities, and specially with the capacity of that age, that could not otherwise conceive of spirituall things, than by such corporall demonstrations.'[25] Scot used the same hermeneutic in the far more crucial narrative of the fall of humanity in Eden. He suggested that the language of Satan entering into the body of the serpent, which earlier writers had used as a proof-text to demonstrate that demons could possess corporeal creatures, was also figurative. He added (forestalling modern historians' suspicions no less than those of contemporaries): 'although I abhorre that lewd interpretation of the Family of Love . . . as would reduce the whole Bible into allegories: yet (me thinks) the creeping there is rather metaphorically or significately spoken, than literally.'[26]

So long as most Protestant thinkers remained governed by post-Aristotelian scholastic metaphysics, it was to be expected that the language of 'spirits' would continue to be couched in familiar terms, based ultimately on Aquinas and his contemporaries. In the seventeenth century a few bold thinkers would embrace a quite different metaphysic.[27] This alternative way of thinking would challenge the actual existence of spiritual creatures, and therefore the whole cosmic idea of spiritual harm and superstitious remedies against it. That belongs to a later chapter.

15

Reformed Catholicism: Purifying Sources, Defending Traditions

T he Catholic Church did not remain passive while the theologians of the Protestant Reformation accused it of demonic superstitions. An elaborately argued and vigorously written polemical literature emerged to rebut the claims of the Protestants and tried to stabilize the 'official' position of the Church on these matters. However, the post-Reformation Catholic perspective on the theology of superstition was necessarily a very complex one. It used to be accepted wisdom that the Roman Catholic Church after the Council of Trent embarked on a campaign to suppress the traditional, popular abuses of the official cult, and to bring popular religion more strictly under the control of the seminary-educated priesthood. Jean Delumeau described how the midsummer bonfires for St John Baptist's day, around which all sorts of superstitious beliefs had accrued, were domesticated. The clergy presided over the fires, prevented people from taking brands from the fire to use as talismans, ensured that the fire was thoroughly burned to ashes, and then saw to the ashes being raked into the earth.[1] This story has become a sort of emblem of the Counter-Reformation at village level. Yet the story of the Catholic response to popular belief may be a great deal more complex than the stereotype of intellectual domination of popular belief suggests.

Catholic theology had in fact to achieve three separate things in its systematic and pastoral responses to superstition after c.1560, in order to be true to its image of itself and of the Church's mission. First of all, Catholic thought had to preserve and continue those aspects of late medieval thought that were still held to be valid. No amount of 'Catholic reform' could be allowed to overwhelm the Church's belief in its own continuous witness to apostolic truth. Secondly, Catholic theologians sought to purge their tradition of the accumulations and accretions of supposititious and apocryphal elements that had established themselves, not only in the popular mind but also among many leading members of the clergy. In one sense they here aspired merely to continue the work of the later medieval pastoral writers and the confessional theorists and canonists before them. However, the atmosphere had changed. The Church was committed to catechizing and correcting its people. Clarity now became more important, for clergy and laity alike. Yet in practice, one finds that Catholic theologians not infrequently disagreed and contradicted each other on this subject.

Despite the considerable amount of work done in the Council of Trent, there was still nothing like unanimity over where devotion and piety ended and superstition and 'vain observances' began. The Council had given very little lead on this subject. It condemned the abuse of scripture where it was 'turned and twisted to scurrilous use, to wild and empty fancies, to flattery, detractions, superstitions, godless and devilish magical formulae, fortune telling, lotteries, and also slanderous pamhplets'.[2] Another decree ordered that the ordinaries must prohibit and remove from the mass 'anything that has been brought in, either by greed which is the service of idols, or by irreverence which can hardly be distinguished from impiety, or by superstition which is the counterfeit mimic of true devotion'.[3] Still on the mass, the council decreed that ordinaries should 'banish from the Church any idea of a particular number of masses and candles which derives more from the cult of superstition than from true religion', thus apparently dealing a blow to the trental and other similar devotions.[4] In general, the council called for 'superstition' to be eschewed in such matters as prayers for the dead, the cult of images, or the issuing of indulgences, but hardly specified where the lines were to be drawn.[5] The conciliar decrees established pious principles rather than laying down usable guidelines for purging and cleansing local practice.[6]

Thirdly, Catholic polemical theologians fervently and at times furiously defended many traditional aspects of the old cult that the Protestants had attacked. It was unthinkable to leave unanswered the Protestant critique of consecrations, with its implication that all Catholic worship derived from demonic perversions of true Christianity. Social historians might have interpreted the work of Catholics and Protestants as running along parallel tracks, but in the eyes of contemporaries these systems of belief were very different. The Catholic polemical programme aspired to dig deep and broad trenches to separate orthodox piety on the one hand from superstitious abuses on the other, over a terrain where the boundaries were neither clearly marked nor widely agreed.[7] In the medieval past, not only had there been no clear distinction at parish level between those things; even among the learned, significant disagreements forced clergy to be careful how they preached against ordinary people's customs and beliefs.[8]

Consequently the Catholic literature presents problems of interpretation and exposition: it is traditional and yet innovative, authoritarian yet also controversialist and partisan. The situation becomes slightly more complicated still if one includes in consideration some of the treatises on magic and witchcraft written by laymen. Neither Nicolas Remi nor Jean Bodin was a trained theologian, yet both wrote works on demonology that were widely read and debated, not least by Protestants.[9] Coherent demonological theory mattered much less for these authors than demolishing the sceptics and reporting the most sensational stories of demonic activity. They tended to amplify the physical causes of sorcery and minimize the power of the Church against it. Since such 'witchmongers' (as Reginald Scot called them) do not fit comfortably within what is essentially a discussion of historical theology, they will not receive extensive treatment within the present survey.[10] On the other hand, certain Catholic authors from the theological academy will figure prominently in what follows: the Ingolstadt academic theologian Albrecht Hunger (1545–1604); the Jesuit demonologist, biblical exegete, and historian Martín Delrio (1551–1608); the early seventeenth-century bishop of Hebron and suffragan bishop of Bamberg, Friedrich Förner (c.1570–1630); the Observant Franciscan Girolamo Menghi of Viadana (1529–1609), one of the most prominent writers on exorcism; and the Portuguese Inquisitor Manuel do Vale de Moura (c.1564–1650).[11] Use will also be made of the work entitled *Flagellum Diaboli, oder Dess Teufels Gaisl*, attributed to the Spanish mystic Francisco de Osuna (d. 1540/1) but published only in German in 1602 in a translation by Egidius Albertinus, Secretary to the Bavarian *Hofrat*.[12] Given that the work draws largely on the early sixteenth-century German nominalist theologian Martin Plantsch, and that where it departs from Plantsch it displays a very German-centred focus on rebutting Lutheran heresy, there are reasons to treat this writing, at least in its surviving form, as a German work of the early 1600s rather than anything earlier.[13]

Continuity with the medieval superstition-critique

Nothing had happened in the course of the Reformation to make the Thomist-Aristotelian analysis of demons and magic obsolete: so not surprisingly, a great deal of what was written on the subject in late sixteenth-century Catholicism remained quite familiar from earlier decades and centuries. Albrecht Hunger, in the set of theses on magic that he prepared for a student disputation in 1574, accounted for the existence and properties of demons in conventional scholastic terms. He ran through the existence of demons (theses 11–17), the evil origin of magic (theses 18–32), the natural powers of demons and their limitations (theses 33–63), divination (theses 66–74), and sorcery (theses 75–8).[14] Similarly conventional demonological theories were incorporated in Girolamo Menghi's *Compendio dell'arte essorcistica*, in the first two books of Martín Delrio's *Magical Disquisitions*, and at the beginning of the second part of Manuel do Vale de Moura's treatise on incantations.[15] Delrio's treatment represented both the most thorough and the most rationalistic of these critiques: he argued against the supposed power of bodies to influence each other remotely and rejected the powers claimed for special forms of words. He attacked Felix Hemmerli's views on helpful charms with particular venom.[16] Several of these writers, as they argued that demons did not and could not know the future, took the occasion to attack judicial astrology. The Jesuit Benito Pereira wrote at length against divination by dreams and by the stars in his *Against the Deceptive and Superstitious Arts* of 1591.[17] The *Flagellum Diaboli* expounded in detail how demons could not possibly know the future; the author then rather spoilt the point by elucidating all the allegedly bad signs in Martin Luther's horoscope, as though these were conclusive signs of trouble.[18]

A number of entirely traditional pastoral themes reappeared with extensive and detailed treatment in the post-Tridentine Catholic treatises. Martín Delrio dedicated the second part of his third book to 'vain observances'.[19] To call something a 'vain observance' constituted the mildest form of reproach that a medieval theologian could inflict on a supposedly helpful practice that failed the test of rationality or authoritative tradition.[20] For that very reason the label was a dangerous one to use, since it was most likely to attach itself to something that others thought was innocuous or even orthodox. Such observances might be either mortal or only venial sins, depending on the intention and knowledge of the person using them. Typically they were done to acquire goods or benefits of some kind, either physical benefits such as the well-being of crops or livestock, or bodily health for oneself, or they were performed for the sake of intellectual or spiritual benefits, knowledge, or even remission of sins.[21] A vain observance could be diagnosed when the rite either clearly failed to conform to scripture or tradition, or added superfluous details and circumstances that had no spiritual or moral purpose.[22] Unlike some of his medieval predecessors, Delrio then expended a great deal of space on examples of superstitious vain observances. Many of these related to customary circumstances for fasts, the wearing of amulets, the observance of omens, and the use of the ecclesiastical calendar for a variety of irrational purposes. Of all the critics of the 'Egyptian Days', Delrio was possibly the first ecclesiastical writer actually to publish which twenty-four days of the year these actually were.[23] He also suggested a highly intricate etymology, derived from the Hebrew, for the omnipresent medieval charm-word *Ananisapta*.[24] In possibly his most intriguing piece of didactic ethnography, Delrio gave truncated versions of a large arsenal of verbal charms, designed to cure illnesses, identify the thieves of lost goods, or to cure those supposedly afflicted with sorcery.[25] The list had nothing particularly surprising except for its source. Beyond any doubt Delrio copied these formulae from Johann Weyer's *De Praestigiis*, despite the disapproval that he elsewhere expressed for 'the heretic Wierus' and all that he stood for.[26]

One pastoral priority apparently remained urgent. Ordinary people still had to be dissuaded from using superstitious remedies against bodily misfortunes and threats to their well-being. Albrecht Hunger imagined the sort of protest that confronted theological critics of curative techniques:

Look, they exclaim, this man is sick to the great distress of himself and all his family, or even of some entire people; he is despaired of by the physicians; why may he not be cured by superstitious means, especially if it is supposed that the key to his health lies in the superstitious methods? Is it not lawful to resist vain things with other vain things, as with a key? Surely health and help may be sought from any source, from words as much as from herbs, from the power of spirits as much as from the power of corporeal things?[27]

Such an objection, however, was 'clearly unworthy of a Christian person . . . evil things are not to be done in order that good things may come of them; therefore sorcery may not be repelled with sorcery.'[28]

Girolamo Menghi's *Compendio* largely followed Silvestro Mazzolini's arguments (sometimes to the extent of plagiarism) in arguing that 'one may not repel one vain and superstitious thing with another.'[29] Both Menghi and Delrio picked up the medieval dispute between Dominican and Franciscan writers, especially around the relatively lax position on counter-magic attributed to Peter Aureoli. Both these writers came down on the rigorist side of the dispute and condemned what they saw as Aureoli's dangerously lenient stance.[30] Delrio also attacked an even more obvious target, the prescriptions of Theophrastus Paracelsus for curing illness caused by sorcery. Here again the Jesuit borrowed extensively from a Protestant author, this time the Lutheran Johann Georg Godelmann, whose work on sorcery had appeared some years earlier.[31] Friedrich Förner echoed Delrio's warnings against superstitious preservatives, and even claimed the mantle of Paul at Athens: 'Men of Bamberg, in everything I see that you are exceedingly superstitious: I gather this from you not only today, on the day you call St Walburga's day, when you practise innumerable superstitions, but that the whole year round you do and observe similar things, which lead people away from the worship of God and hope in his mercy.'[32]

Catholic writers of the later sixteenth century generally did not delve into the more subtle disputes about the precise way in which divine power worked in sacraments and sacramentals and other holy things.[33] Friedrich Förner suggested that the mere utterance of the names of Jesus or the Virgin Mary had remarkable preservative powers.[34] Förner and Delrio both proposed frequent use of the sign of the cross as a preservative technique, citing a range of authorities ancient, medieval, and modern.[35] In these texts one still breathes the same air as Johannes Nider in the early fifteenth century. In their world the correct performance of a sacred gesture or rite could turn away misfortune; the mistaken or wrongheaded omission of approved rites or use of forbidden ones could bring calamity. Such writers did not actually claim that divine power was delegated down into sacred objects and gestures; but they did not deny it either, and the drift of their rhetoric rather suggested it. Their world was not providentialist in so far as it mattered very much, for one's temporal and eternal well-being, to use ritual correctly.

The purging of Catholic traditions

It is extremely difficult at times to draw any sort of boundary between the continuation of the medieval superstition-critique and the purging or cleansing of the sources of tradition more commonly associated with the Counter-Reformation. As some recent authors have observed, it is often hard to distinguish between pre- and post-Tridentine objectives in many issues of pastoral theology: the Reformation divide does not always mark a paradigm shift.[36] In this subject, more than almost anywhere else, continuity and 'reform' merge into one another, since many of the aims of the Catholic reformers can be identified in an earlier form among late medieval rationalists like Gerson or Plantsch. Both Girolamo Menghi and Martín Delrio urged extreme caution in the matter of amulets, but the prescriptions that they offered to make a 'safe' amulet resembled those of the medieval Thomists very closely.[37] When Delrio criticized the practice of submerging the images of saints in rivers to bring good growing rains for the coming year, 'for instance of St Martin or St Urban and others in Germany, and in Aquitania', he was only echoing the criticism made by Martín of Arles early in the sixteenth century.[38] Neither can one detect any greater intellectual thoroughness, legal precision, or administrative control about this process. Individual writers passed verdicts on popular beliefs and practices, with appeals to ancient and medieval authorities, very much as before.

However, in some respects the 'purging' of popular customs started to strike home at some 'folklorized' elements of popular Catholicism. Martín Delrio swept aside all the traditional arguments about the evil eye except the explanation that it was caused by demonic pact: this was in effect to condemn all curative methods other than appeal to the protection of the Church.[39] Delrio also took a particularly stern line over the practitioners of charismatic healing known in Spanish as *saludadores*.[40] These people had never been entirely orthodox in the eyes of the Church, but received widespread credence in local culture. A well-travelled writer, Delrio remarked that such people were known as the 'Gentiles S. Catharinae' or of St Paul in Italy; or the 'children of the Saturday of *Parasceve*' among the Belgians. Delrio opined that the *saludadores* could not be absolutely and indiscriminately condemned, nor entirely approved of either. There was much that was suspect about how they worked; for example, their claim that they needed to drink a lot of wine for their cures to be successful, or that they could not function in the presence of another more powerful healer. Delrio thought that other Catholic theologians who had written on the subject were too generous towards them.[41] He showed particular stringency on the subject of a technique for curing wounds allegedly used by healers active among the Spanish soldiers in the Low Countries during the Dutch Wars. These healers used a long formula in Spanish which involved repeating most of the words of the institution of the Eucharist, including the consecration, words supposedly too holy to be known or heard by laypeople. It concluded with the prayer that 'by these most holy words, and by their power, and by the merit of your most holy passion, this wound (and this evil) may be healed'.[42] The practice was investigated just before Delrio published his treatise, and debated in the presence of the bishop of Ypres, Pierre Simons (1584–1605), and his advisers. The resulting condemnation seemed unduly harsh to many, as Delrio remarked; but they were mistaken. It was wrong to expect miraculous cures regularly from God; the strict verbal formula should be unnecessary; unauthorized formulae were suspect of demonic pact; finally, the formula misused the words of the mass, words above all held in reverence in the Church, spoken only in the mass itself or in academic disputation. Delrio's detailed reporting of the terms of the condemnation suggests strongly that he was himself instrumental in bringing it about.[43]

Manuel do Vale de Moura took a much more aggressive approach to spurious traditions in his exhaustive exploration of the subject of healing charms and incantations. The ruling principle of his treatise dictated that all *ensalmas* that claimed to achieve an effect by the mere fact of being uttered or expressed—'constitutive' *ensalmas*—were illicit; only in certain circumstances might 'invocative' *ensalmas*, that contained a prayer to God, be permitted.[44] This rigid rationalistic principle led Moura to investigate a range of thinkers from both inside and beyond the theological academy and to criticize their views. Like others he attacked Hemmerli and Paracelsus at some length.[45] Unlike others, he broadened his critique to the otherwise respectable medical writer Juan Bravo, who had claimed that curative spells might operate through some natural but occult property inhering in the words themselves.[46] Moura began by enumerating and summarizing at great length the arguments made in favour of the mechanical effectiveness of *ensalmas*, apparently to forestall objections. He listed, especially in the first part of his treatise, a great many Catholic customs and beliefs that appeared to betray a belief in the 'constitutive' power of a healing or protective charm.[47] He cited the claims made for the *Bulla Sabbathina*, by which it was believed that the Carmelites who observed particular devotions to the Virgin would be released from purgatory by a personal appearance of the Virgin on their behalf on the first Saturday after their death.[48] He related from Ortelius and Majoli the stories of 'St Patrick's Purgatory' in Ireland, an island in Lough Derg supposedly endowed with particular spiritual vices and virtues; there supposedly lived there a religious community of such virtue that no-one who died there was ever assigned more than one night in purgatory.[49] Discussions of these beliefs later in the book would dissect and dismantle the arguments and seek to establish Moura's own highly rationalistic and rigorous position. Whether this was Moura's intention or not, his exhaustive enumeration of conflicting authorities actually demonstrated two things: first, there was a great range of folkloric Catholic customs that, according to popular belief, had what he called 'constitutive' effects; second, there was a real muddle of opinions among theologians as to what to think about these customs. Both Moura and Delrio confronted a passage in Tommaso de Vio Cajetan's commentary on Aquinas's *Summa* that appeared to create space for customs with slightly suspicious conditions:

Many observances are done both with holy words and the requirement of certain conditions which in themselves seem vain, and for which no reason can be given by which they might be sufficiently excused.... Therefore they are not condemned, but rather are to be tolerated, because they are done out of the devotion of the faithful; it is possible, that God may have revealed them to some saint, and thus from things that otherwise would be indifferent and vain, they were made holy.[50]

Moura's text documented the very confused and conflicted response of later sixteenth-century Catholic theologians to a wide range of popular customs that supposedly had specific apotropaic effects. He challenged Nicolaus Serarius and Francisco Valles over the power allegedly infused into the liver of the fish that was burned to drive away a demon in the book of Tobit.[51] He quoted with partial disapproval a letter on the subject of charismatic cures written by the Jesuit Pablo Ferrer, chancellor of Évora and Moura's former teacher, in 1606.[52] Many other theologians, basing themselves on Aquinas's carefully phrased permission to wear texts as amulets, had in Moura's view been too generous in the things that they allowed.[53] Pastoral authors who appeared at least to betray some degree of uncertainty included confessional writers such as Toletus and Azor.[54] Moura did not hesitate to dissect and challenge near-contemporary and highly respectable authors on spiritual guidance such as Gerónimo Llamas and Leonardus Lessius SJ. He argued that these authorities were not consistent, and that the reasons that they offered for admitting the power of charismatic curative practices did not bear examination.[55] Moura vehemently opposed any private form of words or ceremony which claimed to secure certain physical or spiritual benefits for the user or anyone else to whom it was applied. After analysing all the stories of special graces granted to saints' cults, certain prayers, or anything like, he finally concluded that any ritual, the mere performance of which was supposed to ensure benefits (for instance the certainty of not dying in mortal sin), was to be rejected.[56]

Defending Catholic rites against their critics

Manuel do Vale de Moura, as a Portuguese inquisitor little troubled by the events of the Reformation, could afford the luxury of taking a single-minded rationalistic approach to 'superstitious' cults. He was quite unusual, as his own work demonstrated. Much more typically, early modern Catholic writers faced both ways and struck out to their right and their left. They might still condemn vulgar superstitions, and certainly anything savouring of demonic involvement; but they also needed to defend the rites and practices of the Catholic Church against the demonizing assaults of Protestant polemic. The rebuttal of Protestant critiques did not occupy the greater part of Counter-Reformation superstition treatises; it did, however, evoke the most vigorous language and the most obviously original elaborations of the tradition. The typical sequence of propositions ran as follows:

1. Misfortunes can be caused by sorcery through the agency of demons;
2. Superstitious means to resist sorcery are dangerous and forbidden;
3. Catholic methods to resist sorcery are entirely lawful and helpful;
4. Protestant attacks on these methods are heretical.

Catholic defenders of the Church's methods for repelling sorcery and demonic vexation needed to respond to the two very specific arguments devised in Protestant polemic: that the 'consecration' of holy objects as sacramentals to resist misfortune was an improper and illicit use of physical materials; and that the 'exorcism' of people and places to drive away the forces of evil was itself a form of demonic magic. To rebut the first argument, nearly all Catholics continued to cite as proof-text the passage in I Timothy 4: 4–5, 'for every creature of God is good and nothing is to be rejected that is received with thanksgiving; for it is sanctified by the Word of God and prayer', despite Protestant attempts to prove that this passage had nothing to do with the consecration of sacramentals.[57]

Albrecht Hunger of Ingolstadt, after a series of theses on magic that overlapped considerably with Johann Heerbrand's Lutheran theses of a few years earlier, concluded his propositions with a vigorous and polemical defence of Catholic preservatives against sorcery that rebutted Heerbrand item by item. Thesis 88 read:

Sorcery is also repelled without doubt by the merits and intercessions of the saints; it is repelled by the signing of the holy cross, by adjuration, exorcisms, prayers, and by the most holy blessings of the Church, which is the column and foundation of the truth (although the heretics may deride this) if we use, in complete faith and entire devotion of the mind, these and the other things called sacramentals of the Church, as for instance sprinkling with holy water, and bravely resist the wickedness of demons.[58]

It was 'not at all vain' to think that God might respond positively to the words of the Church's exorcisms. Sacramentals were not infallibly powerful; but neither were they magical as the 'innovators of our time' claimed. Hunger then mocked the criticisms Heerbrand had levelled at the consecration of the Eucharist, and responded to his jibes at the Agnus Dei amulet and the poem associated with it (already mocked by Weyer). Hunger's rebuttals had a somewhat scholastic, pedantic quality: he tried to pick holes in the Protestant criticisms by identifying technical errors in their descriptions of Catholic rites and customs. As a concluding stroke he likened the Protestants' resistance to 'Catholic truth' to the resistance offered Moses by the Egyptian sorcerers Jannes and Mambres.[59] Protestants were like stubborn magicians.

Martín Delrio personified the ambivalences of the Catholic intellectual response to Protestant criticisms of 'superstitious' consecrations. With an even but occasionally confusing hand he both criticized and defended Catholic customs, sometimes within the same passage. When discussing amulets, Delrio remarked that not only 'the heretic Wier' but also Nicolas Remi condemned the use of amulets on the basis of patristic texts that they misapplied or misunderstood. Amulets were perfectly licit, but only provided that they avoided any of the danger signs suggesting unknown names, mysterious symbols, or precise conditions for the materials used, all of which suggested demonic involvement. He warned against the superstition of collecting the spurious names of angels, as found in the text called 'Arbatel' ("ארבעהאל").[60] He pointed out that the passage from the *Opus Imperfectum in Matthaeum*, a text which Protestant authors loved to cite against amulets, was not by St John Chrysostom as previously supposed, and did not condemn all wearing of holy things around the neck, as was claimed.[61] On sacramentals and their use in exorcisms Delrio was even more carefully balanced: he wrote that 'I do not assent to the heretics who remove all supernatural power from exorcisms and all consecrated and blessed things . . . nor does the credulity or superstition of certain Catholics please me, who ascribe this power even to things which are not consecrated, as hypericum, rue, the horns and dung of goats, also to baths and beatings.'[62]

On balance, as the *Magical Disquisitions* unfolded the desire to defend the Church against the Protestants appeared to take over from other objectives in Delrio's writing. In the sixth book he back-pedalled against an earlier critique of popular practice by the fifteenth-century theologian Nicholas of Cusa. Cusanus had described as a 'superstitious practice' the use of consecrated things for a purpose other than their intended use, 'as for instance if holy water is drunk to cure illness, or sprinkled for fertility, or sometimes given to animals'. Delrio responded that to use holy water thus as though it had a natural property to that end, or to add superstitious rites to its use would be evil indeed. However, to use it as a *sacramentale*, to expect that God might work a miracle through the sacramental for the confirmation of faith, and to remove the assaults and deceits of demons, was pious and lawful for Catholics.[63] The same logic applied to quite a number of practices involving consecrated things so long as the intention was good. A physical substance might have power over demons when used as part of a Catholic ritual, because the supernatural cause, from God or a good angel, concurred in its working: thus exorcisms using physical apparatus could torment and drive out demons.[64] The third section of the second chapter of Delrio's sixth book enumerated, praised, documented, and advertised a whole array of 'supernatural, divine, or ecclesiastical remedies'.[65] These always helped the soul, and at worst never harmed the body. Faith, all the seven sacraments, the help of holy people (who might even work miracles), exorcism, works of penance, invocation of Christ and the saints, the sign of the cross, relics, and of course the sacramentals, amulets, and holy bells: all these were proven in specific instances to have been helpful in repelling physical illness, demonic possession, and other misfortunes.[66]

Positive advertising of the benefits of Catholic rituals against misfortune was accompanied by a fierce attack on Protestant critics, usually on the grounds of some technical error in their hostile descriptions. It was, Delrio claimed, a slander to accuse Catholics of 'baptizing' rather than blessing bells, as was alleged by Brenz, Calvin, and Weyer. Heretics who alleged this were attributing to the Church the mistaken ideas of the uneducated 'to give colour to their schism'.[67] At the very end of his monumental work Delrio gave an entire chapter to defend Catholic remedies against the attacks of Johann Georg Godelmann. Godelmann ignorantly accused Catholic exorcists of being like enchanters, on the evidence of other heretics such as Aretius (Marti), Chemnitz, Lavater, and Weyer. Regarding sacramentals, Delrio insisted that good Catholics did not attribute the curative power to the physical consecrated objects themselves but to God using these things as 'a moral instrument'. The benign effects of all ecclesiastical preservatives lay not in their physical nature but in their moral effects: they gave a sign to the demon, forcing it to remember the victory of Christ and to retreat. Delrio then rejected the claim that the early Fathers used only prayer, without the application of physical materials. Delrio's rebuttals acquired a somewhat spluttering, repetitive quality towards the end: like Hunger he accused Godelmann and the others of misunderstanding Catholic ritual. He objected to the claim that the works of 'Dionysius the Areopagite' were spurious and pseudonymous, insisting on their authenticity.[68] Delrio clearly found the *in hominem* argument more useful than a structured philosophical answer to the Protestants. By proving that they were ignorant of what they criticized, and outrageous heretics into the bargain, he could at least strengthen wavering Catholics. Reclaiming convinced Protestants was not on the agenda.

Delrio wrote a relatively educated and rationalistic defence of Catholic preservative practices. Not all other writers were so technically correct: often the argument depended more on the allegedly successful outcomes of the rites, rather than from a precise theological explanation of how they worked. The second part of the *Flagellum Diaboli*, published in German in 1602, contained a point-by-point advocacy of each of the Church's remedies against hostile sorcery.[69] Most of this text, in addition to the first part of the book, was paraphrased in translation from Martin Plantsch's *Short Work on Witches* of 1507.[70] However, the *Flagellum* departed from its source to apostrophize holy water and its benefits, and to excoriate those Protestants who claimed that 'all waters are equally blessed by God at the creation'. After a whole series of arguments from the symbolic significance of holy water, the text added: 'Who is there, who does not know that this our holy water will remain uncorrupt for a whole year and more, while ordinary water will not remain good for more than about a month? What can be the origin of that other than the blessing? . . . [Protestants] are like dogs which bark at everything they do not know or do not wish to know.'[71] The belief that holy water was physically less corruptible than ordinary water was not, in fact, a theological claim: it was a popular belief without theological sanction, yet widely diffused in later medieval culture.[72]

Bishop Friedrich Förner offered the most elaborate and extensive defence of the Church's remedies in his *Panoply of the Armour of God*. Sermons 14 to 35 of his cycle were devoted entirely to extolling the resources of the Church, largely in the same order and with some of the same arguments as those used by Delrio in book 6, chapter 2 of *Magical Disquisitions*. On one hand Förner was slightly more of a moralist: the afflicted were to fast, give alms, pray fervently, scourge themselves, and do penance after lapses.[73] On the other side, although Förner broadly followed Delrio's arrangement of the material and copied many of his sources, he indulged more freely in reporting ecclesiastical folklore. He related the story that the power of the sign of the cross was so great that the Emperor Julian the Apostate, after his reversion to paganism, still used the sign of the cross to drive away demons. This argument appeared to claim automatic or mechanical effects for Christian rites, if even a pagan could make them 'work'.[74] 'Holy water' he continued, 'is like a beam in the eye to both Lutherans and Calvinists: they rave against it, and complain of a thousand superstitions and insane idol-worship, when they hear that we sanctify whatsoever created things for spiritual effects, to drive away demons.'[75] Sermons 31 and 32 were devoted entirely to stories of the powerful effects of holy water.[76] He concluded his sermon-cycle with eclectic and anecdotal evidence of the good effects of the Agnus Dei and other amulets, and of consecrated bells.[77]

Catholic polemics repelled Protestant attacks not only on the issue of consecrations, but also on two other issues: the reality of apparitions of souls in purgatory, and the Church's power to exorcize evil spirits. Ghosts figured occasionally in the superstition literature and also generated a sub-genre of writing on their own. Albrecht Hunger and Martín Delrio sought first and foremost to disentangle the issue of apparitions of the dead from the enchantments of magicians. For these careful and orthodox theologians, magicians could not cause or compel the spirits of the dead to appear. By this reasoning they reached essentially the same conclusion as the Protestants over the apparition of Samuel at Endor. However, they could not accept the Protestant corollary that all and every apparition of a dead soul was in fact a demonic deceit. Souls might well be released from purgatory to ask for the prayers of the living; souls could not be released from hell, and such release would serve no purpose.[78] Delrio allowed himself quite an amount of space to describe and summarize stories of apparitions of the dead from classical antiquity and philosophical writers. He refuted the arguments of Lutheran and reformed authors including Melanchthon, Rivius, Marbach, and Lavater. Delrio occasionally allowed his polemical edge to get the better of clarity. Where it was polemically convenient, apparitions of souls could be assumed to be demons. Delrio alleged that Melanchthon had claimed to have had conversations with spirits, which he then reported in his *De Anima*. Delrio commented wryly, 'is this holiness, bare curiosity, or occult pact? I pass no judgement, I leave the matter there.'[79]

Lavater's reformed critique of ghosts and apparitions provoked controversy with several specialist Catholic works on the subject. The Capuchin Noel Taillepied (1540–89) published in 1588 a *Treatise of the Apparition of Spirits* that dissected Lavater's work minutely, even to the extent of copying his title and arrangement, but reversing the theological conclusions that he had drawn.[80] Pierre le Loyer (1550–1634) published in 1586 a two-volume treatise on spectres and apparitions, reissued several times.[81] Petrus Thyraeus of Mainz (1546–1601) published in 1594 a series of treatises on apparitions of spirits, on those possessed by demons, and on haunted places. His works were widely used and cited by other Catholics such as Delrio.[82]

Catholic writers insisted with particular vigour on the Church's power to exorcize spirits, not just with the rite of exorcism itself but with the infused holiness of all the rites and ceremonies of the Church. As Hunger insisted, 'the Church from Christ's authority has power over demons.'[83] Delrio quoted a litany of examples where demons afflicted people, Protestant clerics attempted to cast them out and failed, but Catholic priests exorcized them easily.[84] In the midst of an attack on 'superstitious' incantations, he insisted that the arguments used against charms did not apply to the exorcisms of the Church: 'the prayers of the Church . . . work both as cause and sign at once.'[85] In the last section of his magnum opus Delrio related a variety of stories of successful exorcisms, several of which were taken by Friedrich Förner for his Bamberg sermon-cycle.[86] For Förner, exorcism presented the ultimate proof of the truth of Catholicism:

It is the true Church, and has the teaching of Christ, and the true Gospel, in which there is the power of compelling demons, driving them out, and destroying their illusions. This power is not found either among Lutherans or Calvinists, as has already been proved elsewhere *ad nauseam*, rather it is only the Catholic priests, remaining in the unity of the Catholic Church [who can do this]. Therefore only the Catholic Church to which we hold is the true Church of Christ, militant on earth, and in that true faith, outside which there is no salvation.[87]

The *Flagellum Diaboli*, not usually a text given to original reasoning, defended Catholic exorcism against some of the attacks of Protestant rationalists. Protestants who criticized the physical performances used in exorcism, such as taking the possessed person and pulling him by the hair or the ears, or striking him on the head, did not understand that this sort of humiliation was deeply offensive to the devil. Lucifer 'having thought that he had overcome Christ, is overwhelmed by the power of his servants ... the devil is obliged to bear patiently the contumely and mockery which is inflicted upon him by the exorcists, as servants of Christ.'[88] The text assumed that Protestants must be failed exorcists because of their exclusion from the true Church: 'Luther ... regardless that he had not the power of faith, attempted nevertheless to drive out the devil; but how it came about with him because of that, everyone knows well.'[89]

Catholic propagandists reported with particular delight the successes of Catholic rituals against demons when these were used in the mission field, whether in America or Asia among those who had never known Christianity, or in Europe where the question was of converting sceptical Protestants. Baptism had freed a Peruvian prince called Tamaracunga from the assaults of demons; the power of the Eucharist had recently driven demons out of Netherlandish Calvinists.[90] Delrio reported how the power of the sign of the cross was attested by a range of miracles.[91] Lopez de Gómara reported that among the American Indians the deceits and apparitions of demons amongst the Indians were best dispelled with the presence of the Eucharist, the image of the crucifix, and the sprinkling of holy water, 'and the very evil spirits have themselves confessed this to the Indians'.[92] Even the super-rationalist Manuel do Vale de Moura reported from Joannes dos Santos the story that a missionary priest had forced a devil to carry water and cut down wood for the brethren for seven years.[93] The Jesuit Antonio Possevino told a story of a successful exorcism in the Baltic regions. A leading Calvinist at one time complained bitterly to one of the Jesuit Fathers that he could not catch wolves as he used to do in his district, claiming the pits in which they were to be captured were impeded by country folk by means of enchantments. The priest offered to sprinkle holy water over the place, so that these enchantments might be dissolved. The Calvinist then laughed and added, that 'if he saw that these enchantments of this sort could be dissolved with holy water, and that wolves could be captured by that means, then he would believe at once, that water of this sort was a divine thing.' For good measure the Calvinist had a haunted house on his estate called Parnomoiisa, which had become uninhabitable. The priest successfully repaired the wolf-traps with holy water and exorcized the house, sprinkling holy water and erecting a cross on a hill overlooking the village. These rites solved the problem for good.[94]

Catholic exorcisms

To seize the experience and physical reality of exorcism, one has to turn to the published manuals for exorcists, which proliferated towards the end of the sixteenth century in Catholic publishing houses. While it is possible that some actual exorcists used even more elaborate or arcane rituals, they were unlikely to have been any more restrained in their ceremonial than the published manuals recommended. Probably the most influential practical guides for exorcists in the later sixteenth century, though by no means the only ones, were those written by the Observant Franciscan Girolamo Menghi. These exorcism manuals, known by various titles, were anthologized and republished through to the late seventeenth century.[95] Menghi's writings typically comprised a discursive part which conveyed the theology of sorcery and its remedies, followed by a liturgical part containing prescriptions for a successful exorcism. In his *Compendium of the Exorcist's Art*, published in Italian, Menghi specified the nature of ecclesiastical remedies rather more fully than his predecessors. Herbs, as such, had no natural power to drive away demons; yet if they were combined with ecclesiastical consecration and exorcism, one could make medicines and potions from them.[96] There was unease about amulets which contained unknown names of God; so Menghi helpfully supplied etymologies (often erroneous) for some of the most impressive ones. The acceptable names of God included 'El, Eloym, Eloa, Sabaoth, Elyon, Esereheie, Adonay, Ya, Thetragramaton ('il qual gli Hebrei Iehova, cioè ineffabile hanno esposto'), Saday' and 'Agla, Homousion, Heheye', and also 'Agios, Otheos, Ischiros, Athanatos'. The latter was nothing more than the ancient Greek Orthodox invocation known as the *Trisagion* ('Holy God, Holy and Strong, Holy and Immortal . . .'): Menghi, knowing no Greek, seems to have assumed that it was a list of the names of God.[97]

The exorcisms in Menghi's *Flagellum Daemonum* must have reinforced, rather than diminished, the impression that the Church believed in the power of words and rituals to heal all ills. Several of these invoked God in a list of impressive, powerful, and essentially incomprehensible names;[98] they exorcized the demon several times 'through the virtue of all the holy, ineffable, and most powerful names . . . and through the power of all those ineffable names'.[99] Earth, air, fire, and water were all to be conjured individually, to prevent them from containing the devil; fire was conjured before it was used to burn an image of the devil, to torment the demon.[100] In the appendix entitled *Most Efficacious Remedies for Expelling Malign Spirits*, Menghi supplied a series of formulae for blessing holy oil. For curing ailments in the body caused by demons, he gave this recipe:

Take white hellebore, hypericum, rose-sugar, and incense [in specified quantities], and boil them in a pound of white wine until they are reduced to half their volume; then have the boiled wine blessed and exorcized by a priest according to the form as below, and give it to the patient at a suitable time for three days; each day, notwithstanding vomiting, the sick person being duly contrite and confessed, and being in a state of grace, is to be exorcized for the space of three or four hours; because thus he will be healed, if the grace of God is favourable.[101]

Similar prescriptions were supplied for the preparation of holy salt, incense of blessed herbs, and for the conjuration of parchment on which amulets were to be written. One could tell whether or not a person was vexed by evil spirits, by writing a list of the holy names of God (supplied by Menghi) on blessed parchment, and placing it on the patient when he or she was unaware of it.[102] Some of Menghi's more exotic exorcisms supplied ammunition for Protestant critics, and Delrio did not seem overly enthusiastic to defend all 'private exorcisms by diverse exorcists'.[103] Other manuals of exorcism showed a rather more cautious approach. Pietro Antonio Stampa, priest at Chiavenna in the Valtelline, published at Como in 1597 an exorcism manual entitled *Fuga Satanae*, written to equip exorcists who aspired to cure the victims of witchcraft.[104] This work was much more chaste and simple than Menghi's. There was no invoking of God in elaborate lists of names; the prayers and readings were almost entirely scriptural. The burning of the instruments of sorcery used fire and sulphur rather than unusual herbs. Nevertheless, Stampa proposed burning effigies of the demon and the witch, and gave directions for preparing a cross with texts to be hung up as an amulet. Numerous other exorcism manuals appeared around the same period and appear to have been commercially successful for their publishers.[105] Over time, with the consolidation of Counter-Reformation liturgical texts in the *Rituale Romanum* of 1614, the

Church hierarchy hoped and expected that other forms of exorcism would fall into disuse. In fact the older semi-official forms of ritual were a very long time dying.[106]

However, Menghi had not actually trespassed very far, if at all, beyond the bounds of Catholic orthodoxy with his exorcism manuals, which continued to be published. He drew his 'names of God' from respectable traditional sources, even if his command of Greek and Hebrew words was rather feeble. The issue went deeper than merely 'purging' exorcism formulae of spurious names of unknown spirits or apocryphal folkloric additions to the rite. Either it was legitimate to utter long and impressive verbal formulae in Latin over physical substances to turn them into instruments of supernatural violence against evil spirits, or it was not. The question was at root a theological one: did the Church have the authority to use verbal formulae and physical materials to humiliate and torment evil spirits in the name of God? Protestants denied it; Catholic theologians, equally rationally by their own lights and principles, asserted that the Church assuredly did have such authority. Menghi's impressive formulae and recipes for the use of herbs, wax, fire, and all the rest of the apparatus presented the visible practice that had already been justified and theologized in the rationalizing theoretical treatises of Delrio and his colleagues. In practice, the best evidence suggests that the elaborate rituals of exorcism were psychologically very impressive. An exotically furnished ritual had a better chance of impressing and altering the mental state of a distressed person than the rather chaste and limited prayers that orthodox Protestants allowed themselves.[107]

Demonizing the Protestants

Finally, just as Protestants demonized the Catholics, in exactly the same way Catholics accused the Protestants of being playthings of demons and sorcerers, and blamed them for the perceived rise of sorcery in the contemporary world. Polemical theologians claimed that Protestants, while they attacked the true Church (Catholicism) with unrestrained ferocity, showed themselves weak or unreliable in regard to attacking magic and sorcery. The supposed leniency of Protestants against witches and their scepticism about magic formed, in fact, an important accusation for Catholics to use against them. Hector Wegman, the student whose degree promotion provided the occasion for Albrecht Hunger's theses on magic, threw in the faces of the Protestants the lack of censorship in their publishing houses: 'the "Evangelicals" edit openly and spread abroad things which not only encourage pestilent dissensions about the holy faith, and also (as it were) heresies summoned back from hell, but... also teach manifest magic and execrable idolatry... From their publishing-houses there have recently appeared many books of magic.'[108] Martín Delrio, in the *Proloquium* to his *Disquisitions*, presented a demonizing history of the religious strife of his own age. It was so clear that it was perverse to deny the proposition that magic followed heresies 'as the shadow does the body'. All the leading heretics of the past were also magicians. The Hussites appeared in Bohemia and then the Lutherans in Germany: as the *Malleus Maleficarum* showed, a great crowd of witches followed them. Witches in Trier admitted that they only learned their craft after a Lutheran prince invaded the territory; the abundance of witches in the Alps was explained by the persistence of the Waldensian heresy there. As Delrio's fellow Jesuit Juan de Maldonado had explained, demons made their home in heretics; heresy could not sustain its first energy, but must either dissolve into atheism or turn into magic.[109] Witches, like the Protestant 'beggars' in the Low Countries, promised never to venerate the Eucharist or the saints, to destroy relics and images, and to despise the consecrated things of the Church.[110]

Catholic gossip and folklore, as one might term it, contributed to this demonizing legend around the conflict with the Protestants. At Geila in Brabant it was reported that the demons suddenly left all the possessed people, so that they could attend Luther's funeral. Similarly they were supposed to have left the demoniacs to be present with the Calvinists during the iconoclasm and hedge-preaching of 1566. At St Medard's Church in Paris the Calvinist iconoclasts allegedly broke all the windows except that 'in gratitude' they left one which showed a red devil. In several other places, including St Paul's in London, iconoclastic mobs left only the depictions of devils untouched.[111] Friedrich Förner preached Delrio's apostrophes to the people of Bamberg. He argued that the rise of magic and sorcery in the current age offered an opportunity to prove the truth of Catholicism. 'Which age has been as calamitous, as rich in heresies as our own century? Did not atheism spread around from the root of Calvin? Do they not deny all the efforts of the demon? Do they not turn all the malice of witches into vain and futile delusions and dreams?'[112] Protestants were the friends of sorcerers because they shared an enemy in the Catholic

Church. On the other hand Förner argued in the following sermon that the demons attacked Catholics through sorcery much more than they did the Protestants. Did this mean that evil magic was more common among Catholics than among Protestants? Not so, argued Förner, since the devil does not believe in wasting his time:

> If the Catholics lacked the true faith, if they did not have that faith without which it is impossible, as St Paul says, to please God, then the devil would not make such effort to seduce them. Since on the other hand all those who are estranged from the Catholic faith lack the true faith which saves all who believe, the devil leaves them in their state of unfaithfulness: because no one seeks anxiously for that which he already knows he possesses in all security.[113]

Tragically, in the confessional atmosphere of the late sixteenth and seventeenth century, the supposed prevalence of magic, superstition and witchcraft could be used to support any polemical argument. The arguments were of course elliptical and self-reinforcing. It is improbable that many more people became victims of trials for sorcery or witchcraft as a result of these polemical exchanges, though the possibility existed for local excesses of zeal in some of the German prince-bishoprics.[114] Rather the conviction, among Protestants and Catholics alike, that the other side was doing the devil's work made dialogue of any kind effectively impossible. The debate over superstition did not just 'demonize' the opposing side as a rhetorical device, as an analogy or a throw-away line. It supplied precise theological arguments, grounded in evidence of the other side's behaviour, to justify regarding one's confessional opponents as in league with the powers of darkness. The Reformation debates transformed the cosmic battle against evil: from being a top–downwards conflict of the theologically learned against the ignorant, it became both a vertical struggle and a lateral combat waged amongst the educated, a struggle between different kinds of theologians. The wretched inheritance of the 'confessional orthodox' period of European religious history consisted, in part, of the readiness of rival confessions to treat each other as the literal servants of Satan. Only when the Almighty signally failed to award victory to any one side over the other would the implausibility of these assumptions sink into the religious mind of the seventeenth century.

PART IV

The Cosmos Changes Shape:
Superstition is Redefined

The last section showed how Protestant and Roman Catholic polemics adapted the discourses of 'superstition' that they had inherited from the Middle Ages to suit the propaganda needs of their rival confessions. In so doing the rival religious blocs of early modern Europe literally—not figuratively, not rhetorically—'demonized' each other. In the fourteenth and fifteenth centuries theologians had excoriated 'superstition' in a cultural struggle along a vertical social axis, between the rationalized views of the theologically educated and the instinctive and intuitive folklore of the majority. In the sixteenth century that former struggle continued and in some ways intensified, but it came to be overlaid with a lateral conflict between two rival concepts of the proper use of ritual and religious ceremony in the cosmos. In the seventeenth century, as is well known, the lines of confessional antagonism deepened and hardened between the major religious groupings of Western Europe. Lutheran and 'Calvinist' Protestants eviscerated each other in theological print while they formed and as quickly broke fragile alliances with the resurgent military forces of Spanish and German Catholicism on the battlefield of Central Europe in the Thirty Years War. It might have been expected that in these circumstances the seventeenth century would see little more than the reiteration of old arguments in the debate around superstitions.

In fact the seventeenth century witnessed a crucial transition in the whole debate over what 'superstitions' were and why they were to be avoided, because what had previously been agreed between the disputants now became a controversial and open field of speculation. The medieval and sixteenth-century debates had largely been conducted on the basis of agreement between theologians, who nearly monopolized the discussion of popular superstitions, about the basic workings of the universe. Late scholastics, Protestants, and Roman Catholics had essentially shared the language and the concepts of medieval Christian Aristotelianism as laid down in Peter Lombard and especially Thomas Aquinas. The principles of scholastic metaphysics dictated that rituals, symbols, and messages could influence intelligent substances, but could not transform inert material ones. Matter could not influence matter remotely. Those same principles postulated that invisible spirits existed, both as human souls separated from bodies and as incorporeal intelligences active in the physical world. The whole discourse of superstition depended on agreement over demonology, even amidst its most bitter disagreements over ritual and theology.

In the seventeenth century the parameters of the metaphysical debate suddenly opened up considerably, even as the traditional demonologies continued to be published.[1] Alternatives to scholastic-Aristotelian metaphysics had already existed, most notably among Neoplatonists; but these alternatives had not really influenced the dialogue over superstitions, not least because Neoplatonists tended to be cultural elitists who had nothing to gain by intervening in the theological analysis of folkloric practices. In the seventeenth century many committed Christian thinkers openly challenged the prevailing orthodoxy on the existence and nature of invisible spirits. Such critiques began on the margins of the mainstream confessions but then proliferated especially among Anglican and other Protestant thinkers. One of the curious aspects that the literature on this subject presents is the sudden emergence of England as the milieu for so much that was most important and most controversial in metaphysical thought. To a limited degree this prominence of England may reflect the extreme difficulties of living and working in continental Europe in a century racked by warfare and disrupted by passing armies: England may have emerged simply because other countries were so distressed. However, the internal political stresses of Great Britain, in many ways just as traumatic as those of continental Europe, seem to have had an energizing rather than depressing effect on religious and philosophical thought within England itself. The rise of philosophical 'virtuosi', first in the Commonwealth and Protectorate and then under the restored Stuart monarchy, provoked an unprecedented level of creative reflection and debate on the workings of the invisible universe, among intellectual and religious professionals and amateurs alike.

If demons did not exist, or did not have the powers previously claimed for them, then much of the debate over the workings of superstitions needed to be recast. Cartesianism, in particular, opened up the question of the influence of intellectual and spiritual essences on the material world in an especially disturbing way. Mechanical and materialistic philosophies seemed if anything worse, since they appeared to offer the prospect of explaining the cosmos without the pressing need for spiritual beings of any kind. Scholarly orthodoxy now typically observes that adepts of the new proto-'scientific' philosophies of the seventeenth century did not hold inherently irreligious or secularizing attitudes; indeed many were deeply and even conventionally devout. The evidence for this claim is abundant and incontestable. However, in the area of superstitions, it seems equally clear that changing attitudes to religion and cosmology aroused a fear of materialism and scepticism out of proportion to its reality. The later seventeenth century presented, especially in England and the Netherlands, the spectacle of extreme concern among many thinkers that the spiritual realm was being lost altogether. Attacks on 'Saducism' and 'Atheism', not entirely unknown in the sixteenth century, proliferated in the seventeenth in far greater abundance than the unity, clarity, or abundance of their alleged targets would seem to require or justify. Defenders of the existence of an 'invisible realm' researched all kinds of evidence, including the lore of what had previously been termed 'superstition', to prove their points. Paradoxically, as the fear of outright materialism supplanted the fear of vulgar magic, theological writers rather lost what had been the defining attitude of medieval theologians to the subject. They no longer regarded evidence of spirit activity as an abomination to be warned against and cast out from Christian culture. Rather, they saw it as a helpful proof-text to be exploited in a metaphysical debate. Superstition lost much of its terror as investigators grasped at the rapidly vanishing will-o'-the-wisp. Meanwhile it became not only possible, but common, to argue something that had rarely been argued in previous times: one could claim that the things reported in tales of the supernatural simply had never occurred. Faced with incredulity based often on ridicule rather than reasoning, the defenders of the supernatural found themselves obliged to collect proofs and garner evidence just to establish that there was a subject to be discussed at all.[2]

Around the same time, confessional uniformity and the apparatus for its enforcement, formerly vital prerequisites of the censure of superstition and magic, began not only to weaken, but to fall into disrepute among the educated. To be sure, Catholic powers especially continued to persecute and occasionally to exile their Protestant subjects; Protestant regimes aspired with ever-diminishing success to enforce confessional unity on their populations and continued to deny full civil rights to minorities and dissenters. However, religious totalitarianism and the accompanying persecution, as it became increasingly ineffective, came to be seen in many quarters as absurd. Protestants denounced the expulsion of the Huguenots from France in 1685 as an act of cruelty and obscurantism. Two generations later, educated people of all sorts ridiculed the expulsion of the Lutherans from Salzburg as a bizarre anachronism.[3]

The decline in religious absolutism prepared the way for the characteristic use of the term 'superstition' associated with the Enlightenment. While relatively few of the philosophes actually held and expressed explicitly secularizing or atheistic opinions, many more criticized what one might term the principle of the arbitrary location of the divine in the physical world, and the consequences that flowed from such arbitrariness. 'Superstition' in the Enlightenment became the shorthand term to describe a particular religious cast of mind. It designated the attitude that identified the holy in specific things, people, and places, and that believed that the honour of God located in such things must be defended against blasphemers and infidels. The Enlightenment critique of 'superstition' drew on, and consciously echoed, much of what had already been said about the wrongs of traditional Catholicism by Protestant theologians and by Renaissance humanists before them. However, Enlightenment thinkers did not confine their criticism to 'superstitious' priestcraft. They balanced that critique with censure of dogmatic militancy in all its forms, including those of doctrinaire or sectarian Protestantism. The various follies of religion gone wrong shared the same basic vice: they led to partisanship, violence, and a neglect of basic ethics. Honouring God could not justify dishonouring the human being. Consequently wrong belief was necessarily located in human folly and ignorance, absolutely not—as for the developed Reformation critique—in demonic deception. It was not just philosophes, but many clergy of whatever stamp, who embraced such views, and therefore in a sense suspended much of their confessional identities in the interests of 'rational' religion.

Within another few generations, as is well known, the sometimes affected cosmopolitan rationalism of the Enlightenment generated a reaction against itself in the shape of Romanticism. That reaction forms a fundamental precondition for the final episode in this story, the absorption of superstitions and their associated lore into the work of the folklorists in the early nineteenth century. Late eighteenth- and early nineteenth-century thought concluded that humanity could not exist forever in abstract realms of reason. The traditions and inherited cultures of individual people constituted an indispensable substrate of the diverse humanities. Romanticism and its cultivation of the folkloric and the 'superstitious' past can appear as an *anti-Enlightenment, especially in those countries and cultures where it involved a conscious revival of medieval modes of thought and behaviour. In another sense, however, it demonstrated how completely Europe's intellectuals had lost their fear of the old 'superstitious' cultures. Romantic medievalism stood in relation to original medievalism as secondary epic stands to primary epic, as the library-bound poet Virgil to the semi-mythical Homer. It amounted to self-conscious revivalism through choice, rather than the instinctive and authentic expression of a culture that knew no other way. Moreover, Romantic folklorism treated beliefs about spirits and spells as specific, and therefore relative, to particular human cultures, in the same way as languages, folk tales, or national costumes. The legends of spirits and ghosts did not point through to a metaphysical reality. The only reality was the very human business of distinct ethnic cultures.*

In all this literature we are, of course, dealing with the intellectual superstructure of European thought. Neither the Enlightenment nor its antecedents or successors spoke for all or even a majority of Europe's people. One influential historical school has argued that during the early modern period the bourgeoisie and intelligentsia of Europe became detached as not before from folk-culture through civility, manners, and cosmopolitan education.[4] To the extent that this claim may be true, one would expect the beliefs and assumptions of the majority of Europe's peoples, including the 'superstitions', to have persisted with little alteration through to industrialization and urbanization or indeed beyond.[5] In fact, given the enormous effort expended in medieval and early modern European religion to try to modify people's attitudes to the invisible world and its supposed forces, it would be as implausible to insist that absolutely nothing ever changed, as it would undoubtedly be absurd to claim that ordinary Europeans believed at all times exactly as their intellectual leaders told them to do. The question for this essay relates to the cognitive distance between the educated and the majority. When both the theological elites and the mass of the people believe in spirits—even if they disagree about the ethical and metaphysical systems governing those spirits—the distance between the preacher and the congregation is not so great. When a considerable gulf opens up between the two, as appears to have been the case in the eighteenth and nineteenth centuries, the cultural profile of society and the attitudes of one part of society to another are altered in significant ways.

Eventually, of course, some people do not cease to be superstitious, and others certainly do not cease writing about the fact. A relatively abundant literature of sociology and anthropology continues to explore the phenomena of 'superstition' in modern industrial society.[6] Comparison of this modern literature with medieval and early modern equivalents gives the impression of an even more disjointed body of beliefs and attitudes, profoundly disconnected from the prevailing world-view, than was the case in previous centuries. Yet perhaps the difference is more of degree than kind. The essential quality of superstitious belief is that it is fragmentary, eclectic, pragmatic, disjointed. It perpetually resists confinement within a consistent system of causation or metaphysics.

16

Demonology Becomes an Open Subject in the Seventeenth Century

A considerable amount of this last section of the book will focus on the contested subject of demons and spirits in the seventeenth century. It should already be clear that the traditional critique of superstitions in Western Europe, from Christian late antiquity onwards, depended on a belief in evil spirits. Evil spirits devised superstitious rites, and then gave them whatever spurious effectiveness they appeared to have. Superstitious rituals must be avoided because they were inventions of evil spiritual beings. Superstitious folklore turned creatures that were truly evil into merely mischievous or potentially helpful spirit-friends, servants, or lovers. Participation in such rituals was supposed to be the first stage on a slippery slope towards ever-greater demonic evil: superstition was the 'novitiate of the devil'.[1] These arguments worked sufficiently well, at least for those who wrote and preached them, so long as there was a reasonably broad agreement about the existence of evil spirits, their natures and potentialities. As the second part of the book showed, across the Middle Ages a consensus solidified that explained the powers and limitations of evil spirits according to Christian Aristotelian principles. The 'aery bodies' of the Platonist spirit world gave way to the rationalistic demonology of Aquinas's *Summa against the Pagans*.[2]

In the sixteenth century some thinkers had already begun to challenge some of the outgrowths of conventional demonology, but on a very small scale and on the margins of theological thought. The Family of Love, a movement derived from the Dutch freethinker Hendrik Niclaes, acquired a reputation for reducing much of what was said in scripture to allegory or symbolic language. Consequently, much of the language used about people being possessed of spirits, or spirits being driven out of people, could be explained as metaphor.[3] The Familists reputedly gained significant influence and fashionable cachet in the court of Elizabeth I, notably through the patronage of certain members of the Queen's guard. As Nicodemites who felt no difficulty whatsoever in conforming outwardly to the rules and practices of the Church of England, they were much less offensive to the Queen or her court than they were to some Puritan critics.[4] However, the Familist opinion gained far more notice through the parodies of its critics than through being expressed by its own advocates. All sorts of writers—including Reginald Scot—could mock the symbolic reading of scripture as a 'Familistical' idea.[5] In the mainstream of sixteenth-century religious thought, Protestant as well as Catholic, it was still taken for granted not only that spirits and demons existed, but that they existed within fairly strictly defined metaphysical rules and principles.[6]

This consensus broke down comprehensively in the seventeenth century. Especially in England and the Netherlands, debate opened up over what, if anything, the language of spirits and demons denoted. Much of this debate related only in a tangential and secondary way to the issue of superstitions. Many of the most vigorous debates revolved around the question of witchcraft: only if demons existed, and if pacts could be made with them to achieve prodigious effects, could the legal prosecution and punishment of witches be justified. This study will try to steer around the details of that debate, as belonging to another subject. Yet it cannot be avoided completely, since the same metaphysical arguments affected the early modern response to popular superstitions. Essentially, if one continued to believe in spirits, then superstitions remained pernicious and potentially effective wrong actions. However, if one regarded spiritual beings as impossibly remote, ineffective, or even non-existent, then 'superstitious' activities became merely acts of foolishness and ignorance. Moreover, the seventeenth-century debate promised eventually to turn around the meaning of the word 'superstitious' itself. Ultimately, 'superstition' came to consist in thinking that charms, healing spells, or divinatory techniques achieved anything at all, as opposed to being utterly futile. 'Superstition' moved from being defined as an evil action practised by the incurably ignorant, to become a misconception about the workings of the universe held by perversely misguided but often very well-educated thinkers.

This chapter will review a number of writers who in various ways opened up or challenged the description of superstition and the world of spirits, especially in seventeenth-century England. The chapter following will consider those writers who vigorously defended the idea of an 'invisible world' of spirits. It is not intended to portray the thought of this period as neatly divided between the 'sceptics' and 'credulous', even though some contemporary thinkers depicted it that way.[7] Indeed, some of the most important breaches in the metaphysical consensus were made by those who, like Thomas Browne, held relatively traditional views. Moreover, *both* sides in the debate, whether they minimized the role of spirits in the cosmos or defended and enhanced that role, helped to break down the traditional discourse about superstition. 'Credulous' writers like Joseph Glanvill or John Aubrey caused just as much chaos, if not more, in the theology of superstition as did 'sceptics' such as Thomas Hobbes or Balthasar Bekker. They simply achieved their effects, whether intentionally or not, by a different set of rhetorical positions.

Modifications to traditional demonology: Burton and Browne

Signs of a potential breach in the former broad consensus over demonology appeared, in a modest way, in the encyclopedic work of the Oxford academic and clergyman Robert Burton (1577–1640), *The Anatomy of Melancholy*, first published pseudonymously in 1621.[8] The subject of melancholy would become enormously important in the controversies of the seventeenth century: it was increasingly argued that 'melancholy', meaning a common and rather diverse and widely diffused mental disorder, might explain many of the visions and other supposedly 'supernatural' experiences reported by the common people. Burton supplied an extensive 'Digression of the Nature of Spirits, bad Angels, or Devils, and how they cause melancholy' in the second section of his work.[9] Burton observed that the nature of spirits was controversial: the subject was difficult, and some doubted the existence of spirits altogether. Various Neoplatonist writers argued that spirits were corporeal and mortal, although orthodox theologians had refuted this claim.[10]

Burton then added typically erudite discussions, overloaded with copious and not always precise references, of demons in the universe below the circle of the moon. These he distinguished into species by their presence in the elements of fire, air, water, and earth: in this respect he evoked more overtly magical writers like Paracelsus or Weyer. Burton demonstrated the same tendency that would appear in later sixteenth-century writers, to accumulate references from theological writers and popular folklore and to assimilate each to the other. He also assimilated, compared, and contrasted evidence from writers across different parts of Europe.[11]

Burton followed Protestant theology and demonology sufficiently close-ly to incorporate several key reformed arguments. Catholic writers, he observed, cultivated stories of demonic possession to justify their spuri-ous rites of exorcism.[12] The 'vain and frivolous superstitious forms of exorcisms' to be found among Catholics were 'not to be tolerated, or endured'. Catholic saints hardly differed from pagan deities with their specialist assignments to different diseases. Their exorcisms had sometimes turned out to be frauds, as in the recent case of those perpetrated by the Jesuit Weston.[13] However, Burton devoted even more space to the theme of 'religious melancholy' in general, than he did to the by then rather trite theme of the evils of Catholicism. Superstition and schism, he believed, afforded more examples of disordered human minds than any other area of human conduct or behaviour.[14] Drawing upon the Protestant critique of degraded religion, but extending it beyond its original boundaries, Burton expounded on the evil of superstition with a rhetorical flourish:

A lamentable thing it is to consider, how many myriads of men this idolatry and superstition (for that comprehends all) hath infatuated in all ages, besotted by this blind zeal, which is religion's ape, religion's bastard, religion's shadow, false glass. For where God hath a temple, the devil will have a chapel: where God hath sacrifices, the devil will have his oblations: where God hath ceremonies, the devil will have his traditions: where there is any religion, the devil will plant superstition; and it is a pitiful sight to behold and read, what tortures, miseries it hath procured, what slaughter of souls it hath made.[15]

Most of world was superstitious in some form or another: pagans, Eastern Orthodox, Roman Catholics, and sectarian dissenters within Protestantism were all at fault. On one hand superstitious religions derived from the devil's desire to mimic and to mock true religion and divert people from it; on the other they arose when politicians wished to use religion as a means of social control. Some priests were as manipulative as politicians, or more so: the leaders of Roman Catholicism were sceptics themselves, but strove to make other people more superstitious by fostering belief in stories that they did not credit themselves.[16] Burton expanded at some length on the mechanisms for mental and spiritual control deployed by evil spirits and corrupt religious leaders to keep people in awe. People were kept in ignorance, since ignorance fostered superstition. Threatening and fearsome stories—such as those of purgatory—were told to impress them. Disciplines and mortifications, such as flagellation, severe fasting, and sensory deprivation would not only keep people under the domination of their religious leaders: they might actually stimulate the spurious visions and the mental disturbance that would make people easy to control and to mislead.[17] Superstition provoked an inordinate affection towards one's own opinion and deep hatred of its rivals: from this ensued the bloody persecutions of the inquisitions and the religious wars. 'This is common to all superstition, that there is nothing so mad and absurd, so ridiculous, impossible, incredible, which they will not believe, observe, and diligently perform, as much as in them lies; nothing so monstrous to conceive, or intolerable to put into practice, so cruel to suffer, which they will not willingly undertake.'[18]

Burton was careful, by his lights, to strike out both at right and left. He blamed sectarian Protestants for their fancies of divine inspiration and obsessive avoidance of even the slightest Catholic practice, as much as he criticized Catholics for their legends and traditions. He also denounced irreligion or atheism as religious melancholy 'by defect', whereas superstition represented the same disease 'by excess'.[19] The atheists, however, formed for Burton a rather smaller target: they chiefly comprised Italian philosophers such as Pomponazzi, Cardano, Bruno, or Vanini who (he claimed) questioned the entire world of spirits and explained all miraculous and prodigious events as part of the ordinary course of nature.[20] By later in the century, the number of those either alleged to be atheists or to promote atheism by their disbelief in spirits would multiply considerably from Burton's rather brief list. On the whole, Burton modified the sixteenth-century picture only modestly. He stepped sufficiently out of the mode of confessional antagonism to criticize deviant Protestantisms as well as Catholicism. He derived the evils of 'superstition'—defined rather broadly as religious excess of all kinds—more or less equally from demonic seductions and illusions and from the cynical manipulation of sceptical power-brokers in State and Church. He knew enough about Kepler's cosmology to realize that the traditional concept of the size of the cosmos and the place of spirits within it was problematical, but he did not try to resolve the question.[21]

The exceedingly learned and curious scholar-physician Thomas Browne (1605–82) contributed in various ways to the critique of received wisdom that in due course reframed the debate over superstitions. Around the age of 30 Browne drafted the first version of a masterly essay, *Religio Medici*, 'the Physician's Religion'.[22] Medical writers were notorious for their free thought and pragmatism in religious matters, and Browne approached the topic gently and with some care. Declaring himself a follower of the reformed religion, he mildly admitted to some attraction to 'that which misguided zeal terms superstition'. By this he meant nothing more than an aesthetic or emotive attraction to traditional ritual and ceremony.[23] He encapsulated an unusually explicit mixture of faith and aversion to dogma: he declared himself 'content to understand a mystery, without a rigid definition'; when scripture described something improbable, he concluded that it was 'no vulgar part of faith, to believe a thing not only above, but contrary to, reason, and against the arguments of our proper senses'.[24] He discerned insights into the divine purpose from doctrine, but also from reason and nature, convinced that nature was rationally and providentially governed.[25] In an important, allusive, lyrical passage Browne observed how too much study of nature could lead one to doubt miracles, and to believe that all prodigious accounts from scripture were accomplished by natural skill. 'Thus the devil played at chess with me, and, yielding a pawn, thought to gain a queen of me; taking advantage of my honest endeavours; and, whilst I laboured to raise the structure of my reason, he strove to undermine the edifice of my faith.'[26] Consequently, Browne expressed surprise that 'so many learned heads should so far forget their metaphysicks, and destroy the ladder and scale of creatures, as to question the existence of spirits; for my part, I have ever believed, and do now know, that there are witches. They that doubt of these do not only deny them, but spirits: and are obliquely, and upon consequence, a sort, not of infidels, but atheists.'[27] He was willing to believe, not only in spirits in general, but in tutelary spirits or guardian angels.[28] As an obedient Protestant, he affirmed that apparitions of spirits and ghosts were in truth demons out to cause trouble for people.[29]

Browne expressed, therefore, some conservative and traditional views on the subject of demonology, magic, and witchcraft, for which he has endured some criticism down the years. However, when compared with the sometimes frantic way that some later seventeenth-century authors insisted on evidences of the 'invisible world', Browne made himself more conspicuous by his caution and even his scepticism. Miracles might (or might not) have ceased, but when they did so cease was unclear. Jesuits claimed miracles in the Indies, but these were uncertain based on the available evidence. In addition to individual spirits, 'there may be (for aught I know) a universal and common spirit to the whole world'. He could see almost nothing wrong with the (formally heretical) idea that human souls were generated by traduction rather than specific infusion.[30] 'Many things are true in divinity, which are neither inducible by reason nor confirmable by sense; and many things in philosophy confirmable by sense, yet not inducible by reason.'[31] He observed that by the standards of the religious zealot, no-one could be saved since each church anathematized the other.[32] He warned against dogmatism even in philosophy: 'though our first studies and junior endeavours may style us Peripateticks, Stoicks, or Academicks, yet I perceive the wisest heads prove, at last, almost all Scepticks.'[33]

Above all—and here he touched significantly on the theme of the present book—Browne had no patience with vulgarly received opinion, nor with 'that great enemy of reason, virtue, and religion, the multitude; that numerous piece of monstrosity, which, taken asunder, seem men, and the reasonable creatures of God, but, confused together, make but one great beast, and a monstrosity more prodigious than Hydra'.[34] Browne's greatest contribution to scientific and to ethnographic literature in the mid-seventeenth century lay in his encyclopedic and insatiably curious compendium *Pseudodoxia Epidemica*, 'widely-believed falsehoods', first published in 1646 and revised and enlarged until 1672.[35] The whole premise of the book consisted in the principle that commonly received opinion is fallible: that even if something has been received and reported as truth for a long time, it may yet prove to be false. The learned were prone to depend excessively on the authority of ancient (and often mistaken) writers, even when those writers had no intention or expectation of being treated as infallible.[36] The greatest and original source of error, Browne insisted in conventional terms, was of course the devil. Yet the devil worked, as he had worked for Luther, supremely by disseminating wrong beliefs about God and about the devil's own nature. First, the devil tried to persuade people that there was no God, 'the greatest falsity . . . the highest lie in Nature'. Then the devil proposed that there was not one God, but many; and indeed that the devil himself was a god, able to work miracles, to know and foretell the future, or to raise the spirits of the dead at will. Next—and in contrast to these previous suggestions—the devil made people believe that he was so weak as to be subject to the rites and ceremonies of the magicians. Finally, 'quite to lose us in this maze of Error, he would make men believe there is no such creature as himself: and that he is not only subject unto inferiour creatures, but in the rank of nothing'.[37] The last deception of Satan was to convince contemporary philosophers that he did not exist, and therefore that apparitions and witchcraft were delusions of a melancholy imagination, and that the human soul itself could not survive death.[38]

Much of *Pseudodoxia Epidemica* consisted of short chapters illustrating some widely believed falsehood in mineralogy, botany, zoology, or human biology: these enumerated (for example) mistaken beliefs about the habits and life cycles of exotic animals, or about the existence of mythical ones. In the fifth book, however, Browne took conventional depictions and iconographies as an opportunity to discuss some prevailing cultural beliefs and practices. He listed a variety of popular omens, such as that it was unlucky to meet with a hare, an owl, or a raven, or to spill salt. These beliefs he explained as inheritances from pagan antiquity. The custom of breaking an empty eggshell to defend against witchcraft 'is but a superstitious relict, according to the judgement of *Pliny*'. Browne listed a whole series of habitual customs or superstitions, such as thinking it bad luck to sit cross-legged, or cutting the nails at set and particular days of the week, or allowing hair to grow on a mole on the face. More significantly, Browne noted that the amniotic membrane or caul sometimes found adhering to the head or body of a newborn baby was supposed to act as a talisman not only for the child born with it, but also (quite illogically) to others who preserved it or carried it with them as an amulet.[39] Browne observed that people sometimes divined illness from spots appearing on the fingernails, or discerned the presence of spirits from the guttering of candles. (The latter, Browne thought, might be true if spirits on their appearance exuded sulphurous gases.) The use of the divining rod to find minerals, he thought, was 'a fruitless exploration, strongly scenting of *Pagan* derivation, and the *virgula Divina*, proverbially magnified of old'. To conclude the chapter he declared that 'we are unwilling to enlarge concerning many other; only referring unto sober examination, what natural effects can reasonably be expected, when to prevent the Ephialtes or night-Mare we hang up an hollow stone in our stables; when for amulets against Agues we use the chips of Gallows and places of execution.'[40]

These passages resembled the enumerations of popular beliefs in earlier superstition-treatises, but with some important differences. First, the location of these passages in the rhetorical structure of *Pseudodoxia Epidemica* implied that these beliefs, like those about the unicorn or the amphisbaena, were simply false: not that they were intrinsically ineffective practices that might nevertheless work through the agency of demons. Although traditional in his view of spirits, Browne treated these superstitions as curiosities based on falsehoods rather than threats. Somewhat dismissively, he said that after the cessation or oracles, 'expelled from Oracles and solemn Temples of delusion, [the devil] runs into corners, exercising *minor trumperies*, and acting his deceits in Witches, Magicians, Diviners, and such *inferiour seducers*.'[41] Secondly, Browne's scepticism, literary-critical method, and quest for plausible natural explanations contrasted quite markedly with the attitudes of later seventeenth-century experimenters. The latter would typically report a superstitious charm or divinatory practice, and test its effectiveness by experience, rather than appraising its plausibility according to theology or classical literature.

Dissenting demonologies: Hobbes to Bekker

Burton and Browne in general espoused a conventional demonology, even as they tested the limits of religious consensus on superstitions, their causes, and their origins. A quite different and largely unconnected group of writers in the middle and later seventeenth century took a much more radical approach. They called into question the very existence of 'spiritual beings' as traditionally conceived. This approach derived many of its arguments from the traditional Protestant rhetoric used against Catholic consecrations and legends, though it expanded and extended the scope of this critique very considerably. Such authors argued that the traditional demonology made no sense, whether in terms of natural philosophy or of scripture. They insisted that much of the language of spirits in the Bible was typically if not invariably metaphorical: those invisible, incorporeal spiritual beings, that according to Aquinas and his followers could move the elements around in response to magical charms, did not exist.

One of the most notorious, and most influential, of these radicals was Thomas Hobbes (1588–1679).[42] Hobbes was, of course, primarily a political thinker. The whole thrust of his great work *Leviathan* (1651) sought to prove that sovereignty in human society was by definition indivisible, and that any separation of powers or restraint of the government was illogical and unworkable.[43] However, *Leviathan* contained a considerable amount of theological reasoning, especially in the third and fourth parts, 'Of a Christian Commonwealth' and 'Of the Kingdom of Darkness'. Hobbes denounced the notion that the Church could or ought to subsist as a separate corporation from the secular state. He found this error to be pernicious to the public peace, whether in the hands of Roman Catholics or of Calvinist Protestants. The 'kingdom of God' in the biblical sense of a truly theocratic polity had ceased with the elevation of Saul to the kingdom of Israel, and could not be cited as a justification for a separate ecclesiastical polity in the present age.[44] Ecclesiastical power could not and must not amount to a rival source of legal authority to that of the sovereign.

This driving principle in Hobbes's thought helped to shape his notoriously influential conception of spirits. Hobbes treated Aristotelian philosophy, and metaphysics in particular, with withering contempt. Scholasticism, after all, was the philosophy of the Jesuit Thomists, with their subversive political theories. The scholastic vocabulary used to describe states of being, substances and essences, as Hobbes correctly observed, derived from coined words based on the verb *esse*, 'to be' such as *ens* and *entia*: all such abstractions were 'the names of nothing'.[45] Hobbes extended this linguistic critique to the vocabulary of spirits. In chapter 34 of *Leviathan* Hobbes argued that the universe was made up of bodily matter: 'there is no reall part thereof that is not also body'. Body and substance were in effect the same thing; so to speak of 'incorporeal substance' was to utter a contradiction like an 'incorporeal body'.[46] In common speech 'body' was chiefly used to describe physically palpable or visible matter: the air and such rarefied material were often called breath, wind, or indeed 'spirit'. 'Spirit' either signified tenuous and rarefied matter, or gave a name to the non-existent phantasms of the imagination.

In scripture, 'spirit' was commonly used metaphorically, to mean the qualities of God or of human beings guided by God, including wisdom and submission to the power of God.[47] When the Bible spoke explicitly of 'spirits' as visible beings, it clearly meant creatures endowed with 'aerial bodies', material creatures perceptible to the senses. Hobbes denied that there was any clear evidence about the nature of angels in scripture; he ran through many of the biblical references to show that wherever canonical scripture used the word angel, or messenger, either it indicated a being that had substance and quantity; or it meant a transient apparition to the senses. 'Inspiration' described the state of being guided either by the spirit of God or by evil spirits; the notion of being 'inspired' or 'possessed' by a spirit was a metaphor, and did not mean that virtues or vices were 'bodies to be carried hither and thither, and to be powred into men, as into barrels'.[48] Hobbes dismissed 'demonology' as it was then understood as a mere relic of paganism. Pagans gave the name 'demons' to the sensory impressions formed in their brains, because they did not understand how the senses operated. When Jesus commanded evil spirits to depart, that act was the same as telling the sea to be calm: he was commanding an inanimate entity. The only material 'spirit' that could possess a person was his own spirit or mind. 'To conclude, I find in Scripture that there be Angels, and Spirits, good and evill; but not that they are Incorporeall, as are the Apparitions men see in the dark, or in a dream, or vision; which the Latines call *spectra*, and took for *Daemons*. And I find that there are Spirits corporeall, (though subtile and Invisible;) but not that any mans body was possessed, or inhabited by them.'[49]

Hobbes could appear more conventional in his Protestant critique of Catholic miracles and consecrations. On miracles and magic, Hobbes insisted that only God could work a miracle, for the purpose of demonstrating the power and credibility of his ministers and messengers. No created being, whether angel or devil, could do anything miraculous; magical 'enchantments' could achieve nothing, since words served only to convey intention or meaning. Many bogus 'miracles' were illusions achieved naturally by imposture. The claim that a miracle happened in the consecration of the Eucharist could safely be dismissed on public authority. In language very similar to that of Calvin and other reformed theologians, Hobbes argued that the power of miraculous healing given to the apostles was a temporary gift and soon revoked.[50] Catholic clergy abused scripture when they turned consecrations into 'conjuration or enchantment'. When by the words of consecration it was claimed that the nature or properties of a thing were changed, then consecration became either an extraordinary miracle or a 'vain and impious conjuration'. There was no evidence in the New Testament that the apostles claimed to transform matter in this way. Catholicism used spurious and improper rituals in order to drive away 'phantasms, and imaginary spirits': the futile combated the non-existent.[51]

This apparently conventional Protestant character to Hobbes's rhetoric was, however, mostly misleading. Hobbes's radical materialism prevented him from following received views regarding superstitions and their relationship to the spiritual world. First, he dismissed with almost brutal certainty all tales of the 'supernatural'. Apparitions were typically figments of diseased imaginings, and apparently magical performances, even in the Old Testament, were nothing more than legerdemain and manipulation. Hobbes denied a priori the possibility of a genuine supernatural occurrence through the agency of spirits. This insistence would offer a standing invitation to later seventeenth-century investigators to prove him wrong, whether from scripture or from current experience. Secondly, Hobbes's denial that people could be 'possessed' by incorporeal spirits flew in the face of Protestant as well as Catholic readings of scripture. Protestants were accustomed to denounce the farrago of ritual and consecrated apparatus used in Catholic exorcisms: but it was quite another thing to claim that the evil spirits supposed to possess demoniacs did not exist at all. Thirdly and most dangerously for Hobbes's reputation as a theologian, his doctrine of corporeal spirits required him to be a mortalist. He claimed that the doctrine of the natural immortality of the souls was an import into Christianity from Greek philosophy. Human souls, according to Hobbes, could only be revived with their bodies at the end of time. He suggested that the alien, pre-Christian notion of 'incorporeal souls' had provoked the Catholic Church into inventing purgatory as a place to house these disembodied souls until the Last Judgement.[52] Here again, for many more conventional Protestants this theory, though by no means unprecedented in English Protestantism, represented several steps too far.[53] In Restoration England Hobbes for a brief period entertained somewhat exaggerated fears that he might be tried for heresy. In fact, the prominence given to Hobbes in general and *Leviathan* in particular ensured that he would be a preferred target of the demon- and spirit-mongers of Restoration England.

Other less gifted intellectuals than Hobbes also held and published heterodox views about spirits, and disturbed the discourse over what did or did not happen in the spiritual realm. One of the most interesting contributions to the radical end of the debate came from the hand of the sectarian leader Lodowicke Muggleton (1609–98). With John Reeve, he founded the modest but extraordinarily long-lived sect known as Muggletonianism, that became extinct only with the death of its last adherent in 1979.[54] In 1669 Muggleton published a substantial pamphlet on the story of the witch of Endor in I Samuel 28. Unlike Hobbes, Muggleton was no philosopher: his exegeses and reasonings derived from his knowledge of scripture and his resolute determination to read much of that scripture metaphorically. However, Muggleton shared Hobbes's conviction that life required physical embodiment. In fact, Muggleton went even further than Hobbes: he insisted that even God 'was spirit and body, in form like a Man, from eternity, and his spirit was never divided nor separated from his body, but they were both eternal'.[55] He did not shrink from insisting that human souls were naturally mortal; they were generated naturally when bodies were procreated; they died with the life of the body, and would be revived at the last day with no consciousness of the intervening period since death.[56]

Muggleton's mortalism equipped him to wield a brutal rationalist razor to the whole business of demonology, and in particular to the story of the witch of Endor. First, he held it to be an unscriptural conceit that any creature could subsist as a spirit without a body. When God through Christ or the prophets raised the dead, it was always as spirit and body together. The notion of the appearances of spirits of the dead was a 'vain conceit of most people'.[57] If ghosts were imaginary, so were incorporeal devils. Human reason alone 'hath conceived in his imagination, that God is a spirit without a body. Secondly, he conceiveth in his imagination that the Devil is a spirit flying in the air, which can neither be seen nor felt; yet this Devil or spirit without a body doth tempt man to evil, whereby man is punished, and the tempter he is escaped away without punishment.'[58] The whole notion of an incorporeal devil who was both bound in Hell and yet free to go about tempting people he ridiculed as a misguided conceit of human reason. So, regarding the biblical story of the witch of Endor, Muggleton concluded that the familiar spirit was the woman's own imagination, and the message that Saul heard was the voice of his own conscience recalling the words of Samuel. In other words, the entire story was a psychological metaphor for Saul's remorse and despair.[59] In witchcraft imagination fathered a 'familiar spirit' that was merely a product of the witch's own thought process.[60] In general, Muggleton concluded that the only devil was the human reason separated from the wisdom of God. 'There is no devil nor familiar spirit without them, as people do vainly imagine, but the devil and familiar spirit is all within them, and no where else.'[61] 'The imagination of reason the devil hath created its own soul in its own image and likeness.'[62]

Lodowicke Muggleton wielded strictly limited influence in Restoration England, and presented nothing like so large or so obvious a target to critics as Hobbes did. He argued in an elliptical and often very repetitive fashion, and tended to substitute assertion for demonstration or reasoning. Most of the defenders of the reality of spirits and witchcraft, even those who wrote at greatest length about the witch of Endor, did not trouble to refute him.[63] For those who sought to lower perceptions of the power of demons—and therefore, coincidentally, to dissuade the prosecution of witches—it was unfortunate that the treatises written tending to this effect often came from relatively inexperienced and not always competent disputants, whose arguments were mutually inconsistent and whose reasoning processes were often faulty. In contrast, the defenders of the 'invisible realm' often acted in concert, displayed considerable skill in disputation, and recruited evidence from a range of allegedly 'factual' testimonies that could not easily be refuted, as the next chapter will demonstrate.[64]

The problems that faced the sceptics on the issue of demonology are well illustrated by a work published anonymously in 1676, entitled *The Doctrine of Devils, Proved to be the grand Apostacy of these later Times*. The work is attributed either to Thomas Ady or to N. Orchard, and appeared in one English edition as well as a Dutch translation of 1691.[65] This work attempted to argue down the belief in spirits, and therefore the belief in witchcraft, on grounds drawn partly from scripture and partly from common sense. The author insisted, as his chief argument, that conventional demonology ascribed so much power to demons to achieve miraculous and prodigious effects in the world, that it diminished the splendour of Christ's incarnation and miracles, turning them into rather ordinary feats. To attribute such extraordinary power to evil spirits was, in effect, to turn them into deities and to worship them, at least in the sense that one ascribed power and pre-eminence to them. Demonology therefore (so the argument ran) was not only false but theologically repugnant: it was an 'apostasy' in so far as it denied the unique and supreme power of God.[66] On the face of this the argument seems to have been highly spurious. Medieval theologians had for long known perfectly well how to distinguish between true divine miracles and the 'marvels' produced by demons using natural means.[67] However, the author of *The Doctrine of Devils* had in mind, not the carefully sifted and analysed accounts of traditional demonology, but the much less scrupulously gathered tales drawn from the relatively unregulated world of the English witchcraft trials. As the author claimed:

This Doctrine of Devils tells us, That a Devil can turn himself into a Man or Woman, a Rat, Cat, or Dog at pleasure; and that a Witch can be any creature that she pleaseth to personate: They can cure Madmen, or any other sick Persons at distance; can walk and fly in the Air, yea ride in that fluid element, with Coach and six Horses; can raise Storms of a sudden, and allay them in an instant; can blast, not only a single Tree, but a whole Wood or Forrest; can turn a Town into Ashes in the twinkling of an eye; with a wry look can kill as many as he lists, and raise them again at his pleasure.[68]

The book's argument became plausible only because of the carelessness of its opponents. In their desperate quest to prove the reality of the spirit world, the opponents of 'Saducism' had searched the evidence of the trials of English witches without filtering the information through a theological mesh as their medieval predecessors would have done. Traditional demonologists knew better than to argue that demons, or indeed witches, could know the future with certainty, change people into animals, or raise the dead. Folk-belief did not so discriminate.

The Doctrine of Devils presented a range of other arguments. Probably with conscious intent, the author of the *Doctrine of Devils* echoed the treatise entitled *The apostasy of the latter times* written by Joseph Mede (1586–1638) and published posthumously in 1642. Mede had interpreted the prophecy in I Tim. 4: 1 as foretelling the worship of saints in Catholicism. He understood the 'doctrine of daemons' of the New Testament to refer to the veneration of inferior demigods in paganism. The last great 'apostasy' of the Christian Church was therefore to worship saints alongside God.[69] However, unlike this 1676 treatise, Mede had not deduced any unorthodox theory of evil spirits from his biblical exegesis. Like Mede, the anonymous author insisted that the 'doctrine of devils' foretold in I Tim. 4: 1 meant the teachings *about* devils (i.e. demonology) not teachings *by* devils: after all, who had ever seen a devil in a pulpit?[70] The author argued that the Bible knew nothing of witches making a pact with the devil to do harm; the words used in Hebrew scripture to mean a sorcerer, diviner, or witch could not justify the body of belief about such people then current in England.[71] This argument would trouble his opponents and provoke many angry squabbles over Hebrew words.[72] The supposedly 'universal consent' of past experience counted for nothing, since early modern witchcraft was a relatively recent construct, and many things hallowed by tradition, such as Catholic legends of saints, were now acknowledged as false.[73] Good physicians could diagnose all diseases 'without flying to that absurd Asylum of Ignorance, Laziness, Superstition, or (possibly some thing worse) Witchery, or Possession'.[74] This critique of demonology depended largely on biblical and theological arguments; it extracted (in a way that is sometimes not supposed to have happened) a critique of demonology from the critique of superstition already established in Protestant theology. However, it signally failed to capture the field.

The year after the appearance of *The Doctrine of Devils*, the physician and clergyman John Webster (1611–82) published a work entitled *The Displaying of Supposed Witchcraft*.[75] This book deliberately challenged those writers, chiefly Meric Casaubon and Joseph Glanvill, who had recently argued most strenuously for the reality of demons, apparitions, spirits, and witchcraft.[76] Though profoundly learned in medieval and Protestant scholastic theology, Webster wrote in a vehement, polemical style, giving no quarter to his opponents and leaving no space for compromise. Much of his text concerned witchcraft and witch-trials, topics peripheral to this particular study. However, there were several discussions of themes central to the debate over superstitions. Here Webster's metaphysic posed problems of its own. Webster held a curious mix of opinions: on the one hand he was a vehement Protestant scholastic, and knew the classic authors of reformed theology: he quoted Girolamo Zanchi particularly frequently. Some elements of Webster's arguments derived from fairly classic Protestant rhetoric. He attacked the notion of divine 'permission' to devils on the perfectly orthodox grounds of belief in providence. God did not simply give devils *carte blanche* to harass people (an opinion that Webster denounced as Arminian): on the contrary, every slightest action that evil spirits performed, though evil in itself, achieved some good purpose intended by God.[77] Many stories of spirits told in traditional Catholicism were undoubtedly confected to support belief in purgatory.[78] He accepted that 'miracles are totally ceased as not being any way necessary to confirm the Gospel, which is now established and settled'.[79]

On the other hand, Webster was well-read in the tradition of natural magic and deeply interested in the medical theories of the neo-Paracelsians, especially Johannes Baptista van Helmont (1579–1644). Webster's work sought to unpick most of the premises which underlay traditional demonology. First, he rejected the prevailing assumption that angels and demons were incorporeal. Like Hobbes, he concluded that they were corporeal, but made of a very rarefied, tenuous substance. They were thus immortal only by a specific divine gift, not by nature. Webster rejected any analogies between angelic spirits and human souls.[80] The whole thrust of his work tended to minimize the power and abilities of demons. Their knowledge, limited even before their fall, was much more so afterwards, as were their abilities. Nearly the only way that they could actually affect people was by inciting them to do wrong actions.[81] Demons thus became almost irrelevant to the practice of harmful sorcery, since such sorcery could occur only by the use of natural means such as poisons.[82] The demonic pact he dismissed as fictitious.[83] Many of the creatures of folklore like satyrs, fairies, or mermaids, which in previous centuries had been reclassified as demons, he actually explained away as mistaken reports of real creatures: orang-utans, pygmies, or sea mammals.[84]

Yet Webster was not a materialist like Hobbes. Many stories of the supernatural that were traditionally used to prove demons, tales of apparitions and prodigies, he explained by a curious and individual understanding of the natural world. When the ghosts of murder victims appeared to denounce their murderers, or their bodies bled after death, Webster concluded (after much speculation) either that God acted directly to cause the prodigy, or that the 'astral spirit' or 'sensitive soul' of a person might linger around the body after death and cause the apparition.[85] On charms and spells Webster evinced particular ambivalence. He absolutely rejected the idea that charms worked by the cooperation of demons. He flirted with the Paracelsian idea that the power of the imagination might achieve cures through healing spells. He recalled how as a physician in the North of England he found it necessary to tolerate people's beliefs in bewitchment, and to prescribe amulets so that their own belief would cure them. Cautiously, he considered that there might be some few, rare spells where the words actually contained a curative power, as some medical writers had speculated. However, 'what strange effects soever, that are true and real, that do follow upon the use of words, charms, characters, rhythms, and the like, we do confidently affirm, that they are effected by lawful and natural means, but withal that of this sort in this age, few or none are found out that are efficacious. But that error, credulity, ignorance, and superstition do put great force, and stress upon these things, when really they produce no effects at all.'[86]

Webster was an eccentric figure, who worked on the margins of respectable medicine and theology, though his arguments may appear hardly more fanciful than those of his much more respectable adversaries among the adepts of the Royal Society. He demonstrates most of all that the former consensus among Protestant theological writers about the interrelated subjects of superstition and demonology was breaking down into a confusion of beliefs by the third quarter of the seventeenth century. In the early 1690s there appeared at Amsterdam a much more substantial, more rigorously argued work of Protestant theological writing that mounted a frontal attack on the whole concept of demons and spirits. Balthasar Bekker (1634–98) was a Dutch reformed theologian, teacher, and pastor who served a succession of churches, finally becoming preacher in Amsterdam in 1680. He published a treatise on Cartesian philosophy in 1668: he remained all his life a critical but appreciative student of Descartes.[87] His commentary on the Heidelberg Catechism appeared in 1670, and briefly brought him under suspicion of Socinian sympathies. In 1683 he issued a treatise on comets, his first essay in an area frequently associated with the supernatural. In 1691–3 there appeared his massive, notorious four-part study of demons and witches entitled *The World Bewitched* (*De betoverde Weereld*).[88] This work was almost immediately translated into French and German, and in an abridged version into English.[89]

Bekker's work was so large and so closely argued that almost certainly more people discussed and appraised it than actually read it in its entirety. Bekker himself complained that it was taken for granted that he had simply applied the principles of Cartesian philosophy a priori to the subject of spirits. Descartes's philosophy—so it was supposed—postulated such radical disjunction between spirit and body, that the idea of disembodied spirits communicating with or acting on corporeal natures became unthinkable. As Bekker observed:

The Principle, they say I suppose is, that a Spirit cannot act upon a Body, nor upon other immaterial Spirits. That's the burthen of the Song, and what they make me say over and over every where, and is so confidently published, that even my Friends can scarce forbear crediting it. . . . Thence comes that every Body crys out so differently against me, some saying, that Descartes's Philosophy has spoiled me.[90]

He absolutely denied that he had made any such postulate a principle of his thought; though he did admit to *asking the question* of how such a disembodied spirit might act on a body, or indeed on another spirit.

There were, of course, good grounds to think Bekker a Cartesian, at least of some kind. However, the rhetorical and argumentative structure of his work was much more complex. Bekker insisted, first of all, that his critique relied upon scripture and reason, setting aside 'received wisdom or previous authorities'.[91] However, he absolutely rejected the suggestion that he was a sceptic, or fostered atheism. In particular he distanced himself from what he saw as the pantheism of Spinoza: he believed that this philosophy confused God and creation in a theologically unacceptable way.[92]

The first volume of his work took an ostensibly history-of-religions approach to the question. It reviewed how the doctrines of spirits arose in pagan religions, in the great monotheisms, and in Christianity both Catholic and Protestant. Bekker's primary argument was quite a simple one: the doctrine of 'spirits' originated with the minor deities and demigods of ancient paganism. Pagan magic and divination (which in essence were either natural or fraudulent) also derived from these cultural roots. Present-day paganism, by which Bekker meant the residual folk-beliefs of the peoples of northern Scandinavia, showed the same basic belief-structure.[93] Boldly and a little amateurishly, he then reviewed all the religious beliefs of the major peoples of the world and found basically the same themes: people believed in one supreme God, but habitually assigned parts of the management of human and natural affairs to minor deities or tutelary spirits of various kinds. He discerned this pattern of belief in Asia, Africa, and among the Native Americans.[94] Regarding the major Abrahamic faiths Bekker had to be slightly more careful. He argued that in both Judaism and Islam there had over time been a falling away from the primitive monotheistic beliefs of those religions. With beliefs in spirits there had arisen apocryphal traditions, occult lore, divination, and magic; he seemed, though, to suspect that Islam had suffered from this process rather less than Judaism.[95]

Turning to Christianity, Bekker tactically postponed the question of the essential or 'correct' teachings of Christianity and turned instead to a historical evaluation of its fallings-away from the truth. Quoting the early Fathers in detail, he had little difficulty in demonstrating that they held a wide variety of beliefs about angels and spirits, whether they were corporeal or not, and what their relationship was to human souls. All these ideas, he argued, derived from the intrusion of pagan philosophy into Christian teaching. The main thrust of his argument contended that there was no consensus in patristic 'demonology'; the Fathers had certainly not agreed with the views of contemporary demonologists. He concluded that the doctrine of spirits that established itself in Christianity derived largely from Manichaean dualism.[96] Turning to Roman Catholicism, Bekker more or less abandoned the mask of the religious historian and dissected the demonology found in the *Universal Magic* of the Jesuit Gaspar Schott (1608–66), published in the late 1650s.[97] Ingeniously and perhaps a little unscrupulously, Bekker demonstrated that Schott not only transmitted the full medieval heritage about evil angels, but also passed on the folklore of fairies, goblins and dwarves, spirits of water and woods, and so forth.[98] The implication was clear: the beliefs of learned 'demonology' were as pagan as the folk-beliefs that the demonologists had tried to domesticate and reinterpret. Regarding Protestants, Bekker admitted that many Protestants shared much of Catholic beliefs about spirits. However, he remarked that, because of the greater openness to diversity in Protestantism, one could not identify a single Protestant opinion on the subject. The educated differed from the mass of the people, but the educated also disagreed amongst themselves.[99] The persistent belief in spirits he ascribed to influences as diverse as the folk-tales told in childhood, the prevailing education in classical literature, the teachings of Origen, and Aristotelian metaphysics.[100]

In his second volume Bekker turned from a historical to an overtly biblical and theological approach. Hitherto he had not argued explicitly *that demons did not exist*: rather, he had shown as best he could that the belief in demons and spirits was a pagan invention, intruded into the world's monotheisms over centuries of theological decay and entropy, and never internally consistent. At the outset of book 2 he defined God as spirit, and as pure spirit: there was no validity in inferring the natures of spirits from the nature of God, since God and creatures had nothing in common as to their being. In the third chapter he positively asserted that it was inconsistent with the perfect sovereignty of God for such intermediate demigods or spirits to exist. Human souls were spirits, and indeed immortal spirits; but all other supposed 'spirits' were to be rejected.[101] Bekker explored at considerable length the scriptural lore of angels. Angels were messengers of God and worked by the power of God, but neither reason nor scripture gave any clear information regarding their nature and powers: indeed many biblical accounts of angels (good and bad) could equally well be intended to describe human messengers.[102] Scripture gave no support for the demonologists' claims about what evil spirits could do to people in their physical natures. In the story of the fall, 'nothing is said that ought to carry me to conclude, that the Devil himself can act immediately upon the Soul and Body of Man.' The temptations of Christ were plausibly argued by reformed theologians to have taken place in visions. Therefore, these accounts did not prove that Satan had (for instance) physically carried Christ to the pinnacle of the Temple or to a high mountain.[103] The stories of the expulsion of demons from the possessed proved nothing because, Bekker argued (with rather a bold stroke here), possession by 'daimonia' represented the contemporary description of mental illness, and had nothing to do with the devil, Satan, at all.[104] To drive out *daimonia* signified nothing more (or less) than miraculously to cure an extraordinary and otherwise incurable illness.

Bekker's third book utterly rejected the reality of the contracts with the devil supposedly entered into by witches, and took Joseph Glanvill to task at length for his claims in this area.[105] In general, Bekker argued that magic and sorcery were entirely ineffective, though practitioners of such things might be justly punished in law for their idolatry and even more for their deception and charlatanry.[106] In the fourth book Bekker, at the risk of excessive length, took on the analysis of reports and stories of apparitions, bewitchments, and spiritual creatures—the empirical data on which the late seventeenth-century virtuosi had insisted with such pertinacity. The stories of apparitions and possessions were, for Bekker, all the product of misunderstandings, misapprehensions or deliberate impostures. He was convinced that even celebrated possession cases such as that at Loudun were frauds.[107] From the seventeenth chapter onwards Bekker evaluated a whole array of popular superstitious beliefs concerning spirit-beings, apparitions, and feats of divination, including More and Glanvill's favourite case of the haunted house at Tedworth. He confidently claimed to 'prove that all the Discourses and Narrations made upon that subject, are altogether false'.[108]

After all these sceptical arguments one might ask (and people did) what Bekker actually thought about the Devil. He showed himself slightly evasive on this point: he concentrated rather on the commonly received errors about the power of the Devil and the existence of minor spirits. He aimed to dethrone Satan from what he clearly regarded as an exaggerated position in much contemporary theology. The mainsprings of his determination in this respect appear to have been partly his conviction that contemporary witch-trials were grossly unjust and misguided, and partly real theological objections to a demonology that set up rival deities to the one God. 'I banish from the Universe that abominable Creature to chain him in Hell, that Jesus, our Supream King, may more powerfully and securely reign. Though his Empire that is to endure to the last day, is likewise to subsist in the midst of his Enemies, that are here upon Earth, that is amongst the People of the Devil, or such in whom Sin keeps still *imprinted the Image of the Devil.*'[109]

From the perspective of this study of the theologies of superstition, Bekker's contribution achieved a critical change in the relationship between learned demonology and popular folklore. Previously, among Catholics and Protestants alike, learned demonology defined, analysed, corrected, and reinterpreted what popular 'superstitions' were. Fairies and dwarves were not fairies: they were mischievous demons to be avoided. Magical charms and divination were effective only as far as demons gave them spurious plausibility. Bekker argued, in complete contrast, that *learned demonology and popular superstitions were essentially equivalent.* 'Superstition' consisted in believing that the universe was full of *any* kind of spiritual beings out to cause mischief or to seek alliances with evilly disposed people.

There are no natural Reasons, nor Revelations in the Holy Writ, no certain experiments, that give us cause to ascribe to wicked Spirits, all the Operations and effects that are generally supposed to proceed from the Devil or from Men, his Confederates.... 'Tis not difficult to show, how *wrongfully such a superstition is cherished and increased*, instead of moderating it, or even rooting it out, if possible.... I charge with that fault, Clergy Men and Divines, more than Princes and Magistrates; because the former are more particularly obliged to meditate upon those matters, to watch over the preservation of the Souls committed to their care, and to attempt the cure of a Disease that is so contagious, and feeds upon the very Bowels.[110]

Bekker's work, eccentric and extreme as it was perceived to be, nevertheless developed and extrapolated from arguments that had lain latent in the metaphysics of reformed Protestantism almost from its beginnings. Protestant theology embraced a vision of an utterly sovereign God. It cultivated the belief, as was shown earlier, in rigorous, specific providentialism. It habitually mocked the claims of Catholic liturgy and culture to embody sacred power in consecrated things. It refused to view the world as a cosmic battleground between good and evil spiritual forces, to be fought out with *sacramentalia*, spells, and exorcisms. To that extent, Bekker drew out of Protestant metaphysics the potentialities that had been blocked, so long as most Protestants had remained Aristotelians. Bekker lost no opportunity to evoke and to echo the traditional critique of Catholicism as a species of superstition, and to present his argument as part of that tradition. However, that was not how contemporaries saw the matter. Bekker's book drew howls of protest and criticism from many of his fellow reformed divines in the Netherlands. He was forced to defend himself before the presbytery of Alkmaar and was deposed from his preachership.[111] His first edition provoked a short and fiery rebuttal from Jakob Schuts entitled *Bekker Bewitched*, accusing him of unbelief as well as ineptitude.[112] Some critics accused him of denying any belief in the Devil at all, or even more outrageously of denying that God influenced the lives of people.

Despite the sound and fury that they provoked, the critiques of 'superstitious' demonology in the seventeenth-century Protestant world were thoroughly disjointed, inconsistent, and disconnected. The respective metaphysics of a Hobbes, Webster, or Bekker might seem similar in some respects, but they represented different world-views in search of a new set of principles. In spite of this diffuseness, such views appear to have engendered a real fear that the 'invisible world' was disappearing before people's eyes. It is now time to turn to those thinkers and writers who challenged 'atheism', 'Saducism', and 'Hobbism' in an increasingly furious effort to preserve the reality of the realm of spirits. Their impact on traditional approaches to superstition proved to be almost as chaotic and confusing as that of those whom they attacked.

17

Defending the 'Invisible World': The Campaign against 'Saducism'

For centuries a relatively secure consensus about the existence and even the natures of invisible spirits had prevailed among theological thinkers. That consensus had underpinned the critique of superstitions, even when, as with Protestant attacks on Catholic consecrations, the critique divided Europe's religious thinkers into armed camps. By the mid-seventeenth century, this whole realm of being appeared to have come under sustained intellectual attack from new philosophies. The challenge provoked a response, though not immediately. During the last quarter of the seventeenth century, several important publications purported to show that the world of spirits, demons, ghosts, fairies, and, of course, witches, was real and threatening. The literature on this subject reached a climax in the third edition of *Saducismus Triumphatus* (1688), compiled out of the papers of Henry More and Joseph Glanvill.[1]

It would be an easy and quite mistaken interpretation to read this genre of writing as mere reactionary medievalism. Traditional superstition-treatises had taken the *existence* of superstitious rites and non-human spirits for granted. The challenge in the fourteenth or fifteenth century was to prove that such beings and rites were evil rather than helpful. The anti-Saducism treatises, in contrast, sought to prove that spirits, divination, ghosts, and sorcery really existed in the first place, in the face of what was claimed to be a systematic and 'atheistical' disbelief in spirits among their contemporaries. Consorting with spirits might be evil, and witchcraft certainly was, but evil was no longer the primary focus. Theological fastidiousness was replaced by insatiable and often indiscriminate curiosity. The anti-Saducists often broke the old rules. They did not always conform to the former post-Aristotelian conventions about what demons could or could not do. They certainly did not conform—despite being, in most cases, Anglican clergy—to the traditional Protestant line on the cessation of miracles or the impossibility of real appearances of the spirits of the dead. Reversing the traditional order of priorities, this school of thought actively sought out stories of the weird and the supernatural from traditional culture. They then took the empirical data as received fact, rather than sifting and reinterpreting it (as medieval demonologists had done) in accordance with certain metaphysical presuppositions. No less than their opponents, the anti-Saducists testified to the breakdown of received certainties.

Homes and Casaubon

Most of the following chapter will analyse two particularly emblematic and important works in this genre, More and Glanvill's *Saducismus Triumphatus* and John Aubrey's *Miscellanies*, the latter one of the most remarkable treatises on superstitions to emerge from the early modern era. However, to highlight the differences between the traditional demonological lore and the literature that appeared from 1680 onwards, brief attention will be paid to two other earlier treatises from slightly different ideological perspectives. In 1650 Nathaniel Homes (1599–1678), an independent minister first ordained as an Anglican cleric and a dissenter after the Restoration, published his *Daemonologie*.[2] Homes wrote principally as an apocalyptic prophet, who saw the signs of the last days all around him. Homes, like others, saw his own age as the one foretold in I Tim. 4: 1, when people would forsake the truth and listen to 'doctrines of devils':[3] in this case he identified the 'doctrines of devils' as consisting in charms and enchantments, and especially in the arts of divination. A particular bugbear of his appears to have been judicial astrology, 'that diabolicall Astrologie which is practised by some, in these all-evill times (in sorts of sins) to the great prejudice of truth and godlinesse'.[4] He wished that the interregnum parliament might outlaw it (as the same body did in fact criminalize fornication and adultery).

In classic Protestant vein, Homes saw the deception of the devil in all allegedly supernatural occurrences. He told a somewhat apocryphal

story that Luther saw a vision of the crucified Christ on the wall while
he was praying on Good Friday. Luther denounced the apparition as
a vision of the devil, declaring that he knew no picture of Christ but
his Word and Sacraments, and the vision vanished.[5] Homes proposed a
fairly conventional Protestant theory of demons, derived from medieval
antecedents, emphasizing that the devil lost nothing of his practical skill at
his fall, and spoke through apparitions such as the serpent in the garden
and Samuel in the enchantment of the witch of Endor.[6] He went on
to insist that all dealers in the diabolical arts had some sort of compact
or covenant with Satan.[7] While such a covenant might be explicit, it
could also be merely implicit, through the use of charms: all this precisely
echoed the late medieval analysis.[8] Somewhat leniently, Homes allowed
that among the simple clients of soothsayers, 'they are not reall charmings or
Inchantings in them that use them superstitiously through simple ignorance,
having no Compact expresly or implicitely with the Devil, with desire
and confidence to act from him; although by these they be in a faire way,
as going to Inchanters, is the next doore to Inchanting.'[9] Homes showed
himself progressively more and more interested in those manifestations of
superstition that seemed harmless, but gave the devils space to deceive and
seduce, as in the watching of omens or the use of superstitious divinations.[10]
Worst of all, perhaps, were those sectaries who believed that they heard
voices of direct divine inspiration, since

to turne away from the certaine word, to uncertaine voyces, what and whence
they are, must needs be from the Devil . . . these pretended Protestants that doe (as
I may say in a Figure) give the right hand to voyces, I know not what nor whence,
leaving the Word of God as a surer and more effectuall divine instituted meanes of
salvation, then a voyce from Heaven (2 Pet. 1. 19. Gal. 1. 8, 9. Luke 16. 10.) doe
herein follow Diabolicall lyes.[11]

Homes, in short, combined his demonological critique of superstitious
divinations, astrology included, with a vehement theological condemnation
of sectarian claims to direct inspiration. He adhered to a strict classically
Protestant line on a number of test cases, insisting for instance that the
apparition to the witch of Endor was certainly a devil.[12] His ambition was
a traditional one: to prove that superstitious divinations were not innocent
or respectable, but demonic.

    With the treatises entitled *Of Credulity and Incredulity, in Things Natural,
Civil, and Divine*, two surviving parts of a three-part project by the
classical scholar and ecclesiastic Meric Casaubon (1599–1671) published

in 1668–70, one enters a quite different world, though it is still not quite the world of More and Glanvill.[13] Casaubon wrote his *Of Credulity and Incredulity* towards the end of his life, after a period of illness in the 1660s, and the work presents a bricolage of enormously recondite erudition combined with mostly second-hand (and occasionally first-hand) supernatural tales. Casaubon wrote to provoke reflection and wonderment at the variety of the world, rather than to make a polemical point. He compiled the work largely from memory at a time when poor health restricted his ability to check references. Consequently he adopted a sort of stream-of-consciousness approach, entirely abandoning chapter divisions, and wandering back and forth between related topics without any obvious structure. He warned against both excessive belief and excessive disbelief, although he considered scepticism more of a threat to late seventeenth century thought than excessive credulousness. He feared that 'one prime foundation of Atheism, as by many ancient, and late, is observed, [is] the not believing the existence of spiritual essences, whether good, or bad; separate, or united.'[14] He took particular exception to what he saw as the dogmatic insistence of some authors who (he claimed) wished to be thought philosophers because of their rigorous and dogmatic disbelief in anything supernatural. In his own writing he frequently expressed ambivalence about certain issues, or considered that belief or disbelief might be equally arguable about aspects of a reported event.[15] 'For to believe every thing, that is reported or written, because it is possible, or not at all strange; in case it be true; doth argue as much weakness, as to believe nothing, but what our selves have seen.'[16]

Casaubon seems to have been insatiably curious about allegedly marvellous and strange things that happened in the world, and were related by such respectable and credible witnesses that it was perverse to deny them. Protesting rather too much, he insisted. 'I profess again seriously, as I have done before, this Discourse was never undertaken by me, to tell the Reader strange stories, though true; which might have made it much more both easie and voluminous.'[17] He expressed a fascination with natural monsters, sympathies and antipathies, the occult qualities of things, celestial influences, miracles, chemistry, and alchemy.[18] Casaubon devoted a considerable amount of the work to evaluating tales of magical healing. Such healing usually combined (possibly natural) herbal cures with superstitious and therefore demonic verbal formulae. He adhered to traditional demonological standards. A cure that was *per se* ineffective could only work by implicit demonic pact; even a demonic cure must work by divine permission. He exploited his prodigious learning to compare accounts such as the famous incident of herbal exorcism reported by Josephus with the stories from much more recent demonologists.[19] He showed himself to be fascinated by stories of people who could charm animals by mere words, 'whispering' not only horses but dogs, cats, and even bulls.[20] His work formed a sort of quarry of exotic stories of people able to live long without food, magical transportation of crops from one field to another, marks left in human bodies by thunder, snakes' eggs, the cure of scorpions' bites, and so forth. The latter part of his treatise on credulity of natural things comprised a fairly traditional superstition-treatise on methods of divination, followed by a rather diffuse discussion of prodigies.[21]

In general—and here Casaubon differed from those who wrote just a few years later—he avoided polemic or special pleading. However, in one area Casaubon did allow himself to argue a case. He insisted that disbelief in witches and their activities inevitably led to disbelief in spirits, and thus to outright atheism. He criticized vehemently those authors perceived to be sceptics about witchcraft. He noted (correctly) that Weyer believed in evil spirits and the delusions they caused, but denied the pact and therefore the culpability of witches. Casaubon responded that this made almost any crime excusable by the same argument. Reginald Scot, on the other hand, he bragged of not having read at all, though he quoted some alleged evidence of his lack of learning. Unlike Glanvill, Casaubon did not dilate on, or quote at length, the supposed evidence of vernacular witch-trials. He was more interested in the demonological theory than the alleged testimonies. He regarded it as unthinkable that a purely imaginary crime should have been prosecuted successfully for so long.[22] In this rhetorical stance Casaubon marked the transition between the old superstition-literature and the new. In some parts of his work he sought to show that magical healing was not benign or morally neutral, but dangerous meddling with forbidden forces; in others he tried to argue down the view that all talk of spirits and demons was mere nonsense. A little like Hamlet to Horatio, he argued that 'many things happen supernaturally, which are above the sphere and activity of the believed, and beloved atomes, and can be referred to no other cause, but the operations of Demons, or evil Spirits: which once secured; Atheism hath lost its greatest prop, and the mockers and scoffers of the time, the chiefest object of their confidence and boasting.'[23] In this latter vein, he could go so far as to suggest that a little superstition might actually be a better thing than its opposite:

I think I have read in Julius Scaliger, a man of singular as learning, so piety; some where; (I find it so in my papers, but not the place quoted) *Melior superstitio* (so it do not proceed to a breach of any particular command of Gods revealed word: so I understand it) *nimiâ sobrietate, qua facile degenerat in Atheismum*: that is, Better is superstition, sometimes, than too much sobriety, (or cautelousness) which is apt soon to degenerate into Atheism. At another time, perchance, I should not think so well of it: But now when Atheism doth so prevail, and true Piety, under the name of superstition, subject to derision; I think the advice is not amiss.[24]

More and Glanvill

Homes and Casaubon were individual, not to say isolated writers. The circle of Henry More (1614–87) and Joseph Glanvill (1636–80) was quite the opposite. Here a group of scholar-virtuosi, several of them, like More and Glanvill, Fellows of the Royal Society, maintained an ongoing dialogue over several decades with clerics, judges, and various correspondents about the supernatural, and contributed to the mutually reinforcing character of their various works. Henry More, a Cambridge academic and Anglican priest-theologian, was one of the most heavyweight philosophical minds among the group known as the Cambridge Platonists. His interest in spirits grew out of his enterprise to demonstrate the immortality of the soul and the existence of God, and his strongest contributions to the debate were in the area of abstract principles.[25] Joseph Glanvill, significantly younger than More, embraced many of his ideas but had a more practical and polemical turn of theological mind than his mentor. An admirer of Descartes in his early years, Glanvill turned against materialistic philosophy, probably under More's influence. For Glanvill, experimental philosophy, including the gathering of well-authenticated data, would help to refute materialism and atheism.[26] Glanvill was naturally the collector of stories, and the polemicist who sought to beat down his opponents.

The approach of the More–Glanvill circle would turn the debate on superstition in a radically new direction. Rather than seeking to dampen down beliefs in weird or marvellous occurrences and to confine them within a strict metaphysical system, the investigators of the Royal Society believed in collecting the data first, and then speculating about what interpretation might fit the available testimonies. The largest monument to this school of thought is the book entitled *Saducismus Triumphatus*, published in increasingly elaborate editions from 1681 onwards.[27] In the form that it reached by the 1688 edition after the deaths of both its authors, it represented the work of many hands. It was edited anonymously out of several of More and Glanvill's previous publications, papers, and correspondence. It also incorporated written accounts presented either as witness testimonies at trials or as letters sent to one or other of the principal authors. *Saducismus Triumphatus* was by no means the only work of its kind: substantial contributions to the same general effect appeared around the same time from Richard Bovet,[28] Nathaniel Crouch,[29] and the celebrated independent pastor and spiritual writer Richard Baxter.[30] However, More and Glanvill's work remained the most influential, and it can represent its genre for the purposes of this brief analysis.

Because of its complex genesis, *Saducismus Triumphatus* was an oddly organized and in some ways incoherent work, and themes must be extracted from its text in order to identify its message. The first theme that commands attention is the authors' empirical method. Evidence always took precedence over its interpretation according to theory. Henry More cited at great length the story of a spectral apparition of a murdered woman to a miller near the place she was murdered in County Durham in 1632. This story, drawn ironically from Webster's much-despised sceptical work on witchcraft, fitted no theological interpretation of ghosts. More nevertheless declared it to be 'so considerable, that I make mention of it in my Scholia on my Immortality of the Soul . . . I know by long experience, that nothing rouzes them so out of that dull Lethargy of Atheism and Saducism, as Narrations of this kind.'[31] Glanvill, usually the more pragmatic of the two, gave an even more explicit statement of this approach, answering the foreseen objection of sceptics to the impossibility of some of the prodigies reported in the book:

So that the utmost that any mans reason in the world can amount to in this particular, is only this, That he cannot conceive how such things can be performed; which only argues the weakness and imperfection of our knowledge and apprehensions, not the impossibility of those performances: and we can no more from hence form an Argument against them, than against the most ordinary effects in Nature. . . . Matters of fact well proved ought not to be denied, because we cannot conceive how they can be performed. Nor is it a reasonable method of inference, first to presume the thing impossible, and thence to conclude, that the fact cannot be proved. On the contrary, we should judge of the action by the evidence, and not the evidence by the measures of our fancies about the action. . . . For in resolving natural Phænomena, we can only assign the probable causes, shewing how things may be, not presuming how they are.[32]

One ought to pause a little over Glanvill's method here. Previous demonological theory had insisted quite explicitly that certain things were impossible for spirits, such as transforming one creature into another or raising the dead. Any reports of such things therefore had to result from illusions. The concept that demons could cause illusions armed earlier superstition-theorists to discount or 'reinterpret' any narrative that purported to relate something impossible. More and Glanvill cast these presuppositions out of the window. They largely rejected the concept of something being a priori impossible; they also generally (though not consistently) discounted illusion as a plausible explanation for strange phenomena.[33] Typically, *Saducismus* treated an account as credible if it was reported by a sufficient number of respectable witnesses, not suspect of religious enthusiasm, mental instability, habitual mendacity, or 'credulity'. Their concept of what made a 'respectable' witness had of course a social component, but it was not only aristocratic or bourgeois witnesses who were deemed worthy of credit. Essentially anyone thought credible in a lawcourt seems to have passed More and Glanvill's criteria for truthfulness.

More and Glanvill, having turned aside from conventional Aristotelian metaphysics, devised their own theories of spirits. Recondite as this subject may seem, it was absolutely critical to their response to 'superstitious' phenomena. *Saducismus Triumphatus* handled the issue of spirits in two quite distinct ways. First, the 1688 edition incorporated a translation of part of More's *Enchiridion Metaphysicum* regarding the nature of spirits.[34] More's exposition was not easy to follow, not least because he began by attacking opponents in technical detail—what he called removing 'vast Mounds of Darkness'—before expounding his own ideas. However, in essence he defined spirit as the opposite of body. Bodily substance was made up of particles of matter such that it could be divided into smaller aggregations; it was also impenetrable, in the sense that matter could not pass into or through other matter. Spirit, More claimed, was essentially the opposite. A spirit was an 'immaterial substance intrinsically endued with life and the faculty of motion': it was characterized by being indivisible and 'indiscerpible', that is, it could not be chopped up into smaller parts, and by being penetrable, that is, able to enter into or pass through matter or other spirits.[35] He also postulated a certain quality in spirits, which he called the 'the Hylopathy of Spirits' that allowed them to influence and control matter. Thus he responded to one of the objections of some Cartesians.[36]

More's philosophy of spirits, though arcane, had its own internal logic and sharpened the distinction between material and immaterial. Glanvill, on the other hand, made remarks on the subject quite inconsistent with More's theories. At various points in the book he discussed the nature of spirits and angels. When discussing witches' familiars in his 'Considerations' on witchcraft, Glanvill speculated that 'the Genii . . . are recreated by the reeks and vapours of humane blood, and the spirits that proceed from them: which supposal . . . is not unlikely . . . And that they are not perfectly abstract from all body and matter . . . there are several considerable Arguments I could alledge to render it exceeding probable.'[37] In other words, Glanvill resurrected the Platonic idea that spirits might, after all, be corporeal. Angels were called spirits, 'And Spirit imports as much Substance as Body, though without gross bulk.'[38] He went on to suggest a most bizarre speculation, that the reason why spirits were only rarely seen was because it must cause them pain to compress their bodies to a sufficient density to become visible:

'Tis a very hard and painful thing for them, to force their thin and tenuous Bodies into a visible consistence, and such shapes as are necessary for their designs in their correspondencies with Witches. For in this action their Bodies must needs be exceedingly compress'd, which cannot well be without a painful sense. And this is perhaps a reason why there are so few Apparitions, and why appearing Spirits are commonly in such haste to be gone.[39]

Elsewhere in the work Glanvill repeated this suggestion that spirits were not entirely incorporeal, while rebutting Webster's comments on the witch of Endor.[40] In general, Glanvill's demonology proved almost infinitely flexible. He supposed that lesser demons and even evil ghosts might serve as familiars with witches as well as 'senior' demons.[41] It remained unclear just how the lesser demons differed from the greater, or why a 'departed humane Spirit, forsaken of God and goodness' would be allowed to roam about the world at all.

Not only did More and Glanvill abandon nearly all the traditional restraints on speculation about the natures of spirits: they also challenged a host of principles that had been inherited by the Church of England, with the other reformed churches, since the Reformation. Glanvill had a most curious notion about the nature of divine permission and divine providence. In place of Calvin's minutely provident God, Glanvill thought it undignified for God to manage all of creation directly; more probably

God supervised human affairs indirectly through the ministry of angels, even if it was not necessary for them to appear visibly.[42] Rather than assuming, as most Protestant thinkers had done, that the acts of demons were controlled by a meticulous divine plan and permission, Glanvill seemed to think that demonic malice was partly constrained by a sort of self-government among the demons themselves: 'we may suppose that Laws of their own may prohibit their unlicens'd injuries ... as Generals forbid Plunder, not out of love to their Enemies, but in order to their own Success.' This theory explained why there was not even more demonic malice evident than was actually the case.[43] He questioned explicitly whether miracles had indeed ceased as reformed orthodoxy claimed. He cited the extraordinary healing practices of the 'Irish stroker', the charismatic healer Valentine Greatrakes, as proof that 'such Miracles as are only strange, and unaccountable performances, above the common methods of Art or Nature, are not ceas'd.' The authority that he quoted, however, a letter from the dean of Chester, observed of Greatrakes only that 'there is something in it more than ordinary; but I am convinc'd it is not miraculous.'[44] Glanvill saved the appearances by affirming that demonic marvels were not miracles, but created a new third category of marvellous cures, not quite divine miracles, but marvels that might happen by divine gift or some unknown physical principle.

Saducismus Triumphatus showed itself most theologically and philosophically creative in the matter of ghosts and apparitions of the dead. Protestant orthodoxy held categorically that since purgatory did not exist, all claims of the apparitions of spirits of the departed were demonic apparitions, illusions, or priestly frauds.[45] Consequently, theologians stated categorically that the apparition conjured by the witch of Endor could not possibly have been the real Samuel.[46] More and Glanvill both took exactly the opposite view to traditional theology. As he mercilessly pilloried the unfortunate Webster for his exegesis of the story of Saul and the witch, Henry More insisted that the apparition was indeed the soul of Samuel. He claimed 'that departed Souls, as other Spirits, have ... both a faculty and a right to move of themselves, provided there be no express Law against such ... they have a Power of appearing in their own personal shapes to whom there is occasion.' This power, he argued, was natural and not miraculous.[47] Glanvill similarly asserted that the apparition was indeed Samuel, and saw no reason why blessed spirits should not be able to appear voluntarily and take an interest in human affairs, though not (of course) as being compelled by the demonic magic of a sorcerer. Some ghosts who appeared might even have been those called angels in scripture.[48] Both More and Glanvill re-expounded the story of Samuel at great length and to the same general effect, though chiefly to ridicule the often far-fetched speculations of sceptics who tried to claim that nothing supernatural was implied in the scriptural story.[49]

Having argued that ghosts or apparitions of the souls of the dead might truly appear, and apparently by their own volition, the authors of *Saducismus* then documented a substantial body of recent instances when spirits of the departed had done exactly that. Fourteen 'relations' in the book described at considerable length how ghosts of the dead appeared to denounce their murderers, to confess to otherwise undetected crimes, to prophesy the future fate of those to whom they appeared, or to warn their friends to behave better in this life. Most interestingly, in several of the accounts recorded in the work, ordinary people to whom the ghosts first appeared questioned whether the apparition was really a ghost or a demon, some of them insisting obstinately that it must be a demon.[50] More dramatic than the apparitions of ghosts, however, was the celebrated case of the Tedworth poltergeist. For several years in the early 1660s the house of John Mompesson, of Tedworth in Wiltshire, experienced a range of disturbances and bizarre happenings that caused considerable distress to its inhabitants and generated great curiosity among Glanvill and his circle.[51] In March 1661 Mompesson had confiscated a drum from a vagrant drummer at Ludgershall (presumably a disbanded ex-soldier) and shortly afterwards began to hear mysterious drumming noises all around his own house. Mysterious lights appeared, beds and bed linen were pulled around, and some of the children of the family were thoroughly frightened.

Several of the details of this account stubbornly refused to tally with conventional (or any) demonology. One night the people in the house spread ashes over a haunted bedroom, to find claw-marks, incomprehensible writing, and 'circles and scratches in the ashes' in the morning. The demon was apparently corporeal.[52] The 'demon' seemed to be frightened by being threatened with swords or pistols, so at times weapons were used to calm it down; on one occasion after a pistol was fired in the spirit's direction a drop of blood was found on the floor.[53] While Glanvill visited the place himself to investigate, most of the account he drew from the owner, of whom he wrote 'Mr. Mompesson is a Gentleman, of whose truth in this account, I have not the least ground of suspicion, he being neither vain nor credulous, but a discreet, sagacious and manly person.'[54] Nothing seemed to enrage More and Glanvill more than the repeatedly circulating rumour, put about by Webster among others, that the whole Tedworth apparition had been revealed as a fraud, even that Glanvill had confessed that it was such.[55] The story of the Tedworth haunting had a long afterlife. In 1692 the Dutch preacher Jacobus Koelman issued a Dutch translation of the story.[56] In 1715 Joseph Addison published his play entitled *The Drummer; or, the Haunted House. A comedy*, which went through many editions through the eighteenth century. The original narrative was then reprinted as a pamphlet in English in 1716.[57] Meanwhile, *Saducismus* included ten other stories of poltergeists or similar spirits troubling houses elsewhere in the British Isles.[58]

Saducismus Triumphatus included relatively little on the subject of demonic possession. Prima facie this absence appears surprising. However, given the difficulty experienced in the previous century or so in identifying genuine possession, and all the theological disputes that such stories had provoked, More and Glanvill may have chosen to be wary on this subject. The one relation in the collection explicitly concerned with possession, the sixth part of the continuation, proves the rule by its exceptionality. It describes the possession of the ironically named Robert Churchman, a Quaker, by an evil spirit. During his possession the Quaker displayed knowledge of scripture passages that he had never known or studied before, having trusted to interior light. The intention of the possessing demon was apparently to drive Churchman back to the Quakers and away from the Church of England, whose services he had started to attend under the persuasion of his parish priest.[59]

Finally and most notoriously, *Saducismus Triumphatus* affirmed and insist-ed on the reality of witches, as men and women who made compacts with the devil and performed prodigious acts of malefice, zoomorphic trans-formations, and extraordinary transportations from one place to another. Although the work dealt with many other subjects, witchcraft presented the most obvious and apparently the most compelling factual evidence for the reality of spirits—and even on one occasion for the separate existence of the human soul[60]—because based on testimonies recorded under oath in courts of law. *Saducismus* became popularly known as 'Glanvill on witches' because of the spectacular witchcraft stories included in the collection.[61] It is doubtful whether the publication of the book had much effect on the actual trials of witches in England, which dwindled away under the influ-ence of a succession of highly sceptical judges. One of the last celebrated cases, the trial of Jane Wenham, led to her conviction in 1712 despite the judge's doubts: she was promptly reprieved.[62] It seems more likely, in fact, that *Saducismus Triumphatus* depended for its evidence on the continuing thread of witch prosecutions under a small number of magistrates who remained fascinated by the subject. Robert Hunt, JP for the county of Somerset, apparently supplied Glanvill with a significant proportion of the witch testimonies from England included in the collection, and conducted some of the preliminary investigations himself.[63] Since the cases documented in the book consisted chiefly of unedited narrations and trial testimonies, folkloric elements such as the alleged transformation of witches into small animals were incorporated in the accounts. Only exceptionally did the authors edit or reinterpret what was reported.[64] Symptoms typical of the Paracelsian understanding of bewitchment, such as the voiding by the bewitched of hard or sharp objects invisibly introduced into the body, appeared frequently.[65] Most curiously of all, the authors reported in some detail the folkloric methods used to diagnose and reverse bewitchment. Rather than condemning such counter-magical ploys unambiguously, the editors remarked that 'the benignity of Providence is to be acknowledged in that the villanies of witchcraft lie obnoxious to such a natural or ratified way of discoveries and counter-practices as these.'[66]

Aubrey

In 1696 a work entitled *Miscellanies upon Various Subjects* was published from the papers of the antiquarian and biographer John Aubrey FRS (1626–97). This collection largely completed the dismantling of *any* intellectual or theological basis for the analysis and critique of superstitions.[67] Yet in a sense Aubrey's treatise, more precisely focused on issues of superstition than *Saducismus Triumphatus*, grew out of the same empirical cast of mind, the same refusal to sort and sift evidence by dogmatic criteria, that had animated the authors of the former work. The *Miscellanies* marked the culmination of many years' inquiry into folk culture, an inquiry evidently marked by no particular religious or polemical cast except insatiable curiosity.[68] In the late 1680s Aubrey had compiled a manuscript treatise entitled 'Remaines of gentilisme and Judaisme'. This work embodied the same methodology as the *Miscellanies*, in so far as Aubrey believed that contemporary folk-beliefs could best be understood by reference to their nearest analogues in classical antiquity.[69]

Miscellanies presented a rather random and intriguing collection of weird and surprising phenomena, generally without analysis, explanation, or critique. Aubrey discussed 'fatalities' at length, meaning circumstances in which particular days, times, places, or things had proved to be spectacularly unlucky. This included discussion of the 'Egyptian Days', although his list drawn from 'an old Romish prayer book' differed from Delrio's.[70] Most of the work comprised reports of various kinds of supernatural communications and insights, usually unsought by those who received them. Portents and omens occurred before significant events in nations, especially the fall of monarchies or monarchs. People received insights about future events in dreams: Aubrey even described how he himself saw in a dream the profile of the island of St Helena before he arrived there, and subsequently reported the vision to the Royal Society.[71] Captain Henry Bell had a dream that foretold that he would have leisure (it turned out to be in a debtors' prison) to translate Luther's *Table Talk* into English.[72] Aubrey related some of the stories of informative ghosts from *Saducismus* and a few others reported by Elias Ashmole.[73] Richard Napier, a quack physician known to Ashmole, practised medicine with the aid of angels.[74] More unusually, Aubrey reported stories from Wales and Scotland that had not formed part of the received lore on superstitions. In Wales, so Aubrey learned from Richard Baxter, mysterious lights known as 'corpse-candles' appeared to light the way towards their graves for people about to die.[75] In parts of Scotland (Aubrey's information came chiefly from the Moray and Beauly Firth areas, though the phenomenon was known across the Highlands) people were gifted or cursed with 'second sight' by which they could foresee the future, predict the outcomes of illnesses, and describe events far distant.[76]

Aubrey also reported stories of magical divination and even witchcraft, though for a correspondent of Glanvill and Baxter he showed very restrained interest in these phenomena. Women used methods of divination to see their future husbands. The word 'abracadabra' could be used as an amulet against illness, and Aubrey helpfully provided a diagram for drawing it up. Various superstitious cures were described, often with the proviso that they must be performed under the correct astral signs. Various folk-remedies against hostile sorcery were reported, including the since long-familiar one involving a shed horseshoe found by chance.[77] Demonic spirits occasionally lifted people in the air, not just voluntary witches but also the horrified victims of bewitchment. A story, deemed 'fabulous' (mythical) by Aubrey's correspondent, reported the charm ('Horse and Hattock') supposedly used by Scottish witches to initiate magical flight. A child tried using the spell to make his top fly away into the distance, and succeeded.[78]

Compared to More and Glanvill, Aubrey showed little interest in theorizing about demons, and even less in engaging in polemics with sceptical writers. The bulk of his work majestically ignored one of the core principles of traditional demonology, that spirits, especially evil spirits, could not know the future with certainty. Nearly all his stories of apparitions, portents, and presages would have fallen foul of the theological principles of earlier decades. However, Aubrey was not interested in passing judgement or crafting a philosophy about the phenomena that he reported. As with his antiquarian investigations into stone circles, or his natural history of Wiltshire, he simply collected the evidence that seemed interesting, and used his network of correspondents to discern what seemed the most intriguing and authenticated data. Aubrey stood in the same tradition as a small number of Renaissance collectors of esoteric lore, such as Pierre Breslay, Simone Majoli, or even Girolamo Cardano.[79] The vital difference is that the earlier collectors of the exotic usually incurred the suspicion of the theological authorities of their day. By the 1690s the loudest theological voices—at least in England and elsewhere in Protestant Europe—were actually *encouraging* the collecting of whatever stories might prove the existence of the 'invisible world' of spirits.

Clearly, the 'anti-Saducist' movement of the late seventeenth century did not simply perpetuate or defend the medieval demonological world-view, let alone its Protestant equivalent. More and Glanvill drew the accusation of crypto-Catholicism or Arminianism from some of their opponents,[80] but their abandonment of traditional demonology went much further than rejecting Protestant providentialism, the cessation of miracles, or disbelief in ghosts. Medieval demonology had imposed a whole set of restraints on the abilities of invisible spirits: on that basis it condemned as 'superstitious' the belief that evil spirits could (for instance) heal serious diseases or accurately foretell the future. The anti-Saducists abandoned the Aristotelian metaphysic that had domesticated and contained popular beliefs about the spirit world: in its place they put a strange brew of Neoplatonism, astrology, chemical speculation, empiricism, or even a complete lack of theoretical principles. This whole movement did not *continue* the medieval and early modern discourse over superstition; it actually *discarded* it in the name of empirical research, so as to disprove the Hobbists and Cartesians.

Therefore, the sceptical thinkers in the previous chapter and the credulous ones in this chapter impacted the metaphysical analysis of superstition in ways far more similar than has been thought. Between them, the sceptics and the credulous completely dismantled the long-standing architecture of the theological critique of superstitions, one group by arguing that almost nothing was real, and the other by insisting that almost anything could be real if the evidence seemed plausible enough. More and Glanvill's views seemed at the time to command the field in English religious thought, though within a generation or two they would become obsolete among the educated. Their very inclusiveness and eclecticism, supposed to convince doubters, only exposed them to the greater ridicule and satire. By a bizarre irony, it would be among the Methodists that the views of these latitudinarian and anti-Calvinist Anglicans would have the longest afterlife.[81]

18

Towards the Enlightenment

Within barely two generations the debate on superstitions opened up still further and transformed itself again. In the sixteenth century the label of 'superstition' had flown back and forth as an insult in inter-confessional polemics. In the seventeenth century 'superstitions' had become entangled in debates over new ways to explain the workings of the cosmos. In the eighteenth century 'superstition' became a shorthand term used by disputants about the role of religion in society, and its relationship to philosophy and ethics. These transformations opened the way, ultimately, for sceptics to use 'superstition' as a pejorative term to denote *any* religious notion or belief. However, the trajectory by which 'superstition' changed its meaning followed anything but a straightforward course. The basic meaning of the term remained the same as before: superstition was religion gone bad, religion practised wrongly. In one sense, changing understandings of 'superstition' simply reflected changing values and priorities: as assumptions about how religion might 'go wrong' changed, the applications of this rather loosely pejorative term shifted and adjusted themselves.

However, even that explanation is too simple. The eighteenth century did not discard the heritage of previous centuries wholesale, whatever the statements of propagandists for the 'Enlightenment' might at times imply. Some 'superstition-treatises' emerged from the movement known as 'baroque Catholicism' that embodied a firm belief in the continuity of traditional metaphysics and traditional pastoral theology. In Protestant Europe, the seventeenth-century debate over the reality of spirits continued into the era of the Enlightenment with no clearly discernible winners or losers. The persistence of beliefs in demons and witches in southern

Germany exacerbated the split between traditional baroque Catholics and the rationalist movement known as 'reform Catholicism'. The exponents and propagandists of *lumières* drew heavily from previous debates. They cited Protestants and Catholic predecessors alike as they broadened the critique of 'superstition' to include all claims to locate the divine in the arbitrary and irrational, whether these comprised material manifestations or metaphysical dogmas. 'Superstition' represented for them the belief in a God unworthy of a rational, enlightened philosopher. In the course of these disputes a new form of rhetoric entered the discourse. Rather than appealing directly to metaphysical reasoning, the disputants increasingly used satire and ridicule as a ploy against the credulous and the traditionalists.

Baroque Catholicism at its most rational: Thiers and his successors

In 1679 the first edition appeared of the *Treatise on Superstitions according to Holy Scripture, the Decrees of the Councils and the Opinions of the Holy Fathers and Theologians*, compiled by the French pastoral theologian and cleric Jean-Baptiste Thiers (1636–1703), curé of the country parish of Champrond-en-Gâtine.[1] A much fuller, definitive four-volume edition of the work emerged in 1697–1704, and in this form the work was republished in 1712 and within a collection of similar works in 1733–6 and subsequently.[2] Thiers took controversial and polemical stances on a whole range of subjects, but, despite some official disapproval, his work continued to be read and republished through the eighteenth century. It has been widely used as a repertoire of rural religious beliefs and practices ever since.[3] The work exemplifies traditional and innovative features in proto-Enlightenment thought in almost equal and confusing measure. First of all, Catholic theologians remained firmly committed to the continuity of traditional pastoral theology and traditional metaphysics. Thiers acknowledged little or nothing of the furious debates conducted across the Channel over the nature of spirits, and was as committed to the validity of precedent traditions as his radical Protestant counterparts were not.

Thiers's first book comprised an enormously detailed list of conciliar decrees against superstition, including numerous French provincial councils.[4] It concluded with a set of criteria for distinguishing superstitions, drawn almost entirely from the late medieval demonological analysis. A rite

was superstitious if the effects it claimed to produce could not naturally be
expected from the things that were done, and if it was therefore suspect of
a pact, whether overt or tacit, with demonic forces.[5] The remainder of the
first volume, in five further books, presented a fairly traditional taxonomy
of different forms of superstitious practice. Worship became superstitious
if it was directed to an inappropriate object—such as a false relic—or to
an excessive or superfluous degree.[6] Idolatry, diabolical magic, and sorcery
were of course forbidden.[7] The third to sixth books of the first volume dealt
respectively with divinations, 'vain observances', phylacteries and amulets,
and incantations for curing illnesses and other purposes.[8] Thiers demonstrated his traditionalism by his profound and largely unquestioning respect
for precedent authority, in the form of previous councils and theologians.
He manifested his conservatism also by his uncomplicated acceptance of
the existence of demons. Yet one could not quite write in the 1670s or
1690s as though nothing had changed. He declared that to wish to prove
the existence of black, or demonic, magic, was to 'try to brighten the sun'.[9]
However, having just deemed the task quite redundant, he proceeded to
explain how demonic magic was documented at great length in law, in
theology, and in history.

Thiers then confronted the fact that the *parlement* of Paris no longer
accepted the existence of witchcraft, and had in effect ceased to endorse
such prosecutions.[10] He responded that the decree of the *parlement* should
not take precedence over the established scripture, laws, and doctrine
of the Church. He cited without criticism some of the most extreme
demonological texts from previous centuries. He then affirmed the reality
of *malefice*, of harmful sorcery, and enumerated its many forms.[11] He warned
the faithful against an extraordinarily long list of preservative charms and
rituals commonly used to defend against hostile sorcery or bewitchment,
such as using herbs dug in a particular way, spitting on the shoes or
one's chest, or using wolf-skin as an amulet.[12] Despite these concessions to
tradition, quite evidently Thiers did not regard witchcraft or its prosecution
as a worthwhile subject to pursue. His discussion of hostile sorcery took
minimal space in an otherwise extensive work. He made no attempt
to fight the sort of rearguard action in defence of witch-trials that was
being mounted in England or Germany around the same period. His chief
concern seems to have been pastoral and practical. The rural populace
served by the Catholic priesthood believed in hostile sorcery; priests must
try to dissuade them from using superstitious means of self-protection.

Thiers showed his more modernizing, enlightened side in other ways also. As a product of the movement to achieve a more educated parish clergy, Thiers regarded 'superstition' as a disease afflicting especially the less educated rural lower classes. His approach manifested the social distance that the post-Tridentine push for a learned clergy had established between parish priests and their peoples.[13] Moreover, he approached the task of enumerating popular superstitions with a vast encyclopedic curiosity. Previous theological critics of superstition had habitually listed a few examples only: Weyer's extended list of charms, borrowed by Delrio, had been an exception.[14] Even in the first volume of the *Traité* Thiers tended to list instances more heavily than previous authors; from the second to the fourth volume this tendency manifested itself to excess. He corresponded with fellow clergy to request even more ample documentation than his own extensive reading and experience provided.[15] Thiers was not an ethnographer: he made no attempt to locate beliefs within their cultural context, or to distinguish between current and ancient practices.[16] Yet his curiosity was indefatigable.

Thiers differed from earlier Catholic superstition-critics in a third important aspect. From the second volume onwards he organized his analysis and polemic around those particular superstitious rituals, customs, or beliefs that adhered to the sacraments of the Church. Having dismissed the traditional themes of divination and incantation in the first volume, he focused intensely and at prodigious length on purging the ecclesiastical cult of apocryphal accretions imposed on it by popular credulity. It was superstitious to think that a pregnant woman who received the Eucharist thereby baptized her unborn infant such that it needed no further baptism.[17] It was superstitious to insist on communicating in a large rather than a small wafer, or to bury a Eucharistic wafer with the dead, or to use unconsecrated hosts as though they were a medicine.[18] Like the sixteenth-century Spanish academic Pedro Ciruelo, Thiers disapproved of the many multiple masses supposed to bring special benefits to the dead, of which the most famous was the Trental of St Gregory.[19] Thiers devoted an entire book—the seventh—to the subject of the infinite variety of indulgences offered in the Catholic Church, especially those attached to particular devotions, relics, or altars. Several of these claimed, wrongly, infallibly to deliver souls from purgatory or to ensure that they never went there.[20] To this extent Thiers's work somewhat resembled earlier works on casuistry; some practices that encrusted the cult might be truly superstitious, others indifferent or acceptable.[21] Rarely, however, had a casuistic treatment of superstitions been compiled in such obsessive detail.

Thiers wrote the most copious of the superstition-treatises to emerge from late baroque Catholicism, but by no means the only one. Pierre Lebrun (1661–1729), an Oratorian priest, published in 1702 a *Critical History of Superstitious Practices: which have seduced the people and embarrassed the learned.*[22] Lebrun partook rather more of the spirit of the scientific virtuosi. He warned against excessive incredulity as well as credulity. He focused on attempting a scientific analysis of the divining rod, and decided that anything that relied on the special powers of the individual using it must risk involving the demonic. He then discussed at length tests for discerning witchcraft, then listed charms and other aspects of superstition in a manner similar to Thiers and his medieval forebears.[23] Like Thiers, Lebrun subscribed to fairly traditional beliefs about demons. So did Dom Augustin Calmet (1672–1757), who published *Dissertations* on the apparitions of angels, demons, and spirits and on returning spirits and vampires in 1746.[24] Calmet's work dwelt chiefly on the problem apparitions of spirits and departed souls, and on the allied question of whether the bodies of dead people might rise again. However, Calmet inevitably became drawn into the realm of broader superstition-critique: he wrote about magic, witchcraft, and demons as well as ghosts and vampires. Calmet concluded that most stories were fables or illusions, and of course affirmed that only God could truly raise the dead. However, he belonged to the traditional Catholic culture when he insisted that angels and spirits had their own realm of free action to influence the sublunary world.[25] He belonged to an even more traditional realm when he speculated that goblins 'seem ... to be of a middle nature between good and evil angels; for it is very seldom that they do any harm'.[26]

Similarly, abbé Nicolas Lenglet Dufresnoy (1674–1755) incorporated much accumulated lore in his multi-part *Collections of Dissertations, Ancient and Modern, on Apparitions, Visions and Dreams* of 1751.[27] The relative credulity of these Catholic collectors and commentators—even when they were far more selective in what they believed than, say, the early Fellows of the Royal Society—would provoke the satirical amusement of later Enlightenment authors. Abbé Laurent Bordelon, in his satirical novel about beliefs in superstition, listed Thiers's work on superstitions as a source and quoted it extensively. He remarked of the book that 'it contains a prodigious Mass of Learning, employ'd to prove that Superstitious Practices are condemnable. 'Twere to be wish'd that such a Learned Man had labour'd in the same manner to shew that they are fallacious in their Pretences.'[28]

Of Lebrun, Voltaire remarked that 'he wishes to oppose the absurdity of witchcraft, yet he himself commits the absurdity of believing in its power.'[29] Unlike the seventeenth-century English anti-Saducists, the Catholic clerics of the early Enlightenment largely stayed within the metaphysical limits laid down in medieval demonology: but that did not spare them the ridicule of the *philosophes*.

Protestants and Catholics on spirits, ghosts, witches, and possession

Just as Catholic writers in France continued but subtly modified the traditional demonological discourses about charms, apparitions, and spirits, so in England the theological and metaphysical debates of the seventeenth century continued into the eighteenth. In Protestant Europe, scripture typically commanded authority in a way that tradition did not; so many of the continuing debates concerned the interpretation of scriptural texts used to prove the existence of spirits and the real possibility of superstitious performances. In 1715–16 one Richard Boulton, who may be identical with the author of a number of medical works and controversial pieces, published in two volumes *A Compleat History of Magick, Sorcery, and Witchcraft*.[30] The work of itself added little to the debate except provocation. It comprised a large collection of trial testimonies in witchcraft cases, in the manner of *Saducismus Triumphatus*. In between these accounts were interleaved chapters on the history of witchcraft, on apparitions and ghosts appearing by night, on apparitions of spirits, and the misfortunes of those who consulted them.[31] The work had an air of plagiarism about it, and probably derived much of its material from Glanvill and Aubrey. However, it did provoke an important rejoinder and began one of the last witchcraft debates in the early eighteenth century. In 1718 Francis Hutchinson (1660–1739), then a parish priest at Bury St Edmunds, published his *Historical Essay Concerning Witchcraft*.[32] Hutchinson had already revealed himself as something of a rationalist in his attack on the 'pretended spirit of prophecy' that had attracted notice in parts of Europe from 1688 onwards, chiefly in the form of Catholic prophecies against Protestantism.[33]

Most of Hutchinson's argument sought to prove the falsity of accusations of witchcraft, and to discredit those who sought to revive trials for the crime in England, following his encounter with one of the last defendants in 1712.[34] The rhetoric of Hutchinson's piece rather resembled that of Reginald Scot over a century earlier. Rather than taking on the scholastic demonologies, he looked down with disdain on the unruly and folkloric details found in the trials of witches in English and Scottish lawcourts. He demonstrated to his own satisfaction that the celebrated witch-trials so prized by Glanvill and Boulton, were misguided either through misunderstanding or deliberate fraud. He could also claim that the methods popularly used to detect witchcraft, such as 'swimming', were in themselves 'superstitious' and moreover criminal in English law. He applauded the judicial decision in 1712 that made 'swimming' a witch an act of murder if the victim died.[35] Following on earlier sceptical writers, Hutchinson argued that witchcraft in the Bible did not resemble that described by Boulton and others, though he also warned against fruitless debates over the precise meaning of Hebrew words.[36] Needless to add, Hutchinson's piece did not end the debate. Richard Boulton responded in 1722 with *The Possibility and Reality of Magick, Sorcery, and Witchcraft, demonstrated*.[37] A year later an émigré Huguenot and Anglican cleric named Jacques Daillon, who styled himself the Comte du Lude, published a reply to Boulton in defence of Hutchinson.[38] In 1726 Hutchinson's treatise appeared in a German translation with a preface from the sceptical legal authority on witch-trials, Christian Thomasius.[39]

As the disputes about witches gradually dwindled, another furious debate arose over the interpretation of spirit possession, and by implication over the existence of 'spirits' in general. In 1737 Arthur Ashley Sykes (*c*.1684–1756), Cambridge graduate and rector of Rayleigh in Essex, published his *An Enquiry into the Meaning of Demoniacks in the New Testament*.[40] Sykes deployed arguments that were by this stage becoming somewhat familiar in contemporary Protestant theology of a critical tendency. First, he argued that Christian beliefs had become contaminated by the ideas of classical paganism. The ancient Greeks and Romans had believed that the souls of dead people became δαιμόνια (daimonia), and that such spirits could be the 'true causes of extraordinary distempers amongst Mankind' including diseases such as epilepsy.[41] Severe diseases were attributed to the actions of these evil spirits; so, when Christ 'cast out demons', it signified that he cured otherwise hopeless diseases that had supposedly been inflicted by such demons. Sykes then demonstrated that the ancient belief, that a demon caused such an illness, was of course false, and the idea of 'demonic possession' was therefore both a misunderstanding and a relic of paganism.[42] This heavily exegetical approach inevitably provoked reams of controversy. It was not difficult for critics to argue that scripture did in fact conceive of personal demons possessing, rather than just afflicting, human beings. The concept of applying critical distance to scripture and interpreting its language as rooted in its cultural context, though known in the eighteenth century, posed many risks for Protestant exegetes.[43] Sykes's pamphlet provoked a huge storm of controversy, and over a dozen other pamphlets were published either for or against his arguments within the succeeding two years.[44]

Perhaps the most interesting impact of the English debate occurred when it was revived in Protestant and Catholic Germany in the third quarter of the century. In 1760 the great Lutheran theologian of Halle, Johann Salomo Semler, published a short treatise on demoniacs in the New Testament.[45] Semler borrowed Sykes's arguments more or less wholesale. He argued that the idea that demons could 'possess' someone and thereby cause illness and insanity derived from pagan and antique Jewish mythology. The disciples adopted the language and concepts of their time, and supposed that Jesus really cast out an actual demon when he cured someone afflicted with a terrible disease. This reading preserved the notion of a Gospel miracle, since Jesus' healing was itself miraculous even if the presence of the 'demon' was imaginary.[46] In the mid-1770s Semler's views on demons spilled over from the mostly Protestant north of Germany to the Catholic south. A parish priest named Johann Joseph Gassner acquired notoriety as a charismatic religious healer of people suffering from diseases allegedly inflicted by demonic possession.[47] Gassner divided both Protestants and Catholics, some insisting that his cures were true and real, others convinced that he was at best misguided. Semler became drawn into the debate as the most prominent Protestant demonologist of the age.

A reform Catholic theologian, the Theatine priest Ferdinand Sterzinger, also attacked the procedures used in Gassner's exorcisms. He objected in particular to so-called probative exorcisms. In these the healer-exorcist asked the demon inside the person to give a spectacular sign of its presence: he thus aggravated the patient's symptoms before relieving them by the expulsion of the demon.[48] Unlike the Protestants, Sterzinger did not entirely deny the existence or power of demons, but he interpreted the traditional understanding of possession in the narrowest possible sense. Only those afflicted people who showed the very specific symptoms of possession laid down in the 1614 *Rituale Romanum*, such as the use of languages previously unknown to them or the wielding of superhuman strength, could be deemed to be possessed.[49] Catholic rationalists such as Sterzinger deployed different exegetical tools and applied different assumptions from their Protestant counterparts. However, they argued to a very similar end result. They believed that demonic possession always or nearly always equalled mental or physical illness, and that to think that it was caused by the presence of an indwelling, intelligent, incorporeal evil spirit was itself a 'superstitious' opinion. However, these theological debaters shared one premise in common with earlier seventeenth-century rationalists. They remained committed to the principle of authority, whether authoritative scripture or authoritative Church. Reason remained a tool with which to interpret the sacred texts, rather than an independent source of insight. Among thinkers closer to the heart of 'Enlightened' thought, the order of priorities would be reversed. Reason would suggest independent criteria by which to discern what the creator might or might not choose to do in the universe, and further redefine what should be included within the term 'superstition'.

Proto-Enlightenment thought: Bayle and the Comet

Pierre Bayle (1647–1706), academic theologian and philosophical contro-versialist, moved the debate on superstitions on to a new level, several generations before some of the theological disputants discussed in the last section. He became most famous for his massive critical *Dictionnaire*, as well as for his trenchant and fervently argued polemic against religious persecution in his *Commentaire Philosophique*.[50] As a reformed Protestant Huguenot, Bayle experienced at first hand the evils produced by state-sponsored religious persecution, as well as by doctrinaire restraints on thought. He taught in the French Protestant academy in Sedan, but on its suppression took refuge in Rotterdam, there to suffer constant criticism from his fellow Huguenot, Pierre Jurieu. This context of fierce criticism and state persecution contributed to Bayle's chronic tendency to wrap and overlay his ideas under layers of irony, anonymity, reported speech, or attribution to others of some of his own ideas. The vastness and richness of Bayle's work makes a thorough treatment at this stage of a broad outline survey impractical. However, one fairly compact work, well known to the debaters about superstition in the eighteenth century, fairly commands attention: Bayle's *Various Thoughts on the Occasion of a Comet*, published first in 1682 and definitively in 1683.[51]

In the cosmos as understood before Copernicus and Kepler, comets were believed to be deeply significant. Ptolemaic cosmology envisaged the universe as a hollow sphere, with the earth at the centre and the planetary bodies revolving around it. At the outermost edges were the concentric spheres of the heavens; the 'firmament' of fixed stars was the innermost of these and the one visible from earth. The earth was both the centre and the low point of creation, the domain of the fall, sin, decay, and corruption. The heavens were presumed to be naturally perfect and unchangeable, as their greater proximity to the dwelling of God and the angels implied.[52] Therefore, whenever something did appear to disrupt the perceived perfection and stability of the heavens, it was assumed that this event presented an intentional and deliberate sign from the Almighty, usually a sign of dire warning of misfortunes to come. Appearances of novas, which were quite rare, and comets, which were quite frequent, aroused concern and speculation beyond the circles of professional astrologers. Philipp Melanchthon, an amateur speculator about astrology rather than an astrologer, expressed real concern about the appearance of a comet (later recognized as what we now know as Halley's comet) in 1531.[53]

Pierre Bayle wrote his treatise in the wake of the appearance of a comet in Europe from November 1680 into the following January. This comet occasioned the by now conventional flood of cheap print pamphlets prompted by any perceived prodigy or portent. Several of these predicted, in a range of self-serving ways, political disruptions and disasters to the states and kingdoms of Europe. Historical treatises claimed that after each appearance of a comet terrible and momentous things had happened.[54] Apocalyptic Protestant preachers such as Increase Mather (1639–1723) preached and wrote pieces with titles like *Heaven's Alarm to the World*.[55] Works of this kind abounded particularly in England and Germany, though fear of comets was discerned in France as well.[56] Among philosophical and scientific investigators the notion was already current that comets might simply be planetary objects that were only visible for small parts of their orbit.[57] However, only after the appearance of the comet that bears his name in 1682 would Edmund Halley conclude that the periodic orbits and reappearance of comets could be demonstrated experimentally; he published his results only after 1705. The accuracy of his predictions was not established until 1758–9, after Halley's death.[58] The astrological and portentous understanding of comets still prevailed in the 1680s. The study of portents and marvels was not classified as a 'superstition' by the learned in Protestant or Catholic Europe. Indeed, Kaspar Peucer's treatise on divination treated the study of marvels as a legitimate investigation of the purposes of God.[59]

Bayle therefore displayed some boldness in challenging this very broad if loose consensus that comets portended something, even though there was never any agreement as to what that something was. He published his *Thoughts* in the form of a series of letters supposedly written by a moderate and thoughtful French Catholic to a doctor of the Sorbonne. The anonymity of the treatise and the disguising of his theological views enabled him to disavow aspects of the arguments later, but there was little doubt over the main thrust of his argument. Bayle challenged the wonder- and portent-mongers not in the realm of science, but of theology. He asked whether it was rational to regard comets as portents on religious grounds. There was no plausible *natural* reason why the appearance of a comet should cause, or be associated with, particularly dire events in the world, any more than was the case with an eclipse of the sun: both were naturally harmless.[60] Therefore, if comets 'signified' dire events to come without being the natural causes of those events, they must necessarily be instituted as miraculous signs by God, who alone knew the future with certainty.[61] Yet comets gave an extremely imprecise and inefficient guide to future events. Effective presages ought to be clear, exceptional, and highly visible; comets were intermittent but quite common, and were often very hard to see for any save professional astronomers.[62] Moreover, God could hardly be expected to perform a major miracle knowing that the only foreseeable consequence was that people might commit even worse sins than before. Since most of humanity were idolaters, and even more had been so in the past, all that previous comets could have done was to confirm people in their bad habits.[63] Furthermore, comets were supposedly indiscriminate and general signs of misfortune; yet rarely indeed did misfortune to one people not also mean good fortune or at least opportunities to another.[64] On purely rational grounds, therefore, comets could not be divine signs, since that would require God to be at best obscure, at worst a promoter of sins and a liar.

Bayle also deployed arguments from history in order to assimilate belief in comets to a whole range of other ancient beliefs. The belief in the portentous nature of comets was 'an old superstition of the pagans, introduced and preserved in Christianity by the predisposition in favour of antiquity'.[65] Bayle showed with little difficulty that comets and other astral signs had been exploited quite cynically in classical times by political leaders and their panegyrists, sometimes in contradictory ways.[66] Early Christians, he argued (here following a typical Protestant argument developed more than a century before by Bullinger), absorbed great chunks of classical culture and lore into their belief-systems, removing only the explicitly idolatrous aspects.[67] Consequently, the belief about comets belonged to this same classical baggage that was imported into Christianity, and was indeed a type of superstition in itself. It was not condemned in antiquity like some others, but was inherently superstitious nevertheless.[68] Protestants who had criticized papal superstitions had failed to include the inspection of prodigies with the other kinds, as Bayle observed in a passage very critical of Kaspar Peucer and others of his ilk.[69] He mocked the persistent notion of lucky and unlucky days, lucky and unlucky names, and other sub-pagan beliefs. To criticize these was relatively traditional in the theological critique of superstitions, though ironically Bayle denounced the investigation of 'fatalities' just as John Aubrey was enthusiastically collecting them.[70]

Bayle developed in the *Thoughts* a profounder and more important argument that anticipated the developed ideas of the eighteenth-century Enlightenment. He turned against the conventional argument that opposed the work of nature and the work of God. He rejected the whole notion that a 'prerogative instance' or abnormality in nature was a special sign of the presence of the divine.[71] Previously, those who wished to assimilate abnormal happenings to 'nature' had usually incurred the suspicion that they denied miracles and therefore the action of God. Bayle argued that nature showed God acting according to the laws that the divine will had instituted; therefore the works of nature were the works of God just as much as any allegedly 'miraculous' manifestations.[72] A misbirth or a monster was a natural occurrence, not a prodigy or a miracle; indeed, God would need to perform a miracle to prevent such abnormalities from occurring.[73] In principle, Bayle saw the hand of the divine in the regular and ordered working of nature. 'Nothing gives us a loftier idea of a monarch than seeing that, having wisely established a law, he maintains it strictly in regard to all without permitting particular prejudice or the interested recommendations of a favourite to bring any restriction thereto.'[74] God, the supreme lawgiver, had least need of all to violate laws already established by the divinity. This argument would find its most famous echo in the article 'Miracles' in Voltaire's *Philosophical Dictionary*. Voltaire summarized, as it were in reported speech, the arguments of some 'physicists' that it was absurd to suppose that God needed to subvert the order of nature, 'to disorder the mechanism in order to make it work better'. To suppose that God worked miracles was to insult God, to imagine that the Almighty could not work out the divine plan without making adjustments that breached the natural laws.[75] Bayle was not, of course, Voltaire. Nevertheless, he initiated the line of argument that turned any attribution to God of an arbitrary, specific, or exceptional use of power into a 'superstition'. If God suffuses the whole everyday business of the physical world, then God is not confined to the exceptional.

Bayle, notoriously, resisted classification and deliberately made it difficult to pin him down to one set of opinions. Elements in the *Thoughts* echoed very conservative beliefs, while other sections were astonishingly bold. Unlike other Protestant modernizers, Bayle allowed the existence of demons to pass without explicit comment. The devil fulfilled for him the role that he had played since the later Luther: he perverted true religion and took pleasure in aggravating human beings' innate and persistent tendency to twist and deprave their worship. Demons were, for instance, responsible for bogus oracles or bad religion.[76] On the other hand, Bayle demolished one of the stock arguments of cautious theists by hypothesizing that atheism might make for better citizens than idolatry. Bayle borrowed extensively from Plutarch's critique of vain religion, though he rejected some aspects of his argument. He claimed that the evidence simply did not support the belief that any religion was better than none.[77] Depending on one's taste or preference, Bayle was either the most extreme of the Protestant providentialists or one of the earliest deists. In either case, his notorious little treatise on the comet brought the whole business of inspecting marvels and special providences within the scope of the superstition-critique.

The rhetoric of ridicule from Shaftesbury to Voltaire

One misunderstands the eighteenth century if one views its responses to superstition solely in terms of learned metaphysical arguments. The philosophical disintegration of the seventeenth century had left the metaphysicians no secure ground on which to argue. All kinds of things might be possible; it was no longer satisfactory to argue that ghosts, portents, or miraculous cures could not exist simply because they did not fit the prevailing theology. Argument from authoritative scripture offered no better route to agreement, since it buried one in tendentious and tedious exegesis of doubtful passages or obscure Hebrew words. If one even deigned, for instance, to engage someone like Glanvill in debate over evidence of an apparition, one had in a sense sold the argument out before it began. Many of the more radical disputants resorted to satire and ridicule rather than syllogism. In an atmosphere where there was less to fear from ecclesiastical authoritarianism, the first generation of what one might call religious journalists employed mockery in place of reason, or as an adjunct to it.[78] An articulate exponent of the value of reasoned ridicule in the debates over religion was Anthony Ashley Cooper, third Earl of Shaftesbury (1671–1713). In the 1700s Shaftesbury assembled a collection of essays that appeared in 1711 under the title *Characteristicks of Men, Manners, Opinions, Times.*[79] The first of these essays, 'On Enthusiasm', appeared first in 1708. It argued at length and with considerable philosophical erudition for the value of ridicule, and formed a sort of *Praise of Folly* for the early Enlightenment. Shaftesbury remarked that in the ancient world visionaries and enthusiasts were tolerated, but so were philosophers: while some sects joined with the 'superstition and enthusiasm of the times', others, more sceptical, stood out against it. So everyone benefited from the resulting free flow of ideas.[80] In his 'Essay on the Freedom of Wit and Humour' Shaftesbury explained that he took ridicule seriously enough to use it with responsibility. ''Tis in reality a serious study, to learn to temper and regulate that humour which Nature has given us, as a more lenitive remedy against vice, and a kind of specifick against superstition and melancholy delusion.'[81] In a sense the satirists appealed to an instinctive sense of the way the world worked that lay below the claims of metaphysics. In any event, ridicule of 'superstition' entered the debate in the late seventeenth and early eighteenth century, and has never really left it.

Though not directly addressed to the issue of popular superstitions, the satirical piece entitled *The Count of Gabalis*, written by the abbé Nicolas-Pierre-Henri Montfaucon de Villars (1635–73) helped to popularize the deliberate use of ridicule as a means to handle overwrought investigations into metaphysical mysteries.[82] The work claimed to satirize Kabbalism and the beliefs of the Rosicrucians about spirits, which allegedly included the system of belief in nymphs, sylphs, salamanders, gnomes, and demons, inherited from Paracelsus.[83] The preface to the English edition of 1680 observed that

the secret sciences of the Cabal, are of the number of those Chymaeras, to which we give most Authority, when we dispute against them soberly; . . . we should not therefore undertake to baffle and destroy them, but by jeering . . . the secret sciences are dangerous, if we meddle not with them in such a manner, as may inspire us with contempt against them; by painting out their ridiculous mysteries, and preventing the world's losing time in search after them.[84]

The text narrated a series of bizarre encounters between the narrator and the Count of Gabalis, an apparently distinguished individual who nevertheless related extraordinary tales of meetings and associations with spirit-creatures.[85]

However, the most copious and—in a certain manner—scholarly satire against superstitions in general came from the pen of the abbé Laurent Bordelon (1653–1730) in the form of the *History of the Ridiculous Extravagancies of Monsieur Oufle*. This work appeared in French in 1710 and was almost immediately translated and published in English in the following year.[86] *Monsieur Oufle* began with a premise almost certainly derived from Cervantes' *Don Quixote*. Its eponymous central character, a prosperous and leisured individual, suffered from the permanent obsession with reading every possible work of literature on the subject of magic, witchcraft, demonology, and superstition, and believing all of the most fantastic claims made for it. The novel's plot revolved around the misadventures that M. Oufle's obsessions and delusions provoked, and the attempts of various members of his large and diverse household either to restore him to common sense or to exploit his fantasies to their own advantage. In the most genuinely comic episode of the novel, after a dinner and much wine Oufle discovers a carnival costume including a bear's head and decides to scare his wife with it. In this way he hopes to shock her out of her sceptical attitude to werewolves and such beliefs. However, rather than calling on his wife Oufle simply falls asleep; wakened by the breaking of a chamber-pot in the room above, he sees himself in the mirror, still wearing the bear's head, and thinks that he has really been turned into a werewolf. He rushes out into the street and begins to howl like a wolf, chasing and frightening everyone in sight, until members of his family capture him and take him home in a coach.[87]

In the remainder of the work Bordelon depicted the confusion created in Oufle's family life by his doubts about his wife's fidelity and his attempts to use divination to discover whether she was faithful or not. He followed that with the chaos created when an astrological horoscope suggested that the contented Oufle ought to be a great lover, and Oufle insisted on falling in love without the slightest idea as to why or with whom.[88] Thereafter the pedantic aspects of Bordelon's project—for despite the satire his purpose was definitely quite serious—rather took over from the comic. Oufle delivers a long, reference-encumbered speech in defence of the existence of apparitions, to be met with a rebuttal from his sceptical brother Noncrede.[89] A figure claiming to be Oufle's 'genius' writes a lengthy and futile treatise to try to dissuade him from using judicial astrology.[90] The second part consisted largely of extensive discourses between the various characters for and against the existence and supposed powers of devils.[91] Bordelon remembered his literary objectives towards the end, when he depicted Oufle as convinced that small animals and butterflies were really demons in disguise, and conceiving the farcical belief that his horse was bewitched.[92] His son borrows his father's horse without permission and over-exhausts it; the following morning it is unwell, and Oufle remembers a long stare given the horse the previous day by an old woman. Oufle goes to confront the woman to ask her to remove the supposed bewitchment of the horse. They argue, and to counter her magic he steals her watch, at which she protests loudly to the family. The conniving son admits his illicit riding of the horse, and the 'witch' becomes a good friend to Oufle's wife. 'The Horse, after some days rest, recover'd his former Strength; and Monsieur Oufle continued as whimsical and superstitious as ever.'[93]

Bordelon's purpose clearly encompassed more than mere entertainment. He included in the work an extensive bibliography of works on the subject of superstition and magic (ostensibly the contents of Oufle's library) and demonstrated by his copious and often very extensive footnotes that he had read a great deal of it.[94] His citation policy sometimes displayed little scruple: Bordelon cited even relatively sceptical writers, such as Weyer, chiefly as sources for the most bizarre tales of apparitions and transformations. Nevertheless, Bordelon clearly knew well the sceptical as well as the credulous literature—he quoted Bekker many times—and regarded his satire as contributing to the same enterprise as that of Bayle and Bekker. In a more frivolous spirit Joseph Addison (1672–1719) wrote his comic drama *The Drummer; or, the Haunted House*, for his friend the actor-manager Richard Steele, and first published it in 1715.[95] As mentioned earlier, the farcical comedy *The Drummer* based itself loosely around the story of the demon of Tedworth, the poltergeist story that dominated the pages of *Saducismus Triumphatus*. In *The Drummer* the poltergeist turns out to be a living man called Fantome. He steals around the 'haunted' country house of a rich widow, pretending to be the lady's late husband's ghost and hoping to scare her out of making what Fantome and his female accomplice fear will be an unwise second marriage. The lady's suitor, Tinsel, turns out to be a sceptic, an urban rationalist imbued with the most fashionable scientific ideas and incredulous of spirits.[96] The lady's husband Sir George then turns up, the report of his death having been a mistake. He arrives disguised as a conjurer offering to exorcise the spirit. The bogus drummer scares away the adventurer Tinsel; the husband then scares away the false ghost by shedding his disguise and appearing as his supposedly-dead self.[97] Addison thus deployed all the themes of a haunting and an exorcism as a scenario for a domestic farce. Though the play was not a huge dramatic success on its London performance, it merited numerous reprintings through the eighteenth century, both on its own and as part of the author's collected works.[98]

Ridicule continued to be used as a rhetorical device through the century to address debates over superstition that had run into the sand as far as serious controversy was concerned. During the controversy over Johann Joseph Gassner's campaign of healing by exorcism in southern Germany in the mid-1770s, a work appeared describing his activities entitled *A Merry Adventure of a Spiritual Don Quixote, Father Gassner the Conjurer of Devils in Ellwangen*.[99] The short octavo pamphlet purported to consist of reports from a Prussian officer sent back to his friend in Berlin. More satirical, but also far more biting, was William Hogarth's brutal engraving, entitled 'Credulity, Superstition and Fanaticism: A Medley' published in 1762. Hogarth depicted in the engraving the famous Methodist preacher George Whitefield (1714–70) who preached a Calvinistic form of Methodism characterized by hellfire sermons.[100] Hogarth showed Whitefield ranting in the pulpit, his wig falling off the back of his head in his agitation. A harlequin costume was visible beneath his preacher's gown. In his hands he held up figurines of a witch flying on a broomstick, and a winged and horned devil brandishing a gridiron. The pulpit was surrounded with statues depicting famous apparitions, such as the alleged appearance of the ghost of the Duke of Buckingham's father shortly before the duke's own murder in 1627.[101] Various books lay around the hall, including James VI's *Daemonlogie*, *Saducismus Triumphatus* (described as 'Glanvil on witches'), and Wesley's sermons. The Drummer of Tedworth stood in statuette form above a sort of thermometer of psychological morbidity ranging from 'raving' to 'suicide'. A woman swooned on the floor while a procession of rabbits issued from between her legs, a reference to the claims made in 1726 by Mary Toft to be able to give birth to rabbits.[102] Hogarth clearly took for granted, first that his readers and customers would be able to decode many of the references to the alleged superstitious beliefs that had become stock-in-trade of the Methodist anti-Enlightenment; and secondly that the majority opinion would share his willingness to treat these beliefs as matters for ridicule rather than serious discussion.

Enlightenment views of 'superstition' in Hume and Voltaire

At the height of the Enlightenment, philosophers could certainly use ridicule as freely as their less intellectual counterparts.[103] However, the arguments of the philosophers of the mid-eighteenth century on superstition embodied far more than just ridicule. 'Superstition' acquired in their hands different layers of meaning, and different textures of reference to the world of religion and belief. In this brief survey it is only possible to sample some of the ideas of the Enlightenment in order to discern the broad outlines of its critique. Use will be made of two key texts: David Hume's essay 'Of Superstition and Enthusiasm' from *Essays Moral and Political* (1741–2), and Voltaire's *Philosophical Dictionary*.[104] These two important philosophers actually read 'superstition' in substantially different ways. However, in each case the concept of what was 'superstitious' served, as it had done for centuries, to define by negation what was legitimate in the sphere of religion itself.

David Hume (1711–76) wrote some of the boldest and most challenging philosophical inquiries on human knowledge ever written; he also presented some of the most cogent critiques of conventional religion, especially in his *Natural History of Religion*, offered in earnest by a serious thinker to that date.[105] His *History of England* presented a learned critique of the role played by religious disputes in the history of the sixteenth and seventeenth centuries.[106] His essay on 'superstition and enthusiasm' forms a small part of a much larger enterprise. It appeared as the twelfth essay in the first volume of *Essays Moral and Political* (1741), Hume's first venture in publishing his collected essays.[107] Nevertheless, its clarity and symmetry made it one of Hume's most accessible contributions to the subject. Hume argued that superstition and enthusiasm represented polar opposites, ideal-types of two extremes in the psychology and political sociology of religion. Hume began by suggesting that those with a low spiritual self-esteem conceived a morbid need of rituals and intermediaries to encounter the divine, and such people naturally became superstitious. On the other hand, those with an excessively exalted sense of their spiritual worth and access to God conceived that they could know and approach the divinity without intermediaries, without ritual, and without dogma, and so became 'enthusiasts'. The superstitious naturally felt the need to have priests, perceived to be holier and purer than themselves, who could speak for them; so superstition favoured priestly power. Enthusiasts naturally felt no need of priestly leadership: the Quakers, the most pronounced enthusiasts, dispensed with it entirely. Enthusiasm tended to begin with a turbulent and alarming emotional flourish, but over time calmed down and became peaceable and politically inoffensive. Superstition appeared highly disciplined at the start, but with the increase in priestly power typically became ever more contentious, subversive, and dangerous. In politics, enthusiasts tended to resist all impositions of authority whether ecclesiastical or secular and to favour civil liberty. Superstitious people tended to be authoritarians, like the Catholics, high Tories, and Jacobites of Hume's own time. Hume concluded the essay by comparing the Jesuits in France (whom he called 'Molinists', that is, followers of the Jesuit theologian Luis de Molina, 1535–1600) with the Jansenists. The Jesuits, the 'superstitious', adhered rigidly to ritual forms and upheld tyranny; the Jansenists, Hume claimed, were enthusiasts who favoured the inward life, and preserved 'the small sparks of the love of liberty' in France.

Needless to say, Hume's contrast was a great deal too neat. An obvious implausibility hung around the idea of associating idealized psychological states with the religious affiliations of vast numbers of people. The two poles of superstition and enthusiasm deliberately left most of Protestant Christianity untouched. Hume's polemic served to demonstrate, as he later proved in his *History*, that fanatical ritualism among the Laudians and fanatical sectarian independency were both injurious to civil peace, and therefore inferior to a moderate civil Protestantism.[108] His claim that superstition derived from a low estimate of human spiritual worth sat very oddly with the Reformation doctrine of total human depravity on one hand or Molina's melioristic theology of human nature on the other. Nevertheless, Hume's typology of superstition contained some suggestive and important elements. Like Bayle sixty years earlier, he identified superstition with the belief that divine power is delegated down into certain special, arbitrary, positive people, things and activities in the human realm, and that the superstitious naturally favour the extension of such priestly activities and the power that goes with them. Hume could also use the term 'superstition' dismissively; for example to refer to the belief in witches.[109] However, the emphasis of the term had shifted to encompass what, in the eyes of the rationalists, was a disordered mode of religious thought found at the heart of the major faiths, not just on their margins.

This more developed, broader concept of what 'superstition' means received its authoritative exposition in the essays in Voltaire's *Philosophical Dictionary*. Voltaire (1694–1778) compiled the *Dictionary* from 1752 onwards, first published it in 1764, and continued to enhance it in successive editions. After Voltaire's death the editors of the *Œuvres complètes* published at Kehl in 1785–9 amalgamated the original 118 articles of Voltaire's *Dictionnaire philosophique* with numerous other pieces on the same subject published elsewhere, creating a much larger corpus with many additional articles from Voltaire's other works and contributions, relevant to the present subject.[110] Although alphabetically arranged, Voltaire's texts (and those of his guest contributors) followed a discernible programme, such that one can legitimately extract from several of the articles a systematic presentation of Voltaire's critique of 'superstitious' religion. The article 'Superstition' in the Kehl edition of the *Dictionnaire* constituted of one of the longer items, in five sections of nearly 4,000 words. The themes of this article overlapped and interlaced with those of many others; here Voltaire's approach will be treated as a more or less integrated whole. First, Voltaire proposed what might be called a cosmological argument against superstition. 'Superstition' consisted in the erroneous belief that God manifested the divine presence and power through exceptional and extraordinary manifestations of the holy. French people boasted of no longer being superstitious after the lessons learned from the reformers. Yet they continued to believe in bizarre miracles such as the annual liquefaction of the blood of St Janvier. French churches still preserved relics such as the robe, hair-clippings, or milk of the Virgin, or the foreskin of Jesus. Supposedly possessed people were exorcized on Maundy Thursday by being presented with a relic of the true cross. 'I could quote twenty similar examples: blush, and change your ways.'[111] Voltaire quoted with contempt the story of a miraculous apparition of Jesus in a church in Brittany, and the letter that the Saviour supposedly left on the altar warning everyone to be good Catholics.[112]

In the article 'Miracles', as already noted, Voltaire presented the philo-sophical argument that to expect miracles was in effect to insult God, to claim that the divine being needed constantly to interfere in the mechanism of the universe to make it work properly. Voltaire quoted Chrysostom to the effect that miracles were no longer necessary in the Church; then con-trasted that opinion with the belief of Jesuit missionaries that they were still performing them.[113] Given the enormous scale of the universe, it displayed human myopia and self-centredness to imagine that God would repeatedly subvert the natural order for the inhabitants of one small planet. 'Is it not the most absurd of follies to imagine that the Infinite Being would intervene on behalf of three or four hundred ants on this mass of mud?'[114] God 'has thousands and thousands of other suns, planets, and comets to govern. His immutable laws and his eternal plan cause all of nature to move; everything is bound to his throne by an infinite chain of which no single ring may ever be out of place.'[115] This cosmic metaphysical perspective moved Voltaire to look with condescension on the people of past ages, or less educated contemporaries, who could not see so far. That bogus miracles and relics were accepted by the people of provincial France showed their ignorance and primitivism. At the time of the execution of the priest Gaufridi for sorcery in 1611, 'most of our provincials had not progressed much above Caribs and Negroes [sic]'. However, 'let us not mock the ancients, poor people as we are, barely emerged from barbarism'.[116] Even great spirits such as Newton could waste their time on apocalyptism.[117]

Voltaire made a second major point in his critique of bad religion: superstition tended to fan the flames of sectarian hatred, and caused people to commit acts of terrible violence in the name of religion. He returned to this point again and again. In 1771 a group of political agitators had taken communion before attempting to assassinate the king of Poland. They took an oath before the image of the Virgin of Częstochowa to 'avenge God, religion, and country', outraged by the 'favourer of atheists and heretics'. Against the suggestion that freethinkers were bad subjects, Voltaire insisted that 'superstition sets the world on fire; philosophy puts out the flames'.[118] Religious enthusiasm, like that of the Jesuits in Japan, ended in a destructive civil war.[119] The notion that one could appease God by massacring the perceived enemies of God spread with frightening completeness through all religions. Fanaticism destroyed empires and set people against each other in the name of religion.[120] 'Fanaticism is to superstition what a fit is to a fever, or rage is to anger.'[121] The Catholic religion, despite teaching its people that in the Eucharist they absorbed the real body of Christ into their own physical bodies, could not dissuade them from committing atrocious murders.[122] Most lyrical of all was the vision that Voltaire described in 'Religion'. An angel brought him to a place where bones were heaped up in vast mounds, the remains of those killed in religious strife down the years. After meeting with a series of humane leaders of pagan religions, Voltaire met Jesus, who showed him the terrible wounds of his passion. Jesus explained the simplicity of his teaching, pleaded his respect for his own traditions, and disowned the violence done in his name.[123] Although it was agreed that every individual who persecuted his neighbour for disagreeing with him was a monster, states were allowed to persecute for religion even when they did so with inconsistency and hypocrisy. François I 'paid [Protestants] in Saxony out of policy; he burned them in Paris out of policy.' 'You monsters, who need superstitions as a crow's gizzard needs carrion! . . . If you have two religions among you, they will cut each others' throats; if you have thirty, they will live in peace.'[124] 'The superstitious person is governed by the fanatic, and becomes one. . . . the less superstition, the less fanaticism there will be; and the less fanaticism, the less misery.'[125]

Although passionate about his own religious views, Voltaire warned that a measure of relativism was needed to evaluate the accusation of 'superstition' made by the followers of one religion against another. Half of Europe thought that the other half was superstitious. French Catholics regarded Italian Catholics as superstitious 'and were barely mistaken'; Anglicans thought the same of French Catholics, and Quakers the same of Anglicans. However, Voltaire noted that the absence of elaborate rituals might not excuse one of superstition, if one replaced rituals with a set of absurd dogmas.[126] Voltaire appeared fascinated by the Quakers: he devoted the first of the *Philosophical Letters* to retelling in great detail the story of their origins and practices. The notion of a religious group with almost no ritual and almost no dogma intrigued him, though it was clear that Quakerism fell some way short of the philosophical ideal religion that Voltaire wished could prevail over the existing faiths.[127] Yet he did believe that in their simplicity, in their belief in the guidance of the spirit, in their lack of distinctions between members, the Quakers resembled the primitive Christians more than any other group.[128]

In a third major argument, Voltaire suggested that superstition entered the Church from pagan sources, especially during the early centuries of conversion. This argument was by no means new in the Enlightenment. Protestant historians had argued something similar for two centuries, and Balthasar Bekker deployed the claim to good effect. However, the *philosophes* gave the notion its greatest dissemination. Voltaire quoted Cyril of Alexandria to the effect that the cult of the saints and martyrs had a pagan origin. When the temples of the pagan gods were abolished, people instead went to the saints and asked for material benefits and protection against misfortune. Theodoret had described how the temples of the gods were demolished and the materials used to build the churches of the saints. 'The populace is superstitious, and it is by superstition that one keeps it in chains.' Relics were ascribed all sorts of implausible miracles. 'Freshly out of paganism, and delighted to find in the Christian Church—under other names—human beings who had been deified, the common people honoured them just as they had honoured their false gods.'[129] Voltaire amused himself with the Catholic notion of purgatory. It was attributed to the Maccabean period according to a dubious legend; but much more probably it derived from Virgil's description of souls undergoing purgation in the *Aeneid* via Simonian and Origenian heretics, with the later support of Gregory the Great.[130]

Like Bekker (but unlike Hume), Voltaire claimed that religions were all monotheistic in their origins, and that they gradually decayed as human weakness required a multiplicity of minor deities to supply individual needs. The notion of spirit-beings entered Christianity as it had paganism before it. As the pagan religions believed in the power of words as magical incantations, so Christians began to drive away demons through the power of words in rites of exorcism.[131] Specifically, Voltaire was convinced that the notion of demons came from the religions of the Middle East. The story of Tobias's exorcism of the demon Asmodeus by the fumigation of the heart and liver of a fish, told in the book of Tobit (and a proof-text for Catholic exorcism) derived from Persian magical lore.[132] Balthasar Bekker, as Voltaire observed in a whimsical and rather arch article about him, had observed that the notion of the devil came from Persian and Chaldean religions; it was 'an imitation of ancient mythology, just a warmed-over dish . . . we are just plagiarists.'[133] Even the most revolting of the elements in the early modern myth of witchcraft, the notion of witches copulating with the devil in the shape of a goat at the sabbat, could be traced to stories reported of Egyptian worship by Herodotus. From this garbled notion of antiquity emerged the witches' sabbat. 'Only philosophy has finally cured people of this abominable chimera, and taught judges that one must not burn imbeciles.'[134]

Finally, superstition served as the tool to the unscrupulous and those trying to control the simple by deceit. Dubious relics kept the people in chains, and the early Fathers thought that it was vital not to endanger their faith by asking too many questions about them.[135] 'To enchant a dead person, to raise them up, was the simplest thing in the world ... One only needs to have a spirit of divination, and to make this spirit of divination work, one needs only to be a deceitful scoundrel, and to be dealing with a weak-minded person: and no-one can deny that those two things have been extremely common.'[136] Voltaire summed up his arguments thus: 'the superstitious person is to the scoundrel what the slave is to the tyrant. . . . Superstition, born in paganism, adopted by Judaism, infected the Christian Church from the very first ages.'[137] One might ask if Voltaire used the term 'superstition' so broadly that he drained it of any specific meaning. Superstition was associated with fanaticism, with ignorance, with deceit; in short, it represented all the antitheses of the 'reason' that Voltaire and the *philosophes* aspired to put in the place of, or at least alongside, the traditional systems of belief. However tempting the accusation, it would not be entirely just. All the enlightened versions of 'superstition' shared the same basic point. Superstition postulated what might be called the divine arbitrary: that God was in *this* and not in *that*. The arbitrary and selective location of the divine in miracles, and not in nature; in specific cults, images, words, and people, and not in the rational contemplation of the divine in the cosmos; the defence of that very selective vision of the holy and the sacred, without regard to neighbourly charity and even at the expense of basic human moral standards: all these represented either the essence of superstition or its inevitable effects. The *philosophes* reworked elements of the arguments that Protestantism had devised more than two centuries earlier, but peeled them away from the Reformation's cosmology and its preoccupation with dogma. They could do so with far greater clarity and consistency than the reformers, since they had abandoned both the scholastic Aristotelian cosmology and the superhuman authority of scripture. 'Superstition' in Enlightenment thought was by no means the same thing as 'religion', at least not for the major thinkers. They almost certainly aspired to a purified, rational contemplation of the divine as they claimed to do, with perhaps a handful of exceptions like Jean Meslier and the Baron d'Holbach.[138] However, they had cut the anchor cables of religious certainty one by one. Believers who have tried, with them, to eschew belief in the divine arbitrary have been adrift with that uncertainty ever since.

Counter-currents and conclusion

It has been wisely said that, while the Enlightenment was a product of the eighteenth century, the eighteenth century was not the product of the Enlightenment.[139] Those who read the intelligent and often very earnest as well as satirical critiques of the *philosophes* may too easily be tempted to assume that they won their arguments, at least among the educated. Voltaire himself was not so sanguine. He documented very clearly that in the France of his time a vigorous and enthusiastic taste for edifying religious prodigies continued to hold sway even among the bourgeoisie, never mind the peasantry.[140] Scholarly martyrologists like Thierri Ruinart would strive to rehabilitate those legends of apocryphal saints that a more learned hagiography wished to purge from the canon.[141] In both Protestant and Catholic Europe the modernizing faiths of Latitudinarian Anglicanism, doctrinal Lutheranism, and reform Catholicism generated reactions against themselves. In the case of some Pietists and Catholics, and certainly among the Methodists, these reactions provoked a renewed quest for evidences of the supernatural. Hogarth's satires on Wesley and Whitefield did not completely miss the mark. The Gassner controversy in 1770s Germany proved that, while many Lutherans and Catholics were sceptics about charismatic healing by exorcism, some Pietists and conservative Catholics found the whole affair extremely attractive. A satirical journalist who strayed into the wrong territory after poking fun at Gassner's patrons found himself imprisoned.[142] When the Prussian Friedrich Nicolai travelled through southern Germany in 1781, he found one of Girolamo Menghi's more florid exorcisms still in use, though he did not recognize it as such.[143] In much of Europe, the forcible 'dechristianization' that followed on the French Revolution contributed to give Enlightened critiques of Christianity and the early versions of a history-of-religions school a bad reputation.[144]

However, one very important shift in attitudes had occurred. Whether they believed in demons or superstitious rites or not, Europe's intellectuals appeared to have lost their fear of them. Medieval pastoral theologians, and many of their early modern counterparts, had expressed an apparently genuine pastoral concern that superstitious activities would entangle people with demons and harm or even destroy souls. The 'anti-Saducists' seemed, on the other hand, far more concerned to prove their 'atheist' opponents wrong than to dissuade people from, for instance, superstitious cures for bewitchment or even techniques for divining sorcery.[145] Curiosity and the desire for evidence took precedence over a consistent metaphysic or even a consistent pastoral ethic. The experimental and investigative response to the Gassner phenomenon provided yet another instance of this attitude. Once intellectual theologians lost their fear and alarm at invisible demonic powers, they would cease to be concerned about waging a pastoral campaign against superstitions. In a curious way, the trajectory of scientific and Enlightenment thought may actually have caused the pastoral pressure on popular superstitions to *lessen* rather than increase in the eighteenth and even the nineteenth centuries. One does not struggle mightily to wean hearts and minds away from a rival that one has long since ceased to fear or respect.

Curiosity took quite another turn in the early nineteenth century. As is well known, post-Enlightenment thinkers abandoned the quest for a fully rational, cosmopolitan humanity. They not only acknowledged, but positively embraced the notion of folk-cultures, ethnic traditions, and national identities. Where Rousseau had already pointed the way, the philosophers of Romanticism re-envisaged humanity as consisting of a diverse set of 'peoples' with their own temperaments, traditions, and defining beliefs.[146] Out of this movement emerged the collection of folklore. Goethe, the Grimm brothers, and Ludwig Bechstein in their different ways collected, conserved, and transmitted folk tales that typically included elements of spirit beings, charms and spells, divination and soothsaying, and popular magic, including artfully reworked versions of the lore of the superstition-treatises described in the first four chapters of this book.[147] Arnim and Brentano collected and edited traditional ballads in *Des Knaben Wunderhorn* in the 1800s.[148] These included many tales of the supernatural that had already in the early modern period provided fodder for chapbook verse. However, the high culture of the Romantic era depended fundamentally on the wistful recreation of magical and supernatural worlds that, ironically, no longer troubled Europe's leading religious intellectuals at all. 'Superstitions' had ceased to be a source of fear or condemnation and had become a necessary cultural ornament. They even received their bibliographer and encyclopedist in Jacques-Albin-Simon Collin de Plancy (1794–1881), who issued the first edition of his whimsically named *Infernal Dictionary* in 1818.[149]

Meanwhile theologians learned increasingly to do without the devil and to live with the insights of the cultural historians of antiquity. In the thought of F. D. E. Schleiermacher (1768–1834) Protestant theology began progressively to detach itself from metaphysical or historical statements about the world. Religion did not have to depend on, or postulate as its necessary accessories, statements about how the cosmos worked, or about how human society worked. All religious statements were in truth merely manifestations of what lay at the heart of religious experience, 'the immediate consciousness of the universal existence of all finite things in and through the Eternal'.[150] Schleiermacher proceeded confidently to dismiss many of the metaphysical cruces that had so troubled his predecessors:

The conflict about which event is actually a miracle and wherein the character of a miracle properly consists, over how much revelation there might be and the extent to which and the reasons why one might believe in it, and the obvious effort to deny and to push aside as much as may be done with propriety and discretion in the foolish opinion of thereby doing a service to philosophy and reason, all of these are the childish operations of the metaphysicians and moralists in religion. They confuse all points of view and bring religion into the disrepute of encroaching upon the totality of scientific and empirical judgments.... However loudly religion demands back all those defamed concepts, it leaves you, your physics, and, may it please God, your psychology inviolate.[151]

In such a climate metaphysical, let alone 'scientific', statements about the world ceased to be the proper province of theology: one was irrelevant to the other. While Schleiermacher was a little ahead of his time in some of his bolder statements, by the middle and later nineteenth century Protestant theology had become increasingly confident that a vital residuum of religious truth would still be left, even when all the metaphysics of the late antique world or the Middle Ages were set aside. The embodiment of Christianity in the philosophical garb of the ancient Greeks, which Bekker had already blamed for introducing the notion of demons into Christian theology, became the original sin and the primordial distraction of Christian theologians, according to a liberal church historian such as Adolf von Harnack (1851–1930).[152]

By the end of the nineteenth century, the main tenets of the Enlight-enment critique of traditional religion had been embraced by modernist theologians in mainstream Protestantism and even by some brave souls in Roman Catholicism. It was accepted that sacred texts are human docu-ments with both a cultural and a textual history. The cosmological myths of the Hebrew Bible bear obvious and important relationships to other myths of the cultures of the Near East. Christianity as it developed inherited and exchanged many ideas with the cults and philosophies of pagan late antiqui-ty. The transcendent claims of faith could only be discerned in and through this very human cultural matrix. On the other side of the confessional divide, Roman Catholicism cultivated and nurtured across the nineteenth century a repristinated Thomism, in philosophy as in theology. It pursued this goal with unprecedented scholarly rigour, and with deliberate rather than unconscious rejection of the historical distance that separated the thirteenth century from the nineteenth.[153] However, its metaphysical focus tended to be directed more and more towards the correcting and refining of the Church's own practices, which was more or less where Jean-Baptiste Thiers had left it in the eighteenth century.

With the mid-nineteenth century came the final abandonment of any attempt by states to enforce religious discipline on their subjects, and thus of any practical sanctions that the churches might hope to impose on belief and practice outside the forum of conscience. Consequently, there has been a widespread and predictable diversification, fragmentation, and disintegration in the area of views of the supernatural. The late nineteenth and twentieth centuries saw the rise of more or less systematic revivals and reconstructions of 'occult' philosophies and even religious cults, many based loosely or closely on the ideas of Edward Alexander 'Aleister' Crowley (1875–1947).[154] These notions belong more properly to the decadent afterlife of Renaissance occultism, rather than to popular superstition: they were as bookish as they are eclectic and artificial. Spiritualism and converse with the dead enjoyed a period of vogue in the Victorian and Edwardian periods, though even the patronage of Arthur Conan Doyle could not remove its persistent associations with charlatanry and fraud.[155] More recently the quest for experimental proof of the existence of spirits, undertaken in a mental climate entirely familiar to Glanvill and his kind, continues to generate a subset of popular entertainment.[156] Astrology, perhaps most absurdly of all, has continued to be practised and to give employment to many people. It is now several centuries since the cosmology that made plausible the notion of stellar influences on the physical world was exploded. Any educated person knows that the universe is vast, not a confined hollow sphere. Cosmic matter is as unstable in the farthest galaxy as here: it does not become more perfect, unchangeable, and spiritual the farther one leaves the earth. How exactly the casual and conventionally interpreted patterns created by vastly distant masses of exploding gas, patterns specific to a few global cultures, and which in any case appear only accidentally because viewed from the earth's perspective, can still be thought significant for the lives of human beings is a mystery which, fortunately, this book does not have to solve.

Genuine 'superstition' does survive of course in the classic sense in which it has been discussed in this book. In parts of rural Europe especially, folk-healers long continued to practise their art on the margins of traditional religion. Researchers have discovered such people relatively recently in rural Spain.[157] In the extreme south of Italy, where the pastoral visitations and the administrative uniformity prescribed by the Council of Trent had failed to take root, the exuberant medieval diversity of ecclesiastical sacramentals, unofficial saint cults, and folk-healers persisted with little obvious modification up to the nineteenth century.[158] On a recent visit to the Dordogne region of France a tour guide advised me that folk-healers still practised in that area, although for an outsider it was extremely difficult to make contact with them. In urban industrialized society there is still a rich field of inquiry for the ethnographer, and books continue to be published about superstitions.[159] In the latter case, however, one is typically dealing with utterly disjointed and incoherent bodies of ideas. Charms for good luck, small private rituals to ensure success in sport or in love, the discernment of good or bad days from entirely chance occurrences, persist despite or even because of the fact that no coherent explanation of any causal rationale can be given. One researcher, who expected to find it difficult to conduct anthropological fieldwork on the area of superstitions, was surprised by how ready and open all sorts of highly educated people were to describe their favourite superstitions to him.[160] It is precisely this incoherence and disjointedness that modern superstition shares with its medieval and ancient equivalents. The whole point about 'superstitions' is that they do not require or wish for a consistent or rational metaphysic. They live and breathe on the irrational association between perceived effect and assumed cause. It was the peculiar and perhaps inherently self-defeating ambition of theologians and philosophers from the Middle Ages to the

Enlightenment to try to make rigorous sense of human thought, to reduce all meaning, causes, and effects in the cosmos to a coherent and rational set of ideas. The quest to control and domesticate superstition was, in the end, a futile one; philosophers and theologians have long since abandoned it. Nevertheless it remains a profoundly instructive lesson and case study in humanity's efforts to make sense of our predicament.

Notes

INTRODUCTION

1. Christine Shaw, *Julius II: The Warrior Pope* (Oxford: Blackwell Publishers, 1993), 102 ff. Michael Tavuzzi, *Prierias: The Life and Works of Silvestro Mazzolini da Prierio, 1456–1527* (Durham, NC: Duke University Press, 1997), 25–6, dates the event to Lent 1494, though 1495 seems to fit the chronology of the military context slightly better, unless of course Tavuzzi means 1494 Old Style.

2. Silvestro Mazzolini, da Prierio (Silvester Prierias) *De Strigimagarum Demonumque Mirandis libri tres* (Rome: Antonius Bladis de Asula, 24 Sept. 1521), sig. ff iii^v–iv^r.

3. Kaspar Peucer, *Commentarius de Praecipuis Divinationum Generibus: in quo à prophetijs diuina autoritate traditis, et physicis praedictionibus, separantur diabolicae fraudes & superstitiosae obseruationes, & explicantur fontes ac causae physicarum praedictionum, diabolicae et superstitiosae confutatae damnantur* (Wittenberg: Johannes Crato, 1553).

4. Kaspar Peucer, *Commentarius, de Praecipuis Divinationum generibus, in quo a prophetiis, authoritate divine traditis, et a Physicis conjecturis, discernuntur artes et imposturae diabolicae, atque observationes natae ex superstitione, et cum hac conjunctae: Et monstrantur fontes ac causae Physicarum praedictionum: Diabolicae vero ac superstitiosae confutatae damnantur* (Frankfurt: Wechel, Claudius Marnius & heirs of Ioannes Aubrius, 1607), 727–8. The 1607 edition will be cited throughout this work. For further discussion see Ch. 12 below.

5. For discussion of the etymology see Dieter Harmening, *Superstitio: Überlieferungs- und theoriegeschichtliche Untersuchungen zur kirchlich-theologischen Aberglaubensliteratur des Mittelalters* (Berlin: E. Schmidt, 1979), 26–32.

6. For a survey of some of the debate over its etymology and the multiplicity of uses to which the term was put in Roman antiquity, see Michele R. Salzman, ' "Superstitio" in the "Codex Theodosianus" and the Persecution of Pagans' in *Vigiliae Christianae*, 41/2 (1987), 172–188, esp. 173–5; also Dale B. Martin, *Inventing Superstition: From the Hippocratics to the Christians* (Cambridge, MA., and London: Harvard University Press, 2004).

7. For an early example see Augustine, *De Doctrina Christiana*, book 2, chs 20–24; see Augustine, *On Christian Teaching*, ed. and trans. R. P. H. Green (Oxford: Oxford University Press, 1997), 48–51. The modern Latin edition is Augustine, *De Doctrina Christiana*, ed. and trans. R. P. H. Green, Oxford Early Christian Texts (Oxford; New York: Clarendon Press, 1995). See also articles by D. Grodzynski, '*Superstitio*', *Revue des Études Anciennes*, 76 (1974), 36–60, and Salzman (above, n. 6) on the term in late antique culture. The early history of the term is explored in Ch. 5 below.

8. See Harmening, *Superstitio, passim* but esp. 72 ff.

9. See below, Ch. 4.

10. For examinations of the divide that occasionally opened up between inquisitorial literature and the evidence of individual testimonies, see e.g. my *Waldenses: Rejections of Holy Church in Medieval Europe* (Oxford: Blackwell, 2000).

11. Rare exceptions might be the heresies of the Free Spirit and the Luciferans, which were almost entirely imaginary constructions of the ecclesiastical writers on heresy. See e.g. Robert E. Lerner, *The Heresy of the Free Spirit in the Later Middle Ages* (Berkeley: University of California Press, 1972).

12. See below, Chs. 6–8.

13. The belief that some demons might be morally neutral was condemned as error 22 in the 'Decretum Facultatis Theologiae Parisiensis contra superstitiosos Errores Artis Magicae' of 1398, cited in H. Institoris and J. Sprenger, *Malleus Maleficarum*, 2 vols in 3 (Lyons: Sumptibus Claudii Bourgeat, 1669), ii, part II [separate title-page and pagination], 172 ff.

14. Wilhelm Dilthey, 'Auffassung und Analyse des Menschen im 15. und 16. Jahrhundert', in *Wilhelm Diltheys gesammelte Schriften*, ii. *Weltanschauung und Analyse des Menschen seit Renaissance und Reformation*, 8th edn (Stuttgart and Göttingen, 1969), 39–42 and 53–63, and as trans. in L. W. Spitz (ed.) *The Reformation: Basic Interpretations* (Lexington, MA: D. C. Heath, 1972) 11–24.

15. See Adolf von Harnack, *What is Christianity?* trans. T. B. Saunders (Philadelphia: Fortress Press, 1986), 268: 'the greatest movement and the one most pregnant with good was the Reformation in the sixteenth century; . . . today there are thirty millions of Germans, and many more Christians outside Germany, who possess a religion without priests, without sacrifices, without 'fragments' of grace, without ceremonies—a spiritual religion!'

16. See Ernst Troeltsch, 'Renaissance and Reformation', from his *Gesammelte Schriften*, iv (Tübingen, Mohr, 1925), 261–96 and as trans. in Spitz (ed.) *The Reformation*, 25–43; but compare also Ernst Troeltsch, *Die Bedeutung des Protestantismus für die Entstehung der modernen Welt: Vortrag, gehalten auf der IX. Versammlung deutscher Historiker zu Stuttgart am 21. April 1906* (Munich: R. Oldenbourg, 1906).

17. See e.g. Max Weber, *The Sociology of Religion*, trans. Ephraim Fischoff (Boston: Beacon Press, 1963). See discussion in M. M. W. Lemmen, *Max Weber's Sociology of Religion: Its Method and Content in the Light of the Concept of Rationality* (Hilversum: Gooi en Sticht, 1990)

18. 'That great historic process in the development of religions, the elimination of magic from the world (*Entzauberung der Welt*) which had begun with the old Hebrew prophets and, in conjunction with Hellenistic scientific thought, had repudiated all magical means to salvation as superstition and sin, came here [in Puritanism] to its logical conclusion . . . there was not only no magical means of attaining the grace of God for those to whom God had decided to deny it, but no means whatever.' Max Weber, *The Protestant Ethic and the Spirit of Capitalism*, trans. Talcott Parsons (New York and London: Scribners, Allen & Unwin, 1930), 105; see also ibid., 117, 149. Further elaboration of the thesis may be found in *From Max Weber: Essays in Sociology*, ed. H. H. Gerth, C. Wright Mills, and Bryan S. Turner (London: Routledge, 2009).

19. See the various theses on the alleged material and social causes of the success of the Reformation in my *The European Reformation* (Oxford: Clarendon Press, 1991), ch. 17, 293–304.

20. See e.g. R. Po-Chia Hsia, *Social Discipline in the Reformation: Central Europe 1550–1750* (London: Routledge, 1989), esp. 122–73; Ernst Walter Zeeden, *Die Entstehung der Konfessionen: Grundlagen und Formen der Konfessionsbildung im Zeitalter der Glaubenskämpfe* (Munich: R. Oldenbourg, 1965).

21. See the influential and controversial thesis of Jean Delumeau, *Catholicism between Luther and Voltaire: A New View of the Counter-Reformation* (London: Burns & Oates; Philadelphia: Westminster Press, 1977); also his *Un chemin d'histoire: chrétienté et christianisation* (Paris: Fayard, 1981) and discussion in J. K. Powis, 'Repression and Autonomy: Christians and Christianity in the Historical Work of Jean Delumeau', *Journal of Modern History*, 64 (1992), 366–74.

22. See below, Part III introduction and n. 4.

23. The classic work on this thesis remains Norbert Elias, *The Civilizing Process: The History of Manners and State Formation and Civilization*, trans. E. Jephcott (Oxford: Blackwell, 1994); a recent full exploration of the thesis is in Peter Burke, Brian Harrison, and Paul Slack (eds), *Civil Histories: Essays presented to Sir Keith Thomas* (Oxford: Oxford University Press, 2000).

24. Edward Gibbon, *The Decline and Fall of the Roman Empire*, 'General Observations on the Fall of the Roman Empire in the West': 'Europe is secure from any future irruption of Barbarians; since, before they can conquer, they must cease to be barbarous. Their gradual advances in the science of war would always be accompanied, as we may learn from the example of Russia,

with a proportionable improvement in the arts of peace and civil policy; and they themselves must deserve a place among the polished nations whom they subdue.'

25. The fullest exploration of this abundant subject is Alexandra Walsham, *Providence in Early Modern England* (Oxford: Oxford University Press, 1999).

26. The classic article on this subject is R. W. Scribner, 'The Reformation, Popular Magic, and the "Disenchantment of the World"', *Journal of Interdisciplinary History*, 23 (1993) 475–94; reprinted in C. Scott Dixon (ed.) *The German Reformation: The Essential Readings* (Oxford: Blackwell, 1999), 262–79. For a schematic presentation of his view see also R. W. Scribner, 'Elements of Popular Belief', in T. A. Brady, H. A. Oberman, and J. D. Tracy (eds), *Handbook of European History 1400–1600: Late Middle Ages, Renaissance and Reformation* 2 vols (Leiden and New York: E. J. Brill, 1994–5), i. *Structures and Assertions*, 231–62.

27. A key statement of this thesis is 'Incombustible Luther: The Image of the Reformer in Early Modern Germany', in R. W. Scribner, *Popular Culture and Popular Movements in Reformation Germany* (London: Hambledon Press, 1987), 323–53.

28. These visions were discovered by Jürgen Beyer, a pupil of Dr Scribner, and published in Jürgen Beyer, 'A Lübeck Prophet in Local and Lutheran Context', in Bob Scribner and Trevor Johnson (eds), *Popular Religion in Germany and Central Europe 1400–1800* (Basingstoke: Macmillan, 1996), 166–82; id., 'Lutherische Propheten in Deutschland und Skandinavien im 16. und 17. Jahrhundert. Entstehung und Ausbreitung eines Kulturmusters zwischen Mündlichkeit und Schriftlichkeit', in Robert Bohn, ed., *Europa in Scandinavia: Kulturelle und soziale Dialoge in der Frühen Neuzeit* (Frankfurt am Main: P. Lang, 1994), 35–55.

29. See esp. Trevor Johnson. 'The Reformation and Popular Culture', in Andrew Pettegree (ed.), *The Reformation World* (London and New York: Routledge, 2000), 555 ff. and 557 for the quotation. See also Helen Parish and William G. Naphy (eds) *Religion and Superstition in Reformation Europe* (Manchester: Manchester University Press, 2002).

30. The results were often picturesque. One of Dr Scribner's articles explored the intricate legal processing of a minor offence of politically imprudent 'careless talk' by a drunken German villager who was subsequently banned from alehouses for life.

31. As is argued e.g. by Ulinka Rublack, *Reformation Europe* (Cambridge: Cambridge University Press, 2005).

32. See Owen Chadwick, *The Early Reformation on the Continent* (Oxford: Oxford University Press, 2001), 151–80.

33. See Margo Todd, *The Culture of Protestantism in Early Modern Scotland* (New Haven and London: Yale University Press, 2002), esp. 205 ff.

34. It may, just possibly, be significant that Dr Scribner was raised as a Roman Catholic in Australia and reportedly rediscovered his Catholic faith near the end of his life while at Harvard Divinity School.

35. Alexandra Walsham, 'The Reformation and "the Disenchantment of the World" Reassessed', *Historical Journal*, 51/2 (2008), 527–8.

36. Ibid. 501 and notes 11–12.

37. See below, Ch. 5; on Caesarius see William E. Klingshirn, *Caesarius of Arles: The Making of a Christian Community in Late Antique Gaul* (Cambridge: Cambridge University Press, 1994).

38. See below, Ch. 5, nn. 33–4.

39. Peter Lombard, *Book of Sentences*, bk 4, dist. 34, chapter 'De his qui maleficiis impediti coire nequeunt'. This passage was commented on by nearly all scholastic commentators.

40. e.g. Aquinas's *Summa contra Gentiles*: see below, Ch. 6, nn. 14–15.

41. Examples of expositions of the Decalogue are Nikolaus von Dinkelsbühl, in Karin Baumann, *Aberglaube für Laien: zur Programmatik und Überlieferung spätmittelalterlicher Superstitionenkritik*, 2 vols [continuously paginated] (Würzburg: Königshausen & Neumann, 1989); *Dives and Pauper*, ed. Priscilla Heath Barnum, 3 vols, Early English Text Society, nos. 275, 280, 323 (London: Oxford University Press, 1976–2004); Luther's *Exposition of the Ten Commandments* follows on in this genre: see *Decem Praecepta wittenbergensi predicata populo. Per P. Martinum Luther Augustinianum* (Wittenberg: Johann Rhau-Grunenberg, 1518).

42. See e.g. Jean Gerson, 'Opusculum adversus doctrinam cuiusdam medici delati in Montepessulano, sculpentis in numismate figuram leonis cum certis caracteribus', in J. Gerson, *Joannis Gersonii Doctoris Theologi & Cancellarii Parisiensis Opera Omnia*, ed. Ludovicus Ellies du Pin, 5 vols, 2nd edn (The Hague: P. de Hondt, 1728), i, cols. 206–8; Heinrich von Gorkum (*c.*1386–1431) *Tractatus de supersticiosis quibusdam casibus* (Esslingen: Conrad Fyner, 1473), which dealt with four instances of popular religious practices on the margins of respectability; Isidoro Isolani OP's *Libellus adversus Magos: Divinatores: Maleficos: eosque qui ad religionem subeundam maleficis artibus quempiam cogi posse asseverant* (Milan, 1506), which addressed the claim that people could be moved to enter a religious order as a result of sorcery; Martinus de Arles, *Tractat[us] insignis et exquisitissimus de Superstitionibus contra maleficia seu sortilegia, que hodie vigent in orbe terrarum* (Paris: [P. Gromors], 1517), which investigated whether local people who submerged a statue of St Peter to bring rain were committing a sin by doing so.

43. Martín de Castañega, *Tratado de las supersticiones y hechizerias y de la possibilidad y remedio dellas (1529)*, ed. Juan Robert Muro Abad (Logroño: Gobierno de La Rioja, Instituto de Estudios Riojanos, 1994); Pedro Ciruelo, *Reprouacion delas supersticiones y hechizerias. Libro muy vtile y necessario a todos los buenos christianos*, etc. (Salamanca: P. de Castro, a costa del honrrado varon G. de Milis, 1539)

44. On this subject see two excellent articles by Michael D. Bailey, 'The Disenchantment of Magic: Spells, Charms and Superstition in Early European Witchcraft Literature', *American Historical Review*, 111/2 (2006), 383–404; id., 'Concern over Superstition in Late Medieval Europe', in S. A. Smith and Alan Knight (eds), *The Religion of Fools: Superstition Past and Present, Past and Present* Supplement 3 (Oxford: Oxford University Press, 2008), 115–33: on the surge in pastoral theological literature see esp. 127 ff.

45. Bailey, 'Disenchantment of Magic', 387 ff. However, this present work does not draw as heavily on the *Malleus Maleficarum* as other recent works, especially Hans Peter Broedel, *The Malleus Maleficarum and the Construction of Witchcraft: Theology and Popular Belief* (Manchester: Manchester University Press, 2003) and Henricus Institoris and Jacobus Sprenger, *Malleus Maleficarum*, ed. and trans. Christopher S. Mackay, 2 vols (Cambridge : Cambridge University Press, 2006). The *Malleus* was more closely and specifically devoted to the issue of witchcraft than most of the other works cited here, and it was largely derivative from other sources that are discussed extensively in this work. Accordingly it was decided not to add substantially to the already copious literature on the *Malleus*.

46. Johann Weyer, *De praestigiis daemonum, et incantationibus ac veneficiis, libri V* (Basle: Ioannes Oporinus, 1563).

47. Martinus Delrio SJ, *Disquisitionum Magicarum Libri Sex*, 3 vols (Louvain: Gerardus Rivius, 1599–1600)

48. Instances are e.g. Pedro Ciruelo (1470–1560), *Pedro Ciruelo's A treatise reproving all superstitions and forms of witchcraft: very necessary and useful for all good Christians zealous for their salvation*, trans. E. A. Maio and D. W. Pearson (Rutherford, NJ: Fairleigh Dickinson University Press, 1977); Johann Weyer, *Witches, Devils, and Doctors in the Renaissance*, ed. George Mora and Benjamin Kohl, trans. John Shea, Medieval & Renaissance Texts & Studies, 73 (Binghamton, NY: Medieval & Renaissance Texts & Studies, 1991; repr. 1998); Martín del Rio, *Investigations into Magic*, ed. and trans. P. G. Maxwell-Stuart (Manchester and New York: Manchester University Press, 2000).

49. This is the general conclusion, though carefully nuanced, of Stuart Clark, *Thinking with Demons: The Idea of Witchcraft in early modern Europe* (Oxford: Clarendon Press, 1997).

50. Andreas Althamer, *Eyn Predig von dem Teuffel, das er alles unglueck in der welt anrichte* ([Nuremberg: Jobst Gutknecht], 1532); Johann Spreter, *Ein kurtzer Bericht, was von den abghotterischen Sägen vn[nd] Beschweren zühalten: wie der etlich volbracht, vnnd das die ein Zauberey, auch Greüwel vor Gott dem Herren seind* (Basle: Bartholomeus Westheymer, 1543).

51. John Martiall, *A treatyse of the Crosse gathred out of the scriptures, councelles, and auncient fathers of the primitive church* (Antwerp: John Latius, 1564); James Calfhill, *An aunswere to the Treatise of the crosse* (London: Henry Denham, for Lucas Harryson, 1565); John Martiall, *A replie to M. Calfhills blasphemous answer made against the treatise of the crosse* (Louvain: John Bogard, 1566); [Jacobus Heerbrandus], *De Magia Disputatio ex cap. 7. Exo.,... praeside reverendo et clarissimo viro Jacobo Heerbrando, sacrae theologiae Doctore eximio, ac eiusdem in Academia Tubingensi Professore publico... Nicolaus Falco Salueldensis... respondere conabitur* (Tübingen: [Ulrich Morhart], 1570); Albrecht Hunger (1545–1604), *De Magia Theses Theologicae, in celebri et catholica academia Ingolstadiana An. S. N. M.D.LXXIIII, die 21 Junii per Reverendum et eruditum virum M. Hectorem Wegman Augustanum, SS. Theologiae Baccalaureum formatum, Divae Virginis apud eandem Academiam Parochum, pro impetrando Licentiae gradu, ad publicam disputationem propositae: Praeside Reverendo et Clarissimo viro Alberto Hungero, SS. Theologiae Doctore et Professore ordinario, Collegii Theologici pro tempore decano* (Ingolstadt: Weissenhorn, 1574).

52. As observed in my 'For Reasoned Faith or Embattled Creed? Religion for the People in Early Modern Europe', in *Transactions of the Royal Historical Society*, 6th series, 8 (1998), 165–87, and note 18.

53. See e.g. Stuart A. Vyse, *Believing in Magic: The Psychology of Superstition* (New York and Oxford: Oxford University Press, 1997). Note also the intentional absence of chronological narrative in Stephen Wilson, *The Magical Universe: Everyday Ritual and Magic in Pre-modern Europe* (London and New York: Hambledon and London, 2000).

54. Eamon Duffy, *The Stripping of the Altars: Traditional Religion in England, c.1400–c.1580* (New Haven; London: Yale University Press, 1992), and esp. 266–87.

55. For an important refutation of the argument that Catholic reform 'homogenized' religious culture, see esp. the works of Simon Ditchfield, e.g. *Liturgy, Sanctity and History in Tridentine Italy: Pietro Maria Campi and the Preservation of the Particular* (Cambridge : Cambridge University Press, 1995).

56. See e.g. John Redwood, *Reason, Ridicule, and Religion: The Age of Enlightenment in England, 1660–1750* (London: Thames & Hudson, 1976).

57. Elizabeth Labrousse, *Pierre Bayle*, 2nd edn, 2 vols (Dordrecht and Boston: M. Nijhoff, 1985).

58. See below, Ch. 18, nn. 1–3.

59. See Lyndal Roper, *Witch Craze: Terror and Fantasy in Baroque Germany*, (New Haven and London: Yale University Press; new edn, 2006), esp. chs. 9–10; H. C. Erik Midelfort, *Exorcism and Enlightenment: Johann Joseph Gassner and the Demons of Eighteenth-Century Germany* (New Haven and London: Yale University Press, 2005); Jane Shaw, *Miracles in Enlightenment England* (New Haven and London: Yale University Press, 2006).

I. THE PROBLEMS OF PRE-MODERN LIFE

1. The older, more pessimistic history of family life and the emotions is represented by such classic works as Philippe Ariès, *Centuries of Childhood: A Social History of Family Life*, translated from the French by Robert Baldick (London: Jonathan Cape, 1962); also ed. with a new introduction by Adam Phillips (London: Pimlico, 1996); Lawrence Stone, *The Family, Sex and Marriage in England 1500–1800* (London: Weidenfeld & Nicolson, 1977); Edward Shorter, *The Making of the Modern Family* (New York: Basic Books, 1975).

2. The emotional intensity of early modern family life is ably documented e.g. in Ralph A. Houlbrooke, *The English Family, 1450–1700* (London: Longman, 1984); Ralph A. Houlbrooke, *Death, Religion, and the Family in England, 1480–1750* (Oxford: Clarendon Press, 1998); Keith Wrightson, *English Society, 1580–1680*, new edn (London: Routledge, 2003).

3. See Johannes Nider, *Preceptorium Divine Legis* (Basle: Berthold Ruppel, c.1470), prec. 1, ch. 11, sect. 15. Nider's *Preceptorium* appeared in many incunabular editions. As this edition has neither quire signatures nor page numbering of any kind, reference is made here to the minutely subdivided chapter-divisions of the work. Compare Silvestro Mazzolini, da Prierio (Silvester Prierias) *De Strigimagarum Demonumque Mirandis libri tres* (Rome: Antonius Bladis de Asula, 24 Sept. 1521), sigs. R ii^v and following.

4. Compare with the superstition-literature the material collected in Stephen Wilson, *The Magical Universe: Everyday Ritual and Magic in Pre-Modern Europe* (London: Hambledon, 2000), 311 ff, though Wilson intentionally does not classify his material chronologically.

5. Ecclesiasticus 38: 1 and following.

6. Martín of Arles y Andosilla, *Tractatus insignis et exquisitissimus de superstitionibus contra maleficia seu sortilegia que hodie vigent in orbe terrarum: in lucem nuperrime editus* (Paris: [P. Gromors], 1517); another edition (Rome: Vincentius Luchinus, 1559); reference is here made to the edition in *Tractatus Universi Juris*, xi, pt. 2 (Lyons, 1584), fos. 402^v–8^r, sect. 104, based on Nider, *Preceptorium*, precept 1, ch. 9.

7. See Jean Gerson's critique of a physician for using an emblem of a lion for healing an illness of the kidneys, in 'Opusculum adversus doctrinam cuiusdam medici delati in Montepessulano, sculpentis in numismate figuram leonis cum certis caracteribus', in J. Gerson, *Joannis Gersonii Doctoris Theologi & Cancellarii Parisiensis Opera Omnia*, ed. Ludovicus Ellies du Pin, 5 vols 2nd edn (The Hague: P. de Hondt, 1728), i, cols. 206–8. For recent works on the history of pre-modern medicine see e.g. Andrew Cunningham, *The Anatomical Renaissance: The Resurrection of the Anatomical Projects of the Ancients* (Aldershot: Scolar, 1996); Ole Peter Grell and Andrew Cunningham (eds) with Jon Arrizabalaga, *Health Care and Poor Relief in Counter-Reformation Europe* (London and New York: Routledge, 1999).

8. Martin Plantsch, *Opusculum de sagis maleficis* (Pforzheim: Thomas Anshelm, 1507), sig. c iv; Johannes Geiler von Kaisersberg, *Die Emeis, dis ist das büch von der Omeissen* (Strasbourg: Johannes Grieninger, 1517), ch. 34 on fos. 55v ff. Note that the same reference to discovery of foreign matter appeared in *Saducismus Triumphatus*, below, Ch. 17 n. 65.

9. Mazzolini, *De Strigimagarum . . . Mirandis*, bk 1, ch. 15, sigs. Riiv ff.

10. Theophrastus Bombast von Hohenheim ['Theophrastus Paracelsus'], *Opera Omnia*, 3 vols (Geneva: Ioannes Antonius & Samuel de Tournes, 1658), sect. 49 'De Occulta Philosophia', ii. 494.

11. Johann Weyer, *Witches, Devils, and Doctors in the Renaissance*, ed. George Mora and Benjamin Kohl, trans. John Shea, Medieval & Renaissance Texts & Studies, 73 [a scholarly edition and translation of Johann Weyer, *De Praestigiis Daemonum*] (Binghamton, NY: Medieval & Renaissance Texts & Studies, 1991; repr. 1998), 154–6.

12. See Wilson, *Magical Universe*, 402 ff.; for a discussion of the modern phenomenon see e.g. Michelle Gonzalez Maldonado, 'If It Is Not Christian, Is it Theology? Espiritismo, Evil Eye, and Santería: A Dialogue with Latino/a Theology' presented to the Drew Transdisciplinary Theological Colloquium, VII, Drew University Theological School, Madison, NJ, 20–23 November 2008. http://depts.drew.edu/tsfac/colloquium/2008/abstracts.html#Maldonado.

13. Galatians 3: 1, in the Vulgate 'o insensati Galatae quis vos fascinavit ante quorum oculos Iesus Christus proscriptus est crucifixus'. Aquinas quoted the text as 'quis vos fascinavit veritati non obedire?' and was largely followed thus by his copiers and imitators.

14. Thomas Aquinas, *Summa Theologica*, Ia q. 117 a. 3 arg. 2.

15. *Summa Theologica*, Ia q. 117 a. 3 ad 2; quoted by Martín of Arles, *Tractatus de Superstitionibus*, sects. 35–6. This explanation may derive from Plutarch's *Symposium* (V.7), which has a separate chapter περὶ τῶν

καταβασκαίνειν λεγομένων, καὶ βάσκανον ἔχειν ὀφθαλμόν. The ὀφθαλμὸς βάσκανος is mentioned e.g. by Pliny the Elder, *Historia Naturalis*, VII.2, where the power to 'fascinate' is ascribed to certain barbarian peoples. For some of the classical lore on the subject, see Matthew W. Dickie, 'Heliodorus and Plutarch on the Evil Eye', *Classical Philology*, 86/1 (Jan. 1991), 17–29.

16. Nider, *Preceptorium*, prec. 1, ch. 11, q. 24; Geiler, *Die Emeis*, ch. 27, on fos. 47ʳ ff. See also Bernhardus Basin, 'Opusculum de artibus magicis, ac Magorum Maleficiis', in [Heinrich Institoris (1430–1505)], *Malleus Maleficarum: Maleficas et earum hæresim frameâ conterens, ex variis auctoribus compilatus, & in quator tomos iustè distributus*, 2 vols in 3 (Lyons: Claudius Bourgeat, 1669), ii, part I, 1–17 and especially 7 for eighth proposition.

17. Martín de Castañega, *Tratado de las supersticiones y hechizerias y de la possibilidad y remedio dellas, 1529* (Madrid: Sociedad de Bibliofilos Espanoles, 2nd series, 17, 1946), 71 ff (ch. 14); translation in David H. Darst, 'Witchcraft in Spain: The Testimony of Martín de Castañega's Treatise on Superstition and Witchcraft (1529)', *Proceedings of the American Philosophical Society*, 123/5 (1979), 298–322; this reference on 309. Modern edn by Juan Robert Muro Abad, 3rd edn (Logroño: Gobierno de La Rioja, Instituto de Estudios Riojanos, 1994).

18. Pedro Ciruelo (1470–1560), *Reprovación de las supersticiones y hechizerías (1538)*, ed. José Luis Herrero Ingelmo (Salamanca: Diputación de Salamanca, 2003), translated as *Pedro Ciruelo's A treatise reproving all superstitions and forms of witchcraft: very necessary and useful for all good Christians zealous for their salvation*, trans. E. A. Maio and D. W. Pearson (Rutherford, NJ: Fairleigh Dickinson University Press, 1977), bk 3, ch. 5, 234 ff and specifically 237–8.

19. Martín of Arles, *Tractatus de Superstitionibus*, section 26; *Dives and Pauper*, ed. Priscilla Heath Barnum, 3 vols, Early English Text Society, nos. 275, 280, 323 (London: Oxford University Press, 1976–2004), commandment 1 ch. 50 in vol. i, 186–7.

20. Martin Luther, *Decem Praecepta wittenbergensi predicata populo* (Wittenberg: Johann Rhau-Grunenberg, 1518), sig Aiiiᵛ; also ed. in *WA* 1, 394 ff. Johann Spreter, *Ein Kurtzer Bericht was von den Abgötterischen Sägen vnd Beschweren zuhalten wie der etlich volbracht vnnd das die ein Zauberey auch greüwel vor Gott dem Herren seind* (Basle: Bartholomeus Westheymer, 1543), sig. Aivʳ.

21. The classic text to this effect is *Malleus Maleficarum* (1669), pt. 1, q. 6, in i. 40–7, but here it largely borrows from earlier remarks by other theological writers.

22. For soldiers, see e.g. 'Opusculum adversus doctrinam cuiusdam medici', in *Opera*, ed. du Pin, I, cols. 206–8, proposition 12; Mazzolini, *De Strigimagarum . . . Mirandis*, for the story of an infantry commander called 'Marzocchio': on sig. ff iiiᵛ ff, as above in the Introduction, n. 2.

23. Discussion of the healing of wounds with plain linen cloth 'which they call "St Anselm's art"' appears in Martinus Delrio SJ, *Disquisitionum Magicarum Libri Sex*, 3 vols (Louvain: Gerardus Rivius, 1599–1600), i. 33–7, 42; also ii. 114.

24. The binding of the weapon or 'weapon-salve' is found e.g. in Benedictus Aretius, *Problemata theologica* (Lausanne: Franciscus Le Preux, 1578), article 'Magia' in part II, fo. 42^v; also Johann Georg Godelmann, *Tractatus de Magis, Veneficis et Lamiis, deque his recte cognoscendis et puniendis* (Frankfurt: Nicolaus Bassaeus, 1601), 86. The weapon-salve would become famous later in the seventeenth century as a result of the experiments of Sir Kenelm Digby, documented in Kenelm Digby, *A late discourse made in a solemne assembly of nobles and learned men at Montpellier in France … touching the cure of wounds by the powder of sympathy; with instructions how to make the said powder; whereby many other secrets of nature are unfolded*, trans. R. White (London: R. Lownes, and T. Davies, 1658).

25. Such techniques included the 'Lady Fasts' discussed (with evident disapproval) in *Dives and Pauper*, ed. Barnum, commandment 1, ch. 42 in i. 172–4. Note also the stories and rhymes about Christopher, reported by Luther, *Decem Praecepta*, sigs. Cii^v–iii^r. Rituals supposed to ensure freedom from dying suddenly and unprepared are also enumerated and criticized in Emanuele do Valle de Moura, *De Incantationibus seu Ensalmis Opusculum Primum* (Évora: Laurentius Crasbeeck, 1620), 132.

26. Compare Wilson, *Magical Universe*, 115–214.

27. On Burchard's 'Corrector' see Ludger Körntgen, 'Canon Law and the Practice of Penance: Burchard of Worms's Penitential', in *Early Medieval Europe*, 14/1 (2006), 103–17.

28. Quoted in Joseph Hansen (ed.), *Quellen und Untersuchungen zur Geschichte des Hexenwahns und der Hexenverfolgung im Mittelalter* (Hildesheim: G. Olms, 1963, reprint of the original edition, Bonn: C. Georgi, 1901), 42. See quotation and discussion of this text in Burchard in Catherine Rider, *Magic and Impotence in the Middle Ages* (Oxford and New York: Oxford University Press, 2006), 44–5.

29. For Hincmar's discussion of impotence by sorcery, see Rider, *Magic and Impotence*, pp 31 ff.

30. Peter Lombard, *Libri IV Sententiarum*, bk 4, dist. 34, 'de his qui maleficis impediti coire non possunt'. The text is included in *Joanni Duns Scoti … Opera Omnia*, ed. L. Wadding, 26 vols, (Paris: Ludovicus Vives, 1891–5), xix. 399. It is discussed in Thomas Aquinas, *Scriptum super Sententiis*, bk 4, dist. 34 q. 1, proemium and art. 2 s. c. 1 and corollary; also article 3, 'Utrum maleficium possit matrimonium impedire'. For the canon law text, see

Decretum part 2, causa 33, qu. 1 c. iv: *si per sortiarias vel maleficas*, in *Corpus Juris Canonici*, ed. Aemilius Ludouicus Richter and Aemilius Friedberg (Graz: Akademische Druck- u. Verlagsanstalt, 1959), i, col. 1150, as cited e.g. by Aquinas, *Super Sententiis*, lib. 4 d. 34 q. 1 a. 3 s. c. 1. For canonical discussion of impotence see Rider, *Magic and Impotence*, 53 ff; also the *Liber Extra, De frigidis et maleficiatis*, Decretals IV tit. 15, in Friedberg (ed.), *Corpus Juris Canonici*, ii, cols. 704–8, although the *Liber Extra* does not discuss the sources of the impotence except implicitly, in the title of the section.

31. See Duns Scotus, *Lectures on the Sentences*, bk 4, q. 34, in *Duns Scoti . . . Opera Omnia*, vol. xix. 403–4 and commentary on 406–7, for a particularly influential discussion of whether one could lawfully remove or destroy sorcerers' emblems. Duns Scotus was widely discussed and quoted by nearly all late scholastic authors. See Geiler, *Die Emeis*, ch. 33, fos. 54^v ff; also quoted by Jacobus van Hoogstraten (*c.*1460–1527), *Tractus magistralis declarans quam graviter peccent querentes auxilium a maleficis; Contra petentes remedia a maleficis* (Cologne: Martinus de Werdena, 1510), ch. 2; and Mazzolini, *De Strigimagarum . . . Mirandis*, bk 2, ch. 10, sig. ee ii^v.

32. See e.g. the discussion of this topic in Petrus de Palude, *Scriptum in librum quartum sententiarum* (Venice: Bonetus Locatellus and Octauianus Scotus, 1493), fo. 171^r.

33. The primary source of this explanation is *Malleus Maleficarum* (1669), part I, q. 9, at i. 59–62. For a detailed modern discussion see Walter Stephens, *Demon lovers: Witchcraft, Sex, and the Crisis of Belief* (Chicago: University of Chicago Press, 2002), 300–8.

34. Felix Hemmerli, 'Tractatus III de Credulitate Daemonibus Adhibenda', published in some editions of the *Malleus Maleficarum* (Frankfurt: Nicolaus Bassaeus, 1588 and 1600), ii. 429.

35. See a reference to this in Carl Lindahl, John McNamara, and John Lindow (eds) *Medieval Folklore: A Guide to Myths, Legends, Tales, Beliefs, and Customs* (Oxford: Oxford University Press, 2002), 321, with indications of where such 'nests' were depicted in popular imagery.

36. On the subject in general, see Rider, *Magic and Impotence, passim*.

37. Nider, *Preceptorium*, prec. 1, ch. 11, sect. 25; Laurent Joubert, *Popular Errors*, trans. Gregory Rocher (Tuscaloosa: University of Alabama Press, 2006) and *The Second Part of the Popular Errors* (Tuscaloosa: University of Alabama Press, 2007)

38. Natalie Zemon Davis, 'Proverbial Wisdom and Popular Errors', in her *Society and Culture in Early Modern France: Eight Essays* (Stanford, CA: Stanford University Press, 1975), 227–67.

39. On midwives in the era of the witch-hunts, see e.g. Alison Rowlands, 'Monstrous Deception: Midwifery, Fraud and Gender in Early Modern Rothenburg ob der Tauber', in Ulinka Rublack (ed.), *Gender in Early Modern German History* (Cambridge and New York: Cambridge University Press, 2002), 71–101.

40. On the involvement of lying-in maids in witchcraft trials, see Lyndal Roper, 'Witchcraft and Fantasy in early Modern Germany', in her *Oedipus and the Devil: Witchcraft, Sexuality and Religion in Early Modern Europe* (London and New York: Routledge, 1994), 199–225.

41. Luther, *Decem Praecepta*, sigs Aiv^{r-v}.

42. William of Auvergne, *De Universo*, pt. 2, sect. 3, ch. 25, in *Guilelmi Alverni . . . Opera Omnia*, 2 vols (Aurelia: F. Hotot; London: Robertus Scott, 1674), i. 1072–3; for a detailed history of the changeling, emphasizing the aspect of literary and theological transmission, see C. F. Goodey and Tim Stainton, 'Intellectual Disability and the Myth of the Changeling Myth', *Journal of the History of the Behavioral Sciences*, 37/3 (2001), 223–40.

43. Jacob of Jueterbogk (also known as Jacobus de Clusa, *c*.1381–1465), 'De Potestate Daemonum, Arte Magica, Superstitionibus et Illusionibus eorundem', in Cornell University Archives, MS. 4600 Bd. Ms. 4, fos. 183^{r}–257^{v}, here on fo. 248r; Nider, *Preceptorium*, precept 1, ch. 11, qq. 10–14; Geiler von Kaisersberg, *Die Emeis*, fo. 43^{r}; Mazzolini, *De Strigimagarum . . . Mirandis*, sigs. S iii^{r}; ff iv^{v}. See also the extract from Nicolaus von Jauer in Hansen, *Quellen*, 69, and an anonymous *Tractatus de daemonibus* of *c*.1415, ibid. 86.

44. Luther, *Decem Praecepta*, sig. Ci^{r}. Luther reportedly repeated the story in his *Table Talk*.

45. 'Frenzy' is discussed in John Pecham's catechetical manual of 1281 'Ignorantia Sacerdotum' under the heading of the sacrament of extreme unction. On the *Ignorantia Sacerdotum*, a classic text of late medieval catechesis, see Decima L. Douie, *Archbishop Pecham* (Oxford: Clarendon Press, 1952), 134–42.

46. [Johannes Nider], *Johannis Nideri theologi olim clarissimi De visionibus ac revelationibus: opus rarissimum historiis Germaniæ refertissimum, anno 1517, Argentinæ editum* (Helmstedt: Paulus Zeisingius, Salomon Schnorrius, 1692) [the accessible early modern printed edition of Nider's *Formicarius*], 290–2. On Kalteisen see Thomas Prügl, *Die Ekklesiologie Heinrich Kalteisens OP in der Auseinandersetzung mit dem Basler Konziliarismus* (Paderborn: F. Schöningh, 1995) and the editions of Kalteisen's sermons issued in several volumes ed. by Bernhard D. Haage and Helga Haage-Naber. On possession in general in the Middle Ages and early modern period, see Nancy Caciola, *Discerning Spirits: Divine and Demonic Possession in the Middle Ages* (Ithaca, NY; London: Cornell University Press, 2003); also Moshe Sluhovsky, *Believe not Every Spirit: Possession,*

Mysticism, & Discernment in Early Modern Catholicism (Chicago: University of Chicago Press, 2007); Sarah Ferber, *Demonic Possession and Exorcism in Early Modern France* (London and New York: Routledge, 2004).

47. See book 5 of Johannes Nider's *Formicarius*, found in *Malleorum quorundam maleficarum, tam veterum quam recentiorum authorum, tomi duo* (Frankfurt: Nicolaus Bassaeus, 1582), i. 694 ff. Ch. 5, 728 ff is devoted entirely to the issue of inordinate love and desire arising out of sorcery; see also Guido Ruggiero, *Binding Passions: Tales of Magic, Marriage, and Power at the End of the Renaissance* (New York: Oxford University Press, 1993).

48. See Aquinas, *Super Sententiis*, 2 dist. 8, q. 1, art. 5, on the limits of the devil's ability to control the human will. Aquinas concludes that demons can plant impressions in the imagination, angels in the understanding, but only God in the will.

49. And compare also Wilson, *Magical Universe*, 3–111.

50. Felix Hemmerli, 'Tractatus I de exorcismis', in *Malleus Maleficarum* (Frankfurt: Nicolaus Bassaeus, 1600), ii. 378.

51. Geiler, *Die Emeis*, ch. 33, at fos. 54^v ff; compare e.g. Plantsch, *Opusculum de sagis maleficis*, sig. c ii^r; Mazzolini, *De Strigimagarum . . . Mirandis*, book 2, ch. 7, sigs. bb ii^v ff.

52. *Malleus Maleficarum* (1669), pt. II, q. 2, at i. 176; copied in Mazzolini, *De Strigimagarum . . . Mirandis*, pt. 2, ch. 10, sigs. ee iii ff; also quoted by Girolamo Menghi, *Compendio dell'arte essorcistica, et possibilita delle mirabili, et stupende operationi delli demoni, et dei malefici. Con li rimedii opportuni alle infirmità maleficiali* (Bologna: Giovanni Rossi, 1582), bk 3 ch. 2, 537. See discussion in Michael Bailey, 'The Disenchantment of Magic: Spells, Charms, and Superstition in Early European Witchcraft Literature', *American Historical Review*, 111/2 (2006), 383–404 at 399.

53. Nider *Preceptorium*, prec. 1, ch. 11, sect 34; Nider, *Formicarius*, book 5, *Malleorum quorundam maleficarum* (1582), i. 727, reflecting the story of the sorcerer Staedelin; followed in Mazzolini, *De Strigimagarum . . . Mirandis*, bk 2 ch. 7, sigs. bb ii^v ff; Geiler, *Die Emeis*, fo. 44^r.

54. The charming of storms is discussed in Castañega, *Tratado de las supersticiones*, ch. 19, 117 ff, and in Darst, 'Witchcraft in Spain', 316 ff; Ciruelo, *Reprobación*, ed. Maio, bk 3, ch. 9, 291 ff; Martín of Arles, *Tractatus de Superstitionibus*, sect. 45.

55. Martín of Arles, *Tractatus de Superstitionibus, passim*, but especially the introduction and early sections that discuss the concern with drought.

56. Ibid., sect. 42; compare Luther, *Decem Praecepta*, sig Aiv^v on conjuring flocks against attack by wolves.

57. Felix Hemmerli, 'Tractatus I de exorcismis', in *Malleus Maleficarum* (Frankfurt: Nicolaus Bassaeus, 1600), ii. 384.

58. The theological argument postulated that the adjuration was directed not to the pests but to the demons directing them. See Thomas Aquinas, *Summa Theologica*, II^a–IIae, q. 90, art. 3. However, for a hostile view of this procedure see Castañega, *Tratado de las supersticiones*, ch. 18 on 89 ff, and in Darst, 'Witchcraft in Spain', 312 ff; also Ciruelo, *Reprobación*, ed. Maio, bk 3, ch. 10, 305, where informal practices to exorcise pests are condemned and the story of Gregory of Ostia's cleansing of the fields is recounted. On the practice see Walter Woodburn Hyde, 'The Prosecution and Punishment of Animals and Lifeless Things in the Middle Ages and Modern Times', *University of Pennsylvania Law Review and American Law Register*, 64/7 (May 1916), 696–730; Hampton L. Carson, 'The Trial of Animals and Insects: A Little Known Chapter of Mediæval Jurisprudence', *Proceedings of the American Philosophical Society*, 56/5 (1917), 410–15.

59. On a celebrated legal opinion on behalf of the rats of Autun, see Bartholomaeus a Chassanaeo, *Catalogus gloriae mundi libr. XII.* (Lyons, 1529, and many subsequent editions) based on a legal *consilium* that Chasseneux produced early in his career. It was cited e.g. in John Foxe, *The Acts and Monuments*, ed. Joseph Pratt, 8 vols (London: Religious Tract Society, 1877), iv. 488; see also David Murray, *Lawyers' Merriments* (Glasgow, n.p.: 1912), 128–30.

60. Geiler, *Die Emeis*, ch. 23, fos. 43^{r-v}, based on Nider, *Preceptorium*, prec. 1, ch. 11, sect. 11.

2. A DENSELY POPULATED UNIVERSE

1. Jean Gerson, 'De Erroribus circa Artem Magicam et Articulis Reprobatis', in J. Gerson, *Joannis Gersonii Doctoris Theologi & Cancellarii Parisiensis Opera Omnia*, ed. Ludovicus Ellies du Pin, 5 vols, 2nd edn (The Hague: P. de Hondt, 1728), i, cols. 210–19; also ed. in *Malleus Maleficarum: Maleficas et earum hæresim frameâ conterens, ex variis auctoribus compilatus, & in quator tomos iustè distributus*, 2 vols in 3 (Lyons: Claudius Bourgeat, 1669), ii, pt. II, [with separate title-page and pagination], 163–75: references are here to the *Malleus* edition.

2. Gerson, 'De Erroribus circa Artem Magicam', in *Malleus Maleficarum* (1669), ii pt. II, 174.

3. Alphonsus de Spina [Alfonso de Espina], *Fortalitium fidei* (Lyons: Gulielmus Balsarin, 1487), bk 5, consideration 10, difference 2, sig. L i^v; Gustav Henningsen, '"The Ladies from Outside": An Archaic Pattern of the Witches' Sabbath', in Bengt Ankarloo and Gustav Henningsen (eds), *Early*

Modern European Witchcraft: Centres and Peripheries (Oxford: Oxford University Press, 1990), 191–215.

4. Martin Luther, *Decem Praecepta wittenbergensi predicata populo* (Wittenberg: Johann Rhau-Grunenberg, 1518), sigs. Bii^v–Biii^r.

5. Johann Weyer, *Witches, Devils, and Doctors in the Renaissance*, ed. George Mora and Benjamin Kohl, trans. John Shea, Medieval & Renaissance Texts & Studies, vol. 73 (Binghamton, NY: Medieval & Renaissance Texts & Studies, 1991; repr. 1998), 72.

6. Olaus Magnus, *Historia de gentibus septentrionalibus* (Rome: Ioannes Maria de Viottis, 1555); English edition as *Description of the Northern Peoples*, trans. Peter Fisher and Humphrey Higgens, ed. Peter Foote, 3 vols, Hakluyt Society; 2nd ser., nos. 182, 187–8 (London, 1996–8).

7. Magnus, *Description*, i.162.

8. Ibid., i.164–5.

9. Ibid., i. 170–7.

10. Ibid., i. 182 and quotations in e.g. Benedictus Aretius, *Problemata theologica* (Lausanne: Franciscus Le Preux, 1578), article 'Satan', part II, fos. 19^v–20^r.

11. Weyer, *Witches, Devils, and Doctors*, bk 1, ch. 22, 74–6; the original of the story is in Johannes Trithemius, *Chronicon insigne Monasterij Hirsaugiensis, ordinis S. Benedicti* (Basle: Apud Iacobum Parcum, 1534); later edition, Johannes Trithemius, *Johannis Trithemii . . . Primae partis opera historica*, ed. Marquard Freher, (Frankfurt: Wechel, 1601); on the story of Hutgin or Hödeken see G. L. Kittredge, 'The Friar's Lantern and the Friar Rush', *PMLA*, 15/4. (1900), 415–41. Reginald Scot (1538?–1599), *The Discovery of Witchcraft: . . . Whereunto is added an excellent Discourse of the nature and substance of devils and spirits* (London: A. Clark and Dixy Page, 1665) [the *Discourse* is separately paginated], ch. 21, though Scot does not give the story in full.

12. This piece of folklore has an interesting history. See W. D. Paden, 'Mt. 1352: Jacques de Vitry, the Mensa Philosophica, Hödeken, and Tennyson', *Journal of American Folklore*, 58/227 (1945), 35–47.

13. Weyer, *Witches, Devils, and Doctors*, 73; see also Scot *Discourse of Devils*, ch. 21, on *Daemones montani*.

14. On *Sylvestres*, see See Johannes Nider, *Preceptorium Divine Legis* (Basle: Berthold Ruppel, *c.*1470), prec. 1, ch. 11, sect. 6.

15. Joseph Hansen (ed.), *Quellen und Untersuchungen zur Geschichte des Hexenwahns und der Hexenverfolgung im Mittelalter* (Hildesheim: G. Olms, 1963, reprint of the original edition, Bonn: C. Georgi, 1901), 41. Walter Stephens, *Demon Lovers: Witchcraft, Sex, and the Crisis of Belief* (Chicago: University of Chicago Press, 2002) provides a very detailed coverage of the relationship between

demonology and sexuality, but chiefly in the context of the witch literature of the fifteenth century onwards.

16. Nider, *Preceptorium*, prec. 1 ch. 11, sect. 3; Johannes Geiler von Kaisersberg, *Die Emeis, dis ist das büch von der Omeissen* (Strasbourg: Johannes Grieninger, 1517), ch. 19, on fos. 39ᵛ ff. For the *Venusberg* compare Theophrastus Bombast von Hohenheim, ['Theophrastus Paracelsus'], *Opera Omnia*, 3 vols (Geneva: Ioannes Antonius & Samuel de Tournes, 1658), section 32 'De nymphis, sylvis, Pygmaeis, salamandris et caeteris spiritibus', ii. 395.

17. Paracelsus, *Opera Omnia*, ii. 395–6.

18. *Wahrhafte Geschichte Herrn P. v. St.* (Strasbourg: B. Jobins Erben, 1598). A 1588 edition of the poem was ed. by Fischart, a Protestant writer. In connection with the Stauffenberg legend see Gerhild Scholz Williams, *Ways of Knowing in Early Modern Germany: Johannes Praetorius as a Witness to his Time* (Aldershot: Ashgate, 2006), 26–7, 42–5.

19. Ludwig Achim, Freiherr von Arnim and Clemens Brentano (eds), *Des knaben Wunderhorn: Alte deutsche Lieder*, 3 vols (Heidelberg: Ben Mohr und Zimmer, 1808); Jaroslav Kvapil, *Divadlo Jaroslava Kvapila, Souborné dílo Jaroslava Kvapila*, vol. iii (Prague: Dr. Václav Tomsa, 1948).

20. Paracelsus, *Opera Omnia*, ii. 396.

21. Ibid. 393–5.

22. Jacob of Jueterbogk (also known as Jacobus de Clusa, c.1381–1465), 'De Potestate Daemonum, Arte Magica, Superstitionibus et Illusionibus eorundem', in Cornell University Archives, MS. 4600 Bd. Ms. 4, fo. 208ᵛ.

23. Nider, *Praeceptorium*, prec. 1 ch. 11 qq. 10–14; Johannes Nider's *Formicarius*, in *Malleorum quorundam maleficarum, tam veterum quam recentiorum authorum, tomi duo* (Frankfurt: Nicolaus Bassaeus, 1582), bk 5 ch. 2, at i. 703–12; Geiler von Kaisersberg, *Die Emeis*, fo. 43ʳ, item vi; De Spina, *Fortalitium*, book 5, consideration 10, difference 2, sig. L iʳ.

24. Nider, *Praeceptorium*, prec. 1, ch. 10, also ch. 11, q. 10; Geiler, *Die Emeis*, ch. 23 fo. 43ʳ; Martín of Arles y Andosilla, *Tractatus insignis et exquisitissimus de superstitionibus*, in *Tractatus Universi Juris*, xi, pt. 2 (Lyons, 1584), fos. 402ᵛ–8ʳ, section 13. For reference to legends of apparitions at Ember seasons see also Scot, *Discourse of Devils*, ch. 28.

25. Nider, *Praeceptorium*, prec. 1, ch. 11, q. 5, drawing on William of Auvergne, *De Universo*, part 2, sect. 3, ch. 24, in *Guilelmi Alverni . . . Opera Omnia*, 2 vols (Aurelia: F. Hotot; London: Robertus Scott, 1674), i. 1065; Thomas Aquinas, *Scriptum super Sententiis*, lib. 4 dist. 45 q. 1 a. 1 quaestiuncula 3, corollary. As William of Auvergne told the stories of spectral armies and apparitions of the dead in the same chapter, this probably inspired Nider's ordering of the material.

26. Alfonso de Spina, *Fortalitium*, book 5, consideration 10, diff. 4; Geiler *Die Emeis*, fos. 38ᵛ-9ʳ; Caspar Peucer, *Commentarius, de Praecipuis Divinationum generibus, in quo a prophetiis, authoritate divine traditis, et a Physicis conjecturis, discernuntur artes et imposturae diabolicae, atque observationes natae ex superstitione, et cum hac conjunctae: Et monstrantur fontes ac causae Physicarum praedictionum: Diabolicae vero ac superstitiosae confutatae damnantur, ea serie, quam tabella praefixa ostendit* (Frankfurt: Wechel, Claudius Marnius & heirs of Ioannes Aubrius, 1607), 735 ff.

27. For Regino, see Wilfried Hartmann, *Das Sendhandbuch des Regino von Prüm*, Ausgewählte Quellen zur deutschen Geschichte des Mittelalters, 42 (Darmstadt: Wissenschaftliche Buchgesellschaft, 2004).

28. Burchard in Hansen, *Quellen*, 40; For Burchard's *Decretum*: Greta Austin, 'Jurisprudence in the Service of Pastoral Care: The *Decretum* of Burchard of Worms', *Speculum*, 79 (2004), 929-59 and her *Shaping Church Law around the year 1000: The Decretum of Burchard of Worms* (Aldershot; Burlington, VT: Ashgate, 2008).

29. Decreti Secunda pars, Causa xxvi, quest. V c. 12, in *Corpus Juris Canonici*, ed. Aemilius Ludouicus Richter and Aemilius Friedberg (Graz: Akademische Druck- u. Verlagsanstalt, 1959), i, cols. 1030-1. On the history of the *Decretum* see Anders Winroth, *The Making of Gratian's Decretum* (Cambridge: Cambridge University Press, 2001) though Winroth only addresses this particular canon in the tabular appendix. For examples of the canon being quoted see Hansen, *Quellen*, 70, and Martín of Arles, *Tractatus de Superstitionibus*, section 11.

30. [Johannes Nider], *Johannis Nideri theologi olim clarissimi De visionibus ac revelationibus: opus rarissimum historiis Germaniæ refertissimum, anno 1517, Argentinæ editum* (Helmstedt: Paulus Zeisingius, Salomon Schnorrius, 1692), bk 2 ch. 4, 200-1. See discussion in Michael D. Bailey, *Battling Demons: Witchcraft, Heresy, and Reform in the Late Middle Ages* (University Park: Pennsylvania State University Press, 2003), 47 and nn.

31. Nider, *Praeceptorium*, prec. 1, ch. 10, also ch 11, q. 10; Geiler, *Die Emeis*, ch. 18. See also Luther, *Ten Commandments*, sig. Bivʳ⁻ᵛ, quoting Geiler.

32. Martín of Arles, *Tractatus de Superstitionibus*, sections 11-12.

33. Hansen, *Quellen*, 76.

34. Carlo Ginzburg, *I benandanti: ricerche sulla stregoneria e sui culti agrari tra Cinquecento e Seicento* (Turin: G. Einaudi, 1966).

35. Stories of people apparently turned into animals by sorcery figure prominently in *Malleus Maleficarum: Maleficas et earum hæresim frameâ conterens, ex variis auctoribus compilatus, & in quator tomos iustè distributus*, 2 vols in 3, (Lyons: Claudius Bourgeat, 1669), i. 63 ff. See also Silvestro Mazzolini, da Prierio

(Silvester Prierias) *De Strigimagarum Demonumque Mirandis libri tres* (Rome: Antonius Bladis de Asula, 24 Sept 1521), bk 2, ch. 11, at sigs. ee iv[r] ff. Augustine, *De Genesi ad Litteram libri duodecim*, bk 7, chs. 11 (16–17) in Migne, *Patrologia Latina*, (*PL*) vol. 34, scorned the idea of human beings being turned into animals as a fiction or a demonic illusion.

36. Palladius, *Lausiac History* chapters 19-20 in *Patrologia Latina*, *PL* vol. 73, cols. 1110–11 (chapters 17: 6–9 in some numerations), contains one version of the story, the one current in the later Middle Ages. There was an alternative version in Rufinus's *Historia Monachorum*, (21.17) in *PL*, vol. 21, col. 451. See David Frankfurter, 'The Perils of Love: Magic and Countermagic in Coptic Egypt', *Journal of the History of Sexuality*, 10/3–4 (2001), 480–500.

37. Luther *Ten Commandments*, sig. Biv[v].

38. Nider *Formicarius*, bk 5, ch. 4, 720–2.

39. Nider *Preceptorium* prec. 1, ch. 11, sects. 8–9.

40. Geiler, *Die Emeis*, chapters 21–2, fos. 41[v]–42[v], with references to Vincent of Beauvais and William of Auvergne. A classic story of a man deluded by demons into thinking himself turned into a wolf appears in William of Auvergne's *De Universo*, pt. 2, sect. 3, ch. 13, in *Guilelmi Alverni...Opera Omnia*, i. 1043. See also the article 'Freud, the Wolf-Man, and the Were-wolves', in Carlo Ginzburg, *Clues, Myths, and the Historical Method* (Baltimore: Johns Hopkins University Press, 1989); and Darren Oldridge, *Strange Histor-ies: The Trial of the Pig, the Walking Dead, and Other Matters of Fact from the Medieval and Renaissance Worlds* (London and New York: Routledge, 2005), ch. 6, 'Werewolves and Flying Witches'.

3. HELPFUL PERFORMANCES: THE USES OF RITUAL

1. Jacobus van Hoogstraten (*c*.1460–1527), *Tractus magistralis declarans quam graviter peccent querentes auxilium a maleficis; Contra petentes remedia a maleficis* (Cologne: Martinus de Werdena, 1510).

2. Gerson, J., *De Directione Cordis*, in Jean Gerson, *Œuvres complètes*, ed. Palémon Glorieux (Paris, New York: Desclée, 1960–), viii (1971), sect. 37–8, 108–9.

3. Johann Spreter, *Ein kurtzer Bericht, was von den abghotterischen Sägen un[nd] Beschweren zühalten: wie der etlich volbracht, unnd das die ein Zauberey, auch Greüwel vor Gott dem Herren seind* (Basle: Bartholomeus Westheymer, 1543); Emanuele do Valle de Moura, *De Incantationibus seu Ensalmis Opusculum Primum* (Évora: Laurentius Crasbeeck, 1620). Pedro Ciruelo, *Reprobación*, bk 3, ch. 3, refers to healers who used enchantments as *ensalmadores*: see *Pedro Ciruelo's A treatise reproving all superstitions and forms of witchcraft: very necessary*

and useful for all good Christians zealous for their salvation, trans. E. A. Maio and D. W. Pearson (Rutherford, NJ: Fairleigh Dickinson University Press, 1977), 198, and see also 202.

4. Robert E. Lerner, 'Werner di Friedberg intrappolato dalla legge', in J.-C. Maire Vigueur and A. Paravicini Bagliani (eds) *La parola all'accusato* (Palermo: Sellerio, 1991), 268–81, and specifically 269–70 for the details above.

5. Ibid. 279–80.

6. Nicholas Magni of Jauer's 'Tractatus de supersticionibus' of 1405 survives in over 80 manuscript copies. It is partially edited in Joseph Hansen (ed.), *Quellen und Untersuchungen zur Geschichte des Hexenwahns und der Hexenverfolgung im Mittelalter* (Hildesheim: G. Olms, 1963, reprint of the original edition, Bonn: C. Georgi, 1901), 67 ff. See Adolph Franz, *Der Magister Nikolaus Magni de Jawor* (Freiburg im Breisgau: Herder, 1898); also Friedrich Wilhelm Bautz and Traugott Bautz (eds), *Biographisch-bibliographisches Kirchenlexikon* (Hamm [Westf.]: Bautz, 1970–), article 'Nikolaus Jauer', by Ansgar Frenken.

7. Felix Hemmerli, 'Tractatus II de exorcismis' in *Malleus Maleficarum* (Frankfurt: Nicolaus Bassaeus, 1600), ii. 398–400. Hemmerli criticizes 'Frater Johannes' who may be Johann of Erfurt, the Franciscan author of a summa on confessions, and 'a certain Doctor in a certain little treatise on superstitions' who is probably Nicholas Magni of Jauer.

8. On amulets, see especially the extensive discussion in Ciruelo, *Reprobación*, bk 3, ch. 4, as in *Treatise reproving all superstitions*, ed. Maio and Pearson, 212 ff.

9. Lerner, 'Werner di Friedberg', 280: 'Christus wart geborn, Christus wart verlorn, Christus wart widerfunden, des gesegen diese wonden in nomine patris et filii et spiritus sancti'. Also quoted almost identically in Hemmerli, 'Tractatus II de exorcismis', ii. 399–400.

10. Felix Hemmerli, 'Tractatus I de exorcismis' in *Malleus Maleficarum* (Frankfurt: Nicolaus Bassaeus, 1600), ii. 378: 'Ob das sey | dass Maria Magd oder Jungfrauw | ein Kind Jesum gebahr | so komme diesem Thier das Blatt ab | im Namen des Vatters | etc.' Again, on ibid., ii. 416–17: 'Ich beschwere euch Wuerme bey dem Allmaechtigen GOTT | dass euch diese Statt oder Hauss als unmaehr seye | als unmaehr GOTT ist der Mann | der ein falsch Urteil spricht | unnd ein rechtes kan | In Namen dess Vatters | etc.'

11. Ibid., ii. 393.

12. For the use of the first chapter of St John's Gospel see [Heinrich Institoris (1430–1505)], *Malleus Maleficarum: Maleficas et earum hæresim frameâ conterens, ex variis auctoribus compilatus, & in quator tomos iustè distributus*, 2 vols in 3 (Lyons: Claudius Bourgeat, 1669), pt. II, q. 2, ch. 7, at i. 206; Silvestro Mazzolini, da Prierio (Silvester Prierias), *De Strigimagarum Demonumque Mirandis libri tres* (Rome: Antonius Bladis de Asula, 24 Sept 1521), sig. ff ii^{r-v}. Johann Weyer,

Witches, Devils, and Doctors in the Renaissance, ed. George Mora and Benjamin Kohl, trans. John Shea, Medieval & Renaissance Texts & Studies, 73 [a scholarly edition and translation of Johann Weyer, *De Praestigiis Daemonum*] (Binghamton, NY: Medieval & Renaissance Texts & Studies, 1991; repr. 1998), 391.

13. Weyer, *Witches, Devils, and Doctors*, 373 ff., 387 ff. Note that the Vulgate numbering of the Psalms differs from that now commonly used.

14. Martín de Castañega, *Tratado de las supersticiones y hechizerias y de la possibilidad y remedio dellas*, 1529 (Madrid, Sociedad de Bibliofilos Espanoles, 2nd series, 17, 1946) ch. 19, on 117 ff.; translation in David H. Darst, 'Witchcraft in Spain: The Testimony of Martin de Castañega's Treatise on Superstition and Witchcraft (1529)', *Proceedings of the American Philosophical Society*, 123/5 (1979), 316 ff; also [John Hooper]. *Early writings of John Hooper, D.D., Lord Bishop of Gloucester and Worcester, Martyr, 1555: Comprising The declaration of Christ and his office. Answer to Bishop Gardiner. Ten commandments. Sermons on Jonas. Funeral sermon*, ed. Samuel Carr, Parker Society (Cambridge: Cambridge University Press, 1843), 328–9: 'not many years sith I was borne in hand of an old man that erred by ignorance, that this medicine could heal all diseases, + Jesus + Job + habuit + vermes + Job + patitur + vermes + in + nominee + Patris + et + Filii + et + Spiritus Sancti + Amen + lama zabacthani +. God opened his heart afterwards to know the truth'.

15. See *The key of Solomon the king/Clavicula Salomonis*, translated and edited by S. Liddell MacGregor Mathers. (London: Kegan Paul, Trench, Trübner, 1909).

16. Martín of Arles y Andosilla, *Tractatus insignis et exquisitissimus de superstitionibus*, in *Tractatus Universi Juris*, xi, pt. 2 (Lyons, 1584), fos. 402^v–8^r, section 45.

17. [Girolamo Menghi], *Compendio dell'arte essorcistica, et possibilita delle mirabili, et stupende operationi delli demoni, et dei malefici. Con li rimedii opportuni alle infirmità maleficiali. Del R. P. F. Girolamo Menghi da Viadana Minore Osservante* (Bologna: G. Rossi, 1582), 582. The words quoted are simply a slightly garbled version of the Eastern invocation 'Holy God, Holy and Strong, Holy and Immortal, [have mercy on us].' Also cited by Castañega, *Tratado de las supersticiones*, chapter 19 on 117 ff. (as above, n. 14); compare also Menghi's own use of the formula (among others) in *Remedia Efficacissima*, 65.

18. Menghi, *Compendio*, 112, 133, 140 ff., 201.

19. Ibid., bk 1, chs. 8–9.

20. Weyer, *Witches, Devils, and Doctors*, 387 ff.

21. Werner Karl, 'Ananizapta—eine geheimnisvolle Inschrift des Mittelalters', *Sammelblatt des Historischen Vereins Ingolstadt*, 105 (1996), 59 ff. See also Werner Karl, 'Ananizapta und der Middleham Jewel', *Sammelblatt des Historischen Vereins Ingolstadt*, 110 (2001), 57 ff. *Anazapta*, a variant of the word, was used

as the title of a film centred on the mid-14th-century outbreak of the plague in Europe, directed by Alberto Sciamma and released in 2001.

22. Hemmerli, 'Tractatus I de exorcismis', ii. 395–6.

23. Martín of Arles, *Tractatus de Superstitionibus*, sections 52–3; Weyer, *Witches, Devils, and Doctors*, 393.

24. Delrio, *Disquisitions*, bk 3, pt. 2, q. 4, sect. 8, at ii. 117 ff; *Encyclopédie*, article 'Ananisapta' follows Delrio on this question.

25. Weyer, *Witches, Devils, and Doctors*, 388–9.

26. See edition in Karin Baumann, *Aberglaube für Laien: zur Programmatik und Überlieferung spätmittelalterlicher Superstitionenkritik*, 2 vols [continuously paginated] (Würzburg: Königshausen & Neumann, 1989), 521, lines 602 ff.

27. Jean Gerson, 'De Erroribus circa Artem Magicam et Articulis Reprobatis', in *Malleus Maleficarum: Maleficas et earum hæresim frameâ conterens, ex variis auctoribus compilatus, & in quator tomos iustè distributus*, 2 vols in 3 (Lyons: Claudius Bourgeat, 1669), ii, pt. II. [with separate title-page and pagination], 168 ff. Gerson is quoted in Martín of Arles, *Tractatus de Superstitionibus*, sections 38 and 80. For the Key of Solomon reference see above. For other references to virgin parchment see Castañega, *Tratado de las supersticiones*, ch. 16, 81 ff; Darst, 'Witchcraft in Spain', 310 ff.

28. Baumann, *Aberglaube für Laien*, 548; compare Martín of Arles, *Tractatus de Superstitionibus*, sections 38–9; Plantsch, *Opusculum*, sig. e viii^r.

29. Martín of Arles, *Tractatus de Superstitionibus*, sections 93 and 100, cites the popular approval of chastity, as does Jacob of Jueterbogk (also known as Jacobus de Clusa, *c*.1381–1465), 'De Potestate Daemonum, Arte Magica, Superstitionibus et Illusionibus eorundem', in Cornell University Archives, MS. 4600 Bd. Ms. 4, fo. 248^r; Nider *Preceptorium* prec. 1, ch. 11 q. 2, based on William of Auvergne, *De Universo*, part 2 sect. 3, ch. 18, in *Guilelmi Alverni . . . Opera Omnia*, 2 vols (Aurelia: F. Hotot; London: Robertus Scott, 1674), i. 1049; Geiler, *Die Emeis*, fo. 39^v. Nider is extravagant in his praise of chastity in the *Formicarius* (but does not say so much about the devil wishing to praise it).

30. e.g. Hansen, *Quellen*, 41–2 item 2, Martín of Arles, *Tractatus de Superstitionibus*, section 9.

31. Hoogstraten, *Tractatus magistralis*, ch. 3.

32. Heinrich von Gorkum (*c*.1386–1431) *Tractatus de supersticiosis quibusdam casibus* (Esslingen: Conrad Fyner, 1473), fos. 2^r–4^r; for Agatha and fires compare Martín of Arles, *Tractatus de Superstitionibus*, section 14.

33. Gorkum, *De supersticiosis quibusdam casibus*, fos. 4^r–5^r.

34. Ibid., fos. 6^r–7^r.

35. Ibid., fos. 8^v–9^r.

36. Castañega, *Tratado de las supersticiones*, ch. 16, 81 ff; Darst, 'Witchcraft in Spain', 310 ff. Compare Castañega, *Tratado*, ch. 21, 127–31 and Darst, 'Witchcraft in Spain', 318 for further endorsement of this practice.

37. Gerson, 'De Erroribus circa Artem Magicam' as above, n. 27, vol. ii part II, 169; compare Manuel do Vale de Moura as below, chapter 15. nn. 47–56.

38. An exception was made for baptism in the case of an emergency.

39. The list comes from Plantsch, *Opusculum*, sigs. f i^r–g i^v. Compare the work of Friedrich Förner below, chapter 15. nn. 73–7. For modern discussions of sacramentals see R. W. Scribner, 'Cosmic Order and Daily Life: Sacred and Secular in Pre-Industrial German Society', in K. von Greyerz (ed.), *Religion and Society in Early Modern Europe 1500–1800* (London: German Historical Institute; Boston: Allen & Unwin, 1984), 20–1, also id., *The German Reformation* (London: Macmillan, 1986), 11–12; also id., 'Ritual and Popular Religion', in R. W. Scribner, *Popular Culture and Popular Movements in Reformation Germany* (London: Hambledon Press, 1987), 36–41.

40. Geiler, *Die Emeis*, chapters 30–1.

41. Plantsch, *Opusculum*, sig. g i^v–ii^r. For the letter of Jesus to Abgar of Edessa, see J. K. Elliott (ed. and trans.), *The Apocryphal New Testament: A Collection of Apocryphal Christian Literature in an English Translation* (Oxford: Clarendon Press, 1993), 538–42.

42. e.g. Hoogstraten, *Tractatus magistralis*, chapter 10; Plantsch, *Opusculum*, sig. e viii^r.

43. Nider, *Preceptorium*, prec. 1, ch. 11, sect. 27, as quoted by Mazzolini, *De Strigimagarum . . . Mirandis*, bk 2, ch. 12, sig. gg i^{r-v}; compare Jacob of Jueterbogk, 'De Potestate Daemonum', fos. 252^r ff.

44. This from Nider, *Preceptorium*, prec. 1, ch. 11, sect. 26, amplifying Aquinas's conditions for the proper form of an amulet, from *Summa Theologica* II^a–IIae, q. 96, a. 4, also quoted in Mazzolini, *De Strigimagarum . . . Mirandis*, bk 2, ch. 12, sect. I, sigs. gg i^v–ii^v and in Martín of Arles, *Tractatus de Superstitionibus*, sects. 40–1.

45. Compare here also Ciruelo, *Reprobación*, bk 3, ch. 8, as in *Treatise reproving all superstitions*, ed. Maio and Pearson, 274 ff: Ciruelo contrasts the restrained and disciplined behaviour of 'true exorcists' with those who use arcane words, hold long conversations with the devils, and bring a level of theatricality to the whole performance.

46. Mazzolini, *De Strigimagarum . . . Mirandis*, bk 2, ch. 12, sect. 2, sigs. gg ii^v ff.

47. Girolamo Menghi, *Flagellum Daemonum, exorcismos terribiles, potentissimos, et efficaces: Remediaque probatissima, ac doctrina singularem in malignos spiritos expellendos, facturasque et maleficia fuganda de obsessis corporibus complectens* (Bologna, 1589).

48. Menghi, *Flagellum*, 173 ff.

49. Menghi, *Fustis Daemonum, adiurationes formidabiles, potentissimas, et efficaces in malignos spiritus fugandos de oppressis corporibus humanis . . . auctore R. P. F. Hieronymo Mengo Vitellianensi* (Bologna, 1589), including his *Remedia efficacissima*.

50. Castañega, *Tratado de las supersticiones*, chapter 1, 17–22; Darst, 'Witchcraft in Spain', 301–2.

51. Martín of Arles, *Tractatus de Superstitionibus*, sections 70, 91, 94. Note also ibid., section 57, on soothsayers celebrating the Eucharist on the same day as offering magical services.

52. On these parallel sources of assistance see especially the idea of a 'system of the sacred' in David Gentilcore, *From Bishop to Witch: the System of the Sacred in Early Modern Terra d'Otranto* (Manchester: Manchester University Press, 1992). See also William E. Klingshirn, *Caesarius of Arles: The Making of a Christian Community in Late Antique Gaul* (Cambridge: Cambridge University Press, 1994), 167 and 222.

53. Jean Gerson, 'Triologium Astrologiae Theologizatae', in J. Gerson, *Joannis Gersonii Doctoris Theologi & Cancellarii Parisiensis Opera Omnia*, ed. Ludovicus Ellies du Pin, 5 vols, 2nd edn (The Hague: P. de Hondt, 1728), i, col. 202: 'Qualis mihi cura est quis me sanet, quis victoriam, quis honorem, quis divitias det, quis denique adjuvet? Sit Deus, sit diabolus, dummodo proveniat mihi illud quod opto.'

4. INSIGHT AND FORESIGHT: TECHNIQUES OF DIVINATION

1. For some of the pre-modern evidence, see Stephen Wilson, *The Magical Universe: Everyday Ritual and Magic in Pre-Modern Europe* (London: Hambledon, 2000), 375 ff.

2. Note that the early modern edition of Nider's *Formicarius* was entitled *On Visions and Revelations*: [Johannes Nider], *Johannis Nideri theologi olim clarissimi De visionibus ac revelationibus: opus rarissimum historiis Germaniæ refertissimum, anno 1517, Argentinæ editum* (Helmstedt: Paulus Zeisingius, Salomon Schnorrius, 1692).

3. Isidore, *Etymologies*, VIII, 9; edited in Migne, *PL*, vol. 82, cols. 9–728; the relevant passage on divination is on cols. 310–14. See also Isidore of Seville, *The Etymologies of Isidore of Seville*, ed. and trans. Stephen A. Barney, W. J. Lewis, J. A. Beach, and Oliver Berghof (Cambridge: Cambridge University Press, 2006), 181–2.

4. Thomas Aquinas, *Summa Theologica*, II^a–IIae, q. 95, a. 3.

5. See citation of Isidore's list in Nikolaus von Dinkelsbühl, in Karin Baumann, *Aberglaube für Laien: zur Programmatik und Überlieferung spätmittelalterlicher*

Superstitionenkritik, 2 vols [continuously paginated] (Würzburg: Königshausen & Neumann, 1989), 530 ff; Jakob of Jüterbogk (also known as Jacobus de Clusa, *c*.1381–1465), 'De Potestate Daemonum, Arte Magica, Superstitionibus et Illusionibus eorundem', in Cornell University Archives, MS. 4600 Bd. Ms. 4, fo. 231^r, in almost the same order as Thomas; likewise Johannes Nider, *Preceptorium Divine Legis* (Basle: Berthold Ruppel, *c*.1470), prec. 1, ch. 11.

6. William of Auvergne, *De Universo*, pt. 2, sect. 3, ch. 18, in *Guilelmi Alverni... Opera Omnia*, 2 vols (Aurelia: F. Hotot; London: Robertus Scott, 1674), i. 1049 ff, and compare Jacob of Jueterbogk, 'De Potestate Daemonum', fos. 248^r ff. On divinatory techniques see also [Pedro Ciruelo], *Pedro Ciruelo's A treatise reproving all superstitions and forms of witchcraft: very necessary and useful for all good Christians zealous for their salvation*, trans. E. A. Maio and D. W. Pearson (Rutherford, NJ: Fairleigh Dickinson University Press, 1977), 146 ff.

7. Caspar Peucer, *Commentarius, de Praecipuis Divinationum generibus, in quo a prophetiis, authoritate divine traditis, et a Physicis conjecturis, discernuntur artes et imposturae diabolicae, atque observationes natae ex superstitione, et cum hac conjunctae: Et monstrantur fontes ac causae Physicarum praedictionum: Diabolicae vero ac superstitiosae confutatae damnantur, ea serie, quam tabella praefixa ostendit* (Frankfurt: Wechel, Claudius Marnius & heirs of Ioannes Aubrius, 1607) For earlier editions see Introduction, n. 3.

8. Johann Weyer, *Witches, Devils, and Doctors in the Renaissance*, ed. George Mora and Benjamin Kohl, trans. John Shea, Medieval & Renaissance Texts & Studies, vol. 73 [a scholarly edition and translation of Johann Weyer, *De Praestigiis Daemonum*] (Binghamton, NY: Medieval & Renaissance Texts & Studies, 1991; repr. 1998), bk 2, ch. 12, 134 ff.

9. *Dives and Pauper*, ed. Priscilla Heath Barnum, 3 vols, Early English Text Society, nos. 275, 280, 323 (London: Oxford University Press, 1976–2004), commandment 1, ch. 36, at i. 162–5.

10. Weyer, *Witches, Devils, and Doctors*, 378 and 380; cf. Martinus Delrio SJ, *Disquisitionum Magicarum Libri Sex*, 3 vols (Louvain: Gerardus Rivius, 1599–1600), bk 3, pt. 2, q. 4, sect. 9, no. 15, at ii. 125 ff.

11. Weyer, *Witches, Devils, and Doctors*, 381 ff; Delrio, *Disquisitionum Magicarum*, bk 3, pt. 2, q. 4, sect. 9, no. 15, fifth part, though he abbreviates the curse. Compare with Lester K. Little, *Benedictine Maledictions: Liturgical Cursing in Romanesque France* (Ithaca, NY: Cornell University Press, 1993), esp. 255–6; and the Excommunication in Laurence Sterne's *Tristram Shandy*, discussed in Little, 1 ff. See also Henry Charles Lea, *Materials toward a History of Witchcraft*, ed. Arthur C. Howland, 3 vols continuously paginated (New York: T. Yoseloff, 1957), 514.

12. Martín of Arles y Andosilla, *Tractatus insignis et exquisitissimus de superstitionibus*, in *Tractatus Universi Juris*, xi, pt. 2 (Lyons, 1584), fos. 402^v–8^r, section 31, also quoted by Johann Georg Godelmann, *Tractatus de Magis, Veneficis et Lamiis, deque his recte cognoscendis et puniendis* (Frankfurt: Nicolaus Bassaeus, 1601), 114. On calendar divination, see also Wilson, *Magical Universe*, 25 ff.

13. Sources for these include Godelmann, *Tractatus de Magis*, 114–15. An even fuller list of weather saints is found in Henry B. Wheatley, 'Saint Swithin's Day', *The Antiquary* (July 1882), 1–4.

14. *Dives and Pauper*, ed. Barnum, commandment I, chs. 47–8, at i. 182–5.

15. Ciruelo, *Reprobación*, bk 3, ch 6, ed. Maio, 245–6.

16. Eric Plumer, *Augustine's Commentary on Galatians: Introduction, Text, Translation, and Notes* (Oxford: Oxford University Press, 2003), 186–7.

17. Joseph Hansen (ed.), *Quellen und Untersuchungen zur Geschichte des Hexenwahns und der Hexenverfolgung im Mittelalter* (Hildesheim: G. Olms, 1963, reprint of the original edition, Bonn: C. Georgi, 1901), 43.

18. For other mentions of the Egyptian Days see Martín of Arles, *Tractatus de Superstitionibus*, sections 15 and following; Jean Gerson, 'Tractatus Contra Superstitionem praesertim Innocentium', in J. Gerson, *Joannis Gersonii Doctoris Theologi & Cancellarii Parisiensis Opera Omnia*, ed. M. Lud. Ellies du Pin, 5 vols, 2nd edn (The Hague: P. de Hondt, 1728), i, cols. 203–6: describes belief in Innocents' Day as well as in Egyptian Days; Gerson, 'De Observatione Dierum quantum ad Opera', written against a physician at Montpellier, in *Opera*, ed. du Pin, i, cols. 208–10; Heinrich von Gorkum (*c.*1386–1431) *Tractatus de supersticiosis quibusdam casibus* (Esslingen: Conrad Fyner, 1473), fols 7^v–8^v; Nikolaus von Dinkelsbühl in Baumann, *Aberglaube für Laien*, 541 lines 897 ff. The days are actually listed by Delrio, *Disquisitionum Magicarum*, ii. 110–11: Delrio's cited source is Pierre Breslay, *L'Anthologie ou Recueil de plusieurs discours notables, tirez de diuers bons autheurs Grecs & Latins* (Paris: Chez I. Poupy, 1574), bk 1, c. 53.

19. Gerson, 'Tractatus Contra Superstitionem praesertim Innocentium', in *Opera*, ed. du Pin, i, cols. 203–6 as above.

20. Martín of Arles, *Tractatus de Superstitionibus*, section 15.

21. Ibid. section 29. Compare *Dives and Pauper*, ed. Barnum, commandment I, ch. 46, at i. 181–2. Note that in the life of St Bernard it was reported that Bernard blessed animals in the countryside such that they could not be caught by hunters: see *The Cistercian World: Monastic Writings of the Twelfth Century*, trans. and ed. Pauline Matarasso (London: Penguin, 1993), 40.

22. *Dives and Pauper*, ed. Barnum, commandment I, ch. l, at i. 186–7.

23. Desiderius Erasmus, *Praise of Folly*, in: *Collected Works of Erasmus*, xxvii. *Literary and Educational Writings*, 5 (ed. A. H. T. Levi; Toronto: University of Toronto Press 1986), 131.

24. *Dives and Pauper*, ed. Barnum, commandment I, ch. 46, at i. 181–2.

25. Nikolaus von Dinkelsbühl, in Baumann, *Aberglaube für Laien*, 542–5.

26. Delrio, *Disquisitionum Magicarum*, facing ii. 109. On omens, see also Ciruelo, *Reprobación*, ed. Maio, 153 ff.

27. Augustine, *De Doctrina Christiana*, ed. and trans. R. P. H. Green, Oxford Early Christian Texts (Oxford; New York: Clarendon Press, 1995), II. xx (31), 48–9; part of this (not all) was also cited by Thomas Aquinas in *Summa Theologica* II^a–IIae, q. 92, a. 2, and again in II^a–IIae, q. 96, a. 2, as quoted by Martín of Arles, *Tractatus de Superstitionibus*, sections 28–9.

28. Hansen, *Quellen*, 42 ff; *Dives and Pauper*, ed. Barnum, commandment I, ch. 34, at i. 157–9.

29. On the *sortes biblicae* see also William E. Klingshirn, *Caesarius of Arles: the Making of a Christian Community in late antique Gaul* (Cambridge: Cambridge University Press, 1994), 220.

30. William E. Klingshirn, 'Defining the Sortes Sanctorum: Gibbon, Du Cange, and Early Christian Lot Divination', *Journal of Early Christian Studies*, 10/1 (2002), 77–130.

31. *Dives and Pauper*, ed. Barnum, commandment I, ch. 38, at i. 166–7.

32. Jean Gerson, 'Triologium Astrologiae Theologizatae' (Lyons, 1419), in *Opera*, ed. du Pin, i, cols. 189–203.

33. Gerson, 'Tractatus Contra Superstitionem praesertim Innocentium', in *Opera*, ed. du Pin, i, cols. 203–6, extract on col. 204, and as quoted in Martín of Arles, *Tractatus de Superstitionibus*, sections 16–17.

34. For a simpler and more aggressive distinction between 'true' and 'false' (i.e. judicial) astrology see Ciruelo, *Reprobación*, ed. Maio, 137 ff. Philipp Melanchthon's horoscope was cast by Virdung von Hasfurt: see Euan Cameron, 'Philipp Melanchthon: Image and Substance', *Journal of Ecclesiastical History*, 48/4 (1997), 711–12 and references.

35. Felix Hemmerli, 'Tractatus II de exorcismis' in *Malleus Maleficarum* (Frankfurt: Nicolaus Bassaeus, 1600), ii. esp. 407–8; for the refutation of the legends see Jean Gerson, 'Opusculum adversus doctrinam cuiusdam medici delati in Montepessulano, sculpentis in numismate figuram leonis cum certis caracteribus' in *Opera*, ed. du Pin, I, cols. 206–8 at col. 208.

36. Delrio, *Disquisitionum Magicarum*, bk 3, sect. 2, q. 8, at ii. 115–25.

37. See the 'Opus paramirum', in Theophrastus Bombast von Hohenheim, ['Theophrastus Paracelsus'], *Opera Omnia*, 3 vols (Geneva: Joannes Antonius & Samuel de Tournes, 1658), i. 137–40.

38. Paracelsus, 'De Occulta Philosophia', in *Opera Omnia*, ii. 494.

39. Paracelsus, 'Archidoxis Magicae Libri vii', in *Opera Omnia*, ii. 695.

40. Ibid., ii. 695–700.

41. Marvin W. Meyer and Richard Smith (eds) *Ancient Christian Magic: Coptic Texts of Ritual Power* (Princeton: Princeton University Press, 1999), *passim*, and for description of the sources, 6–8.

42. See e.g. Jeffrey Spier, 'Medieval Byzantine Magic Amulets and their Tradition', *Journal of the Warburg and Courtauld Institutes*, 56 (1993), 25–62. See 51 ff for the catalogue of the surviving amulets and after 62 for illustrations.

43. See Don C. Skemer, *Binding Words: Textual Amulets in the Middle Ages* (Philadelphia: Pennsylvania State University Press, 2006). For examples of relatively long elaborate amulets in textual form, see ibid. 285–310.

44. See the great variety of texts issued by Penn State University Press under the series title *Magic in History*: http://www.psupress.psu.edu/books/series/book_SeriesMagic.html.

45. Richard Kieckhefer, *Forbidden Rites: A Necromancer's Manual of the Fifteenth Century* (Stroud, Glos.: Sutton Publishing, 1997), based on Bayerische Staatsbibliothek. Manuscript. Clm 849. The text itself is edited in the original Latin on 190–346.

46. See article on this subject by Dieter Harmening in his *Zauberei im Abendland: vom Anteil der Gelehrten am Wahn der Leute. Skizzen zur Geschichte des Aberglaubens* (Würzburg: Königshausen & Neumann, 1991), 90 ff; on magic rings see also more recently Dieter Harmening, *Wörterbuch des Aberglaubens* (Stuttgart: Reclam, 2005), 359–60.

47. See Peter Murray Jones and Lea T. Olsan, 'The Middleham Jewel: Ritual, Power, and Devotion', *Viator*, 31 (2000), 249–90.

48. Eamon Duffy, *The Stripping of the Altars: Traditional Religion in England, c.1400–c.1580* (New Haven; London: Yale University Press, 1992), 266–87.

49. W. P. Reeves, 'Shakespeare's Queen Mab', *Modern Language Notes*, 17/1. (1902), 10–14 epitomizes a quite extensive scholarly literature on fairies in Shakespeare around 100 years ago. There are comparatively few modern equivalents; but see e.g. Roger Lancelyn Green, 'Shakespeare and the Fairies' *Folklore*, 73/2 (1962), 89–103.

50. Christopher Marlowe's *Doctor Faustus* assumes that the different theological perspectives on the conjuring of demons, i.e. whether they were truly compelled by magical rites or only obliged the conjurer to entrap him, would be fully understood by the audience. Marlowe's play was derived from the *Faustbuch*, a late sixteenth-century German compilation referred to below in Ch. 3 n. 43.

51. See Valerie I. J. Flint, *The Rise of Magic in Early Medieval Europe* (Princeton: Princeton University Press, 1991).
52. See e.g. John T. Noonan, *The Scholastic Analysis of Usury* (Cambridge, Mass: Harvard University Press, 1957); James A. Brundage, *Law, Sex, and Christian Society in Medieval Europe* (Chicago: University of Chicago Press, 1987).

5. THE PATRISTIC AND EARLY MEDIEVAL HERITAGE

1. For the life of Augustine, see Peter Brown, *Augustine of Hippo: A Biography* (new edn, London: Faber; Berkeley: University of California Press, 2000); Augustine, *Confessions*, ed. and trans. Henry Chadwick (Oxford and New York: Oxford University Press, 1991).
2. See Augustine, *Confessions*, ed. Chadwick, e.g. 24, 47, 115, 123–4, 127, 183–5 for allusions to or echoes of Plotinus in the *Confessions*.
3. For the Latin text of *City of God* see *Sancti Aurelii Augustini . . . Opera Omnia*, ed. the Benedictines of St-Maur, 11 vols (Paris: 1841–2), vol. vii, incorporated in the *Patrologiae Cursus Completus, Series Latina*, (PL) ed. Jacques-Paul Migne, vol. 41, cols. 12–804. A modern translation is Augustine, *The City of God against the Pagans* ed. and trans. R. W. Dyson (Cambridge: Cambridge University Press, 1998).
4. For Augustine's polemical works against Donatism, Manichaeism, and Pelagianism see Migne, *PL*, vols 42–4; extracts in translation are found in P. Schaff et al. (eds), *A Select Library of the Nicene and Post-Nicene Fathers*, 1st series (Grand Rapids, MI: Eerdmans, 1956), vol. iv (writings against the Manichaeans and against the Donatists) and vol. v (anti-Pelagian writings).
5. Note also the association with the term στοιχεία (stoicheia): see Clinton E. Arnold, 'Returning to the Domain of the Powers: "Stoicheia" as Evil Spirits in Galatians 4: 3,9', in *Novum Testamentum*, 38/1 (1996), 55–76 and refs.
6. See Cyprian of Carthage, 'On the Vanity of Idols' as trans. in *The Ante-Nicene Fathers: Translations of the Writings of the Fathers down to A.D. 325*, ed. and trans. Alexander Roberts and James Donaldson, 10 vols (Edinburgh: T. & T. Clark; Grand Rapids, MI: Eerdmans, 1989–90), v. 465–9 and esp. 467: '[demons] are impure and wandering spirits, who, after having been steeped in earthly vices, have departed from their celestial vigour by the contagion of earth, and do not cease, when ruined themselves, to seek the ruin of others; and when degraded themselves, to infuse into others the error of their own degradation . . . These spirits, therefore, are lurking under the statues and consecrated images: these inspire the breasts of their prophets with their afflatus, animate the fibres of the entrails, direct the flights of birds, rule the lots, give efficiency to oracles, are always mixing up falsehood with truth, for they are both deceived and they deceive.'

7. *City of God*, ii in general and for the quotation. ii.10, Dyson edn 61.

8. Ibid., ii. 14, Dyson edn 66–7.

9. Ibid, ii. 17–22, Dyson edn 69–82.

10. Ibid., ii. 24–5, Dyson edn 84–8. Compare also Augustine's refutation of Apuleius on the demons in *City of God*, viii. 22.

11. Augustine, *On the Holy Trinity*, in P. Schaff et al. (eds), *A Select Library of the Nicene and Post-Nicene Fathers* (Grand Rapids, MI: Eerdmans, 1956), 1st series, vol. iii, bk 4 chs 10–13, 76–8.

12. Augustine, *On the Holy Trinity*, in *Nicene and Post-Nicene Fathers*, 1st series, vol. iii, bk 3 ch. 11, 65–8.

13. *City of God*, xv. 23, Dyson edn 680–1 and compare iii. 5, Dyson edn 98.

14. Compare *City of God*, vii *passim*, Dyson edn 267–311, containing Augustine's critique of Varro's accounts of the ancient Gods leading up to his discussion of the story of Numa Pompilius and the nymph Egeria.

15. For Augustine's attitude to miracles, see Augustine, 'On the Trinity', in *Nicene and Post-Nicene Fathers*, 1st series, vol. iii, bk 3 chs 5–8; for quotation see ch. 8, 60–1.

16. Augustine 'De divinatione daemonum liber unus', in Migne, *PL*, vol. 40, cols. 581–91.

17. Ibid., ch. 3, cols. 584–5.

18. Ibid., ch. 4, cols. 585–6.

19. Ibid., chs 5–6, cols. 586–7.

20. For *On Christian Doctrine* see the Latin original in Migne, *PL*, vol. 34, cols. 15–122; modern edition, Augustine, *De Doctrina Christiana*, ed. and trans. R. P. H. Green, Oxford Early Christian Texts (Oxford; New York: Clarendon Press, 1995).

21. Augustine *De Doctrina Christiana*, ii. xx.

22. Ibid., ii. xxi–xxii (31–4).

23. Ibid., ii. xxiii (36): 'ex quadam pestifera societate hominum et daemonum, quasi pacta infidelis et dolosae amicitiae constituta.'

24. *City of God*, x. 9–11, Dyson edn 370–2.

25. Augustine *De Doctrina Christiana*, ii. xxiii (35).

26. The quotation is derived from [ps-Michael Psellus], *Psellus' dialogue on the operation of daemons: now, for the first time translated into English from the original Greek*, trans. Marcus Collisson (Sydney: James Tegg, 1843), 18–49. One of several early modern Latin editions is *Michaelis Pselli De Operatione Daemonum Dialogus*, ed. and trans. Gilbertus Gaulminus Molinensis (Paris: H. Drouart, 1615).

27. The work appeared in Iamblichus of Chalcis, *Iamblichus de mysteriis Aegyptiorum* (Lyons: Tornæsius, 1549), 334–61; and in Marsilius Ficinus, *M. Ficini ... Opera*, 2 vols (Basle: Henricpetri, 1576).

28. On Caesarius see especially William E. Klingshirn, *Caesarius of Arles: The Making of a Christian Community in Late Antique Gaul*, Cambridge Studies in Medieval Life and Thought, 4th series, 22 (Cambridge: Cambridge University Press, 1994), chs 7–8 and esp. 210–26. Compare Valerie I. J. Flint, *The Rise of Magic in Medieval Europe* (Oxford: Clarendon Press, 1991), 147 ff.

29. See Carl Paul Caspari (ed.), *Martin von Bracara's Schrift De Correctione Rusticorum, zum ersten Male vollständig und in verbessertem Text herausgegeben* (Christiania: Mallingschen Buchdruckerei, 1883).

30. Dieter Harmening, *Superstitio: Überlieferungs- und theoriegeschichtliche Untersuchungen zur kirchlich-theologischen Aberglaubensliteratur des Mittelalters* (Berlin: E. Schmidt, 1979), in general but esp. 72 ff. On early medieval Europe compare Bernadette Filotas, *Pagan Survivals, Superstitions and Popular Cultures in Early Medieval Pastoral Literature* (Toronto: Pontifical Institute of Mediaeval Studies, 2005), 42–51 for a different assessment.

31. Isidore, *Etymologies*, VIII, 9; edited in Migne, *PL*, vol. 82, cols. 9–728; the relevant passage on divination is on cols. 310–14. See also above, Ch. 4, n. 3.

32. Hrabanus Maurus's *De Universo* is ed. in Migne, *PL*, vol. 111, cols. 9–614; the passage under discussion is found on cols. 422–5.

33. Regino of Prüm, *Libri duo de synodalibus causis et disciplinis ecclesiasticis*, ed. Friedrich G. A. Wasserschleben, (Leipzig: Engelmann, 1840, repr. 1964); see also *MGH Capitula episcoporum* I, 1984, 53–6; Burchard's *Decretum* is published as *Decretorum libri XX*, in Migne, *PL*, vol. 140, cols. 537–1053. Ivo's *Decretum*, in Migne, *PL*, vol. 161, cols. 47–1036.

34. For Gratian see *Corpus Juris Canonici*, ed. Aemilius Ludouicus Richter and Aemilius Friedberg (Graz: Akademische Druck- u. Verlagsanstalt, 1959), i, cols. 1019–36.

35. Ibid., cols. 1019–26.

36. Ibid. cols. 1030–1; on the authentic council of Ancyra of 314, see http://www.ccel.org/ccel/schaff/npnf214.viii.iii.html and his sources.

37. *Corpus Juris Canonici*, i, 1032–6. The remainder of Causa xxvi does not appear to address the issue of sorcery.

38. For the sources for the life of Germanus see the Bollandist *Acta Sanctorum* for July, vii. 200 ff.; Boninus Mombritius, *Sanctuarium seu Vitae sanctorum*, 2 vols (Hildesheim and New York: Georg Olms, 1978), i. 572–83. However, these sources do not appear to contain the story reported by Nider.

39. [Johannes Nider], *Johannis Nideri theologi olim clarissimi De visionibus ac revelationibus: opus rarissimum historiis Germaniæ refertissimum, anno 1517, Argentinæ editum* (Helmstedt: Paulus Zeisingius, Salomon Schnorrius, 1692), 201 ff.

40. On the cult of Habundia see Joseph Hansen (ed.), *Quellen und Untersuchungen zur Geschichte des Hexenwahns und der Hexenverfolgung im Mittelalter*

(Hildesheim: G. Olms, 1963, reprint of the original edition, Bonn: C. Georgi, 1901), 69, 84.

41. Besides Nider's *Formicarius*, as n. 39 above, see Johannes Geiler von Kaisersberg, *Die Emeis, dis ist das büch von der Omeissen* (Strasbourg: Johannes Grieninger, 1517), ch. 17, fos. 35 ff; Jacob of Jueterbogk (also known as Jacobus de Clusa), 'De Potestate Daemonum, Arte Magica, Superstitionibus et Illusionibus eorundem', in Cornell University Archives, MS. 4600 Bd. Ms. 4, fo. 205^r; Martin Plantsch, *Opusculum de sagis maleficis* (Pforzheim: Thomas Anshelm, 1507) sigs. cii^r–iii^v; and Alphonsus de Spina [Alfonso de Espina], *Fortalitium fidei* (Lyons: Gulielmus Balsarin, 1487), book 5, consideration 10, diff. 5, sig. L ii^r.

42. Athanasius's *Life of Antony* is ed. in *Patrologiae Cursus Completus*, Series Graeca (*PG*), ed. Jacques-Paul Migne, vol. 26, cols. 835–978; Palladius, *Historia Lausiaca* is found in Migne, *PL*, vol. 73, cols. 1066–1234; Cassian, *Conlationes*, in Cassian's *Opera*, ed. M. Petschenig, in Corpus Scriptorum Ecclesiasticorum Latinorum, 2 (Vienna, 1886). See also Athanasius, *The life of Antony and the letter to Marcellinus*, trans. Robert C. Gregg (New York: Paulist Press, 1980); Cuthbert Butler (ed.), *The Lausiac History of Palladius: A Critical Discussion Together with Notes on Early Egyptian Monachism*, 2 vols in 1 (Hildesheim: Olms, 1967); Robert T. Meyer (ed. and trans.), *Palladius: The Lausiac History* (New York: Newman Press, 1964); Cassian, *Conferences*, ed. in P. Schaff et al. (eds), *A Select Library of the Nicene and Post-Nicene Fathers*, 2nd series (Grand Rapids, MI: Eerdmans, 1956), vol. xi.

43. Nider refers to Cassian in the *Formicarius* many times: see e.g. *De visionibus ac revelationibus* 293 ff., and in book 5 in *Malleorum quorundam maleficarum, tam veterum quam recentiorum authorum, tomi duo* (Frankfurt, Nicolaus Bassaeus, 1582), i. 711, 734, 743, 767.

44. Nider cites Vincent in the *Formicarius*, e.g. in *De visionibus ac revelationibus* 252; and in *Malleorum quorundam maleficarum* (1582), 735.

45. Two of the most famous representations of the temptation of St Anthony appear in a side panel of Matthias Grünewald's Isenheim altarpiece now in the Unterlinden Museum in Colmar, and in Martin Schongauer's *Saint Anthony Tormented by Demons* (*c*.1470–75) of which copies exist in the Metropolitan Museum of Art in New York and in the Art Institute of Chicago.

46. Nider, *Formicarius*, book 4 chapter 2, in *De visionibus ac revelationibus* 415–24. For Potamiaena see Eusebius, *Ecclesiastical History*, vi. 5; also Palladius, *Lausiac History*, ch. 3, though Palladius does not report the story related by Nider. On Paphnutius see *The Life of St Humphrey (Saint Onofrius), Hermit*, trans. Dean Kavanagh (London: Burns and Oates, 1906).

6. SCHOLASTIC DEMONOLOGY IN THE TWELFTH
AND THIRTEENTH CENTURIES

1. On Lombard, see Marcia L. Colish, *Peter Lombard* (Leiden and New York: E. J. Brill, 1994).

2. The text of the *Sentences* is edited in [Peter Lombard], *Sententiarum libri quatuor, per Joannem Aleaume . . . pristino suo nitori vere' restituti*, 4 vols (Paris: J.-P. Migne, 1853) and in an electronic version in CLCLT–2 : CETEDOC library of Christian Latin texts (Turnhout: Brepols, 1994).

3. Key commentaries on the *Sentences* were compiled by Bonaventure, Duns Scotus, Francis of Marchia, Gabriel Biel, Gilles of Rome, John Capreolus, John of Mirecourt, Richard of Middleton, Peter of Candia, Peter of Tarentaise, Peter Aureoli, Petrus de Palude, Thomas Aquinas, William of Ockham, and many others.

4. *Sentences*, bk 2, dists. 2–11. For scholastic demonology from Lombard onwards see Alain Boureau, *Satan the Heretic*, trans. Teresa Lavender Fagan (Chicago: University of Chicago Press, 2006), 94 ff; also Robert Muchembled, *A History of the Devil: From the Middle Ages to the Present*, trans. Jean Birrell (Cambridge: Polity Press, 2003), ch. 1.

5. *Sentences*, bk 2, dist. 2.

6. Ibid., dist. 8.

7. Ibid., dist. 3

8. Ibid., dists. 4–5.

9. Ibid., dist. 6.

10. Ibid., dist. 7.

11. Alexander Murray, *Reason and Society in the Middle Ages* (Oxford: Clarendon Press, 1978), esp. 110 ff; see also R. W. Southern, *Medieval Humanism and Other Studies* (Oxford: Blackwell, 1970); and *Scholastic Humanism and the Unification of Europe*, 2 vols (Oxford: Blackwell, 1995–2001).

12. For the controversies after Aquinas's death see e.g. a brief discussion in Anthony Kenny, *Aquinas* (Oxford: Oxford University Press, 1980), 26–7.

13. For a more general discussion of medieval scholastic angelology, see David Keck, *Angels and Angelology in the Middle Ages* (Oxford and New York: Oxford University Press, 1998), esp. 71–114. Keck discusses extensively the angelology of Bonaventure and the Franciscan tradition. Since most of the late medieval superstition-treatises cited Aquinas very extensively and rarely mentioned Bonaventure at all, this study focuses on the metaphysical theories of Aquinas.

14. The citations from the works of Thomas Aquinas here are derived from http://www.corpusthomisticum.org/iopera.html: Corpus Thomisticum, subsidia studii ab Enrique Alarcón, collecta et edita (Pampilona: Ad

Universitatis Studiorum Navarrensis, 2000–) a database transcribed from a range of standard Latin printed editions.

15. Thomas Aquinas, *Summa contra Gentiles*, 3: 108–10 as below. See chapter 109: 'Quod autem in Daemonibus sit peccatum voluntatis, manifestum est ex auctoritate sacrae Scripturae. Dicitur enim I Ioan. 3[-3], quod *Diabolus ab initio peccat*. Et Ioan. 8[-44], de Diabolo dicitur quod *est mendax, et pater mendacii* et quod *homicida erat ab initio*. Et Sap. 2[-24] dicitur quod *invidia Diaboli mors introivit in orbem terrarum*.'

16. Accessible texts of these works are found at http://www.corpusthomisticum. org/qds.html and http://www.corpusthomisticum.org/qdm01.html.

17. Jakob of Jüterbogk (also known as Jacobus de Clusa, *c*.1381–1465), 'De Potestate Daemonum, Arte Magica, Superstitionibus et Illusionibus eorundem', in Cornell University Archives, MS. 4600 Bd. Ms. 4, fo. 184^v, quoting John of Damascus: *Exposition of the Orthodox Faith*, book 2, chapter 3.

18. Thomas Aquinas, *Summa Theologica*, I^a q. 44 a. 2, I^a q. 45 a. 4, I^a q. 46 a. 3. See also *Summa Theologica*, I^a q. 61 articles 1–4.

19. *Summa Theologica*, I^a q. 50 a. 1. Compare *Summa contra Gentiles*, 2: 46–50, and, for more extended arguments that spiritual creatures were truly incorporeal and not endowed with 'aery bodies' or any other kind, see *Quaestio disputata de spiritualibus creaturis*, articles 6 and 7; and *De Malo*, question 16 art. 1.

20. *Summa contra Gentiles*, 2: 91. Compare *Quaestio disputata de spiritualibus creaturis*, article 5.

21. *Summa contra Gentiles*, 2: 52–4.

22. *Summa Theologica*, I^a q. 50 a. 5; *Summa contra Gentiles*, 2: 55.

23. *Summa Theologica*, I^a q. 50 a. 2 and 4; *Summa contra Gentiles*, 2: 93–95. Compare *Quaestio disputata de spiritualibus creaturis*, articles 1 and 8.

24. *Summa Theologica*, I^a q. 50 a. 3; *Summa contra Gentiles*, 2: 92.

25. *Summa Theologica*, I^a q. 62, arts. 1–3, 5–6, 8.

26. Gregory the Great, *Homilia in Evangelia* xxxiv, in *Patrologiae Cursus Completus, Series Latina (PL)*, ed. Jacques-Paul Migne, vol. 76, cols. 1249–55; ps-Dionysius, *Celestial Hierarchy* chs. 3–7, and Aquinas, *Summa Theologica*, I^a q. 108 on the hierarchies.

27. *Summa Theologica*, I^a q. 106 art. 1, and art. 4

28. *Summa Theologica*, I^a q. 54 a. 4, I^a q. 54 a. 5, I^a q. 55 a. 1, I^a q. 56, I^a q. 58 a. 3; *Summa contra Gentiles*, 2: 96–101.

29. *Summa Theologica*, I^a q. 57 a. 3; compare *De Malo*, q. 16, art. 7.

30. *Summa Theologica*, I^a q. 57 a. 4; compare *De Malo*, q. 16, art. 8.

31. *Summa Theologica*, I^a q. 57 a. 5.

32. *Summa Theologica*, I^a q. 110 a. 4; *Summa contra Gentiles*, 3: 99–100.

33. *Summa Contra Gentiles*, 3: 101.

34. *Summa Contra Gentiles*, 3: 103.

35. *Summa Theologica*, Iᵃ q. 111 a. 3−4; compare *De Malo*, q. 16, art. 11.

36. *Summa Theologica*, Iᵃ q. 48 a. 2, 49 a. 2.

37. *Summa Theologica*, Iᵃ q. 63 art. 1−2.

38. *Summa Theologica*, Iᵃ q. 59 a. 4.

39. *Summa Theologica*, Iᵃ q. 63 art. 3; compare *De Malo*, q. 16, art. 3.

40. *Summa Theologica*, Iᵃ q. 63 arts. 5−9; compare *De Malo*, q. 16, art. 4.

41. *Summa Theologica*, Iᵃ q. 64 art. 4.

42. *Summa Contra Gentiles*, 3: 105−6. Compare also Aquinas's rescript entitled *De operationibus occultis naturae ad quendam militem ultramontanum*, in http://www.corpusthomisticum.org/opo.html for a similar point: 'Apparent etiam nigromanticarum imaginum quidam effectus, qui procedunt non ex aliquibus formis quas susceperint praedictae imagines, sed a Daemonum actione qui in praedictis imaginibus operantur.'

43. *Summa contra Gentiles*, 3: 107−8; compare *Summa Theologica*, Iᵃ q. 63 art. 4.

44. *Summa contra Gentiles*, 3: 109.

45. *Summa Theologica*, Iᵃ q. 64 a. 1; q. 109 art. 1, 2, 4; q. 111; compare *De Malo*, q. 16, art. 11.

46. *Summa Theologica*, Iᵃ q. 58 a. 5. Aquinas elaborated considerably on this point in *De Malo*, q. 16, art. 6: in general fallen angels could not be deceived about natural things but could be in error about divine things.

47. *Summa Theologica*, Iᵃ q. 114 a. 4

48. *Summa Theologica*, Iᵃ q. 64 art. 2, and more extensively *De Malo*, q. 16, art. 5; compare John of Damascus, *Exposition of the Orthodox Faith*, book 2, chapter 4, with reference to Nemesius, *On the Nature of Man*: see trans. by Philip van der Eijk and R. W. Sharples (Liverpool: Liverpool University Press, 2008), ch. 1.

49. *Summa Theologica*, Iᵃ q. 114 art. 3, 5.

50. *Summa Theologica*, IIᵃ−IIae q. 92 a. 1, 2; 93 a. 1, 2.

51. *Summa Theologica*, IIᵃ−IIae q. 94.

52. *Summa Theologica*, IIᵃ−IIae q. 95 a. 2.

53. See Ch. 4 above.

54. *Summa Theologica*, IIᵃ−IIae q. 95 a. 4.

55. *Summa Theologica*, IIᵃ−IIae q. 95 arts. 5−8.

56. *Summa Theologica*, IIᵃ−IIae q. 96 a. 1.

57. *Summa Theologica*, IIᵃ−IIae q. 96 a. 2. For Aquinas's rejection of the natural causality attributed to magical shapes or spells, see also *De operationibus occultis naturae ad quendam militem ultramontanum* as cited above, n. 42.

58. *Summa Theologica*, IIᵃ−IIae q. 96 a. 3.

59. *Summa Theologica*, IIᵃ−IIae q. 96 a. 4.

60. See above, n. 41.

61. For Aquinas's critique of the argument from astral causation, see esp. *Summa Theologica*, I^a q. 115 art. 4.

62. *Summa contra Gentiles*, 3:104–6.

63. For a particularly clear example of Thomist influence, outside the Dominican order, see the demonology in the Carthusian Jacob of Jueterbogk, 'De Potestate Daemonum', fos. 183–99 esp.; compare also Joseph Hansen (ed.), *Quellen und Untersuchungen zur Geschichte des Hexenwahns und der Hexenverfolgung im Mittelalter* (Hildesheim: G. Olms, 1963, reprint of the original edition, Bonn: C. Georgi, 1901), pp. 82 ff. for the anonymous *Tractatus de daemonibus*.

64. *Super Sent.*, lib. 4 d. 34 q. 1 a. 3 co.: 'Quidam dixerunt, quod maleficium nihil erat in mundo, nisi in aestimatione hominum, qui effectus naturales, quorum causae sunt occultae, maleficiis imputabant. Sed hoc est contra auctoritates sanctorum, qui dicunt, quod Daemones habent potestatem supra corpora, et supra imaginationem hominum, quando a Deo permittuntur; unde per eos malefici signa aliqua facere possunt. Procedit autem haec opinio ex radice infidelitatis, sive incredulitatis, quia non credunt esse Daemones nisi in aestimatione vulgi tantum, ut terrores quos homo sibi ipsi facit ex sua aestimatione, imputet Daemoni; et quia etiam ex imaginatione vehementi aliquae figurae apparent in sensu tales quales homo cogitat, et tunc creduntur Daemones videri. Sed haec vera fides repudiat, per quam Angelos de caelo cecidisse, et Daemones esse credimus, et ex subtilitate suae naturae multa posse quae nos non possumus; et ideo illi qui eos ad talia facienda inducunt, malefici vocantur.'

65. On providence see *Summa contra Gentiles*, 3: 64 ff.

7. THE DEMONOLOGICAL READING OF SUPERSTITIONS IN THE LATE MIDDLE AGES: AREAS OF CONSENSUS

1. On confessional manuals see above all T. N. Tentler, *Sin and Confession on the Eve of the Reformation* (Princeton: Princeton University Press, 1977); leading examples of the confessors' manual include Angelo Carletti, *Summa angelica de casibus conscientiae* (Chivasso: Jacobinus Suigus, de Suico, 1486, and many subsequent editions); Silvestro Mazzolini da Prierio, *Summa Summarum, que Sylvestrina dicitur* (Bologna: Hector, 1515, and many subsequent editions).

2. This argument was adumbrated in Thomas Aquinas, *De operationibus occultis naturae ad quendam militem ultramontanum*, at http://www.corpusthomisticum. org/opo.html : 'Sicut autem imagines ex materia naturali fiunt, sed formam sortiuntur ex arte; ita etiam verba humana materiam quidem habent naturalem, scilicet sonos ab hominis ore prolatos, sed significationem quasi formam

habent ab intellectu suas conceptiones per huiusmodi sonos exprimente. Unde pari ratione nec verba humana habent efficaciam ad aliquam immutationem corporis naturalis ex virtute alicuius causae naturalis, sed solum ex aliqua spirituali substantia. Hae igitur actiones quae per huiusmodi verba fiunt, vel per quascumque imagines vel sculpturas, vel quaecumque alia huiusmodi, non sunt naturales, utpote non procedentes a virtute intrinseca, sed sunt empericae; et ad superstitionem pertinentes'. However, it was left to the later medieval authors to apply the principle specifically.

3. Dinkelsbühl, *Ain Tractat*, in Karin Baumann, *Aberglaube für Laien: zur Programmatik und Überlieferung spätmittelalterlicher Superstitionenkritik*, 2 vols [continuously paginated] (Würzburg: Königshausen & Neumann, 1989), 533, lines 623 ff.

4. Johannes Nider, *Preceptorium Divine Legis* (Basle: Berthold Ruppel, *c*.1470), prec. 1, ch. 11, sect. 16.

5. Bernhardus Basin, 'Opusculum de artibus magicis, ac Magorum Maleficiis', in [Institoris], *Malleus Maleficarum: Maleficas et earum hæresim frameâ conterens, ex variis auctoribus compilatus, & in quator tomos iustè distributus*, 2 vols in 3 (Lyons: Claudius Bourgeat, 1669), ii, pt I, 4–5; the story of Virgil's bronze mouse may be found in Felix Hemmerli, 'Tractatus Secundus exorcismorum seu adiurationum', in *Malleus Maleficarum* (Frankfurt: Nicolaus Bassaeus, 1600), ii. 415.

6. Martin Plantsch, *Opusculum de sagis maleficis* (Pforzheim: Thomas Anshelm, 1507) sigs. b vi^v–vii^v.

7. See Jean Gerson, 'Opusculum adversus doctrinam cuiusdam medici delati in Montepessulano, sculpentis in numismate figuram leonis cum certis caracteribus', in J. Gerson, *Joannis Gersonii Doctoris Theologi & Cancellarii Parisiensis Opera Omnia*, ed. Ludovicus Ellies du Pin, 5 vols, 2nd edn (The Hague: P. de Hondt, 1728), i, cols. 206–8, proposition 7. Compare discussion in Basin, 'Opusculum de artibus magicis' as above note 5.

8. *Pedro Ciruelo's A treatise reproving all superstitions and forms of witchcraft: very necessary and useful for all good Christians zealous for their salvation*, trans. E. A. Maio and D. W. Pearson (Rutherford, NJ: Fairleigh Dickinson University Press, 1977), 205. The editors' reading that rhubarb counteracted 'cholera' should be corrected to 'choler' by analogy with 'phlegm' in the next phrase.

9. See the discussion of Paracelsus and his healing techniques above, Ch. 4 at nn. 38–9.

10. Emanuele do Valle de Moura, *De Incantationibus seu Ensalmis Opusculum Primum* (Évora: Laurentius Crasbeeck, 1620), 21–9, citing 'Bravus Chamisius', probably Joannes Bravus, *De curandi ratione per medicamenti purgantis exhibitionem libri III* (Salmantica: Cornelius Bonardus, 1588).

11. Baumann, *Aberglaube*, 524, lines 327 ff: 'Und wie es geschicht in allerlay ungelauben, so kumbt es doch alles aus ainem gedingen, das man hat oder macht mit dem tewfel haimlich oder offentlich.'

12. Jean Gerson, 'De Erroribus circa Artem Magicam et Articulis Reprobatis', in *Malleus Maleficarum*, ii, part II, 163–75, at 165.

13. Ibid. 165–7, and compare 172.

14. Gerson, 'Triologium Astrologiae theologizatae', proposition 21, in *Opera*, ed. du Pin, i, cols. 196, 200; 'Opusculum adversus doctrinam cuiusdam medici delati in Montepessulano', ibid., col. 206.

15. Jacobus van Hoogstraten (*c.*1460–1527), *Tractus magistralis declarans quam graviter peccent querentes auxilium a maleficis; Contra petentes remedia a maleficis* (Cologne: Martinus de Werdena, 1510), chapter 1.

16. Martín de Castañega, *Tratado de las supersticiones y hechizerias y de la possibilidad y remedio dellas*, 1529 (Madrid, Sociedad de Bibliofilos Espanoles, 2nd series, 17, 1946), ch. 4, 33–7; David H. Darst, 'Witchcraft in Spain: The Testimony of Martin de Castañega's Treatise on Superstition and Witchcraft (1529)', *Proceedings of the American Philosophical Society*, 123/5 (1979), 304. Compare Nider, *Preceptorium*, prec. 1, ch. 9, from which Castañega may be deriving this analysis of gravity of sins.

17. On the canon law of marriage see James A. Brundage, *Law, Sex, and Christian Society in Medieval Europe* (Chicago: University of Chicago Press, 1987); Ralph A. Houlbrooke, *The English Family, 1450–1700* (London; New York: Longman, 1984). The intricate canonical processes surrounding Henry VIII's multiple marriages and divorces offer extreme examples of this mode of reasoning.

18. *Dives and Pauper*, ed. Priscilla Heath Barnum, 3 vols, Early English Text Society, nos. 275, 280, 323 (London: Oxford University Press, 1976–2004), commandment 1, ch. 36, i. 162.

19. Gerson, 'Triologium Astrologiae', proposition 21, col. 196 as above. Compare Martín, of Arles y Andosilla, *Tractatus insignis et exquisitissimus de superstitionibus* in *Tractatus Universi Juris*, xi, pt. 2 (Lyons, 1584), fos. 402^v–8^r, sect. 93.

20. Nider, *Preceptorium*, prec. 1, ch. 11 sect. 19; Johannes Geiler von Kaisersberg, *Die Emeis, dis ist das büch von der Omeissen*, (Strasbourg: Johannes Grieninger, 1517), ch. 27, fos. 47^r ff; Martín of Arles, *Tractatus de Superstitionibus*, sect. 58. Compare also Plantsch, *Opusculum de sagis maleficis*, sig. b vi^v.

21. Heinrich von Gorkum (*c.*1386–1431) *Tractatus de supersticiosis quibusdam casibus* (Esslingen: Conrad Fyner, 1473); see more specific discussion of the phenomena described in this treatise in Ch. 3 above at notes 32–5.

22. Gorkum, *Tractatus*, fos. 3^r–4^r.

23. Gorkum, *Tractatus*, fo. 5^v.

24. Ibid., fo. 6^{r-v}.

25. Geiler, *Emeis*, ch. 25, fo. 45^v.

26. Castañega, *Tratado de las supersticiones*, chs 1–3 on 17–32, and in Darst, 'Witchcraft in Spain', 301–3.

27. Stuart Clark, *Thinking with Demons: The Idea of Witchcraft in Early Modern Europe* (Oxford: Clarendon Press, 1997), chs 5–6, 69–93.

28. See the discussions of animal transformations in Ch. 1 above.

29. On the classic tale of illusory transformation into a wolf in William of Auvergne, see above, Ch. 2 n. 40. See Geiler, *Emeis*, ch. 21, fos. 41^v ff, drawing on Nider, *Preceptorium*, prec. 1, ch. 11, sect. 9.

30. Geiler, *Emeis*, ch. 22, fos. 42^v ff, drawing on Nider, *Preceptorium*, prec. 1, ch. 11, sect. 8.

31. See discussion of *dusii* and above, Ch. 5 at n. 13.

32. Thomas Aquinas, *Summa Theologica*, I^a q. 51 a. 3 ad 6. For detailed discussion of this theme, see Walter Stephens, *Demon Lovers: Witchcraft, Sex, and the Crisis of Belief* (Chicago: University of Chicago Press, 2002), 61 ff.

33. Nider *Formicarius*, book 5, ch. 9, as in *Malleorum quorundam maleficarum, tam veterum quam recentiorum authorum, tomi duo* (Frankfurt: Nicolaus Bassaeus, 1582), i. 765–9. Note ibid., book 5 ch. 10, i. 770 ff for more incubus lore.

34. Ibid. v. 10, i. 775–7.

35. Jacob of Jueterbogk (also known as Jacobus de Clusa, *c*.1381–1465), 'De Potestate Daemonum, Arte Magica, Superstitionibus et Illusionibus eorundem', in Cornell University Archives, MS. 4600 Bd. Ms. 4, fos. 205^v ff, 252^r ff.

36. e.g. Martín of Arles, *Tractatus de Superstitionibus*, sect. 13; note that before Martín used the scholastic quotations on incubi he revealed a pastoral insight (sect. 12): he heard the story of an experience of temptation by an incubus from a respectable woman whom he regarded as an entirely innocent victim of the delusion.

37. Plantsch, *Opusculum de sagis maleficis*, sig c iii^{r-v}; Geiler, *Emeis*, ch. 34 part 2, fos. 55v ff.

38. Castañega, *Tratado de las supersticiones*, ch. 11 on 57 ff; and in Darst, 'Witchcraft in Spain', 307.

39. Silvestro Mazzolini, da Prierio (Silvester Prierias) *De Strigimagarum Demonumque Mirandis libri tres* (Rome: Antonius Bladis de Asula, 24 Sept 1521), book 2, ch. 3, 'that there are *striges* or *lamiae* in nature', sigs. X i^r ff. Compare also sig. Y iv^r ff, and *Malleus Maleficarum* I, q. iii.

40. Pius II [Enea Silvio Piccolomini], *Pii II Commentarii rerum memorabilium que temporibus suis contigerunt*, ed. Adrianus van Heck, 2 vols, Studi e testi, 312–13 (Città del Vaticano: Biblioteca apostolica vaticana, 1984), 443 ff

and esp. 444: 'nisi me fallit opinio, ex incubo prognatus spiritu'. Alain de Coëtivy, Cardinal of Avignon (d. 1474), was arguing (in vain) that Jean Jouffroy, Bishop of Arras (*c.*1412–73), should under no circumstances become a cardinal.

41. See Ch. 1 above, at n. 48.

42. Petrus de Palude, *Scriptum in quartum sententiarum*, bk 4, dist. 34 (Venice: Bonetus Locatellus, 1493), fos. 169^r–171^v.

43. Nider *Formicarius*, book 5, ch. 5 as in *Malleorum quorundam maleficarum* (1582), i. 728–35.

44. Ibid., ch. 6, 736–45.

45. *Malleus Maleficarum*, especially I. 7–8 and II. 5–7.

46. See Ch. 1 above, at nn. 12–18.

47. See above, Ch. 1 n. 42.

48. Johann Georg Godelmann, *Tractatus de Magis, Veneficis et Lamiis, deque his recte cognoscendis et puniendis* (Frankfurt: Nicolaus Bassaeus, 1601), pp. 37–8. The story was apparently reported by Martin Luther to his elector.

49. Alphonsus de Spina [Alfonso de Espina], *Fortalitium fidei* (Lyons: Gulielmus Balsarin, 1487), sigs. L i^r–iii^v, also partially quoted by Joseph Hansen (ed.), *Quellen und Untersuchungen zur Geschichte des Hexenwahns und der Hexenverfolgung im Mittelalter* (Hildesheim: G. Olms, 1963, reprint of the original edition, Bonn: C. Georgi, 1901), 146–8.

50. For an early version of this anti-feminist cliché see William of Auvergne, *De Universo*, part 2, section 3, chapter 24, in *Guilelmi Alverni . . . Opera Omnia*, 2 vols (Aurelia: F. Hotot; London: Robertus Scott, 1674), i. 1066–7; see also Michael D. Bailey, *Battling Demons: Witchcraft, Heresy, and Reform in the Late Middle Ages* (University Park: Pennsylvania State University Press, 2003), 48 ff.

51. Nider, *Preceptorium*, prec. 1, ch. 11, q. 21. This explanation would be considerably elaborated and exaggerated by Heinrich Krämer in the *Malleus Maleficarum*: see Stephens, *Demon Lovers*, 32–57, with specific reference to Krämer's theory of the relationship between witchcraft and female sexuality.

52. Nider, *Preceptorium*, prec. 1, ch. 11, q. 25.

53. Geiler, *Emeis*, ch. 26, fo. 46^v.

54. *Malleus Maleficarum*, part I, question vi.

55. Castañega, *Tratado de las supersticiones*, chapter 5 on 37 ff.; and in Darst, 'Witchcraft in Spain', 304–5.

56. See above, Ch. 3 nn. 50–1.

57. For theory see Gerson, twelfth proposition of 'Opusculum adversus doctrinam cuiusdam medici', *Opera*, ed. du Pin, i, cols. 206–8: 'such things, finally, are

sought for to be used, not just by old witches, but by many following [*the profession of*] arms'; Mazzolini tells the story of a soldier who sought a charm to cure his lame horse in Mazzolini, *De Strigimagarum . . . Mirandis*, book 2 chapter 11, sigs. ff. iii ff., as above in the Introduction; compare Luther's observations on swords and weapons being enchanted, as discussed above, Ch. 1 at n. 20.

58. See Ch. 3 above, at nn. 38–41.

59. Geiler, *Emeis*, chs 30–1, fos. 50^r–52^v.

60. Mazzolini, *De Strigimagarum . . . Mirandis*, book 2 chapter 9, sigs. dd ii^v and ff; but compare below, chapter 11, sigs. ee iv^r ff, where Mazzolini differs from Plantsch and echoes sections of the *Malleus Maleficarum*.

61. See reference *Summa Theologica*, II^a–IIae q. 96 a. 4. These conditions for the proper use of amulets are cited e.g. in Baumann, *Aberglaube*, 548, lines 1134 ff; Nider, *Preceptorium*, prec. 1, ch. 11, q. 26; Martín of Arles, *Tractatus de Superstitionibus*, sects. 40–1 (quoting Nider).

62. Thomas Aquinas, *Summa Theologica*, II^a–IIae q. 93 a. 2 co.

63. Nider *Preceptorium*, prec. 1, ch. 11, q. 23.

64. Mazzolini, *De Strigimagarum . . . Mirandis*, sigs. ff iii^r, and Martín of Arles, *Tractatus de Superstitionibus*, sects. 4–5.

8. THE DEMONOLOGICAL READING OF SUPERSTITIONS IN THE LATE MIDDLE AGES: AREAS OF DIFFERENCE AND DISAGREEMENT

1. *Joanni Duns Scoti . . . Opera Omnia*, ed. L. Wadding, 26 vols (Paris: Ludovicus Vives, 1891–5), xix. 403: 'Si per orationes sanctorum virtus demonis impediatur, bene fit; si tamen deus illas non exaudiat, tunc si maleficium sciretur et destrueretur, demon non fatigaret eum amplius, quia ex pacto non assistit nisi dum durat aliquod signum. Et ex hoc patet quod trufatica est illa quaestio an liceat tollere maleficium intentione curandi maleficiatum: non enim solum licet, sed est meritorium destruere opera diaboli: nec est in hoc aliqua infidelitas: quia destruens non acquiescit operibus malignis: sed credit demonem posse et velle fatigare, dum tale signum durat: et destructio talis signi imponit finem tali vexationi.' See discussions in Jacobus van Hoogstraten (*c*.1460–1527), *Tractus magistralis declarans quam graviter peccent querentes auxilium a maleficis; Contra petentes remedia a maleficis* (Cologne: Martinus de Werdena, 1510), ch. 2, and Silvestro Mazzolini, da Prierio (Silvester Prierias) *De Strigimagarum Demonumque Mirandis libri tres* (Rome: Antonius Bladis de Asula, 24 Sept 1521), sig. ee ii^v; and in its scholastic and legal context in Catherine Rider, *Magic and Impotence in the Middle Ages* (Oxford and New York: Oxford University Press, 2006), 144 ff and 151.

2. Hoogstraten, *Tractus magistralis*, ch. 2; Mazzolini, *De Strigimagarum . . . Mirandis*, sig. ee ii^v.

3. Peter Aureoli, in Aureolus, Petrus [*c.*1280–1322], *Commentariorum in primum [-quartum] librum Sententiarum*, 2 vols (Rome: Zannetti, 1596–1605) on *Sentences* bk 4, dist. 34, qq. 2–3, and Angelus [Carletti] de Clavasio, *Summa Angelica* (as below, note 5), article 'Maleficium': that it is lawful to seek of a sorcerer who is prepared to do this, to lift the sorcery with sorcery. These texts are reviewed in Martinus Delrio SJ, *Disquisitionum Magicarum Libri Sex*, 3 vols (Louvain: Gerardus Rivius, 1599–1600), iii. 193 ff. Aureoli himself as quoted in Catherine Rider, *Magic and Impotence in the Middle Ages* (Oxford and New York: Oxford University Press, 2006), 151–2, does not appear to deserve the Dominicans' censures; but it is clear that theological and legal opinion could slide into acceptance of curative counter-magic.

4. These arguments are here summarized from Delrio, *Disquisitionum Magicarum*, iii. 198 ff.

5. Angelo Carletti, *Summa angelica de casibus conscientiae* (Chivasso: Jacobinus Suigus, de Suico 1486, and many subsequent editions); there are reported to have appeared at least thirty-one editions of this text from 1476 to 1520.

6. A long list of conflicting civil, theological, and canonical authorities is enumerated and discussed by Delrio, *Disquisitionum Magicarum*, iii. 193 ff and 200–29.

7. Hoogstraten, *Tractus magistralis*, ch. 4 *passim*.

8. Mazzolini, *De Strigimagarum . . . Mirandis*, bk 2, ch. 10 *passim*.

9. Delrio, *Disquisitionum Magicarum*, bk 6, ch. 2, sect. 1, questions 1 and 2, iii. 173 ff. Note also Mazzolini, *De Strigimagarum . . . Mirandis*, as quoted (with less independence of mind) in Girolamo Menghi, *Compendio dell'arte essorcistica, et possibilita delle mirabili, et stupende operationi delli demoni, et dei malefici. Con li rimedii opportuni alle infirmità maleficiali* (Bologna: Giovanni Rossi, 1582), book 3, ch. 2, 528 ff.

10. Delrio, *Disquisitionum Magicarum*, iii. 195 ff.

11. Thomas Aquinas, *Summa Theologica*, II^a–IIae q. 96 a. 4 arg. 1, II^a–IIae q. 96 a. 4 arg. 2;

12. *Summa Theologica*, II^a–IIae q. 96 a. 4 ad 2.

13. Thomas Aquinas, *Scriptum super Sententiis*, lib. 4 d. 3 q. 1 a. 2 qc. 1 ad 5.

14. Nider *Formicarius*, book 5, as in *Malleorum quorundam maleficarum, tam veterum quam recentiorum authorum, tomi duo* (Frankfurt: Nicolaus Bassaeus, 1582), i. 740.

15. Jacob of Jueterbogk (also known as Jacobus de Clusa, *c.*1381–1465), 'De Potestate Daemonum, Arte Magica, Superstitionibus et Illusionibus eorundem', in Cornell University Archives, MS. 4600 Bd. Ms. 4, fo. 222^r–v.

16. Mazzolini, *De Strigimagarum . . . Mirandis*, sig. ff ii^r and following.
17. Ibid., sig. ff iii^r.
18. Hoogstraten, *Tractus magistralis*, ch. 3, response to objection 2.
19. See Ch. 7 above, at note 23.
20. Heinrich von Gorkum (*c.*1386–1431) *Tractatus de supersticiosis quibusdam casibus* (Esslingen: Conrad Fyner, 1473), fo. 5^v.
21. Ibid., fo. 7^r.
22. See above, Ch. 7, at note 6.
23. Martin Plantsch, *Opusculum de sagis maleficis* (Pforzheim: Thomas Anshelm, 1507) sigs. b vii^v–c i^r.
24. On this principle in late scholastic theology, see Berndt Hamm, *Promissio, Pactum, Ordinatio: Freiheit und Selbstbindung Gottes in der scholastischen Gnadenlehre*, Beiträge zur historischen Theologie, 54 (Tübingen: Mohr, 1977).
25. Johannes Geiler von Kaisersberg, *Die Emeis* (Strasbourg: Johannes Grieninger, 1517), sermon 24, fos. 44^v–45^r; Martín de Castañega, *Tratado de las Supersticiones y Hechicerias* (Madrid: Sociedad de Bibliofilos Espanoles, 2nd series, 17, 1946), 25–33, and esp. as follows: 'Dios concurre con los Sacramentos; porque los Sacramentos son señales eficaces, esto es, que son de tanta eficacia por pacto divino, que no faltara Dios de concurrir, si de otra parte no hubiere falta.'
26. Mazzolini, *De Strigimagarum . . . Mirandis*, bk 1, chs 3–5.
27. Ibid., bk 1, chs 6–12.
28. Ibid., bk 2, chs 2–7.
29. Ibid., bk 3 *passim*.
30. Ibid., bk 2, ch 3, sig X i^r. Compare Aquinas as above, Ch. 7 n. 32.
31. Ibid., bk 2, ch. 7, sig. bb ii^v. Note, however, that some other Dominican writers such as Nicolas Jacquier were more explicit about divine permission: see chapters 14 and 25 of his *Flagellum hæreticorum fascinariorum*, in the collected volume of the works of Nicolas Jacquier, Joannes Myntzenbergius, Nicolas Bassée, Lambert Daneau, Joachim Camerarius, Martín de Arles y Andosilla, Johannes Trithemius, and Thomas Erastus, *Flagellum hæreticorum fascinariorum* (Frankfurt: Nicolaus Bassæus, 1581), 95 ff, 167 ff.
32. Plantsch, *Opusculum*, sig a ii^v.
33. Ibid., sig. a iv^r.
34. Ibid., sigs. a iv^r–viii^r.
35. Ibid., sigs. biii^{r-v}.
36. Ibid., sigs. b iv^v–c i^r.
37. Ibid., sigs. c i^v–v^r.
38. Ibid. sigs. c v^v–e v^r.

39. Plantsch, *Opusculum*, sigs. e vii^r–g ii^v.

40. Jean Gerson, *De Directione Cordis*, in Jean Gerson, *Œuvres complètes*, ed. Palémon Glorieux (Paris, New York: Desclée, 1960–), vol. viii (1971), para. 42, 110–11.

41. Jean Gerson, 'De Erroribus circa Artem Magicam et Articulis Reprobatis', in *Malleus Maleficarum: Maleficas et earum hæresim frameâ conterens, ex variis auctoribus compilatus, & in quator tomos iustè distributus*, 2 vols in 3 (Lyons: Claudius Bourgeat, 1669), ii, part II [with separate title-page and pagination], 169.

42. Gerson, *De Directione Cordis*, in *Œuvres complètes*, ed. Glorieux, viii, sect. 35, 108. See fuller discussion of Gerson's rhetoric in the next chapter.

43. Jean Gerson, 'Triologium Astrologiae Theologizatae', in J. Gerson, *Joannis Gersonii Doctoris Theologi & Cancellarii Parisiensis Opera Omnia*, ed. Ludovicus Ellies du Pin, 5 vols, 2nd edn (The Hague: P. de Hondt, 1728), I, col. 196.

44. Johann of Frankfurt, in Joseph Hansen (ed.), *Quellen und Untersuchungen zur Geschichte des Hexenwahns und der Hexenverfolgung im Mittelalter* (Hildesheim: G. Olms, 1963, reprint of the original edition, Bonn: C. Georgi, 1901), 71 ff; passage cited on 77. Compare Caroline Walker Bynum, *Wonderful Blood: Theology and Practice in Late Medieval Northern Germany and Beyond* (Philadelphia: University of Pennsylvania Press, 2007), 25–45, for the theological debates over the status of the most famous field-shrine, the Eucharistic host shrine at Wilsnack.

45. Hansen, *Quellen*, 104.

46. *Dives and Pauper*, ed. Priscilla Heath Barnum, 3 vols, Early English Text Society, nos. 275, 280, 323 (London: Oxford University Press, 1976–2004), i. 172–3.

47. Martín of Arles y Andosilla, *Tractatus insignis et exquisitissimus de superstitionibus*, in *Tractatus Universi Juris*, xi, pt. 2 (Lyons, 1584), fos. 402^v–8^r, sect. 78.

48. Plantsch, *Opusculum*, sig. g iv^{r–v}.

49. Pedro Ciruelo, *Reprovación de las supersticiones*, translated as *Pedro Ciruelo's A treatise reproving all superstitions and forms of witchcraft: very necessary and useful for all good Christians zealous for their salvation*, trans. E. A. Maio and D. W. Pearson (Rutherford, NJ: Fairleigh Dickinson University Press, 1977), 321–5.

50. [Johannes Nider], *Johannis Nideri theologi olim clarissimi De visionibus ac revelationibus: opus rarissimum historiis Germaniæ refertissimum, anno 1517, Argentinæ editum* (Helmstedt: Paulus Zeisingius, Salomon Schnorrius, 1692), 417–22.

51. Mazzolini, *De Strigimagarum . . . Mirandis*, ii. 11. vi. v, sig. ff iii^r. R. W. Scribner, 'Ritual and Popular Religion in Catholic Germany at the time of the Reformation', in R. W. Scribner, *Popular Culture and Popular Movements*

in Reformation Germany (London: Hambledon Press, 1987), 35–6, discusses synodal criticisms of weather-processions in the fifteenth century, especially those that involved carrying the Eucharist in procession.

52. See above, Ch. 2 n. 29; Decreti Secunda pars, Causa xxvi, quest. V c. 12, in *Corpus Juris Canonici*, ed. Aemilius Ludouicus Richter and Aemilius Friedberg (Graz: Akademische Druck- u. Verlagsanstalt, 1959), i, cols. 1030–1.

53. For examples of the canon being quoted see Hansen, *Quellen*, 70, and Martín of Arles, *Tractatus de Superstitionibus*, section 11.

54. Luther, *Ten Commandments*, sig. Biv ᵛ, following Geiler, *Die Emeis*, chapter 18 based on *Formicarius*, ii. 4.

55. Giordano da Bergamo, *Quaestio de strigis*, as excerpted in Hansen, *Quellen*, 195–200; Alphonsus de Spina [Alfonso de Espina], *Fortalitium fidei* (Lyons: Gulielmus Balsarin, 1487), book 5, consideration 10, difference 10, sig. L iiiʳ and as excerpted in Hansen, *Quellen*, 147–8; Samuel, Cassinensis, *Questione de le strie: questiones lamearum* ([Pavia?], 1505), excerpted in Hansen, *Quellen*, 262 ff; Joannes Franciscus de Ponzinibio, *Tractatus subtilis et elegans de lamiis* (Pavia: Iacobus de Burgo Franco, 1511), excerpted in Hansen, *Quellen*, 313 ff; Martín of Arles, *Tractatus de Superstitionibus*, section 11 as above.

56. Hansen, *Quellen*, 133–45, and Jacquier, *Flagellum*, chapters 7–9, in *Flagellum hæreticorum fascinariorum*, as above, note 31.

57. Hansen, *Quellen*, 200–7.

58. Bernhardus Basin, 'Opusculum de artibus magicis, ac Magorum Maleficiis', in *Malleus Maleficarum: Maleficas et earum hæresim frameâ conterens, ex variis auctoribus compilatus, & in quator tomos iustè distributus*, 2 vols in 3 (Lyons: Claudius Bourgeat, 1669), ii, pt I, 8–10.

59. Vincenzo Dodo of Pavia, *Apologia contra li defensori dele strie* (Pavia, 1506) as excerpted in Hansen, *Quellen*, 273 ff; Bartolomeo Spina, *Quaestio de strigibus: una cum tractatu de praeeminentia sacrae theologiae & quadruplici apologia de lamiis contra Ponzinibium* (Rome, 1576) and as excerpted in Hansen, *Quellen*, 326 ff; Mazzolini, *De Strigimagarum . . . Mirandis*, ii. 1, sig. S iiiʳ ff.

60. Arnaldus Albertini, *Tractatus solemnis et aureus de agnosendis assertionibus Catholicis, et haereticis* (Venice, 1571) and as excerpted in Hansen, *Quellen*, 344 ff.

61. *Malleus Maleficarum*, (Lyons, 1669), pt. I, q. i, in i. 1–6.

9. THE PASTORAL USE OF THE SCHOLASTIC CRITIQUE OF SUPERSTITIONS

1. Martin Plantsch, *Opusculum de sagis maleficis* (Pforzheim: Thomas Anshelm, 1507) was based on sermons preached in the parish Church of St George's in Tübingen in 1505, the year that a witch was burned in the town: see sig. a ivʳ. Johannes Geiler von Kaisersberg, *Die Emeis, dis ist das büch von*

der Omeissen (Strasbourg: Johannes Grieninger, 1517) was based on a cycle of sermons delivered in Lent 1508 by Geiler at the *Hochstift* in Strasbourg, transcribed by Johannes Pauli, warden of the discalced Carmelites.

2. J. Gerson, *De Directione Cordis*, in Jean Gerson, *Œuvres complètes*, ed. Palémon Glorieux (Paris, New York: Desclée, 1960–), vol. viii (Paris, 1971), section 35, 108: 'fiant innumerae particulares observantiae quae nullam videntur habere institutionis rationem; et ita talis ritus transit in superstitionem quae nihil aliud est quam vana religio. Dicitur autem vana, quia caret ratione vel effectu.'

3. Ibid., sects. 36–8, 108–9: see the extended quotation in Ch. 3 above and n. 2.

4. Ibid., sects. 39–41, 109–10.

5. Ibid., sects. 42–8, 110–12.

6. Ibid., sects. 48–9, 112–13.

7. See above, Ch. 3 at note 4, and Robert E. Lerner, 'Werner di Friedberg intrappolato dalla legge', in, J.-C. Maire Vigueur and A. Paravicini Bagliani (eds) *La parola all'accusato* (Palermo: Sellerio, 1991), 268–81.

8. Felix Hemmerli, 'Tractatus I de exorcismis' in *Malleus Maleficarum* (Frankfurt: Nicolaus Bassaeus, 1600), ii. 378, 390.

9. Ibid, ii. 387, 392.

10. See above Ch. 3 at note 32.

11. The preface to the *Treatise on Superstitions* is found in Nicolas Jacquier, Joannes Myntzenbergius, Nicolas Bassée, Lambert Daneau, Joachim Camerarius, Martín de Arles y Andosilla, Johannes Trithemius, and Thomas Erastus, *Flagellum hæreticorum fascinariorum* (Frankfurt: Nicolaus Bassæus, 1581), 351–3. Lumbier is approximately 20 km ESE of Pamplona in present-day Spain. Labiano, also mentioned by Martín, is much closer to Pamplona but also on the ESE side of the city.

12. Martín of Arles y Andosilla, *Tractatus insignis et exquisitissimus de superstitionibus*, in *Tractatus Universi Juris*, xi, pt. 2 (Lyons, 1584), fos. 402ᵛ–8ʳ, sections 9 and 45 refer explicitly to things that he learned during pastoral visitations.

13. See Caroline Walker Bynum, *Wonderful Blood: Theology and Practice in Late Medieval Northern Germany and Beyond* (Philadelphia: University of Pennsylvania Press, 2007), 25–45.

14. See Keith Thomas, *Religion and the Decline of Magic: Studies in Popular Beliefs in Sixteenth- and Seventeenth-Century England* (London: Weidenfeld and Nicolson, 1971), 47: 'The medieval Church thus did a great deal to weaken the fundamental distinction between a prayer and a charm, and to encourage the idea that there was virtue in the mere repetition of holy words'; also 56: 'The leaders of the [late medieval] Church thus abandoned the struggle

against superstition whenever it seemed in their interest to do so.' For the claim of self-interest on the part of the clerical patrons of field-shrines, see Martin Luther's 'To the Christian Nobility of the German Nation', in Martin Luther, *Luthers Werke: Kritische Gesamtausgabe* (Weimar: Böhlaus Nachfolger 1883–1948), vi. 447 ff.; translated as Martin Luther, *Luther's Works*, XXXVI: *Word and Sacrament II*, edited by J. J. Pelikan, H. C. Oswald, and H. T. Lehmann (Philadelphia: Fortress Press, 1959), xliv. 185 ff. and nn.

15. See above, in the Introduction, and below, the introduction to Part III.
16. See the arguments of John W. O'Malley and others below, Ch. 15 note 36.

PART III INTRODUCTION

1. For catechesis, see e.g. G. Strauss, *Luther's House of Learning: Indoctrination of the Young in the German Reformation* (Baltimore: Johns Hopkins University Press, 1978); Ian Green, *The Christian's ABC: Catechisms and Catechizing in England c.1530–1740* (Oxford: Oxford University Press, 1996); on the Roman Catholic side, the works of Peter Canisius, *Summa doctrinae christianae* (Vienna: Zimmermannus, 1555), *Catechismus Minimus* (Ingolstadt, 1556), and *Catechismus minor* (Cologne, 1558), and also the Tridentine Catechism, published as *Catechismus, ex decreto Concilii Tridentini, ad parochos, Pii Qvinti Pont. Max. iussu editus* (Rome: Paulus Manutius, 1566).

2. On pastoral visitations, see Umberto Mazzone and Angelo Turchini, *I Visiti Pastorali: Analisi di una fonte* (Bologna: Il Mulino, 1985); on confessional discipline see R. Po-Chia Hsia, *Social Discipline in the Reformation: Central Europe 1550–1750* (London: Routledge, 1989), esp. 122–73. See also B. Tolley, *Pastors and Parishioners in Württemberg during the Late Reformation 1581–1621* (Stanford, CA: Stanford University Press, 1995), 64 ff.

3. For typical Erasmian satire of vulgar superstitions, see *The Colloquies of Erasmus*, ed. C. R. Thompson (Chicago: University of Chicago Press, 1965), esp. 'A Pilgrimage for Religion's Sake' and 'The Shipwreck'. These works are analysed in more detail below. Erasmus's works were initially placed on the Index in the Counter-Reformation and then extensively expurgated, restricting Catholic access to some works; in contrast they were extensively used as school-texts in Protestantism.

4. For acculturation, see J. Delumeau, *Catholicism between Luther and Voltaire: A New View of the Counter-Reformation*, trans. Jeremy Moiser (London: Burns & Oates; Philadelphia: Westminster Press, 1977), and R. Muchembled, *Popular Culture and Elite Culture in France, 1400–1750*, trans. Lydia Cochrane (Baton Rouge: Louisiana State University Press,1985); also the discussion in J. K. Powis, 'Repression and Autonomy: Christians and Christianity in

the Historical Work of Jean Delumeau', *Journal of Modern History*, 64 (1992), 366–74; for the separation of elite and popular cultures see P. Burke, *Popular Culture in Early Modern Europe*, 3rd edn (Farnham: Ashgate, 2009) and his sources, also the more recent work of R. Muchembled, especially his *L'Invention de l'homme moderne: Sensibilités, mœurs et comportements collectifs sous l'ancien régime* (Paris: Fayard, 1988).

5. Stuart Clark, *Thinking with Demons: The Idea of Witchcraft in Early Modern Europe* (Oxford: Clarendon Press, 1997), esp. chapters 29–34.

6. See above, Introduction, notes 26–9.

7. Compare Richard van Dülmen, 'Reformation und Neuzeit: ein Versuch', *Zeitschrift für historische Forschung*, 14 (1987), 1–25, translated as 'The Reformation and the Modern Age', in Scott Dixon (ed.), *The German Reformation: The Essential Readings* (Oxford: Blackwell, 1999), 193–223 and references.

8. See e.g. Jane Shaw, *Miracles in Enlightenment England* (New Haven and London: Yale University Press, 2006).

9. Alexandra Walsham, 'The Reformation and the "Disenchantment of the World" Reassessed', *Historical Journal*, 51/2 (2008), 501 and notes 11–12.

10. See e.g. Jean Delumeau, 'Les Réformateurs et la superstition', in *Actes du colloque l'Amiral de Coligny et son temps (Paris, 24–28 octobre 1972)* (Paris: SHPF, 1974), 451–87.

11. See Robin Briggs, 'Embattled Faiths', in Euan Cameron (ed.), *Early Modern Europe: An Oxford History* (Oxford: Oxford University Press, 1999), 188–9, on the 'decline of the devil' in seventeenth-century culture.

12. On the relatively lenient treatment meted out by officials of organized inquisitions to the purveyors of low-level magical services, see e.g. Mary Rose O'Neil, 'Discerning Superstition: Popular Errors and Orthodox Response in Late Sixteenth Century Italy' (Ph.D. thesis, Stanford University, 1981); Mary O'Neil, 'Magical Healing, Love Magic and the Inquisition in Late Sixteenth-Century Modena', in Stephen Haliczer (ed.), *Inquisition and Society in Early Modern Europe* (Totowa, NJ: Barnes & Noble, 1987), pp 88–114; Mary O'Neil, '*Sacerdote ovvero strione*: Ecclesiastical and Superstitious Remedies in 16th century Italy', in S. Kaplan (ed.), *Understanding Popular Culture: From the Middle Ages to the Nineteenth Century* (Berlin and New York: Mouton, 1984), 53–83. See also John Tedeschi, 'The Inquisitorial Law and the Witch', in B. Ankarloo and G. Henningsen, *Early Modern European Witchcraft: Centres and Peripheries* (Oxford: Clarendon Press, 1990), 83–118, for the prevalence of cases of minor sorcery in the inquisition records.

13. However, some thinkers such as Niels Hemmingsen did suggest that implicit pact might well lead down the road to a more explicit demonic involvement.

10. SOME RENAISSANCE CHRISTIAN HUMANISTS
AND 'SUPERSTITION'

1. For some discussion of this diversity see E. Cameron, 'The Impact of Humanist Values', *Historical Journal*, 36/4 (1993) 957–64.

2. On Iamblichus, see Christopher S. Celenza, 'The Search for Ancient Wisdom in Early Modern Europe: Reuchlin and the Late Ancient Esoteric Paradigm', *Journal of Religious History*, 25/2 (2001), pp 115–33; his works were published in *Iamblichus de Mysteriis Aegyptiorum, Chaldaeorum, Assyriorum. Proclus in Platonicum Alcibiadem de anima atque daemone. Idem de sacrificio & magia. Porphyrius de diuinis atq; daemonib. Psellus de daemonibus. Mercurii Trismegisti Pimander* (Lyons: J. Tornaesius, 1577).

3. The classic study of Renaissance Hermetic Neoplatonism remains Frances A. Yates, *Giordano Bruno and the Hermetic Tradition* (Chicago: University of Chicago Press, 1964, repr. 1991). See also Lenn Evan Goodman (ed.), *Neoplatonism and Jewish Thought* (Albany: State University of New York Press, 1992); and Ingrid Merkel and Allen G. Debus (eds), *Hermeticism and the Renaissance: Intellectual History and the Occult in Early Modern Europe* (Washington: Folger Shakespeare Library; London: Associated University Presses, 1988).

4. Richard M. Cameron, 'The Charges of Lutheranism Brought against Jacques Lefèvre d'Etaples (1520–1529)', *Harvard Theological Review*, 63/1. (1970), 119–149, and esp. 132 and references. On the religious environment of Paris in Lefèvre's time, see James K. Farge, *Orthodoxy and Reform in Early Reformation France: The Faculty of Theology of Paris, 1500–1543*, Studies in Medieval and Reformation Thought, 32 (Leiden: E. J. Brill, 1985); Denis Crouzet, *La Genèse de la réforme française 1520–1560*, Regards sur l'histoire, 109, Histoire moderne (Paris: SEDES, 1996).

5. On Renaissance natural magic, see e.g. Richard Kieckhefer, *Magic in the Middle Ages* (Cambridge: Cambridge University Press, 1989), 144–50, with discussion of Lefèvre and others. See also the conventional but positive description of natural magic in e.g. [Jacobus Heerbrandus], *De Magia Disputatio ex cap. 7. Exo., ... praeside reverendo et clarissimo viro Jacobo Heerbrando, sacrae theologiae Doctore eximio, ac eiusdem in Academia Tubingensi Professore publico ... Nicolaus Falco Salueldensis ... respondere conabitur* (Tübingen: [Ulrich Morhart], 1570), theses 1–4.

6. For the *Paraphrases* see Jacques Lefèvre d'Étaples, *In hoc opere continentur totius philosophie naturalis paraphrases: adiecto ad litteram familiari commentario declarate* (Paris: Wolfgang Hopyl, 1502).

7. [Jacques Lefèvre d'Étaples (ed.)], *Divini Dionysii Areopagite Caelesti hierarchia; Ecclesiastica hierarchia; Divina nomina; Mystica theologia; Undecim epistolae:*

Ignatii Undecim epistolae. Polycarpi Epistola una. Theologia viuificans Cibus solidus (Venice: Joannes Tacuinus, 1502).

8. The following remarks draw upon Lewis W. Spitz, 'The Conflict of Ideals in Mutianus Rufus: A Study in the Religious Philosophy of Northern Humanism', *Journal of the Warburg and Courtauld Institutes*, 16/1–2. (1953), 121–43 esp at. 129 ff. See also Robert W. Scribner, 'The Erasmians and the Beginning of the Reformation in Erfurt', *Journal of Religious History*, 9 (1976/7), 3–31; Jean-Claude Margolin, 'Mutian et son modèle erasmien', in *L'humanisme allemand (1480–1540). XVIIIe Colloque international de Tours* (Munich and Paris: Fink, Vrin, 1979) 169–202. The correspondence is edited in Karl Krause (ed.) *Der Briefwechsel des Mutianus Rufus* (Kassel: A. Freyschmidt, 1885).

9. Spitz, 'Conflict of Ideals', 131.

10. Ibid. 131–3.

11. For modern biographies of Erasmus, see e.g. Léon-E. Halkin, *Erasmus: A Critical Biography* (Oxford and Cambridge, MA: Blackwell, 1993); Richard J. Schoeck, *Erasmus of Europe*, 2 vols (Edinburgh: Edinburgh University Press, 1990–3); James D. Tracy. *Erasmus of the Low Countries* (Berkeley: University of California Press, 1996).

12. *Collected Works of Erasmus* (Toronto; Buffalo: University of Toronto Press, 1974–) vol. 66: *Spirituala; Enchiridon; De Contemptu Mundi; De Vidua Christiana*, ed. John W. O'Malley (1988), 65.

13. References are made here to the translation in Desiderius Erasmus, *Praise of Folly*, in *Collected Works of Erasmus*, vol. 27: *Literary and Educational Writings*, 5, ed. A. H. T. Levi (Toronto: University of Toronto Press 1986); see also M. A. Screech, *Ecstasy and The Praise of Folly* (London: Duckworth, 1980).

14. Erasmus, *Praise of Folly*, ed. Levi, 114.

15. See above, Ch. 5, at note 46, also ch. 8, at note 44.

16. Erasmus, *Praise of Folly*, ed. Levi, 114.; For the story of St Bernard and the saving verses of the Psalms, see Peter Phillips, 'Broadening Horizons', *Musical Times*, 139/1859 (1998), 18–23, which cites Erasmus's mention of this legend on 19. See also George Steel, 'Notes on Robert Parsons' Latin Works' at http://www.millertheatre.com/parsons/latinpdf/notes_latin.pdf. The peculiar text of *O Bone Jesu*—a group of different psalm verses interleaved with 'O' acclamations in Latin, Hebrew, and Greek—is a special devotional collection known as 'St. Bernard's Verses.' The pious legend surrounding the origin of the text runs thus: While reading his Bible, St. Bernard was approached by the Devil, who taunted him. The Devil claimed that there existed a secret formula of psalm verses that, if recited daily, would hold the Devil powerless. However, the Devil understandably refused to divulge these

verses to Bernard. Determined to learn the magic verses, Bernard threatened that if the Devil did not reveal these apotropaic verses, he would recite the *entire* Psalter every day. When confronted with this threat of piety, the devil divulged the secret verses to Bernard and to posterity.

17. Erasmus, *Praise of Folly*, ed. Levi, 115.

18. Ibid., 130–1.

19. Jean Gerson, 'De Directione Cordis', in Jean Gerson, *Œuvres complètes*, ed. Palémon Glorieux (Paris, New York: Desclée, 1960–) vol. viii (1971), section 49, 113: 'such as we see in certain religious [orders] concerning some particular observances not necessary to salvation, which are preferred to the laws of God and the Gospels: we even see this in the decretum and the decretals; indeed, sometimes a monk is more severely punished for going about without his cowl than one who commits adultery or sacrilege, and going against one decree of the pope than against the precepts of the Gospel, as Christ criticized the Pharisees: "you have made God's law null and void because of your traditions." '

20. Erasmus, *Praise of Folly*, ed. Levi, 126–30 (theologians), 132–5 (preachers). Compare Larissa Taylor, *Soldiers of Christ: Preaching in Late Medieval and Reformation France* (New York: Oxford University Press, 1992), for a more sympathetic and realistic picture of the more successful of late medieval preachers.

21. For the *Colloquies*, see *Collected Works of Erasmus* (Toronto; Buffalo: University of Toronto Press, 1974–), vols 39–40: *Colloquies*, trans. and ed. Craig R. Thompson (1997).

22. For the astonishing publishing success of the *Colloquies* see *Colloquies*, ed. Thompson, *Collected Works of Erasmus*, 39, xx–xxvii, xxxi–xxxvi.

23. *Colloquies*, ed. Thompson, *Collected Works of Erasmus*, 40, 619–21 (introduction) 621–74 (text and notes). The shrine of the Virgin Mary at Walsingham was destroyed in the destruction of abbeys and pilgrimage sites in 1538 but was revived by Anglo-Catholic devotees in the early twentieth century.

24. *Colloquies*, ed. Thompson, *Collected Works of Erasmus*, 40, 624–8, 632–3. On pilgrimages and Erasmus see J. van Herwaarden, *Between Saint James and Erasmus: Studies in Late-Medieval Religious Life: Devotion and Pilgrimage in the Netherlands* (Leiden: Brill, 2003).

25. *Colloquies*, ed. Thompson, *Collected Works of Erasmus*, 39, 351–2 (introduction), 352–67 (text and notes).

26. Ibid. 355–6, and commentaries on 362–5.

27. Ibid. 531–3 (introduction), 533–44 (text and notes).

28. The term δεισιδαιμονία derived from a character in Theophrastus. See Theophrastus, *Characters*, trans. James Diggle (Cambridge: Cambridge

University Press, 2004), 110–13 (text) and 349–75 (commentary). Although the term referred to those who were excessively pious in classical pagan religion rather than the 'superstitious' in the medieval sense, it was used in both senses in Renaissance literature. See also Hendrik Bolkestein, *Theophrastos' Charakter der Deisidaimonia, als religionsgeschichtliche Urkunde* (Giessen: A. Töpelmann, 1929); Samson Eitrem, 'Zur Deisidämonie', *Symbolae Osloenses*, 31 (1955), 155–69.

29. There does not appear to be any systematic discussion of superstition anywhere in the *Adages*: the word itself does not figure in the large thematic indexes compiled for the later sixteenth- and seventeenth-century editions.

30. See W. Deonna, 'The Crab and the Butterfly: A Study in Animal Symbolism', *Journal of the Warburg and Courtauld Institutes*, 17/1–2. (1954), 47–86, and esp. 64, 82 and note 300, with references to multiple other early modern appearances of the story. For Erasmus's version see *Opus Epistolarum Des. Erasmi Roterdami*, ed. P. S. Allen, 12 vols (Oxford: Clarendon Press, 1906–58), vii, 462–3f, no. 2037.See discussion in Johann Weyer, *Witches, Devils, and Doctors in the Renaissance*, ed. George Mora and Benjamin Kohl, trans. John Shea, Medieval & Renaissance Texts & Studies, 73 (Binghamton, NY: Medieval & Renaissance Texts & Studies, 1991; repr. 1998), 51–2.

11. MAGIC, THE FALLEN WORLD, AND FALLEN HUMANITY: MARTIN LUTHER ON THE DEVIL AND SUPERSTITIONS

1. For the Fourth Lateran Council see Norman P. Tanner (ed.), *Decrees of the Ecumenical Councils*, 2 vols (London and Washington: Sheed & Ward, Georgetown University Press, 1990), 227–71. On the unique status of the Catholic Church see Constitution 1, 230–1. On Innocent III and his context, see Colin Morris, *The Papal Monarchy: The Western Church from 1050 to 1250* (Oxford: Clarendon Press, 1989), 417 ff.

2. For the decree of Lateran IV regarding auricular confession see Constitution 21, in Tanner (ed.), *Decrees*, 245. On the late medieval theory of confession See esp. T. N. Tentler, *Sin and Confession on the Eve of the Reformation* (Princeton: Princeton University Press, 1977).

3. Lateran IV, Constitution 21, in Tanner (ed.), *Decrees*, 245, specifies that those who refuse to make confession should be denied Christian burial. For purgatory, see J. Le Goff, *The Birth of Purgatory*, trans. A. Goldhammer (Chicago: University of Chicago Press, 1984).

4. See the debates around Hus's *De Ecclesia*, as analysed in H. A. Oberman, *Forerunners of the Reformation: The Shape of Late Medieval Thought* with documents trans. by Paul L. Nyhus (Philadelphia: Fortress 1981), 208–37.

5. On the plurality of late medieval schools, see Jaroslav Pelikan, *Reformation of Church and Dogma (1300–1700)* (Chicago: University of Chicago Press, 1984), 10–12; J. H. Overfield, *Humanism and Scholasticism in Late Medieval Germany* (Princeton: Princeton University Press, 1984), 49 ff.; A. Renaudet, *Préréforme et humanisme à Paris pendant les premières guerres d'Italie, 1494–1517*, 2nd edn (Paris, Librairie d'Argences, 1953), 53–94.The fullest exposition of the developed Ockhamist position is still H. A. Oberman, *The Harvest of Medieval Theology: Gabriel Biel and Late Medieval Nominalism* (Cambridge, MA: Harvard University Press, 1963).

6. See e.g. the extracts from Wessel Gansfort and Staupitz in Oberman, *Forerunners*, 93–120, 175–203, where theological inquiry does not challenge official religious practice in any significant way.

7. On nominalism, see especially Oberman, *Forerunners*, 121–203, and e.g. Heiko A. Oberman, '*Facientibus quod in se est Deus non denegat gratiam*: Robert Holcot O.P. and the Beginnings of Luther's Theology', in Oberman, *The Dawn of the Reformation* (Edinburgh: T. & T. Clark, 1992), 84–103 and esp. 90 ff.

8. See the discussion of this point in my *The European Reformation* (Oxford: Clarendon Press, 1991), 121–3 and references.

9. Ibid., 123–8 and references. It is fair to add that this distinction is not uncontroversial in Reformation theological history: not all historians agree that the distinction between justification and regeneration is as clear-cut in Luther as this summary suggests.

10. Ibid., 144–55 and references.

11. See Euan Cameron, 'Martin Luther', in Adrian Hastings, Alistair Mason, and Hugh Pyper (eds), *Key Thinkers in Christianity* (Oxford: Oxford University Press, 2003), 53–63.

12. The text of the sermons appears (with some modifications) in Martin Luther, *Luthers Werke: Kritische Gesamtausgabe* (Weimar: Böhlaus Nachfolger 1883–1948), i. 398–521; the original pamphlet edition is *Decem Praecepta wittenbergensi predicata populo. Per P. Martinum Luther Augustinianum* (Wittenberg: Johann Rhau-Grunenberg, 1518). The latter edition is visible at http://luther.hki.uni-koeln.de/luther/pages/suche2_5.html. The pamphlet, which contains material not in the Weimar edition, is here used for references.

13. Luther, *Decem Praecepta*, Rhau-Grunenberg edition, sig. Aii^v.

14. Ibid., sigs. Aiii^v–iv^r. The *Enchiridion Leonis papae* was traditionally attributed to Pope Leo III (795–816), who supposedly presented it to Charlemagne. See *Manuel ou enchiridion de prières* (Lyons: no imprint, 1584); *Enchiridion Leonis Papae, serenissimo imperatori Carolo Magno in munus pretiosum datum, nuperrimè mendis omnibus purgatum* (Mainz: no imprint, 1633).

15. Luther, *Decem Praecepta*, Rhau-Grunenberg edition, sig. Aiv^{r-v}.

16. Ibid., sig Bi^r.

17. Ibid., sigs. Bi^r–Bii^r.

18. Ibid., sigs. Bii^v–Ci^r. Many authors imply that Luther believed entirely conventionally in witches, but compare Sigrid Brauner, *Fearless Wives and Frightened Shrews: The Construction of the Witch in Early Modern Germany* (Amherst: University of Massachusetts Press, 1995), for a more measured and learned treatment of Luther.

19. Luther was fairly clearly drawing here on Johannes Geiler von Kaisersberg, *Die Emeis, dis ist das büch von der Omeissen* (Strasbourg: Johannes Grieninger, 1517), chapter 33, fos. 54^v ff.; and in turn on Geiler's source, Martin Plantsch, *Opusculum de sagis maleficis* (Pforzheim: Thomas Anshelm, 1507), sigs. b iv^v ff.

20. Luther, *Decem Praecepta*, Rhau-Grunenberg edition, sigs. Bii^v–Biii^r. See above, Ch. 2 note 4.

21. Ibid., sig. Biii^{r-v}.

22. Ibid., sig. Biv^r.

23. Note that Luther accepted the authority of the Canon *Episcopi* and showed no awareness that its authenticity or relevance on this question had ever been disputed. That point alone strongly suggests that he could not have read the *Malleus Maleficarum*.

24. Luther, *Decem Praecepta*, Rhau-Grunenberg edition, sig. Ci^r.

25. For Luther's humanism see Lewis William Spitz, *Luther and German Humanism* (Aldershot: Variorum, 1996); also Timothy P. Dost, *Renaissance Humanism in Support of the Gospel in Luther's Early Correspondence: Taking all Things Captive* (Aldershot: Ashgate, 2001).

26. Luther, *Decem Praecepta*, Rhau-Grunenberg edition, sig. Ci^v.

27. Ibid., sigs. Cii^r–Civ^r.

28. Ibid., sig. Civ^{r-v}.

29. Compare almost identical passage in Erasmus, *Enchiridion*, CWE edition, 65–72.

30. Luther, *Decem Praecepta*, Rhau-Grunenberg edition, sigs. Di^r–Dii^v.

31. Note that some of these etymologies were in a part of the text that Luther later excised for publication, realizing that his conjectures were mistaken. (Notes in *WA* edition make this clear.)

32. Luther, *Decem Praecepta*, Rhau-Grunenberg edition, sig. Civ^r.

33. Ibid., sigs. Diii^r–Div^r.

34. Ibid., sig. Div^{r-v}.

35. Ibid., sig. Div^v–Ei^r. Note that the attack on field-shrines and new devotions was repeated in a more succinct way in *To the Christian Nobility* in 1520, and cite references.

36. Compare Bynum *Wonderful Blood*, 27–45 for the theological disarray over new shrines. Luther was not breaking new ground here.

37. Luther, *Decem Praecepta*, Rhau-Grunenberg edition, sigs. Ei^v–Eii^v.

38. Ibid., sigs. Eii^v–Eiv^v.

39. Some scholars would argue that this process took place even earlier. My own exposition follows that of Martin Brecht, *Martin Luther: Sein Weg zur Reformation, 1483–1521* (Stuttgart: Calwer, 1981), translated as the first volume of Martin Brecht, *Martin Luther*, trans. James L. Schaaf, 3 vols (Philadelphia: Fortress Press, 1985–93), at present the definitive biography of its subject.

40. *Luthers Werke*, xlii. 25–7; Martin Luther, *Luther's Works*, ed. Jaroslav Pelikan and H. T. Lehmann, 55 vols (St Louis: Concordia, and Philadelphia: Fortress Press, 1955–86), i. 33–6: commentary on Genesis 1: 9–10.

41. *Luthers Werke*, xlii. 38–9; *Luther's Works*, i. 51–2, commentary on Genesis 1: 21–2.

42. *Luthers Werke*, xlii. 50; *Luther's Works*, i. 67, commentary on Genesis 1: 27.

43. *Luthers Werke*, xlii. 79; *Luther's Works*, i. 104–5, commentary on Genesis 2: 16; and compare *Luthers Werke*, xlii. 140–7; *Luther's Works*, i. 188–98, commentary on Genesis 3: 15.

44. *Luthers Werke*, xlii. 40; *Luther's Works*, i. 54, commentary on Genesis 1: 22; Ibid., 1: 13 and 1: 24; compare *Luthers Werke*, xlii. 58; *Luther's Works*, i. 77, commentary on Genesis 2: 2. Luther was obviously unaware of the usefulness of thistles to the Scots before the Battle of Largs in 1263.

45. *Luthers Werke*, xlii. 74–7; *Luther's Works*, i. 97–101, commentary on Genesis 2: 11–13.

46. *Luthers Werke*, xlii. 138–9; *Luther's Works*, i. 185–6, commentary on Genesis 3: 15.

47. *Luthers Werke*, xlii. 152–4; *Luther's Works*, i. 204–6, commentary on Genesis 3: 17–19.

48. *Luthers Werke*, xlii. 154–6; *Luther's Works*, i. 207–9.

49. *Luthers Werke*, xlii. 17–18; *Luther's Works*, i. 22–3; commentary on Genesis 1: 6.

50. *Luthers Werke*, xlii. 85; *Luther's Works*, i. 111–12, commentary on Genesis 2: 17.

51. The supreme exploration of the demonic in Luther's make-up is of course Heiko A. Oberman, *Luther: Man between God and the Devil*, trans. Eileen Walliser-Schwarzbart (New Haven: Yale University Press, 1989); see also more specifically Jörg Haustein, *Martin Luthers Stellung zum Zauber- und Hexenwesen*, Münchener kirchenhistorische Studien, 2 (Stuttgart: W. Kohlhammer, 1990).

52. Luther defended against the criticisms of Johannes Oecolampadius the fact that in *That these Words* . . . (see below, note 64) he had referred to the devil at least 77 times: see Brecht, *Martin Luther*, ii. 319.

53. John 16: 11.

54. 2 Cor. 4: 4

55. *Luthers Werke*, xl pt. 1, 313–14; *Luther's Works*, xxvi. 189–90, commentary on Galatians 3: 1.

56. Martinus Delrio SJ, *Disquisitionum Magicarum Libri Sex, in tres tomos partiti* (Louvain: Gerardus Rivius, 1599–1600), ii. 28.

57. Galatians 3: 1: 'O insensati Galatae quis vos fascinavit ante quorum oculos Iesus Christus proscriptus est crucifixus.' Note that the version used by Luther says 'Who has bewitched you so that you do not obey the truth?' 'Quis vos fascinavit non obedire veritati' (following the then current Vulgate version, *Luthers Werke*, xl pt. 1, 313). This reading is important for his exegesis of the passage.

58. See above at note 24.

59. *Luthers Werke*, xl pt. 1, 315: 'Quando vult discedere per suas illusiones, tum facit, ut abeat: non fuit lesio vero, alioqui non posset restitui.'

60. *Luthers Werke*, xl pt. 1, 315; *Luther's Works*, xxvi. 190–1, commentary on Galatians 3: 1. The story of Macarius was used by Luther in the *Decem Praecepta*, Rhau-Grunenberg edition, sig. Biv^v. This is a version of a story in Palladius's *Historia Lausiaca*, chapters 19-20 in *Patrologia Latina*, vol. 73, cols. 1110–11, though in the Palladius version the girl appears as a mare rather than a cow. Luther may be citing the story in the version from Rufinus's *Historia Monachorum*, in *Patrologia Latina*, vol. 21, col. 451, though Rufinus also recorded the girl being turned into a horse. Luther made the same mistake in 1516–18 and subsequently.

61. See the *Book of Concord*, as *Die Bekenntnisschriften der evangelisch-lutherischen Kirche: herausgegeben im Gedenkjahr der Augsburgischen Konfession 1930*, 10th edn (Göttingen: Vandenhoeck & Ruprecht, 1986), 564–5.

62. *Bekenntnisschriften der evangelisch-lutherischen Kirche*, 420: purgatory is described in Latin and German as 'mera diaboli larva' and 'ein lauter Teufelsgespenst'.

63. For an analysis of this work see Peter Matheson, *The Rhetoric of the Reformation* (Edinburgh: T. & T. Clark, 1998), 199–214.

64. *Luthers Werke*, xxiii. 64–283; Luther's *Works*, xxxvii. 13–150.

65. *Luthers Werke*, xxiii. 64–5; *Luther's Works*, xxxvii. 13.

66. *Luthers Werke*, xxiii. 64–9; *Luther's Works*, xxxvii. 13–17.

67. *Luthers Werke*, xxiii. 70–1; *Luther's Works*, xxxvii. 17.

68. See Heiko A. Oberman, 'Martin Luther: Forerunner of the Reformation', in Oberman, *The Reformation: Roots and Ramifications*, trans. A. C. Gow (Edinburgh: T. & T. Clark, 1994), 40 ff.

69. Reference to 2 Cor. 4: 9.

70. Reference to 2 Cor. 2: 14.

71. *Luthers Werke*, xl pt. 1, 318; *Luther's Works*, xxvi. 193, commentary on Galatians 3: 2.

72. Mark U. Edwards, Jr., *Luther and the False Brethren* (Stanford, CA: Stanford University Press, 1975), esp. 200 ff; for Luther's early response to Zwingli's Eucharistic ideas, see Euan Cameron, *The European Reformation* (Oxford: Clarendon Press, 1991), 164 and note 49.

73. *Luthers Werke*, xviii. 139; *Luther's Works*, xl. 149.

74. *Luthers Werke*, xl pt. 1, 318–22; *Luther's Works*, xxvi. 194–7, commentary on Galatians 3: 1.

75. *Luthers Werke*, xxiii, 72–5; *Luther's Works*, xxxvii. 19–20.

76. See Cameron, *European Reformation*, 84–5 and references.

77. Oberman, *Luther*, 218–20.

78. Luther, *Decem Praecepta*, Rhau-Grunenberg edition, sig. Biv^r.

79. Luther's *De Servo Arbitrio* is ed. in *Luthers Werke*, xviii. 551–99 (introduction), and 600–787 (text); *Luther's Works*, xxxiii. 3–295.

80. For the 'hidden God' in Luther's theology, see especially *Luthers Werke*, xviii. 684 ff.; *Luther's Works*, xxxiii. 138 ff. See also Paul Althaus, *The Theology of Martin Luther*, trans. Robert C. Schultz (Philadelphia: Fortress Press, 1966), 274–86.

81. *Luthers Werke*, xviii. 685–6; *Luther's Works*, xxxiii. 140.

82. *Luthers Werke*, xviii. 615–17; *Luther's Works*, xxxiii. 37–9.

83. Compare Plantsch, *Opusculum*, sig. cv^v–ei^v; also Geiler, *Die Emeis*, chapters 35–41.

84. *Luthers Werke*, l. 488–509 (introduction), 509–653 (text); *Luther's Works*, xl. 5–177; the title of the German 1539 edition is *Von den conciliis und Kirchen*, sometimes variously translated as the singular or the plural.

85. This motif would have a long succession. See, for instance, Richard Bancroft's sermon *Of the Church* from 1588, possibly following Luther in this passage: 'Where Christ erecteth his church, the divell in the same church-yarde will have his chappell', *Tracts of the Anglican Fathers*, part III, Andrews and Bancroft (London: W. E. Painter, 1839); a parallel quotation occurs in Robert Burton, *The Anatomy of Melancholy* (London: Chatto and Windus, 1927), 667. See also below, Ch. 16 at note 15. It also appeared in George Herbert's *Jacula Prudentum*, where it ran, 'No sooner is a temple built to God but the Devil builds a chapel hard by'. See also Daniel Defoe, 'The True Born Englishman', pt. I: 'Whenever God erects a house of prayer | The devil always builds a chapel there; | And 'twill be found, upon examination, | The latter has the largest congregation.' See [Daniel Defoe], *The Earlier Life and the Chief Earlier*

Works of Daniel Defoe, ed. Henry Morley (London: George Routledge and Sons, 1889), 184.

86. *Luthers Werke*, l. 644; *Luther's Works*, xl. 167–8.

87. Compare the concept of the 'devil's sacraments' as discussed above, Ch. 7 at notes 25–7.

88. Luther here referred to, but did not quote, a rhyme in German that claimed spectacular effects for the Agnus Dei, including the notorious couplet that it was as good as God's blood for destroying sin: 'Zu Verstörunge der Sünden ist es gut | Gleich als das zarte ware Gottes blut'. Shortly afterwards Luther published the rhyme about the Agnus, in a short pamphlet entitled *Von den geweihten Wasser und des Papsts Agnus Dei*, published in *Luthers Werke*, l. 668–73; see discussion in Johann Weyer, *Witches, Devils, and Doctors in the Renaissance*, ed. George Mora and Benjamin Kohl, trans. John Shea, Medieval & Renaissance Texts & Studies, 73 (Binghamton, NY: Medieval & Renaissance Texts & Studies, 1991; repr. 1998), bk 5 ch. 9, 392.

89. *Luthers Werke*, l. 644–5; *Luther's Works*, xli. 168–9.

90. *Luthers Werke*, l. 646–7; *Luther's Works*, xli. 169–71.

91. *Luthers Werke*, l. 649; *Luther's Works*, xli. 173–4.

12. PRODIGIES, PROVIDENCES, AND POSSESSION: THE SIXTEENTH-CENTURY PROTESTANT CONTEXT

1. See above, Ch. 10 n. 3.

2. See Robin Briggs, 'Embattled Faiths', in Euan Cameron (ed.) *Early Modern Europe: An Oxford History* (Oxford: Oxford University Press, 1999), 197.

3. On the drive towards 'social control' see e.g. R. Po-Chia Hsia, *Social Discipline in the Reformation: Central Europe 1550–1750* (London, 1989); foundational works in this area are e.g. Ernst Walter Zeeden, *Die Entstehung der Konfessionen: Grundlagen und Formen der Konfessionsbildung im Zeitalter der Glaubenskämpfe* (Munich: R. Oldenbourg, 1965).

4. See the classic depiction of the regulation of midsummer bonfires in J. Delumeau, *Catholicism between Luther and Voltaire*, trans. Jeremy Moiser (London: Burns & Oates, 1977), 177–9 and below, Ch. 15 note 1.

5. Compare Stuart Clark, *Thinking with Demons: The Idea of Witchcraft in Early Modern Europe* (Oxford: Clarendon Press, 1997), chs 29 and following for this point.

6. This point is made by Robin Bruce Barnes, *Prophecy and Gnosis: Apocalypticism in the Wake of the Lutheran Reformation* (Stanford, CA: Stanford University Press, 1988), 96 ff.

7. On Melanchthon see Sachiko Kusukawa, *The Transformation of Natural Philosophy: The Case of Philip Melanchthon* (Cambridge and New York: Cambridge

University Press, 1995). See also Euan Cameron, 'Philipp Melanchthon: Image and Substance', *Journal of Ecclesiastical History*, 48/4 (1997), 705–22.

8. Cameron, 'Philipp Melanchthon', 707 and references.

9. Clark, *Thinking with Demons*, chs 16–17.

10. [Philipp Melanchthon], *Philippi Melanthonis Opera quae supersunt omnia*, ed. Carolus Gottlieb Bretschneider, Corpus Reformatorum, vols 1–28 (Halle: C. A. Schwetschke and Son, 1834–60), vol. 13 (1846), cols. 179–412. See discussion in Kusukawa, *Transformation*, 144–60.

11. *Melanthonis Opera*, CR, vol. 13, cols. 179–85.

12. Ibid., cols. 189–92.

13. Ibid., col. 292.

14. Ibid., cols. 306 ff.

15. Ibid., col. 323.

16. Ibid., cols. 325–6.

17. This explanation is cited by Clark, *Thinking with Demons*, 298.

18. Pietro Martire Vermigli (1499–1562), *In duos libros Samuelis prophetae . . . commentarii doctissimi*, 2nd edn (Zurich: Froschouerus, 1567), fos. 162^v–168^r.

19. Ibid. fos. 164^v–165^r.

20. Ibid., fos. 165^{r-v}.

21. Benedictus Aretius, *Problemata theologica continentia præcipuos christianae religionis locos, brevi et dilucida ratione explicatos* (Lausanne: Franciscus Le Preux, 1578), article 'Satan', part 2, fos. 19^r–20^r.

22. Johann Georg Godelmann, *Tractatus de Magis, Veneficis et Lamiis, deque his recte cognoscendis et puniendis* (Frankfurt: Nicolaus Bassaeus, 1601) 7–15; the first Latin edition appeared in 1591 and the German translation in 1592.

23. 'Augustin Lercheimer' [= Hermann Wilken or Witekind, d. 1603], *Ein Christlich Bedencken unnd Erinnerung von Zauberey*, published in *Theatrum de veneficis: Das ist: Von Teufelsgespenst, Zauberern und Gifftbereitern, Schwartzkünstlern, Hexen und Unholden, vieler fürnemmen Historien und Exempel* (Frankfurt am Main: Nicolaus Bassaeus, 1586), 262–4.

24. George Gyfford, *A Discourse of the subtill Practises of Devilles by Witches and Sorcerers. By which men are and have bin greatly deluded* (London: [T. Orwin] for Toby Cooke, 1587), sigs. C4^v–F4^r.

25. See the introduction to Johann Weyer, *Witches, Devils, and Doctors in the Renaissance*, ed. George Mora and Benjamin Kohl, trans. John Shea (Medieval & Renaissance Texts & Studies, 73) (Binghamton, NY: Medieval & Renaissance Texts & Studies, 1991; repr. 1998), xxxvi–xlv. For Weyer's religious affiliations, see also Friedrich Wilhelm Bautz and Traugott Bautz (eds), *Biographisch-bibliographisches Kirchenlexikon* (Hamm [Westf.]: Bautz, 1970–), article 'Weyer, Johann' and references.

26. For Weyer's minimally coded approval of the Reformation, see e.g. *Witches, Devils, and Doctors*, 76–7: 'a purer and more fervent preaching of the gospel has been ringing in men's minds . . .'; 470: 'the example of the purer and newly-emergent church . . .'; 149–50: 'this pestilence [*magical divination, practised especially by priests*] steals frightfully along and rages against the whole Christian world, especially where the voice of the Gospel sounds forth less clearly and the truth of divine worship seems to be stained by all sorts of superstitious pagan rites, invented by the cunning of the Devil, no doubt.'

27. Ibid. 3–22.

28. On Familism in general, see Christopher W. Marsh, *The Family of Love in English Society, 1550–1630* (Cambridge and New York: Cambridge University Press, 1993); for Scot's possible affiliations, see discussion in Clark, *Thinking with Demons*, 544–5; for Scot's disavowal of Familism see Reginald Scot (1538?–1599), *The Discovery of Witchcraft: . . . Whereunto is added an excellent Discourse of the nature and substance of devils and spirits* (London: A. Clark and Dixy Page, 1665), [the *Discourse* is separately paginated] chapter 31, 27–8.

29. Scot, *Discourse . . . of devils and spirits*, chs. 2–3, 2–4.

30. Ibid., chs. 6–7, 6–7.

31. Ibid., ch. 33, 29.

32. Ibid., ch. 32, 28–9.

33. On Althamer's career see Bautz, *Biographisch-bibliographisches Kirchenlexikon*, art. 'Althamer, Andreas'; Andreas Althamer, *Eyn Predig von dem Teuffel, das er alles unglueck in der welt anrichte* ([Nuremberg: Jobst Gutknecht], 1532)

34. Althamer, *Predig*, sigs. Aii^v–iii^v.

35. Ibid., sigs. Aiv^r–Bi^r.

36. Ibid., sigs. Bi^v–Biii^v.

37. Philipp Melanchthon, *Initia Doctrinae Physicae*, in *Melanthonis Opera*, CR, vol. 13 (Halle, 1846), col. 323.

38. Aretius, *Problemata*, part II, fos. 19^v–20^r.

39. Weyer, *Witches, Devils, and Doctors*, 33–4.

40. Ibid., book 3, chs. 19–31, 231–60.

41. Aretius, *Problemata*, art. 'fascinatio", part III, fos. 47^r–48^r; Nicolaus Hemmingius [= Niels Hemmingsen], *Admonitio de superstitionibus magicis vitandis, in gratiam sincerae religionis amantium* (Copenhagen: Iohannes Stockelman and Andreas Gutterwitz, 1575), sigs. K3^r–K8^v.

42. Lercheimer, *Christlich Bedencken*, 270. Note that the term *Gaukelei* in German at this period signified the demonic illusion, yet is the cognate and source of the English word 'jugglery': demonic magic and simple mountebanks' tricks tended to be run together in common speech.

43. See the anonymous *Historia von D. Johann Fausten* (Frankfurt: Spies, 1587); the German text is presented on the site 'Bibliotheca Germanica:

Frühneuhochdeutsche Literatur', on http://www.hs-augsburg.de/~harsch/ germanica/Chronologie/16Jh/Faustus/fau_dfo.html. The haycart story appears in ch. 37, the pigs in ch. 44.

44. Aretius, article 'Magia', part II, fos. 41^v–43^v contains the stories; but cf. allusions in Lercheimer, *Christlich Bedencken*, 271; Godelmann, *Tractatus de Magis*, ch. 3, 22 ff., item 17; and cf. reference in Martin Luther, *Decem Praecepta wittenbergensi predicata populo. Per P. Martinum Luther Augustinianum* (Wittenberg: Johann Rhau-Grunenberg, 1518), sig. Biv^v (though not attributed to Faust by name in this case).

45. For the life of Peucer see Jürgen Moltmann, *Christoph Pezel (1539–1604) und der Calvinismus in Bremen*, (Bremen: Verlag Einkehr, 1958), 11 ff., 167 ff. On Peucer, Lavater, and Weyer, see Michael Heyd, *Be Sober and Reasonable: The Critique of Enthusiasm in the Seventeenth and Early Eighteenth Centuries*, Brill's Studies in Intellectual History, 63 (Leiden and New York: E.J. Brill, 1995) esp. ch. 2.

46. Kaspar Peucer, *Commentarius, de Praecipuis Divinationum generibus, in quo a prophetiis, authoritate divine traditis, et a Physicis conjecturis, discernuntur artes et imposturae diabolicae, atque observationes natae ex superstitione, et cum hac conjunctae: Et monstrantur fontes ac causae Physicarum praedictionum: Diabolicae vero ac superstitiosae confutatae damnantur, ea serie, quam tabella praefixa ostendit* (Frankfurt: Wechel, Claudius Marnius & heirs of Ioannes Aubrius, 1607), chs. 1, 12, 17.

47. Peucer, *Commentarius, de . . . Divinationum generibus*, 286–93.

48. Ibid. 299–302.

49. Weyer, *Witches, Devils, and Doctors*, book 2, chs. 12–17, 134–50.

50. Hemmingsen, *Admonitio*, sigs. G4^r–K1^r.

51. Girolamo Zanchi, *De diuinatione tam artificiosa, quam artis experte, et utriusque variis speciebus tractatus, olim studiosae iuuentuti in Schola Argentinensi publicè prælectus; nunc verò in gratiam eiusdem ab hæredibus primùm in lucem editus. Accessit tractatus Thomæ Erasti medici clarissimi De astrologia diuinatrice* (Hanouiae: Apud Guilielmum Antonium, 1610).

52. Weyer, *Witches, Devils, and Doctors*, bk 5, ch. 39, 469–70; see also quotations from these in Godelmann, *Tractatus de Magis*, bk 1, ch. 6.

53. See T. Freeman, 'Demons, Deviance and Defiance: John Darrell and the Politics of Exorcism in Late Elizabethan England', in P. Lake and M. Questier (eds), *Conformity and Orthodoxy in the English Church, c.1560–1660* (Woodbridge, Suffolk; Rochester, NY: Boydell Press, 2000), 34–63. See also the works of John Darrell: *A detection of that sinnful, shamful, lying, and ridiculous discours, of Samuel Harshnet. entituled: A discouerie of the fravvdulent practises of Iohn Darrell* (England, no place or printer, 1600); *The replie of Iohn Darrell, to the answer of Iohn Deacon, and Iohn Walker, concerning the doctrine of the*

possession and dispossession of demoniakes (England, no place or printer, 1602), and Harsnett's attack as below.

54. Samuel Harsnett, *A Declaration of Egregious Popish Impostures to withdraw the harts of her Maiesties subiects from their allegeance, and from the truth of Christian religion professed in England, under the pretence of casting out devils* (London: James Roberts, 1603).

55. See James Sharpe, *The Bewitching of Anne Gunter: A Horrible and True Story of Deception, Witchcraft, Murder and the King of England* (London: Routledge, 2000); on possession especially in Protestant Germany, see Clark, *Thinking with Demons*, 389 ff.

56. Scot, *Discourse . . . of devils and spirits*, chs. 14–18.

57. Melanchthon, *Initia Doctrinae Physicae*, in CR, 13 (Halle, 1846) cols. 320 ff., 350 ff.

58. Peucer, *Commentarius, de . . . Divinationum generibus*, 735.

59. Melanchthon, *Initia Doctrinae Physicae*, in CR, 13, col. 350.

60. Peucer, *Commentarius, de . . . Divinationum generibus*, 722–3.

61. Ibid. 724–7. In Peucer especially, medical and theological arguments combined and overlapped frequently.

62. Philipp Melanchthon, *Deuttung der czwo grewlichen Figuren Bapstesels czu Rom und Munchkalbs zu Freyberg ynn Meysszen funden* (Wittenberg: Johann Rhau-Grunenberg, 1523). See also Peucer, *Commentarius, de . . . Divinationum generibus*, 727–8, and discussion in R. W. Scribner, *For the Sake of Simple Folk: Popular Propaganda for the German Reformation* (Cambridge and New York: Cambridge University Press, 1981), 127–32.

63. Melanchthon, *Initia Doctrinae Physicae*, in CR, 13 (Halle, 1846), col. 353.

64. Peucer, *Commentarius, de . . . Divinationum generibus*, 729–30.

65. Ibid. 728–9.

66. Ibid. 728; Andrew Cunningham and Ole Peter Grell, *The Four Horsemen of the Apocalypse: Religion, War, Famine and Death in Reformation Europe* (Cambridge: Cambridge University Press, 2000), 172; Alexandra Walsham, 'Vox Piscis, or The Book-Fish: Providence and the Uses of the Reformation past in Caroline Cambridge', *English Historical Review*, 114/457 (1999), 581 and refs.

67. Walsham, 'Vox Piscis', 574–606. On prodigies, see also Alexandra Walsham, *Providence in Early Modern England* (Oxford: Oxford University Press, 1999), ch. 4; Norman R. Smith, 'Portent Lore and Medieval Popular Culture', *Journal of Popular Culture*, 14 (1980), 47–59; Katharine Park and Lorraine J. Daston, 'Unnatural Conceptions: The Study of Monsters in Sixteenth- and Seventeenth-Century France and England', *Past and Present*, 92 (1981), 20–54; Dudley Wilson, *Signs and Portents: Monstrous Births from the Middle Ages to the Enlightenment* (London and New York: Routledge, 1993); Julie

Crawford, *Marvelous Protestantism: Monstrous Births in Post-Reformation England* (Baltimore: Johns Hopkins University Press, 2005).

68. Peucer, *Commentarius, de . . . Divinationum generibus*, 733.

69. Ibid. 733–6, and 734 for the extract.

70. Ibid. 736–8.

71. One of the earliest and transitional pieces on this subject was Johannes Rivius of Attendorn (1500–53), *Joannis Rivii Athendoriensis De spectris et apparitionibus umbrarum seu de vetere superstitione liber* ([Leipzig?], 1541). In the same year he published *De Instaurata renovataque doctrina ecclesiastica libellus*, marking the beginnings of the Reformation in Albertine Saxony.

72. Peucer, *Commentarius, de . . . Divinationum generibus*, 294.

73. Ludwig Lavater (1527–86), *De spectris, lemuribus et magnis atque insolitis fragoribus, variisque praesagitionibus quae plerunque obitum hominum, magnas clades, mutationesque imperiorum praecedunt, liber unus* (Geneva: Anchora Crispiniana, 1570). Subsequent editions appeared in 1575, 1580, and in the seventeenth century. An English translation was produced, entitled *Of ghostes and spirites, vvalking by night and of straunge noyses, crackes, and sundrie forewarnings: which commonly happen before the death of men: great slaughters, and alterations of kingdoms*, trans. Robert Harrison (London: Thomas Creede, 1596).

74. Lavater, *De spectris*, part 2 chapter 15; *Of ghostes and spirites*, 163.

75. Lavater, *De spectris*, part 2, chapters 15–18.

76. Weyer, *Witches, Devils, and Doctors*, bk 1, ch. 12, 33, and ch. 13 *passim*, also ch. 17, 56; Aretius, article 'Spectra', part I, fos. 54^v–56^v; Godelmann, *Tractatus de Magis*, 35. See also *Book of Concord*, as *Die Bekenntnisschriften der evangelisch-lutherischen Kirche: herausgegeben im Gedenkjahr der Augsburgischen Konfession 1930*, 10th edn (Göttingen: Vandenhoeck & Ruprecht, 1986), 419 ff; Hemmingsen, *Admonitio*, sigs. H6^v, K6^r; Jean Delumeau, 'Les Réformateurs et la superstition', in *Actes du colloque l'Amiral de Coligny et son temps (Paris, 24–28 octobre 1972)* (Paris: SHPF, 1974), 451–87 and esp. 454 ff. For modern literature on the subject, see B. Gordon, 'Malevolent Ghosts and Ministering Angels: Apparitions and Pastoral Care in the Swiss Reformation', in *The Place of the Dead: Death and Remembrance in Early Modern Europe*, ed. B. Gordon and P. Marshall (Cambridge: Cambridge University Press, 2000), 87–109; P. Marshall, *Beliefs and the Dead in Reformation England* (Oxford: Oxford University Press, 2002); the articles collected in *Early Modern Ghosts: The Proceedings of the 'Early Modern Ghosts' Conference held at St. John's College, Durham University on 24 March 2001*, ed. by J. Newton and J. Bath (Durham: Centre for Seventeenth-Century Studies, 2002).

77. Vermigli, *In duos libros Samuelis*, fos. 155^v–162^v.

78. Ibid., fo. 161^{r-v}.

79. Vermigli, *In duos libros Samuelis*, fo. 162^r.

80. Vermigli, *In duos libros Samuelis*, fo. 162^{r-v}; Gratian, *Decretum*, II, causa 26, question v, c. xiv, *nec mirum*, in *Corpus Juris Canonici*, ed. Aemilius Ludouicus Richter and Aemilius Friedberg (Graz: Akademische Druck- u. Verlagsanstalt, 1959), i, cols. 1034–5 (which is chiefly a quotation from Augustine's *Questions on the Old and the New Testament*, as quoted also by Weyer, *Witches, Devils, and Doctors*, 130–1).

81. Weyer, *Witches, Devils, and Doctors*, bk 2, chs 9–10, 127–33. Compare also Aretius, article 'Spectra', part I, fo. 57^r; Lavater, *De Spectris*, bk 2, ch. 7; Godelmann, *Tractatus de Magis*, 33–4.

82. See Helen Parish and William G. Naphy (eds) *Religion and Superstition in Reformation Europe* (Manchester: Manchester University Press, 2002), 17–18.

83. Melanchthon, *Physics*, cols. 323 ff; Peucer, *Commentarius, de . . . Divinationum generibus*, ch. 17, 642–719.

84. Heinrich Bullinger, *Wider die Schwartzen Künst, Aberglaeubigs segnen, unwarhafftigs Warsagen, und andere dergleichen von Gott verbottne Künst*, in *Theatrum de veneficis: Das ist: Von Teufelsgespenst, Zauberern und Gifftbereitern, Schwartzkünstlern, Hexen und Unholden, vieler fürnemmen Historien und Exempel* (Frankfurt am Main: Nicolaus Bassaeus, 1586), 298–306, ch. 3.

85. John Calvin, *Avertissement contre l'astrologie judiciaire*, ed. Olivier Millet, (Geneva: Droz, 1985), *passim*.

86. Jean Gerson, 'Triologium Astrologiae theologizatae', in *Joannis Gersonii Doctoris Theologi & Cancellarii Parisiensis Opera Omnia*, ed. Ludovicus Ellies du Pin, 5 vols, 2nd edn (The Hague: P. de Hondt, 1728), i, cols. 189–203; Benedictus Pererius Valentinus, SJ [= Benito Pereira], *Adversus Fallaces et Superstitiosas Artes, Id est, De Magia, de Observatione somniorum, et de Divinatione Astrologica, Libri tres* (Ingolstadt: Sartorius, 1591), book 3, 163 ff.

87. See Euan Cameron, 'Protestant Identities in the Later Reformation in Germany', in Ole Peter Grell and Bob Scribner (eds), *Tolerance and Intolerance in the European Reformation* (Cambridge: Cambridge University Press, 1996), 116 ff. and references.

88. Barnes, *Prophecy and Gnosis*, 50–1, based on Luther's *Supputatio annorum mundi*. See also ibid. 100 ff.

89. See John Foxe, *The Acts and Monuments*, ed. Joseph Pratt, 8 vols (London: Religious Tract Society, 1877), ii. 724–6 for his exposition of Rev. 20: 1–3. On the interpretation of this text in Protestant theories of history, see Euan Cameron, 'Medieval Heretics as Protestant Martyrs', in *Martyrs and Martyrologies: Papers Read at the 1992 Summer Meeting and the 1993 Winter Meeting of the Ecclesiastical History Society*, ed. D. Wood, Studies in Church History, 30 (Oxford: Blackwell, 1993) 185–207 and esp. 190, 195 ff.

90. See Pierre Viret, *Le Monde a l'Empire et le Monde Demoniacle* (Geneva: Jaques Bres, 1561), part 2 ch. 1, entitled 'Le diable deschainé'; Gyfford, *A Discourse*, sig. D1ᵛ; William Perkins, *A Discourse of the Damned art of Witchcraft; so farre forth as it is revealed in the scriptures, and manifest by true experience*, in *Works* (London: Cantrell Legge, Printer to the Universitie of Cambridge, 1618), 649; and compare Clark, *Thinking with Demons*, 321 ff. on this subject. Thomas Becon, 'The Acts of Christ and Antichrist', in John Ayre (ed.), *Prayers and other Pieces of Thomas Becon*, Parker Society (Cambridge: Cambridge University Press, 1844), 498–539, interprets the Reformation conflict in the same terms of apocalyptic oppositions between Christ and the pope.

91. [Jacobus Heerbrandus], *De Magia Disputatio ex cap. 7. Exo., . . . praeside reverendo et clarissimo viro Jacobo Heerbrando, sacrae theologiae Doctore eximio, ac eiusdem in Academia Tubingensi Professore publico . . . Nicolaus Falco Salueldensis . . . respondere conabitur* (Tübingen: [Ulrich Morhart], 1570); [Albertus Hungerus], *De Magia Theses Theologicae, in celebri et catholica academia Ingolstadiana An. S. N. M.D.LXXIIII, die 21 Junii per Reverendum et eruditum virum M. Hectorem Wegman Augustanum, SS. Theologiae Baccalaureum formatum, Divae Virginis apud eandem Academiam Parochum, pro impetrando Licentiae gradu, ad publicam disputationem propositae: Praeside Reverendo et Clarissimo viro Alberto Hungero, SS. Theologiae Doctore et Professore ordinario, Collegii Theologici pro tempore decano* (Ingolstadt: Weissenhorn, 1574).

92. Weyer, *Witches, Devils, and Doctors*, bk 2, ch 1, 93 ff. Cf. also Gyfford, *A Discourse*, ch 3, sig. B3ʳ; Lambert Daneau, *Dialogus de Veneficis*, in Nicolas Jacquier, Joannes Myntzenbergius, Nicolas Bassée, Lambert Daneau, Joachim Camerarius, Martín de Arles y Andosilla, Johannes Trithemius, and Thomas Erastus, *Flagellum hæreticorum fascinariorum* (Frankfurt: Nicolaus Bassæus, 1581), 193 and 197 ff.; see Reginald Scot, *The Discoverie of Witchcraft: wherein the lewde dealing of witches and witchmongers is notablie detected* (London: By William Brome, 1584) bk 6, ch. 1 for expositions of Hebrew terms.

93. Weyer, *Witches, Devils, and Doctors*, 98.

94. Thomas Erastus, *Repetitio Disputationis de lamiis seu strigibus, in qua solide et perspicue, de arte earum, potestate, itemque poena disceptatur* (Basle: Petrus Perna, 1578), 15.

95. Ibid. 14; Hemmingsen, *Admonitio*, sig. B7ʳ⁻ᵛ.

96. Godelmann, *Tractatus de Magis*, 85–6.

97. Ibid. 106–7.

98. See, for instance, Hemmingsen, *Admonitio*, sig. C4ʳ for this argument.

99. Story amalgamated from versions in Johann Spreter, *Ein kurtzer Bericht, was von den abghotterischen Sägen unnd Beschweren zühalten: wie der etlich volbracht, unnd das die ein Zauberey, auch Greüwel vor Gott dem Herren seind* (Basle:

Bartholomeus Westheymer, 1543), sig. Aiv^v and Hemmingsen, *Admonitio*, sig. C2^r. Compare another version of the story in Weyer, *Witches, Devils, and Doctors*, 416; also quoted in Martinus Delrio SJ, *Disquisitionum Magicarum Libri Sex, in tres tomos partiti* (Louvain: Gerardus Rivius, 1599–1600), iii. 191. According to Friedrich Förner, *Panoplia armaturae Dei, adversus omnem superstitionum, divinationum, excantationum, demonolatriam, et universas magorum, veneficorum, et sagarum, et ipsiusmet Sathanae insidias, praestigias et infestationes* (Ingolstadt: Gregorius Haenlinius, 1626), 23–5, this comes from the *Speculum exemplorum*, tom. 2, dist. 10, num. 16. The source text has not yet been traced.

100. On auto-suggestion, see Weyer, *Witches, Devils, and Doctors*, bk 5, ch 18, 416 ff.

101. See above Ch. 4 note 36.

102. Weyer, *Witches, Devils, and Doctors*, 153.

103. Thomas Erastus, *Disputationum de medicina nova Philippi Paracelsi pars prima* [. . . *quarta*]: *in qua, quae de remediis superstitiosis & magicis curationibus ille prodidit, praecipuè examinantur*, 4 parts in 2 vols (Basle: Petrus Perna, 1571–3).

104. Godelmann, *Tractatus de Magis*, ch. 8, 75 ff.

105. Ibid. 80, for example.

106. Godelmann, *Tractatus de Magis*, 92 ff. and compare Delrio to the same effect, bk 6, ch. 2 sect. 1 q. 1, at iii. 175 ff, as discussed below.

107. A fuller treatment of confessional issues in the witch literature is found in Clark, *Thinking with Demons*, chs 29 and following, and especially ch. 35.

108. Daneau, *Dialogus de Veneficis*, 241–64. Note that Daneau casts his treatise in the form of a dialogue that gives space to the argument that these phenomena were merely illusions, even though that position is quite strongly rejected.

109. Weyer, *Witches, Devils, and Doctors*, 173–9.

110. Ibid., bk 3, *passim*.

111. Ibid., bk 6, *passim* and esp. translation 561 ff. On Weyer's arguments and the response to them see H. C. Erik Midelfort, 'Johan Weyer and the Transformation of the Insanity Defense', in R Po-chia Hsia, *The German People and the Reformation* (Ithaca, NY: Cornell University Press,1988), 234–61.

112. Lercheimer, *Christlich Bedencken*, chs. 9–14.

113. Ibid., chs. 16, 19.

114. Antonius Praetorius, *Gründlicher Bericht von Zauberey und Zauberern, deren Urpsrung, Unterscheid, Vermögen und Handlungen, Auch wie einer Christlichen Obrigkeit, solchen schändlichen Laster zu Begegnen* (Frankfurt: Stoltzenberger, 1629), 73–82. The first edition appeared in 1598: see Bautz, *Biographisch-bibliographisches Kirchenlexikon*, art. 'Prätorius, Anton'.

115. Godelmann, *Tractatus de Magis*, books 2 and 3, *passim*. Samuel Harsnett, *A Declaration of Egregious Popish Impostures* (London: James Roberts, 1605), 136, contains a blistering attack on vulgar witch-beliefs highly reminiscent of Reginald Scot.

116. See for discussion of the theological issues Lyndal Roper, *Witch Craze: Terror and Fantasy in Baroque Germany* (New Haven: Yale University Press, 2004), 37–9; also Wolfgang Behringer, 'Demonology: 1500–1660', in R. Po-chia Hsia, *Christianity: Reform and Expansion, 1500–1660*. The Cambridge History of Christianity, vol. vi (Cambridge and New York: Cambridge University Press, 2007), 406–24. For a brave essay in a hitherto unpopular line of argument see Lisa Jacqueline Watson, 'The Influence of the Reformation and Counter Reformation upon Key Texts in the Literature of Witchcraft' (Ph.D. thesis, University of Newcastle upon Tyne, 1997).

117. See discussion of this point in Clark, *Thinking with Demons*, 530–2.

13. THE PROTESTANT CRITIQUE OF CONSECRATIONS: CATHOLICISM AS SUPERSTITION

1. See above, Ch. 8.

2. See above on Luther, Ch. 11 at notes 84–6.

3. Martin Plantsch, *Opusculum de sagis maleficis* (Pforzheim: Thomas Anshelm, 1507), sigs. f i^v–g i^r; on sacramentals, see also R. W. Scribner, 'Cosmic Order and Daily Life: Sacred and Secular in Pre-Industrial German Society', in Kaspar von Greyerz (ed.), *Religion and Society in Early Modern Europe, 1500–1800*, (London, German Historical Institute; Boston: Allen & Unwin, 1984), 20–1; R. W. Scribner, 'Ritual and Popular Religion in Catholic Germany at the Time of the Reformation', in R. W. Scribner, *Popular Culture and Popular Movements in Reformation Germany* (London: Hambledon, 1987), 36–41. See above, Ch. 3 note 39.

4. Plantsch, *Opusculum* sig. g ii^v and g iv^r.

5. Andreas Bodenstein von Karlstadt, *Von geweychtem Wasser vnd Saltz . . . Wider den vnuerdienten Gardian Franciscus Seyler* (Wittenberg: Johann Grunenberg, 1520); other editions appeared at Strasbourg: Martin Flach, 1520; Leipzig: Wolfgang Stöckel, 1520; Leipzig: Valentin Schumann, 1520. References are here to the Leipzig edition printed by Stöckel. See also Andreas Bodenstein, *Antwort Andres Bo. von Carolstad Doctor geweicht wasser belangend: wider einen bruder Johan. Fritzhans genant: holtzuger ordens.* (Wittenberg: Melchior Lotter, 1521).

6. Karlstadt, *Von geweychtem Wasser* (Leipzig: Stöckel, 1520), sigs. Aii^v–iv^v.

7. Ibid., sigs. $Biii^r$–iv^r.

8. Ibid., sigs. Bii^v–Cii^r.

9. Ibid., sig. Ciii^{r-v}: 'Dartzu beken ich | das vorbedalkter briff | etzlichen zeu-
berischen hendeln ursach gegeben hat. derhalben wol ein yglicher Christ-
glaubiger trewlich gewarnet sey | das er nit nach betriegischer und vorbotner
weyd graesen gehe und fal mit den blinden furern | in die grube | die | die
eygen gesetzmacher graben | als Matthei. xv. geschrieben steet.'

10. But see an alternative view on Karlstadt in Peter Matheson, *The Rhetoric of
the Reformation* (Edinburgh: T. & T. Clark, 1998), 59–80.

11. Text in Martin Luther, *Luthers Werke: Kritische Gesamtausgabe* (Weimar:
Böhlaus Nachfolger 1883–1948), xviii: 62–125, 134–214; translation in
Martin Luther, *Luther's Works*, ed. Jaroslav Pelikan and H. T. Lehmann, 55
vols (St Louis: Concordia, and Philadelphia: Fortress Press, 1955–86), xl.
79–223.

12. Johann Eberlin von Günzburg, *Wider die schender der Creaturen Gottes, durch
Weyhen, oder segnen, des Saltzs, Wasser, Palmen, kraut, wachss, fewr ayer, Fladen
&c: nit zür achtung der Creatur, allain meldung der gotslesterlichen betrüglichen
falsch glaubigen yrrsalen* (Augsburg: Heinrich Steiner, 1525). For extended
discussion, see Geoffrey Dipple, *Antifraternalism and Anticlericalism in the
German Reformation: Johann Eberlin von Günzburg and the Campaign against the
Friars* (Aldershot: Scolar, 1996), 122–30.

13. Eberlin, *Wider die schender der Creaturen Gottes*, sigs. Aii^v–iii^v.

14. Ibid., sigs. Bi^{r-v}.

15. See above, Ch. 7; also Luther's use of the same argument, see above, Ch. 11
at note 59.

16. Eberlin, *Wider die schender der Creaturen Gottes*, sig. Bii^v.

17. Ibid., sigs. Biii^v–iv^r.

18. Ibid., sig. Cii^r.

19. Ibid., sigs. Cii^v–iii^v: 'mer ain zauberey dann ain segen'.

20. Johann Spreter, *Ein kurtzer Bericht, was von den abghotterischen Sägen vn[nd]
Beschweren zühalten: wie der etlich volbracht, vnnd das die ein Zauberey, auch
Greüwel vor Gott dem Herren seind* (Basle: Bartholomeus Westheymer, 1543).
On the author, see Theo Spreter von Kreudenstein, *Johann Spreter von Kreuden-
stein. Doktor beider Rechte, Rottweiler Bürger im 16. Jahrhundert* (Sigmaringen:
Jan Thorbecke Verlag, 1988).

21. See Johann Spreter, *Form vnd Ordnung wie vo[n] dem Pfarrer zu Sant Steffan
in Costanz vnd sinen Curaten, mit Touffen. richten Infuren vn[d] den abgestorbnen
gehalten würt* (Constance?: s.n., 1526); id., *Christenlich instruction uñ frintlich erma-
nung, Götlichs wort anzenemen, der kirchen Christi in der stat Rotwil* (Constance?,
1527).

22. Besides *Ein kurtzer Bericht*, in 1543 Johann Spreter published *Von Renndten,
Gülten, Zinsen, Zehenden, Neüwbrüchen und Wücher des neüwen und alten Tes-
taments* (Basle: Bartholomeus Westheymer, 1543); id., *Vonn Weltlicher vnd*

Geistlicher Oberkeyt, Adel vnd Ritterschafft, Kriegen vnnd Kriegßleüten, zweyen Schwertern, wem die zugestelt, wann, wo und von wem die zu gebrauchen seyen (Basle: Bartholomeus Westheymer, 1543); id., *Christenlich Instruction und ware erklärung fürnemlicher artickel des Glaubens, von händel, art, wort, werck* (Basle: Bartholomeus Westheymer, 1543); id., *Von heiligen Biblischer Gschrifft, unnd ihrem Geyst, wie die ein vass, oder werckzeug der warheit, vnd bisshär verhalten, Was auch vn wölche Biblische, oder Apocryphische bücher seyen* (Basle: Bartholomeus Westheymer, 1543); id., *Von der waren Christenlichen, vn erdachten Entchristische Kirche, dere Haubs Stadthelter, Gwalt vn Schlüssel* (Basle: Bartholomeus Westheymer, 1543); id., *Von der Fürsehung, Beruffung, vnnd Ordnung Gottes. Item Gottes forcht Widergeburt des menschen, Freien vnd Eygnen wille* (Basle: Bartholomeus Westheymer, 1543). All of these works were quite short.

23. Spreter, *Ein kurtzer Bericht,*, sig. Ai^v.

24. Ibid., sigs. Aii^v–iii^v.

25. Ibid., sigs. Aiii^v–iv^r.

26. Ibid., sigs. Aiv^v–vi^v.

27. Caspar Peucer, *Commentarius, de Praecipuis Divinationum generibus* (Frankfurt: Wechel, Claudius Marnius & heirs of Ioannes Aubrius, 1607), 303–8.

28. See Heinrich von Gorkum and Martin Plantsch on this issue as above, Ch. 8, at nn. 19–24.

29. Peucer, *Commentarius, de . . . Divinationum generibus*, 309–10.

30. Ibid. 318–21.

31. Ibid. 326–7.

32. Johann Weyer, *Witches, Devils, and Doctors in the Renaissance*, ed. George Mora and Benjamin Kohl, trans. John Shea (Medieval & Renaissance texts & studies, 73) (Binghamton, NY: Medieval & Renaissance Texts & Studies, 1991; repr. 1998), bk 5, ch. 3, 370.

33. Ibid. 370 ff., 373 ff.

34. Ibid. 391 ff.

35. e.g. [Jacobus Heerbrandus], *De Magia Disputatio ex cap. 7. Exo., . . . praeside reverendo et clarissimo viro Jacobo Heerbrando, sacrae theologiae Doctore eximio, ac eiusdem in Academia Tubingensi Professore publico . . . Nicolaus Falco Salueldensis . . . respondere conabitur* (Tübingen: [Ulrich Morhart], 1570), thesis 89, 14 ff.; Johann Georg Godelmann, *Tractatus de Magis, Veneficis et Lamiis, deque his recte cognoscendis et puniendis* (Frankfurt: Nicolaus Bassaeus, 1601), 57.

36. For Luther, see above, Ch. 11 notes 87–8, and *Luthers Werke*, l, 668–73;

37. Weyer, *Witches, Devils, and Doctors*, bk 5, ch. 9, 392. Weyer cited as his source a work entitled *Ceremonies of the Roman Church*, 1, 7, ch. 3, 'On the Consecration of the Agnus Dei'. This exact source has not been traced,

but Melchior Hittorpius, *De divinis Catholicae Ecclesiae officiis ac ministeriis, varii vetvstorvm aliqvot ecclesiae patrum ac scriptorum libri, videlicet B. Isidori Hispaleñ Episcopi, Albini Flacci Alcvini, Amalarii Trevirens. Episcopi, Hrabani Mavri Moguntineñ Episcopi, VValafridi Strabonis Abbatis, B. Ivonis Episcopi Carnotensis, & quorundā aliorum* (Cologne: Gervinus Calenius & haeredes Iohannis Quentel, 1568), in the section devoted to Albinus Flaccus Alcuinus's *De Divinis Officiis*, 61–2, presents a description of the making and distribution of the Agnus Dei. A similar passage is found in Amalarius of Trier's *De Ecclesiasticis Officiis*, bk 1, ch. 17 on the blessing of *agni* made from consecrated wax, ibid. 130.

38. Weyer, *Witches, Devils, and Doctors*, 424 ff.

39. Heerbrand, *De Magia Disputatio*, theses nos. 82–97.

40. 'Augustin Lercheimer' [= Hermann Wilken or Witekind, d. 1603], *Ein Christlich Bedencken unnd Erinnerung von Zauberey*, published in *Theatrum de veneficis: Das ist: Von Teufelsgespenst, Zauberern und Gifftbereitern, Schwartzkünstlern, Hexen und Unholden, vieler fürnemmen Historien und Exempel* (Frankfurt am Main: Nicolaus Bassaeus, 1586), 289 ff.

41. Godelmann, *Tractatus de Magis*, 56–8.

42. Heinrich Bullinger, *The Decades of Henry Bullinger*, ed. Thomas Harding, Parker Society, 4 vols (Cambridge: Cambridge University Press, 1849–52), iv. Fifth Decade (1852), 254–67 and esp. 260, 264 for the extract; Bullinger's argument here echoes exactly the same argument against the power of blessings and consecrations to change matter that was discussed earlier. Similarly Bullinger, *Wider die Schwartzen Künst, Aberglaeubigs segnen, unwarhafftigs Warsagen, und andere dergleichen von Gott verbottne Künst*, in *Theatrum de veneficis: Das ist: Von Teufelsgespenst, Zauberern und Gifftbereitern, Schwartzkünstlern, Hexen und Unholden, vieler fürnemmen Historien und Exempel* (Frankfurt am Main: Nicolaus Bassaeus, 1586), 300, argued that there was no power to bless embedded in the words.

43. *The Works of John Knox*, ed. David Laing 6 vols (Edinburgh: T. G. Stevenson, 1854–64), iii. 50–1; for traditional beliefs about the the 'five words' of consecration see Eamon Duffy, *The Stripping of the Altars: Traditional Religion in England, 1400–1580* (New Haven and London: Yale University Press, 1992), 95 ff.

44. Knox, *Works*, iv. 186–8.

45. Ibid., iii. 196–7, 212. This paragraph draws on my 'Frankfurt and Geneva: The European Context of John Knox's Reformation', in R. A. Mason (ed), *John Knox and the British Reformations*, in the St Andrews Studies in Reformation History (Aldershot: Ashgate/Scolar Press, 1998), 51–73 and for the specific point 62–5.

46. Antonius Praetorius, *Gründlicher Bericht von Zauberey und Zauberern, deren Urpsrung, Unterscheid, Vermögen und Handlungen, Auch wie einer Christlichen Obrigkeit, solchen schändlichen Laster zu Begegnen* (Frankfurt: Stoltzenberger, 1629), 56–62.

47. Ibid. 62–6.

48. On possession and exorcism and their inter-confessional aspects, see esp. D. P. Walker, *Unclean Spirits: Possession and Exorcism in France and England in the Late Sixteenth and Early Seventeenth Centuries* (Philadelphia: University of Pennsylvania Press, 1981); Sarah Ferber, *Demonic Possession and Exorcism in Early Modern France* (London and New York: Routledge, 2004); also Philip M. Soergel, *Wondrous in his Saints: Counter-Reformation Propaganda in Bavaria* (Berkeley: University of California Press, 1993).

49. Correctly cited from Josephus, *Jewish Antiquities*, bk 8, ch. 2, sect. 5: 'And he [Solomon] left behind him the manner of using exorcisms, by which they drive away demons, so that they never return; and this method of cure is of great force unto this day; for I have seen a certain man of my own country, whose name was Eleazar, releasing people that were demoniacal in the presence of Vespasian, and his sons, and his captains, and the whole multitude of his soldiers. The manner of the cure was this: He put a ring that had a root of one of those sorts mentioned by Solomon to the nostrils of the demoniac, after which he drew out the demon through his nostrils; and when the man fell down immediately, he adjured him to return into him no more, making still mention of Solomon, and reciting the incantations which he composed. And when Eleazar would persuade and demonstrate to the spectators that he had such a power, he set a little way off a cup or basin full of water, and commanded the demon, as he went out of the man, to overturn it, and thereby to let the spectators know that he had left the man.' Compare discussion of the same text in Weyer, *Witches, Devils, and Doctors*, bk 5, ch. 22, and Reginald Scot, *The Discoverie of Witchcraft: wherein the lewde dealing of witches and witchmongers is notablie detected* (London: By William Brome, 1584) bk 15, ch. 33.

50. Mark 5: 7.

51. Benedictus Aretius, *Problemata theologica continentia præcipuos christianae religionis locos, brevi et dilucida ratione explicatos* (Lausanne: Franciscus Le Preux, 1578), article 'exorcistae', part II, fos. 66^v–68^r.

52. Martin Chemnitz, *Examination of the Council of Trent*, trans. Fred Kramer, 4 vols (St Louis: Concordia, 1971–86), ii. 689. Compare also Peucer, *Commentarius, de . . . Divinationum generibus*, 321–2, and also Weyer, *Witches, Devils, and Doctors*, bk 5, chs. 23–7, for a more anecdotal critique of Catholic exorcisms.

53. Ludwig Lavater (1527–1586), *De spectris, lemuribus et magnis atque insolitis fragoribus, variisque praesagitionibus quae plerunque obitum hominum, magnas clades, mutationesque imperiorum praecedunt, liber unus* (Geneva: Anchora Crispiniana, 1570), part III, ch. 10, *Of ghostes and spirites, vvalking by night*, trans. Robert Harrison (London: Thomas Creede, 1596), 207.

54. Bullinger, *Wider die Schwartzen Künst*, 301.

55. Scot, *Discoverie*, bk 15, ch. 22. Compare ibid., ch. 29.

56. Godelmann, *Tractatus de Magis*, 55–7.

57. For the traditional arguments on the cessation of miracles, see e.g. Carlos M. N. Eire, *War Against the Idols: The Reformation of Worship from Erasmus to Calvin* (Cambridge: Cambridge University Press, 1986), 221–4. For a particularly thoughtful revisionist article on this particular theme, see Mark Greengrass, 'Miracles and the Peregrination of the Holy in the French Wars of Religion' in José Pedro Paiva (ed.), *Religious Ceremonials and Images: Power and Social Meaning (1400–1750)*, (Coimbra: Palimage Editores, 2002), 389–414.

58. The classic article on this subject is R. W. Scribner, 'The Reformation, Popular Magic, and the "Disenchantment of the World"', *Journal of Interdisciplinary History*, 23 (1993), 475–94; reprinted in C. Scott Dixon (ed.), *The German Reformation: The Essential Readings* (Oxford: Blackwell, 1999), 262–79.

59. See e.g. Luther's ambiguous use of the term 'Wunder' in *To the Christian Nobility of the German Nation*, in *Luthers Werke*, vi. 447: 'Es hilfft auch nit, das wundertzeychen da geschehen, dan der bosze geyst kan wol wunder thun, wie unns Christus vorkundigt hat Matt. xxiiii.' See also *Luther's Works*, xliv. 186; on the miracles/marvels distinction see Stuart Clark, *Thinking with Demons: The Idea of Witchcraft in Early Modern Europe* (Oxford: Clarendon Press, 1997), 153.

60. Calvin, *Institutes*, preface to François I, in *Ioannis Calvini Opera quae supersunt, Omnia*, ed. Guilielmus Baum, Eduardus Cunitz, Eduardus Reuss, 59 vols Corpus Reformatorum, 29–87 (Brunswick, Berlin: Schwetschke, 1863–1900), i, cols. 9–26 and esp. cols. 14–16 on the issue of miracles.

61. [John Hooper], *Later writings of Bishop Hooper: together with his letters and other pieces*, ed. Charles Nevinson, Parker Society (Cambridge: Cambridge University Press, 1852), 44–5. For detailed discussion of the Protestant theological critique of miracles see Jane Shaw, *Miracles in Enlightenment England* (New Haven and London: Yale University Press, 2006), 22–31. Shaw draws attention to the possibility that non-theologians in Protestant England may not wholly have embraced the learned theological position on this issue.

62. James Calfhill, *An Answer to John Martiall's Treatise of the Cross*, ed. Richard Gibbings, Parker Society (Cambridge: Cambridge University Press, 1846), 333.

63. Calvin, *Institutes*, IV. xix. 18–19; this passage was quoted in Scot, *Discoverie*, bk 8, ch. 1.

64. Lavater, *De spectris*, part III chapter 9; *Of ghostes and spirites*, 206.

65. William Perkins, *A Discourse of the Damned Art of Witchcraft; so farre forth as it is revealed in the scriptures, and manifest by true experience*, in *Works* (London: Cantrell Legge, Printer to the Universitie of Cambridge, 1618), ch. 7, pt III, sect. 5, 650 ff.

66. Ibid. 649.

67. For Erasmus and the cult of saints, see above, Ch. 10 at notes 14 and 25–6; for Luther, see above, Ch. 11 notes 27–32.

68. Heinrich Bullinger, *De Origine Erroris Libri Duo: in priore agitur de Dei veri iusta invocatione & cultu vero, de Deorum item falsorum religionibus & simulachrorum cultu erroneo: in posteriore disseritur de institutione & vi sacrae Coenae domini, & de origine ac progressu Missae papisticae, contra varias superstitiones pro religione vera antiqua & orthodoxa* (Zurich: Froschauer, 1539), fos. 32^r–45^r.

69. Ibid., fo. 56^v.

70. Ibid., fos. 113^v–114^v.

71. Ibid., ch. 33, fo. 160^v.

72. Ibid., fos. 164^v–167^r.

73. Ibid., fos. 167^v–172^r.

74. Bullinger, *The Decades*, i (1849), 221.

75. [John Hooper]. *Early writings of John Hooper, D.D., Lord Bishop of Gloucester and Worcester, Martyr, 1555: Comprising The declaration of Christ and his office. Answer to Bishop Gardiner. Ten commandments. Sermons on Jonas. Funeral sermon*, ed. Samuel Carr, Parker Society (Cambridge: Cambridge University Press, 1843), 312–14.

76. Aretius, *Problemata*, article 'Magia', part II, fo. 42^r; Godelmann, *Tractatus de Magis*, 21f; cf. Lercheimer, *Christlich Bedencken*, 273 ff.

77. Weyer, *Witches, Devils, and Doctors*, bk 5, ch. 2, 367 ff.

78. Lercheimer, *Christlich Bedencken*, fo. 279^v. [Note: leaves 277–82 of the *Theatrum* are foliated rather than paginated]

79. Godelmann, *Tractatus de Magis*, 86.

80. Nicolaus Hemmingius [= Niels Hemmingsen], *Admonitio de superstitionibus magicis vitandis, in gratiam sincerae religionis amantium* (Copenhagen, 1575), sigs. Bviii^v–Ci^r.

81. John Bale, *The Latter Examination of Mistress Anne Askewe*, in *Select Works of John Bale, D.D., Bishop of Ossory*, ed. Henry Christmas, Parker Society (Cambridge: Cambridge University Press, 1849), 236.

82. Calfhill, *Answer to John Martiall's Treatise of the Cross*, 338; italics are mine.

83. George Gyfford, *A Discourse of the subtill Practises of Devilles by Witches and Sorcerers. By which men are and have bin greatly deluded* (London: [T. Orwin] for Toby Cooke, 1587), sig. G2ʳ.

84. Pietro Martire Vermigli (1499–1562), *In duos libros Samuelis prophetae... commentarii doctissimi*, 2nd edn (Zurich: Froschouerus, 1567), fo. 35ᵛ.

85. Lercheimer, *Christlich Bedencken*, 276.

86. Reginald Scot, *The Discovery of Witchcraft:... Whereunto is added an excellent Discourse of the nature and substance of devils and spirits* (London: A. Clark and Dixy Page, 1665) [the *Discourse* is separately paginated], ch 18.

87. Hemmingsen, *Admonitio*, sigs. Fiiʳ–iiiʳ.

14. THE PROTESTANT DOCTRINE OF PROVIDENCE AND THE TRANSFORMATION OF THE DEVIL

1. See above, Ch. 8, at nn. 30–8.

2. [Philipp Melanchthon], *Philippi Melanthonis Opera quae supersunt omnia*, ed. Carolus Gottlieb Bretschneider, Corpus Reformatorum, 1–28 (Halle: C. A. Schwetschke and son, 1834–60), xiii, (Halle, 1846), cols. 190–1.

3. Ibid., cols. 203–6.

4. Sachiko Kusukawa, *The Transformation of Natural Philosophy: The Case of Philip Melanchthon* (Cambridge and New York: Cambridge University Press, 1995), pp 160–7.

5. Jean Calvin, *De la predestination eternelle de Dieu, par laquelle les uns sont eleuz à salut, les autres laissez en leur condemnation; Aussi de la providence par laquelle il gouverne les choses humaines* (Geneva: Jehan Crespin, 1552). The text also appeared in Latin as the *De Aeterna Dei Praedestinatione, qua in salutem alios ex hominibus elegit, alios suo exitio reliquit: item de providentia qua res humanas gubernat, consensus pastorum Genevensis Ecclesiae a Io. Calvino expositus* (Geneva: Joannes Crispinus, 1552), ed. in *Ioannis Calvini Opera quae supersunt Omnia* ed. Guilielmus Baum, Eduardus Cunitz, Eduardus Reuss, 59 vols Corpus Reformatorum, 29–87 (Brunswick, Berlin: Schwetschke, 1863–1900), viii (1870): the section on providence is found in cols. 347–66.

6. *Calvini Opera*, viii, cols. 347–51.

7. Ibid., cols. 351–4. The reference to the unbroken bones of Jesus alludes to John 19: 33–6.

8. *Calvini Opera*, viii, cols. 355–7.

9. Ibid., col. 358.

10. Ibid., cols. 358–63 and col. 363 for the quotation.

11. Ibid., col. 364: 'Denique quoties mirifica Dei consilia et profundas cogitationes praedicat, non de praeceptis loquitur, quae ante oculos patent

exposita: sed potius inaccessam illam lucem commendat, in qua reconditum est consilium, quod mentis nostrae captu altius suspicere et adorare cogimur.'

12. See most recently Bruce Gordon, *Calvin* (New Haven and London: Yale University Press, 2009), 161–80 for instances of how Calvin had to negotiate very sensitively with Swiss allies whom he could not overawe.

13. Benedictus Aretius, *Problemata theologica continentia præcipuos christianae religionis locos, brevi et dilucida ratione explicatos* (Lausanne: Franciscus Le Preux, 1578), article 'Providentia', part II, fo. 34^{r-v}.

14. Ibid, fos. 34^v–35^r.

15. Heinrich Bullinger, *Wider die Schwartzen Künst, Aberglaeubigs segnen, unwarhafftigs Warsagen, und andere dergleichen von Gott verbottne Künst*, in *Theatrum de veneficis: Das ist: Von Teufelsgespenst, Zauberern und Gifftbereitern, Schwartzkünstlern, Hexen und Unholden, vieler fürnemmen Historien und Exempel* (Frankfurt am Main: Nicolaus Bassaeus, 1586), 303–4. For a Lutheran version of the reasons why divine providence might allow demonic assaults, see Nicolaus Hemmingius [= Niels Hemmingsen], *Admonitio de superstitionibus magicis vitandis, in gratiam sincerae religionis amantium* (Copenhagen: Iohannes Stockelman and Andreas Gutterwitz, 1575), sigs. E8^r–G3^r.

16. See above, Ch. 11, at nn. 25–38, 61–71.

17. For an example of this metaphorizing process, see the discussion of Lodowick Muggleton, Ch. 16, at nn. 54–62.

18. Pierre Viret, *Le Monde a l'Empire et le Monde Demoniacle* (Geneva: Jaques Bres, 1561), translated into English as *The Worlde Possessed with Deuils: conteinyng three dialogues*, (London: J. Kingston, 1583). cf. also Stuart Clark's comments in *Thinking with Demons: The Idea of Witchcraft in Early Modern Europe* (Oxford: Clarendon Press, 1997), 420–1.

19. *Theatrum Diabolorum, das ist, Ein sehr nützliches verstenndiges Buch: darauss ein jeder Christ sonderlich vnnd fleissig zu lernen wie dass wir in dieser Welt nicht mit Keysern, Königen, Fürsten, und Herrn oder andern Potentaten, sondern mit dem allermechtigsten Fürsten dieser Welt dem Teuffel zukempffen vnd zustreiten . . . : allen frommen Christen, so ihrer Seelen Heil und Seligkeit angelegen in diesen letzten Zeiten da allerley Laster grausamlich im Schwang gehn mit gantzem Ernst vnnd Fleiss zubetrachten* (Frankfurt am Main: Peter Schmid, Hieronymus Feyrabend, 1569)

20. Ria Stambaugh (ed.), *Teufelbücher in Auswahl*, 4 vols (Berlin: De Gruyter, 1970–); note also Keith L. Roos, *The devil in 16th century German literature: The Teufelsbücher*, Europäische Hochschulschriften, 1st series: Deutsche Literatur und Germanistik, 68 (Bern: Herbert Lang; Frankfurt am Main: Peter Lang, 1972). Note discussion (to slightly different effect) in Robert

Muchembled, *A History of the Devil: From the Middle Ages to the Present*, trans. Jean Birrell (Cambridge: Polity, 2008) 111 ff.

21. Reginald Scot, *The Discovery of Witchcraft: . . . Whereunto is added an excellent Discourse of the nature and substance of devils and spirits* (London: A. Clark and Dixy Page, 1665) [the *Discourse* is separately paginated], chapter 13.

22. See above, Ch. 12 note 31.

23. Scot, *Discourse . . . of devils and spirits*, ch. 16.

24. Scot probably derived the idea of scriptural language as 'accommodation' to human capacities from Calvin, where it plays a key role in his theology. See for example Calvin, *Institutes*, I. xvii. 13; II. xi. 13; II. xvi. 2; III. xviii. 9.

25. I Kings 22: 19–23; Scot, *Discourse . . . of devils and spirits*, ch. 16.

26. Scot, *Discourse . . . of devils and spirits*, ch. 31.

27. See Chs. 16–17 below and also Nathan Johnstone, *The Devil and Demonism in Early Modern England* (Cambridge: Cambridge University Press, 2006).

15. REFORMED CATHOLICISM: PURIFYING SOURCES, DEFENDING TRADITIONS

1. J. Delumeau, *Catholicism between Luther and Voltaire: A New View of the Counter-Reformation* (London: Burns & Oates; Philadelphia: Westminster Press, 1977), 177–9. Some parts of this paragraph are based on my article 'For Reasoned Faith or Embattled Creed? Religion for the People in Early Modern Europe', *Transactions of the Royal Historical Society*, 6th series, 8 (1998), 165–87.

2. Norman P. Tanner (ed.), *Decrees of the Ecumenical Councils*, 2 vols (London and Washington: Sheed & Ward and Georgetown University Press, 1990), 665: 'ad profana quaeque convertuntur et torquentur verba et sententiae sacrae scripturae, ad scurrilia scilicet, fabulosa, vana, adulationes, detractationes, superstitiones, impias et diabolicas incantationes, divinationes, sortes, libellos etiam famosos.'

3. Decree on things to be observed and to be avoided in celebrating mass, Session 22, 17 September 1562, in Tanner (ed.), *Decrees*, 736: 'quae vel avaritia, idolorum servitus, vel irreverentia, quae ab impietate vix seiuncta esse potest, vel superstitio, verae pietatis falsa imitatrix, induxit.'

4. The same decree, in Tanner (ed.), *Decrees*, 737: 'Quarundam vero missarum et candelarum certum numerum, qui magis a superstitioso cultu quam a vero religione inventus est, omnino ab ecclesia removeant.' Compare with Pedro Ciruelo's critique of Trentals and other similar devotions: Pedro Ciruelo, *Reprovación de las supersticiones*, translated as *Pedro Ciruelo's A treatise reproving all superstitions and forms of witchcraft: very necessary and useful for all good Christians*

zealous for their salvation, trans. E. A. Maio and D. W. Pearson (Rutherford, NJ: Fairleigh Dickinson University Press, 1977), 321–2.

5. Tanner (ed.), *Decrees*, 774–6, 796–7.

6. The term 'superstition' appears only once in the *Catechismus Romanus*, in relation to the name of God. Here the Catechism criticizes Jewish practice, in the exposition of the 2nd commandment: stressing that honour was due to the meaning of the name of God and not the forms of the letters, it added 'hence we easily infer the superstition of those among the Jews who, while they hesitated not to write, dared not to pronounce the name of God, as if the divine power consisted in the four letters, and not in the signification'.

7. See the complex typologies, with diagrams, proposed in R. W. Scribner, 'Ritual and Popular Religion in Catholic Germany at the time of the Reformation', in R. W. Scribner, *Popular Culture and Popular Movements in Reformation Germany* (London: Hambledon Press, 1987), 17–47.

8. See above, Ch. 9, in particular with reference to the case of Werner of Friedberg and the varying advice given by Jean Gerson at different periods.

9. Nicolas Remi, *Nicolai Remigii daemonolatreiae Libri tres, Ex Iudiciis Capitalibus Nongentorum plus minus hominum* (Cologne: Henricus Falckenburg, 1596; also Frankfurt: Palthen, 1596); Jean Bodin, *De la démonomanie des sorciers* (Paris: Du Puys, 1580). Note also that Bodin's *Universæ naturæ theatrum: in quo rerum omnium effectrices causæ & fines contemplantur, & continua series quinque libris discutiuntur* (Lyons: Jacques Roussin, 1596) contains his eccentric demonology.

10. See the Introduction, note 45, for a comparable decision in respect of the *Malleus Maleficarum*.

11. Albrecht Hunger (1545–1604), *De Magia Theses Theologicae, in celebri et catholica academia Ingolstadiana An. S. N. M.D.LXXIIII, die 21 Junii per Reverendum et eruditum virum M. Hectorem Wegman Augustanum, SS. Theologiae Baccalaureum formatum, Divae Virginis apud eandem Academiam Parochum, pro impetrando Licentiae gradu, ad publicam disputationem propositae: Praeside Reverendo et Clarissimo viro Alberto Hungero, SS. Theologiae Doctore et Professore ordinario, Collegii Theologici pro tempore decano* (Ingolstadt: Weissenhorn, 1574); Martinus Delrio SJ (1551–1608), *Disquisitionum Magicarum Libri Sex*, 3 vols (Louvain: Gerardus Rivius, 1599–1600); Friedrich Förner (*c.*1570–1630), *Panoplia armaturae Dei, adversus omnem superstitionum, divinationum, excantationum, demonolatriam, et universas magorum, veneficorum, et sagarum, et ipsiusmet Sathanae insidias, praestigias et infestationes* (Ingolstadt: Gregorius Haenlinius, 1626); Girolamo Menghi of Viadana (1529–1609), *Compendio dell'arte essorcistica, et possibilita delle mirabili, et stupende operationi delli demoni, et dei malefici. Con li rimedii opportuni alle infirmità maleficiali* (Bologna: G. Rossi, 1582), and for other

works by this author, see below, note 95; Emanuele do Valle de Moura (*c*.1564–1650), *De Incantationibus seu Ensalmis: Opusculum Primum* (Évora: Laurentius Crasbeeck, 1620).

12. Franciscus de Osuna [attrib.], *Flagellum Diaboli, oder Dess Teufels Gaisl, darin gar lustig und artlich gehandelt wird: Von der Macht und Gewalt dess boesen Feindts: von den effecten und Wirckungen der Zauberer Unholdter und Hexenmaister* (Munich: Adam Berg, 1602).

13. The real Francisco de Osuna (*c*.1492–*c*.1540) was born in Andalucia and entered the Order of Observant Franciscans during the reform programme associated with Cardinal Jimenez de Cisneros. He wrote a series of maxims as a practical guide for recollection, arranged into a series of 'Spiritual Alphabets' which had a profound influence on Carmelite spirituality. He seems an implausible author for the *Flagellum Diaboli*. For Plantsch's work see Martin Plantsch, *Opusculum de sagis maleficis* (Pforzheim: Thomas Anshelm, 1507).

14. Hunger, *De Magia Theses Theologicae*, theses 11–78.

15. Menghi, *Compendio dell'arte essorcistica*, books 1 and 2; Delrio, *Disquisitionum Magicarum*, books 1 and 2; Valle de Moura, *De Incantationibus*, section II chapter 1.

16. Delrio, *Disquisitionum Magicarum*, i. 32 ff., 51 ff.; ii. 115 ff.

17. Benedictus Pererius Valentinus, SJ [= Benito Pereira], *Adversus Fallaces et Superstitiosas Artes, Id est, De Magia, de Observatione somniorum, et de Divinatione Astrologica, Libri tres* (Ingolstadt: Sartorius, 1591), *passim*.

18. Osuna, [attrib.], *Flagellum Diaboli*, part II, fos. 70 ff.

19. Delrio, *Disquisitionum Magicarum*, book 3, part II, in ii. 98 ff.

20. Compare Ciruelo, *Reprobación*, as in *Treatise reproving all superstitions*, ed. Maio and Pearson, part III, ch. 11, 312–27, where the chapter is entitled 'concerning supplications made with vain and superstitious ceremonies'.

21. Delrio, *Disquisitionum Magicarum*, book 3, pt 2, questions 1–3.

22. Ibid., question 4, sections 1–2.

23. Delrio, *Disquisitionum Magicarum*, ii. 110–11.

24. Ibid., ii. 123–5 approx.

25. Ibid., ii. 125–33.

26. Compare Johann Weyer, *Witches, Devils, and Doctors in the Renaissance*, ed. George Mora and Benjamin Kohl, trans. John Shea, Medieval & Renaissance Texts & Studies, 73 (Binghamton, NY : Medieval & Renaissance Texts & Studies, 1991; repr. 1998), bk 5, ch. 4, 373–91. Delrio's quotations are of course selective and eliminate Weyer's anticlerical and anti-Catholic rhetoric. For Delrio's hostility to Weyer, see e.g. i. 58.

27. Hunger, *De Magia Theses Theologicae*, thesis 86.

28. Ibid., theses 86–7.

29. Menghi, *Compendio*, 528 ff.; compare Silvestro Mazzolini da Prierio (Silvester Prierias), *De Strigimagarum Demonumque Mirandis libri tres* (Rome: Antonius Bladis de Asula, 24 Sept 1521), sigs. dd iv^r, ee ii^v, and following.

30. Menghi, *Compendio*, 531 (and parallel passage in *Fustis Daemonum* ch 5); Delrio, *Disquisitionum Magicarum*, iii. 196 ff. and 203 ff. (for discussion of the 'Scotus question').

31. Delrio, *Disquisitionum Magicarum*, iii. 175; compare Johann Georg Godelmann, *Tractatus de Magis, Veneficis et Lamiis, deque his recte cognoscendis et puniendis* (Frankfurt: Nicolaus Bassaeus, 1601), 80-3.

32. Förner, *Panoplia*, sermon 5, 49 ff. The allusion is to Acts 17.

33. Compare above, Ch. 4.

34. Förner, *Panoplia*, sermons 25-6.

35. Ibid., sermons 29-30; Delrio, *Disquisitionum Magicarum*, iii. 276.

36. Michael Mullett, *The Catholic Reformation* (London: Routledge, 1999), argues that most of the initiatives of the Catholic reform continued policies already adumbrated or actually initiated in the late Middle Ages: see *passim*, and explicitly in the preface, ix-x. John W. O'Malley points out that the original objectives of the Society of Jesus addressed the improvement of pastoral care in the Church, not something called 'reform', far less a specific response to the Protestant movements. See John W. O'Malley, 'Was Ignatius Loyola a Church Reformer? How to Look at Early Modern Catholicism', in David M. Luebke (ed.) *The Counter-Reformation: The Essential Readings* (Oxford, Blackwell, 1999), 65-82 and the extended historiographical and thematic treatment in John W. O'Malley, *Trent and all That: Renaming Catholicism in the Early Modern Era* (Cambridge, MA: Harvard University Press, 2000).

37. Menghi, *Compendio*, book 3, ch. 8; Delrio, *Disquisitionum Magicarum*, book 3, part II, question 4, section 3.

38. Delrio, *Disquisitionum Magicarum*, i. 113, 156.

39. Ibid., ii. 27; compare with discussion above in Ch. 2.

40. On these healers, see Ciruelo, *Treatise reproving all superstitions*, 255-6; for the cult of St Quiteria see also W. A. Christian, *Local Religion in Sixteenth-Century Spain* (Princeton: Princeton University Press, 1981), 108-9.

41. Delrio, *Disquisitionum Magicarum*, i. 37-42, with reference to other discussions in Francisco Vitoria, *Reverendi patris F. Fracisci Victoriae ... relectiones vndecim ... [ed.] Per R.P. praesentatum F. Alfonsum Muñoz* (Salamanca: Ioannes a Canoua, 1565); Alphonsus de Veracruz, *Physica speculatio* (Salamanca: Ioannes Baptista à Terranoua, Simon à Portonarijs, 1569); Martin de Azpilcueta [= Navarrus], *Enchiridion sive manuale confessariorum et poenitentium* (Antwerp: C. Plantinus, 1581).

42. Delrio, *Disquisitionum Magicarum*, ii. 114 ff.; the authorities for keeping the words of consecration of the Eucharist both obscure and inaudible are cited in Heinrich Bullinger, *De Origine Erroris Libri Duo: in priore agitur de Dei veri iusta invocatione & cultu vero, de Deorum item falsorum religionibus & simulachrorum cultu erroneo: in posteriore disseritur de institutione & vi sacrae Coenae domini, & de origine ac progressu Missae papisticae, contra varias superstitiones pro religione vera antiqua & orthodoxa* (Zurich: Froschauer, 1539), fos. 208^v–9^r: the most important was Guillaume Durand's *Rationale*.

43. Delrio, *Disquisitionum Magicarum*, ii. 114.

44. Valle de Moura, *De Incantationibus*, section II, chapters 7–14, 228–360. Moura's distinction between supplicatory prayer and coercive spell is similar to that proposed (and rejected) in Richard Kieckhefer, *Magic in the Middle Ages* (Cambridge: Cambridge University Press, 1989), 14–15.

45. Valle de Moura, *De Incantationibus*, fo. 4^{r-v}, 11^{r-v}.

46. Valle de Moura, *De Incantationibus*, pt I, ch. 2; pt II, ch. 4; Moura addresses particularly the thought of the medical writer Juan Bravo, (fl. 1546–96), in such works as the *De curandi ratione per medicamenti purgantis exhibitionem libri III* (Salmanca: Cornelius Bonardus, Joannes Pulmannus, 1588).

47. Valle de Moura, *De Incantationibus*, pt I, ch. 4.

48. Ibid., fo. 9^v–12. [The work is foliated to 11, then paginated 12–552.]

49. Ibid., pt. I, ch. 1, sect. 54, 19–20; compare later in the same work, pt. II, ch. 12, sect. 12; pt. II, ch.13, sect.19; pt II, ch.15, sect. 6. He refers to Ortelius's atlas, plate 14 of Ireland; and to Simone Majoli, *Dies caniculares* (Rome: J. A. Ruffinelli, 1597), i. colloq. 15.

50. Tommaso de Vio Cajetan, *Commentarii in Summam theologiæ S. Thomæ Aquinatis* (Venice: Nicolinus, 1593), on *Summa Theologica*, II^a–IIae q. 96; and also in his *Summula*, art. 'Superstitio'; quoted by Valle de Moura, *De Incantationibus*, pt I, ch. 4, sect. 2, 34–5; Compare Delrio, *Disquisitionum Magicarum*, book 3, q. 4, sect. 2: Delrio quotes a slightly different text, perhaps from two treatments of the same subject. Note that on 63 Valle de Moura quotes Petrus de Ledesma, *Summa*, pt. 2, tract. 11 *de iuramento*, cap 7, end of conclusion 6, as quoting Cajetan in Spanish.

51. Valle de Moura, *De Incantationibus*, pt. I, ch. 2, sect. 11; pt. I, ch. 3, sects. 3–4; compare pt. II, ch. 4 and see Tobit 6: 3–8: 3.

52. Valle de Moura, *De Incantationibus*, 32–4.

53. Ibid., pt. I, ch. 4, sects. 15–19, 42–3.

54. Valle de Moura refers, amongst others, to Franciscus Toletus, *Instructio Sacerdotum* (Cologne: Gymnicus, 1621), bk 4, ch. 16, and to Johannes Azor, *Institutionum moralium* (3 vols in 2, Lyons: Jacques Cardon & Pierre Cauellat, 1602–22), bk 9, ch. 26, sect. 6.

55. Valle de Moura, *De Incantationibus*, pt I, ch. 6, sects. 4–5; pp 64–5.

56. Ibid. 132.

57. The Vulgate reads: 'quia omnis creatura Dei bona et nihil reiciendum quod cum gratiarum actione percipitur; sanctificatur enim per verbum Dei et orationem'.

58. Hunger, *De Magia Theses Theologicae*, thesis 88.

59. Ibid., theses 89–95; for Jannes and Mambres, see 2 Tim. 3: 8, a post-biblical tradition based on Exod. 7: 11. The names are preserved in various forms. 'Iannes et Mambres' is the Vulgate version.

60. Note that the text entitled 'Arbatel' continues to be edited by occult publishers. See Joseph H. Peterson (ed.), *Arbatel: Concerning the Magic of the Ancients* (Lake Worth, FL: Ibis Press, 2009).

61. Delrio, *Disquisitionum Magicarum*, i. 58 ff. The text is in *Opus imperfectum in Matthaeum*, homily 43. It was extensively quoted in Protestant polemics even though it was already widely known not to be by Chrysostom, as in e.g. Heinrich Bullinger, *The Decades of Henry Bullinger*, ed. Thomas Harding, Parker Society, 4 vols (Cambridge: Cambridge University Press, 1849–52), iv, Fifth Decade (1852). 260–1; James Calfhill, *An Answer to John Martiall's Treatise of the Cross*, ed. Richard Gibbings, Parker Society (Cambridge: Cambridge University Press, 1846), 285; [John Hooper], *Later Writings of Bishop Hooper: together with his letters and other pieces*, ed. Charles Nevinson, Parker Society (Cambridge: Cambridge University Press, 1852), 407; [John Jewel], *The Works of John Jewel, Bishop of Salisbury*, ed. John Ayre, 4 vols, Parker Society (Cambridge: Cambridge University Press, 1845–50), i. 327–8; iii. 445. The text had already been quoted in Aquinas *Summa Theologica*, II^a–II ae q. 96 art 4.

62. Delrio, *Disquisitionum Magicarum*, i. 370.

63. Ibid., iii. 191–2; in this passage Delrio felt it necessary to step back from particularly critical opinions on the use of holy water expressed previously by Nicholas of Cusa.

64. Ibid., iii. 229 ff.

65. Note that Delrio was not as coy about using the word 'supernatural' as some modern theorists.

66. Delrio, *Disquisitionum Magicarum*, iii. 235–96.

67. Ibid. 294–5: the reference is to Stanislaus Hosius's argument that bells are not baptized, but blessed in Stanislaus Hosius, *Confutatio prolegomenon Brentii: quae primum scripsit aduersus venerabilem virum Petrum à Soto, deinde verò Petrus Paulus Vergerius apud Polonos temerè defendenda suscepit* (Cologne: Maternus Cholinus, 1560), book 5.

68. Delrio, *Disquisitionum Magicarum*, iii. 296–320.

69. Osuna, [attrib.], *Flagellum Diaboli*, fos. 33^v ff.

70. Ibid., fo. 33^v corresponds to Plantsch, *Opusculum*, sig. f i^r; Ibid., fos. 37^v−38^r corresponds to Plantsch, *Opusculum*, sig. f iii^r; Ibid., fos. 50^r−51^r corresponds to Plantsch, *Opusculum*, sigs. b vii^v−c i^r.

71. Ibid., fos. 38^v−40^v.

72. Note that this belief was even admitted by Waldensian heretics in fourteenth-century Germany, otherwise proverbially sceptical about holy water: see Dieter Kurze (ed.) *Quellen zur Ketzergeschichte Brandenburgs und Pommerns* (Berlin: Veröffentlichungen der historischen Kommission zu Berlin, 45, Quellenwerke, 6, 1975), 120, 223.

73. Förner, *Panoplia*, sermons 16−18.

74. Förner, *Panoplia*, 242−3, reports the story from Theodoret, *Ecclesiastical History*, bk 3, ch. 1 [actually in book 3, ch. 3], that even Julian the Apostate used the sign of the cross to drive away demons *after his apostasy*. Theodoret related how Julian crossed himself from habit in the presence of demons called up by a soothsayer in a pagan temple, and the demons promptly disappeared. His apostasy was not public at that time.

75. Förner, *Panoplia*, 259.

76. Ibid. 258−71.

77. Ibid. 272−90.

78. Hunger, *De Magia Theses Theologicae*, theses 22−8; Delrio, *Disquisitionum Magicarum*, bk 2, questions 26−7.

79. Delrio, *Disquisitionum Magicarum*, bk 2, question 38, in i. 349−50.

80. Noël Taillepied, O.F.M. Cap., *Traité De L'Apparition Des Esprits. A Scavoir, Des ames separees, Fantosmes, prodiges, & accidents merveilleux, qui precedent quelquefois la mort des grands personnages, ou signifient changemens de la chose publique* (Rouen: Romain de Beauuais, 1600). On this work and the ensuing controversies, see Stuart Clark, 'The Reformation of the Eyes: Apparitions and Optics in Sixteenth- and Seventeenth-Century Europe', *Journal of Religious History*, 27/2 (2003), 143−60. See also Stuart Clark, *Vanities of the Eye: Vision in Early Modern European Culture* (Oxford: Oxford University Press, 2007).

81. Pierre Le Loyer, sieur de La Brosse (1550−1634) *IIII. livres des spectres, ov apparitions et visions d'esprits, anges et démons se monstrans sensiblement aux homes* (Angers: G. Nepueu, 1586).

82. Petrus Thyraeus, *De variis tam spirituum, quam vivorum hominum prodigiosis apparitionibus, & nocturnis infestationibus libri tres* (Cologne: Cholinus, 1594); *De daemoniacis liber unus in quo daemonum obsidentium conditio, obsessorum hominum status, rationes item & modi, quibus ab obsessis daemones exiguntur . . . & explicantur*

(Cologne: Cholinus, 1594); *Loca infesta: hoc est, De infestis, ob molestantes daemoniorum et defunctorum hominum spiritus, locis, liber unus* (Cologne: Cholinus, 1598).

83. Hunger, *De Magia Theses Theologicae*, thesis 89.

84. Delrio, *Disquisitionum Magicarum*, bk 3 part I, question 7, ii. 74 ff. Compare Förner, *Panoplia*, 94 ff.

85. Delrio, *Disquisitionum Magicarum*, bk 3 part II, question 4, section 8, ii. 117 ff.

86. See e.g. Delrio, *Disquisitionum Magicarum*, iii. 261, 285, taken up by Förner, *Panoplia*, 268.

87. Förner, *Panoplia*, 194−5.

88. Osuna, [attrib.], *Flagellum Diaboli*, fos. 35^{r-v}.

89. Ibid., fos. 36^r−7^r.

90. Delrio, *Disquisitionum Magicarum*, iii. 237 ff, 253.

91. Ibid., iii. 276−8 and refs. including Tommasso Bozio, *De Signis Ecclesiae libri xxiii* (Cologne: Joannes Gymnicus, 1592) bk 2, ch. 8; bk 15, ch. 1; Jakob Gretser, *De Cruce Christi* (Ingolstadt: Adam Sartorius, 1598), bk 3, chs 18−19; Thyraeus, *De daemoniacis*, pt III, ch. 44.

92. Delrio, *Disquisitionum Magicarum*, iii. 282−6.

93. Valle de Moura, *De Incantationibus*, fo. 4^v, apparently based on João dos Santos, *Etiópia oriental* (modern edition: Lisbon: Publicações Alfa, 1989).

94. Förner, *Panoplia*, 268−9; possibly derived from Delrio, *Disquisitionum Magicarum*, iii. 285 ff. A likely source for the story is Possevino's *Moscovia*: see *The Moscovia of Antonio Possevino, S.J.*, trans. Hugh F. Graham (Pittsburgh: University Center for International Studies, University of Pittsburgh, 1977).

95. Girolamo Menghi, *Compendio dell'arte essorcistica, et possibilita delle mirabili, et stupende operationi delli demoni, et dei malefici. Con li rimedii opportuni alle infirmità maleficiali* (Bologna, 1582); Girolamo Menghi, *Flagellum Daemonum, exorcismos terribiles, potentissimos, et efficaces: Remediaque probatissima, ac doctrina singularem in malignos spiritos expellendos, facturasque et maleficia fuganda de obsessis corporibus complectens; cum suis benedictionibus, et omnibus requisitis ad eorum expulsionem; Accessit postremo Pars secunda, quae Fustis daemonum inscribitur, quibus novi exorcismi, et alia nonnulla, quae prius desiderabantur, superaddita fuerunt* (Bologna, 1589); [second part entitled] *Fustis Daemonum, adiurationes formidabiles, potentissimas, et efficaces in malignos spiritus fugandos de oppressis corporibus humanis* (Bologna, 1589); [the latter includes a separately paginated section entitled] *Remedia Efficacissima in malignos spiritus expellendos, facturasque et maleficla [sic] effuganda de obsessis corporibus; cum suis benedictionibus.*

96. Menghi, *Compendio*, 570−3.

97. Ibid. 574−84.

98. Menghi, *Flagellum*, 112, 125, 147–8, 214, 217, 220, 225, 227.

99. Ibid. 112, 133, 140 ff., 201.

100. Ibid. 173, 175, 179, 189.

101. *Remedia*, 25–6.

102. Ibid. 36–66; for further amulets, see ibid. 89–90.

103. Delrio, *Disquisitionum Magicarum*, iii. 300.

104. Pietro Antonio Stampa, *Fuga Satanae: exorcismus ex sacrarum litterarum fontibus, pioque S. Ecclesiae instituto exhaustus* (Como: H. Froua, 1597).

105. See e.g. Valerio Polidoro, *Practica Exorcistarum* (Padua: Paulus Meietus, 1587); Maximilian van Eynatten, *Manuale Exorcismorum: continens instructiones, et exorcismos ad eiiciendos e corporibus obsessis spiritus malignos* (Antwerp: Plantin-Moretus, 1626); a collection entitled *Thesaurus Exorcismorum sique coniurationum terribilium, potentissimorum, efficacissimorum cum practica probatissima: quibus spiritus maligni, daemones maleficiaque omnia de corporibus humanis obsessis, tanquam flagellis, fustibusque fugantur* . . . combined several of the most successful manuals; it was published in 1608 (Cologne: Lazarus Zetzner, 1608) and subsequently.

106. H. C. E. Midelfort, *Exorcism and Enlightenment: Johann Joseph Gassner and the Demons of Eighteenth-Century Germany* (New Haven: Yale University Press, 2005), 56.

107. For works on possession and exorcism, see above, Ch. 12 note 48.

108. Hunger, *De Magia Theses Theologicae*, preface addressed by Hector Wegman of Augsburg to Philipp Fugger, Lord of Kirchberg and Weissenhorn.

109. Delrio, *Disquisitionum Magicarum*, i. 1–6.

110. Ibid. 112.

111. Ibid., ii. 75 ff.; Delrio cites Guilelmus Damasus Lindanus (1525–88), *De fugiendis nostri seculi idolis* (Cologne: Cholinus, 1580), ch. 14, and Tilmann Bredenbach, (1544–87), *Collationum Sacrarum libri VIII* (Cologne: Gosuinus Cholinus, 1592), bk 7, chs. 37 and 39.

112. Förner, *Panoplia*, 94 ff.

113. Ibid. 108–9.

114. Robin Briggs, *Witches and Neighbours: The Social and Cultural Context of European Witchcraft* (London: HarperCollins, 1996, 2nd edn, 2002) stresses that the triggers for accusation and prosecution of individual witches were nearly always rooted in the conditions of local society rather than larger institutional issues. Occasionally some prince-bishoprics in the Empire (e.g. Trier) witnessed hunts for witches that may have had a more structural origin in ecclesiastical policy or the fascinations of particular ecclesiastics.

PART IV INTRODUCTION

1. Catholic demonological treatises continued to proliferate with the emergence of new witchcraft texts by Delancre and Guazzo in the early 1600s, the appearance of Gaspar Schott's *Physica curiosa, sive, Mirabilia naturæ et artis libris XII. comprehensa quibus plera[que], quæ de angelis, dæmonibus, hominibus, spectris, energumensis, monstris, portentis, animalibus, meteoris, &c. rara, arcana, curiosa[que] circumferuntur* (Würzburg: Johannes Andreæ Endterus, Wolff-gangus Jun. Hæredus, Jobus Hertz, 1662) and the republication of the *Malleus Maleficarum* in 1669 in an expanded edition, with many other texts added.

2. See e.g. John Redwood, *Reason, Ridicule, and Religion: The Age of Enlightenment in England, 1660–1750* (London: Thames & Hudson, 1976) and Jane Shaw, *Miracles in Enlightenment England* (New Haven and London: Yale University Press, 2006): much more concern was expended in this period to prove that the events cited had actually happened, than was the case in previous works.

3. On the revocation of 1685 in France, see e.g. Elisabeth Israels Perry, *From Theology to History: French Religious Controversy and the Revocation of the Edict of Nantes* (The Hague: M. Nijhoff, 1973); on the Salzburg expulsion, see Gerhard Florey, *Geschichte der Salzburger Protestanten und ihrer Emigration 1731–32*, Studien und Texte zur Kirchengeschichte und Geschichte, 1/2, (Vienna, Cologne, and Graz: Böhlau, 1977).

4. See above, Part III n. 4.

5. Alexandra Walsham, 'The Reformation and the "Disenchantment of the World" Reassessed', *Historical Journal*, 51/2 (2008), 501 and notes 11–12.

6. See Stuart A. Vyse, *Believing in Magic: The Psychology of Superstition* (New York and Oxford: Oxford University Press, 1997), discussed below, Ch. 18.

16. DEMONOLOGY BECOMES AN OPEN SUBJECT
IN THE SEVENTEENTH CENTURY

1. For the phrase 'devil's novitiate' see Friedrich Förner, *Panoplia armaturae Dei* (Ingolstadt: Gregorius Haenlinius, 1626), 62; compare Nicolaus Hemmingius [= Niels Hemmingsen], *Admonitio de superstitionibus magicis vitandis, in gratiam sincerae religionis amantium* (Copenhagen: Iohannes Stockelman and Andreas Gutterwitz, 1575), sig. B7^v, for a similar argument.

2. See above, Ch. 6, at nn. 6, 17, 19-23.

3. On the Family of Love in the Low Countries, see Alastair Hamilton, *The Family of Love* (Cambridge: J. Clarke, 1981); Alastair Hamilton (ed.),

Documenta Anabaptistica Neerlandica, vi., *Cronica. Ordo sacerdotis. Acta HN* (Leiden and New York: Brill, 1988); Alastair Hamilton, *Hendrik Niclaes* (Baden-Baden: Koerner, 2003).

4. On Familism in England, see Christopher W. Marsh, *The Family of Love in English Society, 1550–1630* (Cambridge and New York: Cambridge University Press, 1993), esp. 140–97.

5. For Reginald Scot, see above, Ch. 12 note 28. See also Joseph Glanvill and Henry More, *Saducismus Triumphatus: Or, Full and Plain Evidence Concerning Witches and Apparitions,* 3rd edn (London: S. Lownds, 1688), 35.

6. See above, Ch. 12, at nn. 18-32.

7. e.g. Robert Burton, *The Anatomy of Melancholy* (London: Chatto and Windus, 1927), 131.

8. Robert Burton (1577–1640), *The Anatomy of Melancholy, what it is: With all the kindes, causes, symptomes, prognostickes, and severall cures of it* (Oxford: John Lichfield and James Short, for Henry Cripps, 1621). The third edition appeared in 1628. The modern critical edition is ed. Thomas C. Faulkner, Nicolas K. Kiessling, and Rhonda L. Blair, 6 vols (Oxford: Clarendon Press; New York: Oxford University Press, 1989–2000).

9. Robert Burton, *The Anatomy of Melancholy* (London: Chatto and Windus, 1927), Section I, Memb. 1, subj. 2, 115–30.

10. Ibid. 117–19.

11. Ibid. 123–6.

12. Ibid. 129–30.

13. Ibid. 295–9.

14. Ibid. 660 ff.: 661 for the specific quotation.

15. Ibid. 667.

16. Ibid. 669–75.

17. Ibid. 678–83.

18. Ibid. 683–6.

19. Ibid. 704 ff.

20. Ibid. 708–13.

21. Ibid. 320–7.

22. For Browne's life, see R. H. Robbins, 'Browne, Sir Thomas (1605–1682)', in *Oxford Dictionary of National Biography* (Oxford: Oxford University Press, 2004); the early bibliography of *Religio Medici* includes Thomas Browne, *Religio medici* (London: Andrew Crooke, 1642); *A True and Full Coppy of that which was most imperfectly and surreptitiously printed before under the name of Religio Medici* (London: Printed for Andrew Crook, 1643).

23. Browne, *Religio Medici,* part 1, section 3.

24. Ibid., sections 9–10.

25. Ibid., sections 14–17.

26. Ibid., section 19.

27. Ibid., section 30.

28. Ibid., section 33.

29. Ibid., section 37.

30. Ibid., sections 27, 32, 36.

31. Ibid., section 48.

32. Ibid., section 56.

33. Ibid., part 2, section 8.

34. Ibid., part 2, section 1

35. Thomas Browne, *Pseudodoxia Epidemica, or, Enquiries into very many received tenents and commonly presumed truths* (London: Printed by T.H. for E. Dod, 1646); revised and enlarged editions appeared in 1650, 1658, and 1672. There also appeared translations of the work into German, French, and Italian in the seventeenth and eighteenth centuries.

36. Browne, *Pseudodoxia Epidemica*, book 1, chs. 4, 6–7.

37. This dictum was later echoed by Baudelaire: see Nathan Johnstone, *The Devil and Demonism in Early Modern England* (Cambridge: Cambridge University Press, 2006), 1 and n.

38. Browne, *Pseudodoxia Epidemica*, book 1, ch. 10.

39. Ibid., book 5, ch. 22

40. Ibid., book 5, ch. 23.

41. Ibid., book 7, ch. 12. Italics mine.

42. See Noel Malcolm, 'Hobbes, Thomas (1588–1679)', in *Oxford Dictionary of National Biography*.

43. Thomas Hobbes, *Leviathan*, ed. C. B. Macpherson (Harmondsworth and New York: Penguin, 1968).

44. Ibid. 521 ff., 627 ff., 704–15.

45. For his critiques of scholasticism, see e.g. ibid. 688 ff.

46. Ibid. 428–9.

47. Ibid., 429–32.

48. Ibid. 432–42.

49. Ibid. 657–64.

50. Ibid. 469–78, 664–5.

51. Ibid. 633–6.

52. Ibid. 637–9.

53. See Norman T. Burns, *Christian Mortalism from Tyndale to Milton* (Cambridge, MA: Harvard University Press, 1972).

54. See Christopher Hill, Barry Reay, and William Lamont, *The World of the Muggletonians* (London: T. Smith, 1983).

55. Lodowick Muggleton, *A True Interpretation Of the Witch of Endor. Spoken of in 1 Sam. 28, begin, at the 11. Verse* (London: [s.n.], 1669), ch. 9, 26–30.

56. Ibid. 48.

57. Ibid., chs. 8-9, 22–30 and compare ch. 5, 13–15.

58. Ibid., ch. 9, 26–30.

59. Ibid., chs. 2-3, 6, 8, 3–9, 15–18, 22–5. Muggleton's exposition tends to be elliptical and repetitive.

60. Ibid., chs 1, 4, 1–3, 10–12.

61. Ibid., ch. 2, 3–5.

62. Ibid., ch. 9, 26–30.

63. See in the next chapter the discussion of the witch of Endor in More and Glanvill, *Saducismus Triumphatus* (1688), with rebuttal of other authors, in 42 ff., 113–15, 296–7.

64. See below, Ch. 17.

65. Thomas Ady, *The Doctrine of Devils, Proved to be the grand Apostacy of these later Times. An Essay tending to rectifie those Undue Notions and Apprehensions Men have about Daemons and Evil Spirits* (London: Printed for the Author, 1676). The arguments in this work may be compared with the broadly similar work of John Wagstaffe (1633–77), *The Question of Witchcraft Debated. Or a Discourse against their Opinion that affirm Witches, Considered and enlarged*, 2nd edn (London: Edw. Millington, 1671). In a striking anticipation of Bekker, Wagstaffe argued that the belief in demons derived from pre-Christian dualistic theologies.

66. Ady, *Doctrine of Devils*, 26 ff, 41 ff., 52 ff., 62 ff, 101.

67. See above, Ch. 6, notes 33–4.

68. Ady, *Doctrine of Devils*, 53–4.

69. Joseph Mede (1586–1638), *The apostasy of the latter times: in which (according to divine prediction) the world should wonder after the beast, the mystery of iniquity should so farre prevaile over the mystery of godlinesse, whorish Babylon over the virgin-church of Christ, as that the visible glory of the true church should be much clouded, the true unstained Christian faith corrupted, the purity of true worship polluted: or, the gentiles theology of dæmons, i.e. inferious divine powers, supposed to be mediatours between God and man: revived in the latter times amongst Christians, in worshipping of angels, deifying and invocating of saints, adoring and templing of reliques, bowing downe to images, worshipping of crosses, &c.: all which, together with a true discovery of the nature, originall, progresse of the great, fatall, and solemn apostasy are cleared* (London: Richard Bishop and Samuel Man, 1642).

70. Ady, *Doctrine of Devils*, 7–9, 14, 18. Compare Mede, *Apostasy*, 8.

71. Ady, *Doctrine of Devils*, 104–12, 157–76.
72. See discussion of Glanvill in Ch. 17 below.
73. Ady, *Doctrine of Devils*, 188–95.
74. Ibid. 176–7.
75. John Webster, *The Displaying of Supposed Witchcraft. Wherein is affirmed that there are many sorts of Deceivers and Impostors, And Divers persons under a passive Delusion of Melancholy and Fancy. But that there is a Corporeal League made betwixt the Devil and the Witch, Or that he sucks on the Witches Body, has Carnal Copulation, or that Witches are turned into Cats, Dogs, raise Tempests, or the like, is utterly denied and disproved. Wherein also is handled, The Existence of Angels and Spirits, the truth of Apparitions, the Nature of Astral and Sydereal Spirits, the force of Charms, and Philters; with other abstruse matters* (London: 'J. M.', 1677). For Webster's life and other works see http://www.oxforddnb.com/view/article/28944?docPos=18
76. These issues will be discussed in the next chapter.
77. Webster, *Displaying*, 183–93.
78. Ibid. 44, 58, 72, 123, 291.
79. Ibid. 290.
80. Ibid. 197–215.
81. Ibid. 215–36.
82. Ibid. 241–61.
83. Ibid. 63, 99, 117–20.
84. Ibid. 280–5.
85. Ibid. 288–320.
86. Ibid. 321–46.
87. On his critique of Cartesianism when applied to excess, see Balthasar Bekker, *De Philosophia Cartesiana, admonitio candida et sincera* (Wesel: A. ab Hoogen-huysen, 1668) and discussion in Balthasar Bekker, *The World Bewitch'd, or, An examination of the common opinions concerning spirits: their nature, power, administration and operations, as also the effects men are able to produce by their communication* (London: Printed for R. Baldwin in Warwick-Lane, 1695), 253.
88. Balthasar Bekker, *De betoverde weereld, zynde een grondig ondersoek van't gemeen gevoelen aangaande de geesten, deselver aart en vermogen, bewind en bedrijf: als ook 't gene de menschen door derselver kraght en emeenschap doen*, 4 vols (Amsterdam, D. van den Dalen, 1691–3). The German translation appeared immediately: *Die bezauberte Welt, oder, Eine gründliche Unter-suchung des allgemeinen Aberglaubens*, 4 vols (Amsterdam: Daniel von Dahlen, 1693); *Le monde enchanté: ou, Examen des communs sentimens touchant les esprits, leur nature, leur pouvoir, leur administration, & leurs operations*, 4 vols

(Amsterdam: P. Rotterdam, 1694) followed, with a partial English translation (above) in 1695. See Friedrich Wilhelm Bautz and Traugott Bautz (eds), *Biographisch-bibliographisches Kirchenlexikon* (Hamm [Westf.]: Bautz, 1970–), article 'Bekker, Balthasar', and references.

89. On Bekker, see also Andrew Fix, *Fallen Angels: Balthasar Bekker, Spirit Belief, and Confessionalism in the Seventeenth Century Dutch Republic*, Archives internationales d'histoire des idées, 165 (Dordrecht and Boston: Kluwer, 1999); Auke Jelsma, 'The Devil and Protestantism', in A. Jelsma, *Frontiers of the Reformation* (Aldershot: Ashgate, 1998), 25–39. Han van Ruler, 'Minds, Forms, and Spirits: The Nature of Cartesian Disenchantment', *Journal of the History of Ideas*, 61/3. (2000), 381–95. See also Willem Pieter Cornelis Knuttel, *Balthasar Bekker, de bestrijder van het bijgeloof* (The Hague: M. Nijhoff, 1906).

90. Bekker, *World Bewitch'd*, 1695 English edition, abridgement, sig. c5^v–6^r. Compare ibid., sig. c11^v.

91. Ibid., preface, sig. b5^r. For Bekker's aversion to excessive respect for precedent authorities and tradition, see ibid., 263.

92. Ibid., preface, sig. b6^{r-v}.

93. Bekker, i, chs 2–6, 8–50.

94. Ibid., chs 7–11, 51–99.

95. Ibid., chs 12–14, 100–39.

96. Ibid., chs 15–18, 140–82.

97. Ibid. 184; Bekker refers here to Gaspar Schott's *Magia Universalis*, 4 vols (Würzburg: Schönwetter and Pigrin, 1657–9), to demonstrate the continuing prevalence of Catholic arguments in those areas, although given Schott's interest in natural magic of the scientific variety, more appropriate reference might have been to the *Physica Curiosa*.

98. Bekker, i, chs 19–20, and esp. 194–8.

99. Ibid. 211, 220–3.

100. Ibid. 249–59.

101. Bekker, ii, chs 1–5.

102. Ibid., chs 8–15.

103. Ibid., chs 20–1, and abridgement, sig. c9^r for the quotation.

104. Ibid., chs 26–30.

105. Ibid., iii, chs 2–7.

106. Ibid., chs 13–17.

107. Ibid., iv, chs 5–11.

108. Ibid., chs 17–23; abridgement, sig. d6^{r-v}.

109. Ibid., abridgement, sig. b6^v.

110. Ibid., iv, chs 33–4; sig. d8^v for the quotation.

111. For the biographical details, see Bautz, *Biographisch-bibliographisches Kirchen-lexikon*, article 'Bekker', as above.

112. Jacobus Schuts, *De betoverde Bekker, ofte, Een overtuygent bewijs dat het boek vande Heer Bekker, genaemt De betoverde weerelt, doorsaeyt is met de onredelijkste redenering, notoirste onwaarheeden, en andere schadelijcke gevolgen: waar door de waare reeden verlogent, de waarheyt vervalst, en de deught ontsenuwt wert* (The Hague: Barent Beek, 1691). However, soon afterwards the Mennonite preacher and physician Antonius Van Dale (or Dalen: 1638-1708) issued his *Dissertationes de origine ac progressu idololatriae et superstitionum, de vera ac falsa prophetia: uti et de divinationibus idololatricis Judaeorum* (Amsterdam: Boom, 1696), which sought, like Bekker, to reinterpret the Old Testament texts that allegedly proved the existence of demons.

17. DEFENDING THE 'INVISIBLE WORLD': THE CAMPAIGN AGAINST 'SADUCISM'

1. [Henry More and Joseph Glanvill], *Saducismus Triumphatus: Or, Full and Plain Evidence Concerning Witches and Apparitions. In Two Parts. The First treating of their Possibility; The Second of their Real Existence. The Third Edition. The Advantages whereof above the former, the Reader may understand out of Dr H. More's Account prefixed thereunto. With two Authentick, but wonderful Stories of certain Swedish Witches; done into English by Anth. Horneck, D.D.* (London: S. Lownds, 1688).

2. Nathanael Homes, *Dæmonologie, and Theologie. The first, The Malady, Demonstrating the Diabolicall Arts, and Devillish hearts of Men. The Second, The Remedy: Demonstrating, God a rich Supply of all Good* (London: Thomas Roycroft, John Martin, and John Ridley, 1650). For Homes's life, see http://www.oxforddnb.com/view/article/13599.

3. Homes, *Daemonologie*, 16.

4. Ibid., Epistle in prefatory matter.

5. Ibid. 18–19.

6. Ibid. 23–4.

7. Ibid. 24–30.

8. Ibid. 36–7.

9. Ibid. 41.

10. Ibid. 53–61.

11. Ibid. 62.

12. Ibid. 84–6.

13. Meric Casaubon, *A Treatise Proving Spirits, Witches, and Supernatural Operations, by Pregnant Instances and Evidences* (London: Brabazon Aylmer, 1672); the title of this reprinted edition was not the one chosen by the author.

14. Ibid. 2, 7. Compare also 28–9 for similar points.

15. Ibid., e.g. 60, 75.

16. Ibid. 27.

17. Ibid. 132.

18. Ibid. 8–20.

19. Ibid. 77–99.

20. Ibid. 100–18.

21. Ibid. 133–50.

22. Ibid. 35–41.

23. Ibid. 133.

24. Ibid. 152.

25. For More's life see http://www.oxforddnb.com/view/article/19181?doc Pos=20 and sources. For sources on the Cambridge Platonists, see http://www.oxforddnb.com/view/theme/94274?&back=10790 and references.

26. For Glanvill's biography see http://www.oxforddnb.com/view/article/ 10790?docPos=2

27. See note 1 above for the main edition used here. Other important editions were: Joseph Glanvill and Henry More, *Saducismus triumphatus, or, Full and plain evidence concerning witches and apparitions in two parts: the first treating of their possibility, the second of their real existence* (London: J. Collins and S. Lownds, 1681); the second edition of the same title, but with additional material relating to witchcraft cases in Sweden, appeared a year later (London: Tho. Newcomb, for S. Lownds, 1682); the third and definitive edition appeared in near-identical imprints in 1688 and 1689. The English edition was reprinted in 1700 and 1726; a German translation appeared in 1701: *Saducismus triumphatus, oder, Vollkommener und klarer Beweiss von Hexen and Gespenstern, oder, Geister-Erscheinungen*, 3 vols (Hamburg: Gottfried Liebernickel and Nicolaus Spieringk, 1701).

28. Richard Bovet, *Pandaemonium, or, The devil's cloyster: being a further blow to modern sadduceism, proving the existence of witches and spirits, in a discourse deduced from the fall of the angels, the propagation of Satans kingdom before the flood, the idolatry of the ages after greatly advancing diabolical confederacies, with an account of the lives and transactions of several notorious witches: also, a collection of several authentick relations of strange apparitions of dæmons and spectres, and fascinations of witches, never before printed* (London: J. Walthoe, 1684).

29. Nathaniel Crouch, *The Kingdom of Darkness: or The History of Dæmons, Specters, Witches, Apparitions, Possessions, Disturbances, and other wonderful and supernatural Delusions, Mischievous Feats, and Malicious Impostures of the Devil. Containing near Fourscore memorable Relations, Forreign and Domestick, both*

Antient and Modern. Collected from Authentick Records, Real Attestations, Credible Evidences, and asserted by Authors of Undoubted Verity (London: [Printed for the Author], 1688)

30. Richard Baxter, *The certainty of the worlds of spirits fully evinced by unquestionable histories of apparitions and witchcrafts, operations, voices, &c. proving the immortality of souls, the malice and miseries of the Devil and the damned, and the blessedness of the justified. Written for the conviction of sadduces & infidels* (London: T. Parkhurst and J. Salusbury, 1691). The writings of the Mathers on the New England witch trials also form part of this movement.

31. More and Glanvill, *Saducismus Triumphatus* (1688), 17–19, 23.

32. Ibid. 72–3.

33. For a case where illusion was considered a necessary explanation, see Henry More's glosses on a Taunton witchcraft case, ibid. 392–5.

34. Ibid. 133–253.

35. Ibid. 161–5.

36. Ibid. 183.

37. Ibid. 75 ff.

38. Ibid. 277.

39. Ibid. 91.

40. Ibid. 318.

41. Ibid. 77, 270.

42. Ibid. 93–6.

43. Ibid. 82.

44. Ibid. 124 ff. See Jane Shaw, *Miracles in Enlightenment England* (New Haven and London: Yale University Press, 2006), especially ch. 4, 74–96.

45. See treatment of ghosts above, esp. in Ch. 12, at nn. 71–82.

46. See the discussion of Pietro Martire Vermigli's commentaries on Samuel above, Ch. 12, at nn. 77–80.

47. More and Glanvill, *Saducismus Triumphatus* (1688), 42 ff. and esp. 47–8.

48. Ibid. 114–15, and compare e.g. 311–13 for the same general point.

49. For Glanvill's exegesis see ibid. 296–320.

50. Ibid., 'relations' ix–xix, xxvi–xxvii, 399–429, 453–63. For witnesses suspecting ghosts to be demons, see e.g. 417.

51. See esp. Joseph Glanvill, *A Blow at Modern Sadducism in Some Philosophical Considerations about Witchcraft: to which is added the relation of the fam'd disturbance by the drummer in the house of Mr. John Mompesson, with some reflections on drollery and atheisme* (London : Printed by E.C. for James Collins, 1668).

52. More and Glanvill, *Saducismus Triumphatus* (1688), 328.

53. Ibid., e.g. 330–2.

54. Ibid. 334.

55. Ibid., 5, 16, 23, 27, 260, 262–5, and compare John Webster, *The Displaying of Supposed Witchcraft* (London: 'J.M.', 1677), 278.

56. *Den duyvel van Tedworth*, trans. Jacobus Koelman (Amsterdam: by Johannes Boekholt, 1692).

57. Joseph Addison, *The Drummer; or, the Haunted House. A comedy. As it is acted at the Theatre-Royal in Drury-Lane, by His Majesty's servants* (London, 1715); *The drummer of Tedworth containing, the whole story of that dæmon, on which is founded, the new comedy of The drummer: or, the haunted house. . . . To which is added, a large relation of the Marlborough-ghost* (London: J. Roberts, 1716).

58. More and Glanvill, *Saducismus Triumphatus* (1688), relations xx–xxv, 429–53, continuation relat. i, iii–v, 486–520.

59. Ibid., continuation relation vi, 521–8.

60. See Glanvill's remark on 372.

61. In Hogarth's satirical print on George Whitefield, entitled 'Credulity, Superstition, and Fanaticism', Glanvill's book is so described in an illustration in the bottom right-hand corner. Witchcraft cases in *Saducismus Triumphatus* comprise the eight relations ii–viii, xxviii.

62. For the sceptical attitudes displayed by the judge at the trial of Jane Wenham, see Keith Thomas, *Religion and the Decline of Magic: Studies in Popular Beliefs in Sixteenth- and Seventeenth-Century England* (London: Weidenfeld and Nicolson, 1971), 548–9 and 689.

63. Robert Hunt appears as a source for a long sequence of witchcraft narratives in More and Glanvill, *Saducismus Triumphatus* (1688), 339–70.

64. See More's glosses in More and Glanvill, *Saducismus Triumphatus* (1688), 392–5 as referred to above, note 33.

65. See ibid., e.g. 83, 378.

66. Ibid. 396–8.

67. The original edition was J. Aubrey, *Miscellanies upon the following subjects . . .* (London: Edward Castle, 1696). See note 70 below for the edition cited here.

68. See http://www.oxforddnb.com/view/article/886?docPos=2 for the recent life of Aubrey, and reference to his manuscript collections.

69. British Library, Lansdowne MS 231, John Aubrey, 'The Remaines of Gentilisme and Judaisme', believed to date from 1687–9, was also printed in *John Aubrey: Three Prose Works*, ed. John Buchanan-Brown (Fontwell: Centaur Press, 1972).

70. John Aubrey, *Miscellanies upon Various Subjects*, 4th edn (London: John Russell Smith, 1857), 1–32. Compare above, Ch. 4 note 17, for the Egyptian Days and the sources that referred to them.

71. Aubrey, *Miscellanies*, 33–68.

72. Ibid. 91−2; compare *Colloquia mensalia: or, Dr. Martin Luther's divine discourses at his table, &c*. . . . Collected first together by Dr. Antonius Lauterbach, and afterward disposed into certain common places by John Aurifaber. Translated out of the high Germane into the English tongue by Capt. Henrie Bell (London, 1652).

73. Aubrey, *Miscellanies*, 70−120 in general.

74. Ibid. 159−61. The medical and astrological papers of Dr Richard Napier (1559−1634) are conserved in the Ashmole Manuscripts in the Bodleian Library in Oxford. See http://www.archiveshub.ac.uk/news/02120301. html.

75. Ibid., 165−7.

76. Ibid., 174−94. On second sight, see also Jane Dawson, 'Calvinism and the Gaidhealtachd in Scotland', in *Calvinism in Europe, 1560−1620*, ed. A. Duke, G. Lewis, and A. Pettegree, (Cambridge: Cambridge University Press, 1994), 231−53 and esp. 250−2.

77. Aubrey, *Miscellanies*, 130−41. Aubrey was interested in astrological healing and also in occult magic: he worked with Elias Ashmole in copying of *Key of Solomon* in 1674.

78. Aubrey, *Miscellanies*, 142−53.

79. Pierre Breslay, *L'Anthologie ou Recueil de plusieurs discours notables, tirez de divers bons autheurs Grecs & Latins* (Paris: J. Poupy, 1574); Simone Majoli, *Simonis Maioli . . . Dies caniculares: seu, Colloquia tria, & viginti. Quibus pleraque naturae admiranda, quae aut in aethere fiunt, aut in Europa, Asia, atque Africa, quin etiam in ipso orbe nouo, & apud omnes antipodas sunt, recensentur* (Rome, J.A. Ruffinelli, 1597); on Cardano see Anthony Grafton, *Cardano's Cosmos* (Cambridge, MA: Harvard University Press, 1999) and *Hieronymi Cardani mediolanensis medici De rerum varietate libri XVII* (Basle: Henrichus Petri, 1557); and *Hieronymi Cardani Medici Mediolanensis De subtilitate Libri XXI* (Nuremberg: Iohannes Petreius, 1550).

80. Webster, *Displaying*, prefatory material, sig. a4^r.

81. See below, Ch. 18, at nn. 100−2 on Methodists and the supernatural see also Alexandra Walsham, 'The Reformation and the "Disenchantment of the World" reassessed', *Historical Journal*, 51/2 (2008), 526.

18. TOWARDS THE ENLIGHTENMENT

1. The first edition was: J.-B. Thiers, *Traité des superstitions selon l'Ecriture sainte, les décrets des conciles et les sentimens des saints Pères et des théologiens* (Paris, A. Dezallier, 1679, in-12, 454 p.): for an extremely thorough discussion and evaluation of this text see Daniel T. Penney, 'J.-B. Thiers and the Repression

of Superstition in Late-Seventeenth-Century France', Oxford University D.Phil. thesis, 1997; also see the modern abridged edition, Jean-Baptiste Thiers, *Traité des superstitions: croyances populaires et rationalité à l'Âge classique*, ed. Jean Marie Goulemot (Paris: Le Sycomore, 1984).

2. The details are found in Penney, 'J.-B. Thiers', chapter 2 section C, and Thiers, *Traité des superstitions*, ed. Goulemot, 33.

3. Penney, 'J.-B. Thiers', chapter 2 section D; Thiers, *Traité des superstitions*, ed. Goulemot, 25–7.

4. Thiers, *Traité des superstitions*, i, bk 1, chs 1–8.

5. Ibid., bk 1, chs 9–10.

6. Ibid., bk 2, chs 1–2.

7. Ibid., bk 2, chs 3–5.

8. Ibid., bks 3–6 *passim*.

9. Thiers, *Traité des superstitions*, ed. Goulemot, 81

10. Ibid. 82 ff.

11. Ibid. 85–90.

12. Ibid. 91–4.

13. Point made by both Penney, 'J.-B. Thiers', chapter 2 section C.4, and Thiers, *Traité des superstitions*, ed. Goulemot, 19.

14. See above, Ch. 15 at note 26.

15. Thiers, *Traité des superstitions*, ed. Goulemot, 16–17.

16. Ibid. 17.

17. Thiers, *Traité des superstitions*, ii, bk 1, ch. 1.

18. Ibid., bk, 3, ch. 2.

19. Ibid., bk 4, ch. 4. Compare Pedro Ciruelo on vain observances as above, Ch. 8 note 49.

20. Thiers, *Traité des superstitions*, iv, bk 7, *passim*.

21. Compare e.g. Henry of Gorkum as above, Ch. 3 notes 32–5.

22. Pierre Lebrun, *Histoire critique des pratiques superstitieuses: qui ont seduit les peuples, & embarassé les sçavans: avec la methode et les principes pour discerner les effets naturels d'avec ceux qui ne le sont pas* (Rouen and Paris: Jean de Nully, 1702; also Amsterdam, H. Schelte, 1702).

23. Penney, 'J.-B. Thiers', chapter 1, 10–11 and notes 79–82.

24. Augustin Calmet, *Dissertations sur les apparitions des anges, des démons & des esprits et sur les revenans et vampires de Hongrie, de Boheme, de Moravie & de Silesie* (Paris, De Bure l'aîné, 1746); note also English translation: *Dissertations upon the apparitions of angels, dæmons, and ghosts, and concerning the vampires of Hungary, Bohemia, Moravia, and Silesia. By the Reverend Father Dom Augustin Calmet,... Translated from the French* (London: M. Cooper, 1759).

25. Calmet, *Dissertations*, conclusion to part I.

26. Ibid., part I, chapter 91.

27. Nicolas Lenglet Dufresnoy, *Recueil de dissertations, anciennes et nouvelles: sur les apparitions, les visions et les songes*, 2 vols (Avignon; Paris: Jean-Noel Leloup, 1751).

28. Laurent Bordelon (1653–1730), *L'Histoire des imaginations extravagantes de Monsieur Oufle, causées par la lecture des livres qui traitent de la magie, du grimoire, des démoniaques, sorciers . . . des fées, ogres . . . phantômes & autres revenans, des songes de la pierre philosophale, de l'astrologie judiciaire . . . Le tout enrichi de figures, & accompagné d'un tres-grand nombre de nottes curieuses, qui rapportent fidellement les endroits des livres, qui ont causé ses imaginations extravagantes, ou qui peuvent servir pour les combattre*, 2 vols (Paris: N. Gosselin, 1710); here cited in the English translation, *A History of the Ridiculous Extravagancies of Monsieur Oufle; Occasion'd by his reading Books treating of Magick, the Black-Art, Daemoniacks, Conjurers, Witches, Hobgoblins, Incubus's, Succubus's and the Diabolical-Sabbath; of Elves, Fairies, Wanton Spirits, Genius's, Spectres and Ghosts; of Dreams, the Philosopher's-Stone, Judicial Astrology, Horoscopes, Talismans, Lucky and Unlucky Days, Eclipses, Comets, and all sorts of Apparitions, Divinations, Charms, Enchantments and other Superstitious Practices . . .* Written originally in French, by the Abbot B—; and now translated into English (London: J. Morphew, 1711), 11.

29. Voltaire (1694–1778), *Dictionnaire philosophique*, in Voltaire, *Œuvres complètes*, 55 vols (Paris: Renouard, 1819–21), vols 33–38, art. 'Enchantement', at vol. 35, 375–84. For the editorial history of the *Dictionnaire*, see below at note 110.

30. Richard Boulton, *A Compleat History of Magick, Sorcery, and Witchcraft*, 2 vols (London: E. Curll . . . J. Pemberton . . . and W. Taylor . . ., 1715–16).

31. Boulton, i, chapters 1–2, 7–8.

32. Francis Hutchinson, *An Historical Essay concerning Witchcraft* (London: R. Knaplock [etc.], 1718). A German translation followed: see below, note 39.

33. Francis Hutchinson, *A short view of the pretended spirit of prophecy, taken from its first rise in the year 1688, to its present state among us* (London, 1708); a subsequent edition appeared in Edinburgh in 1709.

34. See Keith Thomas, *Religion and the Decline of Magic: Studies in Popular Beliefs in Sixteenth- and Seventeenth-Century England* (London: Weidenfeld and Nicolson, 1971), 689, for Hutchinson's encounter with the convicted and then reprieved witch Jane Wenham.

35. Hutchinson, *Historical Essay*, ch. 11.

36. Ibid., ch. 12.

37. Richard Boulton, *The Possibility and Reality of Magick, Sorcery, and Witchcraft, demonstrated; or, a Vindication of a Compleat History of Magick . . . in answer to Dr. Hutchinson's Historical Essay, etc.* (London: J. Roberts, 1722).

38. Jacques Daillon, 'Comte du Lude', Δαιμονολογια: *or, a Treatise of spirits. Wherein several places of Scripture are expounded, against the vulgar errors concerning witchcraft, apparitions, &c. To which is added, an appendix, containing some reflections on Mr. Boulton's answer to Dr. Hutchinson's Historical Essay; entitled The Possibility and Reality of Magick, Sorcery and Witchcraft demonstrated* (London: Printed for the Author, 1723).

39. *Francisci Hutchinsons . . . Historischer Versuch von der Hexerey: in einem Gesprach . . . einer Vorrede des Herrn Geheimden Raths Thomasii; aus dem Englischen in Teutsche übersetzet, auch mit kurtzen Summarien und vollstandigen Registern versehen von Theodoro Arnold* (Leipzig: Johann Christoph Martini, 1726).

40. [Arthur Ashley Sykes], *An Enquiry into the Meaning of Demoniacks in the New Testament.* The second edition, corrected and amended. (London, 1737). Sykes identified himself on the title page only by an acronym. The first edition does not appear to be known and may be fictitious. For Sykes, see http://www.oxforddnb.com/view/article/26867?docPos=4

41. Sykes, *An Enquiry*, 5–6.

42. Ibid., 12 ff.

43. See H. C. Erik Midelfort, *Exorcism and Enlightenment: Johann Joseph Gassner and the Demons of Eighteenth-Century Germany* (New Haven and London: Yale University Press, 2005), 106–7, for the problems this line of argument posed.

44. See discussion in Midelfort, *Exorcism and Enlightenment*, 91 ff. and note 16, with full references on 179–80.

45. Johann Salomo Semler, *Joannis Salomonis Semleri commentatio de Daemoniacis quorum in N.T. fit mentio* (Halle: J. C. Hendel, 1769), described as 'editio auctior'. The first edition reputedly appeared in 1760.

46. Semler, *Commentatio*, and see discussion in Midelfort, *Exorcism and Enlightenment*, 89–93.

47. Midelfort, *Exorcism and Enlightenment, passim*.

48. Ibid. 67 ff.

49. Ibid. 96–7.

50. Pierre Bayle (1647–1706), *Dictionaire historique et critique*, 2 vols (Rotterdam: R. Leers, 1697); 2nd edition (Rotterdam, 1702); [Pierre Bayle], *Commentaire philosophique sur ces paroles de Jésus-Christ: Contrain-les d'entrer*, 'tr. de l'angl. du sieur Jean Fox de Bruggs par M.J.F.', 4 vols ('Canterbury', 1686–8). On Bayle see esp. Elisabeth Labrousse, *Pierre Bayle*, 2nd edn (Dordrecht and Lancaster: Nijhoff, 1985).

51. [Pierre Bayle], *Lettre à M.L.A.D.C., docteur de Sorbonne, où il est prouvé par plusieurs raisons tirées de la philosophie, & de la theologie que les cometes ne sont point le presage d'aucun malheur* (Cologne [i.e. Rotterdam]: P. Marteau, 1682); *Pensées diverses, écrites à un docteur de Sorbonne, à l'occasion de la cométe qui parut au mois de Decembre 1680* (Rotterdam: R. Leers, 1683).

52. For examples of this sort of cosmology, see e.g. Petrus Apianus, *Petri Apiani Cosmographia, per Gemmam Phrysium... restituta. Additis de adem [sic] re ipsius Gemmæ Phry. libellis*, etc. (Antwerp: A. Berckmanus, 1539).

53. See the discussion of the 1531 comet and Melanchthon's response to it in Sachiko Kusukawa, *The Transformation of Natural Philosophy: the Case of Philip Melanchthon* (Cambridge and New York: Cambridge University Press, 1995), 124–34.

54. See e.g. William Green, *Memento's to the world; or, An historical collection of divers wonderful comets and prodigious signs in Heaven, that have been seen, some long before the birth of Christ, and many since that time... Together, with ample discourses, and profitable observations, upon that admirable star which appeared at the birth of Christ, to the eastern magi. As also upon that comet which appeared in the constellation of Cassiopea, after the horrid massacre of the French-Protestants, anno 1572. And several other comets, with their effects to this present time* ([London]: T. Haly, for T. Passinger, 1680).

55. On Increase Mather's contributions, see *Heavens alarm to the world, or, A sermon wherein is shewed that fearful sights and signs in heaven are the presages of great calamities at hand* (Boston: John Foster, 1681); *Kometographia. Or A discourse concerning comets wherein the nature of blazing stars is enquired into: with an historical account of all the comets which have appeared from the beginning of the world unto this present year, M. DC. LXXXIII. : Expressing the place in the heavens, where they were seen, their motion, forms, duration; and the remarkable events which have followed in the world, so far as thay have been by learned men observed: As also two sermons occasioned by the late blazing stars* (Boston: [Samuel Green for Samuel Sewall], 1683).

56. Jacqueline de La Harpe, *L'abbé Laurent Bordelon et la lutte contre la superstition en France entre 1680 et 1730*, University of California Publications in Modern Philology, 26/2 (Berkeley and Los Angeles: University of California Press, 1942), 131–2.

57. This possibility was even known to Bayle: see Pierre Bayle, *Various thoughts on the Occasion of a Comet*, ed. and trans. Robert C. Bartlett (Albany: State University of New York Press, 2000), 18, 24 ff.

58. On this subject in general see Sara Schechner, *Comets, Popular Culture, and the Birth of Modern Cosmology* (Princeton: Princeton University Press, 1999); on Halley's comet and the debates over it see 156–78.

59. Caspar Peucer, *Commentarius, de Praecipuis Divinationum generibus, in quo a prophetiis, authoritate divine traditis, et a Physicis conjecturis, discernuntur artes et imposturae diabolicae, atque observationes natae ex superstitione, et cum hac conjunctae: Et monstrantur fontes ac causae Physicarum praedictionum: Diabolicae vero ac superstitiosae confutatae damnantur, ea serie, quam tabella praefixa ostendit* (Frankfurt: Wechel, Claudius Marnius & heirs of Ioannes Aubrius, 1607), 722 ff.; discussed above, Ch. 12 at note 60.

60. Bayle, *Various thoughts*, ed. Bartlett, 24 ff., 49 ff., 64 ff.

61. Ibid. 76, 131.

62. Ibid. 73 ff.

63. Ibid. 75–6, 88–9.

64. Ibid. 91–3.

65. Ibid. 97 ff.

66. Ibid. 99–104.

67. Ibid. 105–7.

68. Ibid. 113–15.

69. Ibid. 118–19.

70. Ibid. 41–8, and compare with Aubrey above.

71. On the concept of 'prerogative instances', see Stuart Clark, *Thinking with Demons: The Idea of Witchcraft in Early Modern Europe* (Oxford: Clarendon Press, 1997), chapters 16–17.

72. Bayle, *Various thoughts*, ed. Bartlett, 115–16.

73. Ibid. 83.

74. Ibid. 272.

75. Voltaire, *Dictionnaire philosophique*, article 'Miracles', section I, in *Œuvres complètes* (1819–21), vol. 37, 295–302; also in Christiane Mervaud, Andrew Brown and others (eds), *The Complete Works of Voltaire*, vols 35–36 (Oxford: Voltaire Foundation, 1994), vol. 36, 373–84.

76. Bayle, *Various thoughts*, ed. Bartlett, 63, 77–8, 143–4.

77. Ibid. 144 ff., 200 ff.

78. On the role of ridicule see esp. John Redwood, *Reason, Ridicule, and Religion: The Age of Enlightenment in England, 1660–1750* (London: Thames & Hudson, 1976).

79. Anthony Ashley Cooper, Third Earl of Shaftesbury, *Characteristicks of men, manners, opinions, times. In three volumes, i. I. A letter concerning enthusiasm. . . .* ([London], Anno 1711).

80. Ibid. 18.

81. Ibid. 128.

82. [N. P. H. de Montfaucon de Villars], *The Count of Gabalis: or, The extravagant mysteries of the Cabalists exposed, in 5 discourses on the secret sciences*, translated by [Philip Ayres] (London: s.n., 1680).

83. For Paracelsus's system, see above, Ch. 2 at notes 16–17.

84. *The Count of Gabalis*, sigs. A3ʳ–A4ᵛ.

85. Ibid., 28 ff.

86. For the early editions of Bordelon, see above, note 28; see also de la Harpe, *L'abbé Laurent Bordelon*, as above note 56.

87. Bordelon, *Ridiculous Extravagancies of Monsieur Oufle*, book 1, chapters 4–6.

88. Ibid., chapters 8–11.

89. Ibid., chapters 12–15.

90. Ibid., chapter 19.

91. Ibid., book 2, chapters 1–4.

92. Ibid. chapters 5–6.

93. Ibid. chapter 10.

94. Ibid., book 1, chapter 2.

95. Joseph Addison, *The Drummer; or, the Haunted House. A comedy: As it is acted at the Theatre-Royal in Drury-Lane, by His Majesty's servants* (London: Jacob Tonson, 1715).

96. Ibid. 10–11.

97. Ibid. 43–58.

98. Further editions appeared in 1725, 1735, and in Addison's collected works from 1750 onwards, in multiple editions.

99. [Anon.], *Lustiges Abentheuer eines geistlichen Don Quixotte Pater Gassners Teufels-beschwörer in Ellwangen* (Berlin: Christian Ulrich Ringmacher, 1776).

100. Reference for Whitefield: see http://www.oxforddnb.com/view/article/29281?docPos=2 and bibliography.

101. This story is told in John Aubrey, *Miscellanies upon Various Subjects*, 4th edn (London: John Russell Smith, 1857), 79–80.

102. For a detailed interpretation of the engraving, see Bernd Krysmanski, 'We see a ghost: Hogarth's satire on Methodists and Connoisseurs', *Art Bulletin*, 80/2 (1998), 292–310.

103. See e.g. Voltaire, *Dictionnaire philosophique*, articles 'Vampires', 'Apparition' and 'Possédés' in *Œuvres complètes* (1819–21), vol. 38, 447–52; vol. 35, 469–75; vol. 38, 32–4 respectively.

104. For the *Dictionnaire philosophique*, see above, note 29 and below, note 110; David Hume, *Essays, Moral and Political*, 2 vols (Edinburgh: Printed by R. Fleming and A. Alison for A. Kincaid, 1741–2).

105. David Hume, *Four dissertations: I. The natural history of religion. II. Of the passions. III. Of tragedy. IV. Of the standard of taste* (London: printed for A. Millar, 1757).

106. David Hume, *The History of England: From the Invasion of Julius Cæsar to the Revolution in 1688*, 8 vols (London: T. Cadell, 1778).

107. Hume, *Essays, Moral and Political*, i. 141–51.

108. See Hume, *History of England*, chapters 46, 51–2.

109. See e.g. David Hume, *Dialogues Concerning Natural Religion and Other Writings*, ed. Dorothy Coleman (Cambridge: Cambridge University Press, 2007), 12: 'There is indeed a kind of brutish and ignorant scepticism, which gives the vulgar a general prejudice against that which they do not understand . . . This species of scepticism is fatal to knowledge, not to religion; since we find, that those who make greatest profession of it, give often their assent . . . even to the most absurd tenets which a traditional superstition has recommended to them. They firmly believe in witches; though they will not give believe or attend to the most simple proposition of Euclid.'

110. Voltaire, *Œuvres complètes de Voltaire*, 70 vols (Kehl: Société littéraire-typographique, 1785–9). For the story of the expansion of the *Dictionnaire*, see the introduction by A. J. Q. Beuchot in Voltaire, *Œuvres complètes*, 52 vols (Paris: Garnier, 1877–85). The modern edition, ed. by Christiane Mervaud, Andrew Brown and others, *The Complete Works of Voltaire*, vols 35–6 (Oxford: Voltaire Foundation, 1994), preserves only those articles that appeared in Voltaire's own redaction, omitting many of those most useful for this subject.

111. Voltaire, *Dictionnaire philosophique*, art. 'Superstition', sect. 1., in *Œuvres complètes* (1819–21), vol. 38, 304–6; also in *Complete Works*, ed. Mervaud, vol. 36, 536–9.

112. Sect. 2, in *Œuvres complètes* (1819–21), vol. 38, 306–11; also in *Complete Works*, ed. Mervaud, vol. 36, 539–44.

113. Voltaire, *Dictionnaire philosophique*, art. 'Miracles', in *Œuvres complètes* (1819–21), vol. 37, 295–319; 300 for the reference to Chrysostom.

114. Ibid. 296 for the quotation.

115. Voltaire, *Dictionnaire Philosophique*, art. 'Providence' in *Œuvres complètes* (1819–21), vol. 38, 87–9.

116. Ibid., art. 'Enchantement' in *Œuvres complètes* (1819–21), vol. 35, 375–84.

117. Ibid., art. 'Fanatisme', section 5, in *Œuvres complètes* (1819–21), vol. 36, 35–8.

118. Ibid., art. 'Superstition', section 3, in *Œuvres complètes* (1819–21), vol. 38, 311–14.

119. Ibid., art. 'Enthousiasme', in *Œuvres complètes* (1819–21), vol. 35, 400–6.

120. Ibid., art. 'Fanatisme', section 1, in *Œuvres complètes* (1819–21), vol. 36, 19–24.

121. Ibid., section 2, in *Œuvres complètes* (1819–21), vol. 36, 24–30, 27 for the quotation.

122. Ibid., art. 'Eucharistie', in *Œuvres complètes* (1819–21), vol. 35, 523–7.

123. Ibid., art. 'Religion', section 2, in *Œuvres complètes* (1819–21), vol. 38, 151–60.

124. Ibid., art. 'Tolérance', section 2, in *Œuvres complètes* (1819–21), vol. 38, 406–9.

125. Ibid., art. 'Superstition', section 5, in *Œuvres complètes* (1819–21), vol. 38, 316–19; 319 for the quotation.

126. Ibid., esp. 316–17.

127. *Lettres philosophiques*, letters 1–4, in *Œuvres complètes* (1819–21), vol. 24, 3–22.

128. Voltaire, *Dictionnaire Philosophique*, art. 'Tolérance', section 3, in *Œuvres complètes* (1819–21), vol. 38, 409–14.

129. Ibid., art. 'Réliques', in *Œuvres complètes* (1819–21), vol. 38, 174–84.

130. Ibid., art. 'Purgatoire', in *Œuvres complètes* (1819–21), vol. 38, 103–11.

131. Ibid., art. 'Religion', questions 2 and 3, in *Œuvres complètes* (1819–21), vol. 38, 162–9.

132. Ibid., art. 'Asmodée', in *Œuvres complètes* (1819–21), vol. 34, 1–4.

133. Ibid., art. 'Bekker', in *Œuvres complètes* (1819–21), vol. 34, 176–85.

134. Ibid., art. 'Bouc', in *Œuvres complètes* (1819–21), vol. 34, 253–8.

135. Ibid., art. 'Réliques', in *Œuvres complètes* (1819–21), vol. 38, 181.

136. Ibid., art. 'Enchantement', in *Œuvres complètes* (1819–21), vol. 35, 379.

137. Ibid., art. 'Superstition', section 5, in *Œuvres complètes* (1819–21), vol. 38, 316.

138. For this movement in thought see e.g. Paul Henri Thiry, baron d'Holbach (1723–89), *Le bon sens puisé dans la nature. Suivi du Testament du curé Meslier*, 2 vols (Paris: Bouqueton, An 1er [1792/3]).

139. Norman Hampson, 'The Enlightenment', in Euan Cameron (ed.) *Early Modern Europe: An Oxford History* (Oxford: Oxford University Press, 1999), 276.

140. As in Voltaire, *Dictionnaire philosophique*, art. 'Superstition', section 2, in *Œuvres complètes* (1819–21), vol. 38, 306–11.

141. Ibid., art. 'Martyrs', in *Œuvres complètes* (1819–21), vol. 37, 237–55; see also *Acta martyrum: P. Theodorici Ruinart opera ac studio collecta, selecta, atque illustrata* (Verona: ex typographia Tumermaniana, 1731).

142. Midelfort, *Exorcism*, pp 102 ff, 132 ff.

143. Ibid. 143–4 and references; compare Menghi, *Fustis Daemonum, adiurationes formidabiles, potentissimas, et efficaces in malignos spiritus fugandos de oppressis corporibus humanis . . . auctore R. P. F. Hieronymo Mengo Vitellianensi* (Bologna, 1589), later section separately paginated entitled *Remedia Efficacissima*, 65, for the original text, slightly misquoted by Nicolai or his source.

144. See Michelle Vovelle, 'Dechristianization in Year II: Expression or Extinction of a Popular Culture', in Kaspar von Greyerz (ed.), *Religion and Society in Early*

Modern Europe, 1500–1800 (London: German Historical Institute; Boston: Allen & Unwin, 1984), 79–94 and references.

145. See above, Ch. 17 note 66.

146. One of the earliest works to focus single-mindedly on the exceptionality of different races of peoples was Rousseau's *Du Contrat Social*. For developed Romantic-era ethnic theories of history, see e.g. Johann Gottfried Herder (1744–1803), *On World History: An Anthology*, ed., Hans Adler and Ernest A. Menze; trans. Ernest A. Menze with Michael Palma (Armonk, NY: M. E. Sharpe, 1997).

147. See Harm-Peer Zimmermann, *Ästhetische Aufklärung: zur Revision der Romantik in volkskundlicher Absicht* (Würzburg: Königshausen & Neumann, 2001). For collections of folklore, see Jacob Grimm (1785–1863), Wilhelm Grimm (1786–1859) (eds), *Kinder- und Haus-Märchen* 2 vols (Berlin : in der Realschulbuchhandlung, 1812–15); Ludwig Bechstein (1801–60), ed. *Der Sagenschatz und die Sagenkreise des Thüringerlandes*. 4 vols in 2 (Hildburghausen: Kesselring, 1835–38)

148. Ludwig Achim, Freiherr von Arnim (1781–1831), Clemens Brentano (1778–1842) (eds), *Des Knaben Wunderhorn: Alte deutsche Lieder* 3 vols (Heidelberg: Mohr und Zimmer; Leipzig: Breitkopf und Härtel, 1806–8).

149. Jacques-Albin-Simon Collin de Plancy, *Dictionnaire infernal, ou, Recherches et anecdotes, sur les démons, les esprits, les fantômes, les spectres, les revenants, les loup-garoux, les possédés, les sorciers, le Sabbat, les magiciens, les salamandres, les sylphes, les gnomes, etc; les visions, les songes, les prodiges, les charmes, les maléfices, les secrets merveilleux, les talismans, etc.; en un mot, sur tout ce qui tient aux apparitions, à la magie, au commerce de l'enfer, aux divinations, aux sciences secrètes, aux superstitions, aux choses mystérieuses et surnaturelles, etc. etc. etc.* (Paris, P. Mongie aîné, 1818). Collin de Plancy also published a *Dictionnaire critique des reliques et des images miraculeuses*, 3 vols (Paris: Guien, 1821–2); and much later a *Dictionnaire des sciences occultes . . . ou, Répertoire universel des êtres, des personnages, des livres, des faits et des choses qui tiennent aux apparitions, aux divinations, à la magie, au commerce de l'enfer, aux demons, aux sorciers, aux sciences occultes . . . et généralement à toutes les croyances fausses, merveilleuses, surprenantes, mystérieuses ou surnaturelles*, 2 vols (Paris: J. P. Migne, 1860–1).

150. Friedrich Schleiermacher, *On Religion: Speeches to its Cultured Despisers*, ed. and trans. Richard Crouter (Cambridge: Cambridge University Press, 1988), esp. 22 ff.

151. Ibid. 48 for the quotation.

152. See Adolf von Harnack, *Lehrbuch der Dogmengeschichte*, 4th edn, 3 vols (Tübingen: Mohr, 1909–10).

153. Leo XIII's encyclical *Aeterni Patris* gave papal endorsement to a revival of Thomist philosophy and its use in theology on its promulgation on 4 August 1879. For the text see http://www.vatican.va/holy_father/leo_xiii/encyclicals/documents/hf_l-xiii_enc_04081879_aeterni-patris_en.html. An elective course on Thomist demonology was recently taught in the Dominican House of Studies in Washington, DC, under the title MT 718—Angels and Devils (3): see http://www.dhs.edu/academics/moralandspiritualtheology.aspx.

154. On Crowley, see e.g. Lawrence Sutin, *Do what thou wilt: A Life of Aleister Crowley* (New York: St. Martin's Griffin, 2002).

155. For this rather tragic episode, see e.g. Arthur Conan Doyle, *The History of Spiritualism*, 2 vols (London: Cassell, 1926).

156. The *Ghost Hunters* television programme has a website devoted to similar inquiries: see http://www.scifi.com/ghosthunters/

157. See e.g. the works of William A. Christian, including *Person and God in a Spanish Valley*, revised edn (Princeton: Princeton University Press, 1989); *Moving Crucifixes in Modern Spain* (Princeton: Princeton University Press, 1992).

158. This is the central premise of David Gentilcore, *From Bishop to Witch: The System of the Sacred in Early Modern Terra d'Otranto* (Manchester: Manchester University Press, 1992).

159. Stuart A. Vyse, *Believing in Magic: The Psychology of Superstition* (New York and Oxford: Oxford University Press, 1997).

160. Ibid. 219–20.

Bibliography

PRIMARY SOURCES

Addison, Joseph, *The Drummer; or, the Haunted House. A comedy. As it is acted at the Theatre-Royal in Drury-Lane, by His Majesty's servants* (London, 1715)

Ady, Thomas, *The Doctrine of Devils, Proved to be the grand Apostacy of these later Times. An Essay tending to rectifie those Undue Notions and Apprehensions Men have about Daemons and Evil Spirits* (London: Printed for the Author, 1676)

Albertini, Arnaldus, *Tractatus solemnis et aureus de agnosendis assertionibus Catholicis, et haereticis* (Venice: 1571)

Althamer, Andreas, *Eyn Predig von dem Teuffel/das er alles unglueck in der welt anrichte* ([Nuremberg: Jobst Gutknecht], 1532)

Aretius, Benedictus (Benedikt Marti), *Problemata theologica continentia præcipuos christianae religionis locos, brevi et dilucida ratione explicatos* (Lausanne: Franciscus Le Preux, 1578)

Arnim, Ludwig Achim, Freiherr von, and Clemens Brentano (eds), *Des knaben Wunderhorn: Alte deutsche Lieder*, 3 vols (Heidelberg: Ben Mohr und Zimmer; Leipzigs Breitkopf and Härtel, 1806–8)

Ashley Cooper, Anthony, third Earl of Shaftesbury, *Characteristicks of men, manners, opinions, times. In three volumes, i. I. A letter concerning enthusiasm* ([London], 1711)

Athanasius, *Life of Antony*, in *Patrologiae Cursus Completus*, Series Graeca (*PG*), ed. Jacques-Paul Migne, vol. 26, cols. 835–978

—— *The life of Antony and the letter to Marcellinus*, trans. Robert C. Gregg (New York: Paulist Press, 1980)

Aubrey, John, *Miscellanies upon the following subjects . . .* (London: Edward Castle, 1696)

—— *Miscellanies upon Various Subjects*, 4th edn (London: John Russell Smith, 1857)

—— *John Aubrey: Three Prose Works*, ed. John Buchanan-Brown (Fontwell: Centaur Press, 1972)

Augustine of Hippo, *Sancti Aurelii Augustini . . . Opera Omnia*, ed. the Benedictines of St-Maur, 11 vol. (Paris: 1841–2)

Augustine of Hippo, *Confessions*, ed. and trans. Henry Chadwick (Oxford: Oxford University Press, 1991)

—— *De Doctrina Christiana*, ed. and trans. R. P. H. Green, Oxford Early Christian Texts (Oxford: Clarendon Press, 1995)

—— *On Christian Teaching*, ed. and trans. R. P. H. Green (Oxford: Oxford University Press, 1997)

—— *The City of God against the Pagans*, ed. and trans. R. W. Dyson (Cambridge: Cambridge University Press, 1998)

—— *Augustine's Commentary on Galatians: Introduction, Text, Translation, and Notes*, ed. Eric Plumer (Oxford: Oxford University Press, 2003)

Aureolus, Petrus [*c*.1280–1322], *Commentariorum in primum [-quartum] librum Sententiarum*, 2 vols (Rome: Zannetti, 1596–1605)

Bale, John, *The Latter Examination of Mistress Anne Askewe*, in *Select Works of John Bale, D.D., Bishop of Ossory*, ed. Henry Christmas, Parker Society (Cambridge: Cambridge University Press, 1849)

Basin, Bernhardus, 'Opusculum de artibus magicis, ac Magorum Maleficiis', in [Heinrich Institoris (1430–1505)], *Malleus Maleficarum: Maleficas et earum haeresim frameâ conterens, ex variis auctoribus compilatus, & in quator tomos iustè distributus*, 2 vols in 3 (Lyons: Claudius Bourgeat, 1669), ii, part I, 1–17

Baxter, Richard, *The certainty of the worlds of spirits fully evinced by unquestionable histories of apparitions and witchcrafts, operations, voices, &c. proving the immortality of souls, the malice and miseries of the Devil and the damned, and the blessedness of the justified. Written for the conviction of sadduces & infidels* (London: T. Parkhurst and J. Salusbury, 1691)

Bayle, Pierre, *Dictionaire historique et critique*, 2 vols (Rotterdam: R. Leers, 1697); 2nd edn (Rotterdam, 1702)

—— *Lettre à M.L.A.D.C., docteur de Sorbonne, où il est prouvé par plusieurs raisons tirées de la philosophie, & de la theologie que les cometes ne sont point le presage d'aucun malheur* (Cologne [i.e. Rotterdam]: P. Marteau, 1682)

—— *Pensées diverses, écrites à un docteur de Sorbonne, à l'occasion de la cométe qui parut au mois de Decembre 1680* (Rotterdam: R. Leers, 1683)

—— *Commentaire philosophique sur ces paroles de Jésus-Christ: Contrain-les d'entrer*, 'tr. de l'angl. du sieur Jean Fox de Bruggs par M.J.F.', 4 vols ('Canterbury', 1686–8)

—— *Various thoughts on the Occasion of a Comet*, ed. and trans. Robert C. Bartlett (Albany: State University of New York Press, 2000)

Bechstein, Ludwig (ed.), *Der Sagenschatz und die Sagenkreise des Thüringerlandes*. 4 vols in 2 (Hildburghausen: Kesselring, 1835–8)

Becon, Thomas, 'The Acts of Christ and Antichrist', in John Ayre (ed.), *Prayers and other Pieces of Thomas Becon*, Parker Society (Cambridge: Cambridge University Press, 1844), 498–539

Die Bekenntnisschriften der evangelisch-lutherischen Kirche: herausgegeben im Gedenk-jahr der Augsburgischen Konfession 1930, 10th edn (Göttingen: Vandenhoeck & Ruprecht, 1986)

Bekker, Balthasar, *De Philosophia Cartesiana, admonitio candida et sincera* (Wesel: A. ab Hoogenhuysen, 1668)

—— *De betoverde weereld, zynde een grondig ondersoek van't gemeen gevoelen aangaande de geesten, deselver aart en vermogen, bewind en bedrijf: als ook't gene de menschen door derselver kraght en emeenschap doen*, 4 vol. (Amsterdam, D. van den Dalen, 1691–3)

—— *The World Bewitch'd, or, An examination of the common opinions concerning spirits: their nature, power, administration and operations, as also the effects men are able to produce by their communication* (London: Printed for R. Baldwin in Warwick-Lane, 1695)

Bodin, Jean, *De la démonomanie des sorciers* (Paris: Du Puys, 1580)

—— *Universæ naturæ theatrum: in quo rerum omnium effectrices causæ & fines contem-plantur, & continua series quinque libris discutiuntur* (Lyons: Jacques Roussin, 1596)

Bordelon, Laurent, *L'Histoire des imaginations extravagantes de Monsieur Oufle, causées par la lecture des livres qui traitent de la magie, du grimoire, des démoniaques, sorciers ... des fées, ogres ... phantômes & autres revenans, des songes de la pierre philosophale, de l'astrologie judiciaire ... Le tout enrichi de figures, & accompagné d'un tres-grand nombre de nottes curieuses, qui rapportent fidellement les endroits des livres, qui ont causé ses imaginations extravagantes, ou qui peuvent servir pour les combattre*, 2 vol. (Paris: N. Gosselin, 1710)

—— *A History of the Ridiculous Extravagancies of Monsieur Oufle; Occasion'd by his reading Books treating of Magick, the Black-Art, Daemoniacks, Conjurers, Witches, Hobgoblins, Incubus's, Succubus's and the Diabolical-Sabbath; of Elves, Fairies, Wanton Spirits, Genius's, Spectres and Ghosts; of Dreams, the Philosopher's-Stone, Judicial Astrology, Horoscopes, Talismans, Lucky and Unlucky Days, Eclipses, Comets, and all sorts of Apparitions, Divinations, Charms, Enchantments and other Superstitious Practices ...* Written originally in French, by the Abbot B—; and now translated into English (London: J. Morphew, 1711)

Boulton, Richard, *A Compleat History of Magick, Sorcery, and Witchcraft*, 2 vols (London: E. Curll ... J. Pemberton ... and W. Taylor ..., 1715–16)

—— *The Possibility and Reality of Magick, Sorcery, and Witchcraft, demonstrated; or, a Vindication of a Compleat History of Magick ... in answer to Dr. Hutchinson's Historical Essay, etc.* (London: J. Roberts, 1722)

—— *Pandaemonium, or, The devil's cloyster: being a further blow to modern sadduceism, proving the existence of witches and spirits, in a discourse deduced from the fall of the angels, the propagation of Satans kingdom before the flood, the idolatry of the ages after greatly advancing diabolical confederacies, with an account of the lives and transactions of several notorious witches: also, a collection of several authentick relations of strange apparitions of dæmons and spectres, and fascinations of witches, never before printed* (London: J. Walthoe, 1684)

Bozio, Tommasso, *De Signis Ecclesiae libri xxiii* (Cologne: Joannes Gymnicus, 1592)

Bravus, Joannes, *De curandi ratione per medicamenti purgantis exhibitionem libri III* (Salamanca: Cornelius Bonardus, 1588)

Breslay, Pierre, *L'Anthologie ou Recueil de plusieurs discours notables, tirez de diuers bons autheurs Grecs & Latins* (Paris: I. Poupy, 1574)

Browne, Thomas, *Religio medici* (London: Andrew Crooke, 1642); *A True and Full Coppy of that which was most imperfectly and surreptitiously printed before vnder the name of Religio Medici* (London: Printed for Andrew Crook, 1643)

—— *Pseudodoxia Epidemica, or, Enquiries into very many received tenents and commonly presumed truths* (London: Printed by T.H. for E. Dod, 1646)

—— *Pseudodoxia Epidemica, or, Enquiries into very many received tenents, and commonly presumed truths whereunto is added Religio medici, and A discourse of the sepulchral-urnes lately found in Norfolk: together with the garden of Cyrus, or, the quincuncial lozenge, or, Net-work plantations of the ancients, artificially, naturally, mystically considered: with sundry observations* (London: Nathaniel Ekins . . . , 1659)

Bullinger, Heinrich, *De Origine Erroris Libri Duo: in priore agitur de Dei veri iusta invocatione & cultu vero, de Deorum item falsorum religionibus & simulachrorum cultu erroneo: in posteriore disseritur de institutione & vi sacrae Coenae domini, & de origine ac progressu Missae papisticae, contra varias superstitiones pro religione vera antiqua & orthodoxa* (Zurich: Froschauer, 1539)

—— *Wider die Schwartzen Künst, Aberglaeubigs segnen, unwarhafftigs Warsagen, und andere dergleichen von Gott verbottne Künst, in Theatrum de veneficis: Das ist: Von Teufelsgespenst, Zauberern und Gifftbereitern, Schwartzkünstlern, Hexen und Unholden, vieler fürnemmen Historien und Exempel* (Frankfurt am Main: Nicolaus Bassaeus, 1586), 298–306.

—— *The Decades of Henry Bullinger*, ed. Thomas Harding, Parker Society, 4 vols. (Cambridge: Cambridge University Press, 1849–52)

Burton, Robert, *The Anatomy of Melancholy, what it is: With all the kindes, causes, symptomes, prognostickes, and severall cures of it* (Oxford: John Lichfield and James Short, for Henry Cripps, 1621)

—— *The Anatomy of Melancholy* (London: Chatto and Windus, 1927)

—— *The Anatomy of Melancholy*, ed. Thomas C. Faulkner, Nicolas K. Kiessling, and Rhonda L. Blair, 6 vol. (Oxford: Clarendon Press; New York: Oxford University Press, 1989–2000)

Cajetan, Tommaso de Vio, *Commentarii in Summam theologiae S. Thomae Aquinatis* (Venice: Nicolinus, 1593)

Calfhill, James, *An aunswere to the Treatise of the crosse* (London: Henry Denham, for Lucas Harryson, 1565)

—— *An Answer to John Martiall's Treatise of the Cross*, ed. Richard Gibbings, Parker Society (Cambridge: Cambridge University Press, 1846)

Calmet, Augustin, *Dissertations sur les apparitions des anges, des démons & des esprits et sur les revenans et vampires de Hongrie, de Boheme, de Moravie & de Silesie* (Paris: De Bure l'aîné, 1746)

—— *Dissertations upon the apparitions of angels, dæmons, and ghosts, and concerning the vampires of Hungary, Bohemia, Moravia, and Silesia. By the Reverend Father Dom Augustin Calmet, . . . Translated from the French* (London: M. Cooper, 1759)

Calvin, John, *De la predestination eternelle de Dieu, par laquelle les uns sont eleuz à salut, les autres laissez en leur condemnation; Aussi de la providence par laquelle il gouverne les choses humanines* (Geneva: Jehan Crespin, 1552).

—— *De Aeterna Dei Praedestinatione, qua in salutem alios ex hominibus elegit, alios suo exitio reliquit: item de providentia qua res humanas gubernat, consensus pastorum Genevensis Ecclesiae a Io. Calvino expositus* (Geneva: Joannes Crispinus, 1552)

—— *Ioannis Calvini Opera quae supersunt Omnia* ed. Guilielmus Baum, Eduardus Cunitz, Eduardus Reuss, 59 vol. Corpus Reformatorum, 29–87 (Brunswick, Berlin: Schwetschke, 1863–1900)

—— *Avertissement contre l'astrologie judiciaire*, ed. Olivier Millet, (Geneva: Droz, 1985)

Canisius, Petrus, *Summa doctrinae christianae* (Vienna: Zimmermannus, 1555)

Cardano, Girolamo, *Hieronymi Cardani mediolanensis medici De rerum varietate libri XVII* (Basle: Henrichus Petri, 1557)

—— *Hieronymi Cardani Medici Mediolanensis De subtilitate Libri XXI* (Nuremberg: Iohannes Petreius, 1550)

Carletti, Angelo, of Chivasso, *Summa angelica de casibus conscientiae* (Chivasso: Jacobinus Suigus, de Suico, 1486)

Casaubon, Meric, *A Treatise Proving Spirits, Witches, and Supernatural Operations, by Pregnant Instances and Evidences* (London: Brabazon Aylmer, 1672)

Cassian, John, *Opera*, ed. M. Petschenig, Corpus Scriptorum Ecclesiasticorum Latinorum, 2 (Vienna, 1886)

—— *Conferences*, ed. in P. Schaff et al. (eds), A Select Library of the Nicene and Post-Nicene Fathers, 2nd series, 11 (Grand Rapids, MI: Eerdmans, 1956)

Castañega, Martín de, *Tratado de las supersticiones y hechizerias y de la possibilidad y remedio dellas, 1529* (Madrid: Sociedad de Bibliofilos Espanoles, 2nd series, 17, 1946).

—— ed. and trans. David H. Darst, 'Witchcraft in Spain: The Testimony of Martin de Castañega's Treatise on Superstition and Witchcraft (1529)', *Proceedings of the American Philosophical Society*, 123/5 (1979), 298–322

—— *Tratado de las supersticiones y hechizerias y de la possibilidad y remedio dellas (1529)*, ed. Juan Robert Muro Abad (Logroño: Gobierno de La Rioja, Instituto de Estudios Riojanos, 1994)

Catechismus, ex decreto Concilii Tridentini, ad parochos, Pii Quinti Pont. Max. iussu editus (Rome: Paulus Manutius, 1566)

Chassanaeus, Bartholomaeus, *Catalogus gloriae mundi libr. XII.* (Lyons, 1529)

Chemnitz, Martin, *Examination of the Council of Trent*, trans. Fred Kramer, 4 vol. (St Louis, MO: Concordia, 1971–86)

Ciruelo, Pedro, *Reprouacion delas supersticiones y hechizerias: Libro muy utile y necessario a todos los buenos christianos*, etc. (Salamanca: P. de Castro, a costa del honrrado varon G. de Milis, 1539)

—— *Reprovación de las supersticiones y hechizerías (1538)*, ed. José Luis Herrero Ingelmo (Salamanca: Diputación de Salamanca, 2003),

—— *Pedro Ciruelo's A treatise reproving all superstitions and forms of witchcraft: very necessary and useful for all good Christians zealous for their salvation*, ed. and trans. E. A. Maio and D. W. Pearson (Rutherford, NJ: Fairleigh Dickinson University Press, 1977)

Corpus Juris Canonici, ed. Aemilius Ludouicus Richter and Aemilius Friedberg, 2 vol. (Graz: Akademische Druck- u. Verlagsanstalt, 1959)

Collin de Plancy, Jacques-Albin-Simon, *Dictionnaire infernal, ou, Recherches et anecdotes, sur les démons, les esprits, les fantômes, les spectres, les revenants, les loup-garoux, les possédés, les sorciers, le Sabbat, les magiciens, les salamandres, les sylphes, les gnomes, etc.; les visions, les songes, les prodiges, les charmes, les maléfices, les secrets merveilleux, les talismans, etc.; en un mot, sur tout ce qui tient aux apparitions, à la magie, au commerce de l'enfer, aux divinations, aux sciences secrètes, aux superstitions, aux choses mystérieuses et surnaturelles, etc. etc. etc.* (Paris, P. Mongie aîné, 1818)

Crouch, Nathaniel, *The Kingdom of Darkness: or The History of Dæmons, Specters, Witches, Apparitions, Possessions, Disturbances, and other wonderful and supernatural Delusions, Mischievous Feats, and Malicious Impostures of the Devil. Containing near Fourscore memorable Relations, Forreign and Domestick, both Antient and Modern. Collected from Authentick Records, Real Attestations, Credible Evidences, and asserted by Authors of Undoubted Verity* (London: [Printed for the Author], 1688)

Cyprian of Carthage, 'On the Vanity of Idols' as trans. in *The Ante-Nicene Fathers: Translations of the Writings of the Fathers down to A.D. 325*, ed. and trans. Alexander Roberts and James Donaldson, 10 vol. (Edinburgh: T. & T. Clark; Grand Rapids, MI: Eerdmans, 1989–90), v. 465–9

Daillon, Jacques, 'Comte du Lude', Δαιμονολογια: *or, a Treatise of spirits. Wherein several places of Scripture are expounded, against the vulgar errors concerning witchcraft, apparitions, &c. To which is added, an appendix, containing some reflections on Mr. Boulton's answer to Dr. Hutchinson's Historical Essay; entitled The Possibility and Reality of Magick, Sorcery and Witchcraft demonstrated* (London: Printed for the Author, 1723)

Daneau, Lambert, *Dialogus de Veneficis*, in Nicolas Jacquier, Joannes Myntzen-bergius, Nicolas Bassée, Lambert Daneau, Joachim Camerarius, Martín de Arles y Andosilla, Johannes Trithemius, and Thomas Erastus, *Flagellum hæreticorum fascinariorum* (Frankfurt: Nicolaus Bassaeus, 1581), 184–299

Darrell, John, *A detection of that sinnful, shamful, lying, and ridiculous discours, of Samuel Harshnet. entituled: A discouerie of the fravvdulent practises of Iohn Darrell* (England, no place or printer, 1600)

—— *The replie of Iohn Darrell, to the answer of Iohn Deacon, and Iohn Walker, concerning the doctrine of the possession and dispossession of demoniakes* (England, no place or printer, 1602)

Delrio, Martinus (Martín del Rio) SJ, *Disquisitionum Magicarum Libri Sex*, 3 vol. (Louvain: Gerardus Rivius, 1599–1600)

del Rio, Martín, *Investigations into Magic*, ed. and trans. P. G. Maxwell-Stuart (Manchester and New York: Manchester University Press, 2000)

Digby, Kenelm, *A late discourse made in a solemne assembly of nobles and learned men at Montpellier in France . . . touching the cure of wounds by the powder of sympathy; with instructions how to make the said powder; whereby many other secrets of nature are unfolded*, trans. R. White (London: R. Lownes and T. Davies: 1658)

Dives and Pauper, ed. Priscilla Heath Barnum, 3 vols, Early English Text Society, nos. 275, 280, 323 (London: Oxford University Press, 1976–2004)

Duns Scotus, Johannes, *Joanni Duns Scoti . . . Opera Omnia*, ed. L. Wadding, 26 vols (Paris: Ludovicus Vives, 1891–5)

Eberlin, Johann, von Günzburg, *Wider die schender der Creaturen Gottes, durch Weyhen, oder segnen, des Saltzs, Wasser, Palmen, kraut, wachss, fewr ayer, Fladen &c: nit zür achtung der Creatur, allain meldung der gotslesterlichen betrüglichen falsch glaubigen yrrsalen* (Augsburg: Heinrich Steiner, 1525)

Enchiridion Leonis Papae, serenissimo imperatori Carolo Magno in munus pretiosum datum, nuperrimè mendis omnibus purgatum (Mainz: no imprint, 1633)

Erasmus, Desiderius, *Opus Epistolarum Des. Erasmi Roterdami*, ed. P. S. Allen, 12 vols (Oxford: Clarendon Press, 1906–58)

—— *The Colloquies of Erasmus*, ed. C. R. Thompson (Chicago: University of Chicago Press, 1965)

—— *Collected Works of Erasmus* (Toronto; Buffalo: University of Toronto Press, 1974–)

—— *Praise of Folly*, in *Collected Works of Erasmus*, vol. 27: *Literary and Educational Writings*, 5, ed. A. H. T. Levi (Toronto: University of Toronto Press 1986)

Erastus, Thomas, *Disputationum de medicina nova Philippi Paracelsi pars prima [. . . quarta]: in qua, quae de remediis superstitiosis & magicis curationibus ille prodidit, praecipuè examinantur*, 4 parts in 2 vols (Basle: Petrus Perna, 1571–3)

—— *Repetitio Disputationis de lamiis seu strigibus, in qua solide et perspicue, de arte earum, potestate, itemque poena disceptatur* (Basle: Petrus Perna, 1578)

Espina, Alfonso de (Alphonsus de Spina), *Fortalitium fidei* (Lyons: Gulielmus Balsarin, 1487)

Eynatten, Maximilian van, *Manuale Exorcismorum: continens instructiones, et exorcismos ad eiiciendos e corporibus obsessis spiritus malignos* (Antwerp: Plantin-Moretus, 1626)

Ficinus, Marsilius, *M. Ficini . . . Opera*, 2 vols (Basle: Henricpetri, 1576)

Förner, Friedrich, *Panoplia armaturae Dei, adversus omnem superstitionum, divinationum, excantationum, demonolatriam, et universas magorum, veneficorum, et sagarum, et ipsiusmet Sathanae insidias, praestigias et infestationes* (Ingolstadt: Gregorius Haenlinius, 1626)

Foxe, John, *The Acts and Monuments*, ed. Joseph Pratt, 8 vol. (London: Religious Tract Society, 1877)

Geiler, Johannes, von Kaisersberg, *Die Emeis, dis ist das büch von der Omeissen* (Strasbourg: Johannes Grieninger, 1517)

Gerson, Jean, *Joannis Gersonii Doctoris Theologi & Cancellarii Parisiensis Opera Omnia*, ed. Ludovicus Ellies du Pin, 5 vols, 2nd edn (The Hague: P. de Hondt, 1728)

—— *Œuvres complètes*, ed. Palémon Glorieux (Paris, New York: Descleé, 1960–)

Glanvill, Joseph, *A Blow at Modern Sadducism in Some Philosophical Considerations about Witchcraft: to which is added the relation of the fam'd disturbance by the drummer in the house of Mr. John Mompesson, with some reflections on drollery and atheisme* (London: Printed by E.C. for James Collins, 1668)

—— and Henry More, *Saducismus Triumphatus: Or, Full and Plain Evidence Concerning Witches and Apparitions. In Two Parts. The First treating of their Possibility; The Second of their Real Existence. The Third Edition. The Advantages whereof above the former, the Reader may understand out of Dr H. More's Account prefixed thereunto. With two Authentick, but wonderful Stories of certain Swedish Witches; done into English by Anth. Horneck, D.D.* (London: S. Lownds, 1688)

Godelmann, Johann Georg, *Tractatus de Magis, Veneficis et Lamiis, deque his recte cognoscendis et puniendis* (Frankfurt: Nicolaus Bassaeus, 1601)

Gorkum, Heinrich von, *Tractatus de supersticiosis quibusdam casibus* (Esslingen: Conrad Fyner, 1473)

Gretser, Jakob, *De Cruce Christi* (Ingolstadt: Adam Sartorius, 1598)

Grimm, Jacob, and Wilhelm Grimm (eds), *Kinder- und Haus-Märchen*, 2 vols (Berlin: Realschulbuchhandlung, 1812–15)

Gyfford, George, *A Discourse of the subtill Practises of Devilles by Witches and Sorcerers. By which men are and have bin greatly deluded* (London: [T. Orwin] for Toby Cooke, 1587)

Hamilton, Alastair (ed.), *Documenta Anabaptistica Neerlandica*, vi. *Cronica. Ordo sacerdotis. Acta HN* (Leiden and New York: Brill, 1988)

Hansen, Joseph (ed.), *Quellen und Untersuchungen zur Geschichte des Hexenwahns und der Hexenverfolgung im Mittelalter* (Hildesheim: G. Olms, 1963, reprint of the original edition, Bonn: C. Georgi, 1901)

Harsnett, Samuel, *A Declaration of Egregious Popish Impostures to withdraw the harts of her Maiesties subiects from their allegeance, and from the truth of Christian religion professed in England, under the pretence of casting out devils* (London: James Roberts, 1603)

Heerbrandus, Jacobus, *De Magia Disputatio ex cap. 7. Exo.,... praeside reverendo et clarissimo viro Jacobo Heerbrando, sacrae theologiae Doctore eximio, ac eiusdem in Academia Tubingensi Professore publico... Nicolaus Falco Salueldensis... respondere conabitur* (Tübingen: [Ulrich Morhart], 1570)

Hemmerli, Felix, 'Tractatus I de exorcismis', in *Malleus Maleficarum* (Frankfurt: Nicolaus Bassaeus, 1600), ii. 378 ff.; 'Tractatus Secundus exorcismorum seu adiurationum', ibid., ii. 397 ff.; 'Tractatus III de Credulitate Daemonibus Adhibenda', ibid., ii. 422 ff.

Hemmingsen, Niels (Nicolaus Hemmingius), *Admonitio de superstitionibus magicis vitandis, in gratiam sincerae religionis amantium* (Copenhagen: Iohannes Stockelman and Andreas Gutterwitz, 1575)

Herder, Johann Gottfried, *On World History: An Anthology*, ed. Hans Adler and Ernest A. Menze; trans. Ernest A. Menze with Michael Palma (Armonk, NY: M. E. Sharpe, 1997)

Hittorpius, Melchior, *De divinis Catholicae Ecclesiae officiis ac ministeriis, varii vetustorum aliqvot ecclesiae patrum ac scriptorum libri, videlicet B. Isidori Hispalensis Episcopi, Albini Flacci Alcuini, Amalarii Trevirens. Episcopi, Hrabani Mauri Moguntineñ Episcopi, VValafridi Strabonis Abbatis, B. Ivonis Episcopi Carnotensis, & quorundam aliorum* (Cologne: Gervinus Calenius & haeredes Iohannis Quentel, 1568)

Historia von D. Johann Fausten (Frankfurt: Spies, 1587)

Hobbes, Thomas, *Leviathan*, ed. C. B. Macpherson (Harmondsworth: Penguin, 1968)

Holbach, Paul Henri Thiry, baron d', *Le bon sens puisé dans la nature. Suivi du Testament du curé Meslier*, 2 vols (Paris: Bouqueton, An 1er [1792/1793])

Homes, Nathanael, *Dæmonologie, and Theologie. The first, The Malady, Demonstrating the Diabolicall Arts, and Devillish hearts of Men. The Second, The Remedy: Demonstrating, God a rich Supply of all Good* (London: Thomas Roycroft, John Martin, and John Ridley, 1650)

Hoogstraten, Jacobus van, *Tractus magistralis declarans quam graviter peccent querentes auxilium a maleficis; Contra petentes remedia a maleficis* (Cologne: Martinus de Werdena, 1510)

Hooper, John, *Early writings of John Hooper, D.D., Lord Bishop of Gloucester and Worcester, Martyr, 1555: Comprising The declaration of Christ and his office. Answer to Bishop Gardiner. Ten commandments. Sermons on Jonas. Funeral sermon*, ed. Samuel Carr, Parker Society (Cambridge: Cambridge University Press, 1843)

Hooper, John, *Later writings of Bishop Hooper: together with his letters and other pieces*, ed. Charles Nevinson, Parker Society (Cambridge: Cambridge University Press, 1852)

Hosius, Stanislaus, *Confutatio prolegomenon Brentii: quae primum scripsit aduersus venerabilem virum Petrum à Soto, deinde verò Petrus Paulus Vergerius apud Polonos temerè defendenda suscepit* (Cologne: Maternus Cholinus, 1560)

Hume, David, *Essays, Moral and Political*, 2 vols (Edinburgh: Printed by R. Fleming and A. Alison for A. Kincaid, 1741–2)

——*Four dissertations: I. The natural history of religion. II. Of the passions. III. Of tragedy. IV. Of the standard of taste* (London: Printed for A. Millar, 1757)

——*The History of England: From the Invasion of Julius Cæsar to the Revolution in 1688*, 8 vols (London: T. Cadell, 1778)

——*Dialogues Concerning Natural Religion and Other Writings*, ed. Dorothy Coleman (Cambridge: Cambridge University Press, 2007)

Hunger, Albrecht, *De Magia Theses Theologicae, in celebri et catholica academia Ingolstadiana An. S. N. M.D.LXXIIII, die 21 Junii per Reverendum et eruditum virum M. Hectorem Wegman Augustanum, SS. Theologiae Baccalaureum formatum, Divae Virginis apud eandem Academiam Parochum, pro impetrando Licentiae gradu, ad publicam disputationem propositae: Praeside Reverendo et Clarissimo viro Alberto Hungero, SS. Theologiae Doctore et Professore ordinario, Collegii Theologici pro tempore decano* (Ingolstadt: Weissenhorn, 1574)

Hutchinson, Francis, *A short view of the pretended spirit of prophecy, taken from its first rise in the year 1688, to its present state among us* (London: J. Morphew, 1708)

——*An Historical Essay concerning Witchcraft* (London: R. Knaplock [etc.], 1718)

Iamblichus, of Chalcis, *Iamblichus de mysteriis Aegyptiorum* (Lyons: Tornaesius, 1549)

——*Iamblichus de Mysteriis Aegyptiorum, Chaldaeorum, Assyriorum. Proclus in Platonicum Alcibiadem de anima atque daemone. Idem de sacrificio & magia. Porphyrius de diuinis atq; daemonib. Psellus de daemonibus. Mercurii Trismegisti Pimander* (Lyons: J. Tornaesius, 1577)

Institoris, Heinricus, and Jakobus Sprenger (attrib.), *Malleus Maleficarum: Maleficas et earum hæresim frameâ conterens, ex variis auctoribus compilatus, & in quator tomos iusté distributus* 2 vols in 3 (Lyons: Claudius Bourgeat, 1669)

——and Jakobus Sprenger (attrib.), *Malleus Maleficarum*, ed. and trans. Christopher S. Mackay, 2 vol. (Cambridge: Cambridge University Press, 2006)

Isidore, of Seville, *The Etymologies of Isidore of Seville*, ed. and trans. Stephen A. Barney, W. J. Lewis, J. A. Beach, and Oliver Berghof (Cambridge: Cambridge University Press, 2006)

Isolani, Isidoro, *Libellus adversus Magos: Divinatores: Maleficos: eosque qui ad religionem subeundam maleficis artibus quempiam cogi posse asseverant* (Milan, 1506)

Jacquier, Nicolas, Joannes Myntzenbergius, Nicolas Bassée, Lambert Daneau, Joachim Camerarius, Martìn de Arles y Andosilla, Johannes Trithemius, and Thomas Erastus, *Flagellum hæreticorum fascinariorum* (Frankfurt: Nicolaus Bassaeus, 1581)

Jakob, of Jüterbogk (also known as Jacobus de Clusa), 'De Potestate Daemonum, Arte Magica, Superstitionibus et Illusionibus eorundem', in Cornell University Archives, MS 4600 Bd. Ms. 4, fos. 183^r–257^v

Jewel, John, *The Works of John Jewel, Bishop of Salisbury*, ed. John Ayre, 4 vols, Parker Society (Cambridge: Cambridge University Press, 1845–50)

Karlstadt, Andreas Bodenstein von, *Von geweychtem Wasser vnd Saltz . . . Wider den vnuerdienten Gardian Franciscus Seyler* (Wittenberg: Johann Grunenberg, 1520)

—— *Antwort Andres Bo. von Carolstad Doctor geweicht wasser belangend: wider einen bruder Johan. Fritzhans genant: holtzuger ordens.* (Wittenberg: Melchior Lotter, 1521)

The Key of Solomon the King/Clavicula Salomonis, trans. and ed. S. Liddell MacGregor Mathers (London: Kegan Paul, Trench, Trübner, 1909)

Knox, John, *The Works of John Knox*, ed. David Laing, 6 vols (Edinburgh: T. G. Stevenson, 1854–64)

Lavater, Ludwig, *De spectris, lemuribus et magnis atque insolitis fragoribus, variisque praesagitionibus quae plerunque obitum hominum, magnas clades, mutationesque imperiorum praecedunt, liber unus* (Geneva: Anchora Crispiniana, 1570).

—— *Of ghostes and spirites, vvalking by night and of straunge noyses, crackes, and sundrie forewarnings: which commonly happen before the death of men: great slaughters, and alterations of kingdoms*, trans. Robert Harrison (London: Thomas Creede, 1596)

The Lay Folks Mass Book; or, The manner of hearing mass, with rubrics and devotions for the people, in four texts, and office in English according to the use of York, from manuscripts of the Xth to the XVth century, ed. Thomas Frederick Simmons, Early English Text Society, original series, no. 71 (London: N. Trübner & Co., 1879)

Lebrun, Pierre, *Histoire critique des pratiques superstitieuses: qui ont seduit les peuples, & embarassé les sçavans: avec la methode et les principes pour discerner les effets naturels d'avec ceux qui ne le sont pas* (Rouen and Paris: Jean de Nully, 1702; also Amsterdam: H. Schelte, 1702)

Lefèvre, Jacques, d'Étaples, *In hoc opere continentur totius philosophie naturalis paraphrases: adiecto ad litteram familiari commentario declarate* (Paris: Wolfgang Hopyl, 1502)

—— *Divini Dionysii Areopagite Caelesti hierarchia; Ecclesiastica hierarchia; Divina nomina; Mystica theologia; Undecim epistolae: Ignatii Undecim epistolae. Polycarpi Epistola una. Theologia viuificans Cibus solidus* (Venice: Joannes Tacuinus, 1502)

Le Loyer, Pierre, sieur de La Brosse (1550–1634), *IIII. livres des spectres, ou apparitions et visions d'esprits, anges et démons se monstrans sensiblement aux homes* (Angers: G. Nepueu, 1586)

Lenglet Dufresnoy, Nicolas, *Recueil de dissertations, anciennes et nouvelles: sur les apparitions, les visions et les songes*, 2 vols (Avignon; Paris: Jean-Noel Leloup, 1751)

'Lercheimer, Augustin' (= Hermann Wilken or Witekind, d. 1603), *Ein Christlich Bedencken unnd Erinnerung von Zauberey*, published in *Theatrum de veneficis: Das ist: Von Teufelsgespenst, Zauberern und Gifftbereitern, Schwartzkünstlern, Hexen und Unholden, vieler fürnemmen Historien und Exempel* (Frankfurt am Main: Nicolaus Bassaeus, 1586), 261–98

Luther, Martin, *Decem Praecepta wittenbergensi predicata populo. Per P. Martinum Luther Augustinianum* (Wittenberg: Johann Rhau-Grunenberg, 1518)

—— *Colloquia mensalia: or, Dr. Martin Luther's divine discourses at his table, &c.*...Collected first together by Dr. Antonius Lauterbach, and afterward disposed into certain common places by John Aurifaber. Translated out of the high Germane into the English tongue by Capt. Henrie Bell (London, 1652)

—— *Luthers Werke: Kritische Gesamtausgabe* (Weimar: Böhlaus Nachfolger, 1883–1948)

—— *Luther's Works*, ed. J. J. Pelikan, H. C. Oswald, H. T. Lehmann, 55 vols (St Louis: Concordia, and Philadelphia Louis: Fortress Press, 1955–86)

Lyndwood, William, *Lyndwood's Provinciale: The text of the canons therein contained, reprinted from the translation made in 1534*, ed. J. V. Bullard and H. Chalmer Bell (London: Faith Press, 1929)

Magnus, Olaus (Olaf Magnusson), *Historia de gentibus septentrionalibus* (Rome: Ioannes Maria de Viottis, 1555)

—— *Description of the Northern Peoples*, trans. Peter Fisher and Humphrey Higgens, ed. Peter Foote, 3 vols, Hakluyt Society; 2nd series, nos. 182, 187–8 (London, 1996–8)

Majoli, Simone, *Simonis Maioli...Dies caniculares: seu, Colloquia tria, & viginti. Quibus pleraque naturae admiranda, quae aut in aethere fiunt, aut in Europa, Asia, atque Africa, quin etiam in ipso orbe nouo, & apud omnes antipodas sunt, recensentur* (Rome: J. A. Ruffinelli, 1597)

Manuel ou enchiridion de prières (Lyons: no imprint, 1584)

Martiall, John, *A treatyse of the Crosse gathred out of the scriptures, councelles, and auncient fathers of the primitive church* (Antwerp: John Latius, 1564)

—— *A replie to M. Calfhills blasphemous answer made against the treatise of the crosse* (Louvain: John Bogard, 1566)

Martín, of Arles y Andosilla, *Tractatus insignis et exquisitissimus de superstitionibus contra maleficia seu sortilegia que hodie vigent in orbe terrarum: in lucem nuperrime editus* (Paris: [P. Gromors], 1517); another edition (Rome: Vincentius Luchinus, 1559); see also the edition in *Tractatus Universi Juris*, xi, pt. 2 (Lyons, 1584), fos. 402$^\mathrm{v}$–8$^\mathrm{r}$

Martin of Braga, *Martin von Bracaras Schrift De Correctione Rusticorum, zum ersten Male vollständig und in verbessertem Text herausgegeben*, ed. Carl Paul Caspari (Christiania: Mallingschen Buchdruckerei, 1883)

Mazzolini, Silvestro, da Prierio, *Summa Summarum, que Sylvestrina dicitur* (Bologna: Hector, 1515)

—— (Silvester Prierias), *De Strigimagarum Demonumque Mirandis libri tres* (Rome: Antonius Bladis de Asula, 24 Sept. 1521)

Mede, Joseph, *The apostasy of the latter times: in which (according to divine prediction) the world should wonder after the beast, the mystery of iniquity should so farre prevaile over the mystery of godlinesse, whorish Babylon over the virgin-church of Christ, as that the visible glory of the true church should be much clouded, the true unstained Christian faith corrupted, the purity of true worship polluted: or, the gentiles theology of dæmons, i.e. inferious divine powers, supposed to be mediatours between God and man: revived in the latter times amongst Christians, in worshipping of angels, deifying and invocating of saints, adoring and templing of reliques, bowing downe to images, worshipping of crosses, &c.: all which, together with a true discovery of the nature, originall, progresse of the great, fatall, and solemn apostasy are cleared* (London: Richard Bishop and Samuel Man, 1642)

Melanchthon, Philipp, *Deuttung der czwo grewlichen Figuren Bapstesels czu Rom und Munchkalbs zu Freyberg ynn Meysszen funden* (Wittenberg: Johann Rhau-Grunenberg, 1523)

—— *Philippi Melanthonis Opera quae supersunt omnia*, ed. Carolus Gottlieb Bretschneider, Corpus Reformatorum, 1–28 (Halle: C. A. Schwetschke and son, 1834–60)

Menghi, Girolamo, *Compendio dell'arte essorcistica, et possibilita delle mirabili, et stupende operationi delli demoni, et dei malefici. Con li rimedii opportuni alle infirmità maleficiali* (Bologna: Giovanni Rossi, 1582)

—— *Flagellum Daemonum, exorcismos terribiles, potentissimos, et efficaces: Remediaque probatissima, ac doctrina singularem in malignos spiritos expellendos, facturasque et maleficia fuganda de obsessis corporibus complectens* (Bologna: Giovanni Rossi, 1589)

—— *Fustis Daemonum, adiurationes formidabiles, potentissimas, et efficaces in malignos spiritus fugandos de oppressis corporibus humanis . . . auctore R. P. F. Hieronymo Mengo Vitellianensi* (Bologna: Giovanni Rossi, 1589) [usually printed with the *Flagellum Daemonum*]

Mombritius, Boninus, *Sanctuarium seu Vitae sanctorum*, 2 vols (Hildesheim and New York: Georg Olms, 1978)

Montfaucon de Villars, N. P. H. de, *The Count of Gabalis: or, The extravagant mysteries of the Cabalists exposed, in 5 discourses on the secret sciences*, trans. [Philip Ayres] (London: s.n., 1680)

Muggleton, Lodowick, *A True Interpretation Of the Witch of Endor. Spoken of in 1 Sam. 28, begin, at the 11. Verse* (London: s.n., 1669)

Mutianus Rufus, Conradus, *Der Briefwechsel des Mutianus Rufus*, ed. Karl Krause (Kassel: A. Freyschmidt, 1885)

Nemesius, *On the Nature of Man*, trans. Philip van der Eijk and R. W. Sharples (Liverpool: Liverpool University Press, 2008)

Nider, Johannes, *Johannis Nideri theologi olim clarissimi De visionibus ac revelationibus: opus rarissimum historiis Germaniæ refertissimum, anno 1517, Argentinæ editum* (Helmstedt: Paulus Zeisingius, Salomon Schnorrius, 1692)

—— *Preceptorium Divine Legis* (Basle: Berthold Ruppel, *c.*1470)

Osuna, Franciscus de [attrib.], *Flagellum Diaboli, oder Dess Teufels Gaisl, darin gar lustig und artlich gehandelt wird: Von der Macht und Gewalt dess boesen Feindts: von den effecten und Wirckungen der Zauberer Unholdter und Hexenmaister* (Munich: Adam Berg, 1602)

Palladius, *Historia Lausiaca*, in Migne, *PL*, vol. 73, cols. 1066–1234

—— *The Lausiac History of Palladius: A Critical Discussion Together with Notes on Early Egyptian Monachism*, ed. Cuthbert Butler, 2 vols in 1 (Hildesheim: Olms, 1967)

—— *The Lausiac History*, ed. and trans. Robert T. Meyer (New York: Newman Press, 1964)

Paphnutius, *The Life of St Humphrey (Saint Onofrius), Hermit*, trans. Dean Kavanagh (London: Burns and Oates, 1906)

Paracelsus, Theophrastus ('Theophrastus Bombast von Hohenheim'), *Opera Omnia*, 3 vols (Geneva: Joannes Antonius & Samuel de Tournes, 1658)

—— *Paracelsus: Selected Writings*, ed. Jolande Jacobi (Princeton: Princeton University Press, 1979)

Pererius, Benedictus, Valentinus, SJ (Benito Pereira), *Adversus Fallaces et Superstitiosas Artes, Id est, De Magia, de Observatione somniorum, et de Divinatione Astrologica, Libri tres* (Ingolstadt: Sartorius, 1591)

Perkins, William, *Works* (London: Cantrell Legge, Printer to the Universitie of Cambridge, 1618)

Petrus, de Palude, *Scriptum in librum quartum sententiarum* (Venice: Bonetus Locatellus and Octauianus Scotus, 1493)

Petrus, Lombardus (Peter Lombard), *Sententiarum libri quatuor, per Joannem Aleaume . . . pristino suo nitori veré restituti*, 4 vols (Paris: J.-P. Migne, 1853)

Peucer, Kaspar, *Commentarius de Praecipuis Divinationum Generibus: in quo à prophetijs diuina autoritate traditis, et physicis praedictionibus, separantur diabolicae fraudes & superstitiosae obseruationes, & explicantur fontes ac causae physicarum praedictionum, diabolicae et superstitiosae confutatae damnantur* (Wittenberg: Johannes Crato, 1553)

—— *Commentarius, de Praecipuis Divinationum generibus, in quo a prophetiis, authoritate divine traditis, et a Physicis conjecturis, discernuntur artes et imposturae diabolicae, atque observationes natae ex superstitione, et cum hac conjunctae: Et monstrantur fontes ac causae Physicarum praedictionum: Diabolicae vero ac superstitiosae confutatae damnantur, ea serie, quam tabella praefixa ostendit* (Frankfurt: Wechel, Marnius & Aubrius, 1593 and 1607)

Pius II (Piccolomini, Enea Silvio), *Pii II Commentarii rerum memorabilium que temporibus suis contigerunt*, ed. Adrianus van Heck, 2 vols, Studi e testi, 312–13 (Città del Vaticano: Biblioteca apostolica vaticana, 1984)

Plantsch, Martin, *Opusculum de sagis maleficis* (Pforzheim: Thomas Anshelm, 1507)

Polidoro, Valerio, *Practica Exorcistarum* (Padua: Paulus Meietus, 1587)

Praetorius, Antonius, *Gründlicher Bericht von Zauberey und Zauberern, deren Ursprung, Unterscheid, Vermögen und Handlungen, Auch wie einer Christlichen Obrigkeit, solchen schändlichen Laster zu Begegnen* (Frankfurt: Stoltzenberger, 1629)

Psellus, Michael (attrib.), *Michaelis Pselli De Operatione Daemonum Dialogus*, ed. and trans. Gilbertus Gaulminus Molinensis (Paris: H. Drouart, 1615)

—— *Psellus' dialogue on the operation of daemons: now, for the first time translated into English from the original Greek*, trans. Marcus Collisson (Sydney: James Tegg, 1843)

Regino of Prüm, *Libri duo de synodalibus causis et disciplinis ecclesiasticis*, ed. Friedrich G. A. Wasserschleben, 1840 (repr. Graz: Akademische Druck- u.Verlagsanstalt, 1964)

Remi, Nicolas, *Nicolai Remigii daemonolatreiae Libri tres, Ex Iudiciis Capitalibus Nongentorum plus minus hominum* (Cologne: Henricus Falckenburg, 1596; also Frankfurt: Palthen, 1596)

Rivius, Johannes, of Attendorn, *Joannis Rivii Athendoriensis De spectris et apparitionibus umbrarum seu de vetere superstitione liber* ([Leipzig?], 1541)

Schaff, P., et al. (eds), *A Select Library of the Nicene and Post-Nicene Fathers*, 1st series, 14 vols (Grand Rapids, MI: Eerdmans, 1983–6)

Schleiermacher, Friedrich, *On Religion: Speeches to its Cultured Despisers*, ed. and trans. Richard Crouter (Cambridge: Cambridge University Press, 1988)

Schott, Gaspar, *Magia Universalis*, 4 vols (Würzburg: Schönwetter and Pigrin, 1657–9)

Schuts, Jacobus, *De betoverde Bekker, ofte, Een overtuygent bewijs dat het boek vande Heer Bekker, genaemt De betoverde weerelt, doorsaeyt is met de onredelijkste redenering, notoirste onwaarheeden, en andere schadelijcke gevolgen: waar door de waare reeden verlogent, de waarheyt vervalst, en de deught ontsenuwt wert* (The Hague: Barent Beek, 1691)

Scot, Reginald, *The Discoverie of Witchcraft: wherein the lewde dealing of witches and witchmongers is notablie detected* (London: By William Brome, 1584)

—— *The Discovery of Witchcraft: . . . Whereunto is added an excellent Discourse of the nature and substance of devils and spirits* (London: A. Clark and Dixy Page, 1665)

Semler, Johann Salomo, *Joannis Salomonis Semleri commentatio de Daemoniacis quorum in N.T. fit mentio* (Halle: J. C. Hendel, 1769)

Spreter, Johann, *Ein kurtzer Bericht, was von den abghotterischen Sägen vn[nd] Beschweren zühalten: wie der etlich volbracht, vnnd das die ein Zauberey, auch Greüwel vor Gott dem Herren seind* (Basle: Bartholomeus Westheymer, 1543)

Stambaugh, Ria (ed.), *Teufelbücher in Auswahl*, 4 vols (Berlin: De Gruyter, 1970–)

Stampa, Pietro Antonio, *Fuga Satanae: exorcismus ex sacrarum litterarum fontibus, pioque S. Ecclesiae instituto exhaustus* (Como: H. Froua, 1597)

Sykes, Arthur Ashley, *An Enquiry into the Meaning of Demoniacks in the New Testament*. The second edition, corrected and amended (London, 1737)

Taillepied, Noël, *Traité De L'Apparition Des Esprits. A Scavoir, Des ames separees, Fantosmes, prodiges, & accidents merveilleux, qui precedent quelquefois la mort des grands personnages, ou signifient changemens de la chose publique* (Rouen: Romain de Beauuais, 1600)

Tanner, Norman P. (ed.), *Decrees of the Ecumenical* Councils, 2 vols (London and Washington: Sheed & Ward and Georgetown University Press, 1990)

Theatrum Diabolorum, das ist, Ein sehr nützliches verstenndiges Buch: darauss ein jeder Christ sonderlich vnnd fleissig zu lernen wie dass wir in dieser Welt nicht mit Keysern, Königen, Fürsten, und Herrn oder andern Potentaten, sondern mit dem allermechtigsten Fürsten dieser Welt dem Teuffel zukempffen vnd zustreiten . . . : allen frommen Christen, so ihrer Seelen Heil und Seligkeit angelegen in diesen letzten Zeiten da allerley Laster grausamlich im Schwang gehn mit gantzem Ernst vnnd Fleiss zubetrachten (Frankfurt am Main: Peter Schmid, Hieronymus Feyrabend, 1569)

Theophrastus, *Characters*, trans. James Diggle (Cambridge: Cambridge University Press, 2004)

Thesaurus Exorcismorum sique coniurationum terribilium, potentissimorum, efficacissimorum cum practica probatissima: quibus spiritus maligni, daemones maleficiaque omnia de corporibus humanis obsessis, tanquam flagellis, fustibusque fugantur (Cologne: Lazarus Zetzner, 1608)

Thiers, Jean-Baptiste, *Traité des superstitions selon l'Ecriture sainte, les décrets des conciles et les sentimens des saints Pères et des théologiens* (Paris: A. Dezallier, 1679)

—— *Traité des superstitions: croyances populaires et rationalité à l'Âge classique*, ed. Jean Marie Goulemot (Paris: Le Sycomore, 1984)

Thomas Aquinas, *Opera Omnia*, at http://www.corpusthomisticum.org/iopera. html: Corpus Thomisticum, subsidia studii ab Enrique Alarcón, collecta et edita (Pamplona: Ad Universitatis Studiorum Navarrensis aedes, Fundación Tomás de Aquino, 2000–2009):

    Quaestiones disputatae de malo at http://www.corpusthomisticum.org/qdm01. html and following

    Quaestio disputata de spiritualibus creaturis, at http://www.corpusthomisticum. org/qds.html

    Rescriptum De operationibus occultis naturae ad quendam militem ultramontanum, at http://www.corpusthomisticum.org/opo.html

Scriptum super Sententiis, at http://www.corpusthomisticum.org/snp0000.html and following

Summa contra Gentiles, at http://www.corpusthomisticum.org/scg1001.html and following

Summa Theologica, at http://www.corpusthomisticum.org/sth0000.html and following

Thyraeus, Petrus, *De variis tam spirituum, quam vivorum hominum prodigiosis apparitionibus, & nocturnis infestationibus libri tres* (Cologne: Cholinus, 1594)

—— *De daemoniacis liber unus in quo daemonum obsidentium conditio, obsessorum hominum status, rationes item & modi, quibus ab obsessis daemones exiguntur . . . & explicantur* (Cologne: Cholinus, 1594)

—— *Loca infesta: hoc est, De infestis, ob molestantes daemoniorum et defvnctorum hominum spiritus, locis, liber unus* (Cologne: Cholinus, 1598)

Tracts of the Anglican Fathers, part III, Andrews and Bancroft (London: W. E. Painter, 1839)

Trithemius, Johannes, *Chronicon insigne Monasterij Hirsaugiensis, ordinis S. Benedicti* (Basle: Apud Iacobum Parcum, 1534); later edition, *Johannis Trithemii . . . Primae partis opera historica*, ed. Marquard Freher (Frankfurt: Wechel, 1601)

Valle de Moura, Emanuele do, *De Incantationibus seu Ensalmis: Opusculum Primum* (Évora: Laurentius Crasbeeck, 1620)

Vermigli, Pietro Martire, *In duos libros Samuelis prophetae . . . commentarii doctissimi*, 2nd edn (Zurich: Froschouerus, 1567)

Viret, Pierre, *Le Monde a l'Empire et le Monde Demoniacle* (Geneva: Jaques Bres, 1561)

—— *The Worlde Possessed with Deuils: conteinyng three dialogues* (London: J. Kingston, 1583)

Voltaire, *Dictionnaire philosophique*, in Voltaire, *Œuvres complètes*, 55 vols (Paris: Renouard, 1819–21), vols 33–8

—— *Dictionnaire Philosophique*, in *The Complete Works of Voltaire*, ed. Christiane Mervaud, Andrew Brown and others, vols 35–6 (Oxford: Voltaire Foundation, 1994)

Wagstaffe, John, *The Question of Witchcraft Debated. Or a Discourse against their Opinion that affirm Witches, Considered and enlarged*, 2nd edn (London: Edw. Millington, 1671)

Wahrhafte Geschichte Herrn P. v. St. (Strasbourg: B. Jobins Erben, 1598)

Webster, John, *The Displaying of Supposed Witchcraft. Wherein is affirmed that there are many sorts of Deceivers and Impostors, And Divers persons under a passive Delusion of Melancholy and Fancy. But that there is a Corporeal League made betwixt the Devil and the Witch, Or that he sucks on the Witches Body, has Carnal Copulation, or that Witches are turned into Cats, Dogs, raise Tempests, or the like, is utterly denied and disproved. Wherein also is handled, The Existence of Angels and Spirits, the truth of*

Apparitions, the Nature of Astral and Sydereal Spirits, the force of Charms, and Philters; with other abstruse matters (London: 'J.M.', 1677)

Weyer, Johann, *De praestigiis daemonum, et incantationibus ac veneficiis, libri V* (Basle: Joannes Oporinus, 1563)

—— *Witches, Devils, and Doctors in the Renaissance,* ed. George Mora and Benjamin Kohl, trans. John Shea, Medieval & Renaissance Texts & Studies, 73 (Binghamton, NY: Medieval & Renaissance Texts & Studies, 1991; repr. 1998)

William, of Auvergne, *Guilelmi Alverni . . . Opera Omnia,* 2 vols (Aurelia: F. Hotot; London: Robertus Scott, 1674)

Zanchi, Girolamo, *De divinatione tam artificiosa, quam artis experte, et utriusque variis speciebus tractatus, olim studiosae iuventuti in Schola Argentinensi publicè prælectus; nunc verò in gratiam eiusdem ab hæredibus primùm in lucem editus. Accessit tractatus Thomæ Erasti medici clarissimi De astrologia diuinatrice* (Hanouia: Guilielmus Antonius, 1610)

SECONDARY LITERATURE

Althaus, Paul, *The Theology of Martin Luther,* trans. Robert C. Schultz (Philadelphia: Fortress Press, 1966)

Ankarloo, Bengt, and Gustav Henningsen (eds), *Early Modern European Witchcraft: Centres and Peripheries* (Oxford: Oxford University Press, 1990)

Ariès, Philippe, *Centuries of Childhood: A Social History of Family Life,* translated from the French by Robert Baldick (London: Jonathan Cape, 1962); also ed. with a new introduction by Adam Phillips (London: Pimlico, 1996)

Arnold, Clinton E., 'Returning to the Domain of the Powers: "Stoicheia" as Evil Spirits in Galatians 4: 3,9', *Novum Testamentum,* 38/1 (Jan. 1996), 55−76

Austin, Greta, 'Jurisprudence in the Service of Pastoral Care: The *Decretum* of Burchard of Worms', *Speculum,* 79 (2004), 929−59

—— *Shaping Church Law Around the Year 1000: The Decretum of Burchard of Worms* (Aldershot, Hants; Burlington, VT: Ashgate, 2008)

Bailey, Michael D., *Battling Demons: Witchcraft, Heresy, and Reform in the Late Middle Ages* (University Park: Pennsylvania State University Press, 2003)

—— 'The Disenchantment of Magic: Spells, Charms and Superstition in Early European Witchcraft Literature', *American Historical Review,* 111/2 (2006), 383−404

—— *Magic and Superstition in Europe: A Concise History from Antiquity to the Present* (Lanham, MD: Rowman and Littlefield, 2007)

—— 'Concern over Superstition in Late Medieval Europe', in S. A. Smith and Alan Knight (eds), *The Religion of Fools: Superstition Past and Present, Past and Present* supplement. 3 (Oxford: Oxford University Press, 2008), 115−33

Barnes, Robin Bruce, *Prophecy and Gnosis: Apocalypticism in the Wake of the Lutheran Reformation* (Stanford, CA: Stanford University Press, 1988)

Baumann, Karin, *Aberglaube für Laien: zur Programmatik und Überlieferung spätmittelalterlicher Superstitionenkritik*, 2 vols (Würzburg: Königshausen & Neumann, 1989)

Bautz, Friedrich Wilhelm, and Traugott Bautz (eds), *Biographisch-bibliographisches Kirchenlexikon* (Hamm [Westf.]: Bautz, 1970–)

Behringer, Wolfgang 'Demonology: 1500–1660', in R. Po-chia Hsia, *Christianity: Reform and Expansion, 1500–1660*, The Cambridge History of Christianity, vol. vi (Cambridge and New York: Cambridge University Press, 2007), 406–24

Beyer, Jürgen, 'A Lübeck Prophet in Local and Lutheran Context', in Bob Scribner and Trevor Johnson (eds), *Popular Religion in Germany and Central Europe 1400–1800* (Basingstoke: Macmillan, 1996), 166–82

——'Lutherische Propheten in Deutschland und Skandinavien im 16. und 17. Jahrhundert: Entstehung und Ausbreitung eines Kulturmusters zwischen Mündlichkeit und Schriftlichkeit', in Robert Bohn (ed.), *Europa in Scandinavia: Kulturelle und soziale Dialoge in der Frühen Neuzeit* (Frankfurt am Main: P. Lang, 1994), 35–55

Bolkestein, Hendrik, *Theophrastos' Charakter der Deisidaimonia, als religionsgeschichtliche Urkunde* (Giessen: A. Töpelmann, 1929)

Boureau, Alain, *Satan the Heretic*, trans. Teresa Lavender Fagan (Chicago: University of Chicago Press, 2006)

Brauner, Sigrid, *Fearless Wives and Frightened Shrews: The Construction of the Witch in Early Modern Germany* (Amherst: University of Massachusetts Press, 1995)

Brecht, Martin, *Martin Luther: Sein Weg zur Reformation, 1483–1521* (Stuttgart: Calwer, 1981)

——*Martin Luther*, trans. James L. Schaaf, 3 vols (Philadelphia: Fortress Press, 1985–93)

Briggs, Robin, *Witches and Neighbours: The Social and Cultural Context of European Witchcraft* (London: HarperCollins, 1996, 2nd edn, 2002)

Broedel, Hans Peter, *The Malleus Maleficarum and the Construction of Witchcraft: Theology and Popular Belief* (Manchester: Manchester University Press, 2003)

Brown, Peter, *Augustine of Hippo: A Biography* (new edn, London: Faber; Berkeley: University of California Press, 2000)

Brundage, James A., *Law, Sex, and Christian Society in Medieval Europe* (Chicago: University of Chicago Press, 1987)

Burke, Peter, *Popular Culture in Early Modern Europe*, 3rd edn (Farnham : Ashgate, 2009)

——Brian Harrison, and Paul Slack (eds), *Civil Histories: Essays presented to Sir Keith Thomas* (Oxford: Oxford University Press, 2000)

Burns, Norman T., *Christian Mortalism from Tyndale to Milton* (Cambridge, MA: Harvard University Press, 1972)

Bynum, Caroline Walker, *Wonderful Blood: Theology and Practice in Late Medieval Northern Germany and Beyond* (Philadelphia: University of Pennsylvania Press, 2007)

Caciola, Nancy, *Discerning Spirits: Divine and Demonic Possession in the Middle Ages* (Ithaca, NY: Cornell University Press, 2003)

Cameron, Euan, *The European Reformation* (Oxford: Clarendon Press, 1991)

—— 'The Impact of Humanist Values', *Historical Journal*, 36/4 (1993) 957–64

—— 'Medieval Heretics as Protestant Martyrs', in *Martyrs and Martyrologies: Papers Read at the 1992 Summer Meeting and the 1993 Winter Meeting of the Ecclesiastical History Society*, ed. D. Wood, Studies in Church History, 30 (Oxford: Blackwell, 1993), 185–207

—— 'Philipp Melanchthon: Image and Substance', *Journal of Ecclesiastical History*, 48/4 (1997), 705–22

—— 'Frankfurt and Geneva: The European Context of John Knox's Reformation', in R. A. Mason (ed.), *John Knox and the British Reformations*, St Andrews Studies in Reformation History (Aldershot: Ashgate/Scolar Press, 1998), 51–73

—— 'For Reasoned Faith or Embattled Creed? Religion for the People in Early Modern Europe', *Transactions of the Royal Historical Society*, 6th ser., 8 (1998), 165–87

—— (ed.) *Early Modern Europe: An Oxford History* (Oxford: Oxford University Press, 1999)

—— *Waldenses: Rejections of Holy Church in Medieval Europe* (Oxford: Blackwell, 2000)

—— 'Martin Luther', in Adrian Hastings, Alistair Mason, and Hugh Pyper (eds), *Key Thinkers in Christianity* (Oxford: Oxford University Press, 2003), 53–63

Cameron, Richard M., 'The Charges of Lutheranism Brought against Jacques Lefèvre d'Etaples (1520–1529)', *Harvard Theological Review*, 63/1 (Jan. 1970), 119–49

Carson, Hampton L., 'The Trial of Animals and Insects: A Little Known Chapter of Mediæval Jurisprudence', *Proceedings of the American Philosophical Society*, 56/5 (1917), 410–15

Celenza, Christopher S., 'The Search for Ancient Wisdom in Early Modern Europe: Reuchlin and the Late Ancient Esoteric Paradigm', *Journal of Religious History*, 25/2 (2001), 115–33

Chadwick, Owen, *The Early Reformation on the Continent* (Oxford: Oxford University Press, 2001)

Christian, William A., *Local Religion in Sixteenth-Century Spain* (Princeton: Princeton University Press, 1981)

—— *Person and God in a Spanish Valley*, revised edn (Princeton: Princeton University Press, 1989)

——*Moving Crucifixes in Modern Spain* (Princeton: Princeton University Press, 1992)

Clark, Stuart, 'The Rational Witchfinder: Conscience, Demonological Naturalism and Popular Superstitions', in S. Pumfrey, P. L. Rossi, and M. Slawinski (eds), *Science, Culture and Popular Belief in Renaissance Europe* (Manchester: Manchester University Press, 1991), 222–48

——*Thinking with Demons: The Idea of Witchcraft in Early Modern Europe* (Oxford: Clarendon Press, 1997)

——'The Reformation of the Eyes: Apparitions and Optics in Sixteenth- and Seventeenth-Century Europe', *Journal of Religious History*, 27/2 (2003), 143–60.

——*Vanities of the Eye: Vision in Early Modern European Culture* (Oxford: Oxford University Press, 2007)

Colish, Marcia L., *Peter Lombard* (Leiden and New York: E. J. Brill, 1994)

Crawford, Julie, *Marvelous Protestantism: Monstrous Births in Post-Reformation England* (Baltimore: Johns Hopkins University Press, 2005)

Crouzet, Denis, *La Genèse de la réforme française 1520–1560*, Regards sur l'histoire, 109, Histoire moderne (Paris: SEDES, 1996)

Cunningham, Andrew, *The Anatomical Renaissance: The Resurrection of the Anatomical Projects of the Ancients* (Aldershot: Scolar, 1996)

——and Ole Peter Grell, *The Four Horsemen of the Apocalypse: Religion, War, Famine and Death in Reformation Europe* (Cambridge: Cambridge University Press, 2000)

Davis, Natalie Zemon, *Society and Culture in Early Modern France: Eight Essays* (Stanford, CA: Stanford University Press, 1975)

——'Some Tasks and Themes in the Study of Popular Religion', in C. E. Trinkaus and H. A. Oberman (eds), *The Pursuit of Holiness in Late Medieval and Renaissance Religion; Papers from the University of Michigan Conference* (Leiden: Brill, 1974), 307–36

——'From "Popular Religion" to Religious Cultures', in S. E. Ozment (ed.), *Reformation Europe: A Guide to Research* (St Louis: Center for Reformation Research, 1982), 321–41

Dawson, Jane, 'Calvinism and the Gaidhealtachd in Scotland', in A. Duke, G. Lewis, and A. Pettegree (eds), *Calvinism in Europe, 1560–1620* (Cambridge: Cambridge University Press, 1994), 231–53

Delumeau, Jean, 'Les Réformateurs et la superstition', in *Actes du colloque l'Amiral de Coligny et son temps (Paris, 24–28 octobre 1972)* (Paris: SHPF, 1974), 451–87

——*Catholicism between Luther and Voltaire: A New View of the Counter-Reformation*, trans. Jeremy Moiser (London: Burns & Oates; Philadelphia: Westminster Press, 1977)

——*Un chemin d'histoire: chrétienté et christianisation* (Paris: Fayard, 1981)

Deonna, W., 'The Crab and the Butterfly: A Study in Animal Symbolism', *Journal of the Warburg and Courtauld Institutes*, 17/1–2. (1954), 47–86

Dickie, Matthew W. 'Heliodorus and Plutarch on the Evil Eye', *Classical Philology*, 86/1 (Jan. 1991), 17–29

Dilthey, Wilhelm, *Wilhelm Diltheys gesammelte Schriften*, ii. *Weltanschauung und Analyse des Menschen seit Renaissance und Reformation*, 8th edn (Stuttgart and Göttingen, 1969)

Dipple, Geoffrey, *Antifraternalism and Anticlericalism in the German Reformation: Johann Eberlin von Günzburg and the Campaign against the Friars* (Aldershot: Scolar, 1996)

Ditchfield, Simon, *Liturgy, Sanctity and History in Tridentine Italy: Pietro Maria Campi and the Preservation of the Particular* (Cambridge: Cambridge University Press, 1995)

Dixon, C. Scott (ed.), *The German Reformation: The Essential Readings* (Oxford: Blackwell, 1999)

Dost, Timothy P., *Renaissance Humanism in Support of the Gospel in Luther's Early Correspondence: Taking all Things Captive* (Aldershot: Ashgate, 2001)

Douie, Decima L., *Archbishop Pecham* (Oxford: Clarendon Press, 1952)

Duffy, Eamon, *The Stripping of the Altars: Traditional Religion in England, c.1400–c.1580* (New Haven and London: Yale University Press, 1992)

Dülmen, Richard van, 'Reformation und Neuzeit: ein Versuch', *Zeitschrift für historische Forschung*, 14 (1987), 1–25, trans. as 'The Reformation and the Modern Age', in Scott Dixon (ed.), *The German Reformation: The Essential Readings* (Oxford: Blackwell, 1999), 193–223

Edwards, Mark U., Jr., *Luther and the False Brethren* (Stanford, CA.: Stanford University Press, 1975)

Eire, Carlos M. N., *War Against the Idols: The Reformation of Worship from Erasmus to Calvin* (Cambridge: Cambridge University Press, 1986)

Eitrem, Samson, 'Zur Deisidämonie', *Symbolae Osloenses*, 31 (1955), 155–69

Elias, Norbert, *The Civilizing Process: The History of Manners and State Formation and Civilization*, trans. E. Jephcott (Oxford: Blackwell, 1994)

Elliott, J. K. (ed. and trans.), *The Apocryphal New Testament: A Collection of Apocryphal Christian Literature in an English Translation* (Oxford: Clarendon Press, 1993)

Farge, James K., *Orthodoxy and Reform in Early Reformation France: The Faculty of Theology of Paris, 1500–1543*, Studies in Medieval and Reformation Thought, 32 (Leiden: E. J. Brill, 1985)

Ferber, Sarah, *Demonic Possession and Exorcism in Early Modern France* (London and New York: Routledge, 2004)

Filotas, Bernadette, *Pagan Survivals, Superstitions and Popular Cultures in Early Medieval Pastoral Literature* (Toronto: Pontifical Institute of Mediaeval Studies, 2005)

Fix, Andrew, *Fallen Angels: Balthasar Bekker, Spirit Belief, and Confessionalism in the Seventeenth Century Dutch Republic*, Archives internationales d'histoire des idées, 165 (Dordrecht and Boston: Kluwer, 1999)

Flint, Valerie I. J., *The Rise of Magic in Early Medieval Europe* (Princeton: Princeton University Press, 1991)

Florey, Gerhard, *Geschichte der Salzburger Protestanten und ihrer Emigration 1731–32*, Studien und Texte zur Kirchengeschichte und Geschichte, 1/2 (Vienna, Cologne and Graz: Böhlau, 1977)

Frankfurter, David, 'The Perils of Love: Magic and Countermagic in Coptic Egypt', *Journal of the History of Sexuality*, 10/3–4 (July/Oct. 2001), 480–500

Franz, Adolph, *Der Magister Nikolaus Magni de Jawor* (Freiburg im Breisgau: Herder, 1898)

Freeman, T., 'Demons, Deviance and Defiance: John Darrell and the Politics of Exorcism in Late Elizabethan England', in P. Lake and M. Questier (eds), *Conformity and Orthodoxy in the English Church, c.1560–1660* (Woodbridge, Suffolk, Rochester, NY: Boydell Press, 2000), 34–63

Gentilcore, David, *From Bishop to Witch: The System of the Sacred in Early Modern Terra d'Otranto* (Manchester: Manchester University Press, 1992)

Ginzburg, Carlo, *I benandanti: ricerche sulla stregoneria e sui culti agrari tra Cinquecento e Seicento* (Turin: G. Einaudi, 1966)

—— *Clues, Myths, and the Historical Method* (Baltimore: Johns Hopkins University Press, 1989)

Goodey, C. F., and Tim Stainton, 'Intellectual Disability and the Myth of the Changeling Myth', *Journal of the History of the Behavioral Sciences*, 37/3 (2001) 223–40

Goodman, Lenn Evan (ed.), *Neoplatonism and Jewish Thought* (Albany: State University of New York Press, 1992)

Gordon, Bruce, 'Malevolent Ghosts and Ministering Angels: Apparitions and Pastoral Care in the Swiss Reformation', in B. Gordon and P. Marshall (eds), *The Place of the Dead: Death and Remembrance in Early Modern Europe*, (Cambridge: Cambridge University Press, 2000), 87–109

—— *Calvin* (New Haven and London: Yale University Press, 2009)

Grafton, Anthony, *Cardano's Cosmos* (Cambridge, MA: Harvard University Press, 1999)

Green, Ian, *The Christian's ABC: Catechisms and Catechizing in England c.1530–1740* (Oxford: Oxford University Press, 1996)

Green, Roger Lancelyn, 'Shakespeare and the Fairies', *Folklore*, 73/2 (1962), 89–103

Greengrass, Mark, 'The Calvinist Experiment in Béarn', in Andrew Pettegree, A. C. Duke, and Gillian Lewis (eds), *Calvinism in Europe, 1540–1620* (Cambridge; New York: Cambridge University Press, 1994), 119–42

Greengrass, Mark, 'Miracles and the Peregrination of the Holy in the French Wars of Religion', in José Pedro Paiva (ed.), *Religious Ceremonials and Images: Power and Social Meaning (1400–1750)* (Coimbra: Palimage Editores, 2002), 389–414

Grell, Ole Peter, and Bob Scribner (eds), *Tolerance and Intolerance in the European Reformation* (Cambridge: Cambridge University Press, 1996)

—— and Andrew Cunningham (eds) with Jon Arrizabalaga, *Health Care and Poor Relief in Counter-Reformation Europe* (London and New York: Routledge, 1999)

Grodzynski, D., '*Superstitio*', *Revue des Études Anciennes*, 76 (1974), 36–60

Gurevich, Aron, *Medieval Popular Culture: Problems of Belief and Perception*, trans. János M. Bak and Paul A. Hollingsworth (Cambridge: Cambridge University Press, 1988)

Halkin, Léon-E., *Erasmus: A Critical Biography* (Oxford and Cambridge, MA: Blackwell, 1993)

Hamilton, Alastair, *The Family of Love* (Cambridge: J. Clarke, 1981)

—— *Hendrik Niclaes* (Baden-Baden: Koerner, 2003)

Hamm, Berndt, *Promissio, Pactum, Ordinatio: Freiheit und Selbstbindung Gottes in der scholastischen Gnadenlehre*, Beiträge zur historischen Theologie, 54 (Tübingen: Mohr, 1977)

Harmening, Dieter, *Superstitio: Überlieferungs- und theoriegeschichtliche Untersuchungen zur kirchlich-theologischen Aberglaubensliteratur des Mittelalters* (Berlin: E. Schmidt, 1979)

—— *Zauberei im Abendland: Vom Anteil der Gelehrten am Wahn der Leute. Skizzen zur Geschichte des Aberglaubens* (Würzburg: Königshausen & Neumann, 1991)

—— *Wörterbuch des Aberglaubens* (Stuttgart: Reclam, 2005)

Harnack, Adolf von, *Lehrbuch der Dogmengeschichte*, 4th edn, 3 vols (Tübingen: Mohr, 1909–10)

—— *What is Christianity?* trans. T. B. Saunders (Philadelphia: Fortress Press, 1986)

Hartmann, Wilfried, *Das Sendhandbuch des Regino von Prüm*, Ausgewählte Quellen zur deutschen Geschichte des Mittelalters, 42 (Darmstadt: Wissenschaftliche Buchgesellschaft, 2004)

Haustein, Jörg, *Martin Luthers Stellung zum Zauber- und Hexenwesen,* Münchener kirchenhistorische Studien, 2 (Stuttgart: W. Kohlhammer, 1990)

Henningsen, Gustav, ' "The Ladies from Outside": An Archaic Pattern of the Witches' Sabbath', in Bengt Ankarloo and Gustav Henningsen (eds), *Early Modern European Witchcraft: Centres and Peripheries* (Oxford: Oxford University Press, 1990), 191–215

Herwaarden, J. van, *Between Saint James and Erasmus: Studies in Late-medieval Religious Life: Devotion and Pilgrimage in the Netherlands* (Leiden: Brill, 2003)

Heyd, Michael, *Be Sober and Reasonable: The Critique of Enthusiasm in the Seventeenth and Early Eighteenth Centuries*, Brill's Studies in Intellectual History, 63 (Leiden and New York: E. J. Brill, 1995)

Hill, Christopher, Barry Reay, and William Lamont, *The World of the Muggletonians* (London: T. Smith, 1983)

Houlbrooke, Ralph A., *The English Family, 1450–1700* (London: Longman, 1984)

—— *Death, Religion, and the Family in England, 1480–1750* (Oxford: Clarendon Press, 1998)

Hsia, R. Po-Chia, *Social Discipline in the Reformation: Central Europe 1550–1750* (London: Routledge, 1989)

—— *Christianity: Reform and Expansion, 1500–1660*, The Cambridge History of Christianity, vi (Cambridge and New York: Cambridge University Press, 2007)

Hyde, Walter Woodburn, 'The Prosecution and Punishment of Animals and Lifeless Things in the Middle Ages and Modern Times', *University of Pennsylvania Law Review and American Law Register*, 64/7 (May 1916), 696–730

Jelsma, Auke, 'The Devil and Protestantism', in A. Jelsma, *Frontiers of the Reformation* (Aldershot: Ashgate, 1998), 25–39

Johnson, Trevor, 'The Reformation and Popular Culture', in Andrew Pettegree (ed.), *The Reformation World* (London and New York: Routledge, 2000), 555 ff.

Johnstone, Nathan, *The Devil and Demonism in Early Modern England* (Cambridge: Cambridge University Press, 2006)

Jones, Peter Murray, and Lea T. Olsan, 'The Middleham Jewel: Ritual, Power, and Devotion', *Viator*, 31 (2000), 249–290

Joubert, Laurent, *Popular Errors*, trans. Gregory Rocher (Tuscaloosa: University of Alabama Press, 2006)

—— *The Second Part of the Popular Errors* (Tuscaloosa: University of Alabama Press, 2007)

Karl, Werner, 'Ananizapta: Eine geheimnisvolle Inschrift des Mittelalters', *Sammelblatt des Historischen Vereins Ingolstadt*, 105 (1996), 59 ff.

—— 'Ananizapta und der Middleham Jewel', *Sammelblatt des Historischen Vereins Ingolstadt*, 110 (2001), 57 ff.

Keck, David, *Angels and Angelology in the Middle Ages* (Oxford and New York: Oxford University Press, 1998)

Kenny, Anthony, *Aquinas* (Oxford: Oxford University Press, 1980)

Kieckhefer, Richard, *Magic in the Middle Ages* (Cambridge: Cambridge University Press, 1989)

—— *Forbidden Rites: A Necromancer's Manual of the Fifteenth Century* (Stroud, Glos.: Sutton Publishing, 1997)

Kittredge, G. L. 'The Friar's Lantern and the Friar Rush', *Publications of the Modern Language Association of America*, 15/4. (1900), 415–41

Klingshirn, William E., *Caesarius of Arles: The Making of a Christian Community in Late Antique Gaul* (Cambridge: Cambridge University Press, 1994)

Klingshirn, William E., 'Defining the Sortes Sanctorum: Gibbon, Du Cange, and Early Christian Lot Divination', *Journal of Early Christian Studies*, 10/1 (2002), 77–130

Knuttel, Willem Pieter Cornelis, *Balthasar Bekker, de bestrijder van het bijgeloof* (The Hague: M. Nijhoff, 1906)

Körntgen, Ludger, 'Canon Law and the Practice of Penance: Burchard of Worms's Penitential', *Early Medieval Europe*, 14/1 (2006), 103–17

Krysmanski, Bernd, 'We See a Ghost: Hogarth's Satire on Methodists and Connoisseurs', *Art Bulletin*, 80/2 (June 1998), 292–310

Kurze, Dieter (ed.), *Quellen zur Ketzergeschichte Brandenburgs und Pommerns* (Berlin: Veröffentlichungen der historischen Kommission zu Berlin, 45; Quellenwerke, 6, 1975)

Kusukawa, Sachiko, *The Transformation of Natural Philosophy: The Case of Philip Melanchthon* (Cambridge and New York: Cambridge University Press, 1995)

Labrousse, Elizabeth, *Pierre Bayle*, 2nd edn, 2 vols (Dordrecht and Boston: M. Nijhoff, 1985)

La Harpe, Jacqueline de, *L'abbé Laurent Bordelon et la lutte contre la superstition en France entre 1680 et 1730*, University of California Publications in Modern Philology, 26/2 (Berkeley and Los Angeles: University of California Press, 1942)

Lea, Henry Charles, *Materials toward a History of Witchcraft*, ed. Arthur C. Howland, 3 vols (New York: T. Yoseloff, 1957)

Le Goff, J., *The Birth of Purgatory*, trans. A. Goldhammer (Chicago: University of Chicago Press, 1984)

Lemmen, M. M. W., *Max Weber's Sociology of Religion: Its Method and Content in the Light of the Concept of Rationality* (Hilversum: Gooi en Sticht, 1990)

Lerner, Robert E., *The Heresy of the Free Spirit in the Later Middle Ages* (Berkeley: University of California Press, 1972)

—— 'Werner di Friedberg intrappolato dalla legge', in J.-C. Maire Vigueur and A. Paravicini Bagliani (eds), *La parola all'accusato* (Palermo: Sellerio, 1991), 268–81.

Lindahl, Carl, John McNamara, and John Lindow (eds) *Medieval Folklore: A Guide to Myths, Legends, Tales, Beliefs, and Customs* (Oxford: Oxford University Press, 2002)

Little, Lester K., *Benedictine Maledictions: Liturgical Cursing in Romanesque France* (Ithaca, NY: Cornell University Press, 1993)

Margolin, Jean-Claude, 'Mutian et son modèle erasmien', in *L'Humanisme allemand (1480–1540). XVIIIe Colloque international de Tours* (Munich and Paris: Fink, Vrin, 1979), 169–202

Marsh, Christopher W., *The Family of Love in English Society, 1550–1630* (Cambridge and New York: Cambridge University Press, 1993)

Marshall, Peter, *Beliefs and the Dead in Reformation England* (Oxford: Oxford University Press, 2002)

—— and Alexandra Walsham (eds), *Angels in the Early Modern World* (Cambridge: Cambridge University Press, 2006)

Martin, Dale B., *Inventing Superstition: From the Hippocratics to the Christians* (Cambridge, MA, and London: Harvard University Press, 2004)

Matarasso, Pauline (ed. and trans.), *The Cistercian world: Monastic Writings of the Twelfth Century* (London: Penguin, 1993)

Matheson, Peter, *The Rhetoric of the Reformation* (Edinburgh: T. & T. Clark, 1998)

Mazzone, Umberto and Angelo Turchini, *I Visiti Pastorali: Analisi di una fonte* (Bologna: Il Mulino, 1985)

Merkel, Ingrid, and Allen G. Debus (eds), *Hermeticism and the Renaissance: Intellectual History and the Occult in Early Modern Europe* (Washington: Folger Shakespeare Library; London: Associated University Presses, 1988)

Meyer, Marvin W., and Richard Smith (eds) *Ancient Christian Magic: Coptic Texts of Ritual Power* (Princeton: Princeton University Press, 1999)

Midelfort, H. C. Erik, 'Johan Weyer and the Transformation of the Insanity Defense', in R. Po-chia Hsia, *The German People and the Reformation* (Ithaca, NY: Cornell University Press, 1988), 234–61

—— *Exorcism and Enlightenment: Johann Joseph Gassner and the Demons of Eighteenth-Century Germany* (New Haven and London: Yale University Press, 2005)

Moltmann, Jürgen, *Christoph Pezel (1539–1604) und der Calvinismus in Bremen* (Bremen: Verlag Einkehr, 1958)

Morris, Colin, *The Papal Monarchy: The Western Church from 1050 to 1250* (Oxford: Clarendon Press, 1989)

Muchembled, Robert, *Popular Culture and Elite Culture in France, 1400–1750*, trans. Lydia Cochrane (Baton Rouge: Louisiana State University Press,1985)

—— *L'Invention de l'homme moderne: Sensibilités, mœurs et comportements collectifs sous l'ancien régime* (Paris: Fayard, 1988)

—— *A History of the Devil: From the Middle Ages to the Present*, trans. Jean Birrell (Cambridge: Polity Press, 2003)

Mullett, Michael, *The Catholic Reformation* (London: Routledge, 1999)

Murray, Alexander, *Reason and Society in the Middle Ages* (Oxford: Clarendon Press, 1978)

Newton, J., and J. Bath (eds), *Early Modern Ghosts: The Proceedings of the 'Early Modern Ghosts' Conference held at St. John's College, Durham University on 24 March 2001* (Durham: Centre for Seventeenth-Century Studies, 2002)

Noonan, John T., *The Scholastic Analysis of Usury* (Cambridge, MA: Harvard University Press, 1957)

Oberman, Heiko A., *The Harvest of Medieval Theology: Gabriel Biel and Late Medieval Nominalism* (Cambridge, MA: Harvard University Press, 1963)

Oberman, Heiko A., *Forerunners of the Reformation: The Shape of Late Medieval Thought*, with documents trans. by Paul L. Nyhus (Philadelphia: Fortress 1981)

—— *Luther: Man between God and the Devil*, trans. Eileen Walliser-Schwarzbart (New Haven: Yale University Press, 1989)

—— '*Facientibus quod in se est Deus non denegat gratiam*: Robert Holcot O.P. and the Beginnings of Luther's Theology', in Heiko A. Oberman, *The Dawn of the Reformation* (Edinburgh: T. & T. Clark, 1992), 84–103

—— *The Reformation: Roots and Ramifications*, trans. A. C. Gow (Edinburgh: T. & T. Clark, 1994)

Oldridge, Darren, *Strange Histories: The Trial of the Pig, the Walking Dead, and Other Matters of Fact from the Medieval and Renaissance Worlds* (London and New York: Routledge, 2005)

O'Malley, John W., 'Was Ignatius Loyola a Church Reformer? How to look at Early Modern Catholicism', in David M. Luebke (ed.) *The Counter-Reformation: The Essential Readings* (Oxford: Blackwell, 1999), 65–82

—— *Trent and all That: Renaming Catholicism in the Early Modern Era* (Cambridge, MA: Harvard University Press, 2000)

O'Neil, Mary Rose, 'Discerning Superstition: Popular Errors and Orthodox Response in Late Sixteenth-Century Italy' (Ph.D. thesis, Stanford University, 1981)

—— '*Sacerdote ovvero strione*: Ecclesiastical and Superstitious Remedies in sixteenth Century Italy', in S. Kaplan (ed.), *Understanding Popular Culture: From the Middle Ages to the Nineteenth Century* (Berlin and New York: Mouton, 1984), 53–83

—— 'Magical Healing, Love Magic and the Inquisition in Late Sixteenth-century Modena', in Stephen Haliczer (ed.), *Inquisition and Society in Early Modern Europe* (Totowa, NJ: Barnes & Noble, 1987), 88–114

Opie, Iona, and Moira Tatem, *A Dictionary of Superstitions* (Oxford: Oxford University Press, 1989)

Overfield, J. H., *Humanism and Scholasticism in Late Medieval Germany* (Princeton: Princeton University Press, 1984)

Paden, W. D., 'Mt. 1352: Jacques de Vitry, the Mensa Philosophica, Hödeken, and Tennyson', *Journal of American Folklore*, 58/227 (1945), 35–47

Parish, Helen, *Monks, Miracles and Magic: Reformation Representations of the Medieval Church* (Abingdon: Routledge, 2005)

—— and William G. Naphy (eds) *Religion and Superstition in Reformation Europe* (Manchester: Manchester University Press, 2002)

Park, Katharine, and Lorraine J. Daston, 'Unnatural Conceptions: The Study of Monsters in Sixteenth- and Seventeenth-Century France and England', *Past and Present*, 92 (1981), 20–54

Pelikan, Jaroslav, *Reformation of Church and Dogma (1300–1700)* (Chicago: University of Chicago Press, 1984)

Penney, Daniel T., 'J.-B. Thiers and the Repression of Superstition in Late-Seventeenth-Century France', Oxford University D.Phil. thesis, 1997

Perry, Elisabeth Israels, *From Theology to History: French Religious Controversy and the Revocation of the Edict of Nantes* (The Hague: M. Nijhoff, 1973)

Pettegree, Andrew (ed.), *The Reformation World* (London and New York: Routledge, 2000)

Phillips, Peter, 'Broadening Horizons', *Musical Times*, 139/1859. (1998), 18–23

Powis, J. K., 'Repression and Autonomy: Christians and Christianity in the Historical Work of Jean Delumeau', *Journal of Modern History*, 64 (1992), 366–74

Prügl, Thomas, *Die Ekklesiologie Heinrich Kalteisens OP in der Auseinandersetzung mit dem Basler Konziliarismus* (Paderborn: F. Schöningh, 1995)

Redwood, John, *Reason, Ridicule, and Religion: The Age of Enlightenment in England, 1660–1750* (London: Thames & Hudson, 1976)

Reeves, W. P., 'Shakespeare's Queen Mab', *Modern Language Notes*, 17/1 (Jan. 1902), 10–14

Renaudet, A., *Préréforme et humanisme à Paris pendant les premières guerres d'Italie, 1494–1517*, 2nd edn (Paris: Librairie d'Argences, 1953)

Rider, Catherine, *Magic and Impotence in the Middle Ages* (Oxford and New York: Oxford University Press, 2006)

Roos, Keith L., *The Devil in sixteenth Century German Literature: The Teufelsbücher*, Europäische Hochschulschriften, 1st series: Deutsche Literatur und Germanistik, 68 (Bern: Herbert Lang; Frankfurt am Main: Peter Lang, 1972)

Roper, Lyndal, *Oedipus and the Devil: Witchcraft, Sexuality and Religion in Early Modern Europe* (London and New York: Routledge, 1994)

—— *Witch Craze: Terror and Fantasy in Baroque Germany* (New Haven and London: Yale University Press; new edn, 2006)

Rowlands, Alison, 'Monstrous Deception: Midwifery, Fraud and Gender in Early Modern Rothenburg ob der Tauber', in Ulinka Rublack (ed.), *Gender in Early Modern German History* (Cambridge and New York: Cambridge University Press, 2002)

Rublack, Ulinka, *Reformation Europe* (Cambridge: Cambridge University Press, 2005)

Ruggiero, Guido, *Binding Passions: Tales of Magic, Marriage, and Power at the End of the Renaissance* (New York: Oxford University Press, 1993)

Ruler, Han van, 'Minds, Forms, and Spirits: The Nature of Cartesian Disenchantment', *Journal of the History of Ideas*, 61/3. (July 2000), 381–95

Russell, Jeffrey Burton, *Lucifer: The Devil in the Middle Ages* (Ithaca, NY, and London: Cornell University Press, 1984)

Salzman, Michele R., '"Superstitio" in the "Codex Theodosianus" and the Persecution of Pagans', *Vigiliae Christianae*, 41/2 (1987), 172–88

Schechner, Sara, *Comets, Popular Culture, and the Birth of Modern Cosmology* (Princeton: Princeton University Press, 1999)

Schoeck, Richard J., *Erasmus of Europe*, 2 vols (Edinburgh: Edinburgh University Press, 1990–3)

Screech, M. A., *Ecstasy and The Praise of Folly* (London: Duckworth, 1980)

Scribner, Robert W., 'The Erasmians and the Beginning of the Reformation in Erfurt', *Journal of Religious History*, 9 (1976/7), 3–31

—— *For the Sake of Simple Folk: Popular Propaganda for the German Reformation* (Cambridge and New York: Cambridge University Press, 1981)

—— 'Cosmic Order and Daily Life: Sacred and Secular in Pre-Industrial German Society', in K. von Greyerz (ed.), *Religion and Society in Early Modern Europe 1500–1800* (London: German Historical Institute; Boston: Allen & Unwin, 1984), 17–32

—— *The German Reformation* (London: Macmillan, 1986)

—— *Popular Culture and Popular Movements in Reformation Germany* (London: Hambledon Press, 1987)

—— 'The Reformation, Popular Magic, and the "Disenchantment of the World"', *Journal of Interdisciplinary History*, 23 (1993), 475–94

—— 'The Reformation and the Religion of the Common People', in *Die Reformation in Deutschland und Europa: Interpretationen und Debatten, Archiv für Reformationsgeschichte* suppl. (Gütersloh, 1993), 221–42

—— 'Magic, Witchcraft and Superstition', *Historical Journal*, 37/1 (1994), 219–23

—— 'Elements of Popular Belief', in T. A. Brady, H. A. Oberman, and J. D. Tracy (eds), *Handbook of European History 1400–1600: Late Middle Ages, Renaissance and Reformation* 2 vols (Leiden and New York: E. J. Brill, 1994–5), i. *Structures and Assertions*, 231–62

—— and Trevor Johnson, (eds), *Popular Religion in Germany and Central Europe 1400–1800* (Basingstoke: Macmillan, 1996)

Sharpe, James, *The Bewitching of Anne Gunter: A Horrible and True Story of Deception, Witchcraft, Murder and the King of England* (London: Routledge, 2000)

Shaw, Christine, *Julius II: The Warrior Pope* (Oxford: Blackwell Publishers, 1993)

Shaw, Jane, *Miracles in Enlightenment England* (New Haven and London: Yale University Press, 2006)

Shorter, Edward, *The Making of the Modern Family* (New York: Basic Books, 1975)

Skemer, Don C., *Binding Words: Textual Amulets in the Middle Ages* (Philadelphia: Pennsylvania State University Press, 2006)

Sluhovsky, Moshe, *Believe not Every Spirit: Possession, Mysticism, & Discernment in Early Modern Catholicism* (Chicago: University of Chicago Press, 2007)

Smith, Norman R., 'Portent Lore and Medieval Popular Culture', *Journal of Popular Culture*, 14 (1980), 47–59

Smith, S. A., and Alan Knight (eds), *The Religion of Fools: Superstition Past and Present, Past and Present*, suppl. 3 (Oxford: Oxford University Press, 2008)

Soergel, Philip M., *Wondrous in his Saints: Counter-Reformation Propaganda in Bavaria* (Berkeley: University of California Press, 1993)

Southern, R. W., *Medieval Humanism and Other Studies* (Oxford: Blackwell, 1970)

—— *Scholastic Humanism and the Unification of Europe*, 2 vols (Oxford: Blackwell, 1995–2001)

Spier, Jeffrey, 'Medieval Byzantine Magic Amulets and their Tradition', *Journal of the Warburg and Courtauld Institutes*, 56 (1993), 25–62

Spitz, Lewis W., 'The Conflict of Ideals in Mutianus Rufus: A Study in the Religious Philosophy of Northern Humanism', *Journal of the Warburg and Courtauld Institutes*, 16/1-2 (1953), 121–43

—— (ed.) *The Reformation: Basic Interpretations* (Lexington, MA: D. C. Heath, 1972)

—— *Luther and German Humanism* (Aldershot: Variorum, 1996)

Spreter, Theo, von Kreudenstein, *Johann Spreter von Kreudenstein. Doktor beider Rechte, Rottweiler Bürger im 16. Jahrhundert* (Sigmaringen: Jan Thorbecke Verlag, 1988)

Stephens, Walter, *Demon Lovers: Witchcraft, Sex, and the Crisis of Belief* (Chicago: University of Chicago Press, 2002)

Stone, Lawrence, *The Family, Sex and Marriage in England 1500–1800* (London: Weidenfeld & Nicolson, 1977)

Strauss, G., *Luther's House of Learning: Indoctrination of the Young in the German Reformation* (Baltimore: Johns Hopkins University Press, 1978)

Styers, Randall, *Making Magic: Religion, Magic, and Science in the Modern World* (Oxford and New York: Oxford University Press, 2004)

Tavuzzi, Michael, *Prierias: The Life and Works of Silvestro Mazzolini da Prierio, 1456–1527* (Durham, NC: Duke University Press, 1997)

Taylor, Larissa, *Soldiers of Christ: Preaching in Late Medieval and Reformation France* (New York: Oxford University Press, 1992)

Tedeschi, John, 'The Inquisitorial Law and the Witch', *in* B. Ankarloo and G. Henningsen, *Early Modern European Witchcraft: Centres and Peripheries* (Oxford: Clarendon Press, 1990), 83–118

Tentler, T. N., *Sin and Confession on the Eve of the Reformation* (Princeton: Princeton University Press, 1977)

Thomas, Keith, *Religion and the Decline of Magic: Studies in Popular Beliefs in Sixteenth- and Seventeenth-Century England* (London: Weidenfeld & Nicolson, 1971)

Todd, Margo, *The Culture of Protestantism in Early Modern Scotland* (New Haven and London: Yale University Press, 2002)

Tolley, B., *Pastors and Parishioners in Württemberg during the Late Reformation 1581–1621* (Stanford, CA.: Stanford University Press, 1995)

Tracy, James D., *Erasmus of the Low Countries* (Berkeley: University of California Press, 1996)

Troeltsch, Ernst, *Die Bedeutung des Protestantismus für die Entstehung der modernen Welt: Vortrag, gehalten auf der IX. Versammlung deutscher Historiker zu Stuttgart am 21. April 1906* (Munich: R. Oldenbourg, 1906)

—— *Gesammelte Schriften*, iv (Tübingen: Mohr, 1925)

Van Engen, John, 'The Christian Middle Ages as an Historiographical Problem', *American Historical Review*, 91/3 (June 1986), 519–52

van Ruler, Han, 'Minds, Forms, and Spirits: The Nature of Cartesian Disenchantment', *Journal of the History of Ideas,* 61/3 (2000). 381-95

Vovelle, Michelle, 'Dechristianization in Year II: Expression or Extinction of a Popular Culture', in Kaspar von Greyerz (ed.), *Religion and Society in Early Modern Europe, 1500–1800* (London: German Historical Institute; Boston: Allen & Unwin, 1984)

Vyse, Stuart A., *Believing in Magic: The Psychology of Superstition* (New York and Oxford: Oxford University Press, 1997)

Walker, D. P., *Unclean Spirits: Possession and Exorcism in France and England in the Late Sixteenth and Early Seventeenth Centuries* (Philadelphia: University of Pennsylvania Press, 1981)

Walsham, Alexandra, *Providence in Early Modern England* (Oxford: Oxford University Press, 1999)

—— 'Vox Piscis, or The Book-Fish: Providence and the Uses of the Reformation past in Caroline Cambridge', *English Historical Review*, 114/457 (1999), 574–606

—— 'The Reformation and "the Disenchantment of the World" Reassessed', *Historical Journal*, 51/2 (2008), 497–528

Watson, Lisa Jacqueline, 'The Influence of the Reformation and Counter Reformation upon Key Texts in the Literature of Witchcraft' (Ph.D. thesis, University of Newcastle upon Tyne, 1997)

Weber, Max, *The Protestant Ethic and the Spirit of Capitalism*, trans. Talcott Parsons (New York and London: Scribners; Allen & Unwin, 1930)

—— *The Sociology of Religion*, trans. Ephraim Fischoff (Boston: Beacon Press, 1963)

—— *From Max Weber: Essays in Sociology*, ed. H. H. Gerth, C. Wright Mills, and Bryan S. Turner (London: Routledge, 2009)

Wheatley, Henry B., 'Saint Swithin's Day', *The Antiquary*, 6 (1882), 1–4

Williams, Gerhild Scholz, *Ways of Knowing in Early Modern Germany: Johannes Praetorius as a Witness to his Time* (Aldershot: Ashgate; 2006)

Wilson, Dudley, *Signs and Portents: Monstrous Births from the Middle Ages to the Enlightenment* (London and New York: Routledge, 1993)

Wilson, Stephen, *The Magical Universe: Everyday Ritual and Magic in Pre-modern Europe* (London and New York: Hambledon and London, 2000)

Winroth, Anders, *The Making of Gratian's Decretum* (Cambridge: Cambridge University Press, 2001)

Wrightson, Keith, *English Society, 1580–1680*, new edn (London: Routledge, 2003)

Yates, Frances A., *Giordano Bruno and the Hermetic Tradition* (Chicago: University of Chicago Press, 1964, repr. 1991)

Zeeden, Ernst Walter, *Die Entstehung der Konfessionen: Grundlagen und Formen der Konfessionsbildung im Zeitalter der Glaubenskämpfe* (Munich: R. Oldenbourg, 1965)

Zimmermann, Harm-Peer, *Ästhetische Aufklärung: zur Revision der Romantik in volkskundlicher Absicht* (Würzburg: Königshausen & Neumann, 2001)

Index